Using PC DOS

3rd Edition

Chris DeVoney

Revised by David Busch

W9-DDQ-436

que®
CORPORATION
LEADING COMPUTER KNOWLEDGE

Using PC DOS

3rd Edition

Copyright © 1989 by Que® Corporation

All rights reserved. Printed in the United States of America. No part of this book may be used or reproduced in any form or by any means, or stored in a database or retrieval system, without prior written permission of the publisher except in the case of brief quotations embodied in critical articles and reviews. Making copies of any part of this book for any purpose other than your own personal use is a violation of United States copyright laws. For information, address Que Corporation, 11711 N. College Ave., Carmel, IN 46032.

Library of Congress Catalog No.: 89-60356

ISBN 0-88022-419-3

This book is sold *as is*, without warranty of any kind, either express or implied, respecting the contents of this book, including but not limited to implied warranties for the book's quality, performance, merchantability, or fitness for any particular purpose. Neither Que Corporation nor its dealers or distributors shall be liable to the purchaser or any other person or entity with respect to any liability, loss, or damage caused or alleged to be caused directly or indirectly by this book.

92 91 90 89   8 7 6 5 4 3 2 1

Interpretation of the printing code: the rightmost double-digit number is the year of the book's printing; the rightmost single-digit number, the number of the book's printing. For example, a printing code of 89-4 shows that the fourth printing of the book occurred in 1989.

Using PC DOS, 3rd Edition, can be used with PC DOS V3.0 and later.

ABOUT THE AUTHOR

Chris DeVoney

C hris DeVoney received his B.S. degree from the University of Gloucester and has been employed in the microcomputer industry since 1975. Mr. DeVoney has written and edited numerous books and articles about microcomputers. He is the author of *IBM's Personal Computer* and *Using PC DOS* and contributing author of *Managing Your Hard Disk,* all published by Que Corporation.

Publishing Director

David Paul Ewing

Acquisitions Editor

Terrie Lynn Solomon

Product Director

Lois Sherman

Editors

Lisa Hunt
Joseph P. Goodwin
Richard C. Turner

Technical Editors

David Knipsel
Timothy S. Stanley

Book Design and Production

Dan Armstrong
Brad Chinn
Cheryl English
Jennifer Matthews
Dave Kline
Lori A. Lyons

Jon Ogle
Cindy L. Phipps
Joe Ramon
Dennis Sheehan
Louise Shinault
Peter Tocco

Indexers

Sharon Hilgenberg
Carolyn A. Spitler

Composed in Garamond and Universal Monospace
by Que Corporation

CONTENTS AT A GLANCE

v

Part V   Managing Your System

Part VI   DOS Command Reference

TABLE OF CONTENTS

II   Expanding Your Knowledge of DOS and Disks

7   Gaining More Control over Your Files   103

III   Expanding Your Use of DOS

Preface

In August of 1981, IBM® announced its Personal Computer; IBM and Microsoft® announced the IBM Personal Computer Disk Operating System; and the world of micro-computing changed again. Evolution is nothing but change, and revolution is simply fast evolution. On that fateful August day, IBM revolutionized the microcomputer industry to the same degree that Apple Computer revolutionized microcomputing in 1977.

At the madding fast-track pace this industry sets, the Personal Computer and Personal Computer XT have both come and gone. And the astonishing Personal Computer AT has become a commodity with a life of its own.

IBM tried to "retire" AT-style computers by replacing them with the Personal System/2 (PS/2) line, which uses an electronic "architecture" known as Micro Channel™. Recently, a consortium of vendors has given AT-type systems new life. This Enhanced Industry Standard Architecture, or EISA, will form the basis for new AT-class machines. IBM itself has introduced an AT "clone" in the PS/2 Model 30 286. There are now no fewer than eight models in the latest IBM generation alone.

With each generation of personal computers has come an evolution of the operating system. PC DOS V2.0 came about because of the need to address hard disks. DOS V2.1 appeared to utilize the half-height floppy disk drives on the PC*jr*. DOS V3.0 arose when the 1.2-megabyte floppy disk drives and the 30-megabyte hard disk drives of the Personal Computer AT became commonplace. DOS V3.1 is DOS V3.0 with facilities for the IBM PC and Token Ring Networks. V3.1 was the first version of PC DOS released for a peripheral rather than for a computer. DOS V3.2 came out when the first truly portable IBM computer, the IBM Convertible, was announced. DOS V3.3's appearance coincided with the release of the PS/2 family.

Today, we have DOS V4, introduced in mid-1988, but not mated with any IBM computer system. This version's "hardware" connection includes features for computers that have hard disks larger than 32 megabytes, greater amounts of memory, and other enhancements that were scarcely dreamed of when DOS first appeared on the market. The 32-megabyte logical disk barrier has been abolished, and DOS V4 finally supports the Lotus-Intel-Microsoft Expanded Memory Specification (EMS) 4.0.

DOS V4 does have one "revolutionary" innovation of its own. For the first time, DOS sports an officially-supported, menu-oriented user interface, or shell, which can insulate the new user from the dreaded DOS prompt.

New possibilities emerge from each new machine and operating system as one barrier after another falls. Yet, some old problems remain. The chief problem is getting work from your computer. An important part of the solution is learning to use the new operating system. The first edition of this book was written because I thought no one should have to learn an operating system the way I did—the hard way.

This third edition of *Using PC DOS* incorporates the knowledge I have gained since I wrote the first two editions. New commands added to DOS have solved certain problems, and new features of DOS have added some new wrinkles. I will attempt to guide you through both. Throughout the book, I intersperse hints, suggestions, and occasional warnings. I report what DOS finds acceptable and what DOS finds objectionable. I test DOS to its limits and sometimes show when to expect the unexpected. (Actually, DOS never does the unexpected. DOS faithfully executes your commands. The problem arises when the commands you give do not correspond to what you want to do. These "failures of communication" are usually the most frustrating for all users of computers.)

For those of you who have some experience with DOS, don't stop now. DOS V3.3 and V4 have some powerful features that are worth exploiting. The chapters on batch files (Chapters 15 and 16), customizing DOS (Chapter 17), and using your hard disk (Chapter 25) are enlarged. There are also entirely new chapters on the DOS V4 Shell (Chapters 3, 4, 21, and 22) and other new features. The *DOS Command Reference* discusses the old and new DOS commands in detail.

My advice to you is: Don't be intimidated by DOS. When you make a mistake, look at what you typed. Most frequently, a word will simply be misspelled. Find what is wrong with the line and try the command again. The *DOS Command Reference* is helpful for this task. Then experiment. Use practice disks for safety, but *experiment*!

ACKNOWLEDGMENTS

Que Corporation thanks the following individuals for their contributions to this book:

Timothy S. Stanley, for his unstinting efforts to make this book technically accurate and useful for its readers.

Jeff Booher, for providing product demonstrations and general technical assistance on this project.

Stacey Beheler, for cheerfully providing administrative support on this project, frequently without being asked.

TRADEMARK ACKNOWLEDGMENTS

Que Corporation has made every attempt to supply trademark information about company names, products, and services mentioned in this book. Trademarks indicated below were derived from various sources. Que Corporation cannot attest to the accuracy of this information.

ANSI is a registered trademark of American National Standards Institute.

Apple is a registered trademark of Apple Computer, Inc.

dBASE III is a registered trademark and dBASE III Plus is a trademark of Ashton-Tate Corporation.

DisplayWrite 4, IBM PCjr, Micro Channel, and TopView are trademarks and IBM and OS/2 are registered trademarks of International Business Machines Corporation.

Epson Equity is a trademark of Epson America, Inc.

FilePath, FilePaq, SCADHMD, SDADEL, SDADIR, and SDARD are copyrights of SDA Associates.

FLASH is a trademark of Software Masters, Inc.

Lotus and 1-2-3 are registered trademarks and Metro is a trademark of Lotus Development Corporation.

Microsoft, Microsoft BASIC, Microsoft Windows, MS-DOS, and XENIX are registered trademarks of Microsoft Corporation.

MicroSpell is a trademark of Trigram Systems.

MultiMate Advantage is a trademark of Multimate International, an Ashton-Tate Corporation.

Norton Utilities is a trademark of Peter Norton Computing.

PageMaker is a registered trademark of Aldus Corporation.

PC Paintbrush is a registered trademark of ZSoft Corporation.

Pop-Up is a trademark of Popular Programs, Incorporated.

PostScript is a registered trademark of Adobe Systems Incorporated.

ProKey is a trademark of RoseSoft, Inc.

Q&A is a trademark of Symantec Corporation.

RamQuest 50/60 is a trademark of Orchid Technology, Inc.

ScanJet is a trademark of Hewlett-Packard Co.

Seagate is a registered trademark of Seagate Technology.

Turbo Lightning is a trademark and Quattro, SideKick, SideKick Plus, and SuperKey are registered trademarks of Borland International, Inc.

Ventura Publisher is a registered trademark of Ventura Software, Inc.

WordPerfect 5.0 is a registered trademark of WordPerfect Corporation.

WordStar is a registered trademark of MicroPro International Corporation.

UNIX is a trademark of AT&T.

Introduction

Using PC DOS, 3rd Edition, is for anyone who wants to be proficient in using the disk operating system for the IBM PS/2 and Personal Computer family of microcomputers. If you have never used a personal computer, you can use Part I of this book to learn the basic commands you need to know to get started. This part includes hands-on exercises that should give you confidence quickly, even though you are a beginner. If you are an intermediate or advanced user, this book will help you understand and use with ease some of DOS's more sophisticated commands, especially those introduced or extended in DOS V4.

So that there is no misunderstanding about the purposes and goals of this book, it is best to state certain assumptions. Let's look at what you should know before beginning, what materials you should have, and what is and isn't covered.

Before you read this book, you should familiarize yourself with the following: the control and editing keys, the FDISK program (if you have a hard disk system), and the EDLIN line-editing program. If you are using a PS/2 computer, you should be familiar with the configuration program on the Reference floppy disk provided with your computer. If you use a Personal Computer AT, you should be familiar with the SETUP program.

The Quick Reference or Guide to Operations manual provided with your computer is the best source of information on the editing and control keys. Additionally, each computer comes with an excellent tutorial for becoming familiar with the keyboard and layout of the computer. Before proceeding, you should know the cursor-control keys. The DOS editing keys can be learned at your leisure. Appendix F of this book contains some information on the DOS editing and control keys.

The FDISK program configures your hard disk for use. Most dealers run FDISK on your hard disk system before you receive the computer. If FDISK has not yet been run, follow the instructions in Appendix E of this book.

The EDLIN program is a text editor. EDLIN allows you to record and alter text in a disk file. EDLIN is half of a word-processing program. (The other half is the printing process.) As a simple, limited, line-oriented text editor, EDLIN is acceptable. But when compared to other programs, such as WordPerfect® 5, DisplayWrite™ 4, WordStar® 5.0, or Multi-Mate Advantage™, EDLIN is rather pale.

1

You will need a text editor later in this book, starting with Chapter 13. If you want to use EDLIN, read the tutorial in your DOS manual. If you use a word-processing program, use the ASCII text mode, which may also be called the nondocument or programmer mode. Some text editors store and manipulate the characters differently in document and ASCII modes. The text to be used by DOS should always be written in ASCII mode.

What You Should Have

To use this book most effectively, you will need the following:

- Your computer system, connected and working

- The floppy disks provided with your copy of DOS

- Several blank floppy disks, labels, and, if you are using 5 1/4-inch floppy disks, the accompanying protective envelopes

Versions of DOS Covered by This Book

DOS V3 and V4 are covered in this book. When DOS commands work differently between DOS V2 and DOS V3, or between DOS V3 and DOS V4, the differences are mentioned in the chapters. Significant differences in commands between the various versions of DOS after V3 are also mentioned.

Most screen displays in the book are derived from DOS V3.3 programs, using a PS/2 Model 60. Where there is a significant difference in the display with V4, we use that version's screen image. Minor changes are shown on-screen only when they are relevant. (DIR displays a disk serial number with DOS V4 and later, for example.) If you are using a version of DOS other than V3.3 or V4, you may see slight variations in the wording and capitalization of messages on the screen. DOS V4, in particular, has a host of new error messages that say much the same thing as in earlier editions of DOS, but in a different (albeit more complete) manner.

Also, because of the difference in the floppy disks used on the PS/2, Personal Computer AT, and other systems, what you see on your screen may occasionally differ from what the book shows. Be assured that significant differences are explained. The others are cosmetic.

What Is Covered in This Book

Chapter 1 introduces DOS, presents fundamental instructions for getting started, and provides for hands-on practice. You also learn how to start DOS and stop running programs. In Chapter 2 you make working copies of the DOS floppy disks.

Chapter 3 is for DOS V4 users, and shows them how to use the new SELECT program to start up DOS for the first time.

Chapter 4 introduces you to the DOS V4 Shell. You'll learn about how the menus work and other basic techniques for using this important new feature.

Preparing floppy disks and copying files are the topics discussed in Chapter 5. Chapter 6 explains basic DOS concepts and operations, such as getting a list of files, freezing the video screen, naming files, and running DOS commands.

Chapter 7 covers four common operations: copying files, erasing files, changing file names, and copying complete floppy disks. Chapter 8 explores the different parts of DOS and discusses how DOS devices work. Chapter 9 examines floppy disk drives and floppy disks. Chapter 10 examines hard disks and discusses how DOS subdivides and uses all types of disks. Chapter 11 covers naming disk drives and files.

Chapters 12 and 13 cover DOS features borrowed from the UNIX operating system. Chapter 12 discusses the redirection and piping of input and output. Chapter 13 introduces the issue of using hierarchical directories to organize your disks. Chapter 14 expands the concepts of hierarchical subdirectories and shows how to use various DOS commands with subdirectories.

Chapter 15 introduces batch files, which can put DOS to work for you. Chapter 16 examines special commands that can be used with batch files.

Chapter 17 begins the section on customizing DOS. It discusses in detail the CONFIG.SYS file and shows you how to configure the system automatically each time your computer starts. Chapter 18 discusses using DOS in languages other than English. And Chapter 19 shows you how to customize the DOS Shell.

Chapter 20 presents more information on the COPY command and information on the XCOPY command added with DOS V3.2. Chapters 21 and 22 cover the DOS Shell for DOS V4 in more detail. Chapter 23 discusses how to recover a flawed file and presents ways to control your equipment and printer with MODE and PRINT.

The vital subjects of backing up and restoring the hard disk are examined in Chapter 24. Chapter 25 describes four DOS commands that make the hard disk more convenient and faster to use. Chapter 26 presents guidelines on moving information between systems that use different types of floppy disks. Chapter 27 provides a quick summary of the differences between DOS V3.3 and V4. Chapter 28 reviews some of my favorite programs and offers some thoughts on using your computer.

The final section of the book is the *DOS Command Reference*, which lists all DOS commands in alphabetical order and shows the correct phrasing of the command line. The *Command Reference* is a valuable tool for quickly locating and correctly using any DOS command.

What Is Not Covered

PC DOS has so many aspects that no book can be a tutorial on learning DOS, a DOS reference guide, and a system programmer's guide, all at the same time. For this reason, several subjects are omitted from this book:

- EDLIN (the DOS line editor), DEBUG (an assembly language debugger), and LINK (a program linker)

- The Configuration and SETUP programs for the PS/2 and Personal Computer ATs

- An explanation of the ANSI control codes listed in Appendix D

- The DOS function calls and other technical information about DOS

- The writing of device drivers

Most of this information is important to programmers. If you do not program, or if you program only in a higher-level language like BASIC, the absence of this information will not matter to you. If you would like more information on the programming aspects of DOS, see the DOS Technical Reference manual from IBM or the *DOS Programmer's Reference* published by Que Corporation.

Part I

A Short Course on DOS for New Users

Includes

Using DOS the First Time
Copying Disks (DISKCOPY)
Using the DOS V4 SELECT Program
Introduction to the DOS V4 Shell
Preparing Disks and Copying Files
Learning Basic DOS Commands

1

Using DOS the First Time

DOS is the acronym for *disk operating system*. An operating system is a collection of programs that gives control of a computer's resources to the computer's user. These resources are all elements that make up the computer system, including the keyboard, display, printer, and modem. A disk operating system is the software that controls these elements as well as the computer's disk drives for storing and retrieving programs and data.

Introducing DOS

Anyone who uses a personal computer should have some working knowledge of DOS. What you need to know depends on what you want to do with the computer. You may want to know only how to start DOS and issue one or two commands that will get you started using a favorite word-processing program or spreadsheet. Or you may use your computer so much that you need some understanding of all the commands and how they work. Most people fall somewhere in between.

What should you know about DOS? This question has no exact answer. The amount of knowledge you need depends on the use of your computer. All computer users need some fundamental knowledge: how to prepare floppy disks for use, get a list of files on a disk, copy and erase files, and perform other common computer operations. If you can't do these basic things, you'll have to depend on others to do them for you. You will frequently find that outside aid is not always available or reliable and wish you had learned more of your computer's operating system. Even if you plan on using DOS V4's Shell almost exclusively, you'll still need to know something about DOS in order to perform these tasks efficiently. Very few users remain completely unfamiliar with DOS for long.

If you use your computer extensively, or if others depend on your knowledge of computers, you need to know more. Knowing how files are stored on a disk, finding the amount of free space on a disk, establishing and using hierarchical directories, redirecting input and output, and setting up configuration and batch files will be important to you. If you fall into this "frequent user" or "frequent helper" category, you should read about all the features and commands of DOS.

7

DOS has many commands and functions. Fortunately, you are not obligated to use all of them; nor do you need to learn every aspect of each command you use. The first time you encounter a new command, just try to remember its basic function. Later you can return to this book and learn more about the command. The *DOS Command Reference*, Part VI of this book, will be especially helpful as you gain more experience with your computer.

Learning DOS is a circular process. Often, before you can learn one thing, you need to learn something else. But don't be alarmed: DOS is not complicated. As you progress, each piece of DOS falls into place, and you will begin to master the commands you use.

I am a firm believer in learning by doing. I am also an eager person. If you are a new-comer to DOS and are like me, you may want to leapfrog the first few sections of this chapter and immediately try the hands-on exercises. As you do the exercises, be certain to read carefully each step as you work along with the computer—not only in this chapter, but in the next three chapters as well. If you don't, you may miss some small detail, and things may not work the way they should.

This chapter concentrates on the traditional method of starting DOS, a method that can be used for all DOS versions. Chapter 3 explains the optional method of installing DOS V4. This chapter and the next six have hands-on sessions. If you have just started using your computer, go through each chapter step-by-step. If you have already used your computer and are comfortable with it, move on to Chapter 8 for a discussion of how DOS works.

Knowing Your Disk Drives

Before starting out, we'll take a brief tour of your computer and become acquainted with the disk drives. We'll also take a brief look at the floppy disks you use.

Depending on the type of computer you own, you may have one or more floppy disk drives, and one, two, or no hard disk drives. You'll need to know what kind of disk drives you have before you can do the exercises in this chapter and in the next several chapters. The discussion in the next section is limited to floppy disk drives. Hard disk drives are covered in Chapter 10.

Kinds of Floppy Disk Drives

IBM PS/2 computers and IBM Personal Computers and compatibles use two basic types of floppy disk drives: microfloppy and minifloppy. Both types of disk drives use different kinds of disks, come in different capacities, and are used on different computers.

Microfloppy disk drives use 3 1/2-inch floppy disks. These disks each come in a hard plastic shell that measures about 3 1/2 inches by 3 3/4 inches. Microfloppy disks are slightly rectangular, rather than square, so that you can't accidentally insert them side-ways. Additional features of the design prevent you from using disks upside down or backwards. You may be able to insert a microfloppy disk incorrectly, but it will only "click" into place when properly mounted in the disk drive. The designers paid a great deal of attention to making microfloppy disks as foolproof as possible.

Microfloppy disk drives come in two capacities: 720 kilobytes (K) and 1.44 megabytes (M). (A *kilobyte* is roughly a thousand characters; a *megabyte* is roughly a million characters. These terms are described further in Chapter 5.) PS/2 Models 25 and 30, the PC Convertible, and many compatible computers have 720K disk drives. Other PS/2 models have 1.44M disk drives. Figure 1.1 shows a typical microfloppy disk drive.

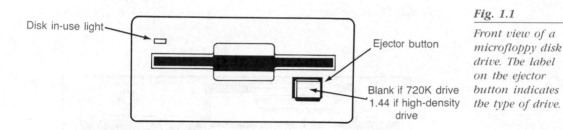

Disk in-use light

Ejector button

Blank if 720K drive
1.44 if high-density drive

Fig. 1.1

Front view of a microfloppy disk drive. The label on the ejector button indicates the type of drive.

To verify the capacity of the disk drive on your PS/2 computer or PC Convertible, look at the blue button on the disk drive. If the button is blank, the disk drive is a 720K disk drive. If you see *1.44*, the drive is a 1.44M disk drive.

Minifloppy disk drives use 5 1/4-inch floppy disks that come in soft plastic envelopes about 5 1/2 inches square.

Minifloppy disk drives come in two forms: *full-height* and *half-height*. The IBM Personal Computer and older IBM PC XT machines use full-height disk drives with a black faceplate. Unless you have a very old PC, the capacity of the drive is 360K. Figures 1.2 and 1.3 show full-height minifloppy disk drives.

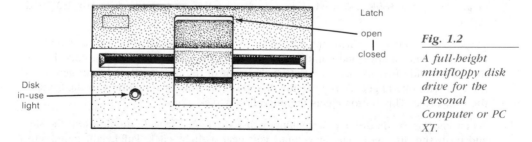

Latch

open
|
closed

Disk in-use light

Fig. 1.2

A full-height minifloppy disk drive for the Personal Computer or PC XT.

Other PCs and compatibles use half-height disk drives—so named because the disk drive is one-half the height of a full-height disk drive. The PC*jr*™, PC XT™, and PC XT™ 286 have half-height drives with a black faceplate. You'll see a tan faceplate on Personal Computer ATs, on external half-height minifloppy disk drives used with the PC Convertible, and on PS/2 computers (see fig. 1.4).

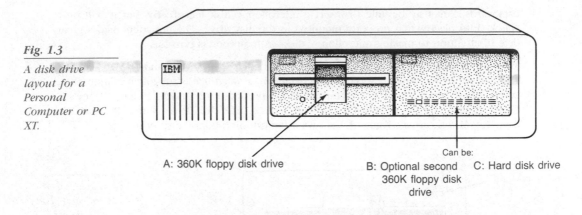

Fig. 1.3

A disk drive layout for a Personal Computer or PC XT.

A: 360K floppy disk drive

Can be:

B: Optional second 360K floppy disk drive   C: Hard disk drive

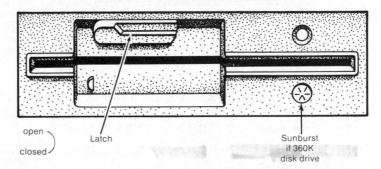

Fig. 1.4

A half-height minifloppy disk drive for the Personal Computer family.

open
closed

Latch

Sunburst if 360K disk drive

Half-height disk drives come in two capacities: 360K and 1.2M HC (high capacity). The PC*jr* and PC XT half-height drives have a capacity of 360K. The PC XT 286, some later models of the PC XT, and the Personal Computer AT use both 360K disk drives and 1.2M high-capacity disk drives. To determine the disk drive capacity of these machines, look for a sunburst symbol on the bottom right of the faceplate. If you see one, the half-height drive is a 360K disk drive. If you do not see the symbol, the drive is a 1.2M HC disk drive.

There are a couple of slight differences in the way you insert disks into and remove them from microfloppy and minifloppy disk drives. To insert a disk into a microfloppy disk drive, slide the disk into the slot on the front of the disk drive and push gently on the disk with one finger. To remove the disk, push the blue or red button on the front of the disk drive. This button ejects the microfloppy disk.

When you insert the disk into a minifloppy disk drive, gently slide the disk into the slot and push the disk with one finger until you hear a slight click. Full-height minifloppy disk drives have a latch located on the top side of the drive. You gently push the latch down to secure a floppy disk. To remove the disk, place your finger under the latch and gently flip the latch up.

Half-height disk drives have a handle rather than a latch for securing the floppy disk in the drive. To close the drive, gently turn the handle down. Turn the handle up to release the disk.

Most half-height disk drives use a spring that pops the disk about half an inch out of the disk drive when you turn the handle up. To remove disks from this kind of drive, simply pull gently. For half-height drives without a spring, and for full-height disk drives, reach into the recessed front plate, grasp the disk between your thumb and forefinger, and pull.

Disk drives with a spring have one peculiarity. If you have just inserted a disk, you can remove it only by closing and opening the handle. There is no place to grasp the disk while it is in the disk drive.

Drive Names

Each disk drive has a name. The name is a single letter of the alphabet, followed by a colon (:)—for example, A: is the name of drive A. If you have more than one floppy disk drive housed in the computer, and your floppy disk drives are placed side by side, the left disk drive is drive A. If the disk drives are stacked, the top disk drive is drive A (see fig. 1.5). The single disk drive housed inside a PC*jr* is drive A.

A: 360K floppy disk drive

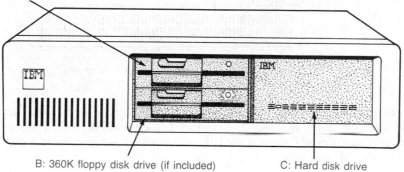

Fig. 1.5

A disk drive layout for newer Personal Computers, PC XTs, and XT 286s.

B: 360K floppy disk drive (if included)   C: Hard disk drive

The next disk drive is usually drive B. On Personal Computers, PC XTs, PC XT 286s, or PS/2 Model 25, 30, 50, 50Z, or 70 machines that have two floppy disk drives, drive B is the rightmost floppy disk drive. On the Personal Computer AT and on PS/2 Model 60 or 80 machines that have two floppy disk drives, drive B is the lower disk drive. Figures 1.6, 1.7, and 1.8 show disk drive layouts for PS/2 Models 30, 50/50Z/70, and 60/80, respectively.

Fig. 1.6

The PS/2 Model 30.

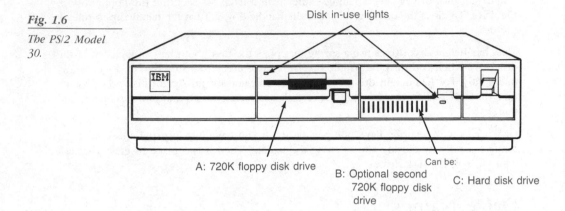

Disk in-use lights

A: 720K floppy disk drive

Can be:

B: Optional second 720K floppy disk drive

C: Hard disk drive

Fig. 1.7

The PS/2 Model 50, 50Z, or 70.

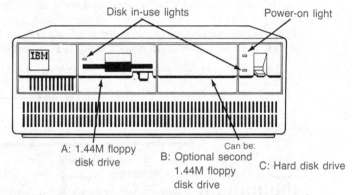

Disk in-use lights

Power-on light

A: 1.44M floppy disk drive

Can be:

B: Optional second 1.44M floppy disk drive

C: Hard disk drive

An external floppy disk drive for the PC family is usually called drive E, regardless of how many internal disk drives are used. The external disk drive for the PS/2 family is drive B if one internal floppy disk drive is used. If the computer has two internal floppy disk drives, the external drive is drive E.

The first hard disk drive is normally called drive C. If your computer is so equipped, the second hard disk drive is often called drive D. Since the hard disk drives get the letters C and D, you can see why the external floppy disk drive is usually called E. As you will see later, a particular hard disk drive also can be divided into separate "imaginary" or *logical* disk drives. In that case, your first hard disk might have logical drives C: and D:, whereas the second hard disk might be E: and F:. This type of arrangement simply enables DOS to access one or more single real or *physical* disk drives in a way that is easier to manage.

Under such a system, each hard disk is like an old brownstone that has been converted to apartments. What was once a single residence is now Apt. A, Apt. B, and Apt. C. When logical drives are used, an external floppy disk drive is called by some drive letter other than E:—perhaps G:. The drive names mentioned are common, but they can vary from system to system.

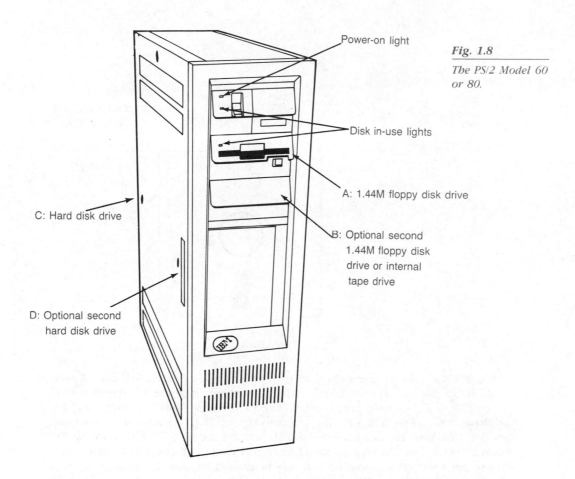

Power-on light

Fig. 1.8

The PS/2 Model 60 or 80.

Disk in-use lights

A: 1.44M floppy disk drive

B: Optional second 1.44M floppy disk drive or internal tape drive

C: Hard disk drive

D: Optional second hard disk drive

Because you do not usually need access to a hard disk drive, many hard disk drives are hidden behind the computer's front cover. This is so on the Personal Computer AT and PS/2 computers. On the PC XT and the XT 286, the hard disk is the visible, rightmost disk drive.

Remember the number and type of floppy and hard disk drives your computer has. Some exercises in this book have different instructions based on the various disk drive setups.

Knowing Your Floppy Disks

Basically, there are two kinds of microfloppy disks and two kinds of minifloppy disks. Microfloppy disks hold either 720K or 1.44M of data. Minifloppy disks hold either 360K or 1.2M of data. There is no visible difference between 360K and 1.2M floppy disks. To tell the difference, you must look at the label on the box or disk. Figure 1.9 shows microfloppy and minifloppy disks.

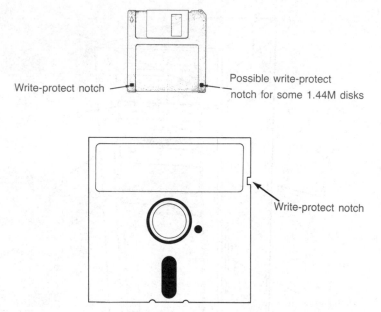

Fig. 1.9

*A 3 1/2-inch
microfloppy and
a 5 1/4-inch
minifloppy disk.*

All floppy disks, mini- or microfloppy, are used on both sides. Hence you'll normally see the letters *2S* (two sided) or *DS* (double sided) on the box or on the disks themselves. If you see *2D* or *DD* (double sided, double density), the floppy disk is a 360K disk. If a minifloppy disk has the letters *HC* (high capacity) or *HD* (high density) on the label, the disk is a 1.2M disk. For microfloppy disks, *2D* or *DD* indicates a 720K disk; *HC* or *HD* means a 1.44M disk. The only visible difference between 720K and 1.44M microfloppy disks is that a second write-protect hole may be present on some 1.44M disks.

For all floppy disks, the side of the disk with the label is "up." When you insert the disk into the disk drive, the label should face up. Or, if the disk drives are mounted on their sides, the label should face left. For microfloppy disks, the end that holds the sliding metal bar is the front of the disk. For minifloppy disks, the oblong opening where the disk itself is visible is the front of the disk. Some manufacturers place a small arrow on the front of the disk to indicate the side that should be inserted into the disk drive. When you insert a floppy disk into a disk drive, remember that the front end goes in with the label facing either up or to the left.

Minifloppy disks, unlike microfloppy disks, *can* be easily inserted the wrong way. Always be careful when putting these disks into your disk drive.

Knowing Your Keyboard

Before you work with DOS, you should know that computers come with several different types of keyboards. You should also know these three very important keys: Enter, Backspace, and Escape (Esc).

Early Personal Computers and some PC XTs have a keyboard similar to the one shown in figure 1.10. Some Personal Computer AT keyboards are like the one shown in figure 1.11. Newer personal computers (the PC XT, XT 286, and Personal Computer AT) and PS/2 computers use a keyboard similar to that shown in figure 1.12. The keyboards function in the same manner, but the layout is different. Become familiar with the position of the keys discussed in the rest of this section.

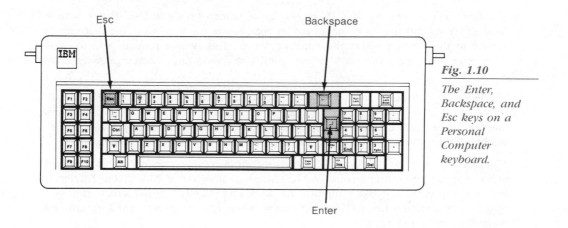

Fig. 1.10

The Enter, Backspace, and Esc keys on a Personal Computer keyboard.

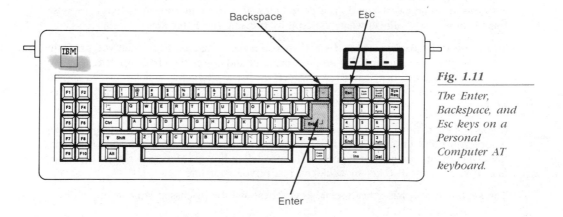

Fig. 1.11

The Enter, Backspace, and Esc keys on a Personal Computer AT keyboard.

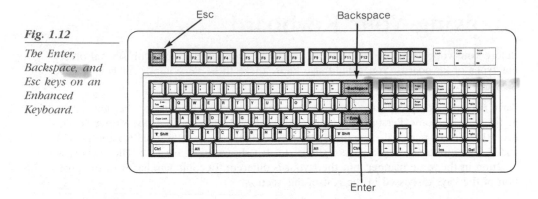

Fig. 1.12

*The Enter,
Backspace, and
Esc keys on an
Enhanced
Keyboard.*

The Enter key is the "go" key. When you press Enter, you signal DOS that you have finished typing and that DOS should act on your command or answer. The first sample session in this chapter shows the Enter key as ↵. This symbol reminds you to press Enter after you type a line. After a few times, you should find yourself pressing Enter automatically.

The Enter key is located to the right of the alphanumeric keys. On Enhanced Keyboards, a second Enter key is located to the right of the numeric keypad. The two Enter keys function identically, although the Enter key on the numeric pad does not have the ↵ symbol. Either key can be used to signal DOS that you have finished entering data.

The Enter key can be the "point of no return." In many cases, once you have pressed Enter, you cannot reenter a command or change an answer you have given. Therefore, before you press Enter, take a moment to check that your typing is correct. After you become acquainted with DOS, you will know when typing mistakes are harmless and when they can cause trouble.

Several programs and DOS commands need only a one-letter answer, such as **Y** for yes or **N** for no. In some cases, you do not press Enter after you type the single-letter response. But for now, always finish what you type by pressing the Enter key.

You can use the Backspace key (←) when you make a mistake. Each time you press the Backspace key, the cursor backs up one character and erases the character. The *cursor* is the flashing underscore that shows where the next character will be placed on the screen. After you move the cursor backward and erase a mistake, you can retype the rest of the line.

If you make a major typing mistake, you can use the Esc key. When you tap the Esc key before you press Enter, DOS puts a backslash (\) on the screen and drops to the next line. DOS ignores what you typed on the preceding line and lets you retype the entire line. If you hit the Esc key by accident, just retype your line.

The keyboard also has other special keys. These will be discussed later in the book.

Knowing What You Type

Take a moment to become familiar with the conventions used throughout this book to distinguish what you type from what the computer displays. What you should type is shown **like this**. What the computer displays is shown `like this`. For example, in this command line

A>DIR

DOS provided the A>, and you would type **DIR**.

The one symbol you don't see is ↵, the symbol for the Enter key. After you type **DIR**, you must press Enter. As mentioned, only the first sample session in this chapter shows the symbol for the Enter key. Remember to press Enter when you finish typing a line.

Getting Ready for Hands-on Practice

To practice using DOS V3 or V4, you will need the following:

- Your PS/2 computer or personal computer, plugged in and ready to go.

- The floppy disks supplied with DOS. For DOS V3, you will have either a single microfloppy disk or two minifloppy disks. DOS V4 is supplied on two microfloppy disks or five minifloppy disks. A list of the disks for each version is shown in table 1.1.

  For DOS V3, the single microfloppy disk labeled "Startup/Operating" is the disk you'll use. For DOS V3.3, the start-up disk is the one that does not read "Supplemental Programs." The DOS V4 floppy disk you will use is labeled "Install."

- One blank microfloppy disk for DOS V3 or two blank microfloppy disks for DOS V4. Those with minifloppies will need two blank minifloppy disks for DOS V3 or five blank minifloppy disks for DOS V4.

Table 1.1
DOS Disks for Versions 3 and 4

DOS Version	3 1/2-Inch Disks	5 1/4-Inch Disks
V3	Startup/Operating	Startup Operating (or Supplemental Programs)
V4	Install Operating	Install Select Operating 1 Operating 2 Operating 3

Find labels for each of the floppy disks. If you are using minifloppy disks, you also need two write-protect tabs. On microfloppy disks, the tab is built into the disk (see figs. 1.13 and 1.14). Labels and write-protect tabs normally come in the box with the blank disks.

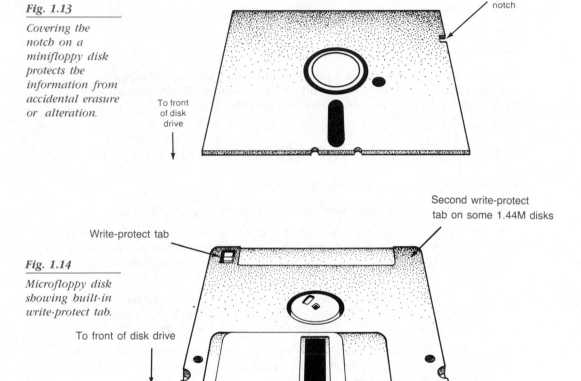

Fig. 1.13

Covering the notch on a minifloppy disk protects the information from accidental erasure or alteration.

Write-protect notch

To front of disk drive

Second write-protect tab on some 1.44M disks

Write-protect tab

Fig. 1.14

Microfloppy disk showing built-in write-protect tab.

To front of disk drive

If you have a PS/2 computer or a Personal Computer AT, you must run the CONFIGURA-TION (PS/2) or SETUP (Personal Computer AT) program before starting the exercise. (See your documentation for directions.) If you have a hard disk drive and have not yet set it up, don't worry. You don't need your hard disk set up properly until Chapter 5. When you finish this chapter, follow the instructions in Appendix E. Then proceed to the next chapter.

Differences between DOS V3 and V4

For the purposes of this first exercise, you need to know about only a few small differences between DOS V3 and V4. Versions of DOS prior to V4 started by loading the key DOS program files into memory and displaying the DOS system prompt (A>, B>, C>).

DOS V4 provides you with a choice. You can install DOS so that it will load, or "boot," in a manner similar to that of earlier DOS versions. Or you can choose to install DOS so that it loads a special program called the DOS Shell when you start your computer. In place of the DOS command line prompt (A>, etc.), your screen displays a menu, like that in figure 1.15.

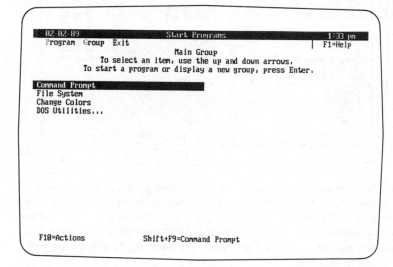

Fig. 1.15

The DOS V4 Shell.

You don't type in commands with this Shell. Instead, you highlight various menu choices with your mouse or with the keyboard's cursor keys. In addition, some of your computer's function keys have special meanings to the DOS Shell. In some respects, the Shell resembles the Presentation Manager, which is a part of OS/2® (Operating System/2). If you have used DOS before, you may also have seen shell-like operations in programs such as Microsoft® Windows or DESQview™.

The DOS Shell is simply a type of user *interface*, or way in which you interact with the computer. The Shell enables you to carry out most of the functions you can perform at the A> or C> prompt, but without the need to learn the detailed syntax of commands. For example, you can load programs, look at a directory (a list of the files on a disk), copy files, prepare disks for use, and do other tasks, all from the DOS Shell. You can set up all the programs you use so that they will return you to the DOS Shell menu when they end. So you may rarely need to access the DOS command line or see an A> or C> prompt.

The DOS Shell provides a series of *pull-down menus* instead of the DOS command line. A menu is just a list of choices or options from which you may select; it can include programs to be run or functions you may need. The DOS Shell menus provide features not readily available from the A> or C> prompt. These include the capability of moving files, sorting directory listings, and even changing the colors of your screen display. Users of "regular" DOS versions need special utilities or batch files (which contain commands for DOS to carry out) to do the same things.

A typical pull-down menu is shown in figure 1.16.

Fig. 1.16

A DOS Shell pull-down menu.

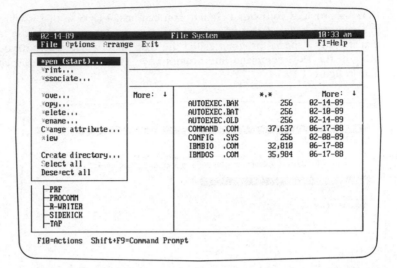

With the DOS Shell you can take advantage of the capabilities provided by a *mouse*, a type of pointing device used to move the cursor around on-screen. You can access menus and their options very quickly with a mouse. Just slide the mouse a few inches across your desktop or mouse pad to position the cursor and then click the button. For some types of functions, such as selecting text, drawing, or moving rapidly among pull-down menus, the mouse is very fast.

The DOS Shell also enables you to work with the keyboard arrow keys if you want to move the cursor around the screen and select menu items without a mouse.

Even if you decide to use the DOS Shell, you will still find some use in learning the DOS commands as described in the first section of this book. Why? First, because many functions and options are not provided by the standard DOS Shell. Second, some functions can be carried out more quickly from the A> or C> prompt. For example, you can automate repetitive tasks through batch files (those lists of commands mentioned earlier) or simply by typing a customized command line at the DOS prompt. Knowing how to use DOS outside the Shell will prove useful to you.

Finally, you may not always be stationed at your "home" computer. If you must borrow someone else's system, even if only for a few minutes, you may find that an earlier version of DOS is installed or that the computer's regular user hasn't installed the DOS Shell. For that reason, I recommend that if you have a system with one disk drive, you learn how to perform key functions on systems with two drives (and vice versa).

Learning DOS's basic commands is a good way for DOS V4 users to decide whether they want to use the DOS Shell or stick with the fast, efficient DOS command line. The following exercises, then, will interest all DOS users. Later on, you'll learn how to carry out some of these functions by using the DOS V4 Shell. Everything in this chapter deals only with the DOS V3 and DOS V4 command line interface.

Starting and Stopping DOS

The first exercise is nothing more than starting and stopping the computer, a procedure performed in the same way whether you are using DOS V3 or DOS V4. Let's begin by starting the computer. This process is called *booting,* from the phrase "pulling oneself up by one's bootstraps." The process has three steps:

1. Putting the DOS disk into the drive

2. Turning on the computer

3. Accepting or changing the date and time

The next section covers the first two steps.

Starting the Computer

Place the start-up disk in the first floppy disk drive, drive A. This disk will be either the Startup or the Startup/Operating floppy disk provided with your copy of DOS V3, or the Install disk provided with DOS V4. If you are using a version of DOS earlier than V3.3, you should use the disk that is not labeled "Supplemental Programs."

The label of the disk should face up, and the side with the sliding bar or oblong opening should be inserted first. If you are using minifloppy disks, secure the disk in the drive. Start your computer by turning the power switch on.

When you power up your computer, the system does a self-test to check whether the computer is working properly. This test is called a *power-on self-test,* or *POST.* The amount of time POST takes depends on the type of computer you have and the amount of *random-access memory* (RAM) in the computer. Users of PS/2 computers, Personal Computer ATs, and XT 286s will see numbers in the message displayed in increments of 64K or 128K—064KB OK, 128KB OK, and so on—while the test runs. The test can take from a few seconds to as long as two minutes.

After the test is finished, your computer will begin to load DOS. This process takes a few more seconds. If you have a version of DOS prior to DOS V4, you will be asked to enter the time and date. If this is not the first time your computer has been started up, someone may have installed a special file called AUTOEXEC.BAT on your computer. When a computer is started up, it looks for a batch file called AUTOEXEC.BAT and attempts to run the commands contained in it. If someone has placed an AUTOEXEC.BAT file on your start-up disk, you might *not* see the Date and Time prompts. Instead, the computer may go directly to the DOS prompt or perform some other tasks included in the batch file.

No DOS Prompt?

DOS V4 users will see neither the date and time questions nor the A> prompt. The DOS V4 Install disk is, in fact, equipped with a special AUTOEXEC.BAT file. This file is run automatically by the computer when DOS is booted. So DOS V4 does not go directly to the DOS prompt; instead, it loads a program called SELECT. This program lets you choose how you want to install DOS (either with a command line or the DOS Shell, for example). For now, however, we simply want to go to the DOS A> prompt.

To do that, DOS V4 users should follow these steps:

Step 1. *After the computer boots, you will see an IBM logo screen that says the SELECT program is being loaded. If you are using 360K disks, you must insert the Select disk when prompted before you see this screen. One line of the screen's message tells you that you can press Enter to continue or Esc to cancel. Press the Esc key.*

Step 2. *Another screen appears, with the message that you have chosen to end SELECT. To confirm this choice, press F3. The DOS A> prompt appears. If you are using 360K drives, put the Install disk back into the drive. If you press Esc when you are asked to insert the Select disk, you get the A> prompt.*

You may now follow the instructions provided for users of DOS V3.3 and earlier versions. Any time you reset the computer, you'll need to go through this same procedure. Once you have made a copy of your Install disk, you'll learn how to remove the AUTO-EXEC.BAT file from the duplicate disk. Removing that file eliminates the need for these steps, so you can boot directly to the DOS prompt if you like.

Resetting the Computer (Ctrl-Alt-Del)

If your computer is already on, you can use the key combination Ctrl-Alt-Del to reboot or reset it. Simply hold down the Ctrl and Alt keys while you press and release the Del key. It makes no difference whether you press the Ctrl key before the Alt key, but you must hold them down together before you press and release Del.

On older Personal Computer keyboards and on the Personal Computer AT keyboard, the Ctrl key is located just to the left of the A key (see figs. 1.17 and 1.18). The Alt key is just to the left of the space bar, which is the longest key on the keyboard. The Del key is on the lower right part of the numeric keypad, on the right side of the keyboard. Del shares a key with the period (.).

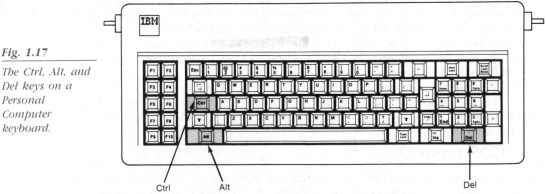

Fig. 1.17

The Ctrl, Alt, and Del keys on a Personal Computer keyboard.

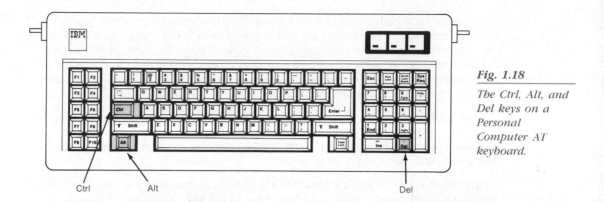

Fig. 1.18

The Ctrl, Alt, and Del keys on a Personal Computer AT keyboard.

Enhanced Keyboards (the ones that have the special-function keys at the top) provide two sets of Ctrl and Alt keys, one set on either side of the space bar. The Ctrl keys are farther from the space bar and have black letters. The Alt keys are located next to the space bar and have green letters. There are two Del keys. The first Del key is located on the six-key editing pad between the alphanumeric keys and the numeric keypad. The second Del key shares a key with the period on the numeric keypad (see fig. 1.19).

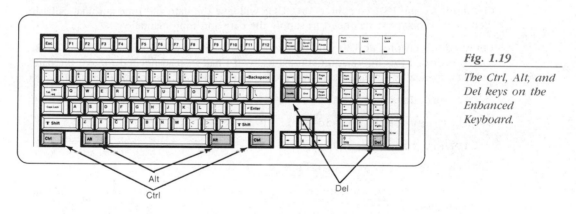

Fig. 1.19

The Ctrl, Alt, and Del keys on the Enhanced Keyboard.

The easiest way to press the Ctrl-Alt-Del key combination is to use your left thumb to hold down the Alt key and your left forefinger to hold down the Ctrl key. (If you have an Enhanced Keyboard, you'll be holding down the left Ctrl and Alt keys.) With your right hand, tap the Del key; then release all three keys. As soon as you press the Del key, the computer starts a system reset.

A *system reset* is slightly different from turning off and on again the power to your computer. Remember that when you turn on the power switch, the system does a full self-test. But when you do a system reset, the computer skips the parts of the self-test, including the lengthy memory test. Given a choice between turning the computer off and on again or doing a system reset, choose the system reset. Resetting usually takes less than 15 seconds and is safe because the computer constantly checks its memory.

You can perform a system reset as one of three "panic buttons" used when something is drastically wrong with the computer. Note that when you do a system reset, what you are working on is lost, for you are restarting the computer from scratch. But what you have saved on the computer's disks is safe.

Another panic button is jokingly named by my friends the "master reset" key. This is the computer's on/off switch, and it is the last resort. You'll learn about the third panic button (which is actually the first in order of preference) later in this chapter.

Entering the Date and Time

You should now see the A> prompt on your screen. You have an opportunity to reset the date and time of your system after the computer has been started or reset.

When DOS starts, the red light on the first floppy disk drive should come on. DOS then asks for the current date and time. If your computer has a built-in clock (the Personal Computer AT and PS/2 computers do), DOS will give the date and time automatically. If there is no clock, you will need to supply the date and time manually.

I finished this chapter at 5:30 p.m. on October 20, 1988. My system has a built-in clock and so provided this information automatically. If I had instead needed to give the date and time manually, I would have answered DOS's request in the following manner:

```
Current date is Tue 1-01-1980

Enter new date (mm-dd-yy): 10-20-88 ↵

Current time is 0:00:13.47

Enter new time: 17:30:42 ↵
```

With DOS V4, the time and date are asked for only if the AUTOEXEC.BAT file is not on the Install disk.

Notice how the current date and time are entered. The date is entered as numbers in the form *mm-dd-yy*, where

mm is the month, 1 to 12

dd is the day, 1 to 31

yy is the last two digits of the year

Note that you can enter months earlier than October with single digits, such as 6 for June, 7 for July, and so forth. You also can use 06, 07, etc. I used hyphens between the numbers, but I could have used slashes instead.

DOS is a little fussier about how you enter the time. You enter the time as *hh:mm:ss.xx*, where

hh is the hour, 0 to 23

mm is the minute, 0 to 59

ss is the second, 0 to 59

xx is the hundredth of a second, 0 to 99

You may use either a colon (:) or a period (.) between the hour, minute, and second; you can use only a period (.), however, between the second and hundredth of a second. DOS gets annoyed if you use any other punctuation.

DOS versions prior to V4 use a 24-hour clock, which is similar to military or universal clocks. To indicate the afternoon hours to DOS, you add 12 to the 12-hour clock time. For example, 2:00 p.m. becomes 14:00.

DOS V4 lets you enter the time according to either a 12- or a 24-hour clock, depending on how the time format is specified by your country code. Country codes are discussed in Chapter 18.

If you do not have a Personal Computer AT or a PS/2 computer, enter the current date and time now. Don't bother entering the hundredth of a second (*xx*), and don't forget to press the Enter key after you finish typing.

If you have a built-in clock, the date and time should be correct. If they are correct, just tap Enter after each is displayed. If the date and time are incorrect, enter the correct information. With DOS V3.3 and DOS V4, entering the date and time resets the system clock.

If you're using a version of DOS earlier than V3.3, setting the date and time does not reset the system clock. The entered date and time values are lost at power-off time. This is a DOS bug. You must use a custom assembler program or the SETUP program on the IBM-provided diagnostic disk to set the clock.

Your screen should now look something like this:

```
Current date is Thu  10-20-1988

Enter new date: ↵

Current time is 17:30:43.47

Enter new time: ↵


The IBM Personal Computer DOS

Version 3.30 (C)Copyright International Business Machines Corp
1981, 1987

          (C)Copyright Microsoft Corp 1981, 1986

A>
```

If you are using another version of DOS, the copyright notice will be different. DOS V4 users won't see this notice unless they have erased AUTOEXEC.BAT from the Install disk.

The A> prompt is the key. If your screen shows nothing at all or does not show an A> prompt (or C> prompt, if you start from the hard disk), you have a problem. If the message Invalid Date or Invalid Time appears on your screen, you did not enter the numbers correctly. You may have typed a nonsense date or time or incorrectly punctuated the date or time. You may also have used the numeric keypad instead of the number keys.

When you reboot a Personal Computer, the keypad is set in the "cursor control/editing" mode. To use the keypad to enter numbers for the date and time, you must either hold down the shift key as you type the numbers or press the Num Lock key once. (PS/2 computers intelligently start with the numeric keypad in the numeric, not the editing, mode.)

If your video screen looks similar to the one just shown, DOS has successfully started and is in control of your computer system. You have completed the booting process. Now everything you type will be handled by DOS.

Don't worry if the numbers after the decimal point are different from those in the example or if the copyright message is slightly different. You have a different revision of DOS, which does not matter for now. The first digit, however, should be 3 or higher. If the first digit is something else, this book does not match your program.

Stopping DOS with Ctrl-Break (or Ctrl-C)

Before you continue, you should learn about the third "panic button" on your computer, which, as mentioned earlier, is the first in order of preference: Ctrl-Break (or Ctrl-C). In this section, you will use Ctrl-Break or its equivalent, Ctrl-C, to interrupt the execution of a DOS command.

If you are using minifloppy disks and DOS V3.3, take the Startup disk out of the disk drive, place the disk labeled "Operating" into the disk drive, and close the disk drive door. Otherwise, make sure that the disk you used to boot the computer is still in drive A and that the door is closed. At the A> prompt, type

DISKCOPY A: A:

Then press Enter. Always press Enter after you finish typing a command. For now, type your commands in capital letters. In most cases, DOS does not care whether you use upper- or lowercase letters.

The red light on the left drive should come on briefly. Then the following message appears:

```
Insert SOURCE disk in drive A:
Press any key when ready . . .
```

Press either Ctrl-Break or Ctrl-C: hold down the Ctrl key and then tap either the Break key or the C key. (On older keyboards, the Break key is the same key as the Scroll Lock key, which is on the upper right side of the keypad. On new keyboards, the Break key is the same as the Pause key, which is also on the upper right side of the keyboard.)

Your screen should now look like this:

```
Insert SOURCE disk in drive A:

Press any key when ready . . .

^C

A>
```

Pressing Ctrl-Break or Ctrl-C initiates the "stop what you are doing" command. Whether you press Ctrl-Break or Ctrl-C does not matter; either key sequence tells DOS to stop the program that is running, exit from the program, and take control again. That's what the ^C on the screen shows.

Ctrl-Break is the first panic button to use if things are drastically wrong—if you put the wrong disk in the drive, for example, invoke the wrong command, or give the wrong file name. You should be able to stop the program by pressing Ctrl-Break or Ctrl-C. Note that this panic button does not always work. DOS typically checks the keyboard for Ctrl-Break or Ctrl-C only when it works with the video display, keyboard, printer, or serial port. You may have to press the keys several times to get DOS to respond. If all else fails, you can use the system reset sequence or turn off the power. Avoid these last two panic buttons whenever possible, however.

Here is one other item to keep in mind: when DOS says Press any key when ready..., it really means that you should press *almost* any key when ready. If you press the Shift, Alt, Caps Lock, Num Lock, Scroll Lock, Pause, Sys Req, or (on the new keyboards) Print Screen key, DOS continues to wait. The system reset sequence, however, is guaranteed to reset your system. Generally, either the Enter key or the space bar is a good choice when DOS says that it wants any key pressed.

✓ Summary

In this chapter, you learned some facts about disk drives, floppy disks, and the keyboard, as well as how to start and stop the computer.

The following are the key points to remember:

❑ The Personal Computer and PS/2 families have two different types of floppy disk drives: microfloppy (3 1/2-inch) and minifloppy (5 1/4-inch). The capacities of the disk drives are different: 720K or 1.44M for microfloppy disk drives, and 360K or 1.2M for minifloppy disk drives.

❑ When you start DOS from a floppy disk, you use the first disk drive, drive A.

❏ Three important keys are the Enter key, which informs DOS that a typed line has been completed; the Backspace key, which erases a single character; and the Escape key, which ignores the current line and enables you to start over.

❏ Three "panic buttons" are Ctrl-Break (Ctrl-C), which stops a running command; Ctrl-Alt-Del, which resets the computer and restarts DOS; and the power switch, which should be turned off if all else fails.

❏ Two frequently used DOS commands are DATE and TIME.

Chapter 2 introduces the DISKCOPY command.

2

Copying Disks (DISKCOPY)

You may have heard from your friends that making copies of disks is important. The statement is true. You should make copies of any program disks before you use the program.

In this chapter, you'll make a copy of the original disk or disks that hold DOS. If you have microfloppy disk drives, you'll make a copy of the single microfloppy disk that comes with DOS. If you use minifloppy disk drives, you'll copy the minifloppy disks that come with DOS (one or two with DOS V3.3 and earlier; five with DOS V4). First, you will make a copy of your DOS V3.3 (or earlier) or DOS V4 start-up disk. This is the disk you used to load DOS. With DOS V2 and V3, using this disk is all you need to do to run DOS from a floppy disk. For DOS V4, you will be able to load DOS from the copy of the disk you will make, but you also have an additional option. You can make a start-up disk with the SELECT program.

Copying the DOS Startup Disk

The disks you'll be copying are those shown in table 1.1 in Chapter 1.

This exercise has two sets of instructions. The first set is for users who have computers with two floppy disk drives. The second set is for users whose computers have one floppy disk drive.

The Personal Computer AT can fit into both groups, however. This computer can have one floppy disk drive, two identical floppy disk drives, or two different ones. If you have an AT with different floppy disk drives, use the instructions for a single disk drive.

Within each set of directions are separate instructions for microfloppy- and minifloppy-disk users. The separate instructions are given at the end of each section.

During this exercise, you may see an unusual message on the screen. Owners of systems that have either high-capacity disk drives (the PC XT 286 and Personal Computer AT) or

1.44M floppy disk drives (PS/2 computers) are most likely to see such a message. If you see something quite different from the screen display, go to the section "Did Something Go Wrong?" for additional instructions.

You may want to skim the directions that do not apply to your computer. Then you'll be familiar with the proper procedure whenever you use a computer with floppy disk drives that are different from your computer's disk drives.

Copying with Two Floppy Disk Drives

The instructions in this section are for users of computers with two identical floppy disk drives. These instructions are for most Personal Computer users and for any PC XT, XT 286, AT, or PS/2 owners whose computers have two identical floppy disk drives.

For the copying process, be sure that the DOS V3 Startup/Operating disk or the DOS V4 Install disk is still in drive A and that the door is closed. (If you are using minifloppy disks, use the DOS V3 Operating or DOS V4 Install disk instead.) Place a new, blank disk in drive B and close the door. Then type

DISKCOPY A: B:

You should see the following message:

A>**DISKCOPY A: B:**

```
Insert SOURCE disk in drive A:

Insert TARGET disk in drive B:

Press any key when ready...
```

The *source* disk is the disk to be copied, which in this case is the DOS V3 Startup or DOS V4 Install disk. The *target* disk is the blank disk in drive B. This disk will become an exact copy of your DOS V3 or V4 disk.

If you are using microfloppy disks, or minifloppy disks and DOS V4, you already have the right floppy disks in the correct disk drives, and you can press any key to begin copying. For minifloppy disks and DOS V3, you must first remove the DOS V3 Operating disk from drive A, place the DOS V3 Startup disk in drive A, and then press any key to begin copying. The light on drive A will go on. If you are using microfloppy disks, you will see this message:

```
Copying 80 tracks

9 Sectors/Track, 2 Side(s)
```

If you are using minifloppy disks, you will see this message:

```
Copying 40 tracks

9 Sectors/Track, 2 Side(s)
```

In 10 to 50 seconds, the light on drive A will go out, and the light on drive B will go on. Afterward, you'll see the following message:

```
Formatting while copying
```

This message tells you that DOS is preparing the blank disk in drive B to hold the information that will be transferred from the DOS disk in drive A.

You'll probably notice that the lights on the drives go on and off several times. The number of times this happens depends on the amount of random-access memory in your computer and the type of floppy disk drives you have.

After DISKCOPY has finished copying the floppy disk, you will see this message:

```
Copy another diskette (Y/N)?
```

If you are using a version of DOS and a disk format that includes additional DOS disks, enter **Y** and repeat the process until all the DOS disks are copied. After you have copied all the DOS disks, enter **N** when asked if you want to copy another.

Skim the instructions in the section "Copying with One Floppy Disk Drive" and do the steps at your leisure. The instructions for machines with one floppy disk drive work on your computer also, but those procedures are slightly less convenient to use.

Be sure to follow the instructions in the section "Labeling and Write-Protecting Your New Diskettes."

Copying with One Floppy Disk Drive

This section is for users of computers that have one floppy disk drive, such as most Personal Computer XTs, XT 286s, Personal Computer ATs, and PS/2s, or for users whose computers have two different types of floppy disk drives. Only one disk drive will be used to copy the disk(s).

At the end of this section, instructions are given first for users whose computers have microfloppy disk drives (who will make one floppy disk copy). Then come instructions for those users whose computers have minifloppy disk drives (who will make two floppy disk copies).

Make sure that your DOS V3 Startup/Operating microfloppy or DOS V4 Install disk is in drive A and that the door is closed. If you have a single minifloppy drive, insert the DOS V3 Operating or DOS V4 Install disk in the drive. Type

    DISKCOPY A: A:

You should see the following message:

```
Insert SOURCE disk in drive A:

Press any key when ready...
```

The source disk is the DOS disk you want to copy, which is already in drive A if you are using microfloppies; just press the space bar. If you are using minifloppies, remove the

Operating disk from drive A and place the Startup disk in drive A and then press the space bar. The light on your floppy disk drive will go on. Users of DOS V4 should leave the Install disk in the drive. If you are using microfloppy disks, you should see this message in a few seconds:

```
Copying 80 tracks

9 Sectors/Track, 2 Side(s)
```

If you are using a minifloppy disk drive, you should see this message:

```
Copying 40 tracks

9 Sectors/Track, 2 Side(s)
```

After 10 to 30 seconds, the following message should appear:

```
Insert TARGET disk in drive A:
Press any key when ready...
```

Take your DOS Startup/Operating or Startup disk (or Install disk, if you are using DOS V4) out of the floppy disk drive, put the blank disk into the same drive, close the door, and press a key. If you are not using DOS V4, you should then see this message:

```
Formatting while copying...
```

For DOS V4 users, if the disk is already formatted, the message will not appear.

DOS is now preparing your blank disk to hold the information from the original DOS Startup disk. After a brief period (anywhere from 20 seconds to about one minute), you may see the following message appear a second time:

```
Insert SOURCE disk in drive A:

Press any key when ready...
```

Take out the second disk and again place your DOS Startup disk in the drive. Close the door and press a key. After another brief period, you should see the following message:

```
Insert TARGET diskette in drive A:

Press any key when ready...
```

Change disks again, close the door, and press a key. These messages may appear once, or they may appear several times. The number of times the messages appear (and the number of times you exchange disks) depends on the type of floppy disk drive you have and the amount of random-access memory in your computer. Each time the messages appear, simply exchange disks and press a key.

Finally, you should see this message:

```
Copy another diskette (Y/N)?
```

If you are using a version of DOS and a disk format that includes additional DOS disks, enter **Y** and repeat the process until all the DOS disks are copied. After you have copied all the DOS disks, enter **N** when asked if you want to copy another.

Labeling and Write-Protecting
Your New Disks

You now have working copies of your system disks. You can boot DOS from the copy of the DOS V3 Startup disk or DOS V4 Install disk if you want. However, if you have DOS V4, you will see the SELECT program each time. (If you are using 5 1/4-inch disks with DOS V4, you will be asked to put the Select disk in drive A.) For now, you can prevent seeing the SELECT program by typing this command at the DOS prompt:

ERASE A:AUTOEXEC.BAT

This command will remove the AUTOEXEC.BAT file from the disk, and DOS will load just as it does for DOS V3 and earlier versions. You can still use your original Install disk to run the SELECT program later on if you wish.

Label each disk with the name corresponding to the disk it was copied from. Double-check against table 1.1 to see that you have copied all the DOS disks. Label the disks with the version number (V3.0, V3.1, V3.2, V3.3, or V4).

Always label a floppy disk after you perform a DISKCOPY operation. The label reminds you that the disk has something useful on it.

If you have microfloppy disks, turn the disk over and locate the sliding tab on the upper left part of the microfloppy disk. Slide the tab up so that you can see through the hole. This action write-protects the disk. Sliding the tab up protects the microfloppy disk from having information erased or changed.

If you have minifloppy disks, you will find a square notch on the right side of the disk (as you look at the front of the disk. See fig. 1.13). Cover this notch with a special paper or plastic tab called a write-protect tab. These tabs are usually supplied with the disk. You can use any opaque tape or label to cover the notch, as long as you are certain it won't come off easily and possibly "gum up" your disk drive.

Keep the copy of the Startup or Install disk handy. You'll need it in later chapters. Store your original DOS disks in a safe place.

Now, unless something went wrong, you can skip to the chapter summary.

Did Something Go Wrong?

If you are using high-capacity disk drives (HC disk drives) and high-capacity disks, this exercise may not work right for you. This exercise may also not work on PS/2 computers that use 1.44M disk drives and 1.44M disks. If you see any messages indicating that something is wrong (the message may say something about invalid media or about track 0 being bad), press the Ctrl-Break sequence when DOS asks you to place a new disk in drive A. To do this exercise properly, you need to begin the copying exercise again, using 360K or 720K disks.

Other potential error messages may be one of the following:

```
Unrecoverable read error on drive A

Unrecoverable write error on drive A

Unrecoverable write error on drive B
```

The next line of the error message will state the side and track of the error. If you see the first message, either your DOS disk is bad, or the drive may be faulty. Stop DISKCOPY by pressing the Ctrl-Break sequence. Take the disks to another computer and try the exercise again. If the exercise works, your disk drive probably has problems. If the exercise still does not work, your copy of DOS is probably faulty. Either way, see your dealer about the problem.

If you see the second or third error message (about a write error), the blank disk you are using may be bad, or your disk drive may be faulty. Most likely, the problem is the disk.

Press the Ctrl-Break sequence to stop the program. Repeat the DISKCOPY directions for the kind of disk you are copying. If you are using two disk drives, before you start, remove and reinsert the floppy disk in drive B. Sometimes a disk does not sit properly on the spindle. Reinserting the disk may correct the problem.

If you get the same error message, repeat the exercise with a different blank disk. If this tactic works, the first disk is bad and should be replaced. If the tactic does not work, you probably have a disk drive problem. Check with your dealer to have the drive repaired.

Summary

In this chapter, you used the DISKCOPY command to make working copies of your original DOS disks. Remember that you use the DISKCOPY command to copy only floppy disks.

Chapter 3 shows you how to set up your system if you have DOS V4.

3

Using the DOS V4
SELECT Program

DOS V4 includes some features designed to make using the operating system easier than in earlier versions of PC DOS. Although the new DOS Shell user interface has received the most attention, other key enhancements are significantly different. If you have DOS V3, you will get a taste in this chapter of what lies ahead if you elect to upgrade to V4.

In this chapter you'll learn about one enhancement of DOS V4—the new start-up procedure for first time users. If you completed the boot-up exercise in Chapter 1, you found that the disks supplied with DOS V4 don't boot directly to the A> prompt, as do disks that come with earlier versions of DOS. Instead, you saw an IBM logo screen and, if you pressed Enter, a Welcome screen that introduced you to the SELECT program. You saw how to bypass this program and go to the DOS A> prompt.

SELECT is a utility that will help you install DOS. SELECT either creates floppy disks you can use to boot from your floppy disk drives (much like DOS V3) or copies DOS to your hard disk. We concentrate on creating a bootable floppy disk in this chapter.

Why Do You Need SELECT?

If you have used versions of DOS prior to V4, you might wonder why an installation program like SELECT is needed at all. For the knowledgeable user, creating a bootable DOS floppy disk is easy enough.

But if you are a new user to DOS, you are more likely to wonder why such a handy utility was seven years in the making! After all, as a new user, you are faced with that cryptic A> prompt when booting your computer for the first time. If you performed the exercises in Chapter 2, you saw that copying the DOS disks required quite a few steps. DOS V4 takes care of all that for you. And, SELECT makes the considerably more complex hard-disk installation procedure just as easy.

Strictly speaking, SELECT is not an all-new utility. With DOS V3, you could employ SELECT to prepare a floppy disk for use with various "country" codes and keyboard combinations. If you had no need to change to a different country code, however, you probably never had occasion to use SELECT. Prior to DOS V3.3, SELECT worked only with floppy disks.

Special Note for OS/2 Users

This chapter shows you how to install DOS V4 to a floppy disk. If you have OS/2 installed on your hard disk, you may want to use these instructions to create a bootable DOS V4 floppy disk. Then, you'll be able to use OS/2 and DOS V4 interchangeably. To start OS/2, boot from your hard disk as usual. To start DOS V4, use the floppy disk you'll create in the exercise that follows. You should also know that some vendors of computers (other than IBM) have implemented a "dual boot" feature that allows both OS/2 and DOS to reside on a single hard disk in bootable form. The system "defaults" to one mode if you do not tell it to boot the other.

Starting SELECT

As you create a bootable disk with SELECT, the program asks you to make some decisions. These choices can affect how efficiently your computer uses DOS, as well as which DOS V4 features are available to you. Don't be alarmed: the decisions you make are not permanent. As you learn more about DOS and how you want to use it, you can modify the set-up, or *configuration*, of DOS.

To do this exercise, you need the following:

- Your computer, turned on and operating.

- The floppy disks supplied with DOS V4. For systems using 3 1/2-inch drives, you will have two 720K floppy disks, labeled "Install" and "Operating." Systems using 5 1/4-inch drives will have five floppies, labeled "Install," "Select," "Operating 1," "Operating 2," and "Operating 3."

- Blank floppy disks. If you have 3 1/2-inch, 720K disk drives, you will need two blank disks, labeled "Startup" and "Shell". If you have a 1.44M drive, you'll need a single high density disk labeled "Startup/Shell". For 360K or 1.2M floppy drives, you will need four blank disks: "Startup," "Shell," "Working 1," and "Working 2."

Insert the DOS 4.0 disk labeled "Install" in drive A and boot your computer. If the computer is already turned on, press Ctrl-Alt-Del as you did in the exercise in Chapter 2. If you have 5 1/4-inch disks, remove the Install disk when prompted to, insert the SELECT disk, and press Enter. If you are using 5 1/4-inch disks, you will have to reinsert the "Install" disk.

At this point, you'll see the opening IBM screen, which displays the IBM copyright notice and instructs you either to press Enter to continue, or Esc to cancel. Press Enter and a screen like the following appears:

```
                         Welcome

Welcome to DOS 4.00 and the SELECT program. SELECT will
 install DOS 4.00 on your fixed disk or diskette.
If you install DOS 4.00 on a diskette, the number of
blank diskettes you need depends on the type and
capacity of your diskette drive:

Drive Type (Capacity)        Number of Diskettes

    5.25Inch Drive (360KB)      four 5.25   (360KB)
    5.25Inch Drive (1.2MB)      four 5.25   (360KB)
    3.5Inch Drive (720KB)       two 3.5     (1MB)
    3.5Inch Drive (1.44MB)      one 3.5     (2MB)

If you install DOS 4.00 onto a fixed disk, you need
one blank diskette:

    5.25Inch Drive              one 5.25    (360KB)
    3.5Inch Drive              one 3.5    (1 or 2MB)

       Press Enter (↵) to continue or Esc to Cancel
-------------------------------------------------------------
       Enter      Esc=Cancel
```

Note that even if your computer has 1.2M disk drives, the DOS V4 SELECT program requires you to have 360K floppy disks available to produce the bootable disk. Ignore the second half of the screen for now. We'll deal with hard disks later.

Press Enter, and you see the Introduction screen to SELECT, which lists the various special key assignments used within the program. That screen looks like this:

```
Introduction

As you view the SELECT displays, you will be asked to make a
choice or type an entry. If you are uncertain about what to
choose or type, you can accept the predefined choice or press the
F1 help key for more information about an item.

You will be using these keys in the SELECT program:

    Enter            To proceed to the next step.
    Esc              To cancel the current display.
    Tab              To move to the next entry field.
    PgUp/PgDn        To scroll information one page at a time.
    Up/Down Arrow    To move the highlight bar to the next item.
    F1               To view the help information.
    F3               To exit SELECT.
    F9               To view key assignments while viewing help.
    Left/Right Arrow To scroll data fields horizontally
                          to the left or right.
```

```
You can press Enter, Esc and the F1 keys when they appear on the
display.

----------------------------------------------------------------

Enter    Esc=Cancel
```

Keep this page handy as you run SELECT in case you want to use these special keys.

The following instructions show selected screens that are displayed as you run the SELECT program. You should keep this book next to your computer as you do the exercise so that you may enter the information requested.

Choosing a Configuration

The next two screens allow you to specify configuration information that DOS will use to set up your system. You don't need to know what the functions or parameters are at this time. They will be explained later. In the Specify Function and Workspace screen, you'll be asked to choose from among three options:

1. Minimum DOS function; maximum program workspace

2. Balance DOS function with program workspace

3. Maximum DOS function; minimum program workspace

Are you puzzled? DOS V4 has been so simple to use up until this point; now you are asked to make a major decision that apparently can have some significant impact on how your system functions. Don't worry. All SELECT has asked is whether you would prefer to set up your system so that some of DOS' specialized functions are enabled, or whether you would prefer to have those functions disabled.

The specific functions include utility programs that can make your system run a tiny bit faster. If you do not enable these DOS functions, more of your computer's memory will be available to run larger programs. Additional memory will also be spared for programs like Lotus® 1-2-3®, which functions better with more memory.

Choosing Option 1 provides you with the maximum amount of free memory. Since DOS V4 uses about twice as much memory as DOS V3.3 (128K), you may need to specify Option 1 to run some of your memory-hungry programs. Lotus 1-2-3, dBASE IV™, and Ventura Publisher® (especially Version 2.0) all can use as much DOS memory as you can provide. In fact, some of these programs may not run under DOS V4 at all if you allocate too much memory to DOS functions or add-on programs. Selecting Option 1 should leave you about 564K of memory free for your applications.

Option 2 enables some of the special DOS functions and leaves a little less memory free—approximately 548K. You can select this option if you don't plan to load up with other programs that permanently grab their own share of memory. The desktop utility SideKick is a typical example of such a program.

Option 3 enables all of the special DOS features, leaving you with about 534K of free memory. This still may be enough for your applications. The only sure way is to try and run each of them and see what happens.

Remember, you can add DOS functions at any later time, either by running SELECT again or by adding statements to a special file (CONFIG.SYS) that is described in Chapter 17.

Once you have chosen your DOS/memory balance, you can proceed to the Select Country and Keyboard menu, which shows you the predefined country (usually United States) and predefined keyboard (None; no special keyboard). You may either accept the predefined country and keyboard or specify a different country and keyboard.

Unless you work extensively in a language other than English, you can accept the predefined country and keyboard. Chapter 18 explains how to determine what other combinations you might need under other circumstances.

Choosing Drive and Printer Information

The next two SELECT screens let you specify where you want to install DOS V4. You may choose between drive C (usually the hard disk) and drive A (the first floppy disk). For this exercise, we will practice installing DOS V4 on a floppy disk, so select Option 2 (drive A).

SELECT will next ask how many printers you have. You can specify from none up to seven. You can only specify as many printers as you have ports. The ports are LPT1, LPT2, LPT3, COM1, COM2, COM3, and COM4. Most users will specify one printer or perhaps two: a letter-quality and a draft-quality printer. For each printer you want to indicate, you can choose from the list that is displayed as SELECT runs.

These options probably cover every printer you might use. If you have an IBM printer and know its model number and whether it is connected to a serial or parallel port, you may select the appropriate option above. If you have another type of printer, you can choose either Other Parallel Printer or Other Serial Printer, depending on the port the printer is connected to. Consult your printer manual to determine which type you have. You need to know this information because for each printer you select you must tell SELECT which port it is attached to.

Once you have entered your printer type, SELECT will give you one last chance to accept or change the current configuration and continue with the installation of DOS V4. The items you can change include code page switching, extended display support, GRAFTABL support, GRAPHICS print screen support, DOS Shell, and RAM Disk. Don't worry about these now. When you are ready to proceed, press Enter.

SELECT will next prompt you for the time and date and then copy the operating system files to a floppy disk. As you recall, you can boot DOS V4 and run it from the floppy disks supplied with DOS V4 as we did in Chapter 2. However, doing so is not a good idea. The original disks should be reserved, and you should use only the working copy that you made in Chapter 2, or the copy produced during this exercise.

When prompted to do so, insert the blank disks you have prepared. SELECT will tell you which disk to insert as the source disk (the disk containing the files to be copied) and which as the destination disk (the disk where the files will be copied to). When SELECT has finished running, you will have from one to four working disks, depending on the type of system you have. You will boot from the disk labeled "Startup" or the disk labeled "Shell." In addition, you may have to insert the disk labeled "Shell" (or, if you have 5 1/4-inch drives, "Working 1" or "Working 2") to access different DOS utility programs.

Summary

In this chapter you learned how to install DOS on a floppy disk using DOS V4's SELECT program. Some of the options for configuring your system were explained briefly, along with details on how to specify a printer.

In the next chapter, you'll learn how to run DOS V4 from the DOS Shell. As you found in Chapter 1, you can also run DOS V4 from the DOS prompt. Read Chapter 4 for an introduction to the Shell. Then proceed with the following chapters in order, so you can learn more about using your computer with hard disks and using more advanced DOS commands.

Once you understand the key features of DOS, the Shell will be even easier to use.

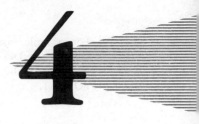

Introduction to the DOS V4 Shell

This chapter and the preceding one apply specifically to DOS V4. DOS V3 users may want to skim this chapter or skip ahead to Chapter 5. This brief introduction to the DOS V4 Shell puts the later explanations of DOS commands in perspective. Once you've read the material in this chapter, you will be able to relate command-line functions and their equivalents on the Shell menus. You will also be equipped to use the Shell options as they are presented in the following chapters.

Why a Shell?

The DOS command line you access from the A> or C> prompt is fast to use, once you have learned the intricacies of DOS command syntax. For example, you can type a command like:

DIR C:\WP | FIND "02-" | SORT /+24 > SORTDIR.WP

That probably doesn't make any sense to you—and that is exactly the point. The DOS command line is very powerful. The preceding line would create a file (SORTDIR.WP) that consists of a list, sorted by date, of the files in a hard disk's WP subdirectory which include "02-" as part of their date. However, at this point you may not know what a "subdirectory" is, nor what the "FIND" or "SORT" commands are. And what is that funny vertical bar character, anyway?

For someone who has learned DOS syntax, typing such a line can be a fast, ad hoc solution. But few of us can recall every DOS command and parameter from memory (I frequently use my own reference books to make sure I am using obscure commands properly). Various add-on user interfaces for DOS, called *shells*, have been created to avoid the problems caused by users' puzzlement at the cryptic A> or C> prompt.

As I noted earlier, Microsoft Windows is such a shell. DOS V4 provides a shell of its own that you can use to carry out many key functions. One of the good things about the DOS Shell is that it is easy to learn to use. It is also simple to modify so that the programs and functions *you* want are included.

41

For example, instead of typing complex strings of commands to copy a disk or a file, you can use the DOS Shell File System. Or, should you want to prepare a disk for use, you may access the DOS Shell Utilities menu, where you will find the program called FORMAT.

Shell Basics

Let's look at the DOS Shell now to see how it works and how it can make using DOS V4 easier.

In Chapter 3, you used the SELECT program to install the Shell automatically, creating a special file called DOSSHELL.BAT. That file is a batch file that contains the commands needed to load the Shell properly. You can load the Shell by typing DOSSHELL from the A> or C> prompt. For now, you should use the DOS Shell in this manner.

If you followed the installation instructions in Chapter 3, you now have at least two floppy disks, one labeled Startup and one labeled Shell. If you are using 5 1/4 inch disks, you also have disks labeled Working 1 and Working 2.

To start DOS without the DOS Shell, insert the disk labeled Startup into drive A and turn on the computer. If the computer is already on, you can boot by pressing Ctrl-Alt-Del.

To start DOS with the DOS Shell, follow the instructions for the kind of disk drives your computer has:

- For 3 1/2-inch microfloppy disk drives, insert the disk labeled Shell in drive A and turn on the computer or press Ctrl-Alt-Del if the computer is already on. Note that some programs you may need while using DOS are not on the Shell disk. You may have to insert the Startup disk from time to time.

- For 5 1/4-inch minifloppy disk drives, insert the disk labeled Startup into drive A and turn on the computer or press Ctrl-Alt-Del. When you see the DOS prompt, type DOSSHELL and press Enter. Utility programs that are not on the Shell disk can be found on the Startup or the Working 1 or Working 2 disks.

The Shell Menu Tree

The DOS Shell has a series of menus that are arranged in branching, tree fashion. You start with the top-most menu. That menu will provide a list of functions from which you may choose. Those choices may include DOS commands, utility programs, or even sub-menus with a list of selections of their own.

For example, the main menu you will work with in the Shell is called the Start Programs/Main Group menu. It is your jumping-off point to each of the other DOS Shell functions and submenus. From this menu, you may load programs or access additional menus. The menu of the Shell looks something like the conceptual structure shown in figure 4.1.

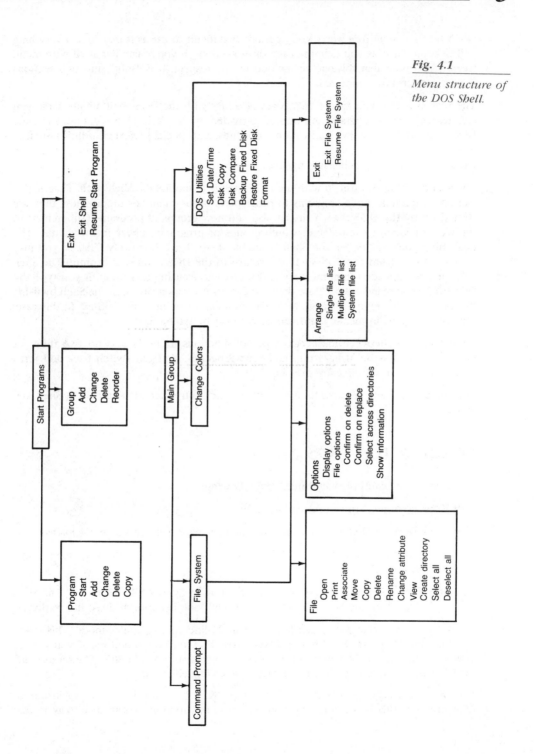

Fig. 4.1

Menu structure of the DOS Shell.

Don't let this menu tree worry you. It is not as difficult to use as it may look. Everything will become clear as you examine each of its sections. If you're familiar at all with menu trees, you'll note that this one seems odd in one respect. It is "split" into two sections that aren't directly connected.

The reason is that you can do two types of things with the DOS Shell menus. First, you can access various programs and utilities provided by the Shell. These functions include DOS commands, your own applications programs, and special DOS Shell utilities, such as the File System or the Change Colors functions. These are all accessed through the Main Group menu and the submenus beneath it.

The second thing you can do with the DOS Shell is to modify the Shell itself. That is, you can add programs, move programs to other parts of the menu, or modify how they are started up by the DOS Shell. You can also add new groups of programs (submenus) to the tree, or change the order in which groups or programs appear in the menus. The final thing you can "do" to the Shell is disable it—or leave it entirely. That is, you may choose to exit from the DOS Shell and return to the DOS command prompt. The Shell will then be unloaded from memory and no longer available to you, until you type the DOSSHELL command again. (Note that you can also "temporarily" exit the Shell by using the DOS Prompt option from the Main Group menu or by pressing Shift-F9. In this case, the Shell remains in memory and can be recalled by typing **Exit**.)

To differentiate between these two types of functions, DOS V4 sets up two different menus for them—the Main Group and Start Programs. You can switch back and forth between them at any time, by pressing F10.

The following exercise provides you with a quick introduction to the DOS Shell key menus.

Loading the DOS Shell

To perform this exercise, you'll need the following.

- Your computer, turned on and operating
- Your DOS V4 Shell and Startup disks, or your hard disk with DOS V4 loaded

First, boot your computer to load DOS. Review the instructions at the beginning of this chapter if you need to.

The DOS Shell will be displayed on your screen, as in figures 4.2, 4.3, or 4.4. The Shell can be displayed in one of four modes, which will look like one of these illustrations.

Figure 4.2 shows what the screen looks like in 25-line color graphics mode. This mode will be used by most DOS V4 users who have EGA or VGA monitors. If you have a monochrome VGA or EGA monitor, your screen will also look like this. The mouse cursor (if you have a mouse) will be displayed as an angled arrow.

The DOS Shell also operates in text mode (see fig. 4.3). If you have a monochrome or CGA monitor, this is the mode for you. You may set up your system to display in text

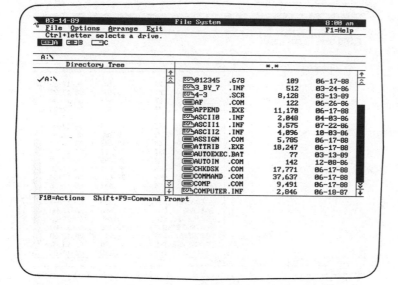

Fig. 4.2

The DOS Shell menu for the 25-line color graphics mode.

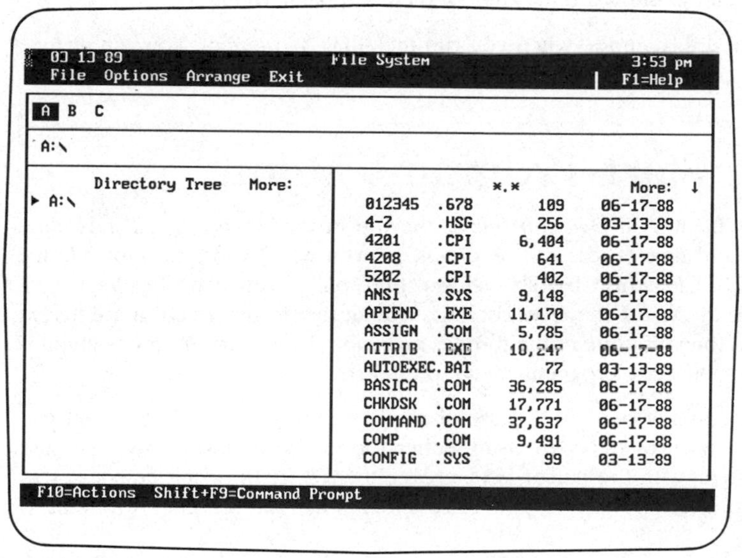

Fig. 4.3

The DOS Shell menu for the text mode.

mode even if you have a VGA or EGA monitor, but there is no advantage to this mode for you. The mouse cursor is displayed as a graphics box in text mode.

A third and fourth mode are available for use with VGA monitors—a 30-line black-and-white or color graphics mode (see fig. 4.4). These modes have the additional advantage of displaying five extra lines on the screen. The text is slightly smaller and may be more difficult to read on some monitors. However, with a good-quality monitor, this mode is

Fig. 4.4

The DOS Shell menu for the 30-line black-and-white graphics mode.

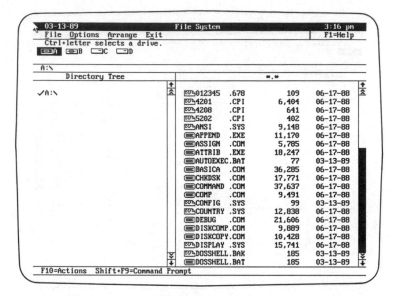

```
 03-13-89                        File System                        3:16 pm
  File  Options  Arrange  Exit                              F1=Help
  Ctrl+letter selects a drive.
  [==]A  [==]B  [=]C  [=]D

 A:\
      Directory Tree                                *.*
                                    ↑     ↑
  ✓A:\                              ☒   012345  .678      109   06-17-88  ↑
                                         4201    .CPI    6,404   06-17-88  ☒
                                         4208    .CPI      641   06-17-88
                                         5202    .CPI      402   06-17-88
                                         ANSI    .SYS    9,148   06-17-88
                                         APPEND  .EXE   11,170   06-17-88
                                         ASSIGN  .COM    5,785   06-17-88
                                         ATTRIB  .EXE   18,247   06-17-88
                                         AUTOEXEC.BAT       77   03-13-89
                                         BASICA  .COM   36,285   06-17-88
                                         CHKDSK  .COM   17,771   06-17-88
                                         COMMAND .COM   37,637   06-17-88
                                         COMP    .COM    9,491   06-17-88
                                         CONFIG  .SYS       99   03-13-89
                                         COUNTRY .SYS   12,838   06-17-88
                                         DEBUG   .COM   21,606   06-17-88
                                         DISKCOMP.COM    9,889   06-17-88
                                         DISKCOPY.COM   10,428   06-17-88
                                         DISPLAY .SYS   15,741   06-17-88
                                    ☒    DOSSHELL.BAK      185   03-13-89  ☒
                                    ↓    DOSSHELL.BAT      185   03-13-89  ↓
  F10=Actions   Shift+F9=Command Prompt
```

well worth using. The chief advantage comes when you display directories, since an additional five files can be shown on a single screen without scrolling.

DOS determines the display mode when you run the SELECT program. You can change to a different mode by modifying the DOSSHELL.BAT file, as described in Chapter 19.

Using the Start Programs Menu

The Start Programs menu is the *action bar* at the top of the screen. It can include a display of the date and time (these can be disabled if you wish) and a prompt offering help if you press F1. The action bar also shows three pull-down menu headings: Program, Group, and Exit. One of these will be highlighted; that is, displayed in a different color or in reversed tones. If none of the three is highlighted, the Start Programs menu is not active. To select the Start Programs menu, press F10.

Pull-down menus are lists of choices that are displayed beneath the headings when you select the heading. You may select by using either the mouse or the cursor keys and Enter. To select a menu with the cursor keys, press either the right or left cursor key to move the highlighting from right to left. Press Enter when the choice you want is selected.

If you have a mouse installed on your computer, you may move the cursor directly to one of the three menu headings. The cursor is a block in text mode and an arrow in graphics mode. Click the left mouse button once to select the Start Programs option you want.

Whether or not you have a mouse attached to your system, you can select a menu by typing the underlined key letter associated with that menu heading: *P*rogram, *G*roup, or *E*xit. The highlighted line will then drop down to the first item on the pull-down menu.

You may now move the highlighting with the up- and down-arrow keys or with the mouse. If you move the highlighting with the cursor keys, the selections will cycle back to the beginning when you reach the bottom of the list or to the bottom when you reach the top of the list.

To *select* one of the submenu items, either press Enter or click the left mouse button. To *exit* a pull-down menu, press Esc.

The following exercise lets you practice using the Start Programs action bar menu. For this exercise, you will select various choices without activating any of them.

To do this exercise, you need your computer up and running and the DOS Shell Start Programs/Main Group menu displayed on the screen.

In case you use a computer that is not equipped with a mouse, you may want to read the next section on using the menus without the mouse. To use the keyboard, follow these directions:

Step 1. If the action bar is not activated (none of the three selections is highlighted), activate it by pressing F10.

Step 2. Use the left- and right-arrow keys to move the highlighting to the Program heading on the action bar. Press Enter, or the down-arrow key. Or, press P to activate the Program menu.

Step 3. When the pull-down menu appears, move the cursor to the Add... selection using the down-arrow key. Or type A and press Enter.

The Add Programs screen appears. You don't wish to add a program at this time. You can press Esc to remove this menu from the screen and return to the Main Group menu.

Step 4. Now, move the cursor to the Group heading on the action bar.

You have two options here:

- You can return from the Program menu to the action bar by pressing Esc. You may then move to the Group menu heading using the right-arrow key or by typing G. Press Enter to pull down the menu.

- You can move *directly* from the Program pull-down menu to the Group pull-down menu by using the right-arrow key. It isn't necessary to first go "through" the Group heading to reach the menu.

Step 5. When the Group menu appears, move the cursor to the Add selection (either with the cursor keys or by typing A). Press Enter.

The Add Group screen appears. Because you don't want to add any groups now, press Esc.

The Main Group menu appears again.

Step 6. Now, move the cursor to the Exit menu on the action bar. You can do this by choosing either of the options in Step 3.

The Exit menu appears with two choices: Exit Shell or Resume Start Programs. Move the cursor to Resume and press Enter.

What Are the Start Programs Menus Good For?

Many of the functions you carry out from the Start Programs menus do something with one of the choices in the Main Group. For example, with the Program menu you can start a program or delete it from the Main Group listing.

To let you know which Main Group entry the Start Programs selection will act upon, one of the items in the Main Group menu will also be highlighted. If you wish to work with a different choice in the Main Group, switch from the Start Programs menu by pressing F10. Move the highlighting in the Main Group to your new choice, using the mouse or cursor keys. Then switch back to the Start Programs action bar by pressing F10 again.

The next exercise introduces you to some of these functions. But first, let's look at the special functions of some of the keys used with the Start Programs menu.

Function Keys and Special Key Definitions

F1

If you need help, press the F1 function key. You will see a series of text screens with useful information. You may page through the help screens using the PgUp and PgDn keys. Within HELP you may use these keys:

Esc	to return to the menu
F1	for instructions on how to use HELP
F9	for a list of the special key definitions
F11 or **Alt-F1**	for an index of available help screens

Shift-F9

This key combination will take you to the DOS command prompt. You may return to the shell by typing **EXIT**.

F10

As noted, this key moves the cursor to the action bar if the cursor is located in the Main Group or to the Main Group if the cursor is located in the action bar.

Now, let's go back to the Start Programs menus and use what we've learned to do something useful.

Using the Program Submenu

First, select the Program menu from the action bar. If the cursor is located in the Main Group, press F10 to move it back to the action bar; then activate the Program menu with the mouse or keyboard. The pull-down menu looks like figure 4.5.

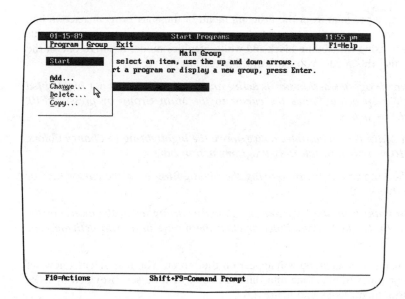

Fig. 4.5

The Program menu.

If you are using the Shell in graphics mode, some of these choices may be dimmed or blurred to indicate they are not presently available. If you are using the text version of the Shell, the underlined key letter will be replaced by an asterisk to indicate that the choice is not available.

Remember that you may choose an item by typing its key letter. You can also move the highlighting with the cursor keys and press Enter. You may also move the highlighting with the mouse and click the mouse button.

We'll explore each of the choices on the Program submenu. The easiest to understand is the Start selection.

Start a Program

This option is used to start the program or utility that is highlighted on the lower part of the screen under the Main Group. If the item is an applications program, DOS will attempt to load the program using the specifications you supplied when the program was added to the Main Group. (Adding programs will be explained shortly.)

For now, you will work with one of the four Main Group selections provided by DOS itself: Command Prompt, File System, Change Colors, or DOS Utilities.

You'll note that the DOS Utilities choice is followed by a series of dots. That is DOS's way of telling you that this selection is not so much a choice of action in itself as a gateway to another menu. That submenu will provide the list of functions (in this case the DOS commands available) that you can choose from. When you are using the Shell, menu items that are themselves headings for submenus will always be indicated by three trailing dots.

To practice starting a program from the Program menu of the Start Programs action bar, you will activate the DOS Shell's Change Colors utility first. (Note: You cannot do this exercise if you are using the 30-line black-and-white graphics mode. If you're one of the few people who use this mode, you can skim this section.)

Step 1. *If the Start Programs action bar is active and Change Colors is* not *highlighted in the Main Group below, move the cursor to the Main Group by pressing F10. Otherwise skip to step 3.*

Step 2. *After the Main Group becomes active, move the highlighting to Change Colors. Then press F10 to return to the Start Programs action bar.*

Step 3. *Select the Program menu by moving the highlighting with the cursor keys or mouse, or by typing* **P**.

Step 4. *Select Program from the Program pull-down menu by using the mouse or the cursor keys or by typing* **S**. *Press Enter or click the mouse button to activate your choice.*

The DOS Shell Change Colors menu will appear on the screen. You may select a new set of screen colors or tones from among four different color or tone sets provided by DOS. The Change Colors menu looks like figure 4.6.

Fig. 4.6

The Change Colors menu.

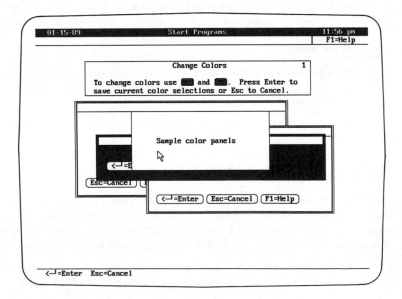

You can preview the new color or tone scheme from the panels displayed. Change from one to another by pressing the left- and right-arrow keys.

When you have chosen the colors you want, press Enter to save the selection. Press Esc to cancel and return to the previous menu. The F1 key will provide you with a Help screen. You can also use the mouse to move the cursor to the [Enter], [Esc = Cancel], or [F1 = Help] boxes and click to choose one of those actions.

Other Program Menu Choices

This chapter does not cover the other choices available from the Program menu. Adding programs to the Main Group, deleting them, or copying them requires a bit more knowledge of how DOS and applications work than you may have at this point. We take up these options in Chapter 21.

A Brief Look at the Group Submenu

The Group menu looks like figure 4.7. It functions somewhat like choices in the Program menu, but instead of adding programs you add new *groups* of programs. The Main Group may have additional groups listed as choices. When you select any of the new groups you may add, you'll be shown an additional menu much like the Main Group menu, with programs that you may add.

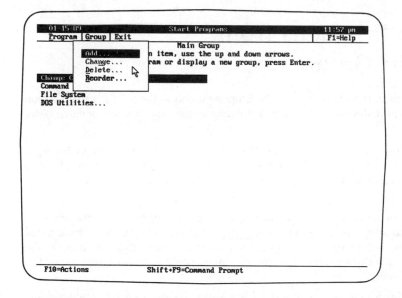

Fig. 4.7

The Group menu.

Why would you want to add groups of programs? After you have added a few programs to the Main Group, you may find that the listing begins to get long and unwieldy. You may add a group as a submenu as a way of moving some of those choices to a new menu listing. The new group can include related programs, such as games, utilities, word processing programs, and so on. You learn how to add groups in Chapter 21.

The Exit Menu

The third pull-down menu in the Start Programs action bar is the Exit menu. Two options are provided. You can either exit the DOS Shell entirely or you can return to the Start Programs action bar.

If you elect to leave the DOS Shell, you will have to reload it using the DOSSHELL command to return. This is in contrast to the Shift-F9 option that is presented along the bottom of the screen, which provides a temporary exit.

Using Shift-F9

Any time you are using the DOS Shell and you want to perform a DOS function, and then return to the DOS Shell, you may press Shift-F9. This key combination provides a DOS command prompt and a reminder that you can return to the Shell by typing **EXIT**.

When you access the DOS prompt in this way, the DOS Shell remains loaded and available for use. You can carry out DOS functions, or even load and run other programs if you have sufficient memory available.

Starting Programs from the Main Group

You don't have to start a program from the Program menu in the Start Programs action bar. In fact, you probably will rarely start a program in this way. There is a much faster method.

You can start programs directly when the Main Group menu is active. Simply highlight the selection you want to start. Then press Enter or click the mouse button. The program will start exactly as if you had chosen it using the Start action from the Program menu.

Why does DOS provide two ways of starting a program? Consider that the Program Menu is set up to allow you to perform some action with the choice that is highlighted in the Main Group below. Starting that program is logically one of those choices. So, the Start option was included for the sake of completeness. You can do anything you need to from that menu.

However, most of the time you will just want to start and run programs. DOS accepts that as a *default* action. Whenever you highlight one of the Main Group choices and press Enter or click the mouse, DOS automatically assumes that you wish to run the program. That's a much faster way of working.

Scrolling Text

You've already practiced moving the cursor around the Shell menus with the mouse. You also saw how you can click the mouse button with the cursor inside a menu box (such as the Esc box in the Add Programs screen). There is one other mouse trick to practice—scrolling text. If you do not have a mouse, you also need to know how to scroll text.

Many of the boxes and screens displayed by the DOS Shell include text. This text may be too long to show in the space allotted. If you don't have a mouse, you can see more text simply by pressing the down- or up-arrow keys to scroll the "window" to a new portion. The PgUp and PgDn keys can also be used.

However, the mouse moves freely beyond the boundaries of the window, and you may not want to take your hand from the mouse to use the keyboard controls. If you are using a mouse in text mode, you have no other choice, however. Graphics-mode mouse users, on the other hand, have a special tool to scroll text. That is the *scroll bar* (see fig. 4.8).

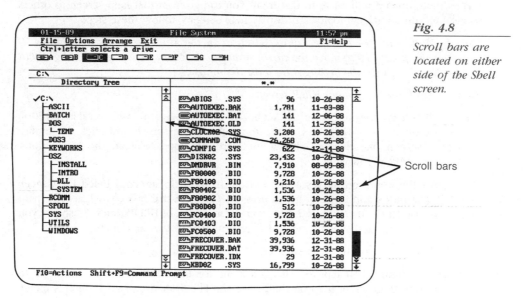

Fig. 4.8

Scroll bars are located on either side of the Shell screen.

The scroll bar is a bar at the right side of a window, as shown in figure 4.8. The bar has the following components:

- A single-line arrow box at the top and bottom. Clicking the cursor inside these boxes will scroll the text up or down one line at a time.

- A page scroll box, indicated by double arrows, located below the top single-line box and above the bottom single-line box. Clicking these boxes will move text up or down one page at a time.

• A slider box moves between the scroll boxes. You can position the cursor on this box, press the left mouse button and, while holding down the button, drag the box up or down. The text window will move with the slider.

You'll use the scroll bar extensively with the DOS Shell File System. But for now, let's put it to work in viewing HELP screens. If you do not have a mouse, use the cursor keys and PgUp and PgDn keys to scroll.

Getting Help

There is one more exercise you should complete to finish your introduction to the DOS Shell. You'll want to know how to get help from DOS whenever you have questions on how to perform a Shell task. HELP screens are readily available whether you have a mouse or not.

HELP is contextual. That is, DOS looks at the menu item currently highlighted as an indication that you are asking for more information about that selection. The HELP screen that pops up will relate to that item. You can go from that help screen to others to get help on additional topics. To display help screens, follow these steps:

Step 1. Make sure the Change Colors selection in the Main Group is highlighted. If necessary, press F10 to move the cursor down to the Main Group and highlight that selection, or move the highlighting with the mouse.

Step 2. Summon the pop-up HELP screen.

Press F1 if you are working from the keyboard. If you have a mouse, you may position the cursor on the F1=Help box at the top right of the screen and click the mouse button. A screen like the one shown in figure 4.9 appears. Read the instructions, scrolling the text if you wish.

Notice that there are four boxes at the bottom of the help screen, labeled Esc-Cancel, F1-HELP, F11-Index and F9-Keys. If you press F1 (or click that box), you'll receive help on how to use HELP. If you choose F11, you see an Index of HELP topics. F9 shows you a list of special key assignments, while Esc returns you to the main menu.

Step 3. Choose F11 or Alt-F1 to view the HELP index.

A screen like figure 4.10 appears. This is a menu for the HELP index, allowing you to choose an introduction, or help on topics like the File System or Start Programs menu. Read any of the index items you wish. When you finish with a given selection, press F11 again to return to the Index menu. Pressing Esc takes you back to the HELP screen from which you called the index.

Step 4. When you finish viewing HELP, press Esc to return to the main menu.

HELP availability will vary, depending on what menus you have on the screen at any given time. Also note that when you add your own programs later on, you can, if you want, type in HELP instructions of your own. Then, anyone accessing that program has the option of pressing F1 and receiving your special tips in the form of a HELP display.

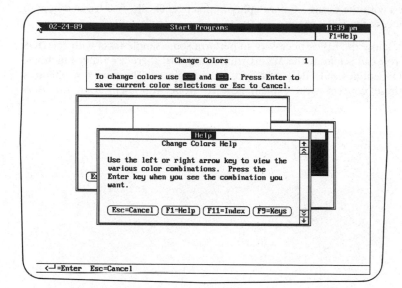

Fig. 4.9

The Change Colors Help screen.

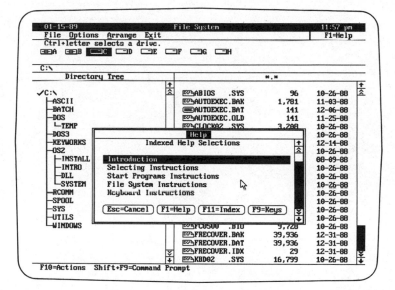

Fig. 4.10

The Help Index.

Summary

This chapter introduced the DOS Shell. You learned how to load the Shell, access HELP screens, and move from the Start Programs menu to the Main Group menu. You also saw how to move the highlighting around within menus and how to select the options you want. You worked with the Change Colors utility as practice. Finally, you learned how to scroll text and access the HELP menu.

At this point, you know the basics necessary to perform some simple tasks with the DOS Shell. However, you can see from the Main Group listing that there are other functions, including the DOS Utilities and File System yet to be explored. The next few chapters will introduce these concepts and explain how to work with them from the DOS prompt.

Preparing Floppy Disks
and Copying Files

In Chapters 2 and 3 you made copies of your DOS start-up disks, using the DISKCOPY command for DOS V3 and SELECT for DOS V4. You also learned about the Enter, Backspace, and Esc keys and about interrupting a DOS command. Chapter 4 introduced the DOS Shell.

This chapter and the next three cover other basic things you need to know to use DOS at the simplest level. These are your "survival" commands and concepts—basic DOS commands and operating techniques that all computer users must know.

You will learn how to prepare a floppy disk for use and how to copy files. Users who own computers with a high-capacity disk drive or a hard disk will make a single copy of the programs that are on the minifloppy DOS disks. Owners of computers with one floppy disk drive, such as PS/2 computers, will see that this kind of computer really has two disk drives. Before you do this copying exercise, we will quickly go over the basic commands and skills you will learn in the next few chapters.

Learning Survival Commands
and Keystrokes

There are seven commands that all DOS users must know. These commands make copies of disks and files, prepare floppy disks for use, change the names of files, erase files, show which files are located on a disk, and show the amount of space that has been used and the amount that is free to be used on a disk. "Survival" keystrokes include sequences for freezing the display and printing the contents of the video screen onto paper.

The key commands and keystrokes are listed in table 5.1. You need not memorize the function of each command or key sequence now. Just glance at the table, paying attention to what the command or key sequence does. In time you will learn the corresponding command's name or keystroke sequence.

Table 5.1
DOS Survival Commands and Keystroke Sequences

Command Function	Name	See Chapter
Copy a floppy disk	DISKCOPY	2
Copy a file	COPY	5
Prepare a disk	FORMAT	5
See the files on a disk	DIR	5
Check free space on a disk	CHKDSK	6
Change a file's name	RENAME	7
Remove a file	ERASE	7
Survival Keystrokes		
Stop a program	Ctrl-Break or Ctrl-C	1
Stop a program and reset the computer	Ctrl-Alt-Del	1
Freeze the video screen	Ctrl-Num Lock, Ctrl-S, or Pause	6
Unfreeze the video screen	Any key	6
Print the contents of the video screen on the printer	Shift-PrtSc	6
Print on the printer and on the video screen at the same time	Ctrl-PrtSc	6
Change the current disk drive	*d:* (drive letter followed by a colon and Enter)	6
Run DOS programs	*programname* (the name of the program, followed by Enter)	6

A trick to gaining control over your computer is to learn what tasks the DOS commands and sequences can do and then remember a key word in the command that performs the task. For example, if I want to copy files from a floppy disk to the hard disk, the key words I remember are "copy files." The command name COPY springs to mind. If I want to get a printed copy of the contents of my screen, I think of "printed screen." I then remember the keystroke sequence Shift-Print Screen or Ctrl-Print Screen.

Table 5.1 is a handy command list for this part of the book. Each command listed in table 5.1 is covered in Part I. You will find an expanded list of commands in Part VI of this book, the *DOS Command Reference*.

Getting Ready for Hands-on Practice

For this session, you will need the following:

- Your Personal Computer or PS/2 computer, plugged in and ready to go.

- The floppy disks used to boot your system (the copy or copies you made in Chapters 2 and 3).

- One blank microfloppy disk and a label if you are using microfloppy disks. If you are using minifloppy disks, one blank HC floppy disk (if you have an HC disk drive) or two 360K minifloppy disks, label(s), and write-protect tab(s).

  If you have a hard disk, it should be set up. If it is not, follow the instructions in Appendix E of this book before you continue.

Preparing Floppy Disks (FORMAT)

When you get a new, blank floppy disk, it is not quite ready to receive information. You must prepare the disk by using the FORMAT command.

Formatting a Boot Floppy Disk (All Users)

Everyone should try the following exercise. Later in the chapter, DOS V4 users will learn how to format a boot floppy disk with the DOS Shell. However, you will still need to know the options and parameters described in this next session. So if you are using the DOS Shell, access the DOS command prompt by pressing Shift-F9 and follow this exercise as shown.

First get the boot-up disk you created in Chapter 2 or Chapter 3. Make sure that a write-protect tab covers the notch on the upper right edge of the minifloppy disk or that the write-protect tab for the microfloppy disk is pushed up (so that you can see through the hole). Then put the disk into drive A.

If you are using microfloppy disks for this exercise, you will need one disk appropriate to the type of disk drive you have. If you have a 720K disk drive, you should have a 720K disk. If you have a 1.44M drive, you should have a 1.44M disk. Users of HC disk drives will need one HC floppy disk, and users of 360K disk drives will need two 360K minifloppy disks. The exercise will not work if you use the wrong type of disk in the HC minifloppy or 1.44M microfloppy disk drive.

Your computer should still be on, with DOS running. If it is not, turn on the computer and start DOS from your floppy disk.

To format the disk, make sure that the start-up disk is in drive A and that the door is closed. If you are using DOS V4 and minifloppy disks, you will have to put the Working 1 disk in the drive. Type

FORMAT A: /S /V

Notice how this command line is phrased. First you type the name of the command (FORMAT). Then you type the name of the disk drive that will hold the floppy disk to be formatted (in this case, A:). Next you enter the two switches, /S and /V. The /S tells DOS to put a copy of the operating system onto the disk you are formatting. The /V tells DOS you want to put a volume label on the disk. DOS V4 users may add an 11-character volume label after the /V switch; the label is separated from the switch by a colon:

FORMAT A: /S /V:MY DOS DISK

If you have DOS V3.3 or earlier versions, you will have to add the volume label later when DOS asks you for it.

The switches used with the FORMAT command are discussed in detail later in the book, but here is a brief overview for now.

Most DOS commands have options that affect the way the command works. A *switch* allows you to select an option. Two options of the FORMAT command are to place a copy of the operating system onto the newly formatted floppy disk and to place a volume label on the disk for identification. To use an option, you must indicate a switch for the option when you use the command. That way, you tell the command to do extra work or to handle things in a different manner.

To use a switch, you type a slash (/) and the character for the switch. A switch is always typed on the same line as that of the DOS command and is usually the last item typed on the line. Some switches require extra information. For now, you will use only the switch character (/) and the single character for the switch.

After you type the FORMAT command line, the red light on the disk drive goes on for a few seconds. You will see the following message:

```
Insert the diskette for drive A:
and strike ENTER when ready
```

Take the DOS Startup disk out of drive A, put your blank disk in the drive, and press the Enter key. DOS V4 users with 5 1/4-inch disks must have the Working 1 disk in drive A. The FORMAT command will not continue until you press Enter. FORMAT is one of the rare commands for which DOS wants you to press a specific key, not just any key.

After you press Enter, the red light on the first disk drive will go on again, and the following message will appear if you have DOS V3:

```
Head:    0 Cylinder:    1
```

If you have DOS V4, you will see this:

```
1 percent of disk formatted
```

You will see the numbers on the screen change constantly. For DOS V3, the number after the word `Head` flips between 0 and 1. The number after `Cylinder` starts at 1 and increases to either 40 (for 360K minifloppies) or 80 (for HC minifloppy disks and for microfloppy disks).

DOS V4 gives you a continual update of what percentage of the disk has been formatted. After 20 to 40 seconds, the line with the numbers disappears, and the following messages appear in its place:

```
Format complete


System transferred
```

Now DOS asks the following:

```
Volume label (11 characters, ENTER for none)?
```

Type **My DOS Disk** and then press Enter.

The floppy disk will spin, and DOS will tell you how much total information the disk can hold, how much space is taken up by DOS, and how much free space is on the disk. For DOS V3.3, the figures are as follows:

360K	362496 bytes total disk space 78848 bytes used by system 283648 bytes available on disk
1.2M	1213952 bytes total disk space 78336 bytes used by system 1135616 bytes available on disk
720K	730112 bytes total disk space 78848 bytes used by system 651264 bytes available on disk
1.44M	1457664 bytes total disk space 78336 bytes used by system 1379328 bytes available on disk

The top set of numbers is for a 360K floppy disk; the second set is for an HC disk; the third set is for a 720K microfloppy disk; and the final set is for a 1.44M microfloppy disk. Remember that the numbers for different versions of DOS V3 will be slightly different.

DOS V4 users see slightly different results, such as the following:

```
1457664 bytes total disk space
  107520 bytes used by system
  1350144 bytes available on disk
```

```
      512 bytes in each allocation unit
      2637 allocation units available on disk
Volume Serial Number is 3952-0BE4
```

Note that DOS V4 reports the number of bytes taken up by each allocation unit, which is the smallest cluster of information that can be stored on a disk. It also tells you the number of these allocation units or clusters available on the disk.

In addition, DOS V4 assigns to each disk a unique serial number, which it calculates from an internal algorithm. This serial number enables DOS to keep track of disks, even if each has the same volume number or name.

To understand the capacity of each floppy disk, you should know two computer terms: *byte* and *kilobyte* (K). A byte is eight *bi*nary digi*ts* (bits) and is the smallest unit of storage on a computer, holding a single computer instruction or character. For example, the word *character* uses nine bytes. *K* stands for *kilo-*, a thousand. A kilobyte is around a thousand bytes; actually, it is 1,024 bytes.

For the 360K minifloppy disk, which is normally used in Personal Computers and PC XTs, the total disk space is 362,496 bytes. Dividing 362,496 by 1,024 produces 354K. For the HC floppy disk, the total disk space is 1,213,952 bytes, which is equivalent to 1,185.5K. The capacity of 720K microfloppy disks is 730,113 bytes, or 713K; for 1.44M microfloppy disks the capacity is 1,457,664 bytes, or 1,423.5K.

The actual storage capacity of floppy disks is higher. DOS does not report on three small sections of a floppy disk that are used exclusively by DOS. The actual capacity of the first minifloppy disk is 368,640 bytes, or 360K. The capacity of the high-capacity disk is 1,228,800 bytes, which is 1,200K, or 1.2M. *M* stands for *megabyte*, which is 1,048,576 bytes (1,024 x 1,024). The capacity of the first type of microfloppy disk is 737,280 bytes, or 720K. The true capacity of the second microfloppy disk is 1,474,560 bytes, or 1,440K.

You may see one of the following messages on-screen:

```
____ bytes in bad sectors
```

or

```
Invalid media or track 0 bad--disk unusable
```

The first line means that DOS found some sectors on the disk that are bad and cannot be used to hold information. If the line stating that there are bytes in bad sectors appears, your disk is usable, but the total amount of free space on the disk is reduced by the number of bytes in bad sectors. If the Invalid media message appears, the areas on the disk that hold key DOS information are bad, and the disk cannot be used at all. If you see either message, answer **Y** to the following question:

```
Format another (Y/N)?
```

Then press Enter. You will see a repetition of the messages that instruct you to insert a floppy disk to be formatted. Do not press Enter yet. First, take the disk out of the drive, reinsert the disk, and close the door if necessary. Press Enter again. Some floppy disks that do not format correctly the first time do so the second time.

If the disk does not format properly the second time, something may be wrong with either the disk drive or the disk (most likely the disk). You can take a disk that has some bad sectors back to the dealer for a replacement, or you can use it, knowing that you will have less storage space than you should have.

The Invalid media message can appear if you use a 360K floppy disk in an HC disk drive or a 720K disk in a 1.44M disk drive. If you used the wrong type of disk, get the right type and try this exercise again. If you used the right type of disk and got this message, take the disk back to your dealer for a replacement.

FORMAT should now be asking the following question:

    Format another (Y/N)?

Answer **N** and press Enter. The A> prompt should reappear. You have now formatted one floppy disk that holds a copy of the disk operating system. Prepare a disk label. If you are using a 360K disk and DOS V3.3 or a later version, write a name like "DOS Master Startup Disk."

If you are using 360K disks, follow the additional directions in the next section. Users of another type of disk should skim the directions on formatting floppy disks without the /S switch and should then go to the section on using the DIR command.

Additional Directions for Users of 360K Disk Drives

If you are using 360K floppy disks, you need to format a second disk. You do not, however, need to place a copy of the operating system on the second disk. Place the start-up disk (or Working 1 disk, for DOS V4 users with 5 1/4-inch disks) back into drive A and type

FORMAT A: /V

Notice that the command is phrased almost the same way as the first FORMAT command, with the exception that you omit the /S switch. When you omit the /S switch, DOS does not place the operating system on the disk. You should see the following message:

    Insert the diskette for drive A:
    and strike ENTER when ready

Take the DOS Startup disk out of drive A; put your second, blank disk in the drive and press Enter. As before, the disk drive light will go on, and the message displaying the head and cylinder numbers will appear. This message will be followed by the Format complete message. You will then be asked for the volume label. Type

2nd Disk

The disk will spin, and DOS will display the statistics on how much information the disk can hold:

```
362496 bytes total disk space
362496 bytes available on disk
```

When the message appears that asks if you want to format another disk, answer **N** and press Enter. The A> prompt should reappear.

Prepare a floppy disk label, using a name like "DOS Master Operating Disk." Take the disk out of the drive and place the label on the disk. For the next exercise, you will need the first disk you formatted. Put the disk labeled "DOS Master Startup Disk" into disk drive A and close the door.

Formatting a Boot Floppy Disk with the DOS Shell

Using the DOS Shell to format a boot floppy disk is much like formatting from the DOS command line. The main difference is that you access the FORMAT program from the Shell instead of directly from the command line. The DOS Shell requires you to type the command line parameters just as you did in the preceding exercise.

To format a floppy disk, follow these steps:

Step 1. *Insert into drive A a fresh disk to be formatted.*

Step 2. *Select the DOS Utilities... choice from the Main Group menu by highlighting the DOS Utilities... selection with the cursor keys or mouse. Press Enter or click the mouse button.*

If DOS Utilities... is highlighted, you can also access this submenu by choosing Start from the Program menu in the Start Programs action bar. If your computer doesn't have a hard disk, you must leave the DOS Shell disk in drive A when selecting utilities.

The DOS Utilities menu appears (see fig. 5.1).

Step 3. *Select the Format option.*

DOS shows you a command line labeled `Parameters`. Since FORMAT is most often used to prepare a floppy disk, DOS supplies the drive name A: as a default value at the beginning of the parameter list. However, in this case, you want to add the /S and /V switches.

Step 4. *Type these switches:*

/S /V

You do not need to type the FORMAT command itself.

Step 5. *Press Enter or click the Enter box.*

If you want to terminate the FORMAT program, press Esc or click the Escape box with the mouse cursor.

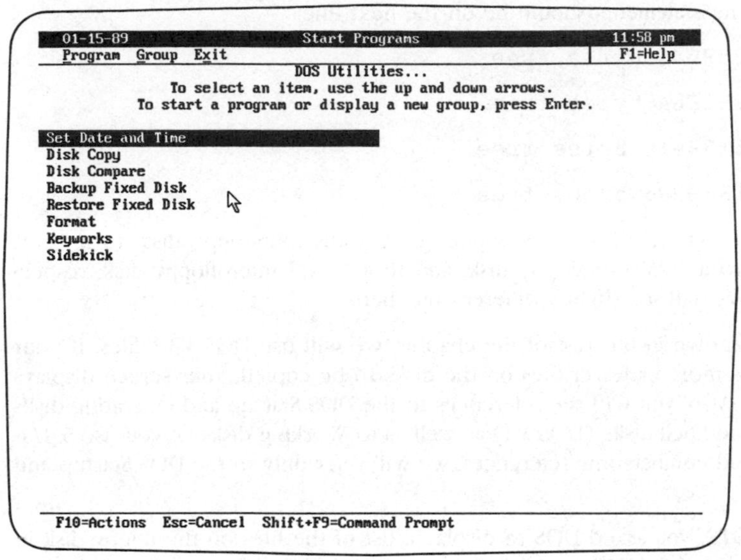
01-15-89
Start Programs
11:58 pm
Program Group Exit
F1=Help
DOS Utilities...
To select an item, use the up and down arrows.
To start a program or display a new group, press Enter.
Set Date and Time
Disk Copy
Disk Compare
Backup Fixed Disk
Restore Fixed Disk
Format
Keyworks
Sidekick
F10=Actions Esc=Cancel Shift+F9=Command Prompt

Fig. 5.1

The DOS Utilities menu.

The menus will be erased from your screen, and you will see much the same screen display as when you format a disk from the DOS command line. When DOS is finished, it will return to the DOS Utilities menu. You can press Esc to return to the Main Group menu. (If you are using floppy disks, you'll have to put the Shell disk back in drive A.)

This method is not much faster than simply pressing Shift-F9 and typing the FORMAT command from the DOS prompt. However, you will find knowing how to perform this task within the Shell helpful.

Looking at a Directory (DIR)

You can see a list of files on a disk by using the DIR command from the DOS command prompt. Or you can use the File System utility from the DOS Shell. First let's look at the command prompt technique.

Be sure that the Master disk or Master Startup disk (the one you created with the FORMAT A:/S/V command) is in drive A. Type **DIR** and press Enter. If you are using DOS V3.3, you should see the following:

```
Volume in drive A is MY DOS DISK
Directory of A:\
COMMAND    COM    25307    3-17-85    12:00P
```

One of the following statements should be on the next line:

```
1 File(s) 283648 bytes free

1 File(s) 651264 bytes free

1 File(s) 1135616 bytes free

1 File(s) 1379328 bytes free
```

The information shown on these lines applies to a 360K minifloppy disk, to a 720K microfloppy disk, to a 1.2M minifloppy disk, and to a 1.44M microfloppy disk, respectively. DOS V4 users will see slightly different numbers.

For the examples shown in the rest of the chapter, we will use DOS V3.3 files. If your version of DOS has more or fewer files on the disks to be copied, your screen displays will look different. Also, you will see references to the DOS Startup and Operating disks or to the Startup and Shell disks (DOS V4) as well as to Working disks (if you use 5 1/4-inch disks). To avoid cumbersome references, we will refer only to the DOS Startup and Operating disks.

When you typed **DIR**, you asked DOS to display a list of the files on the floppy disk in drive A. The purpose of the DIR (*dir*ectory) command is to display the files on a disk.

The first line shown on the screen is the disk's volume label. As indicated previously, this label helps you identify the disk. DOS uses the volume label in two ways: DOS displays the label when you use certain commands, and DOS uses the label to confirm your intention to format a hard disk. The label has no other special uses to DOS.

When you created the volume label, you entered it in upper- and lowercase letters. DOS converted the letters into all uppercase. When you type most names, the case of the letters does not matter. DOS usually converts the characters to uppercase.

The next line on the screen tells you which disk drive and directory path are being displayed. These concepts are discussed in later chapters.

Next, you see one line for every file on the disk. The only file now in the list is COMMAND.COM. The line shows the name of the file, the length of the file in bytes, and the date and time the file was created or last changed. The final line tells you the number of files displayed by the DIR command and the amount of disk space available.

You may remember from the discussion of the FORMAT command that a certain amount of space on the formatted disk was taken up by system files. When you used the DIR command, you saw that the COMMAND.COM file takes up 25K. For DOS V4, COMMAND.COM is a bit larger: 37,637 bytes, or 36.7K.

Is something wrong? Didn't the FORMAT command indicate that many more bytes were used by the system? Where is the rest of DOS?

Nothing is wrong. The remaining space is taken by two files you cannot see: IBMBIO.COM and IBMDOS.COM. These files hold the remaining pieces of the operating system. The files are hidden from you and do not show in the list when you ask for a directory (by using the DIR command).

Literally, there is more to DOS than meets the eye. The DIR command is covered in more detail in the next chapter. And Chapter 8 contains more information on the two hidden files and DOS. For now, remember that the DIR command displays the files on a disk and that when you format a disk with the /S switch, two additional files are placed on the disk.

Viewing Directories with the DOS Shell File System

The DOS Shell File System enables you to perform a long list of functions with your files. Accessing a directory of those files is the most rudimentary of those functions. The directory feature is a good introduction to the File System.

To access the directory, select File System from the Main Group menu. (If you are using floppy disks, the Shell disk needs to be in drive A.) DOS will read the current disk and display the screen shown in figure 5.2.

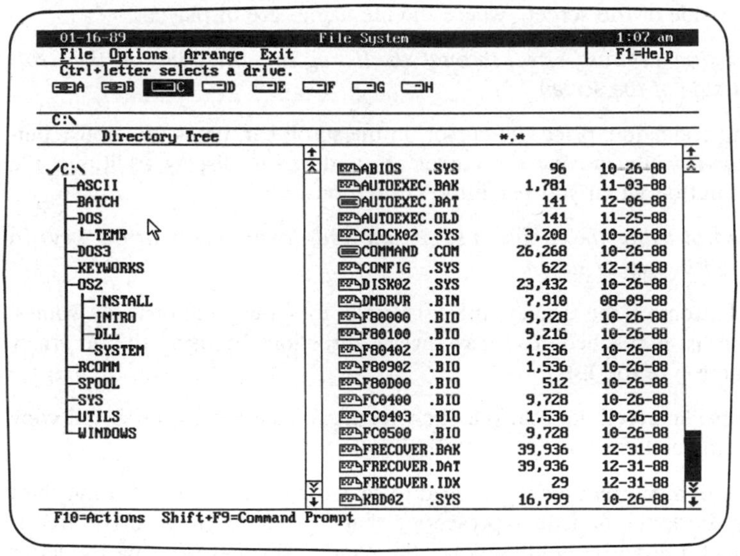

Fig. 5.2

The File System menu.

The menu displayed has four key options: File, Options, Arrange, and Exit. Using most of the features of these menus requires knowledge about files and disk structure, so we will explore those features later in the book. The display shows letters or icons (depending on whether your Shell is graphics- or text-based) representing the disk drives available in your system. The current disk drive is highlighted.

A split-screen display shows you two key pieces of information. At the left is a directory tree that shows how the files are arranged on your disk. DOS's directories and subdirectory structures haven't been discussed yet, so ignore this panel for now.

The right side of the display shows a list of files on the current disk. This list looks much like that shown by the DIR command from the DOS prompt. However, each file will have an icon or character next to it that indicates which type of file it is (if you are not using text mode). For now, you should be concerned only with the same sort of information available from the DOS command line: the file name, extension, size, date, and so forth.

In many cases, not all the files on a disk can be displayed on the screen at once. The DOS Shell provides several ways to scroll back and forth through a listing of file names. If you have a graphics-based system and a mouse, you may use the scroll bar. A *scroll bar* is a Shell icon used to move screen windows up and down so that you can view parts of an area too large to be displayed at one time. If you do not have a mouse or if you are using a text-based Shell, use the cursor keys. Before using either method, you must make sure that the file display panel is active. To scroll through a file listing, follow these steps:

Step 1. *If the action bar is at the top of the screen (if one of the menu headings is highlighted), move down to the file display panel.*

If you are using a mouse, you can simply click the mouse cursor within the area of the panel. If you are not using a mouse, use the Tab key to move the active area to the window at the right side of the screen, where the file names are displayed.

Step 2. *If you are using a mouse, scroll through the listing by "dragging" on the scroll bar at the right side of the screen.*

To use the dragging technique, place the cursor on the scroll bar, press the mouse button, and hold it down while moving the cursor up or down to display additional file names. Release the button when you reach the desired position.

Step 3. *If you are not using the mouse, use the up and down cursor arrow keys to move the highlighting up or down.*

As you reach the bottom of the display, the list scrolls to show additional file names, until the end of the list is reached. You may reverse directions by using the up arrow key to return to the top of the list.

You will use the scrolling technique in the Shell version of the next exercise to copy files from one disk to another.

To view a directory of a different disk, you need to select from the choices in the third line of the display the letter or icon representing that disk drive. If the drive area is active, you can select a drive by holding down the control key and pressing the letter corresponding to that drive (Ctrl-A, Ctrl-B, and so forth) or by clicking on the drive icon or character with the mouse. Press the Tab key to make the drive area active.

Insert your DOS start-up disk in drive A. If the A: letter or icon is already highlighted, just press Enter or click the symbol with the mouse cursor. An updated directory of the disk in that drive will be displayed. To view a disk in a different drive, such as B:, move the highlighting to that symbol and accept it by clicking or pressing Enter.

So far, the directory listing available from the Shell has seemed much like that shown by the DOS DIR command. However, you can also sort directories, display specified files, and do other tasks from the Shell. Those activities are explained in Chapters 21 and 22.

Copying Files with the COPY Command

This section shows you how to copy files between disks by using the COPY command at the DOS command line. If you have DOS V4, you can also copy files by using the Shell's File System (separate instructions appear later in this chapter). If you are using the Shell and want to practice copying from the command line, you must first go to the DOS prompt by pressing Shift-F9. You can then follow the rest of these instructions.

Copying with Two Floppy Disk Drives

This first section is for you if your computer has two disk drives. The drives may be 360K, 720K, 1.2M, or 1.44M in capacity. They do not have to be identical. Note, however, that if you copy from a disk drive with a higher capacity to one with a lower capacity, you may not be able to fit all the files from the larger-capacity disk onto the disk in the lower-capacity drive.

Step 1. *Place into drive A a blank, formatted disk.*

This disk is the *destination disk*, since it is the final destination for the files to be copied.

Step 2. *Place into drive B the disk containing files you want to practice copying.*

This is the *source disk*, since it is the source of the files to be copied. You may use one of your DOS disks or the copies you have made of them. Steps 1 and 2 reverse the usual order for source and destination drives. Here, drive B is the source and drive A is the destination. If your floppy disk drives are not identical, drive A usually has the higher capacity. Thus the disk in drive A, whose capacity equals or is greater than that of drive B, will receive the files.

Step 3. *Type*

COPY B:*.* A: /V

The light on drive B will go on first, then the light on drive A. The lights will alternate for a minute or so while each file is copied from the second disk to the first. The names of each file will appear on the screen as the file is being copied.

Notice the /V switch you typed. This switch tells COPY to verify that the copy being made of each file is correct. /V means something else with another DOS command, but with the COPY command, /V means *verify*.

Shortly, you will see a message like the following:

```
50 File(s) copied
```

The number varies depending on how many files were on the source disk in drive B. This message tells you that DOS has copied the files from the disk in drive B to the disk in drive A. You know that that the copying was successful.

If the source disk has a higher capacity than the destination disk, you might see a different message:

```
Insufficient disk space
```

This message tells you that there were more files on the source disk than would fit on the destination disk. Later in this book you will learn how to use the XCOPY command to copy all the files from a high-capacity disk to two or more lower-capacity disks. For now, just remember that you can't always copy all the files from one disk to another if the disks vary in capacity.

If both your drives have the same capacity and you see the Insufficient disk space message, you are probably copying files to a destination disk that already holds files. In a non-practice session, you may encounter this message rather frequently. Here, too, the XCOPY command will come to your rescue.

Copying between Floppy and Hard Disk Drives

This section, which contains two copying exercises, is for you if your computer has at least one floppy disk and one hard disk drive. Most PS/2, Personal Computer AT, PC XT, and PC XT 286 computers fit this category.

It doesn't matter which disk you use as the source disk for the files to be copied. You may use one of your DOS disks if you like. It also doesn't matter which subdirectory is used as the destination for the files. In the first exercise, you will create a temporary subdirectory called TMP. (Hard disk subdirectories are explained in Chapter 13.)

Before you do this exercise, make sure that your hard disk is set up properly. If it is not, see Appendix E for instructions.

Step 1. Place in drive A the source disk holding files to be copied.

Step 2. Type

    A>**MKDIR C:\TMP**

This command creates on your hard disk a new subdirectory called TMP.

If you see a message that DOS is unable to create the directory, the directory already exists. You may have created the directory earlier for some reason. If so, use another name instead of TMP.

Step 3. *Copy the files from your source disk to the TMP subdirectory by typing*

> **A>COPY A:*.* C:\TMP /V**

You will see lights go on, first on the floppy disk drive and then on the hard disk. The disk drive lights will alternate, and file names will appear on the screen as the files are copied.

Notice the **/V** switch you typed. This switch tells COPY to *verify* that the copy being made of each file is correct. Shortly, you will see the following message:

```
50 File(s) copied
```

The number varies depending on the number of files on the source disk. The message informs you that the copying was successful: DOS has copied 50 files from the source disk to the hard disk subdirectory C:\TMP.

Now try copying from the hard disk onto a floppy disk. Put a blank, formatted disk into drive A and follow these steps:

Step 1. *Type*

> **COPY C:\TMP A: /V**

The disk drive lights will come on alternately, file names will appear on the screen, and within a minute or so you should see the following message:

```
50 File(s) copied
```

The message indicates that the copying of the DOS files was successful.

Step 2. *Remove the practice files from the hard disk. Type*

> **ERASE C:\TMP**

DOS will ask

```
Are you sure (Y/N)?
```

Answer **Y**; all the files in the temporary subdirectory TMP will be erased.

Step 3. *Now remove the TMP subdirectory from your hard disk. Type*

> **RMDIR C:\TMP**

DOS removes the subdirectory without displaying a confirmation message. The next thing you see is the DOS prompt.

You have now copied all the files from a floppy disk to the hard disk and then back to a different floppy disk. These steps form an important file-copying option for those who have a hard disk drive but only one floppy disk drive. To see why this is important, go on to the next section.

Copying Files with One Disk Drive

Today few systems come with just one floppy disk drive as the only mass storage available. Some lap-top computers are furnished with a single disk drive in their entry-level configuration. And a few IBM and compatible computers intended for home or educational use (such as the PS/2 Model 25) may be outfitted with a single floppy disk drive.

For this exercise, you'll need a disk that holds files to be copied and a blank, formatted disk.

Step 1. Insert into drive A the source disk to be copied.

Step 2. Type

COPY A:*.* B:

The disk drive light comes on as DOS reads the first file, or part of it, into memory. The following message appears:

```
Insert diskette for drive B: and strike any key when
ready
```

Step 3. Remove the source disk from drive A and insert the blank, formatted destination disk into the same drive. Press Enter.

The disk drive light comes on again. When the data is written to the disk, you see this message:

```
Insert diskette for drive A: and strike any key when
ready
```

Step 4. Remove the disk and insert the source disk again.

Step 5. Repeat Steps 3 and 4 until all the files on your source disk have been copied to the destination disk.

If you have large files or only a small amount of available memory in your computer, you will find that the number of disk swaps can exceed the number of files on your disk! Even under the best circumstances, copying this way is a tedious task. Some alternatives are provided in a moment. But first, have you been wondering where that drive B came from?

How One Disk Drive Can Be Two

In the preceding exercise, you used the command

COPY A:*.* B: /V

to copy files on a computer that has a single floppy disk drive. Where was drive B? A clue came when DOS prompted you to insert a disk for drive B and you inserted the disk into the same disk drive you had been using. Drive A is the same disk drive as drive B.

When you have only one floppy disk drive, DOS makes two *logical* drives out of the single physical drive. Although you may have only one physical disk drive, DOS treats the real disk drive as though it were two different drives.

DOS keeps track of which logical disk drive you are using. When you request a different logical disk drive, DOS stops the program you are using and instructs you to insert the proper disk and to press a key. If the correct disk is already in the disk drive, just press a key. DOS then permits the program to continue running.

The best use of the second logical disk drive is to copy one or two files between disks. Copying more than a few files this way, however, becomes boring—fast. That's when one of the following alternatives becomes attractive.

COPY Alternatives for Single-Drive Users

If you have only one floppy disk drive and want to copy files to another disk, you have three alternatives:

- If you want to copy all the files from one disk to another and the disks have the same capacity, you can use the DISKCOPY command. DOS will use all available memory to copy large sections of the source disk at one time and reduce the number of disk swaps. Note that you can use this option to copy 360K disks in 1.2M drives or 720K disks in 1.44M drives.

- If you have a hard disk drive, you can copy your files from the source disk to a temporary directory on your hard disk and then back to the new blank disk. This option was described in the section "Copying between Floppy and Hard Disk Drives."

  The main benefit of performing this double-copy step is that you don't have to sit there and swap disks dozens of times. You can type the first command and do something else while DOS copies the files to the hard disk. Then you can type the second command and wait while the files are copied to the second disk.

- If you don't have a hard disk, you can still reduce the number of disk swaps by using the XCOPY command, which is described in Chapter 20. Like COPY, this command copies files to a new disk without erasing any files that are already there. XCOPY reads as many files into memory as it can before asking you to exchange disks. So you may be able to copy a few dozen small files with only a couple of disk swaps.

Using the Shell File System To Copy Files

The preceding exercises are an excellent foundation for using the DOS Shell's File System to copy files. The following exercise will show you how to adapt what you have learned to the Shell. You'll see that copying files can be streamlined by the features built into the Shell.

Copying with Two Floppy Disk Drives

These instructions are for you if your system has two floppy disk drives. You should have the DOS Shell loaded and the Start Programs menu on your screen.

Step 1. *Place into drive A a blank, formatted disk.*

Step 2. *Place into drive B a disk containing files you want to copy.*

Step 3. *Select File System from the Main Group.*

You recall that you select the File System option by highlighting it and pressing Enter or by double-clicking the entry with the mouse.

The File System menu appears on your screen. Make sure that drive B is selected. If it isn't, select it with the mouse or by holding down the Ctrl key and pressing the letter B.

Step 4. *Select the File menu from the action bar.*

Press F10, if necessary, to activate the action bar. You may pull down the File menu with the mouse, or you may type the letter *F* to select the menu, which is shown in figure 5.3. Note that the Copy... option is blurred, shaded, or marked with an asterisk, depending on your display mode.

Fig. 5.3

The File menu.

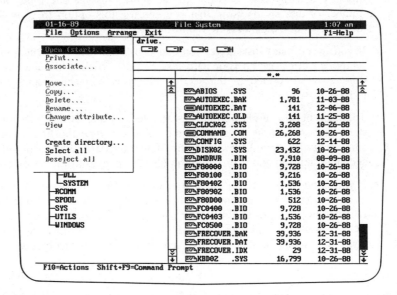

Step 5. *Choose the Select all option from the File menu.*

Now the Copy... option is shown as available.

Step 6. *Choose the Copy... option.*

You see a box like the one shown in figure 5.4.

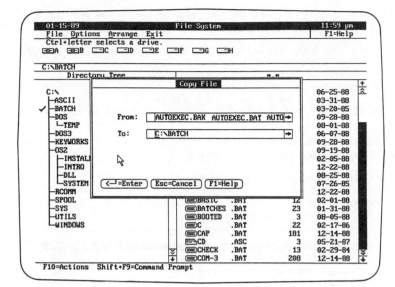

Fig. 5.4

The Copy File box.

The Copy File box has two lines on which you can enter information. The From: line enables you to enter the name of the file(s) to be copied. Because you have chosen the Select all option, each of the file names on the disk will appear one after another on the line. Not all the names will appear at once, since the line has room for just a few. You can use the scroll bar to scroll through the listing, if you want.

On the To: line, you type the name of the destination drive (and more, as you'll see later on). For now, move down to the To: line by using the mouse or pressing Tab. If drive A does not appear on the line, press Del to delete what appears there; type **A:** and press Enter.

The light on drive B will go on first, then the light on drive A. The lights will alternate for a minute or so while each file is copied from the second disk to the first. The names of each file appear on the Copy File screen as the file is being copied. The screen will also tell you that file 1 of 22, or 2 of 22, or 3 of 22, and so on, is being copied. You always know how many files remain to be copied. Finally, a message on the screen tells you that DOS has successfully copied all the files.

Copying with One Floppy Drive or to the Hard Disk

Oddly enough, the DOS Shell won't allow you to copy files from one floppy disk to another floppy disk in the same drive. If you try to copy from drive A to drive B when you have only one drive, the Shell will tell you that two drives are needed for the Copy/ Move commands.

If you have a hard disk, you can get around this limitation by copying your files from drive A to a temporary directory on the hard disk and then back from that directory to a new disk in drive A. The following exercise has you do just that; then you erase the files from the hard disk. After making sure that the DOS Shell is loaded and that the Start Programs menu is on-screen, follow these steps:

Step 1. Place into drive A the copy you made of your DOS Startup/Operating or start-up disk.

Step 2. Select the File System from the Main Group.

You can do this by highlighting the File System selection and pressing Enter or by double-clicking the entry with the mouse. The File System menu will appear on your screen. Make sure that drive A is selected. If it isn't, select it by using the mouse or by holding down the control key and pressing the letter A.

Step 3. Choose the Create directory... option from the File menu.

A box like that in figure 5.5 appears.

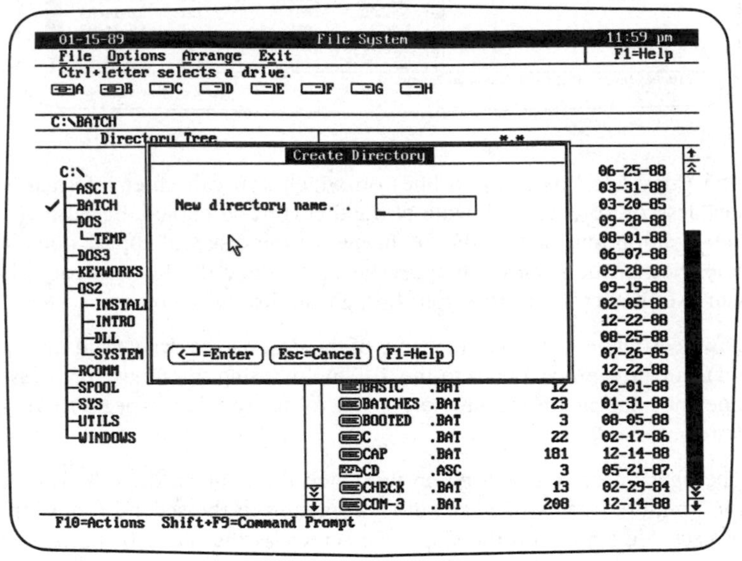

Fig. 5.5

The Create
Directory box.

Step 4. Making sure that the active drive is C:, create a directory by typing

C:\TMP

If DOS tells you there is already another subdirectory by that name, choose another name, such as C:\DOS. Press Enter. Now change back to drive A.

Step 5. Select the File menu from the action bar.

Press F10, if necessary, to activate the action bar. You may pull down the File menu with the mouse, or you may type the letter **F** to select the menu. Note that the Copy... option is blurred, shaded, or marked with an asterisk, depending on your display mode.

Step 6. Choose the Select all option from the File menu.

The Copy... option is now shown as available on the File menu.

Step 7. Choose the Copy... option.

A box like that shown in figure 5.6 appears.

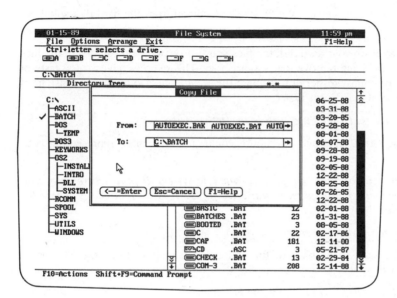

Fig. 5.6

The Copy File box.

The Copy File menu has two lines on which you can enter information. The From: line enables you to enter the name of the file(s) to be copied. Because you have chosen the Select all option, each of the file names on the disk in drive A will appear one after another on the line. (In Chapter 7, you'll learn how to copy multiple files very quickly by selecting any group you want.) Not all the names will appear at once, since the line has room for just a few. You can use the scroll bar to scroll through the listing, if you want. Although the scroll bar is horizontal rather than vertical, it operates exactly like a vertical scroll bar. On the To: line, you type the name of the destination drive (and more, as you'll see later on).

Step 8. Move to the To: line by using the mouse or pressing Tab.

*Step 9. If something appears on the line, delete it with the Del key and type **C:\TMP**. Press Enter.*

The light on drive A will go on first, then the light on drive C (if one is present on the front of your system). The lights will alternate for a minute or so while each file is copied from the floppy disk to the hard disk. The name of each file appears on the Copy File screen as the file is being copied. The screen will also tell you that file 1 of 22, or 2 of 22, or 3 of 22, and so forth, is being copied. You always know how many files remain to be copied. Finally, the message on the screen tells you that DOS has successfully copied all the files.

Step 10. *To copy the files to the second floppy disk, choose Copy... again.*

Step 11. *Type* **C:\TMP** *as the source at the From: prompt and* **A:** *as the destination at the To: prompt.*

Step 12. *Remove the first floppy disk from drive A and replace it with the new, formatted disk.*

Press Enter to accept your entries; the files will be copied from the hard disk subdirectory to the floppy disk.

Since you don't want on your hard disk the files you just copied, you can delete the files in C:\TMP or C:\DOS and remove that subdirectory. This exercise gives you a taste of some tasks that are clumsy to perform through the Shell alone. Doing this exercise from the DOS prompt is actually a lot easier.

Step 13. *Make sure that your hard disk is the active drive.*

If necessary, type Ctrl-C or move the mouse cursor to the symbol representing your drive.

Step 14. *Move the cursor to the left panel of the File System display, where your hard disk's subdirectories are displayed, and select C:\TMP, the subdirectory where the files are located.*

Step 15. *Move back to the File menu.*

Press F10, if necessary, to go back to the action bar, and pull down the File menu. Choose Select all to specify all the files in the C:\TMP subdirectory.

Step 16. *Select the Delete... choice from the File menu.*

The file names in the subdirectory you have chosen will be displayed in the Delete File box. Press Enter to confirm your choice. DOS may ask you to confirm each file before each is deleted. For now, press Enter if you need to confirm each file's deletion. Once the files are deleted, you'll want to remove the subdirectory created to hold the files temporarily.

Step 17. *Exit from the File menu.*

The File System main menu appears on the screen. Move the cursor to the left panel and select the subdirectory you want to remove, C:\TMP. If you have a mouse, you can simply move the cursor to the subdirectory name and click the button. If you do not have a mouse, press the Tab key until the cursor moves to the left panel. Then use the cursor keys to move the highlighting to the correct subdirectory name.

Step 18. *Now pull down the File menu again and select the Delete... option.*

The Delete Directory box appears (see fig. 5.7).

Step 19. *If the directory displayed is the correct directory to be deleted, choose option 2.*

You can cancel the operation by pressing Esc, clicking the Escape box, or choosing option 1.

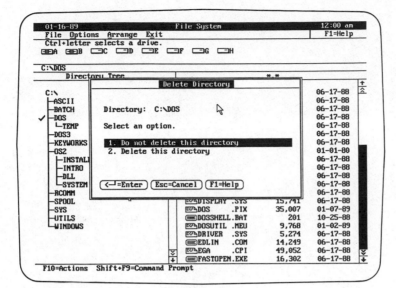

Fig. 5.7

*The Delete
Directory box.*

The directory will be removed. The directory tree display in the left-hand File System panel will be updated to confirm the deletion.

Summary

In this chapter, you used the FORMAT and COPY commands of DOS. You also learned how to perform those tasks in the DOS Shell.

The key points to remember are these:

❏ FORMAT preparcs new disks for use.

❏ COPY copies individual files.

❏ Many DOS commands have switches that affect the way each command works.

❏ To specify a switch, type a slash (/) and then the character for the switch (for example, /V or /S).

❏ Some switches mean different things to different DOS commands. For example, the /V switch means *volume label* to the FORMAT command but *verify* to the COPY command.

❏ On a computer with one floppy disk drive (or an external disk drive), DOS enables you to use that floppy disk drive as though it were two disk drives.

❏ Sometimes the DOS Shell is not the quickest or easiest way to perform a task.

The next chapter reviews most of the commands you have used and provides information about file names.

6

Learning Basic
DOS Commands

In the first five chapters, you used several DOS commands to prepare floppy disks and to copy files and disks. You also were introduced to the Shell of DOS V4. In this chapter and in Chapter 7, you will learn more about the commands you used as well as some additional DOS commands. You will also learn some more key DOS concepts and some basics about file names. This chapter and the next are the most important chapters of this "survival course" on DOS—a quick start if you are just beginning to use a computer. You will find additional information about the commands presented in these chapters later in the book.

This chapter contains additional hands-on exercises for which you will need DOS running on your computer. If your computer is off, place in the disk drive the copy of the DOS Startup disk you made in Chapter 2 and turn on the computer. If your computer is already on, have the DOS Startup disk ready. If you use 360K minifloppy disk drives, have the copy of the Operating disk handy as well. You will use it for some exercises in this chapter.

Getting a List of Files (DIR)

You will use the DOS command line for this exercise. If you are using DOS V4 and the Shell, go to the command prompt by pressing Shift-F9. You can also use the DOS Shell File System to view the directory using the method described in Chapter 5. In that case, what you will see on the screen will differ slightly from the description that follows. However, the key components are the same.

You will recall that you use the DIR command to see a list of the files you have on your disk. The *directory* is the area of the disk where the list of files is kept. DIR is the second most frequently used DOS command. (The most frequently used DOS command is COPY, which is discussed in more detail in Chapter 7.)

With the copy of the DOS Startup disk in drive A, type the following:

A>**DIR**

You should see a list of files appear on your screen. The top part of the list will move off the top of the screen. Do not worry about that now. You will soon learn how to stop the screen's movement.

The following list of files is a full directory of the microfloppy DOS Master disk for V4. (Other versions and disk sizes will show different files and numbers of bytes free.)

A>**DIR A:**

```
Volume in drive A is DOS400
Volume Serial Number is 275F-15DE
Directory of A:\

COMMAND  COM     37637 06-17-88   12:00p
CONFIG   SYS        99 12-26-88    2:26p
AUTOEXEC BAT        77 12-26-88    2:26p
EGA      CPI     49052 06-17-88   12:00p
ANSI     SYS      9148 06-17-88   12:00p
COUNTRY  SYS     12838 06-17-88   12:00p
DISKCOPY COM     10428 06-17-88   12:00p
DISPLAY  SYS     15741 06-17-88   12:00p
DRIVER   SYS      5274 06-17-88   12:00p
FORMAT   COM     22923 06-17-88   12:00p
KEYB     COM     14759 06-17-88   12:00p
KEYBOARD SYS     23360 06-17-88   12:00p
MODE     COM     23040 06-17-88   12:00p
PRINTER  SYS     18946 06-17-88   12:00p
VDISK    SYS      6376 06-17-88   12:00p
4201     CPI      6404 06-17-88   12:00p
5202     CPI       402 06-17-88   12:00p
4208     CPI       641 06-17-88   12:00p
012345   678       109 06-17-88   12:00p
SHARE    EXE     10285 06-17-88   12:00p
IFSFUNC  EXE     21637 06-17-88   12:00p
SYS      COM     11472 06-17-88   12:00p
XCOPY    EXE     17087 06-17-88   12:00p
LCD      CPI     10592 06-17-88   12:00p
APPEND   EXE     11170 06-17-88   12:00p
ASSIGN   COM      5785 06-17-88   12:00p
ATTRIB   EXE     18247 06-17-88   12:00p
BASICA   COM     36285 06-17-88   12:00p
COMP     COM      9491 06-17-88   12:00p
DEBUG    COM     21606 06-17-88   12:00p
DISKCOMP COM      9889 06-17-88   12:00p
EDLIN    COM     14249 06-17-88   12:00p
FIND     EXE      5983 06-17-88   12:00p
```

```
GRAFTABL  COM      10271  06-17-88    12:00p
GRAPHICS  COM      16733  06-17-88    12:00p
GRAPHICS  PRO       9413  06-17-88    12:00p
JOIN      EXE      17457  06-17-88    12:00p
LABEL     COM       4490  06-17-88    12:00p
MEM       EXE      20133  06-17-88    12:00p
MORE      COM       2166  06-17-88    12:00p
NLSFUNC   EXE       6910  06-17-88    12:00p
RECOVER   COM      10732  06-17-88    12:00p
REPLACE   EXE      17199  06-17-88    12:00p
SORT      EXE       5914  06-17-88    12:00p
SUBST     EXE      18143  06-17-88    12:00p
TREE      COM       6334  06-17-88    12:00p
FILESYS   EXE      11125  06-17-88    12:00p
CHKDSK    COM      17771  06-17-88    12:00p
PCIBMDRV  MOS        295  06-17-88    12:00p
PCMSDRV   MOS        961  06-17-88    12:00p
PCMSPDRV  MOS        801  06-17-88    12:00p
SHELL     CLR       4438  12-26-88     2:52p
SHELL     HLP      66977  06-17-88    12:00p
SHELL     MEU       4588  06-17-88    12:00p
SHELLB    COM       3937  06-17-88    12:00p
SHELLC    EXE     153975  06-17-88    12:00p
DOSUTIL   MEU       6660  06-17-88    12:00p
PRINT     COM      14163  06-17-88    12:00p
DOSSHELL  BAT        190  12-26-88     2:51p
59 File(s)      480768 bytes free

A>
```

The first line of the disk directory shows the disk drive whose directory is displayed and the electronic volume label for the disk. This floppy disk has a volume label, DOS400. That label was applied by the SELECT utility. With earlier versions of DOS, if the original DOS Startup/Operating disk does not have a volume label, its copy does not have a label either.

The next line shows the disk drive and directory you are viewing. The directory is A:\. This means that you are viewing the main directory of the floppy disk in drive A. I explain DOS disk directories in Chapter 13.

Now look at the line that begins with COMMAND COM:

```
COMMAND   COM      37637  06-17-88    12:00p
```

For DOS V3.1, the listing is on the tenth line; for other versions of DOS, the listing is on the fourth line.

COMMAND.COM is one of the three files of DOS itself. The listing consists of the *root name* of the file, one or more spaces, and the suffix, or *extension*. The next number is the size of the file, followed by the file's date and time of creation. When an established file is changed, the file's date and time reflect when the file was altered. The date and time in the computer's memory is the basis for the file's date and time "stamp" in the directory.

Now look at the last line of the directory listing. If you are using microfloppy disks and DOS V3.3, the line may be as follows:

```
50 File(s)     128512 bytes free

A>
```

If you are using DOS V3.3 and the minifloppy Startup disk, the line may be the following:

```
22 File(s)      9216 bytes free

A>
```

The first number on each line shows how many files were displayed, and the second number shows how much free space is on the disk. The second figure is usually the most important. It tells you how much room is left on the floppy disk for adding new files or expanding older files.

If you are using the DOS V4 Shell, the File System display does not show the number of files or bytes free. For that information, you need to pull down the Options menu and access the Show Information selection. A box similar to figure 6.1 will appear.

Fig. 6.1

The Show Information screen.

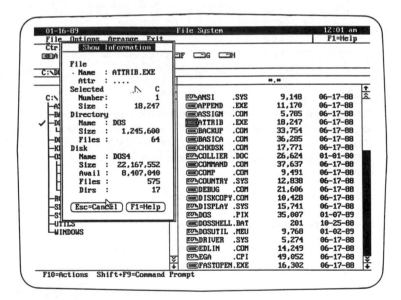

The number of files, the number of bytes free on the disk, and the total capacity of the disk are shown. The Show Information box also displays other information about specific files, which you will learn about later.

Freezing the Screen (Ctrl-S, Ctrl-Num Lock, Pause)

If you are using the DOS command prompt, you noticed that some of the lines of the directory list scrolled off the top of the screen before you could read them. The problem of missing information in this manner is not uncommon. Fortunately, DOS includes several keystroke controls to stop, or freeze, the scrolling of the screen.

To try these controls, type the following:

A>**DIR**

As the list begins to scroll by, hold down the Ctrl key and press the S key. The screen should freeze. If the directory has already gone by, type DIR again and try pressing Ctrl-S again. To start the screen moving again, press any key.

A second way to freeze the screen is to use Ctrl-Num Lock (holding down the Ctrl key and pressing the Num Lock key at the top of the numeric keypad). I find, however, that Ctrl-S is easier to use on the older keyboards because it takes only my left hand to press the key sequence. To press Ctrl-Num Lock, I must use my left hand to hold the Ctrl key while tapping Num Lock with my right hand.

The easiest key sequence that freezes the screen is available on the enhanced keyboards. The Pause key is on the same key with Break, to the immediate left of the green Num Lock indicator light. Pressing this key accomplishes the same freezing action as the Ctrl-S or Ctrl-Num Lock sequence. To restart the screen, press any key.

Making the DIR Command More Convenient (DIR /W, DIR /P)

Ctrl-S, Ctrl-Num Lock, and Pause are helpful in freezing the screen so that you can read the display produced by the DIR command. The DIR command also has two switches that can make the command more convenient to use. The switches are /P for *pause* and /W for *wide*.

The /P switch pauses the listing of the files after 23 lines of files are displayed. When you press a key, the next set of file names is displayed. You use this switch when a directory is long, you do not want the listing to scroll off the screen, and you do not want to use the freeze-screen keys to hold the screen. The disadvantage of using the /P switch is that the top few lines that contain the volume label, disk drive name, and path leave the screen before DIR pauses. You must use the freeze-screen keys to see these lines on long displays.

The /W switch gives a wide display of the directory listing. Five file names are displayed on each line. This switch is useful when you are looking for one file name or a few ones in long directories. The disadvantage is that the file size, the DIR symbol for directories, and the file date and time are not displayed.

Try using these switches by first typing

    A>**DIR** /P

Then type

    A>**DIR** /W

The following screens show what I saw when I used the /P and /W switches with the DIR command on my copy of the DOS V4 microfloppy DOS Startup/Operating disk. Remember that the first few lines of the directory roll off the top of the screen before DIR pauses.

```
A>DIR A: /P
Volume in drive A is DOS400
Volume Serial Number is 275F-15DE
Directory of A:\

COMMAND  COM     37637 06-17-88   12:00p
CONFIG   SYS        99 12-26-88    2:26p
AUTOEXEC BAT        77 12-26-88    2:26p
EGA      CPI     49052 06-17-88   12:00p
ANSI     SYS      9148 06-17-88   12:00p
COUNTRY  SYS     12838 06-17-88   12:00p
DISKCOPY COM     10428 06-17-88   12:00p
DISPLAY  SYS     15741 06-17-88   12:00p
DRIVER   SYS      5274 06-17-88   12:00p
FORMAT   COM     22923 06-17-88   12:00p
KEYB     COM     14759 06-17-88   12:00p
KEYBOARD SYS     23360 06-17-88   12:00p
MODE     COM     23040 06-17-88   12:00p
PRINTER  SYS     18946 06-17-88   12:00p
VDISK    SYS      6376 06-17-88   12:00p
4201     CPI      6404 06-17-88   12:00p
5202     CPI       402 06-17-88   12:00p
4208     CPI       641 06-17-88   12:00p
012345   678       109 06-17-88   12:00p
SHARE    EXE     10285 06-17-88   12:00p
IFSFUNC  EXE     21637 06-17-88   12:00p
SYS      COM     11472 06-17-88   12:00p
XCOPY    EXE     17087 06-17-88   12:00p
Press any key to continue . . .


LCD      CPI     10592 06-17-88   12:00p
APPEND   EXE     11170 06-17-88   12:00p
ASSIGN   COM      5785 06-17-88   12:00p
ATTRIB   EXE     18247 06-17-88   12:00p
BASICA   COM     36285 06-17-88   12:00p
COMP     COM      9491 06-17-88   12:00p
```

```
DEBUG     COM      21606 06-17-88  12:00p
DISKCOMP  COM       9889 06-17-88  12:00p
EDLIN     COM      14249 06-17-88  12:00p
FIND      EXE       5983 06-17-88  12:00p
GRAFTABL  COM      10271 06-17-88  12:00p
GRAPHICS  COM      16733 06-17-88  12:00p
GRAPHICS  PRO       9413 06-17-88  12:00p
JOIN      EXE      17457 06-17-88  12:00p
LABEL     COM       4490 06-17-88  12:00p
MEM       EXE      20133 06-17-88  12:00p
MORE      COM       2166 06-17-88  12:00p
NLSFUNC   EXE       6910 06-17-88  12:00p
RECOVER   COM      10732 06-17-88  12:00p
REPLACE   EXE      17199 06-17-88  12:00p
SORT      EXE       5914 06-17-88  12:00p
SUBST     EXE      18143 06-17-88  12:00p
TREE      COM       6334 06-17-88  12:00p
Press any key to continue . . .


FILESYS   EXE      11125 06-17-88  12:00p
CHKDSK    COM      17771 06-17-88  12:00p
PCIBMDRV  MOS        295 06-17-88  12:00p
PCMSDRV   MOS        961 06-17-88  12:00p
PCMSPDRV  MOS        801 06-17-88  12:00p
SHELL     CLR       4438 12-26-88   2:52p
SHELL     HLP      66977 06-17-88  12:00p
SHELL     MEU       4588 06-17-88  12:00p
SHELLB    COM       3937 06-17-88  12:00p
SHELLC    EXE     153975 06-17-88  12:00p
DOSUTIL   MEU       6660 06-17-88  12:00p
PRINT     COM      14163 06-17-88  12:00p
DOSSHELL  BAT        190 12-26-88   2:51p
59 File(s)      480768 bytes free

C>


A>DIR A: /W

Volume in drive A is DOS400
Volume Serial Number is 275F-15DE
Directory of A:\

COMMAND  COM     CONFIG        SYSAUTOEXEC BATEGA       CPIANSI     SYS
COUNTRY  SYS     DISKCOPY      COMDISPLAY  SYSDRIVER    SYSFORMAT   COM
KEYB     COM     KEYBOARD      SYSMODE     COMPRINTER   SYSVDISK    SYS
4201     CPI     5202          CPI4208     CPI012345    678SHARE    EXE
IFSFUNC  EXE     SYS           COMXCOPY    EXELCD       CPIAPPEND   EXE
```

```
ASSIGN   COM    ATTRIB       EXEBASICA    COMCOMP       COMDEBUG      COM
DISKCOMP COM    EDLIN        COMFIND      EXEGRAFTABL   COMGRAPHICS   COM
GRAPHICS PRO    JOIN         EXELABEL     COMMEM        EXEMORE       COM
NLSFUNC  EXE    RECOVER      COMREPLACE   EXESORT       EXESUBST      EXE
TREE     COM    FILESYS      EXECHKDSK    COMPCIBMDRV   MOSPCMSDRV    MOS
PCMSPDRV MOS    SHELL        CLRSHELL     HLPSHELL      MEUSHELLB     COM
SHELLC   EXE    DOSUTIL      MEUPRINT     COMDOSSHELL   BAT
59 File(s)     480768 bytes free
```

Printing What Appears on the Screen

Often you will need a printed copy of what you see on the video screen. The next two
DOS controls allow you to print the screen display. Before you move on, try the exer-
cises in this section if you have a printer attached to your computer. You must use the
DOS command line; the following techniques will not work properly from the DOS
Shell.

Printing What You Send to the Screen
(Ctrl-PrtSc, Ctrl-P)

You can print what you send to the screen with the PrtSc key (Print Screen on newer
keyboards). The PrtSc key on older keyboards is a tan key that is also an asterisk [*] key
(see figs. 6.2 and 6.3). On the newer keyboards, the Print Screen key is a tan key between the F12 key and the Scroll Lock key on the upper right side of the keyboard (see
fig. 6.4).

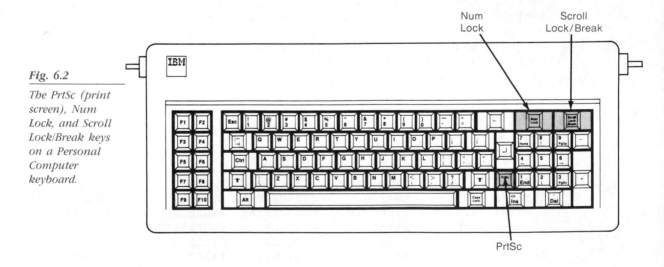

Fig. 6.2

*The PrtSc (print
screen), Num
Lock, and Scroll
Lock/Break keys
on a Personal
Computer
keyboard.*

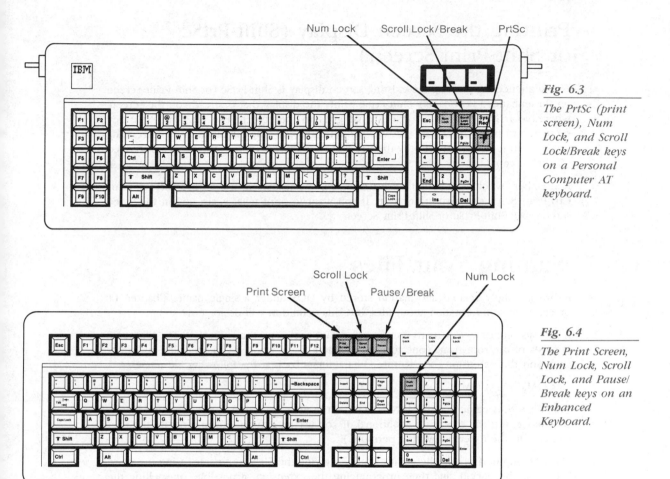

Fig. 6.3

The PrtSc (print screen), Num Lock, and Scroll Lock/Break keys on a Personal Computer AT keyboard.

Fig. 6.4

The Print Screen, Num Lock, Scroll Lock, and Pause/ Break keys on an Enhanced Keyboard.

Make sure that the printer is on and ready to print. Hold down the Ctrl key and press either the PrtSc or Print Screen key. Then type

   A>**DIR**

Notice that whatever appears on the screen is also printed. To turn off the printing, press the Ctrl-PrtSc or Ctrl-Print Screen sequence again.

Ctrl-P works the same way as Ctrl-PrtSc and Ctrl-Print Screen. Any one of the key sequences sends whatever is written to the video display to the printer as well.

To print a long directory listing, turn on the printing with either Ctrl-P (which I prefer), Ctrl-PrtSc (old keyboards), or Ctrl-Print Screen (Enhanced keyboards) and then enter the DIR command. Press Ctrl-P, Ctrl-PrtSc, or Ctrl-Print Screen again to turn off the printing.

Printing the Screen Display (Shift-PrtSc or Shift-Print Screen)

The sequence for printing the existing screen display is Shift-PrtSc (or Shift-Print Screen on the enhanced keyboards). Shift-PrtSc prints the display that is already on the screen, whereas Ctrl-PrtSc or Ctrl-P prints what goes to the screen. Use the Shift-PrtSc key sequence to print the screen that was produced by the DIR command in the preceding section. Notice that you get only the last part of the directory list. The first part scrolled off the screen.

Remember, when you want to print what will be displayed, use Ctrl-P, Ctrl-PrtSc, or Ctrl-Print Screen to turn printing on. If you want to print what is already on the video screen, use Shift-PrtSc or Shift-Print Screen.

Naming Your Files

A *file* is simply related information stored by DOS under a single name. Chapter 11 presents more information about files, but this definition will do for now.

A file has one or two parts to its name: the root name and the extension. The file name consists of the root name (one to eight characters), a period if you are using an extension, and the extension (one to three characters). Look at the following file name:

COMMAND.COM

This file's root name is COMMAND; COM is the file's extension. Every file must have a root name, but the extension is optional. If you use an extension, you separate the root name from the extension with a period (.).

Many "computerists" say file names aloud by giving the file's root name, using the word "dot" for the period, and then pronouncing the extension, if possible, or spelling the extension. For example, I call this file "command dot com."

Although the DIR command lists each file name with one or more spaces between the root name and the extension, you cannot insert a space into a file name. Certain other characters are also not allowed in a file name. For now, use alphabetic characters and arabic numerals. Chapter 11 contains some examples of legal and illegal file-name characters.

Using Wild-Card Characters for Speed and Ease (?, *)

You can use two special characters with file names. These are called *wild-card* characters. The power of wild-card characters is that you can use them to make one file name match a number of files. Wild cards are used most frequently with the DIR command.

You can also use them with the DOS Shell. That application will be covered in the exercise after the next one. First, you will want to learn about how the wild cards work.

The two characters are the following:

?   Matches any one character in the file name

*   Matches any number of characters in the file name

When you name a disk file, you cannot use either ? or * in the file name. These characters are reserved for the many DOS commands that accept wild card characters in a file name that is part of the command line.

When you use a file name that contains one of these characters, your file name becomes *ambiguous*. In other words, the file name you give can match more than one file on the disk. Wild cards are allowed in some programs and DOS commands but not in others.

Both ? and * can even match places in file names where no characters appear. For example, the file name

   WORDS?

matches the files

   WORDS1   WORDST
   WORDSA   WORDS

In the case of the file name WORDS, the ? matches the nonexistent character after the S in the file's root name.

These wild-card characters work with many DOS commands. Try using some wild-card characters with the DIR command. Do not worry about mistakes in typing here. You cannot harm any files by giving the DIR command.

Begin by inserting into drive A the DOS Startup floppy disk you made. Make sure that the door is closed. Now type the following commands:

1. A>**DIR *.COM**

   This command shows a directory listing of any file whose extension is COM.

2. A>**DIR D*.COM**

   This command shows a directory listing of any file whose root name begins with the letter *D* and whose extension is COM.

3. A>**DIR KEY*.***

   This command shows a directory listing of any file whose root name begins with the three letters *KEY*. The file name can have any extension.

4. A>**DIR MO?E.COM**

   This command shows a directory listing for any file whose root name begins with the letters *MO*, whose fourth character in the root name is *E*,

and whose extension is COM. The ? matches any character in the third
position of the root name.

Wild-card characters make many DOS commands easy to use. But wild cards can make a file name match more files than you want. The most common ambiguous file name is *.*, which matches every file in the directory. This file name is most potentially dangerous when it is used with the ERASE command, which is discussed in Chapter 7. You will learn more in Chapter 7 about wild-card characters and when to be especially cautious with them.

Using Wild Cards with the DOS Shell File System

Now let's look at how wild cards can be used with the DOS Shell File System. With the Shell, wild cards work in much the same way as they do with the DOS prompt, but the way they are used is quite different. The Shell gives you new capabilities beyond those of the standard DOS command prompt. For this exercise, you will need your DOS disk in drive A. Reboot the computer if necessary, and make sure the DOS Shell is loaded. You are going to view the disk directory in several different ways, using wild cards and other capabilities of the File System.

Step 1. *Select the File System from the Main Group menu.*

The screen clears, the File System menu appears, and the directory of the currently selected drive is shown in the right panel (see fig. 6.5).

Fig. 6.5

The File System menu, showing the mouse cursor on the currently selected drive.

```
01-16-89                     File System              12:02 am
 File  Options  Arrange  Exit                         F1=Help
 Ctrl+letter selects a drive.
 [=]A  [=]B  [=]C  [=]D  [=]E  [=]F  [=]G  [=]H
 B:\
     Directory Tree                        *.*
 /B:\                         2CR        .ASC        5     08-05-88
                              4201       .CPI    6,404     06-17-88
                              4208       .CPI      641     06-17-88
                              5202       .CPI      402     06-17-88
                              @          .ASC        1     06-07-88
                              AC                 3,000     09-23-88
                              ANSI       .SYS    9,148     06-17-88
                              APPEND     .EXE   11,170     06-17-88
                              APPS       .$$$      172     11-25-88
                              APPS       .ASC      974     09-28-88
                              ASSIGN     .COM    5,785     06-17-88
                              ATTRIB     .EXE   18,247     06-17-88
                              AUTOEXEC   .400       29     12-22-88
                              AUTOEXEC   .BAT       29     12-22-88
                              AUTOEXEC   .INS       60     01-08-89
                              BACKUP     .COM   33,754     06-17-88
                              BASIC      .COM    1,065     06-17-88
                              BASICA     .COM   36,285     06-17-88
                              BOOTED     .ASC       28     06-25-88
                              CD         .ASC        3     05-21-87
                              CHKDSK     .COM   17,771     06-17-88
 F10=Actions   Shift+F9=Command Prompt
```

Now that you have learned about wild cards, you may notice something in the directory display. Above the display should be a line with the *.* wild-card specification. That shows that DOS is currently displaying all of the files that meet that specification, i.e., all of the files.

If you have a graphics-based Shell, the scroll box has a blank space above or below it to indicate that there are additional files that can be viewed by dragging the box. If you have a text-based Shell, the word More: appears in the right-hand column. A down arrow or up arrow (or both, if appropriate) indicates whether additional files appear at the end or beginning of the current screen. If you have a mouse, you can scroll the directory listing by clicking the up or down arrows. If you have a text system and no mouse, you will need to use the cursor keys as described in Chapter 5.

Step 2. *If drive A is not the current disk drive, select it using the mouse or by pressing Ctrl-A.*

The list of files contained on the DOS startup disk is too long to show in a single panel. You can scroll through the listing using the methods described earlier in this book. However, as with the command prompt, you can selectively view files matching a wild-card specification you type in. The Shell has no DIR command, so how do you use the wild cards?

The File System Options menu has a menu choice called Display options. It is here that you can enter the wild cards necessary to limit your directory display.

Step 3. *Pull down the Options menu and select Display options.*

A screen similar to figure 6.6 appears.

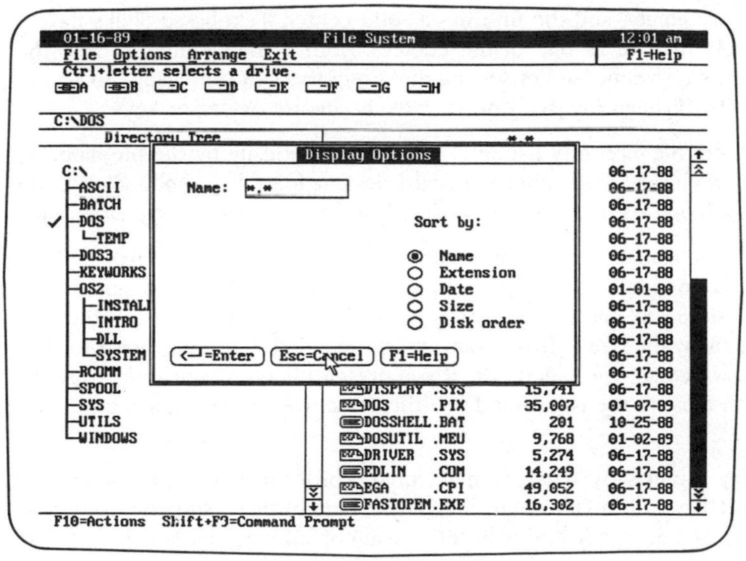

Fig. 6.6

The Display options menu.

The Display Options screen has a place for you to type a file name. This is the equivalent of the file name you type on the command line after the DIR command. The Shell inserts the *.* file specification as a default value so that all files on the current disk directory will be shown (except for hidden files, which we will discuss later).

You may replace the *.* specification with one of your own. The Name: line should be active when you first see the Display options screen. If not, move the cursor to that line with the mouse or by pressing Tab until the cursor stops there.

*Step 4. Type *.EXE and press Enter.*

All of the files on drive A ending with the .EXE extension are displayed. Repeat steps 1-4 a few times, using the various combinations of wild cards you learned earlier in this chapter. Try these variations to see what happens:

> **A???????.***
> **F*.***
> ***.SYS**
> **IBM???.***

You probably noticed the other options shown on the Display options screen. Under the heading Sort by: are five lines:

```
Name
Extension
Date
Size
Disk order
```

If you are using a graphics-based Shell, each of these options is preceded by a circle. Four of the circles are empty, and the fifth has a solid center. Text-based Shells have a right-pointing triangle in front of one of the choices. Both markings indicate that the choice is the currently active method of sorting the directory. You can change to one of the other sort keys by highlighting that option with the mouse or cursor keys.

If Name is highlighted, the directory listing is sorted alphabetically by the file name(s) you have specified using the *.* or other wild-card designations. This mode allows you to find a file quickly if you know its name, because you can scan the list alphabetically.

If Extension is highlighted, the listing is sorted by the file name extensions. This option allows you to group all files together by type, .COM and .EXE files, and so on. Highlighting Date or Size causes the listing to be sorted by the date the file was created or changed or by the size in bytes. Why are these helpful? You may wish to look at your files to see which are the oldest. Or, if you are cleaning up your disk, you may want to know which files are the largest and will therefore free up the most room if you delete them.

You can also display the files by Disk Order, or the order in which they would be shown on your directory with a DIR command. There are not many situations where it is an advantage to view a directory in this order. If you copied files to a new floppy disk using the COPY command, the disk-order display would show you the order in which they were copied. This could prove useful if you copied from several disks in order and wanted to figure out which files on the new disk came from which original disk.

However, as files are deleted from a disk, new file names are inserted in the blank spots first, so the disk order display does not necessarily show you the order in which the files were put on that disk.

You can sort on only one of the five keys; you cannot sort by date and then by size all files created or modified on the same date.

Changing the Current Disk Drive

You can issue any DOS command while you are at the system prompt. The system prompt is the A> or C> symbol that appears on the screen.

The system prompt indicates the current disk drive. The *current disk drive* is the drive where DOS searches for and executes commands.

The letter in the system prompt tells you the current disk drive. When you see A>, the current disk drive is drive A. Because A is the most frequently used disk drive on systems without hard disks, the system prompt is sometimes called the "A prompt." A B> system prompt tells you that drive B is the current drive. And C> indicates that drive C, the hard disk, is the current disk drive.

To change the current disk drive at the command prompt, simply type the letter of the disk drive, followed by a colon, and press Enter. For example, to change the current disk drive to C, you type **C:** and press Enter. The system prompt changes to C>, showing that drive C is the current disk drive. To make drive A the current disk drive again, type **A:** and press Enter.

If you are using the Shell File System, you can change the current disk drive by clicking its symbol with the mouse or by holding down the Ctrl key and typing the letter associated with that disk, e.g., Ctrl-A, Ctrl-C, and so on (see fig. 6.5).

In the hands-on practice session at the end of this chapter, you will practice changing disk drives.

Running DOS Commands

From the DOS Shell, only a few of the DOS commands are available. These commands can be found within the File System (such commands as COPY, DELETE, RENAME) or under DOS Utilities... (DATE, TIME, DISKCOPY, FORMAT, etc.).

You have already used each of those commands both from the DOS Shell and from the DOS command prompt. Now, you will learn how to use some of the others, which can be accessed only from the prompt. If you are using the Shell, access the prompt by typing Shift-F9.

To run any DOS command, you type its root name and press Enter. The only complication in running commands is knowing whether the command is available or whether you must load it from the disk before the command can be run.

DOS has both internal and external commands. *Internal commands* are built into DOS and can be executed at any time. You do not need a floppy disk in the disk drive to start these commands. You can run them whenever the DOS system prompt appears, without having to load a program from a disk.

External commands are disk-based commands that reside on the DOS disk. To execute such a command, the disk that holds the command must be in the disk drive, and you must load the command from the disk. An example is the DISKCOPY command, which you used in Chapter 2.

Internal Commands

DOS has 21 built-in commands. These are listed in table 6.1. For now, do not worry about what each command does. Their functions are discussed in detail later in the book. To use a built-in command, simply type its name at the DOS system prompt. Some commands need more information than the command name. That, too, is explained later.

Table 6.1
Built-in DOS Commands

BREAK	DIR	RMDIR
CHCP	DEL	SET
CHDIR	ERASE	TIME
CLS	MKDIR	TYPE
COPY	PATH	VER
CTTY	PROMPT	VERIFY
DATE	RENAME	VOL

External Commands

To use an external command (a DOS command that is not listed in table 6.1), use the following form:

*d:*dos_command

The *d:* is the name of the disk drive that holds the DOS command. The dos_command is the root name of the DOS command. Typing the name of the disk drive is optional. If the command is on the current disk drive, you can omit the disk drive name. If the command is on a different disk drive, you must give the disk drive, followed immediately by the command's root name. Do not put a space between the name of the disk drive and the root name of the command.

Hands-on Practice: Using an External Command To Check Disk Capacity (CHKDSK)

You have already seen that the DOS Shell File System Options menu will let you see the capacity of a disk by using the Show Information screen. Much of the same information is available from the command prompt using the CHKDSK command.

The following exercise gives separate directions for users whose computers have two floppy disk drives (identical or different) and for users whose computers have one floppy disk drive and one hard disk. If you fit both categories, try both examples.

If your system has two floppy disk drives, put a floppy disk into drive A. The floppy disk should be the one that holds some files. Put a floppy disk that holds the CHKDSK program into drive B. (If drive B is a 360K disk drive, put in drive B the copy of the DOS Operating disk you made in Chapter 2.)

If you are using a hard disk, CHKDSK should be on the hard disk. Put a floppy disk that holds some files into drive A. If drive A is not the current drive (that is, if the system prompt does not say A>), make drive A the current drive. (Type **A:** and press Enter.)

To run the CHKDSK command on a two floppy disk drive system, type

    A>B:CHKDSK

Users who have a hard disk system should type

    A>C:CHKDSK

Notice how the command is phrased. The disk drive name and the root name of the program are given, but the extension COM is not needed.

What happened when you typed the command? Did you see what you expected?

Because you used a disk drive name in front of the command name, DOS was directed to get the CHKDSK program from drive B or from drive C. DOS got the program from one of these disk drives. This is exactly what you told DOS to do.

However, CHKDSK analyzed the floppy disk in drive A. Why? You did not tell CHKDSK which disk to analyze. The explanation is that CHKDSK did not find a disk drive name after the word CHKDSK. Therefore, the current disk drive, drive A, was analyzed.

Unless you tell DOS otherwise, DOS always uses the current disk drive to run a program and to be the object of an action. In this case, the action (CHKDSK) was to analyze the disk. Drive A, the current disk drive, was automatically the object of the action. Understanding this concept is important.

To analyze the disk in drive B or the hard disk (C), you have the following two options:

- Make the drive that holds CHKDSK the current disk drive and then run CHKDSK.

- Tell CHKDSK which disk drive to check.

To use the first option, enter the following:

(For floppy disk users)   (For hard disk users)

A**>B:**   A**>C:**

B**>CHKDSK**   C**>CHKDSK**

To use the second option, enter

(For floppy disk users)   (For hard disk users)

A**>B:CHKDSK B:**   A**>C:CHKDSK C:**

Try both options.

Notice that most DOS commands expect some additional information when you type command lines. The additional information required is called a *parameter* or an *argument*. The two terms have identical meanings and can be freely interchanged. In the following line, **B:** is a parameter.

A**>CHKDSK B:**

It directs CHKDSK to check the floppy disk in drive B. Notice the space between the command CHKDSK and the B. You must put a space between a command name and a parameter. You must also use spaces between any two parameters. If you omit the space, DOS commands do not work the way they should.

DOS V4 users should note that CHKDSK will display the volume serial number and allocation units in its report, an enhancement of previous releases.

Summary

In this chapter, you learned the following key points:

❑ The DIR command gives you a list of files. The DOS Shell gives the same information, with some sorting enhancements.

❑ Ctrl-S, Ctrl-Num Lock, or Pause freezes a screen as it scrolls.

❑ Either Ctrl-P, Ctrl-PrtSc, or Ctrl-Print Screen immediately sends to the printer the same characters that are printed on the screen. You turn off the function by again pressing Ctrl-P, Ctrl-PrtSc, or Ctrl-Print Screen. These functions do not work properly from the Shell.

❑ Shift-PrtSc prints what is already on the screen if you are using the DOS command prompt.

❑ The DIR command has two switches: /P for pausing the screen display and /W for showing a wide display.

❑ A file name has two parts: the root name, which is one to eight characters long, and the optional extension, which is one to three characters long. If you have an extension, you separate the root name from the extension with a period.

❑ The wild-card character ? matches a single character in a file name. The wild-card character * matches all remaining characters in a root name or extension.

❑ Typing the appropriate letter followed by a colon and pressing Enter changes the current disk drive.

❑ To run an internal command, you type the name of the command when the DOS system prompt (such as A>) appears.

❑ For DOS to run an external command, the disk that holds the command must be in a disk drive. If the current disk drive holds the command, you simply type the root name of the command (such as CHKDSK). If the current disk drive does not hold the command, you precede the command name with the name of the disk drive that holds the command (such as A:CHKDSK or C:CHKDSK).

❑ Some commands accept additional information, called parameters or arguments. If you do not supply this additional information, most DOS commands work on the current disk drive.

Chapter 7 introduces the command RENAME and includes more discussion of the commands COPY, DISKCOPY, and ERASE.

Part II

Expanding Your Knowledge of DOS and Disks

Includes

Gaining More Control over Your Files

Understanding DOS and Devices

Understanding Floppy Disks and
Their Drives

Understanding Hard Disks and How
DOS Uses Disks

Naming Disk Drives

7

Gaining More Control over Your Files

This chapter completes your "survival training" and covers the remaining frequently used DOS commands. The new commands discussed are RENAME, the command that changes a file name, and ERASE, the command that removes files from disks. You will also learn more about using the COPY and DISKCOPY commands. All these commands are available from the DOS Shell as well as from the command prompt.

For the hands-on exercises in this chapter, you will need your computer ready to go with DOS running, and you will need a formatted floppy disk. Follow the directions for the FORMAT command in Chapter 5 if you need to prepare a floppy disk. If you like, use the /V switch to make a volume label, such as "Practice." If you do not have a hard disk, you will also need the DOS Master disk (or floppy disks, if you are using the 360K floppy disks) you made in Chapter 5.

More on Copying Files (COPY, /V)

The COPY command copies files. You were introduced to this most frequently used DOS command in Chapter 5. This section presents more information about using the COPY command from the DOS prompt and shows you how to make the command work the way you want it to. Then you will learn ways to use COPY from the DOS Shell. Those of you who use the Shell should go through the next section first. Access the DOS command prompt by pressing Shift-F9.

Understanding the Syntax of the COPY Command

A command's syntax is simply the way the command is phrased. The easiest way to remember the syntax of the COPY command is to think of it in this manner:

COPY *where and what it is now* to *where it is going and what it will be*

The *where it is now* is the name of the disk drive that holds the file you want to copy. The *what it is now* is the name of the file you want to copy. The *where it is going* is the name of the disk drive where the copy of the file will be placed. And the *what it will be* is the new name of the file to be copied.

A more formal way of expressing the command is

> **COPY** *source disk drive and file name* → *destination disk drive and new file name*

The COPY command accepts two file names. The first file name, the *source* file, tells DOS which file to copy. The source file name may be preceded by an optional disk drive name. The source file name can include the wild-card characters ? and *. By using wild cards with a single file name, you can match and copy several files at the same time.

The formal notation for the source disk drive and source file name(s)—the file or files to be copied—is

> *ds:***filenames**.*exts*

ds: (the *s* signifies *source*) is the name of the disk drive that holds the file(s). If the source files are on the current disk drive, you may omit the disk drive name. Remember that if you use a disk drive name, you must place the colon between the disk drive letter and the file name, but you must not put a space before or after the colon.

filenames (the final *s* signifies *source*) is the name of the file or files to copy. You must give the root name, which can contain wild cards. The optional extension is *.exts*. If the file you want to copy has an extension, you must give it. With the COPY command, you may also use wild cards in the extension. Remember to use the period between the root name and the extension and not to use a space between the root name and the extension.

Notice that *ds:* and *.exts* are in italic. When parts of a command appear in italic in this book, they are optional. If the source file is on the current disk drive, you can omit the disk drive name *ds:*. If the file does not have an extension, you omit the extension *.exts*

Although letters or numbers may be added to file names in our notation, the limits on the length of file names remain. Eight characters in the root name and three in the extension are the maximums.

To copy a file, you must type at the very least the command name, **COPY**, and the source file name, **filenames**. Both parts of the command appear in boldface to indicate that you must give these parts.

The second file name, the destination file, tells DOS where to place the file or files that are to be copied. The destination can be just a disk drive name, or a new name for the file or files to be copied, or both. The notation for the destination is

> *dd:**filenamed.extd*

dd: (the second *d* signifies *destination*) is the name of the disk drive to receive the copy of the file or files. If the destination is the current disk drive and the source is another drive, you can omit the disk drive name *dd:*

filenamed.extd is the new name for the file or files copied. *filenamed* is the new root name, and *.extd* is the new extension. You may use wild cards in either part of the destination file name. If you give only *filenamed,* that in itself will be the new name. To give an extension, you must give *filenamed* and specify that the new extension will be *.extd*

The formal syntax for the COPY command is

> **COPY** *ds:***filenames.***exts dd:filenamed.extd* /V

All elements that contain an *s* are part of the source file name. All elements with a *d* are part of the destination file name. COPY also has several switches that affect how files are copied. The most frequently used switch, /V, verifies that the copy of the file is correct. The verify switch is given last.

Only the words **COPY** and **filenames,** which appear in boldface, are mandatory. All other information (disk drive names, the destination file name, and the verify switch) is optional.

Note that when the source and destination drives are the same drive, you cannot copy a file unless *filenames* and *filenamed* are different. In other words, you cannot copy a file onto itself. DOS gives you an error message if you try. Either the source and destination drives must be different, or the source and destination file names must be different.

You give the destination disk drive name when you want to copy files between disk drives. You give a new destination file name when you want the copy of the file to have a different file name.

Now that you have more basic information on how the COPY command works, try using the command several different ways.

Hands-on Practice: Copying Files

For this practice session, make sure that DOS is running on your computer. You will need two disk drives. If your computer has two floppy disk drives, you should put the DOS Master Diskette or Master Operating Diskette into drive A and a formatted floppy disk into drive B. Make sure that the current disk drive is drive A. (If necessary, type **A:** and then press Enter.)

Owners of hard disks should place a formatted floppy disk into drive A. The current disk drive should be drive C. (If necessary, type **C:** and then press Enter.) The current directory should be the one that holds the DOS programs. If you set up your hard disk as shown in Appendix E, issue a **CHDIR \BIN** command to change to the directory that holds the DOS programs. If you have not set up your hard disk by using the instructions in Appendix E, change the BIN to the appropriate name for the directory holding your DOS files.

If you have two floppy disk drives, type

A>COPY CHKDSK.COM B: /V

If you have a hard disk, type

C>COPY CHKDSK.COM A: /V

This command copies the file CHKDSK.COM to the floppy disk in drive B (for users of floppy disk drives) or to the floppy disk in drive A (for users of hard disk drives). You should see the following message:

```
1 File(s) copied
```

If you see any other message, you have the wrong floppy disk in drive A, or you are using the wrong directory on drive C. Either get the right floppy disk or change to the correct directory.

Look at the screen for a few seconds. Do you remember using the COPY command in Chapter 5? When you copied files in that chapter, you used wild-card characters in the file name. When you copied CHKDSK, however, you used a file name without a wild-card character. Do you remember any difference between the video screen now and the video screen as it appeared when you copied with wild-card file names?

The difference is that the COPY command does not display file names when you use an unambiguous file name. If you use a file name that contains wild-card characters, COPY displays the name of each file it copies. If you do not use wild-card characters in the file name, COPY displays only the `File(s) copied` message.

Now copy the Disk BASIC (BASIC.COM) and Advanced BASIC (BASICA.COM) files. First, you need to ensure that the files you want to copy are on the floppy disk or directory you are about to copy from. Use the directory command, DIR, to look. Type

C>DIR BASIC*.*

If you are using floppy disk drives, you will see an A in place of the C. In this example, you see the result from a computer with a hard disk.

To look at the files, you used the name **BASIC*.***. In Chapter 6 you learned that the asterisk wild card matches any characters in a file name. The name **BASIC*** matches all names that start with BASIC and have any other characters in the root name. The asterisk for the extension matches a file with any extension or none. The result is the display of any file name that starts with BASIC.

Your screen should display something like this:

C>DIR BASIC*.*

```
 Volume in drive C is HARD DISK
 Directory of C:\BIN
```

```
BASIC     COM     1063    3-17-87  12:00p
BASICA    COM    36403    3-17-87  12:00p
BASIC     PIF      369    3-17-87  12:00p
BASICA    PIF      369    3-17-87  12:00p
          4 File(s)     228341 bytes free

C>
```

The display lists the two files you wish to copy, BASIC.COM and BASICA.COM. However, two other file names appear in the list: BASIC.PIF and BASICA.PIF. These files are *program information files* that are used by IBM's windowing system software, Top-View™, and Microsoft's windowing system software, Microsoft Windows.

You have a problem. You want to copy the files BASIC.COM and BASICA.COM, but not the two files that have the extension PIF. COPY is an all-or-nothing command. You can use only a single source file name. If you use the same name you gave to the directory command, you will copy too many files. What should you do?

The obvious solution is to use different file names. You could give the COPY command twice, once for each file name. But why give the command twice when one command will do? Look again at the file names shown in the preceding screen. What source file name could we give to COPY that would match the two BASIC program files but omit the two program information files?

Actually, two different names could be used. The possible source file names are

BASIC?.COM

and

BASIC*.COM

Each file name starts with BASIC. BASICA.COM contains one more letter in the root file name than BASIC.COM. Therefore, you can use the ? wild-card character in the sixth position of the root name to match the A in BASICA or the nonexistent character after the C in BASIC. You can also use the asterisk to match all characters in the sixth through eighth positions in the root file name. Hence the file names BASIC?.COM and BASIC*.COM work equally well.

The key to making these names work is that you specify a particular extension, .COM. If you use the * for the extension, you will get all four files. By specifying .COM, you get only files with the extension .COM.

The file names **BASIC?.COM** and **BASIC*.COM** match any file whose first five characters are BASIC and whose extension is .COM. The name BASIC?.COM restricts the match to those files that have no character or any character in the sixth position but do not have any characters in the seventh and eighth positions. **BASIC*.COM** matches files that have any or no characters in the sixth through the eighth positions in the root file name.

Although I can find the * on my keyboard easier than I can the ?, the preferred file name and the one I use is BASIC?.COM. The reason for this choice is that using the asterisk wild card rather than the question-mark character might lead to surprises, because the * matches more files than the ?.

In the case of copying the BASIC files, you know that you want to copy both files that match the name BASIC*.COM. There might be times, however, when you do not check the directory beforehand. When you are not absolutely sure of what files will be copied with a wild-card file name, use as restrictive a file name as possible—in this case BASIC?.COM. When you know what files will be copied, you may use the * wild card with impunity. We will discuss this subject again later in this chapter.

Now that you know the correct file name to use, copy the files. If you use a floppy disk computer, type

A>COPY BASIC?.COM B: /V

If you have a hard disk, type

C>COPY BASIC?.COM A: /V

You will notice that two file names appear on the screen. Because you just used an ambiguous file name, DOS shows the names of the files that match the wild-card name. Your screen should look something like this:

```
C>COPY BASIC?.COM A: /V
BASIC.COM
BASICA.COM

      2 File(s) copied

C>
```

Next, copy the DISKCOPY program to the floppy disk, but change the name of the copied file.

If you have two floppy disk drives, type

A>COPY DISKCOPY.COM B:COPYDISK.COM /V

If you have a hard disk, type

C>COPY DISKCOPY.COM A:COPYDISK.COM /V

Now verify that you have copied your files. Look at the directory of the disk you have been copying from and the directory of the floppy disk you have copied to. If you have a computer with a floppy disk, type the following commands:

A>DIR A: /P

A>DIR B: /P

If you have a computer with a hard disk, type the following commands:

C>DIR C: /P

C>DIR A: /P

Look for the names DISKCOPY.COM and COPYDISK.COM in the directory listings. Notice the date and time for each file. The dates are the same, and so are the times. When you copy a file, DOS gives the copy the date and time of the original file. The file sizes should also be the same.

The next exercise shows what happens when you omit a disk drive name or make a similar mistake. Change the current disk drive to drive B (if you have two floppy disk drives) or to drive A (if you have a hard disk).

If you have two floppy disk drives, type

    B>**COPY COPYDISK.COM B: /V**

If you have a hard disk, type

    A>**COPY COPYDISK.COM A: /V**

You should see the following message:

```
File cannot be copied onto itself

        0 File(s) copied
```

What you attempted to do was to copy COPYDISK.COM on the current disk drive (either drive B or A) back onto drive B or A. DOS correctly informed you that you are really trying to copy the file back to the same floppy disk under the same name. DOS simply gives an error message and does not perform the copying.

Do not remove the floppy disks or turn off your computer yet. You will need this setup for the next hands-on exercises.

Mistakes You Can Make When You Copy Files

As previously suggested, omitting a disk drive name or using the wrong name can be a problem. The problem occurs when the COPY command overwrites a good file with a totally different file. The trap is in the file names.

Using Duplicate File Names

The COPY command can be dangerous if you are not careful about file names. For example, suppose that you have a floppy disk in drive A that holds a file called MYFILE.DAT. This file contains the names and addresses of your clients. You have a floppy disk in drive B that also has a file called MYFILE.DAT, but this file holds the names and addresses of your personal friends. Even though the names of the two files are identical, there is no problem, because each file is on a separate floppy disk.

If, however, you copy MYFILE.DAT from drive A to drive B, DOS first deletes from drive B the file with your friends' names and then copies the file that holds your clients' names to the floppy disk in drive B. You lose the file that holds the information on your friends.

DOS deletes MYFILE.DAT on drive B as a self-defense move. No two files listed in the same directory can have the same name. When you tell DOS to copy files, it checks the names. If a file in the destination directory has a name identical to the name of the file you are copying, DOS deletes the file in the destination directory. No warning is given. The contents of that file are lost. Then DOS executes the COPY command.

This DOS practice is not a problem when you are replacing an outdated version of a file with a new version. The practice *is* a problem when the name of the copied file inadvertently matches another file name, even though the two files are fundamentally different, as in the example of MYFILE.DAT. Mistakes occur most frequently when you use wild cards in a file name. You often "select" more files than you intend. Once the file has been copied over, it is lost. The DOS Shell provides a measure of protection against such errors.

When in doubt about whether you have already used a particular file name, check both directories for duplicate file names before you copy. Use the DIR command on both disks. If file names match, the matching file on the destination floppy disk will be deleted. If you do not want to remove the matching file on the destination disk, you must change the file name. You have two options:

- You can change the name of the file on one of the two disks by using the RENAME command, which is discussed in the next section.

- You can give a unique destination file name so that the names do not match.

Reversing Disk Drive Names

Another "popular" mistake is reversing the disk drive names when attempting to copy files. My hard disk is drive C, and my floppy disk drives are drives A and B. Suppose that I want to replace all the outdated files on my hard disk with the files on a floppy disk I have in drive A. The correct command is

C>**COPY A:*.* C: /V**

This command copies all files from the floppy disk in drive A to the hard disk. If you type the following command, an unpleasant surprise awaits:

C>**COPY C:*.* A: /V**

I call giving this command an "asleep at the switch" error. It replaces the new files on drive A with the old files from drive C. When you copy files, take a second to check your typing. The results are seldom pleasant when you confuse disk drive names.

Copying Files with the DOS Shell

The DOS Shell's ability to copy files quickly and efficiently is one of its most powerful features. You will find that you can perform this type of file management much faster from the Shell than from the DOS prompt, and probably with fewer errors.

For the following exercises, you will need to have the DOS Shell loaded. Select the File System option from the Main Group. You will practice some of the same functions you just completed from the command prompt.

You will need two disk drives for this first exercise. Place your DOS master floppy disk in drive A and a formatted floppy disk in drive B. Make sure that the current drive is drive A. If necessary, select drive A by clicking its symbol with the mouse or by typing Ctrl-A.

If you have a hard disk, insert a formatted floppy disk into drive A. In this case, make sure the current drive is C. Select C by clicking its symbol or typing Ctrl-C.

To copy a file, follow these steps:

Step 1. *Select CHKDSK.COM by moving the highlighting in the right-hand panel to that file. If you have a mouse, you can simply click the file name. If you are using the keyboard, press Tab enough times to make the directory listing active. Then use the cursor keys to move through the files.*

When you have highlighted CHKDSK.COM, click the mouse button or press the space bar to mark it. The file name is highlighted if you have a graphics-based Shell; a right-pointing triangle appears next to the file name if you have a text-based Shell.

Step 2. *Pull down the File menu and select Copy....*

The Copy File box appears on your screen, with the name CHKDSK.COM already shown on the From: line. Move the cursor to the To: line and change that entry. If you have two floppy disk drives, type the following:

B:CHECK.COM

If you have one floppy disk drive and a hard disk, type the following:

A:CHECK.COM

By supplying a name different from that of the source file, you are telling DOS to copy the file and supply a new name at the destination drive.

Step 3. *When you finish, press Enter or click the Enter box with the mouse.*

The Copying File screen appears and reports on the progress of the copy task. You are returned to the File System menu when DOS is finished copying. You can select drive B (or drive C if you have a hard disk) to confirm that CHKDSK.COM has been copied properly.

Copying multiple files is not much more difficult. To copy all files meeting the BASIC*.* specification, follow these steps:

Step 1. *First make sure that drive A or drive C (if you have a hard disk) is the current drive. If it isn't, change to the correct drive.*

There are two ways to copy from drive A or drive C to the floppy all the programs whose file names start with BASIC. In Chapter 6, you used the *.* file specification to copy all the files from a subdirectory or disk to another disk. You could easily substitute in the Copy File box the file specification BASIC*.* as the From: entry. Let's do it another way, however.

Step 2. *Move the cursor to the file listing in the right-hand panel and select the first program that starts with the characters BASIC.*

The first program might be BASIC.COM, BASICA.COM, BASIC.PIF, or BASICA.PIF, depending on your disk. Press the space bar or click the file name to mark the file.

Step 3. Now move through the listing to find the next file, and mark it in the same way. Repeat until all the files are marked.

Step 4. Pull down the File menu and select Copy....

The Copy File box appears on your screen, listing in a horizontal row the names of all the files you have marked. The cursor will be on the To: line.

If you want, you can move the cursor up to the From: line and review the list of files there. Users of graphics-based systems can access the scroll bar. If you have a text-based system, just move the cursor with the right or left arrow keys. The names scroll as you reach the right or left limits of the listing. Move the cursor back to the To: line; change that entry to B: if you have two floppy disk drives or to A: if you have one floppy and a hard disk.

Step 5. When you finish, press Enter or click the Enter box with the mouse.

The Copying File screen appears and reports on the progress of the copy task as each file is copied.

This technique could be applied to files whose names are not similar and that thus do not lend themselves to copying with wild cards. You can mark files quickly and copy them all to the same destination in a few seconds. This capability makes file management with the Shell very easy indeed. You will learn other things that you can do, such as moving files, when you look at the File System in more detail.

Changing File Names

A frequent task of managing disk files is to change the name of a file. You can change the name of a file's copy by using the COPY command, as you just learned. You may, however, sometimes want to change the name of a file without making a copy of the file. The command you use to change a file's name is RENAME. RENAME also has a shorthand form, REN. Either form is acceptable to DOS, and both forms work the same way. The DOS Shell has its own Rename... option in the File menu. First, let's look at the DOS command line equivalent.

Using the RENAME Command (RENAME, REN)

The syntax for RENAME is fairly straightforward:

RENAME *d:*oldfilename.oldext newfilename.newext

d: is the optional disk drive that holds the file you want to rename. The disk drive name must be given when the file whose name will be changed is not on the current disk drive.

oldfilename is the root name of the file whose name will be changed. If the file has an extension (**.oldext**), you must give it.

newfilename is the new root name for the file. When you change the file's name, you can keep the same file extension by giving the current extension for **.newext**; you can change the extension by giving a different name for **.newext**; or you can drop the extension by giving no name for **newext**

Wild-card characters are allowed in the root file names and extensions for the old and new names. Obviously, wild cards are not allowed for disk drive names. (No DOS command uses wild cards for names of disk drives.)

Notice that you do not give a disk drive name with the new file name. You give a disk drive name only with the original file. DOS remembers where the file is (from the original file name) and changes the name but does not move the file, which is why you do not need to (nor should you) give a disk drive designation with the new name.

DOS protects itself from having two files with the same name. If you try to rename a file using a name that is already in the directory, DOS issues an error message. For example, if in a file name you use wild cards that could produce two files with the same name, DOS will give the following error message:

```
Duplicate file name or File not found
```

Any files renamed before the error message appears will have new names, but remaining files are left unchanged. You must use the RENAME command again to change the names of the remaining files.

Remember that the RENAME command does not touch the contents of the file. RENAME changes only the file's name in the appropriate directory. But just as your friends may not immediately recognize you when you wear a different outfit or shave a beard or mustache, DOS does not recognize a new file by its old file name. DOS "sees" the file that has a different file name as a different file. You cannot use the old file name with the new file unless you change the name back to the original name.

Hands-on Practice: Renaming Files

Make sure that the practice floppy disk you are using is in the appropriate disk drive (drive B for two floppy disk drives and drive A for a hard disk). The current disk drive should be the one that holds the floppy disk (drive B and drive A, respectively). In this section, the instructions are the same for users of computers with floppy disk drives and computers with hard disk drives.

Type the following command:

A>**RENAME COPYDISK.COM DISKCOPY.COM**

This command changes the name of the copy you made of DISKCOPY.COM back to its original name. Notice that when you are successful in changing a file's name, DOS does not give you any message. For some DOS commands, no news is good news. You see a message only when an error occurs.

Now type the following:

A>REN CHKDSK.COM CHECK.COM

This renames the check-disk program, CHKDSK.COM, to CHECK.COM. The shorthand form REN is used here. Remember that DOS accepts either REN or RENAME. Because most people prefer to type as few characters as possible, REN is the more popular form.

Next, type these two commands:

A>CHKDSK

A>CHECK

Unless you have another copy of CHKDSK.COM available to DOS (through the PATH command, discussed later), you will see the following message when you type CHKDSK:

```
Bad command or file name
```

This DOS catch-all message states that DOS could not find the command or program you requested. The reason you see the error message when you give the command **CHKDSK** is that the check-disk program is no longer called CHKDSK.COM on the floppy disk. It is now called CHECK.COM. When you type the second line, DOS runs the check-disk program under its new name. Renaming the program does not change what the program does; it changes only the name by which the program is invoked.

Now type the following commands:

A>REN *.COM *.XXX

A>DIR

Notice that all files that had an extension of .COM now have an extension of .XXX. The first wild card in the old file name says, "Match any characters in the root name." The corresponding wild card in the new file name says, "Do not change the root name." A wild-card character is frequently used in the same position in old and new file names to tell DOS not to change that part of the name.

Now try to run the check-disk command by typing **CHECK**. What happened?

DOS is selective about the files it considers to be runable programs. Unless a program ends with a .COM or an .EXE extension, DOS does not execute the file. (A third type of executable file, a batch file, must end in the extension .BAT.)

In this example, the files that had the .COM extension now have the extension .XXX. DOS looks for a file by the name of CHECK.COM, CHECK.EXE, or CHECK.BAT and finds a file CHECK.XXX. Because DOS does not know how to handle a file with an .XXX extension, it keeps looking. Finding no qualifying file, DOS displays an error message.

You know, of course, that the file CHECK.XXX holds a good version of the check-disk program, but DOS does not know that. Be careful when you change the extension of a program file. DOS may not be able to run the program.

To run the check-disk program, you must change the file back to its original name. To do so, type the following:

    A>**RENAME *.XXX *.COM**

This command changes the name of your program files so that they have their original extensions. Now type the following command:

    A>**CHECK**

The check-disk program executes normally.

The last thing you should do is change the check-disk program's name back to its original name. Type the following:

    A>**REN CHECK.COM CHKDSK.COM**

Do not remove the floppy disks or turn off your computer yet. You will need this setup for the next several exercises.

Renaming Files with the DOS Shell

You can rename files just as easily with the DOS Shell, although the procedure is a bit different. The nice thing about the Shell version is that you can mark a number of files and change their names in one batch, if you want. You cannot rename a group of files by using wild cards, however. You must select the files you want to rename, and do them one at a time. Shortly, you will learn a trick to speed up this process, but first, let's rename a list of files. Follow these steps:

Step 1. *Make sure that drive A is the active directory (or drive C if you have a hard disk). Move the cursor to the directory listing.*

Step 2. *Select several files that end with the .COM extension.*

CHKDSK.COM, DISKCOPY.COM, and FORMAT.COM are good examples. Mark each of these by pressing the space bar or clicking the file names with the mouse button.

Step 3. *Now pull down the File menu and choose Rename....*

The Rename File box appears as shown in figure 7.1.

One line says `Current filename:` CHKDSK.COM `1 of 3`; this line means that you are currently working with CHKDSK.COM and that two more files follow it to be renamed. The cursor will be in the New filename... line.

Step 4. *Type* **CHECK.COM** *as the new file name. Press Enter when you're finished, or click the Enter box.*

Fig. 7.1

The Rename File box.

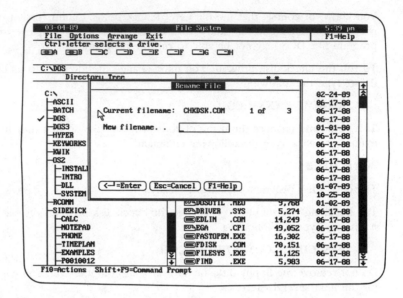

The box will disappear from the screen and reappear with the next file name, DISK-COPY.COM, on the Current filename line. Type in **COPYDISK.COM** as the new file name and press Enter. Repeat this step to change FORMAT.COM to SFORMAT.COM.

When all the files have been renamed, the File System menu appears, and the directory listing is updated to reflect the new names.

Now let's use wild cards as a shortcut for renaming a group of files. Although the DOS Shell's Rename... option does not recognize wild cards, you already know that the directory listing does. You can take advantage of that fact to select a group of files quickly. Just change the directory listing to show only those files, and then select all of them from the File menu.

That procedure is not as complicated as it sounds. Let's assume that you want to rename all the .COM files. Follow these steps:

Step 1. *Pull down the Options menu from the File System action bar and choose Display options....*

The Display Options box appears.

Step 2. *On the Name: line, type the following:*

    *.COM

Step 3. *Press Enter.*

The directory listing changes so that only files ending in the .COM extension are shown.

Step 4. *Now pull down the File menu and choose Select all.*

All the choices in the directory panel are highlighted or marked.

Step 5. *Pull down the File menu again and choose Rename....*

Each of the files ending in .COM is presented in turn for you to supply a new file name. This procedure takes longer than doing the task from the DOS command line, but it is still relatively efficient.

Removing Unwanted Files

Although it seems a waste to destroy work you have done putting files on a disk, there are occasions when you will want to remove a file that is no longer needed. To delete a file, you use the ERASE command. DOS Shell users can accomplish the same thing from the File System's File menu, which has a Delete... option. Let's look at the DOS command line version first.

Using the ERASE or DEL Command (ERASE, DEL)

Like RENAME, ERASE has a short form, DEL, which is short for delete. The syntax for the ERASE command is

> **ERASE** *d:***filename**.*ext*

Users of DOS V4 have one additional option, the /P switch. The ERASE or DEL command looks like this with the switch added:

> **ERASE** *d:***filename**.*ext* /P

d: is the optional disk drive that holds the file or files to be removed. If the file is on the current disk drive, you omit the disk drive name.

filename is the root name of the file to be removed. Giving the root name is mandatory. *.ext* is the extension. You give the extension if the file has one.

When you include the /P switch (with DOS V4 or later), DOS will ask you first whether you want to remove the file:

```
C:\MYFILE.TXT, Delete (Y/N)?
```

You may type **Y** to remove the file or **N** to leave it alone. The /P switch can be used whether you are deleting a single file or, using wild cards, a series of files.

When a file is erased, its name is removed from the list of files on the disk. The disk space used by the file is freed and can be used to store more files or to extend the information in current files.

DOS offers no facility to retrieve files that have been removed. Once a file has been removed, you cannot "unerase" it with a DOS command. The information in the file is lost. Therefore, ERASE is considered a dangerous command, one you should use cautiously. Giving the wrong file name or disk drive name or omitting a necessary disk drive name can result in the removal of the wrong file. Check your typing when you give the ERASE command.

Wild cards are allowed in the root name and the extension when you use the ERASE command. But wild cards make ERASE even more dangerous. When you give the ERASE command an ambiguous file name (a name with wild cards), you may remove more files than you want to. For that reason, DOS V4's /P switch is a good idea whenever you are removing files with a wild-card specification.

Erased files can sometimes, but not always, be recovered with the help of programs that you purchase separately. If you erase a file by accident, follow these three important steps: do not panic, do not record any additional information on the disk, and have a program like Norton Utilities™ on hand. (The utilities are discussed in Chapter 28.)

Hands-on Practice: Erasing Files

For this session, you can use your practice floppy disk. The instructions are the same for users of computers with floppy disk drives and computers with hard disk drives.

Because files you erase are not retrievable, you must be certain that the current disk drive is the correct disk drive for the exercise. The current disk drive is drive B for systems with two floppy disk drives and drive A for hard disk systems. If you inadvertently erase the wrong file, you can copy the erased files from your DOS Master or Master Operating floppy disk. But making sure that you are removing the correct file is always important.

After you give each ERASE command, perform a DIR command to see the results of the erase operation. Notice that the bytes available increase each time you remove a file.

Type the following command:

    A>**ERASE DISKCOPY.COM**

This command removes the DISKCOPY program from your practice floppy disk. Then type

    A>**DEL BASIC*.***

This command deletes all the BASIC language program files from the floppy disk. Note that DEL is interchangeable with ERASE. Finally, type the following:

    A>**ERASE *.***

DOS responds with this message:

```
Are you sure (Y/N)?
```

or

```
All files in directory will be deleted!
```

You are about to erase all the remaining files on the floppy disk. When you give the file name *.* to ERASE, DOS confirms your intentions. If you answer **Y** and then press Enter,

DOS removes all the files on the floppy disk. If you answer **N** and press Enter, DOS does not delete any of the files.

In this example, answer **Y** and press Enter. Issue the DIR command to see that all files have been removed from the directory.

Remember the caution about the ERASE command. If you are in doubt about which files will be erased, use the DIR command first. If a file you do not want erased shows up in the list of files, use a different file name with ERASE.

If you are using DOS V4, you should specify the /P switch when erasing files. First, you must copy some more files to your practice floppy disk. There are several ways to do this. Use one of the methods below:

- If you have a hard disk system, put your practice floppy disk in drive A and type the following line:

    COPY C:\BIN*.* A:

    If your hard disk uses some other directory name (such as C:\DOS) for the DOS files, replace the C:\BIN portion with the correct directory.

- If you have a floppy-disk-based system with two disk drives, insert a disk with some files into drive B and put your practice disk into drive A. Type the following line:

    COPY B:*.* A:

- If you have a system with no hard disk and only one floppy disk, you can also copy files from drive B (the imaginary drive) to A (your real floppy disk). Copying a large group of files requires many disk swaps, however, so copy only a few files. Insert your practice disk into drive A and type the following line:

    COPY B:*.COM A:

DOS will display a message like the following:

    Insert disk for Drive B: in drive and press any key.

You then insert the disk you want to copy from (use your Master DOS disk) into the drive and press Enter. Swap that disk and your practice disk as directed by the messages until all the files have been copied.

Now you are ready to practice using the /P parameter. Make sure that your practice floppy disk is in drive A and type this line:

    ERASE A:*.* /P

You will see each file name displayed in turn, followed by a request to confirm or deny permission to erase the file. Follow through with each file on your practice disk. Erase some, but keep a few to check that the command worked properly.

Now type **DIR** and see whether the files you asked to be deleted were in fact removed.

Erasing Files with the DOS Shell

You can delete groups of files by using the Shell's Delete... option even more simply than you copied or renamed them. First, you need to create some files to delete. Copy a few files from drive A to drive B (if you have two floppy disk drives) or from drive C to drive A (if you have a hard disk).

Step 1. *Select the files you want to remove.*

You can do this by using the Display options... trick explained earlier, so that only files meeting the wild-card specification you enter are displayed in the directory listing. The Select all option in the File menu will choose all of them for deletion.

Or you can mark individual files by highlighting them and pressing the space bar or clicking the mouse button, as always.

Step 2. *When the files you want to delete are marked, pull down the File menu and choose Delete....*

The files you have marked will be shown on a single line in the first of two Delete File screens. You may review this list by scrolling through the names, if you want. Press Enter to accept the list.

DOS will delete the files. You may see a second screen that prompts you to delete or not delete each file. Or DOS may simply delete all of them without asking. What determines whether you are prompted?

The File System lets you determine whether you want to be prompted when a file is deleted, much as DOS V4 has a /P (prompt) switch with the DEL or ERASE commands. You can turn this feature on and off. Try it with the following exercise:

Step 1. *Pull down the Options menu and then the File Options menu.*

The File Options screen, which looks like figure 7.2, appears.

This menu offers three choices:

    Confirm on delete

    Confirm on replace

    Select across directories

If any of the choices has been chosen, it will be highlighted or marked. When `Confirm on delete` is active, the Shell asks you whether you really want to delete each file before removing it. When `Confirm on replace` is active, the Shell prompts you to confirm that you want to copy a new file over an old file with the same name. The final option, `Select across directories`, lets you mark files spanning several disks and directories for even more comprehensive copying, deleting, etc.

If you think you would like to activate any of these choices, you can do it now. If one of them is not to your liking (it becomes tedious, for example, to answer each time you want to copy over an old file), you can quickly switch it off.

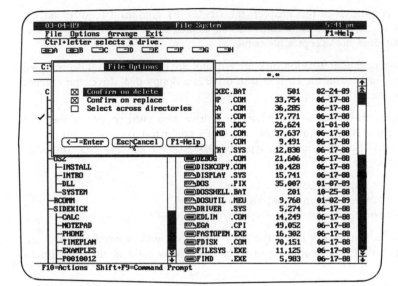

Fig. 7.2

The File Options menu.

More on Copying Complete Disks (DISKCOPY)

In Chapter 2, you used the DISKCOPY command to make a "carbon copy" of your original DOS floppy disk. DISKCOPY copies the entire contents of one floppy disk to another.

DISKCOPY is an external command; that is, it is not built into DOS. It is also available from the DOS Utilities menu that can be selected from the Main Group. When using DISKCOPY from the command line, you must load it from a floppy disk or your hard disk.

Using DISKCOPY from the Command Line

Look at the command line version first. The correct syntax is as follows:

*dc:***DISKCOPY** *ds: dd:*

The notation *dc:* represents the name of the disk drive that holds the DISKCOPY command. If the command is on the current disk drive, you can omit the disk drive name. If DISKCOPY is on a different disk drive, you must give the disk drive name.

ds: is the name of the disk drive that holds the floppy disk to be copied. This is the source floppy disk, indicated by the *s* in the name. *dd:* is the disk drive that holds the floppy disk to receive the information. This is the target (or destination) floppy disk.

Unlike the other commands in this chapter, the DISKCOPY command requires no file name and extension. Some DOS commands use file names; some do not. DISKCOPY is one command that does not accept a file name.

Notice that the source and destination disk drive names are optional. If you do not give a source disk drive name, and the current disk drive is a floppy disk drive, the current disk drive will be used for the copying.

If, however, the current disk drive is the hard disk drive, you must specify at least the source disk drive name. You cannot use the DISKCOPY command to copy a hard disk. If the current disk is the hard disk, and you type the DISKCOPY command, DOS responds with this error message:

```
Invalid drive specification
Specified drive does not exist,
or is non-removable
```

If you specify only a source disk drive, the same disk drive will be used to make the target floppy disk. DISKCOPY prompts you to change floppy disks at the appropriate time.

If the floppy disk you are copying to—the target—is not formatted or is formatted differently, DISKCOPY formats the target floppy disk. The message Formatting while copying indicates that the DISKCOPY command is formatting the floppy disk.

A good practice is to format your floppy disks ahead of time, before you need to use them. Then, if the FORMAT command reports any bad sectors on a floppy disk, you know you cannot use it as the target floppy disk with the DISKCOPY command. The DISKCOPY command would attempt to write to the bad sectors of the target floppy disk and would not produce a good copy.

Like the ERASE command, DISKCOPY is a dangerous command. DISKCOPY destroys whatever information is on the target floppy disk. Obviously, you should never use as the target floppy disk one that contains files you want to keep. When in doubt, use the DIR command on the potential target floppy disk to check the files. If the DIR command shows that files you want are on the floppy disk, use a different target floppy disk.

Because DISKCOPY is a dangerous command, use the write-protect tab to protect your source floppy disk. Move the write-protect tab up (for microfloppy disks) or put a write-protect tab over the notch (for minifloppy disks). This precaution is particularly important when you make a copy of a floppy disk by using only one floppy disk drive. If the source floppy disk is write-protected, you cannot damage it if you accidentally reverse the source and target disk drive names or put the wrong floppy disk into the drive.

Using DISKCOPY from the DOS Shell

You have already accessed the DOS Shell Disk Copy utility, but let's review it here. To access the Disk Copy utility, you must first select the DOS Utilities menu from the Main Group. Disk Copy (two words, not one word) is listed as one of the available utilities.

If you select Disk Copy, you have only a few options. You can enter the source and destination drive letters (in that order). If you have only one disk drive, DOS will prompt you at the appropriate time to load the disk for drive B. You can also abort the process by pressing Esc. DISKCOPY is a very easy utility to use from the DOS Shell, so you will want to put it to work frequently.

Summary

This chapter covered the following key points:

❏ When you use the COPY command, you can give the file a new name or leave it as is.

❏ To change a file's name, you use the RENAME (REN) command.

❏ The ERASE (DEL) command removes files.

❏ DISKCOPY makes a "carbon copy" of a floppy disk.

❏ DISKCOPY, COPY, and ERASE can be dangerous commands if you give the wrong disk drive or file name.

❏ These commands are all available from the DOS Shell. COPY and ERASE, in particular, have some enhancements when used from the Shell.

You are finished with your computer for now. You can put the floppy disks away and relax. In the next few chapters, you will look inside DOS to see how the operating system works.

8

Understanding DOS and Devices

This chapter provides some background about DOS and about how DOS works with *devices*. You will learn what devices are and how to use DOS to control them. The chapter also covers DOS's major parts and explains how these parts work together.

Although this chapter's first sections are somewhat technical, the chapter does lay the foundation for understanding how DOS really works. The section on the Command Processor tells you about COMMAND.COM; this information is the most important technical information about DOS you'll need to know. The sections on devices and device names are also important. In addition, you will learn how to use a device name with the COPY command to create text files quickly.

The Three Parts of DOS

DOS may appear to be one large, nebulous "program," but it actually consists of a multitude of programs. You can classify these programs by function into three major parts: the I/O system, the Command Processor, and the utilities. Although you might think of the DOS Shell as a part of DOS, the Shell is actually just another utility. You may be surprised to learn that you've already used all three parts of DOS in the hands-on practice exercises in Chapters 1 through 7.

To use DOS effectively, you do not need to understand exactly which DOS part performs what function. But an acquaintance with what each part does will help you understand DOS's overall operation.

DOS's first major part is the *input/output* system, abbreviated I/O. The I/O system handles every character typed on the keyboard, displayed on-screen, printed on the printer, and received or sent through communications adapters. The I/O system also contains DOS's disk filing system, a management system that stores and retrieves information from the disk drives.

DOS's second major part, the Command Processor, has several built-in functions, or sub-programs, that handle most of DOS's common tasks—copying files, displaying file lists on-screen, and running programs.

The utilities, DOS's third major part, are not discussed specifically in this chapter, but they are described throughout the book and in Part VI, the *DOS Command Reference*. DOS's utilities are used primarily for housekeeping tasks, such as formatting disks, comparing files, finding the amount of free space on a disk, and printing in background mode. The special utility, the Shell, ties all these functions together.

In the next two sections, we'll take a look at both the I/O system and the Command Processor.

The I/O (Input/Output) System

The I/O system comprises all activities related to the computer's *central processing unit* (CPU—the computer's "brain") and to the computer's memory. When you enter a character from the keyboard, the signal for that character moves from the keyboard to the CPU and to the computer's memory. This activity is *input*. When the computer prints a line on the screen or printer, the signals for the line move out from the CPU and the computer's memory to the screen or printer. This activity is *output*.

Input and output take place between the computer and the computer's *peripherals*, such as the screen, keyboard, printer, and disk drives (see fig. 8.1). Peripherals are used by the computer's CPU and memory, but they are not themselves part of the CPU and memory. Peripherals are important to the computer: without them, the CPU and memory would have no way to communicate to the outside world.

Fig. 8.1

Input and output between the computer's peripherals.

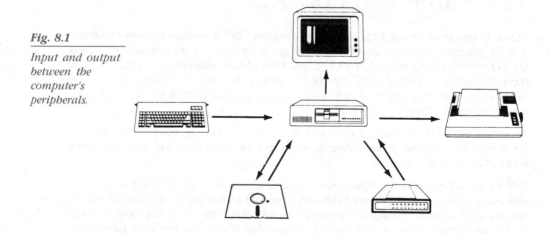

DOS's System for Controlling Peripherals (BIOS)

The part of DOS that communicates with the computer's peripherals is called the *BIOS*, short for Basic Input/Output System. BIOS routines communicate with and provide a standard of control for the keyboard, video display, disk drives, and other peripherals. The BIOS includes the *RIOS* and the *IBMBIO.COM*, each of which is discussed in this section.

The RIOS. The computer's BIOS is located in two places. The first is the computer's system board (or motherboard). On this board, the BIOS is contained in a read-only memory chip called a *ROM*. The nickname for the routines contained in this chip is ROM BIOS, or RIOS (pronounced RYE-ose). The ROM holds the basic routines for communicating with most of the devices used by personal computers.

The IBMBIO.COM. The disk file IBMBIO.COM (called IO.SYS for MS-DOS computers using earlier versions of DOS) is the second location for the BIOS. The file holds the next level of software routines for controlling and communicating with peripherals. These routines build on the routines in the ROM BIOS.

The IBMBIO.COM file is one of the two system files on the disk(s) you created in Chapter 5. You will recall that these files are hidden from you to prevent accidental alteration or erasure. If you unintentionally erase or alter IBMBIO.COM, you cannot properly use the operating system on the altered disk.

The Filing System (IBMDOS.COM)

The final part of the I/O system is the file called IBMDOS.COM (or MSDOS.SYS for MS-DOS computers using earlier versions of DOS). Like IBMBIO.COM, IBMDOS.COM is a system file that cannot be altered or erased. The file contains the major part of the operating system and holds the routines for controlling the information passed between the computer and its peripherals. IBMDOS.COM has two separate filing systems, one for disk drives and one for all nondisk peripherals.

As the control center, IBMDOS.COM communicates its directions to the BIOS. The BIOS, in turn, does the actual "talking" to the devices and transmits the filing system's directions.

The Command Processor (COMMAND.COM)

The Command Processor, COMMAND.COM, is the second major part of DOS. COMMAND.COM is the program with which you communicate, and it, in turn, tells the rest of DOS what to do.

COMMAND.COM displays the system prompt on the video screen when you start DOS. This prompt indicates that you are talking to COMMAND.COM. When you type a command, COMMAND.COM interprets the command and takes the appropriate action.

One of the most important tasks the Command Processor handles is managing critical interrupts. A *critical interrupt* occurs when a hardware device (peripheral) demands attention. At this point, COMMAND.COM diverts the computer's attention to the device. The Command Processor also handles critical errors, usually disk problems or divide-by-zero errors. If you have ever tried to perform the directory command (DIR) on a floppy disk drive that contains no floppy disk, COMMAND.COM is the program that gave the message

```
Not ready error reading drive A
Abort, Retry, Fail?
```

(If this situation should happen to you, you can remedy it by placing a disk into the disk drive and typing **R** for Retry. You can also simply type **A** for Abort to stop the DIR command, and COMMAND.COM will redisplay the system prompt.)

The COMMAND.COM program is operationally organized into two parts. One part is *resident*; once loaded, it remains in memory until you restart DOS or turn off your computer. Most of the COMMAND.COM functions you have just read about are in the resident part of the program.

The second part of COMMAND.COM is *transient* and usually stays in RAM. When a program attempts to allocate memory used by the transient portion of COMMAND.COM, the transient portion is freed. The RAM space formerly occupied by this portion can then be used by other programs.

If one of your programs uses RAM that was occupied by COMMAND.COM, then COMMAND.COM must reload itself from the disk when you have finished with the program. You will know that you must reload COMMAND.COM into RAM if you see the following message:

```
Insert disk with \COMMAND.COM in drive A
and strike any key when ready
```

You'll encounter this message when you start DOS from a disk that does not hold a copy of COMMAND.COM. If you see this message, simply insert a disk that has a copy of COMMAND.COM, such as your DOS Startup disk, and press any key. DOS will reload COMMAND.COM, and the system prompt will reappear.

COMMAND.COM's transient part contains several commonly used DOS commands. These built-in commands are listed in table 6.1 in Chapter 6. When you see the system prompt, you can use any of the commands listed in table 6.1. You don't need to remember which commands are part of the resident or transient part of COMMAND.COM.

COMMAND.COM also processes batch files, executes batch-file subcommands, and redirects input/output. Each of these activities is discussed in later chapters. For now, just remember that you can execute any batch-file or I/O-redirection command when you see the system prompt. You don't have to load a program into memory to use these DOS functions.

The last function of COMMAND.COM mentioned in this section is the most frequently used: loading external DOS commands and applications programs into memory and giving them control of the computer. This book is about DOS, but you spend less than five percent of your computing time interacting directly with DOS. You spend most of your time working with applications programs such as spreadsheets, word-processing programs, accounting programs, and the like. These programs are the real reason you choose to use a microcomputer. Therefore, loading and executing your applications programs are the most important functions of COMMAND.COM.

Learning about Devices

As mentioned previously, a device is a peripheral you connect to your computer. The keyboard, the video screen, and the printer are devices. Each device uses some connection, or *interface*, to talk to the computer. An interface represents both the physical connection (the cable, plugs, and wires) and the electronics that handle communications between the computer and the device.

Some interfaces, such as the one that operates the keyboard unit, are built into the computer. To use a device for which the computer does not have a built-in interface, you have to place a special card or adapter in the computer. (A big difference between Personal Computers and PS/2 computers is that more interfaces are built into PS/2 computers.)

Devices for computers fall into two classes: character-oriented and block-oriented devices. Both types of devices may use either parallel or serial interfaces. The next few paragraphs describe parallel and serial interfaces. Then character-oriented and block-oriented devices are discussed.

The computer and its devices usually communicate with each other one byte at a time. A byte can be transmitted and received in one of two ways. *Parallel* connections transmit the entire byte at one time. A parallel connection uses eight separate wires or lines for the eight bits in a byte, as well as other wires to coordinate the movement of the character. IBM printers use parallel connections.

Serial connections, on the other hand, send the byte one bit at a time. The hardware also sends some additional bits to coordinate the movement of information between the devices. Most modems, the keyboard unit, and the mouse (a menu-selecting and pointing device) use serial connections.

For video displays, the terms *parallel* and *serial* have no real meaning. Video interfaces, either by the adapters or the PS/2 family's Video Graphics Array (VGA), use memory-mapped video. The interfaces project a video image based on the adapter's memory or the array.

Character-oriented devices are peripherals that communicate to the computer one character at a time. Almost all devices that attach to the computer system are character-oriented, including printers, modems, the keyboard, the video display, and selection devices such as a mouse.

Block-oriented devices are peripherals that move information that consists of a group of characters. By this definition, disk drives fit into this category and are the main block devices. In fact, however, disk drives are serial, character-oriented devices. Bytes are stored on the disk, or platter, one bit at a time. The adapter's electronics collect and combine the bits into characters, and the characters into blocks. But this action occurs so fast that you never perceive the work the adapters and disk drives do. It is in this sense that disk drives may be considered block-oriented devices.

Magnetic tape cartridges used for backing up hard disks can be either character- or block-oriented devices. If your tape drive is a *streaming* drive, it is technically a character-oriented device. Otherwise, the tape drive is considered a block-oriented device.

The software used to control these devices (except magnetic tape drives) is in the computer system's BIOS. Higher-level routines are located in DOS's nondisk filing system.

Using Device Names

Every device has a name. PC DOS "knows" several device names. In most cases, the name is based not on the device itself but on the type of adapter the device uses to communicate with the computer.

Device names are three to four characters long. All device names end with a colon. Note, however, that the colon is optional with most commands. When you use a device name in a command, DOS attempts to use the specified adapter or device.

Because of the way DOS is constructed, you can use a device name wherever you can use a file name, meaning that you can direct DOS to get information from a device (such as a modem) or send information to a device (such as a printer).

Each device name is reserved within DOS. You cannot use a device name as the root name of a disk file.

Table 8.1 lists the character-oriented device names that DOS recognizes. This list also includes two additional device names that Disk BASIC and Advanced BASIC (BASICA) use, but DOS does not recognize them. The colon is shown after each device name but is optional.

Beginning with this chapter, you will learn rules for using DOS functions and commands. These rules indicate how to phrase a name or command, what happens when you give or don't give correct command information, and what you can and cannot do with these commands.

The rules in the following list show how you should use device names. Note that if you try to use the root name of a file, and that root name is identical to a device name, DOS will use the device instead of the file.

The following are the rules for character-oriented device names:

1. Valid names for character-oriented devices are CON:, AUX:, COMx:, LPTx:, PRN, and NUL:.

2. The colon after the device name is usually optional.

3. You may use a character-oriented device name wherever you can use file names.

4. If you give an extension with a device name, DOS ignores the extension. For example, DOS treats CON.TXT the same as it does CON:.

5. Do not use a device name for a device that does not exist. For example, if your computer has only one printer, do not use the device LPT2:. You may, however, use NUL:. It is the exception to the rule.

6. When you use NUL: for input, you immediately get an end-of-file condition. When you use NUL: for output, DOS acts as though it is writing information, but it does not record any information. (The data goes into the "bit bucket.")

Rule 5 is especially important. Don't try to use a device you don't have. At best, DOS will give you an error message. At worst, DOS may act erratically.

Table 8.1
Character-Oriented Devices

Name	Device
DOS Device Names	
CON:	The video display and keyboard. Input from CON: comes from the keyboard; output to CON: goes to the video display.
AUX: or COM1:	The first asynchronous communications port.
COM2: COM3: COM4:	The second, third, and fourth asynchronous communications ports, respectively.
LPT1: or PRN	The first line or parallel printer. On PCs, this device is used only for output. PS/2s use LPT1:, LPT2:, and LPT3: for input and output.
LPT2: LPT3:	The second and third parallel printers.
NUL:	A nonexistent (dummy) device.
Disk and Advanced BASIC Device Names	

Name	Device
KYBD:	The keyboard of the system (an input-only device).
SCRN:	The video display (an output-only device).

Using the COPY Command with a Device (COPY CON)

Later in this book, you will be asked several times to create files that hold just a few lines of text. This section shows you a "quick and dirty" way to transfer information from the keyboard directly into a file. You will find that this useful technique is faster than using a text editor for creating short files.

Try the following exercise:

Step 1. *Put a formatted practice disk into a disk drive and type*

> **COPY CON SHOWFILE.TXT**

When you type this line and press Enter, the cursor will move to the beginning of the next line.

Step 2. *Next, type the following line:*

> **This is a file copied quickly between a device and a disk.**

Step 3. *Press Enter at the end of the line.*

Step 4. *After you press Enter, press the F6 function key.*

DOS will display a ^Z on the screen.

Step 5. *Press Enter again.*

You'll see a message indicating that DOS has copied one file.

Step 6. *Now use the TYPE command to see the file you copied. Type the following command:*

> **TYPE SHOWFILE.TXT**

The line that began "This is a file . . ." should appear on your screen.

You have just copied a "file" from the keyboard to a disk file. The letters CON represent a DOS abbreviation for *console*, which is the keyboard and the video screen. In the steps you have just followed, you used the COPY command to take what was typed on the keyboard and put the characters into the disk file called SHOWFILE.TXT.

Does this process work the other way? To find out, type this command:

> **COPY SHOWFILE.TXT CON**

Yes, the process works the other way. This process is identical to using DOS's TYPE command to display the file. You can copy files between the console, serial adapters, printers, or other devices as though you were copying disk files. You cannot use COPY as a general-purpose communications program, but the process illustrates the versatility of both DOS and the COPY command.

To use the COPY command to create text files, follow these three steps:

Step 1. To start the process, use the following command syntax:

COPY CON *d:***filename**.*ext*

The **COPY CON** part of the command copies from the keyboard (CON) to a file. *d:* is the disk drive name (optional). **filename** is the root name of the file you want to create, and *.ext* is the extension for the file (optional).

Be aware that if a file already exists by the same name you use in the COPY process, DOS will erase that file before it creates the new file. Therefore, you should not use a name that is used for another file in the directory unless you want to erase the previously existing file.

Step 2. Type the information you want to place in the file and press Enter at the end of each line.

Be careful as you type lines into the file. Once you have pressed Enter, you cannot correct mistakes made while entering the line. If you make a mistake and have already pressed Enter, omit Step 3 (which saves the file), press Ctrl-Break (or Ctrl-C) to stop the COPY process, and start again at Step 1.

Step 3. After you have entered all the lines, press the F6 function key.

DOS displays a ^Z on-screen. Press Enter; the disk drive light will come on.

Soon DOS will display a message saying that it has copied one file. You have created a text file with the COPY command.

Summary

In this chapter, you learned some important facts about DOS:

- ❏ DOS has three major sections: the input/output system (I/O system), COMMAND.COM, and housekeeping utilities that are stored on disk.

- ❏ The I/O system contains the ROM BIOS, plus IBMBIO.COM and IBMDOS.COM.

- ❏ When you boot the computer, IBMBIO.COM and IBMDOS.COM load into the computer. COMMAND.COM (the Command Processor) also loads into the computer.

- ❏ COMMAND.COM has several built-in functions and DOS commands.

- ❏ DOS has several names that are reserved as device names. You may use these names whenever you would use a file name.

- ❏ You can use the command **COPY CON filename** to create text files quickly.

9

Understanding Floppy Disks and Their Drives

Disk drives are your computer system's most important peripherals. Of course, keyboards and video screens are useful input/output devices; and printers, plotters, and modems extend the capabilities of your system. But with disk drives, the computer can store and retrieve large amounts of information.

A computer uses random-access memory (RAM) to hold temporarily your programs and data, including DOS itself. RAM is volatile, though. When you turn off the computer's power, whatever is in RAM disappears. Disk storage, however, is not volatile. When you turn off the power, whatever is on the disk stays. That is why floppy disks are important.

The next part of this chapter is a tour of the floppy disk.

Understanding Floppy Disks

If you use minifloppy disks, get one of the disks that came with your copy of DOS V3.3 or DOS V4. If you use microfloppy disks, get the microfloppy disk that came with your copy of DOS. We'll start with a look at the minifloppy disk. Then we'll examine the microfloppy disk.

Looking at Minifloppy (5 1/4-Inch) Disks

The floppy disk got its name because the disk and the black, flexible jacket it comes in will "flop" if you flip them back and forth. The disks and their jackets come in protective envelopes. Because the jacket does not provide much protection for your disk, you should handle minifloppy disks with care.

Take your floppy disk out of its envelope. The disk should slide right out. If it looks as if you need to cut something open to get at the disk, you have probably confused the protective envelope with the disk's jacket.

135

The inside of a floppy disk's jacket often has a gauze-like, plastic material glued to it. This material traps small particles of dust and keeps them from contacting the disk as it spins. The material is usually lubricated with silicone so that the disk does not rub as it spins.

Inside the jacket is the disk itself, which is circular and has a diameter of 5 1/4 inches. The disk is usually made of polyurethane coated with metal oxide. Most floppy disks are dark brown and shiny, but some are red, gold, or even green.

Technically, the term *floppy disk* applies to an 8-inch disk. The 5 1/4-inch version is a *minifloppy disk*, and the 3 1/2-inch version is a *microfloppy disk*. Because of sloppy usage, the distinction between these terms has been blurred. This book, however, specifically uses the terms *minifloppy* and *microfloppy* if the difference between the types of disks is important. Otherwise, the term *floppy disk* applies to either minifloppy or microfloppy disks.

Now, to continue the tour, make sure that the side of the disk with the printed label is facing you (see fig. 9.1). This side is the front of the disk. In the middle of the disk is a large *centering hole*. The disk drive grasps the disk by this hole. Sometimes a plastic ring is placed around the centering hole to provide extra strength and to help center the disk on the disk drive.

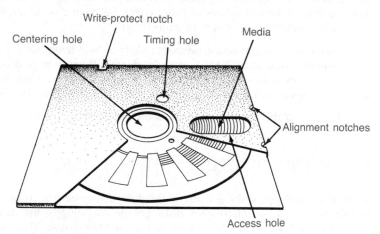

Fig. 9.1

The anatomy of a minifloppy disk.

On both the front and back of the disk jacket, at the bottom, are oblong openings through which you can see the disk. These openings are the *access holes*, where the disk drive's recording heads make contact with the disk.

Now, hold the disk by the edge of the jacket. The top side of the disk has the printed label and should face you. Hold the disk so that the access holes are at the bottom, in the six o'clock position.

You'll notice near the access hole a small hole in the jacket. This is the *index,* or *timing, hole*. Put two fingers in the centering hole and grasp the edge of the disk. Gently rotate the disk until you see a smaller hole, also called the index hole, in the disk itself. The disk drive shines a light through this index hole to help determine where data is stored on the disk. Disks with single index holes are called *soft-sectored* disks. Most personal computers use soft-sectored disks.

Hold the disk vertically and look at the right edge of the jacket near the top. You should see a small notch in the jacket, called the *write-protect notch*. When you leave the notch uncovered, the computer can write information on the disk. When you cover the notch, the disk is *write-protected*: the computer cannot write, change, or erase information on the disk. Technically, we should refer to the notch on the 5 1/4-inch disk as the *write-enable* notch, but careless usage has made the term *write-protect* standard.

Using the write-protect notch is an easy way to protect your disks. If you cover a disk's write-protect notch, no information can be put on the disk, and no files can be erased from it. If you look at the disks provided with DOS V3.3, you'll notice that the IBM DOS disks do not have write-protect notches. The information on these disks is permanently write-protected from alteration or erasure by the computer.

Looking at Microfloppy (3 1/2-Inch) Disks

As you look at a microfloppy disk, you'll notice that it is covered by a plastic shell (see fig. 9.2). The rigid shell protects the disk better than the flimsy plastic cover that protects a 5 1/4-inch disk.

Fig. 9.2

The anatomy of a microfloppy disk, top side.

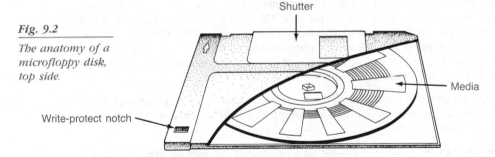

Hold the disk with the label facing you. A sliding metal cover should be at the top. The metal slide, called a *shutter*, covers both the front and the back sides of the disk. Hold the disk in your right hand. With the thumb and forefinger of your left hand, grasp the leftmost part of the metal slide on both sides of the disk. Pull the shutter to the left.

The shutter has two rectangular holes, one on each side of the disk. When you move the shutter to the left, you expose the microfloppy shell's access holes on either side of the disk. Through these access holes you can see both sides of the microfloppy disk inside. The shutter is attached to the shell by a spring. When you release the pressure, the shutter returns to its normal position to cover the access holes.

When you insert the disk into the microfloppy disk drive, the disk drive slides the shutter so that the drive's heads can make contact with the disk. When the disk is not in the drive, the shutter should be closed to protect the disk.

By the way, the microfloppy's hard shell might seem to antiquate the term *floppy*. The disk inside the shell is flexible and "flops" when shaken, however, so the term *floppy* is still appropriate.

Now flip the microfloppy disk over so that the side with the shutter is nearest you. In the center of the disk is the metal spindle, which has two holes (see fig. 9.3). The centering hole is the smaller hole in the center. The *sector-one* hole is the larger, rectangular hole near the edge of the spindle.

Fig. 9.3

The anatomy of a microfloppy disk, bottom side.

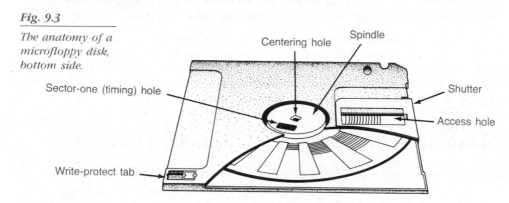

The microfloppy disk drive does not use a light shining through the index hole to determine where the first sector is located on the disk. The timing is done by the disk drive's spindle, which seats itself into the two holes on the disk's spindle. When the disk is placed into the disk drive, the disk drive's spindle turns until the spindle properly seats itself. After the spindle is settled, the hardware of the microfloppy disk drive determines where the first sector is located.

In the upper left corner of the back of the microfloppy disk is the write-protect notch and a small sliding tab. Some disk drives use an infrared light to sense where the tab is; others have a mechanical feeler.

To write-protect a disk, you move the bar up and uncover the hole so that you can see through it from the front. To write to the disk, you move the bar down and cover the hole. If you want to "permanently" write-protect a disk, gently pry the tab out of the slot. (If you later want to write information on the write-protected disk, cover the write-protect hole with black electrical tape or with a write-protect tab that you would use with a minifloppy disk.)

Some 1.44M disks have on the right side a second notch, which certain drives use to determine whether the disk is a 720K or 1.44M disk. IBM disk drives do not sense this notch, however.

A major difference between minifloppy and microfloppy disks is that the microfloppy disk is glued to the metal spindle, whereas the minifloppy disk moves freely within its plastic cover. The microfloppy disk is flexible, however, and slides slightly in the protective shell. Although the microfloppy disk is well protected by its hard plastic shell, you must still handle it with care.

Understanding Floppy Disk Drives

A floppy disk drive has three major sections: a section that holds and spins the disk, a section that moves and controls the disk drive's recording heads, and the electronics that communicate to the computer.

The section that holds and spins the disk is not complicated. On a minifloppy disk drive, when you close the door, two clutches, one on either side of the disk, grasp the disk's centering hole. The bottom clutch is connected by a belt to a motor. The motor, connected to the disk drive's electronics, spins the disk inside its plastic jacket at 300 rpm.

On a microfloppy disk drive, a metal panel pushes the disk onto the spindle. The disk drive's spindle has two nubs to anchor it to the centering hole and to the sector-one hole. The microfloppy disk drive's spindle, like the minifloppy disk drive's spindle, is connected to the motor by a belt.

The second section of both types of disk drive includes two connected, mobile arms that hold the recording heads.

PCs and PS/2s use double-sided disk drives. These drives have a recording head at the end of each arm; the two recording heads face each other. On most minifloppy disk drives, the arms are connected to the disk drive's door or to the knob used to close the disk drive door. In that way, the recording heads clamp onto the disk when you close the disk drive door. Some drives use a magnetic relay to clamp the arms onto the disk. All Personal Computer minifloppy disk drives use the first method. Some microfloppy disk drives use the relay method. The remaining microfloppy disk drives simply use levering systems that clamp the recording heads into position when you insert a disk into the disk drive.

As the arms clamp onto a disk, the disk is held between the recording heads. This positioning keeps the disk from bouncing away from the recording heads and allows the drive to write or read information reliably.

The coordinated mobile arms move back and forth down the center of the drive. A small "stepper" motor connected to a cam or gear moves the arm. Look at the disk's access holes; think about how you insert the disk into the disk drive, and you can imagine how the recording heads move.

The recording heads, the stepper motor, and the magnetic relay (if used) are connected to the disk drive's electronic components. These components, the last section of the disk drive, "talk" to the computer. The write-protect switch is also connected to these circuits. If the switch senses that the disk is write-protected, the disk drive's electronics stop the drive from recording information on the disk's surfaces.

The small light on the front of the disk drive comes on whenever the computer is using the drive. Generally, you should not open a minifloppy disk drive door or eject a microfloppy disk while the light is on.

Other electronic components of the disk drive receive signals from the computer to start the motor that spins the disk, to clamp the recording arm on the disk, to move the recording arm, and to get information from or put information on the disk.

Another piece of electronics on some drives is a *change line*, whose purpose is to inform the computer when the disk may have been changed. Disk drives with change lines have a switch connected to the minifloppy disk drive door or to the microfloppy eject button. When the disk drive door is opened or the eject button is pushed, the disk drive signals the computer that the disk has been changed. It does not matter whether the disk is changed—only that the door has been opened or the button pushed. This change line mechanism is on some 360K disk drives, on all 1.2M drives, and on all microfloppy disk drives.

A floppy disk drive is a fairly "dumb" peripheral. Most of the "intelligence" needed to control the disk drive is on a board or is part of the integrated circuits within the computer itself. This intelligence is located mainly on a disk controller adapter or on a disk controller board. The operating system's BIOS coordinates and governs the floppy disk drive's actions.

The floppy disk drive is more reliable today than it was several years ago. More information (1.2 million or 1.44 million bytes) can be packed into a 5 1/4-inch or 3 1/2-inch disk than could be held in an 8-inch floppy disk only five years ago (241,000 bytes).

Maintaining Your Floppy Disks and Drives

The following sections cover the care of your floppy disks and floppy disk drives. Some suggestions are offered for maintaining your disks and protecting your disk drives from damage.

Taking Care of Your Floppy Disks

Floppy disks are fragile. The plastic jacket provides protection from about 80 percent of the dust, fingerprints, smoke, and other contaminants that can come into contact with the disk. That protection plus a little common sense will ensure a long life for your disks. Treat the disks as you would your personal or business records. In some cases, the disks *are* your records.

Some disk manufacturers put instructions on the back of the envelope about caring for your disks. You may want to read these instructions after you read this section. Some of these instructions are less critical for microfloppy disks than for minifloppy disks because of the greater protection the hard shell gives the microfloppy disk. Note, however, that microfloppies are not immune to damage. Exercising common sense prolongs the life of any disk.

Some Do's for Floppy Disks

Put disks into the disk drive carefully. "Easy does it" is the best advice. Microfloppy disks need a slight push when you finish the move that inserts the disk. When the disk is almost completely inserted, pushing the disk forces the retaining panel to secure the disk into the drive. This securing push takes just slightly more force than you would use when you insert a minifloppy disk.

You should be able to slide a minifloppy disk into the disk drive with little resistance. You may even hear a soft click as the metal bar or write-protect switch slides into place. Minifloppy disk drive doors should close with little resistance.

In a short time, you will know by touch whether you've properly inserted a disk. If you insert a disk or close a disk drive door and sense a problem, remove the disk and put it back in again. You can damage both disk and disk drive if you try to force a disk into a disk drive. The possibility of damaging a minifloppy disk by forcing the drive door closed is especially likely.

When you have finished using a minifloppy disk, put it back in its envelope. The envelope prevents dust and most other contaminants from getting to the surface of the disk.

Putting microfloppy disks back into the clear envelope is not so important. The envelope can, however, protect the disk from liquids, a major danger to microfloppy disks.

Label every disk. Floppy disks seem to multiply like rabbits. Nothing is more frustrating and time-consuming than trying to find one particular disk in a group of 50 disks that appear to be identical. Many computer users buy disks in bulk packaging, and the disks without labels all look alike. Save yourself time by eliminating the need to wade through scores of unlabeled disks to find the one you need.

After you format a disk, put a label on it. You might also include the date you formatted the disk and the version of the program you used or other pertinent information. When you label a disk, use meaningful names and abbreviations so that they will make sense to you at some later date. A disk without a label is fair game for accidental reformatting or erasing and is therefore less useful to you.

Once you have placed a label on a minifloppy disk, use a felt-tipped pen to write on the label. Don't press hard or use a ballpoint pen or pencil; undue pressure can damage the disk under the jacket. To write on a label attached to a microfloppy disk's hard shell, you can use any type of pen or pencil, short of an engraver.

If a label comes loose, remove it and put on a new one. I learned the importance of this lesson the hard way while I was writing the previous version of this book, the *PC DOS User's Guide*.

I took home a disk that held several chapters of the book. When I got home, I stuck the disk into the disk drive and began to work. I noticed that the label was beginning to peel away from the disk, but I didn't think that this fact was important. Later, when I removed the disk from the disk drive, the label came off inside the drive and became lodged on the bottom of the drive. I did not notice that the label was missing.

That evening, I searched for a disk to format and grabbed one from the top of a pile of unlabeled disks. Several hours later, I came back to work on my book again. For 20 minutes, I looked for the disk that held part of the book. A sickening thought struck. I carefully reached inside the disk drive and found the disk label on the bottom of the drive. I had formatted the wrong disk and lost my chapters! Fortunately, I had a day-old backup copy of the disk. All I had lost was one day's work. As I said before, I am an "experienced" computer user.

Another piece of good advice comes from this lesson. *To avoid costly loss of information, always check a disk you are about to format.* Make sure that it is blank or has no useful information on it. Make the DIR command your friend.

Back up disks frequently. What saved me from having to reenter several weeks of work was my backup disk. You should back up vital information daily or at least every two days if you are changing information such as accounting records. You should back up less vital but still important information every couple of days, or at least once a week. Backing up disks is an extremely cheap form of insurance.

Another reason to make backup copies of files is that disks have a finite life. In the past (1978-81), disks had spin lives (the amount of time that a disk drive actually reads or writes information on the disk) of 40 to 80 hours. Newer disks can be used much longer than disks of just a few years ago, but disks do wear out.

Keep infrequently used disks and backup copies of disks away from your computer. Why clutter the place where you work? Why have to dig through disks to find the one you need? Have at hand just the ones you constantly need. When you need a different disk, get it, use it, and put it back. You'll find that managing disks is much easier this way.

Keep your disks "comfortable." Like phonograph records, minifloppy disks can warp if they are not stored perfectly flat or vertical. Warping a disk takes several weeks, but why risk this kind of damage? A number of holders on the market do a good job of storing disks. Although microfloppy disks do not warp, disk holders keep the disks organized and readily accessible.

Keeping disks comfortable also means watching the temperature. Maintain the temperature between 50 and 125 degrees Fahrenheit (10 and 52 degrees Celsius).

If your disks get cold, let them warm up before you use them. This precaution is critical for high-capacity and microfloppy disks. Cold disks become rigid and shrink slightly. On shrunken disks, disk drives record information at a slightly different position. The disk drive does not change its position for recording, but the disk itself is different. As the disk warms up and expands, the disk drive cannot locate the recorded information. This problem is especially true of high-capacity (1.2M) and microfloppy disks and disk drives, in which the "width" of the recording is very narrow.

Be especially careful about excessive heat. On bright, warm days, keep disks you leave in your car out of direct sunlight. The hot summer sun has made roller-coaster rides out of minifloppy disks I left on the back seat of my car. Your car's trunk also can get hot. Microfloppy disks are almost as vulnerable to heat as their minifloppy counterparts. Needless to say, when disks turn into hot Frisbees, the information stored on them is lost.

Buy the right type of disk for your disk drive. If you have a double-sided disk drive, buy double-sided disks. For high-capacity minifloppy and microfloppy disk drives, buy high-capacity disks that undergo a strenuous certification procedure. A bad high-capacity disk can turn up to 1.44 million bytes of information into instant trash.

Floppy disk prices are extremely competitive, and you can buy high-quality disks at good prices. Also, disk manufacturers recently have restored my faith in inexpensive, no-name disks. In the past two years, I have found only four unusable disks out of more than two thousand.

You can tell whether you have a usable disk when you format it: DOS identifies an unusable disk by reporting a large amount of disk space lost to bad sectors. You should always format disks before you use them, even if you use them with the DISKCOPY command. (DISKCOPY and the DOS V4 version of BACKUP will format a disk "on the fly.") Formatting disks individually immediately exposes problem disks.

When you move your computer, take the disks out of the drive. When the disk drive door is closed, the recording heads are in contact with the disk's surface. If the disk drive gets bounced around severely, the heads can scrape the disk and damage it. When you move your computer, particularly if it is a portable, take the disks out of the disk drives. To protect the drives, insert into the drives some unusable disks or the cardboard protectors that came with your computer.

Some Don'ts for Floppy Disks

Don't touch the disk's magnetic surface, particularly the area under the access holes. The oil from your fingers can interfere with the recording heads' ability to read and write information on the disk. Hold minifloppy disks by the jacket. If you need to spin the disk, put your fingers in the centering hole and turn your hand.

For microfloppy disks, leave the shutter closed. If you need to look at the disk, open the shutter and use a pencil or pen in the sector-one hole to rotate the disk.

Don't allow your disks near magnetic fields. Following this instruction can be tricky. You may not keep a magnet by your disks, but what about a video monitor, a fan, a microwave oven, or even your telephone? Each of these appliances generates a magnetic field that has the potential to "clean" your disks and ruin precious information.

Generally, most appliances will not affect your disks unless you keep the disks near the appliance for a long time. As a rule, keep your disks one foot away from any possible offender. Increase the distance for appliances that have very strong electric motors, including everything from pencil sharpeners to heating and air-conditioning motors. The heavier the motor, the farther away you should keep your disks. Plastic holders do not stop magnetic fields. Metal boxes do a better job.

Airport security systems can be a problem for the traveling disk. Generally, the X-ray machines used at airports do not generate a field strong enough to erase disks. If, however, you trigger the metal detector and are carrying disks, ask the security people to hand-inspect the carry-on disks. Don't allow your disks to be placed on top of the X-ray machine, and don't permit examination with a hand scanner. The disks might be too close to damaging magnetic fields. Airport security people, who are now accustomed to traveling disks and computers, are usually happy to cooperate with such requests.

If you are mailing disks or carrying them and want extra protection, wrap them in aluminum foil. This extra precaution will reduce the possibility that magnetic fields will reach your disks.

Don't let your disks take the "Pepsi Challenge" or the "Sanka Break." Be careful with any liquids near disks. That also goes for cigarette, cigar, or pipe smoke and ashes; food; and similar contaminants. If any of these materials gets on your disk and leaves a residue, the recording heads may not be able to retrieve information from the disk. This residue can also lodge on the recording head, making it a menace to other disks.

Although a microfloppy's shell protects the disk from most hazards, the shell is not waterproof. Also, be cautious if you transport microfloppy disks in a shirt pocket. If you perspire, the moisture can reach the disk.

Verbatim Corporation has introduced disks with a Teflon coating that can protect your data from loss caused by foreign matter. The company has invited users to smear peanut butter, oil, and other substances on the surface of the disks. When the material is wiped off, the disk has, in all of the publicized tests, been perfectly readable. Should you buy such disks and use this feature as an invitation to mistreat your floppies? Buy Verbatim disks if you like, but don't suddenly become careless about your media. Consider the Teflon coating an insurance policy on the order of an auto safety belt. If an accident happens, you will be glad for the safety margin, but you still won't be eager to crash-test the feature!

Don't bend disks. Information is tightly packed on a disk. If you put a crease in the disk, the recording head will "jump" over the crease, and you will lose information. Remember the saying for the old punch cards: "Do not fold, spindle, or mutilate."

Don't let your disks get too full. Some programs generate temporary files for your data. If a disk gets too full, you might lose the material on which you are working. For example, WordStar, the word-processing program I use, is not gracious about full disks. If you can't free up some room on the disk, you will lose the last revision of your work. I don't blame WordStar; I curse myself when I let this happen.

Periodically, use the commands CHKDSK or DIR to see how much room is left on a floppy disk or hard disk. To make room, erase files or copy and then erase them.

Taking Care of Your Floppy Disk Drives

Floppy disk drives are fairly rugged pieces of equipment, but they can be damaged. The following general rules about disk drives will help you minimize damage.

When you insert a disk, close the minifloppy drive door carefully. As I previously mentioned, if you jam a disk into the disk drive and try to close the door, you may damage the clutches that clamp down on the disk, the disk itself, or both. With some practice, you will be able to tell when you have jammed a disk.

Clean the recording heads infrequently. Disk recording heads are ceramic and require only infrequent cleaning, perhaps once every three months, or even once a year. Over-cleaning disk drive heads can cause problems. Cleaning solutions and cleaning disks can be abrasive. Alcohol-based cleaning solutions, if overused, can erode the glue that holds the recording head on the arm. If that happens, the recording head will fall off. Generally, the gauzelike material inside the disk jacket will catch and hold most dust and dirt that come along, so frequent cleaning is not necessary.

If you get disk errors, run the diagnostics program that came with your computer. First, format some blank disks on a disk drive you know is good. Then run the diagnostics on the suspect system. If you still get disk errors, use the cleaning disk and rerun the diagnostics. If you still have errors, the disk drive may have other problems, or the disk with the errors may be an unusable disk.

Don't shock your disk drives. In other words, don't give them a strong bump or jar. The arms with the recording head can get out of place, the belt that makes the disk spin can fall off, or the disk drive door or ejector button can break. A floppy disk drive is made of metal and plastic. The plastic can break if you drop the disk drive or slam something into it.

When you move or ship your disk drives long distances, put the cardboard protectors in the drives and close the drive doors. The disk drive recording heads face each other. When the door is closed, the recording-head faces touch each other. If the disk drives receive many bumps or jolts, the recording heads can clap against each other and become damaged. If you put the cardboard protectors in the disk drives and close the doors, the cardboard pieces protect the recording heads. If you have lost your cardboard protectors, you can insert unusable disks in place of the cardboard.

Have your disk drives serviced periodically. Disk drives need a little preventive maintenance every year or two. The belt that spins the disk may stretch. The disk recording heads may move a little out of the track, or the arm mechanism may wear. On minifloppy disk drives, the write-protect switch may also wear. The timing on the disk drives' motors may be off. Usually, a good service technician can test and shape up your disk drives at a reasonable cost. Such maintenance will prevent a small problem from getting bigger.

At the first sign that something is wrong with your disk drives, run your diagnostics. If the disk drive is malfunctioning, get it repaired before you ruin information on good disks.

Summary

In this chapter, you learned the following key points:

❏ Several types of floppy disks are available. The PS/2 family uses microfloppy (3 1/2-inch) disks. The IBM Personal Computer family mainly uses minifloppy (5 1/4-inch) disks.

❏ Floppy disks are fragile and should be handled with care.

❏ Disk drives are fairly rugged, but you can break them if you mishandle them. Disk drives also require occasional maintenance.

❏ You should frequently back up disks that contain important information.

Chapter 10 focuses on hard disk drives and how DOS uses disks.

10

Understanding Hard Disks
and How DOS Uses Disks

This chapter provides a description of hard disks for Personal Computers and for PS/2 computers. The discussion also includes tips for the care of hard disk drives. If you don't have a hard disk yet, skip to the second part of the chapter and read about how DOS uses disks. If you have a hard disk or will be purchasing one soon, read on.

Understanding Hard Disks (Winchesters)

The Winchester disk is the most commonly used hard disk for personal computers. This hard-disk technology was developed at IBM in 1973 under the code name *Winchester*. The disks have since become a practical addition to personal computers.

The Main Parts of a Hard Disk Drive

The recording surface and recording heads of a Winchester disk drive, unlike those of a floppy disk drive, are part of a sealed unit (see fig. 10.1). A hard disk drive uses rigid, circular platters coated with metal oxide. From these platters, the hard disk drive gets its name.

The platters are fixed on a spindle that rotates at approximately 3,600 rpm. This speed is much faster than that of a floppy disk drive. Some Winchester drives use a motor connected directly to the spindle to rotate the platters. Others use a belt-and-spindle arrangement like that of the floppy disk drive.

Because the hard disk is sealed onto the spindle and cannot be removed, the Winchester disk drive and similar drives are called nonremovable disk drives. *Hard disk drive* and *hard file* are the terms IBM usually uses. (By the way, the term *nonremovable disk* also applies to RAM disks, which are discussed in Chapter 17.)

147

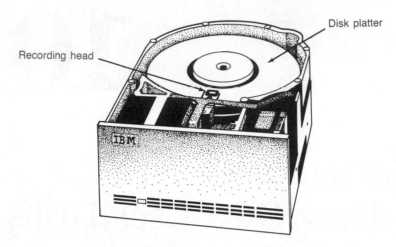

Disk platter

Recording head

Fig. 10.1

An exposed view of a typical full-height hard disk.

A mobile arm within the hard disk holds the recording heads, one at the top and one at the bottom of each platter. The entire arm moves back and forth, as in a floppy disk drive, but in smaller, more precise increments. The Winchester's mobile arm moves faster than the arm of a floppy disk drive, and the recording heads of the hard disk drive are smaller than those of a floppy disk drive. With more controlled movement and smaller recording heads, the hard disk drive can record more information on the surface of the platters.

Winchester disks for personal computers usually have platters whose diameters can range from 3 1/2 to 8 inches. The most common size is the 5 1/4-inch platter, but the 3 1/2-inch platter is gaining popularity, since the smaller platter size makes it easy to build very fast drives. The 5 1/4-inch platter usually holds between 2 1/2 and 10 megabytes of data per side. Hard disk drives with the combination of two sides per platter and two platters have capacities between 10M and 40M. Other hard disks may have more platters and range in capacity from 60M to 100M or more.

The Winchester is an "intelligent" peripheral. Most units have built-in electronics that automatically verify the information written to the hard disk, using sophisticated error-correcting techniques. Because of these capabilities, the writing of information to a Winchester disk is verified routinely.

The Hazards of Hard Disks

Some potential problems are unique to hard disk drives. The air pressure generated by the spinning disk lifts the recording heads just thousandths of an inch off the platter's surface. Should the heads hit any contamination, they will crash into the moving platters and scrape off the disk's metal coating, where information is stored. Fortunately, the Winchester's sealed environment makes such contamination unlikely. A strong blow can also cause the recording heads to crash into the disk surface. For this reason, you should be careful not to bump a Winchester disk, strongly jar the table or desk that holds the disk, or drop the disk.

Winchester disks can take some punishment, however. Newer Winchester disk drives use platters that have a hardened coating called *plated media*, which prevents the loss of information due to physical shock. The coating is often used on Winchester drives mounted into portable computers. While plated-media drives are operating, they can withstand shock levels between 15 and 20 times the force of gravity. Other drives can survive shocks of only 10 times the force of gravity. When a drive is not in use, it can withstand a shock of 20 to 30 times the force of gravity.

Another problem with Winchester disks is disk failure. A hard disk will fail eventually, but that failure is difficult to predict. It can happen at any time during a broad time span, usually between 8,000 and 20,000 hours of use. If you use your computer eight hours a day, five days a week, 50 weeks of the year, that translates into a minimum of a four-year lifetime for your hard disk. However, a problem could also occur a month after you buy the disk drive.

Because a hard disk's failure is unpredictable, you should make a habit of backing up the information on the hard disk. You cannot remove hard disk platters. Therefore, you must transfer information to separate media for backup. Most personal computer users use floppy disks to back up their hard disks. If you have a hard disk, be sure to read about the BACKUP and RESTORE commands in Chapter 24.

You can reduce the danger of damage if you prepare your Winchester disk before you move or ship it. The manufacturer of your disk drive will have included instructions for moving or shipping the hard disk drive. The preparation procedure is usually the reverse of the procedure for installing the disk drive. Note that, as a rule, Winchester drives are more fragile than floppy disk drives.

Most disk operating systems for Winchester drives include a program you must run before you can move or ship the disk. The programs move the recording heads to the edge of the disk, where no information is stored. This process of moving the recording heads into the "safety" zone is called *parking* the heads.

The parking program provided with IBM Personal Computers is called SHIPDISK.EXE and is located on the Diagnostics Disk. Run the program whenever you move the hard disk more than a few feet.

The program for PS/2 computers is called PARKHEAD.COM and is located on the Reference Disk. You do not need to run this program as religiously as you do the program for the standard Personal Computer family. Most of the PS/2 computers use hard disk drives that automatically park their recording heads when you turn off the computer. Still, for safety's sake, you should run PARKHEAD.COM whenever you move the hard disk.

Understanding How DOS Divides Disks

To simplify and speed the handling of a disk, DOS divides the disk into smaller pieces. Notice the use of the word *disk*. This term can apply to a floppy disk or to a hard disk. In this book, the terms *floppy disk* and *floppy disk drive* are used when the reference is specifically to floppy disks and drives.

DOS divides the disk into a series of concentric circles called *tracks* (see fig. 10.2). The number of tracks your disk uses depends on the disk drive. The motor that *steps*, or moves, the recording heads determines the number of tracks. The smaller the step, the more tracks a disk will have.

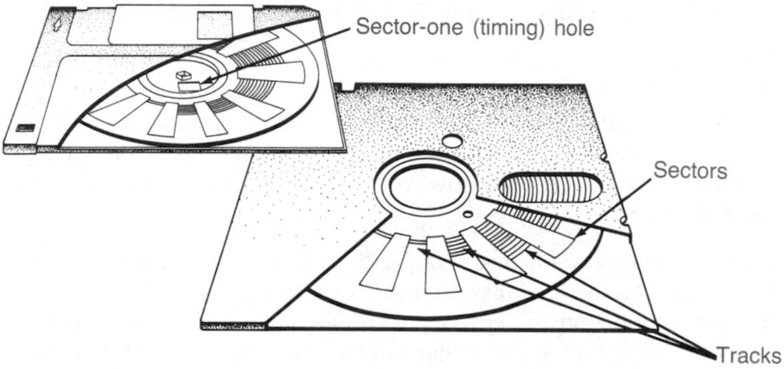

Fig. 10.2

Layout of tracks and sectors on floppy disks.

Sector-one (timing) hole

Sectors

Tracks

Minifloppy disk drives record 48 or 96 tracks per inch. (The standard abbreviation for tracks per inch is *tpi*.) 360K disk drives record 48 tpi, and high-capacity disk drives record 96 tpi. Microfloppy disk drives record 96 tpi.

How DOS Divides Floppy Disks

The entire surface of a floppy disk cannot be used for recording. Disk drives record within a circular band in the middle of the disk. The band is five-sixths of an inch wide. Thus 48-tpi drives can create only 40 tracks. 96-tpi disk drives can create 80 tracks.

The tracks are sliced into *sectors*. DOS V1 used 8 sectors per track. DOS V2, V3, and V4 use 9 sectors on the same 360K disk drive; the 720K microfloppy disk also uses 9 sectors per track. HC disk drives use 15 sectors per track. The 1.44M microfloppy disk uses 18 sectors per track.

How many sectors are on your disks? If you use DOS V3 with IBM double-sided disk drives, you can use disks that have 40 tracks, either 1 or 2 sides, and 8 or 9 formatted sectors per track. A high-capacity disk has 80 tracks, 2 sides, and 15 sectors per track. Both microfloppy disks use 80 tracks per side. A 720K microfloppy uses 9 sectors per track, and the 1.44M disk uses 18 sectors per track. Table 10.1 shows the calculations of total sectors your floppy disks can have.

These figures can also indicate how much information is stored on a disk. Each sector on any disk (including a hard disk) holds 512 bytes. Table 10.2 shows the total bytes each disk can store.

You determine the number of kilobytes (K) on a disk by dividing the disk space by 1,024, as shown in table 10.3.

Table 10.1
Calculating the Number of Sectors on a Floppy Disk

Tracks	Sectors	Sides		Total Sectors
40 x	8 x	1	=	320
40 x	8 x	2	=	640
40 x	9 x	1	=	360
40 x	9 x	2	=	720
80 x	9 x	2	=	1,440
80 x	15 x	2	=	2,400
80 x	18 x	2	=	2,880

Table 10.2
Calculating the Number of Bytes on a Floppy Disk

Total Sectors		Bytes per Sector		Total Disk Space
320	x	512 bytes	=	163,840 bytes
640	x	512 bytes	=	327,680 bytes
360	x	512 bytes	=	184,320 bytes
720	x	512 bytes	=	368,640 bytes
1,440	x	512 bytes	=	737,280 bytes
2,400	x	512 bytes	=	1,228,800 bytes
2,880	x	512 bytes	=	1,474,560 bytes

Table 10.3
Determining the Number of Kilobytes on a Floppy Disk

Tracks	Sectors	Sides	Space in Bytes	Space in K
40	8	1	163,840	160K
40	8	2	327,680	320K
40	9	1	184,320	180K
40	9	2	368,640	360K
80	9	2	737,280	720K
80	15	2	1,228,800	1,200K
80	18	2	1,474,560	1,440K

If you format a minifloppy disk on a regular double-sided IBM disk drive, the disk will have 40 tracks, with 9 sectors per track. DOS uses both sides of the disk. The maximum capacity of the disk is 360K; these disk drives are thus called 360K disk drives.

HC minifloppy disks have 80 tracks, 15 sectors per track, and 512 bytes per sector. DOS uses both sides of the disk. The capacity of such disks is 1,200K, and therefore the capacity of the disk drive is 1,200K, or 1.2M.

Microfloppy disks have 80 tracks and 9 or 18 sectors per track; DOS uses both sides of the disk. The 9-sector disk holds 720K. The 18-sector disk holds 1.440M. These disk drives are called 720K and 1.44M disk drives, respectively.

How DOS Divides Hard Disks

Hard disks are divided much like floppy disks. Each side of a floppy disk has 40 or 80 tracks. Each side of a typical 40M hard disk drive has 731 tracks. The first track on the top side is directly above the first track on the bottom side; the second track on the top is above the second track on the bottom, and so on, for each of the other tracks. If you were to draw a three-dimensional figure that passed through both sides of the disk at any track, you would have a *cylinder* (see fig. 10.3).

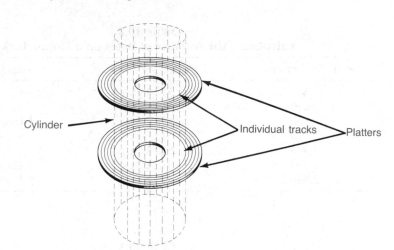

Fig. 10.3

Cylinders of a hard disk drive are created by connecting the corresponding tracks on each side of the platters.

For the hard disk, think of two or more platters stacked on top of each other on the spindle. The tracks for each side of each platter are aligned. If you were to connect any one track through all surfaces, you would again have a cylinder.

The PS/2's 40M hard disk drive has 731 cylinders, meaning that each surface of the eight platters has 731 tracks. The typical PC XT 286 or AT hard disk (20M) has 615 cylinders, which means that each surface of the four platters has 615 tracks. (Each of these computers uses one cylinder for internal purposes. This single cylinder is not available for storing information.)

Hard disk drives use 17 sectors per track. And, as with floppy disks, hard disk sectors have 512 bytes per sector.

To place information on a disk, DOS starts with the first side and the first track. The first side is side 0. The first track is the outermost track, track 0. (Computers use 0 as a real number, not just as a placeholder.)

Although the first side and track are numbered 0, the first sector is called sector 1. DOS starts with sector 1 and fills the remaining sectors in ascending order. The last sector filled is 9, 15, or 18, depending on the type of disk. Then DOS flips to the second side (side 1) and uses track 0, sectors 1 through 9 (or 15 or 18). DOS returns to side 0 and uses track 1, sectors 1 through the highest sector per track, and then goes back to side 1, track 1. This process continues until the entire disk is full. The process works the same way for the hard disk, except that DOS uses each side of the platter (a cylinder) before moving to the next track. (The platter numbering starts at 0.)

Why does DOS work this way? The answer is speed. Switching between the drive's recording heads is faster than moving the recording heads to a new location. This is true for both floppy and hard disk drives.

Understanding How DOS Uses Disks

When you get a new floppy disk or hard disk, it is not ready to be used. DOS must first record some "dummy" information on the disk. This process is called formatting, which you learned to do in Chapter 5.

When you format a floppy disk or a hard disk, DOS records dummy data in each sector. (Additional housekeeping information is also recorded, but this information does not concern us now.) Then DOS sets up three important areas on the disk. The first area is on the first side of the disk in the first sector of the first track (side 0, track 0, sector 1). This area is called the *boot record*. It contains the bootstrap routine DOS uses to load itself.

After the boot record is recorded, the FORMAT command sets up two copies of the file allocation table, or FAT, which will be discussed shortly. The size of each FAT depends upon the capacity of the disk, as shown in table 10.4.

Table 10.4
Size of the FAT for Disks of Various Sizes

Disk Capacity	Size of each FAT (in sectors)
160K	1
180K	2
320K	1
360K	2
720K	3
1.2M	7
1.44M	9

Each copy of the FAT ranges from a size of 1 sector (for DOS V1, 8-sector disks) to 9 sectors (for 1.44M 18-sector microfloppy disks). The larger-capacity disks use larger-sized FATs. One FAT function is to indicate what type of disk you are using: 8-, 9-, 15-, or 18-sector; 40- or 80-track; and single- or double-sided.

After the FAT is set up, DOS lays out the directory. DOS holds six pieces of information about each file in the directory:

- The file's name

- The file's creation date or the date the file was last changed

- The file's creation time or the time the file was last changed

- The file's attributes (characteristics)

- The file's starting cluster entry in the FAT

- The file's size in bytes

The file's attributes tell DOS whether the file needs special handling or protection. The file's attributes can be any combination of the characteristics shown in table 10.5.

Table 10.5
File Attributes Held in the Directory

Attribute	Description
Read-only	A file that may not be altered or erased.
System	A file used by the operating system. This file is normally hidden from view during regular DOS operations.
Hidden	A file hidden from view during normal DOS operations.
Volume label	An 11-character label that helps you identify the disk. You'll see the volume label when you execute DOS commands such as DIR, CHKDSK, or TREE.
Subdirectory	A directory, instead of a file, that holds similar information about other files.
Archive	An attribute that tells DOS a file has not been backed up. This attribute is turned on when DOS creates a file or when you change a file.

Every file you use or create has one directory entry. The entry is 32 bytes long. The directory, which spans several sectors, can hold a fixed number of entries. Table 10.6 indicates how many directory entries various floppy disks can have.

Unlike some other operating-system directories, a DOS directory does not tell you where a particular file is stored on the disk. Instead, each file's entry in the disk directory points to an entry in the FAT. The FAT tells DOS which sectors on the disk actually hold the file. In other words, the FAT guides DOS in finding information stored on the disk. The FAT also indicates the sectors that are not being used.

The FAT is important to DOS—so important that DOS keeps two copies of the FAT for every disk. DOS uses the directory entry to go to the correct part of the FAT for the file you use. DOS then locates your file on the disk by using the entries in the FAT.

When a file grows, DOS checks the FAT to see what sectors are not being used. When the FAT finds a free sector, DOS uses the sector. In filling free sectors, DOS uses a first-

Table 10.6
Maximum Number of Directory Entries for Floppy Disks

Floppy Disk Type	Directory Sectors	Maximum # of Directory Entries
160K	4	64
180K		
320K	7	112
360K		
720K		
1.2M	14	224
1.44M		

found, first-used routine. In other words, DOS takes the first free sector it finds and puts as much of the file as possible in that sector. DOS then looks for the next free sector and places more of the file in the second sector.

The starting place for DOS's search varies according to which version of the operating system is used. With earlier versions, DOS always started to use the most recently freed-up entries first, so that when you deleted a file, its file space was reused immediately the next time a file was created.

Currently DOS uses the "oldest" sectors first. The space occupied by the most recently deleted file is reused last. The significance of this new scheme lies in "unerasing" deleted files. Your chances of success with a special unerase utility are improved because the odds are good that a deleted file's sectors have not been reallocated to another file, even if you created new files since the deletion.

Actually, when DOS looks for free sectors, it looks for a cluster. A *cluster* is the smallest unit of disk space that DOS will work with in the FAT. For a single-sided floppy disk, a cluster is the same as a sector. When DOS searches for a free cluster on a single-sided disk, DOS is looking for a free sector. Double-sided minifloppy disks and 720K micro-floppy disks use two sectors for each cluster. When DOS looks for a free cluster on a double-sided disk, DOS is looking for a free pair of adjacent sectors. For the higher-capacity floppy disks (1.2M or 1.44M), DOS again returns to searching for one sector.

When you instruct DOS to format a floppy disk with system files (with the /S switch), the FORMAT command also places the files IBMBIO.COM, IBMDOS.COM, and COMMAND.COM on your disk. If you use the /V switch, DOS also creates a volume label. DOS places this label into the directory, thus reducing by one the number of files a disk can hold. The volume label has no entry in the FAT, however, and therefore does not take up any disk space.

All DOS programs and utilities automatically deduct the disk space used by the boot record, the FAT, and the directory. Because you cannot use these areas to record your own information, DOS does not count these areas for your total disk space. Thus when you calculate what a disk's capacity should be, the capacities will be larger than those shown by the DIR, FORMAT, and CHKDSK programs.

In Chapter 5, you learned that the disk space that DOS lists is different from what the disk can actually hold. The figures that DOS gives you indicate total user space, not total disk space. There is one more discrepancy between the calculated capacity figures and the "true" capacity of disks. This difference is most apparent with microfloppy disks. You might note that the disks IBM provides with DOS are marked "1.0 MB capacity" for the 720K drive and "2.0 MB capacity" for the 1.44M drive. (Both MB and M stand for megabyte.) Does this mean that the microfloppy disks can hold more information? The answer to this question is yes. The disks do hold more information—but you cannot directly use that additional storage space.

The 720K disks actually hold 1M, and the 1.44M drives hold 2M. The space "reduction" comes from the need to format the disk. When you format a disk, either floppy or hard, additional "dummy" information is recorded that permits the disk drive electronics and DOS to find information on the disk. Some information consists of electronic markings that identify each track and sector. DOS uses this information to ensure that the drive is reading or writing information at the correct disk location. Additional information, called a *cyclic redundancy check* (CRC), is used to verify that the disk information has been recorded correctly.

This additional but vital overhead information is recorded on all disks and occupies approximately 30 percent of the potential storage area. Because of this need for auxiliary information, manufacturers of disk drives quote two capacities: an unformatted capacity (without subtracting the space used by this overhead information) and a formatted (or usable) capacity.

As mentioned earlier, DOS retains some space from a disk's usable storage area to hold data-tracking information. For this reason, a 1M formatted microfloppy disk has a usable data-storage area of 720K. A 2M formatted floppy disk has 1.44M of usable data-storage areas. After DOS dedicates some space for its use, a 2M floppy disk has a usable capacity of only 1.42M, and the 1M microfloppy has a usable capacity of 703K.

When you buy disks for microfloppy drives, you can buy disks marked *DS/DD* or *2S/2D* (both designating double-sided, double-density disks) or those marked *1M* or *1MB* for 720K disk drives. If you have a 1.44M disk drive, you should buy microfloppy disks marked *HC* or *HD* (high-capacity or high-density) or disks marked as having a *2M* or *2MB* capacity.

Summary

In this chapter, you were introduced to the following important points:

❑ Hard disks are high-speed, high-capacity storage devices that are more resistant to problems than other types of disks.

❏ DOS uses certain sections of each disk or hard disk. DOS uses concentric rings called tracks. Each track is divided into sectors. The number of tracks, sectors, sides of a disk or hard disk platter, and platters determines a disk's capacity.

❏ DOS records a directory and a file allocation table (FAT) on each disk when you format the disk. The number of files that a disk's directory can hold is based on the size of the directory.

❏ DOS maintains a list of attributes you can assign to every file. The attributes indicate whether you can alter the file, whether you can list the file in the directory, whether you can back up the file, and whether the file is actually another directory.

❏ Disk drives have two rated capacities: formatted and unformatted. When you format a disk, DOS places on each disk necessary file-tracking, internal information. Storing this information reduces the disk's usable capacity.

Chapter 11 discusses names for disk drives and other devices. You will also learn to use the LABEL command to assign a volume label to a disk, and you'll learn another use for the COPY command.

11

Naming Disk Drives and Files

Part I of this book discussed disks and disk files and how to use them, but said little about what files are. In this chapter, you will learn more about files, particularly how DOS uses them and how to name them. You will also learn how to use the TYPE command to display a file's contents.

Before you learn about disk files, I will give you a list of rules for disk drive names, and you will learn how to use the LABEL command to create or change a disk's volume label.

Naming Disk Drives

A disk drive name consists of two characters—a letter followed by a colon. With DOS V3 and V4, a computer can have up to 26 disk drives. Most computer systems, however, use between two and six disk drives, which are given the names A:, B:, C:, D:, E:, and F:. The following rules govern the use of disk drive names:

1. A disk drive must have a two-character name. The second character must be a colon (:).

2. The first disk drive is A:, the second disk drive is B:, and so on.

3. The character for each additional disk drive is one character higher in the ASCII character set. The final usable letter is Z.

4. You may use either upper- or lowercase letters for disk drive names.

5. When you tell DOS to run a program from a disk, you may precede the program name with the disk drive name.

6. Almost any time you give a file name, you may precede the file name with the disk drive name.

7. Do not try to use a nonexistent disk drive. If you do, DOS displays an error message.

159

Notice rules 5 and 6. These rules govern how you tell DOS where to find your programs and other files. These rules are a more formal statement of the discussion of the current disk drive you encountered in Chapter 6.

Now let's discuss giving a disk a volume name.

Labeling a Disk Electronically

DOS V3 and later versions allow a disk to have a *volume name*, which is an electronic disk label. Volume names have two purposes. First, the volume name helps you to identify the disk. The FORMAT command uses the disk's volume label to confirm your intent to reformat a hard disk. Second, volume names are a convenient way to group floppy disks. The volume name appears when you ask for a directory of a disk, perform a CHKDSK (check disk), display the directory path (using the TREE command), or use a variety of other commands. Volume names are optional. DOS V4 and later also give each disk a non-optional serial number. This serial number gives DOS a unique name for each and every disk that you have. You cannot select the serial number given to a disk, nor can you change it without using a special utility.

When you format a disk with the FORMAT command and use the /V switch, DOS asks you for an 11-character volume name. With DOS V3, the request appears after DOS has physically formatted the disk. With DOS V4, you may bypass this request by typing a colon and a volume name after the /V switch:

FORMAT A: /V:MYDISK

FORMAT is one of two DOS commands that make volume labels. The other command is LABEL. The following list summarizes the rules for volume labels. These rules are almost identical to those for file names, which are discussed later in this chapter.

1. A volume label can be from 1 to 11 characters long.

2. Valid characters for volume labels are the following:

   a. The letters *A* through *Z* or *a* through *z*

   b. The numbers 0 through 9

   c. The special characters and punctuation symbols
      $ # & @ ! & ( ) { } ' _ ~

   d. The space (the use of which is illegal for file names)

3. The following characters cannot be used in a volume label:

   a. Any control character, including Esc (27d or 1Bh) and Del (127d or 7Fh)

   b. The characters
      + = / [] " : , ? * \ <;> | .

4. If you type a label that is too long or use an illegal character, DOS V3.3 and V4 will use the first eleven characters. For versions of DOS before V3.3, DOS asks you to enter the volume label again.

5. A disk drive name cannot precede the volume label when you use the FORMAT command. A disk drive name may precede the volume label when you use the LABEL command.

Remember that each floppy disk or hard disk drive can have only one volume name. And that a volume label, unlike a file name, cannot contain a period. For the most part, the rules for volume names are a little less restrictive than the rules for file names.

With DOS V2, you had only one opportunity to give a volume label—when you formatted the disk. The LABEL command gives you the flexibility to add, change, or delete volume labels at any time.

The syntax for the LABEL command is as follows:

*dc:*LABEL *d:volume_label*

The *dc:* is the disk drive that holds the LABEL command. LABEL is an external command. You may recall from Chapter 6 that an external command must be loaded from a disk before you use the command.

The *d:* is the name of the drive that holds the disk to be labeled. If you do not give a disk drive name, the disk in the current drive will be labeled. If the specified or current disk drive is a floppy disk drive, the floppy disk will be labeled. If the drive is a hard disk, the hard disk will be labeled.

The volume label can contain from 1 to 11 characters. For versions of DOS before V3.3, if you give the volume label on the command line, you cannot use a space in the name. You can use a space with LABEL V3.3. With LABEL before V3.3, the reason for not allowing a space is that DOS interprets the command as having two volume labels (one before the space and another after the space). When that happens, you will get the following message:

```
Illegal characters in volume label
```

When you include a space on the command line, DOS sees the space as a *delimiter* (an item separator), not as a "legal" character. You will get the Illegal characters in volume label message if you enter an improper volume label on the command line when the LABEL command requests a volume name. LABEL V3.3 and V4 know that spaces are legal in a volume label and do not become confused.

If you omit the volume label on the command line, DOS responds with the following:

```
Volume in drive A is current_label
Volume label (11 characters, ENTER for none)?_
```

Here, *current_label* is the existing volume label of the disk. If the disk has no label, DOS displays the message no label.

To add a label to a disk or to replace a current label, type a valid volume label and press Enter. For any version of DOS V3, you may use a space in the label. When you press Enter, DOS replaces the nonexistent or old label with the volume label you entered.

You can use the LABEL command to remove a label from a disk. To delete a volume label, type the following:

   *dc:*__LABEL__ *d:*

Do not give a volume label. When DOS asks for the volume label, just press Enter. DOS will respond as follows:

```
Delete current volume label (Y/N)?_
```

To delete the label, type **Y** and press Enter. If you do not want to delete the label, type **N**, which stops the LABEL command, leaving the current label intact.

Understanding Files

Disk storage is often compared to a filing cabinet that has several drawers. Inside each drawer are file folders (see figs. 11.1 and 11.2). In fact, with a graphics-based DOS Shell, a file folder icon marks each file in the File System directory display (see fig. 11.3). Each folder is used for a particular subject. The folder contains facts about the subject, such as personnel records, charge-card receipts, bank statements, invoices, appliance warranties, automobile repair records, and so on.

A file folder can be empty, or it can hold one or more papers relating to the subject. For example, a folder for a checking account may hold monthly bank statements and the canceled checks returned from the bank.

The person controlling the filing cabinet decides how the files should be arranged. The file folders may be sorted alphabetically or by some other coding system. For example, the folders can also be organized by time, with newer folders placed after older folders as new topics are filed. The arrangement helps the person find a particular file. Of course, the folders can also be left completely disorganized.

Inside each file folder, the information can be organized in some similar manner. Again, the person in control of the filing cabinet decides how the records should be arranged.

Fig. 11.1

Electronic files can be compared to a traditional file cabinet. The drawers are like floppy disks or hard-disk platters. The file folders are like files.

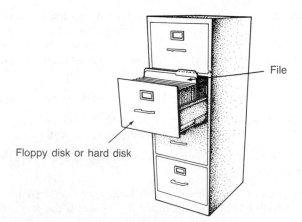

File

Floppy disk or hard disk

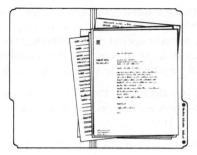

Fig. 11.2

Inside an electronic file, a record is like a sheet of paper. The physical size of the record has little bearing on what information is held in the record or how the information is used.

File folder icon

Fig. 11.3

On the DOS Shell screen, a file folder icon appears beside each file in the directory display.

But if items are not filed in their proper order, either in the cabinet or in the file folders, a lot of work is required to straighten up the cabinet. The same is true if file folders fall out of a drawer or if information is permanently lost from the cabinet through fire or theft. The information is unavailable unless another copy of the records is stored somewhere else.

This analogy fits disk storage. The filing cabinet is the disk drive. The drawers are the floppy disks or hard disk platters.

A file is a set of related items. A disk file is the equivalent of the file folder. You can store any information in a file folder. You can also place any related data in a disk file.

For example, you can place in a disk file any of the following: the programs you use, the names and addresses of your customers or friends, or the orders for your products. The text of this chapter is in a disk file. The only restriction on what can be placed in a disk file is that the information must be data that the computer can process electronically.

A file's smallest allowable size is 0, which is no information at all. The size of the largest disk file depends on the amount of disk storage available. You cannot create a file that is larger than the capacity of your disk. If a file is stored on two floppy disks, it is physically two files, not one. Some programs may place further restrictions on file size.

DOS allows files of up to several *gigabytes* (billions of bytes). At present, no magnetic disk drive can hold this much information (although one-gigabyte hard disks are not far beyond the horizon). Optical disks, the emerging frontier of disk storage, will eventually be able to hold gigabytes of information. Fourteen-inch optical disks that can hold 6.8 gigabytes of data are already available, but they require very expensive disk drives to read them. The current generation of optical disks, including *compact disk ROMs* or *CD ROMs*, can hold just 550 megabytes of information. IBM's optical disk holds 200 megabytes. For the next year, DOS's multigigabyte limit will not be approached.

Just as with a filing cabinet, you determine the information you put in a disk file. You also determine the way information is organized in the file. In other words, you have full control of the filing system and your programs.

Let's carry the analogy further. Each item inside the file folder is called a record. There are two types of records: physical and logical.

A DOS *physical record* is comparable to a sheet of paper. Each sheet is a certain size, 8 1/2 by 11 inches, for instance. Each DOS physical record is 512 bytes. Both records are fixed in size.

A logical record is a set of related items. Each record in the file is organized according to some basic information, such as a person's name, address, city, state, and ZIP code. Each person occupies one record in the file. Most programs use this definition of a logical record. (For more information on both types of records, look at books on assembly language programming, other programming languages, and data management.)

Viewing a File's Contents

If a file can hold anything, how do you know what is in any one disk file? There are several ways to find out. First, every disk file has a name listed in the directory and each file name must be unique. Ideally, if you can remember the file name, you can remember what is in the file.

When you look at the file names in a directory, you may spot a familiar file name. You know that the file holds the names and addresses of your friends. How do you display this information? That will depend on what is really in the disk file. If the file is stored on disk as ASCII text, you can use DOS's TYPE command to display the file's contents on-screen.

ASCII is the acronym for American Standard Code for Information Interchange, the standard way your computer translates its binary ones and zeros into letters, numbers, punctuation, symbols, and special computer characters. Appendix C contains the ASCII chart for characters.

"As ASCII text" means that the program you used took each character as you typed it and put it into the disk file with no changes to the code. The TYPE command "types" on the screen the information from the file. Thus, TYPE is a quick way to display the contents of an ASCII file without your having to use another program.

If your program transforms information and then stores it on disk, you will need a program that can undo this transformation. For example, if your program "crunches" or encrypts information so that a file takes less disk space, the information is not stored character by character as ASCII text. Should you try to use the TYPE command on the file, the information will be gibberish. Generally, the program that crunched the stored information can reverse any encoding.

Remember that DOS stores any bytes on the disk it is told to store. The bytes can be humanly readable text, manipulated data, or program instructions. What these bytes represent is not DOS's concern. DOS is a mindless file clerk that follows your instructions. You and your programs tell DOS what to store.

When you want to use a file, you give DOS the name of the file. DOS goes to the drawer (the floppy or hard disk), searches for a file with the appropriate name, grabs the file, and "opens" it. If there is no file by the name you gave, DOS reports that fact.

You can also tell DOS to create a new file. If a file folder (disk file) with the name you supply already exists, DOS empties the file folder before putting any new information into it. Otherwise, DOS prepares a new file folder (puts the file name into the directory).

On your command, DOS pulls (reads) information from the file or places (writes) information into the file. DOS can be told to start at the beginning of the file or to go to a specific place (record) in the file. In each case, DOS does the hard part of the work. The operating system handles the mundane problems of creating a file, expanding a file, and retrieving information from or placing information into the file. You and your programs just tell DOS what to do.

Viewing a File's Contents with the TYPE Command

To view a disk file's contents, you can use the TYPE command from the DOS prompt. TYPE is built into COMMAND.COM. The TYPE command's syntax is

   TYPE *d:*filename.ext

The *d:* is the optional name of the disk drive that holds the file you want to view. The *filename* is the file's mandatory root name. The *.ext* is the file's optional extension. If the file has an extension, you must type the extension because it is part of the file's exact name. If the file does not have an extension, do not include one.

TYPE does not allow you to use a wild card (* or ?) in the file name. To use TYPE, you must enter an unambiguous file name.

To try the command, first list a file's directory with the DIR command. If you have a file that ends in .BAT or .TXT, try to use the TYPE command to display one of the files. At the DOS system prompt (A>), type the command **TYPE** followed by a space and the name and extension of the file. When you press Enter, you should see the contents of the file on the video screen.

A file's contents will frequently exceed the 24-line limit of the standard video screen. To pause the display to read the lines, use the Ctrl-S, Ctrl-Num Lock, or Pause key. When you have read the screen, press any key to "unfreeze" the screen.

Now try to type a program file. Ask for a directory of a disk again. Do you see any files that end with COM or EXE? At the DOS system prompt, type **TYPE** followed by a space and the complete file name, including the file's extension. The information on the screen should look like nonsense. You may recognize a few words or phrases, but the screen looks mostly incomprehensible. This type of display results when you use the TYPE command to type a program file.

Although TYPE displays any file's contents, you will be able to read only the files that contain ASCII text. Files that are not stored as ASCII text will be unintelligible.

To view a program file's contents, you must use another program. If the program is written in interpretive BASIC (Disk or Advanced BASIC), use BASIC to load and list the program. If the program is in machine language (the native language of the computer's CPU), you will need a disassembler, a program that transforms the binary language of the computer into humanly readable instructions. (DEBUG, a program included with DOS, handles this function and many others. A discussion of DEBUG, however, is beyond the scope of this book.)

Facts about Files

The following list outlines some basic information about files:

- A file holds a set of related information.

- Information in a file is arbitrary. This information can be in a form you can read (ASCII text), can be readable only by programs, or can be a program itself.

- You can use the TYPE command to display a file's contents. If the file holds only ASCII text, the display will be meaningful. If the file holds something else, the display will look like nonsense.

- Every file has a name. The name must be unique in the directory for the disk that holds the file.

- DOS acts as a file clerk, handling the storage and retrieval of files. You are responsible for what the file contains and how its contents are organized.

Understanding File Names

We usually think in terms of names. When a name is understood and accepted, two or more people can use it to identify someone or something. To converse with computers, we also use names. You have already seen how DOS knows a disk file by its name. This name becomes the handle, the common phrase you, your programs, and DOS use to work with a file.

Recognizing Legal File Names

You learned in Chapter 6 that a file name has two parts, a root name and a suffix. The root name can have from one to eight characters. The suffix, or extension, can have from one to three characters. If a suffix is used, it is separated from the root name by a period (.). The suffix is optional.

There are restrictions on the characters you can use in a file name. Some programs may even demand certain names. Some files do not need extensions. Other files need specific root names or extensions. The need for an extension, and the extension's name, depend on what is in the file and how the file will be used.

Why use an extension? In some cases, DOS or your programs force you to use a certain extension. In other cases, your applications programs assume that you will use a certain extension unless you indicate otherwise.

Each program file requires a certain extension. Whenever you want DOS to run a program stored on the disk, the program must have an extension of .COM or .EXE. The abbreviation .COM stands for a machine language *command* file. The extension .EXE stands for a DOS-*executable* file. The program file's extension informs DOS that the file is a program and tells DOS how to execute the file.

A batch file must have the extension .BAT, or DOS will not recognize the file as a batch file. Batch files are discussed in Chapters 15 and 16.

DOS is supplied with a file called MORTGAGE.BAS. This file, a sample program that is written in the BASIC computer language, calculates mortgage payments. Notice that the file's extension is .BAS. Unless you otherwise instruct BASIC, BASIC automatically stores BASIC programs with the .BAS extension. The automatic assignment of this default extension is extremely convenient. If you wanted to load and run the mortgage program from BASIC, you would type **RUN "MORTGAGE"** instead of **RUN "MORTGAGE.BAS"**.

In this case, BASIC allows some shorthand by automatically adding the .BAS extension to the file name. Whenever you load or save the program, BASIC adds the .BAS for you.

Table 11.1 lists some standard extensions. Included are file-name extensions that programs use automatically, extensions that files must have, and some common-sense extensions that will help you identify files. Usually the programs you use will determine the extensions you will need.

Of the extensions listed, four are the most common: .COM, .EXE, .TXT, and .DAT. Beware of the .TMP, .BAK, and .$xx extensions. (This last extension can have any two characters in the place of xx.) Do not use these extensions for your files. If you do, and your programs create files that can use these extensions, you will wipe out files you want to keep.

The following list summarizes the rules for file names:

1. A file name must have

    a. A root name of one to eight characters

    b. An optional extension of one to three characters

    c. A period between the root name and the extension name if an extension is used

Table 11.1
Common File-Name Extensions

Extension	What It Is
.ASM	Assembler source file
.BAK	Backup file
.BAS	BASIC program file
.BAT	Batch file
.BIN	Binary program file
.C	C source file
.CHP	Chapter file (Ventura Publisher®)
.COM	Command (program) file
.CPI	Code page information file (DOS)
.DAT	Data file
.DBF	dBASE III® database file
.DIF	Data Interchange Format file
.DOC	Document (text) file
.DTA	Data file
.EXE	Executable program file
.IDX	Index file (Q&A™)
.HLP	Help file
.KEY	Keyboard macro file (ProKey™)
.LET	Letter
.LST	Listing of a program (in a file)
.LIB	Program library file
.MAC	Keyboard macro file (Superkey®)
.MAP	Linker map file
.MSG	Program message file
.NDX	An index file (dBASE III)
.OBJ	Intermediate object code (program) file
.OVL	Program overlay file
.OVR	Program overlay file
.PCX	A picture file for PC Paintbrush®
.PAS	Pascal source file
.PIF	Program Information File (TopView™/Windows®)
.PRN	Listing of a program (in a file)
.RFT	Revisable Form Text (Document Content Architecture)
.STY	Style sheet (Ventura Publisher)
.SYS	System file or device driver file
.TIF	A picture file in tag image format
.TMP	Temporary file
.TXT	Text file
.$xsx	Temporary or incorrectly stored file
.WK1	Lotus 1-2-3, Release 2 worksheet file
.WKQ	Quattro® spreadsheet file

2. The characters permitted in a file name are

   a. The letters *A* through *Z*. (Lowercase letters are transformed automatically into uppercase.)

   b. The numbers 0 through 9

   c. The special characters and punctuation symbols
      $ # & @ !   ( ) { } ' _ ~

3. The following characters cannot be used in a file name:

   a. Control characters, including Esc and Del

   b. The space character

   c. The characters + = / [] " : ; , ? * \ <> |

4. If DOS finds an illegal character in a file name, DOS stops at the character preceding the illegal one and uses the legal part of the name.

5. A device name can be part of a root name but cannot be the entire root name. For example, CONT.DAT or AUXI.TXT are okay, but CON.DAT or AUX.TXT are not.

6. Each file name in a directory must be unique.

7. A drive name and a path name usually precede a file name. (Path names are discussed in Chapter 13.)

You may notice what seems to be a slight contradiction in the rules for file names. A file name cannot use the wild-card characters ? and *. With some DOS commands, however, you can use file names that contain wild-card characters. The contradiction is simple to explain: no file can use a wild-card character in its name, but file names in DOS commands can contain wild cards when DOS searches for file names.

Table 11.2 lists two sets of file names. Each file name in the first set is correctly phrased and has no illegal characters. The file names in the second list are illegal. An explanation of why the name is illegal follows each name.

The next section explains what happens when you use an illegal file name. But before we get to that discussion, what about good and bad file names? Good file names have two characteristics: the file name is meaningful and related files have similar names.

The file name %$!12.XYZ is perfectly valid, but how can you tell what is in the file? Using an easily remembered file name helps you quickly locate the file you want. For example, the file FRIENDS.DAT is easy to remember as a data file that holds your friends' names and addresses.

Use file names with some common element to name similar files, such as the extension .LET for all files that are letters. Using common elements makes copying and deleting files easier.

Here are two examples of good file names. Every chapter of this book is in a file whose name begins with the letters CHAP, followed by two numbers to indicate the chapter,

Table 11.2
Legal and Illegal File Names

Legal Name	Illegal Name	Explanation
ABCDEFGH.IJK	ABCDEFGHIJ.KLM	Too many characters in the root name
MYLETTER.TXT	.TXT	No root name
TOGO.COM	TO:GO	Cannot use a colon
MYFILE	MY FILE	Cannot have a space in the name
PRINT.EXE	PRN.TXT	PRN is a device name
12-4PM	THIS,WAY	Cannot use a comma
CINDY2	ABCD.EFGH	Too many letters in the extension
(CARL)	?ISIT.CAL	Cannot use a ?

and the extension .PCD (for PC DOS). For example, this chapter has the name CHAP11.PCD. My letter to William Smith is in a file whose name consists of the name SMITH, followed by a letter that indicates order, and the extension .LET for letter. The file names are SMITHA.LET, SMITHB.LET, SMITHC.LET, and so on.

You will see greater advantages to naming files in this fashion when you become familiar with your computer. You will quickly be able to find and remember the contents of the many files you create, and you will be able to perform DOS commands quickly on these files by using wild-card file names.

Avoiding Illegal File Names

When you use an illegal file name, one of two things can happen. DOS will give you an error message and will not perform the operation, or DOS will perform the operation and create a file name, based on what you typed.

How DOS reacts to illegal characters depends on what illegal characters are used and where they are in the file name. Generally, DOS stops forming the root name or extension when it finds the first illegal character. The following list shows what DOS does when it encounters file names whose lengths are illegal:

Illegal File Name	What DOS Does
ABCDEFGHIJ.KLM	Uses the file called ABCDEFGH.KLM
ABCD.EFGH	Uses the file called ABCD.EFG

If you use too many characters, DOS ignores the additional ones. This applies separately to the root name and to the extension. In this first example, DOS ignores the characters *IJ*. In the second example, DOS ignores the fourth character (*H*) in the extension.

If you try to use just an extension (such as .TXT) as a file name, DOS displays an error message. DOS reacts this way because a file must always have a root name.

DOS treats punctuated or separated file names as follows:

Illegal File Name	*What DOS Does*
TO:GO	Uses two names, TO and GO
THIS,WAY	Uses two names, THIS and WAY
MY FILE	Uses two names, MY and FILE

DOS separates file names that contain a colon, semicolon, comma, quotation mark, equal sign, or space. These punctuation marks and the space act as separators, or delimiters, in file names. In each example, DOS sees two names: one name before the delimiter and another after it. The delimiter itself is discarded and does not become part of the file name. What happens next depends on the program you are using. Suppose that you are using the COPY command and you type

A>COPY TO;GO MYFILE

The COPY command will display an error message indicating that you have given too many parameters—three file names (TO, GO, and MYFILE) when you should have given two. (Parameters are discussed in Chapter 15.)

Other programs can react differently. A program expecting only one name may not check for additional file names. In the example just given, such a program would use only the file name TO. GO and MYFILE would simply be ignored.

DOS handles the file name PRN.TXT in the following manner:

Illegal File Name	*What DOS Does*
PRN.TXT	Uses the printer for input or output

PRN is a reserved device name that represents the printer. A reserved name has special meanings to DOS. If you use the name PRN.TXT as a file name, one of three things may happen:

1. DOS attempts to get information from the "file" (that is, tries to get input from the printer) and quickly returns without getting anything. What happens next depends on the program. In most cases, the result is not what you want.

2. If you are putting information into this file and the printer is turned off or not selected, DOS waits for 20 to 30 seconds and then gives an error message telling you that `PRN` (the printer) `is not ready`.

3. If the printer is on and selected, DOS writes the information to the printer and does not save the information to a disk file.

These possibilities apply whenever you use a device name as a root name. DOS uses the device instead of the disk file. If you use such names as AUX.TXT, LPT2.MAC, or NUL.COM as file names, the results will not be what you want.

A word of caution about unique file names: Two files in the same directory cannot have the same name. A file name can be considered the "identity property" of a disk file. You must make sure that each file name is different by adding, subtracting, or changing characters in either the root name or the extension of similarly named files. If you try to use file names that are not different, DOS will not know which file you are designating.

If you try to change a file name to match a name already in the directory, DOS gives you the message:

```
Duplicate file name or File not found
```

and will not rename the file. DOS protects you and itself from having two files with the same name in the same directory.

Remember the caveat from Chapter 7 about the COPY command. When duplicate file names exist on the source and destination disks, the destination file is deleted, and then the source file is copied. In other words, the existing destination file is lost, and DOS gives no warning. When in doubt, you should check both directories for duplicate file names before you copy. Use the DIR command on both disks. This check can keep you from inadvertently losing a good file.

Summary

In this chapter, you learned the following key points:

❏ Certain rules apply when you use disk drive names, create volume labels, or use files.

❏ The LABEL command adds, changes, or deletes volume labels.

❏ A file is a set of related information stored under a common file name.

❏ A file can hold any information.

❏ A valid file name contains legal characters. A good file name is a valid file name that is meaningful to you. Use part of a common name for files that are related.

❏ If you use an invalid file name, the results may vary, but they will seldom be what you want.

In Chapter 12 you will learn about I/O redirection. I will also show you some tricks that make the computer easier to use.

Part III

Expanding Your Use of DOS

Includes

Using Redirection and Piping

Using Hierarchical Directories
To Manage Files

Gaining Better Control with
Hierarchical Directories

Understanding Batch Files

Using Batch Subcommands

12

Using Redirection
and Piping

You do not have to understand redirection and piping to use the computer. But if you know how to use these techniques, you can make several computer-related tasks easier. In this chapter, you will learn how to use redirection and piping. One of the tips you will learn is how to "read" a directory of a disk into a document created by a word processing program. Redirection is a function that you can use only from the DOS command prompt or from batch files that you run from the DOS Shell.

If your system has a printer, turn it on, and make sure that it is ready to print. Press Ctrl-PrtSc (or Ctrl-Print Screen). You learned to use Ctrl-PrtSc in Chapter 6. This sequence prints what you send to the screen.

Now type **DIR**, and press Enter. The directory of the disk prints on your screen and on the printer. Press Ctrl-PrtSc again to turn off the printing.

Now type

   DIR>PRN

What happened? DOS printed on the printer a directory of the disk. DOS did not print the directory on the screen. You have just used an interesting DOS feature: I/O redirection.

The Meaning of Redirection

What is I/O redirection? You know that I/O stands for input and output. In *redirection*, you tell DOS to change the source or destination that is normally used for input and output. Let's look at three new terms that help explain redirection.

DOS has three standard places from which it usually receives or to which it sends characters (see fig. 12.1). *Standard input* is the keyboard, where your programs and DOS normally expect characters to be typed. Typed characters usually come from standard input. *Standard output* is the video screen, where programs and DOS usually display information. Displayed characters normally go to standard output. *Standard error* is also the video screen, where your programs and DOS report any errors that occur. Error messages go to standard error. DOS will only allow you to redirect standard input and output.

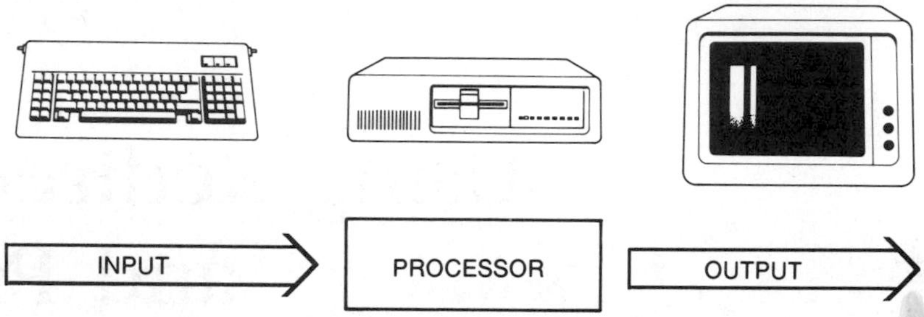

Fig. 12.1

The standards for input and output. The keyboard is used for input, and the video display for output.

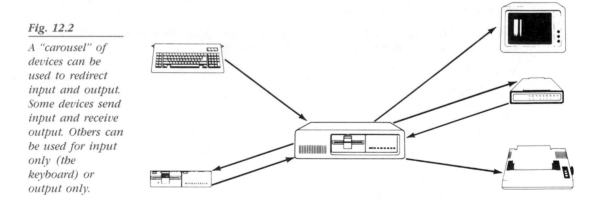

When you redirect I/O, you tell DOS to use a device other than the keyboard or video screen to receive characters or to send the characters somewhere other than where they are normally sent (see fig. 12.2). Instead of letting DOS get characters from the keyboard, you can have DOS get characters from a disk file or from any other device. You also can tell DOS to display characters in a disk file, on a printer, or on another device. Redirection occurred when you typed **DIR>PRN**. When you issued that command, DOS tricked the program into thinking that it was putting information on the standard device: standard output (that is, the screen).

Fig. 12.2

A "carousel" of devices can be used to redirect input and output. Some devices send input and receive output. Others can be used for input only (the keyboard) or output only.

The most frequent use of input redirection is to create a "canned" set of answers to a frequently used program. Programmers often use this trick: they create a disk file that contains a set of standard "answers" for the program with which they are working. When users run the program, DOS is directed to "trick" the program into getting its answers from the file, rather than from a person typing responses at the keyboard. The user runs the program by using input redirection, rather than by remembering the answers that the program requires.

Output redirection is most commonly used to print on the printer information that is normally displayed on the video screen. The other common use for output redirection is to "capture" into a disk file information that is displayed on the video screen. You can then edit the file or print copies of it.

The Symbols for Redirection (<, >, >>)

Redirection uses three reserved symbols:

< redirects a program's input

> redirects a program's output

>> redirects a program's output but adds the text to an established file

You can use these symbols only at the DOS system level when you want them to have their reserved meanings. You add the symbol(s) and the file or device name to the command you type. The syntax is

symbol devicename

or

symbol *d:***filename.***ext*

For the first syntax form, you use the appropriate redirection symbol followed by the name of the device, for example, PRN. In the second syntax form, you use the appropriate redirection symbol followed by a file name. You may *not* use wild cards (* or ?) in the file name. (Although this book has not yet covered the topic of paths, you can place a path name between the disk drive name and the file name. This subject is covered in Chapter 13.) Using a space between the symbol and the device or file name is optional. You *cannot*, however, have a space within the device or file name. The redirection (the symbol, device name, and file name) can appear anywhere on the command line *after* the command name.

Examples of Redirection

The following examples show redirection:

1. DIR>DISKDIR

   This sequence redirects the output of the directory command (DIR) to a disk file called DISKDIR.

2. CHKDSK>COM1

   This command redirects the CHKDSK program's output to the serial port.

3. MYPROG<B:ANSWERS

   This command redirects the input of MYPROG from the file
   ANSWERS on drive B.

In the third example, MYPROG is not expecting you to type anything from the keyboard. Instead, MYPROG will get its input from the disk file called ANSWERS.

Be cautious in using the > symbol. Do not use an existing file name if you want to keep that file. When you use > to redirect output to a disk file, DOS erases any disk file in the directory that has the name you used. DOS then creates a new file to hold the output. In example 1, if a file in the current directory has the name DISKDIR, that file will be erased.

To add redirected output to an established file, use the symbol >>. This symbol *appends* the output to the end of an existing file but does not erase the file's original contents. To change the first example and add the additional copy of the directory to DISKDIR, type

   DIR >>DISKDIR

If you look at the way each symbol points, you will remember how redirection works. The < points away from the device or file and says, "Take the input from here." The > and >> point toward the device or file and say, "Put output there."

Hands-on Practice: Using I/O Redirection with SORT

One of the programs included on your DOS floppy disk is SORT.EXE. SORT sorts lines, items, or characters in ASCII order. You will read more about SORT later in this book, but for now you will use SORT to practice I/O redirection. You will first use SORT without I/O redirection to see how the program works. Then you will try SORT again, first redirecting the input, next redirecting the output, and finally redirecting SORT's input and output.

SORT is an external DOS program, so you must have your master disk in drive A. Or if you have a hard disk, you must use the PATH command to do this exercise. In this example, I will use the hard disk, drive C, which must be the current disk drive. If you use the floppy disk, make sure that the A drive is the current disk drive.

Using SORT and Redirection

In this first example, you will enter lines from the keyboard that SORT will use. SORT will display the lines in an ASCII-sorted order on the video display. Type

   C>**SORT**

The cursor will drop to the next line. Because you did not direct SORT to get its lines from another location, SORT is waiting for you to input lines from the keyboard. Type these lines:

This is the last line.

This is the intermediate line.

This is the first line.

After you have typed the third line, press Enter. Then you must tell DOS you have completed entering lines by pressing F6, the special-function key. Press Enter again.

SORT sorts the lines and displays the lines on the video screen. Because you did not redirect the output, SORT will display the results on the video screen. Your screen should look something like this:

```
C>SORT

This is the last line.

This is the intermediate line.

This is the first line.

^Z

This is the first line.

This is the intermediate line.

This is the last line.

C>_
```

The lines are sorted in ASCII order (similar to alphabetical order).

Using SORT and Redirection on a Disk File

In the next practice session, you will redirect input to the SORT command from a disk file. You will first create a file of lines by using the COPY CON command. Type

C>COPY CON MARY

This line directs the COPY command to take input from the keyboard and place it in the file called MARY. The prompt will disappear, and the cursor will appear on the following line. Now type these lines:

Mary had a little lamb

whose fleece was white as snow

and everywhere that Mary went

the lamb was sure to go

After you have entered the last line, press the F6 key, and then press the Enter key. You should see the message 1 File(s) copied. The DOS prompt will reappear. Now you can use the TYPE command to look at the lines you entered. Type

    C>**TYPE MARY**

The lines you entered will appear on the video screen.

You can sort the lines by entering the command:

    C>**SORT<MARY**

This command instructs DOS to "trick" SORT into getting its input from the file called MARY, rather than getting the input from the keyboard. Instantly, the poem's sorted lines should appear on the display. Here is what you should see:

```
C>TYPE MARY

Mary had a little lamb

whose fleece was white as snow

and everywhere that Mary went

the lamb was sure to go

C>SORT<MARY

and everywhere that Mary went

Mary had a little lamb

the lamb was sure to go

whose fleece was white as snow

C>
```

Again, the lines from the file are sorted in ASCII order.

In the last exercise, you will sort the file MARY that you created, send the result to another file, and then send it to the printer. This technique involves redirecting the SORT output to a disk file. Type the following line:

    C>**SORT<MARY>MARYSORT**

The disk drive light will blink once or twice, and then the DOS system prompt will appear. To see the sorted lines, display the file by using the TYPE command. Type

    C>**TYPE<MARYSORT**

The lines from the file that appear on your screen should be in the same ASCII order you saw when you earlier used SORT. To make a print of the file with its sorted lines, make sure your printer is turned on and ready to print. Then type

    C>**SORT** < **MARY** > **PRN**

This command directs SORT to sort the lines from the file called MARY and then to send the output (the sorted lines) to the printer (PRN).

As mentioned earlier in the chapter, you may use spaces between the redirection symbol and the file or device name. DOS will accept the line

    SORT <MARY> PRN

Try experimenting on your own. First try to redirect the output. Use the > and >> symbols to redirect the output of the DIR and CHKDSK commands. Redirect the output to the printer and to a disk file.

After you have tried a few experiments, move on to the next section on piping, a form of I/O redirection that uses more than one program.

Using Filters and Piping (|)

The concept of using filters and piping goes with I/O redirection. With filters and pipes, you can combine smaller, useful programs to achieve more useful results or simply make using the computer easier.

A *pipe* is a computer-made line that connects two programs. The first program's output becomes the second program's input. A simple example to illustrate piping is a program called MORE. MORE first displays one full screen of information obtained from the standard input; then it displays the message –More–. When you press a key, MORE displays the next full screen of information. MORE repeats this process until the entire input has been displayed on-screen.

MORE is a *filter*: a program that manipulates the stream of standard-input characters, one character after another, as they go to the standard output. A filter gets data from the standard input, modifies it, and then writes the modified data to the standard output (screen). This modification is called *filtering* the data. After MORE filters and displays a full screen of data, the program waits for you to press a key.

Now try the following exercise. If you are wondering how a filter like MORE can be useful, this example will show you.

You can begin this exercise in one of two ways. You can make your BIN subdirectory your current directory by typing CD C:\BIN, or you can place a floppy disk that contains many files, such as the DOS master disk, in drive A. Now type

    DIR | MORE

You will see 23 lines displayed on-screen and then the prompt — More–. When you see the –More– message, press the space bar. Another set of 23 lines appears on-screen. Keep pressing the space bar each time you see the prompt –More– until the system prompt reappears.

Now let's examine the syntax of the example. You remember that DIR displays a listing (directory) of files. MORE presents one screen's worth of information at a time. The vertical bar between the words DIR and MORE is the pipe symbol. If you combine the functions of DIR and MORE through piping, you can view long directory listings one screen at a time.

Piping has more powerful uses, including I/O redirection. You will try more examples later in the chapter, but you must first learn a few details about piping. In this material, you will learn more about the DOS filters MORE and SORT and be introduced to the FIND filter.

Some Details about Piping

Piping, like I/O redirection, works only at the DOS command level. You cannot use piping after you have run a program. You must pipe things when you type the line to run the program.

You are not restricted to using just one pipe at a time. However, only one program name may be on each side of the pipe: you must give the pipe symbol once between each pair of program names. You can also redirect the first program's input and the final program's output in the pipe.

Technically, piping is the chaining together of two or more programs with automatic redirection. DOS creates temporary files for this redirection. When you use piping, make sure your disk has enough room to hold the temporary file(s) that DOS will create. If your disk does not have enough room to hold the temporary files, piping will not work. Take a look at the size of the file on which the piping operation will be working. If you are piping information between two programs, you will generally need at least as much free space as the file's current size. You will need twice as much free space for three or more programs. If your program removes information from the file, you will need less free space. If the program adds more information to the file, you will need more free space.

The Filters

DOS has three standard filters, two of which have already been mentioned:

FIND	Finds a string
MORE	Displays one screen of information and then waits for a keystroke
SORT	Sorts information in ASCII order

This section again discusses MORE and SORT and presents a brief overview of FIND. You will find a more detailed discussion of the filters in Part VI, the *DOS Command Reference*.

The MORE Filter

As mentioned in the earlier discussion, MORE displays one screen's worth of information at a time. If the display has more than 23 lines, MORE displays the prompt -More- and waits for you to press a key. If the display requires fewer than 23 lines, MORE displays all the lines on one screen and returns to the system prompt. Computer users call the full video screen of information that MORE displays a *page* and call what MORE produces a *paged output.*

MORE, FIND, and SORT expect their input from the keyboard (standard input) and place their output on the video screen (standard output). You must use I/O redirection or piping for the filters to work with a disk file or other DOS command.

MORE, FIND, and SORT are external DOS commands, which means you must load these programs from a disk. The syntax to use MORE is as follows:

> *dc:***MORE**

The *dc:* is the name of the disk drive that holds the MORE program. (You can place a path name between the disk drive name and the filter's name. All DOS filters allow the use of path names. This subject is covered in detail in Chapter 13.)

MORE is commonly used to type a file's output one page at a time. For this use, the syntax is as follows:

> *dc:***MORE** *d:***filename.***ext*

The *d:***filename.***ext* is the name of the file you want MORE to display. If you want to display the contents of a file called ACCEPT.LET, the command is

> **MORE < ACCEPT.LET**

MORE will display the contents of the file, one screen at a time. To stop MORE's output on the screen, simply press the Ctrl-Break or Ctrl-C sequence.

The SORT Filter

If you need to sort a file's lines, SORT is the filter to handle the task. SORT's syntax is as follows:

> *dc:***SORT** */R / + c*

The *dc:* is the name of the disk drive that holds the SORT program. SORT has two switches that affect the command's operation. The switches are

/R	*Reverse* the sort (sort in reverse order)
/ + c	Start the sorting at the "*c*th" character (or column) in each line. The *c* is a number ranging from 1 to the length of the longest line.

You will most often want to sort the lines in ascending ASCII order. The ASCII table in Appendix C lists characters in the following order: control characters, characters and punctuation symbols, numbers, more symbols, uppercase letters, more symbols, lowercase letters, and another set of characters and punctuation symbols. SORT follows this order for sorting characters, with two exceptions:

- Lowercase letters are treated as if they are uppercase letters.
- Characters with an ASCII value above 127 are sorted by the specific value based on the current country code.

(Country codes are discussed in Chapter 18, which explains how DOS is used internationally.)

The first exception is beneficial if you want to sort alphabetically rather than by ASCII order. In the ASCII chart, the uppercase A is the first letter, followed by the uppercase letters through Z. Several positions down in the chart come the lowercase letters *a* through *z*. If SORT distinguished upper- and lowercase letters, the first two lines in the sorted poem would have been

> Mary had a little lamb
> and everywhere that Mary went

because the uppercase *M* in Mary comes before the lowercase *a* in the ASCII chart. By ignoring the difference between upper- and lowercase letters, SORT is able to sort letters in true alphabetical order.

The second exception is important if you use PC DOS with a foreign-language character set. The proper sorting order for each foreign language is different. For example, the single German character ß sorts as if it were a two-character *SS*. The Spanish æ sorts as if it were an *a* or an *e*, depending on its use in the word. Many languages do not have a one-to-one sorting sequence for their characters. As discussed later in the book, SORT uses the collating information appropriate to the language used, based on the COUNTRY command in the CONFIG.SYS file.

The /R switch reverses the normal sorting order so that *Z* comes before *A*. This switch is useful when you need to sort something in reverse order.

The second switch, /+c, tells SORT to start the sorting with the character in column c. This switch is most useful when the information on which you are working is aligned in columns, and the column by which you want to sort the file is not the first column. You use /+ followed by the number of the column where sorting should start. SORT skips to the appropriate column to perform its function.

To see how the /+c switch works, try this example:

C>SORT /+8 < Mary

This command will sort the MARY poem based on the characters in the eighth column of each line. The result you will see on your screen is

```
the lamb was sure to go.
Mary had a little lamb
whose fleece was white as snow
and everywhere that Mary went
```

SORT sorted the lines of the poem based on the *d, l, r,* and *b*—the eighth letter in each line. You will try more exercises with the SORT filter later in this chapter.

The FIND Filter

FIND is the DOS filter that automates searching for specific lines in a file. FIND searches a file for lines that match a set of characters you specify, or it finds lines that do not match the specified characters. FIND's syntax is

*dc:*FIND */V/C/N* "**string**" *d:*filename*.ext*

The *dc:* is the disk drive that holds the FIND program. The *d:filename.ext* is the optional name of the file to search. If you do not give a file name, FIND will look for its information from the keyboard.

The set of characters for which you are searching is the "string." In computer terms, a *string* is any set of ASCII characters, including symbols, numbers, and letters. A string can consist of any number of characters, including no characters at all (an *empty string*). To specify a string for FIND, you must surround the string with double quotation marks. FIND searches only for the characters within the double quotation marks.

Unlike the SORT filter, FIND distinguishes between upper- and lowercase characters. With FIND, "THE" is not the same as "the" or "The." To use FIND correctly, you must specify either upper- or lowercase characters.

FIND has three switches:

/V	Displays the lines that do *not* contain the specific string.
/C	*Counts* the lines that have the string, but does not display the lines.
/N	*Numbers* the lines that FIND displays. The numbers appear before the line and are based on the line's position in the file.

If you want to use any of the switches, you have to place them after the command FIND but before the string. FIND is one of the few DOS commands that requires switches to appear directly after the command instead of at the end of the command line.

FIND's most important switch (and the only switch we will cover in detail in this chapter) is /V. This switch directs FIND to search for lines that do not match the string, as opposed to FIND's normal string-matching operation.

Let's use our sample file MARY to test FIND's operation. To find the lines that contain the word "Mary," use the following command:

C>**FIND "Mary" MARY**

Notice that the letters *ary* in the string "Mary" are lowercase. When you run the command, you should see two lines on the screen:

```
Mary had a little lamb

and everywhere that Mary went
```

Now try searching for lines that do not contain the string "Mary." Type

FIND /V "Mary" MARY

The two lines that do not contain "Mary" should appear on your screen.

To see how specifying the wrong case affects FIND's operation, try these two commands:

    C>**FIND "MARY" MARY**

    C>**FIND /V "MARY" MARY**

In the first exercise, no lines should appear. In the second exercise, all the lines will appear. Remember that FIND considers uppercase letters to be different from lowercase letters.

Using I/O Redirection, Piping, and the DOS Filters

When you are challenged to perform some housekeeping task that seems to take longer than the task is worth, you realize the fullest power of redirection, piping, and filters.

The most frequent computer "housekeeping" task is manipulating the output of the DIR command. DOS's capabilities are ideal for demonstrating these operations. Try the exercises in this section on your BIN subdirectory or on the DOS disk. If you are using the DOS V4 Shell, you will find that the directory sorting demonstrated next manipulates the directory much like the File System's sorting features.

First, try sorting DIR's list of files. Although the IBM-provided DOS disks are almost sorted, you will quickly find that most other disks or directories are not. To sort file listings, use the command:

    C>**DIR | SORT**

This command directs DIR's output through the SORT program. The SORT program begins sorting with the first character of the line—the root file name. The DIR | SORT command results in an alphabetized list of files.

Using SORT with the /+c Switch

You can use SORT with the /+c switch to sort the output by other categories of information that the DIR command displays. You can sort the DIR listing by file extension, file size, file date, or any combination of these options. To sort a DIR listing in these ways, you will need the information in table 12.1, which lists the column in which DIR begins the display of file extensions, file size, file date, and so on.

To sort the DIR command's output by file size, use the following command:

    C>**DIR | SORT /+14**

To sort the output by date, use the following command:

    C>**DIR | SORT /+24**

Table 12.1
DIR Information by Column (to be used with SORT)

Information	Columns	Switch
Root file name	1–8	/+1
File extension	10–12	/+10
File size	14–21	/+14
File date	24–31	/+24
File time	34–39	/+34 (24-hour time only)

You can sort the output by more than one column by simply adding another SORT command to the pipe. For example, to sort the DIR command's listing first by extension and then by root file name, use the following command:

C>**DIR | SORT | SORT /+10**

The first time SORT is used, the files are sorted by root name. The second time SORT is used, the output of the first SORT command is sorted by extension. This process produces a list of files sorted by extension, and, within a group of files having the same extension, by file name. You can see, then, that to SORT more than once in a pipe, you must sort in *inverse* order, sorting first on the least important item and then on the most important item.

I do not advocate using SORT on file times that are represented by a 12-hour clock. The technique works correctly only if the directory time is displayed in 24-hour clock style. SORT is "dumb" when it sorts numbers. SORT collates numbers based on the ASCII values of their characters rather than on their real numeric values. To us, 12 is the number 12, but the computer sees 12 as the character 1 followed by the character 2. To illustrate this problem, take a look at the following numbers:

1   2   11   15   21   35   112   241   367

If you use SORT to sort these numbers, it will produce this output:

1   11   112   15   2   21   241   35   367

Since SORT looks at the first character of the number string to start the sort, it ranks 35 after 241. To get the numbers sorted in the proper numeric order, you would need to "pad out" the one- and two-digit numbers with leading zeros:

001   002   011   015   021   035   112   241   367

The following list of times

12:00a   2:25a   10:57a   12:00p   1:45p   5:00p

would be sorted as follows:

1:45p   2:25a   5:00p   10:57a   12:00p   12:00a

This time the sort is not quite in proper time order. (Because a space has an ASCII value less than the character 0, times from 1:00 to 9:59, whether a.m. or p.m., come before 10:00, a.m. or p.m.) With the 24-hour format, the times are sorted correctly because afternoon and evening times are greater than morning times.

Using SORT with a MORE Filter

An annoying aspect of using SORT on the output of the DIR command is that long directory listings scroll off the top of the screen before you can read them. You cannot solve this problem by using the /P (pause) switch with DIR, because DIR's output is fed to SORT. You do not want *this* output delayed. You want, instead, to delay the output of SORT, which is displaying the information you want. If you used a /P switch with DIR, you would have to press a key each time DIR presented a (not displayed) screen of information to SORT. Needless to say, that solution is less than ideal.

The ideal solution to this problem is to force SORT's output through the MORE filter, which you will recall is the one-page-at-a-time filter. To do so, use this set of commands:

   C>**DIR | SORT | MORE**

With this set of commands, the sorted directory listing is displayed one screen at a time. One problem with the DIR | SORT | MORE sorting technique is that the lines listing the volume label, the name of the directory being displayed, the statistics on the number of files being displayed, and the amount of free disk space are listed out of order. Because the DIR command includes displaying the volume label, directory name, and disk statistics, and these displays cannot be suppressed, you must use a different means to remove these lines. FIND offers you the capability of displaying lines that contain or lack certain strings.

To remove the volume label, displayed directory, and disk statistics lines, you have to use an intuitive approach. You must find some information contained in lines for each displayed file that does or does not appear in the other three lines. This information will be a string you feed to the FIND command.

If you look at the output of DIR, you will notice that one character is unique to the lines concerning files. This character does not appear in the other columns. The date separator (-) appears in the date column but does not appear in the other lines. If you add the FIND command to your sorted directory command, the command becomes

   DIR | FIND "-" | SORT

This pipeline first invokes DIR to feed its output to FIND. FIND then looks for lines that contain the hyphen (-). FIND's output is filtered by SORT, which sorts the remaining directory information. If you want to page a long directory listing, you can add MORE to the end of the pipeline, as in the following command:

   DIR | FIND "-" | SORT | MORE

If you want to place the sorted directory listing in a disk file, such as a file named DIRS, the command is

   DIR | FIND "-" | SORT > DIRS

Using Redirection within a Program

In Chapter 8 you learned that COMMAND.COM, the command processor, runs your programs and DOS's built-in functions. Many programs make the capabilities of COMMAND.COM available to you while you are using an applications program. I will use WordStar in this example, but many other applications programs have the ability to run DOS's Shell (COMMAND.COM).

With WordStar Release 4.0, for example, you can run a program while you are working with WordStar's main menu or while you are editing a file. To run another program from within WordStar, you type **R** if you are at the Main Menu and **Ctrl-KF** if you are editing a document. Computer users frequently use WordStar to "merge-print" several files as one lengthy document. To merge-print, you must create a file to hold the individual names of the files you want to merge-print. Rather than remembering the file names, I use I/O redirection to trick the DIR command into placing its results into a disk file. Then I read that file into my WordStar document and edit the document to produce the merge-print commands.

Here is the technique:

Step 1. Begin by typing **R** *from WordStar's Main Menu or Ctrl-KF from within a document.*

Step 2. When WordStar asks you to enter the name of the DOS command you want to run, type

DIR filename.ext > TDIR

Substitute the appropriate file name for **filename.ext**. To get the list of all files that end with .PCD, for example, I use the following command:

DIR *.PCD > TDIR

This command produces a list of the files that end with .PCD and places the output of DIR in a disk file called *TDIR* (for temporary directory) on the current disk drive.

Step 2 is the most important step. In this step, you asked DOS to run the DIR command and place its output in a disk file. Even though you are using an applications program (in this case, WordStar), the applications program allows you to talk to DOS directly. When you talk to DOS, you can run any command, including a built-in DOS command. You can also use I/O redirection and piping.

Step 3. If you are working from WordStar's Main Menu, open the file (WordStar's D option) that will hold the names of the files to be printed.

If you are working within the file, read in the temporary file by using WordStar's Ctrl-KR command. When WordStar asks you the name of the document to be inserted into the file being edited, answer **TDIR**.

Step 4. If the file-name list is short, retype the names and add WordStar's file-include directive (.FI) before each file name; delete the original lines of the directory using WordStar's line-delete command (Ctrl-Y).

If the list is long, first delete the lines that do not contain file names: the ones that show the volume label, directory name, and free-space statistics. Then delete the file size, date, and time information from each line, leaving only the file names and extensions. Replace the blank spaces between the root name and extension with a single period. Insert a **.FI** before each file name. (You might try using a search-and-replace operation, searching for a carriage return and replacing it with a carriage return and .FI. You may need to delete an extra .FI from the bottom of the file.)

You now have a file that holds the merge-print commands for printing the documents. You "printed" the directory to a file, read the list into your document, and cleaned up the lines. Once you have used the technique a few times, you will find it fast and easy.

Remember that with many applications programs you can use any DOS command with or without I/O redirection and piping. Running programs from within other programs has many possibilities. The only limitation is the available RAM to run the second program.

Summary

This chapter introduced redirection, piping, and the DOS filter programs. You can read more about FIND, SORT, and MORE in the *DOS Command Reference* at the back of this book.

Do not forget the caution about redirection. If you use the symbol to redirect a program's output to a disk file, make sure that the disk file's name is unique. If you use a disk file name of a file that already exists, DOS will erase the contents of that file and write the new information into the file. You will have lost the original information. In this chapter, you learned the following important points:

❏ DOS has three standard places to receive and send information: standard input, standard output, and standard error.

❏ By using redirection and piping, you can change where DOS and your programs receive and send information:

        <   receives information from a device or disk file

        >   sends information to a device or disk file

        >>   appends information to a device or disk file

        | takes the output of the program on the left side of the symbol and makes it the input of the program on the right side

❏ The MORE filter displays one screen of information at a time.

❏ The SORT filter sorts information from the keyboard or from a file.

❏ The FIND filter finds lines from the keyboard or in a file that match or do not match a given string.

Chapter 13 introduces the hierarchical directory system.

13

Using Hierarchical Directories To Manage Files

You know that every disk has its own directory. Each disk has one, and only one, directory. This arrangement works well for floppy disks. If, for example, you store 112 or 224 files on a disk (the maximum number of files 360K disks and HC disks can hold, respectively), you can still wade through the directory to find a file. The process is tedious, but not impossible.

Hard disks, on the other hand, are capable of storing hundreds or thousands of files. Storing these file names in a single directory would be inefficient, and working with the files would be awkward. Such storage would be inefficient because when you look for a file, DOS sorts through the directory to find the file you want. From the standpoint of performance, a one-directory solution does not work very well. From the standpoint of usability, locating a perhaps long-forgotten file name from a list of hundreds of files is time-consuming at best. A single directory is an ineffective method of organizing your files.

Fortunately, DOS offers a solution that still allows you to store many files on a disk, but in smaller, more organized, and distinct compartments. Microsoft, the author of DOS, borrowed the concept for the solution from the UNIX operating system: *hierarchical directories*.

Understanding Hierarchical Directories

With hierarchical directories, you can group files on a hard disk the way that most people physically organize disks. Users generally categorize disks by purpose. They arrange each disk so that it contains all the programs and data files they need for a certain task. Such an arrangement, which groups programs and data files logically, works well.

191

How about the hard disk? How can files be organized on the hard disk in the same way that files are organized on disks? The "secret" is the use of subdirectories. For an understanding of this concept, let's look at the directory system as a whole.

Every formatted disk has one directory. The directory is stored on the disk and holds the names of your files, along with other information. The directory itself is really a file in which DOS stores its own data.

The Root Directory and Subdirectories

The starting directory of every disk is the main or root directory. The root directory holds information about programs and data files. More significantly, the root directory holds information about other directories. In fact, the unique feature of the directory system is that each directory can also hold information about other directories. These additional directories are called *subdirectories*.

Think of the root directory as a large box. In this box, you can store file folders. You can also store additional boxes within the larger box. The additional boxes (the subdirectories) can hold file folders and even more boxes (more subdirectories). Each box—the main box (root directory) and smaller boxes (subdirectories)—can hold files and other boxes.

Like the main directory, each subdirectory is a file. The root directory and subdirectories are set up in the same manner and can hold the names of files and other information and the names of other subdirectories.

The only fault with comparing the root directory to a box is that no box can hold more than the main box, and the number of boxes is limited by the size of the main box. With subdirectories, no such fault exists. DOS endows subdirectories with a "magic" property that allows the size of subdirectories to grow larger than the root directory. The number of subdirectories is limited only by the capacity of your disk.

There is one major difference between a root directory and its subdirectories you should know about: restrictions on the root directory. The root directory is fixed in both its size and in the number of files the directory can hold. The maximum number of files a root directory can hold is 112. You cannot store more files than the number listed for the various sizes of disks and hard disks. DOS cannot make the root directory larger. This is because DOS sets aside a certain amount of space for the root directory when the disk is formatted and has no provision for extending this.

Unlike the root directory, a subdirectory can be extended as needed. That's because space for the subdirectory "list" isn't set aside until you actually create the subdirectory. This list is stored as a special kind of DOS file. You can't rename, copy, or delete a subdirectory as you can some other types of files. Yet, because a subdirectory is stored as a file, DOS is able to simply add more sectors onto the subdirectory file as you add files or subdirectories. As long as free disk space exists, you may create additional subdirectories and your existing subdirectories can grow larger.

The Tree Analogy

The terms "parent" and "child" are often used in discussing the directory system. To understand the relationship between directories in a system, imagine a family tree with the founding parents as the base of the tree. Their children are branches on the tree. When the children grow up, marry, and have children of their own, the tree grows more branches. The process continues for each generation, as children marry and have children.

The root directory is like the founding parents. Just as parents have children, the root directory can have subdirectories. Each subdirectory (child) of the root (parent) directory can in turn become a parent to another generation of subdirectories. As you create each new subdirectory, you create a new branch on the tree.

The parent directory "owns" its child subdirectories. Although a parent directory can have many child subdirectories, each child subdirectory is owned by only one parent directory. You can, therefore, trace any subdirectory back to the root directory of the disk.

The terms "up" and "down" describe movement in the directory system. In describing disk structures, it is a convention to refer to the root directory as the "top" of the tree. That's because humans tend to view the outer layer of anything as the top surface, and think of the layers that follow as residing "beneath." So, let's flip the tree upside-down. When you move down, you move from a parent directory to a child subdirectory. When you move up, you move from the child subdirectory to its parent directory. The root directory is the "highest" directory. The subdirectories farthest from the root are the "lowest" branches of the directory tree. Our analogy now more closely resembles the root structure of a tree rather than its branches.

A Sample Hierarchical Directory

Appendix B contains a chart of a sample hierarchical directory. The directory is also illustrated in figure 13.1. The sample directory is used only to demonstrate how the directory system works; it is not intended to show the best way to organize your files.

In the directory in Appendix B, the root directory is at the top. It contains several non-directory files: IBMBIO.COM, IBMDOS.COM, COMMAND.COM, AUTOEXEC.BAT, CONFIG.SYS, VDISK.SYS, COUNTRY.SYS, and KEYBOARD.SYS. You may recognize some of these file names. The root directory also has two subdirectories: DOS and WORDS. The DOS side of the directory contains DOS programs and other program files. The WORDS side has word processing files. In this case, the parent directory owns two children: the DOS and WORDS subdirectories.

Note that there is no directory named ROOT. The root directory uses a special symbol for its name, the backslash (\). If you see only a backslash as the directory name, that backslash signifies the root directory. If you call for the directory of any DOS disk in drive A, you will see the following line:

```
Directory of A:\
```

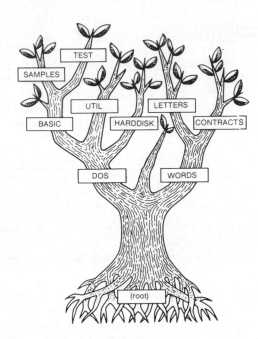

The single backslash tells you that you are getting a directory listing of that disk's root directory.

Let's descend one level on the word-processing side of the directory, down to the WORDS subdirectory. If you are familiar with WordStar, you will recognize the names of several WordStar program files. In addition to these files, WORDS owns two children, the LETTERS and CONTRACTS subdirectories. The LETTERS subdirectory holds letters I have written—letters to IBM, Jack, and Doug. LETTERS also holds the previous revisions of the letters to IBM and Jack (the files that end in .BAK). The CONTRACTS subdirectory holds the drafts of my contracts with Meyer and Anderson. I have used the hierarchical directories to organize word-processing files by purpose: letters and contracts.

Now follow the WORDS subdirectory back to the root directory. Move down one level to the DOS directory. This directory holds several files: the CHKDSK (check disk) program and three other DOS programs, FIND, SORT, and MORE. A copy of the Microsoft Macro Assembler (MASM.EXE) is also in this subdirectory.

DOS owns two children: BASIC and HARDDISK. Two versions of the BASIC language are in the BASIC directory, and programs for the hard disk are in the HARDDISK directory.

Notice that the term directory was used for subdirectory in the preceding paragraph. The two terms are interchangeable when you are referring to any directory other than the disk's root directory. The root directory can be only a directory, but a subdirectory can be thought of as a directory in its own right. From this point on, I'll use the term subdirectory only when it is needed for clarity.

Now follow the BASIC directory down one step further. BASIC owns two directories: a SAMPLES directory, which contains a mortgage program provided with IBM DOS V3.3, and a TEST directory, which contains BASIC programs I created to test disk speed (DSKSPED.BAS) and the screen (SCRNTST.BAS).

Before you start using hierarchical directories, take some time to learn about an important disk-directory term, *path*. A *path* is a chain of directory names. It tells DOS how to maneuver through the directories to find the directory or the file you want. Each directory name is separated by the path character, the backslash (\), which is also the name of the root directory.

Don't let this dual use of the backslash confuse you. Remember that whenever the backslash is the first character of the path, the path starts at disk's root directory. Used otherwise, the backslash just separates directory names. Remember also that whenever you need to use a file name with a path, a path character (\) is also required before the file name.

In Chapter 7, you learned that no two files listed in the same directory can have the same file name. However, the same file name can exist in several directories on the same disk. This duplication does not confuse DOS at all. You just can't use a duplicate file name in the same directory.

A word of warning: for a program or a batch file, avoid using a file name that duplicates the name of a subdirectory in the same directory. For example, in a directory that has a subdirectory called DOIT, don't have a program named DOIT.COM or a batch file called DOIT.BAT.

Here's the reason for the warning: When you execute a program or batch file, you use only the file's root name. If the root name of a program or batch file in a parent directory is identical to a subdirectory name in that same directory, DOS may not know whether you are talking about the program, the batch file, or the subdirectory.

Rules for Directory and Path Names

The following list summarizes rules for directory names. You may notice some similarities among the rules for directory names and rules for file names. They are closely related.

- A directory name has the following:

  a. A root name that contains from 1 to 8 characters.

  b. An optional extension that contains from 1 to 3 characters.

  c. A period separating the root name from the extension.

- Valid characters for a directory name are the following:

  a. The letters A through Z. (Lowercase a to z are changed to uppercase A to Z.)

  b. The numbers 0 through 9.

c. The following special characters and punctuation symbols:

$ # & @ ! ^ ( ) - { } ' ' _ ~

- The following characters cannot be used in a directory name:

a. Control characters, including Esc and Del.

b. A space.

c. The characters

+ = / [ ] " " : ; , ? * \ < > |.

- You cannot create a directory called . (single period) or .. (double period). The single period is DOS's shorthand designation for the current directory, and the double period (..) is the shorthand designation for the parent directory.

- A device name may not be the name of a directory.

- You cannot create a subdirectory called DEV in the root directory.

The following list summarizes the rules for path names.

- A path name can contain from 1 to 63 characters.

- The path is composed of directory names separated by the backslash character (\).

- A drive name may precede a path.

- Generally, a file name may follow a path. When this happens, use a backslash to separate the path name from the file name.

- DOS keeps track of the current path for each drive.

- The characters . (single period for the current directory) and .. (double period for the parent directory) are valid in a path name.

- To start with the root (uppermost) directory, you begin the path name with a backslash. (A drive name before the path character does not contradict this rule.)

- If you don't start with the root directory, DOS starts with the current directory of the disk.

You will recall the notation used earlier in this book for a disk drive and a file name:

*d:***filename**.*ext*

A new notation that includes the path designation is

d:path**filename**.*ext*

This notation is a *full file specification* or a *full file name*. It starts with the optional disk drive name, followed by an optional path name, the mandatory root file name, and finally the optional extension. In the DOS manual, this file specification is called a *filespec*. Almost all DOS commands accept this type of file name: a file name preceded by a drive and path name.

Looking at Subdirectories with the DOS Shell

If you are using the DOS Shell, you can easily view your disk's directory structure. As you've seen in earlier exercises, the File System screen includes a directory tree showing the structure of the current disk. This display is confined to the left panel of the display.

You can move from one subdirectory to another in the tree by highlighting the subdirectory you want. Either click the subdirectory with the mouse or move the highlighting with the cursor keys. A large subdirectory tree can be scrolled just like a list of files. In graphics mode, the tree has its own scroll bar. In text mode, you'll see a More: indicator and up/down arrows in the upper right corner of the panel.

Moving through subdirectories is simple when you use the DOS Shell. It's a bit more complicated for those who work from the DOS command prompt. We'll explore this topic in the next section.

Navigating through Subdirectories

To use DOS effectively with a hard disk or high-capacity floppy disk, you need to know how to navigate through subdirectories. Knowing how to navigate depends principally on understanding path names.

Understanding Path Names

To understand path names, consider the analogy of a major airline's routing system. The airline uses a major city as the central hub for its flights. When the airline cannot offer travelers direct flights between cities, passengers going to different cities go first to the hub city of the routing system. At the hub, the travelers change planes and fly to their final destinations. If a traveler's plane has a stopover at his destination on the way to the hub, the traveler need not go to the central hub. He simply departs the plane at the stopover city. If the airline is large, several cities may serve as minor hubs to other cities. There is, however, a central hub to which these minor hubs connect.

Navigating through subdirectories is like traveling through an airline's routing system. The root directory is the "central hub." The subdirectories are the outlying "cities" on the hub's rim. Subdirectories that contain other subdirectories are minor hubs. DOS is the air-traffic controller. And just as the tower that controls departures and arrivals must be informed about aircraft movements, you must inform DOS when you want to travel to another subdirectory.

The tower (DOS) is always aware of your current position (current directory). If you are located at one city and want to go to another city, you must inform the tower how you will reach that city. If the city is not on the path to the hub, you can restart your journey at the main hub and travel outward to your final destination. If the city is on the way to the hub, you can go directly to the desired destination.

If your destination is on the path to the main hub or is serviced by a minor hub (the current subdirectory), you can use shorthand notations to speed the communication process (the typing of the path). Depending on the location, you may move away from the main hub or toward the main hub and back again. If your destination is the current directory, you can omit almost all the path directions.

In the next section you learn to give DOS directions for moving through the subdirectory system.

Moving through Directories (CHDIR/CD, TYPE)

The following exercises are based on the sample disk directory in Appendix B.

Let's start at the root directory. The objective is to get to the LETTERS directory to see what was written to Doug (DOUG.LET) and then run CHKDSK to see how much space is left on the disk.

You can accomplish this task in two ways: the hard way and the easy way.

The hard way is to move down to the WORDS directory and then to the LETTERS directory. At that point, you could use the TYPE command to display the DOUG.LET file. (TYPE displays a file's contents on-screen.) Then you could return to the root directory of the disk. This procedure involves typing several commands.

The following screen shows the commands you would have to issue to reach DOUG.LET by the first method. These commands begin at the disk's root directory.

A>CHDIR WORDS

A>CHDIR LETTERS

A>TYPE DOUG.LET

**A>CHDIR **

A>

Here is the explanation of the commands. To move to the WORDS directory, you use the DOS command CHDIR (change directories). The command is

A>CHDIR WORDS

DOS checks the root directory to find a subdirectory called WORDS. DOS finds the subdirectory and "moves" there. (You move down one level.) WORDS becomes the disk's current directory. Had DOS not found a subdirectory called WORDS, it would have displayed the following message:

```
Invalid directory
```

This error message indicates that DOS could not find the subdirectory you specified.

CHDIR is a "no news is good news" command. When DOS successfully executes the CHDIR command, no message is given. Only a blank line is printed. Most of DOS's hierarchical directory commands do not return messages when they work properly.

The next command line moves you down one level to the LETTERS directory. The command is

A>CHDIR LETTERS

LETTERS, which holds DOUG.LET, now becomes the current subdirectory. To finish the objective, you would use the TYPE command to display DOUG.LET. Because your word processor may do funny things to a file, the file's display may contain some strange characters when the file is displayed on-screen with TYPE. If, for example, you display a document file created with WordStar (the word processor I use), you will see strange characters.

The last command returns you to the root directory. The command is

**A>CHDIR **

The CHDIR command contains a backslash (\ ). This command is a complete path name that returns you to the root directory. Remember that when you start the path with a backslash, you are instructing DOS to start with the root directory. In the case of CHDIR LETTERS, DOS assumes that you want to start with the directory you were in, because you did not start the path with a backslash character.

The second, and easier, way to move through the directories and display this file is to use the single command line:

A>TYPE WORDS\LETTERS\DOUG.LET

The TYPE command accepts a path name before the file name. DOS interprets this command in the following way:

1. Look in the current directory for the subdirectory called WORDS. Move into this directory.

2. In the WORDS directory, find a subdirectory called LETTERS. Move to the LETTERS subdirectory.

3. In the subdirectory LETTERS, find a file called DOUG.LET. Type the file's contents on-screen.

4. Move back to the beginning directory.

Notice that this command line uses a path character between each directory name. A path character is used also between the last directory name and the name of the file to be typed. You must phrase your command to DOS this way when you use a path name and a file name. If you omit the final path character, DOS sees a large directory name (such as LETTERSDOUG.LET) or two names (WORDS\LETTERS DOUG.LET). The usual result will be an `Invalid path or file name` message from DOS, not the result you want.

Notice also what DOS did after executing the TYPE command. DOS returned to the directory from which the TYPE command was issued. DOS remembers the current directory for every disk you use. If you give DOS a command to go into a different directory to get a file, DOS bounces back to the starting directory after getting the file. The only way you can change the current directory on a disk is to use the CHDIR command.

The second objective in this exercise is to run the CHKDSK (check disk) program on the disk. As before, you have a hard way and an easy way to accomplish this task.

The hard way is to move to the DOS subdirectory, execute the CHKDSK command, and return to the root directory:

A>CD DOS

A>CHKDSK

(DOS displays information about the disk here.)

**A>CD **

CD is an abbreviation for the change directory command. Like RENAME and ERASE, DOS recognizes the shorthand form of CD as CHDIR. This command instructed DOS to move from the root directory to the DOS subdirectory. When the DOS directory became the current directory, DOS ran the CHKDSK program. Then DOS returned to the root directory after CHDIR was complete.

The easy way to accomplish the same thing is to type the following:

A>DOS\CHKDSK

DOS displays information about the disk here and returns to the root directory:

A>

Notice that you can give a path in front of an external command, too. Both a drive name and a path can precede a command name.

You have just seen one of the important differences between DOS versions. In DOS V2, you can execute commands in your current directory only. (The PATH command is an exception; PATH is discussed later in this chapter.) DOS V3 and V4 allow you to execute commands in any directory from any directory. This capability is a major benefit. Many of the tips you'll see later in this book are based on this capability.

CHDIR (or CD) has one additional capability. CHDIR can indicate the current directory. If you type **CHDIR** or **CD** without a path name, you will see the name of the directory for your current disk drive. You can, for example, switch to the LETTERS subdirectory and indicate the current subdirectory and then move back to the root directory and indicate the current directory again. The following commands carry out this activity:

```
A>CD WORDS\LETTERS
A>CD
A:\WORDS\LETTERS
A>CD \
A>CD
A:\
```

You can also use CHDIR to display the current directories of other disk drives. Give the command (CHDIR or CD), followed by a space and a disk drive name. You'll see the current directory for the specified disk drive.

Now that you know the basics of using CHDIR and hierarchical directories, you can try a hands-on practice that will expand your understanding of the CHDIR command and introduce two other hierarchical directory commands.

Hands-on Practice: Using CHDIR/CD, MKDIR/MD, and RMDIR/RD

If you use the DOS Shell, you have already learned how to make and remove directories (Chapter 5). To review, a directory can be created in this way:

1. Go to the File System menu and select the File menu.

2. Choose the Create directory option.

3. Enter the full path name of the directory you wish to create.

4. Confirm your selection when asked by DOS.

To remove a directory follow these steps:

1. Go to the File System menu.

2. Highlight the directory you wish to delete in the tree display shown in the left hand panel.

3. Pull down the File menu from the action bar.

4. Choose Delete from the menu.

5. Confirm that you want to delete the directory.

Command-prompt users have some additional syntax to practice. Because creating and removing directories is a bit tricky without the graphic display of the DOS Shell, you can practice with a few exercises.

In this session, you will use the three hierarchical directory commands CHDIR (change directory), MKDIR (make a new directory), and RMDIR (remove a directory). These commands are also abbreviated CD for CHDIR, MD for MKDIR, and RD for RMDIR. Because DOS recognizes both forms in each case, the abbreviations are used here. For the session, you'll need the following:

- A computer with two disk drives. One drive must be a floppy disk drive (any type); the other drive can be a floppy disk drive or a hard disk drive.

- The DOS Master disk (or Master Operating disk for users of 360K disk drives).

Users with hard disk drives need the DOS disk(s) just mentioned, but these users will need to copy the files from the hard disk to the floppy disk. The files to copy are in the BIN directory on the hard disk.

- If you are using two floppy disk drives, you will also need one formatted disk. Do not put the DOS system files on this disk. (In other words, don't use the /S switch when you format the disk.) Write something like "Practice Directory Disk" on the label of the formatted disk. If you give a volume label (FORMAT /V), call the disk PRACTICE. Owners of hard disk drives do not need an additional disk.

As in earlier chapters, I'll provide separate instructions for users whose computers have two floppy disk drives and for users whose computers have one floppy disk drive and one hard disk. For the demonstration, I'll use 720K floppy disks. If you own a hard disk, use the second set of directions only, regardless of how many floppy drives you have.

Instructions for Two Floppy Disk Drives

Step 1. Put your copy of the DOS Master or Master Operating disk into drive A.

Step 2. Put the practice disk into drive B.

Step 3. Type

MD B:COMS

MKDIR, or its short form MD, makes a new subdirectory called COMS on the disk in drive B.

Step 4. Type

MD B:COMS\SAMPLES

This command makes a new subdirectory called SAMPLES in the subdirectory COMS.

At this point, the root directory owns a directory called COMS, which, in turn, owns a directory called SAMPLES. Notice that you have used a path in this command. DOS moves down through the path. When DOS reaches the last name in the path (SAMPLES), it knows to make a new subdirectory called SAMPLES, instead of trying to move farther in the directory structure.

Many beginning users are confused by path sequences. To keep the path's order and structure clear in your mind, separate the path from the final destination at the last back-slash. The part before the final backslash (B:COMS) tells DOS where the action should take place (make a subdirectory called SAMPLES). The part after the final backslash (SAMPLES) is the object of your action (the subdirectory that DOS is to create).

Step 5. Type

DIR B:

When you ask DOS for a directory of drive B, what you will see on-screen is a listing of the disk's root directory files. Your screen will look something like the following:

```
Volume in drive B is PRACTICE
Directory of  B:\
COMS          <DIR>        2-24-89  10:43p
        1 File(s)    728064 bytes free
```

The appearance of the <DIR> symbol in the second column after a name indicates that the entry is a subdirectory, not a normal file. Because COMS is a subdirectory, COMS has the <DIR> designation following it.

The third column shows the date and time you created the subdirectory or file. Make a note of the time you see on the screen.

Look at the rest of the screen. Notice that the directory listing's first line tells you what disk drive you are using and what directory you are viewing. Study the screen for a few seconds and then move to the next step.

Step 6. *Type*

DIR B:COMS

Now you will see a listing of the COMS subdirectory. The listing will look something like the the following listing:

```
Volume in drive B is PRACTICE
Directory of B:\COMS
.             <DIR>        2-24-89  10:43p
..            <DIR>        2-24-89  10:43p
SAMPLES       <DIR>        2-24-89  10:43p
        3 File(s)    728064 bytes free
```

The SAMPLES directory should hold no surprises, but what are the period and double-period directories? Both are special shorthand symbols used for maneuvering in the directory system. The period represents the subdirectory you are viewing, or the current directory. You can think of it as the subdirectory's "I exist to myself" symbol. The double period represents the parent directory of the COMS subdirectory. In this case, the double period represents the root directory.

Compare the first directory to the second. Notice that the root directory does not contain these symbols. Only subdirectories have the period (.) and double-period (..) symbols. Because the root directory is the base directory, the root directory has no parent.

If you want to tell DOS explicitly to start with the directory you are using, you use the period as the first character in the path. This technique is infrequently used because, unless the path begins with a \, DOS starts movement with the current directory. To tell DOS to move up one level of subdirectories, use the double period. This technique is used more frequently. We'll cover this shorthand symbol again in Chapter 14.

Take a look at the dates and times on the lines with the period and double-period symbols. These dates and times should be the same as those for the COMS entry in the root directory. When DOS creates subdirectories, it not only makes an entry in the parent directory; it also establishes the . and .. files, giving all three items the same date and time.

Step 7. Type

COPY A:*.COM B:\COMS /V

This command copies to the subdirectory COMS on drive B all the files from drive A that have the extension .COM. As you learned earlier, the /V switch tells DOS to verify that it has copied the files correctly.

When you specify a disk drive name in a path, the drive name must appear first. You then specify the path and then the file name. You do not need to specify a path for the disk in drive A because you are currently using the root directory of the disk; that directory contains all the DOS programs you want. For the disk in drive B, you specified a disk drive (**B:**) and a path (**\COMS**). Because you didn't want to give the files new names as they were copied, you didn't use file names.

The usual order of elements is a drive name, followed by a path, and finally, a file name. If you don't need one part, such as the path or the drive name, leave it out.

Step 8. Type

CD B:COMS

This command makes COMS the current directory on drive B.

Step 9. Display the list of files for the root, COMS, and SAMPLES directories. Briefly look at each directory before you display the next one. The required commands are

DIR B:..

DIR B:

DIR B:SAMPLES

The first command tells DOS to step up one level of directories and show the list of files. The second command tells DOS to list the files in the current directory. And the final command tells DOS to list the files in the SAMPLES subdirectory.

For these three commands, I'll show you what I saw on-screen on my computer. If you are using DOS V3.3 and 720K disk drives, you'll see screens identical to mine. If you are using DOS V3.3 with 1.2M or 1.44M disks, you will notice that only the line listing the number of bytes free in the directories will be different. You'll notice more differences in the screens if you are using 360K disks or a different version of DOS, such as V4.

```
A>DIR B:..
Volume in drive B is PRACTICE
Directory of  B:\
COMS         <DIR>      2-24-89   10:43p
     1 File(s)    410624 bytes free
```

```
A>DIR B:
Volume in drive B is PRACTICE
Directory of  B:\COMS
.            <DIR>        2-24-89   10:43p
..           <DIR>        2-24-89   10:43p
SAMPLES      <DIR>        2-24-89   10:43p
COMMAND  COM    25307     3-17-89   12:00p
ASSIGN   COM     1561     3-17-89   12:00p
BACKUP   COM    31913     3-18-89   12:00p
BASIC    COM     1063     3-17-89   12:00p
BASICA   COM    36403     3-17-89   12:00p
CHKDSK   COM     9850     3-18-89   12:00p
COMP     COM     4214     3-17-89   12:00p
DEBUG    COM    15897     3-17-89   12:00p
DISKCOMP COM     5899     3-17-89   12:00p
DISKCOPY COM     6295     3-17-89   12:00p
EDLIN    COM     7526     3-17-89   12:00p
FDISK    COM    48216     3-18-89   12:00p
FORMAT   COM    11616     3-18-89   12:00p
GRAFTABL COM     6128     3-17-89   12:00p
GRAPHICS COM     3300     3-17-89   12:00p
KEYB     COM     9056     3-17-89   12:00p
LABEL    COM     2377     3-17-89   12:00p
MODE     COM    15487     3-17-89   12:00p
MORE     COM      313     3-17-89   12:00p
PRINT    COM     9026     3-17-89   12:00p
RECOVER  COM     4299     3-18-89   12:00p
RESTORE  COM    34643     3-17-89   12:00p
SELECT   COM     4163     3-17-89   12:00p
SYS      COM     4766     3-17-89   12:00p
TREE     COM     3571     3-17-89   12:00p
        28 File(s)     410624 bytes free

A>DIR B:SAMPLES
Volume in drive B is PRACTICE
Directory of  B:\COMS\SAMPLES
.            <DIR>        2-24-89   10:43p
..           <DIR>        2-24-89   10:43p
     2 File(s)     410624 bytes free
```

Step 10. *Copy the BASIC program(s) to the SAMPLES directory.*

If you use 360K disks or a version of DOS before V3.3, the BASIC programs are on a different disk. Take the DOS Master disk out of drive A. Put the Operating disk or the DOS Supplemental Programs disk into drive A. Don't change the disk in drive B.

If you use higher-capacity floppy disks, you should have the BASIC program(s) on the disk you are using.

DOS V3.3 and V4 have a BASIC program, MORTGAGE.BAS, which is a mortgage calculator. Versions of DOS prior to V3.3 have many BASIC programs.

To copy the BASIC programs, you will use a command that will copy simultaneously one or many BASIC programs. To copy the BASIC program files from drive A to the SAMPLES directory, type

A>COPY A:*.BAS B:SAMPLES /V

You'll see the name of each file as DOS copies it from drive A to drive B.

Step 11. Move to the SAMPLES directory by typing

A>CD B:SAMPLES

Step 12. Type:

A>DIR B:

DOS shows the list of files in the SAMPLES directory. Look briefly at the directory, and then go to the next step.

Step 13. Exchange the disk in drive A with the disk in drive B. Use the DIR command to list the directory of drive A; then do the same for drive B.

What happened? In both cases, you got a listing of the files in the root directory. If you change disks and the current directory does not exist on the changed disk, DOS resets the current directory to the root directory.

Step 14. Move back to the SAMPLES directory in drive A by typing

A>CD COMS\SAMPLES

Step 15. Create a new directory called TEST in SAMPLES. Use the following command:

A>MD TEST

Now call for a directory of TEST. (Use the command **DIR TEST**.) You should see only the . and .. entries.

Step 16. Copy BASIC into the TEST directory by typing

A>COPY ..\BASICA.COM TEST /V

This command tells DOS to step up one directory to COMS, get BASICA.COM (Advanced BASIC), and copy it into the TEST subdirectory.

Step 17. Type

RD TEST

Now you should see the following error message:

```
Invalid path, not directory, or directory not empty
```

RD is the remove directory command. You just told DOS to erase the TEST directory. The message you see on your screen tells you that you cannot remove a directory that is not empty. A subdirectory is empty if the only files in the subdirectory are the . and ..

directory symbols. If you want to remove the directory, that directory cannot contain any other files or subdirectories. This precaution is for the safety of the files. DOS assumes that if you want to remove a subdirectory, you will empty it first.

You cannot use RD on the current directory, nor can you remove the root directory of the disk. You will get an error message if you try. On your own, change to the TEST directory and try to remove it. Move back to the SAMPLES directory before going to the next step.

Step 18. *Remove the TEST directory by deleting all files in TEST and using the RD command. Make certain you type the following command correctly before you press Enter:*

ERASE TEST*.*

DOS will ask:

```
Are you sure (Y/N)?
```

DOS V4 will add a message informing you that all files in the directory will be erased. As discussed earlier in the book, these messages are another safety precaution. You have just told DOS to erase all files in the TEST subdirectory. Whenever you tell DOS to erase all files, DOS will ask you to confirm your request.

Because you do want to erase all the files, answer **Y**. If you did not want to erase all of the files, you would answer **N**. The system prompt will reappear.

Next, call for a directory of **TEST** (using DIR TEST). You will see that BASICA.COM was erased but that the . and .. entries remain. You cannot erase a subdirectory with the ERASE command. The only way to remove a subdirectory is to use the RMDIR (or RD) command.

Remove the directory by typing

RD TEST

Now call for a listing of the SAMPLES directory. You will see that the TEST directory has been removed.

Step 19. *Run the MORTGAGE program. First, try to invoke Advanced BASIC, which is in the COMS directory with the mortgage program. Type*

..\BASICA MORTGAGE

Advanced BASIC loads into the computer, executes, and then loads and runs the mortgage calculator program. If you haven't tried the program, try it now.

To exit the program, press the Esc key when you see the menu. You will see an **Ok**. Then type the word **SYSTEM**, and press Enter. The DOS prompt reappears.

The command **..\BASICA** told DOS to move up one directory and get Advanced BASIC. Now try the same command a different way. Type

\COMS\BASICA MORTGAGE

This command also loads and runs Advanced BASIC and the mortgage calculator. At the menu, press the Esc key. Then type **SYSTEM** to get back to DOS.

Now try to load Advanced BASIC without a path name in front of the word BASICA. Type

BASICA MORTGAGE

You'll see the message:

```
Bad command or file name
```

DOS could not find BASICA.COM in the directory you specified. The file is not in the SAMPLES directory; it is in the COMS directory.

You could give a path name whenever you wanted to load Advanced BASIC. However, there is another way: using the PATH command. The PATH command enables you to tell DOS to search in other subdirectories for a program you want to run. If DOS does not find the program in the current directory, DOS will search the directories you named in the PATH command.

Type the following command:

PATH A:\COMS

This command tells DOS to look in the COMS subdirectory if DOS cannot find in the current directory the program you want to run. The last directory named in the path (COMS) is searched, but no other directory is searched (in this case, the root directory of the disk). If you want DOS to search both these directories, you must use the PATH command and type the names of all the directories to be searched, separating the names with semicolons. To have DOS search both the root directory and the COMS subdirectory, you would type

PATH A:\;A:\COMS

Now that the PATH command has been properly set, type

BASICA MORTGAGE

This command will load Advanced BASIC from the COMS directory. BASIC will then load and execute MORTGAGE. Now get out of the menu and back to DOS.

This step was the last instruction for users with two floppy disk drives. You can skim the next section for hard disk users and then skip to the discussion of the PATH command.

Instructions for Floppy and Hard Disk Drives

Step 1. *Put the practice disk into drive A.*

Step 2. *Type CD C:\ to make sure you are at the root directory of the hard disk.*

If your hard disk is not drive C, substitute the appropriate letter of the hard disk drive for the letter C. Also, disconnect the PATH command by typing **PATH**=;. You will need to disconnect the PATH command to see how to run programs from different directories.

Step 3. *Type*

MD A:COMS

This command makes a new subdirectory called COMS on the disk in drive A. MKDIR, or its short form MD, creates a new subdirectory.

Step 4. Type

MD A:COMS\SAMPLES

This command makes a new subdirectory called SAMPLES in the subdirectory COMS.

At this point, the root directory owns a directory called COMS, which, in turn, owns a directory called SAMPLES. Notice that you have used a path name in this command. DOS moves down through the path. When DOS reaches the last name in the path (SAMPLES), DOS knows to make a new subdirectory called SAMPLES instead of trying to move again.

Many beginning hard disk users are confused by path sequences. To keep the path's order and structure clear in your mind, separate the path from the final destination at the last backslash. The part before the final backslash (A:COMS) tells DOS where to do what you've asked (make a subdirectory called SAMPLES). The part after the final backslash (SAMPLES) is the object of your instruction (the subdirectory that DOS is to create).

Step 5. *Type*

DIR A:

What you see is the listing of files in the root directory on the disk. Your screen will look something like this:

```
Volume in drive A is PRACTICE
Directory of  A:\
COMS       <DIR>        2-24-89  10:43p
     1 File(s)    728064 bytes free
```

The <DIR> symbol after a name means that the listed "file" is a directory, not a normal file. The COMS directory has this <DIR> designation following it.

The date and time when you created the directory should also appear on the line with the name. Make a note of the time you see on the screen.

Look at the rest of the screen. Notice the line that tells you what disk drive you are using and what directory you are viewing. Study the screen for a few seconds, and then move to the next step.

Step 6. *Type*

DIR A:COMS

Now you will see a directory of the COMS directory. The listing will look something like the following:

```
Volume in drive A is PRACTICE
Directory of A:\COMS
.           <DIR>        2-24-89   10:43p
..          <DIR>        2-24-89   10:43p
SAMPLES     <DIR>        2-24-89   10:43p
      3 File(s)     728064 bytes free
```

The SAMPLES directory should hold no surprises, but what are the period and double-period directories? Both are special shorthand symbols used for maneuvering in the directory system. The period represents the subdirectory you are viewing, or the current directory. You can think of it as the subdirectory's "I exist to myself" symbol. The double period represents the parent directory of the COMS subdirectory. In this case, the double period represents the root directory, the parent of the COMS subdirectory.

Compare the first directory to the second. Notice that the root directory does not contain these period (.) and double-period (..) directory symbols. Only subdirectories have these symbols. The root directory has no parent; hence, you will not find the . and .. entries in the root directory.

If you want to tell DOS explicitly to start with the directory you are using, you use the period as the first character in the path. This technique is infrequently used because, unless the path begins with a \, DOS starts movement with the current directory. To tell DOS to move up one level of subdirectories, use the double period. This technique is used more frequently. We'll cover this shorthand symbol again in Chapter 14.

Take a look at the dates and times on the lines with the period and double-period symbols. These dates and times should be the same as those for the COMS entry in the root directory. When DOS creates subdirectories, it not only makes an entry in the parent directory; it also establishes the . and .. files, giving all three items the same date and time.

Step 7. *Type*

COPY BIN*.COM A:\COMS /V

This command copies to the subdirectory COMS on drive A **(A:\COMS)** all the files from the subdirectory BIN that have the extension .COM **(BIN*.COM)**. The /V switch tells DOS to verify that it has copied the files correctly.

When you specify a disk drive name in a path, that drive name must appear first. You then specify the path and, finally, the file name. For the **BIN*.COM** portion of the command, you needed to specify a path because the directory that contains all the DOS programs you want is BIN, which is not the current directory. For the disk in drive A, you specified a disk drive **(A:)** and a path **(\COMS)**. Because you didn't want to give the files new names as they were copied, you didn't use file names.

The usual order of elements is a drive name, followed by a path, and finally, a file name. If you don't need one part, such as the path or the drive name, leave it out.

Step 8. *Type*

CD A:\COMS

This command makes COMS the current directory on drive A.

Step 9. *Display the list of files for the root, COMS, and SAMPLES directories. Briefly look at each directory before you display the next one. The required commands are*

DIR A:..

DIR A:

DIR A:SAMPLES

The first command tells DOS to step up one level of directories and show the list of files. The second command tells DOS to list the files in the current directory. And the final command tells DOS to list the files in the SAMPLES subdirectory.

For these three commands, I'll show what I saw on-screen on my computer. If you are using DOS V3.3 and 720K disk drives, you'll see screens identical to mine. If you are using DOS V3.3 with 1.2M or 1.44M disks, you will see that only the line listing the number of bytes free in the directories is different. You'll notice more differences in the screens if you are using a different version of DOS.

```
C>DIR A:..
Volume in drive A is PRACTICE
Directory of  A:\
COMS        <DIR>        2-24-89  10:43p
     1 File(s)     401624 bytes free

C>DIR A:
Volume in drive A is PRACTICE
Directory of  A:\COMS
.           <DIR>      2-24-89   10:43p
..          <DIR>      2-24-89   10:43p
SAMPLES     <DIR>      2-24-89   10:43p
COMMAND  COM    25307   3-17-89   12:00p
ASSIGN   COM     1561   3-17-89   12:00p
BACKUP   COM    31913   3-18-89   12:00p
BASIC    COM     1063   3-17-89   12:00p
BASICA   COM    36403   3-17-89   12:00p
CHKDSK   COM     9850   3-18-89   12:00p
COMP     COM     4214   3-17-89   12:00p
DEBUG    COM    15897   3-17-89   12:00p
DISKCOMP COM     5899   3-17-89   12:00p
DISKCOPY COM     6295   3-17-89   12:00p
EDLIN    COM     7526   3-17-89   12:00p
FDISK    COM    48216   3-18-89   12:00p
FORMAT   COM    11616   3-18-89   12:00p
GRAFTABL COM     6128   3-17-89   12:00p
GRAPHICS COM     3300   3-17-89   12:00p
```

```
KEYB      COM       9056    3-17-89   12:00p
LABEL     COM       2377    3-17-89   12:00p
MODE      COM      15489    3-17-89   12:00p
MORE      COM        313    3-17-89   12:00p
PRINT     COM       9026    3-17-89   12:00p
RECOVER   COM       4299    3-18-89   12:00p
RESTORE   COM      34643    3-17-89   12:00p
SELECT    COM       4163    3-17-89   12:00p
SYS       COM       4766    3-17-89   12:00p
TREE      COM       3571    3-17-89   12:00p
          28 File(s)      410624 bytes free
```

```
C>DIR A:SAMPLES
Volume in drive A is PRACTICE
Directory of  A:\COMS\SAMPLES
.          <DIR>        2-24-89   10:43p
..         <DIR>        2-24-89   10:43p
2 File(s)     410624 bytes free
```

Step 10. *Copy the BASIC program(s) to the SAMPLES directory.*

DOS V3.3 and V4 have a BASIC program, MORTGAGE.BAS, which is a mortgage calculator. Versions of DOS prior to V3.3 come with many BASIC programs. These files are located in the BIN subdirectory. To copy the programs, you will use a command that will copy simultaneously one or many BASIC programs. To copy the BASIC program file(s) from drive A to the SAMPLES directory, type

COPY \BIN*.BAS A:SAMPLES /V

You'll see the name of each file as it is copied from drive C to drive A.

Step 11. *Move to the SAMPLES directory by typing*

CD A:SAMPLES

Step 12. *Type*

DIR A:

DOS shows the list of files in the SAMPLES directory. Look briefly at the directory, and then go to the next step.

Step 13. *Remove the practice disk in drive A, and insert the DOS Master Start-up/Operating or Master Start-up disk into the drive.*

Use the DIR command to list the directory of drive A. What happened? You got a listing of the files in the root directory. If you change disks and the current directory does not exist on the changed disk, DOS resets the current directory to the root directory. This way, DOS does not get confused when you change disks.

Step 14. *Remove the DOS disk from drive A, and put the practice disk back into the drive.*

Make the floppy disk drive the current disk drive, and then make the SAMPLES directory the current directory. The commands are

A:
CD COMS\SAMPLES

Step 15. *Create a new directory called TEST in SAMPLES. Use the following command:*

MD TEST

Now call for a directory of TEST. (Use the command DIR TEST.) You should see only the **.** and **..** entries.

Step 16. *Copy BASIC into the TEST directory by typing:*

COPY ..\BASICA.COM TEST /V

This command tells DOS to step up one directory to COMS, get BASICA.COM (Advanced BASIC), and copy it into the TEST subdirectory.

Step 17. *Type*

RD TEST

Now you should see the following error message:

```
Invalid path, not directory, or directory not empty
```

RD is the remove directory command. You just told DOS to erase the TEST directory. The message you see on your screen tells you that you cannot remove a directory that is not empty. A subdirectory is empty if the only files in the subdirectory are the **.** and **..** directory symbols. If you want to remove the directory, that directory cannot contain any other files or subdirectories. This precaution is for the safety of files. DOS assumes that if you want to remove a subdirectory, you will empty it first.

You cannot use RD on the current directory, nor can you remove the root directory of the disk. You will get an error message if you try. On your own, move to the TEST directory, and try to remove it. Move back to the SAMPLES directory before going to the next step.

Step 18. *Remove the TEST directory by deleting all files in TEST and using the RD command.*

Make certain you type the following command correctly before you press Enter:

ERASE TEST*.*

DOS will ask

```
Are you sure (Y/N)?
```

DOS V4 will also display a message telling you that all files in the directory will be erased. This message is another safety precaution. You have just told DOS to erase all files in the TEST subdirectory. Whenever you tell DOS to erase all files, DOS will ask you to confirm your request.

Because you do want to erase all the files, answer **Y**. If you did not want to erase all of the files, you would answer **N**. The system prompt will reappear.

Next, call for a directory of TEST (using **DIR TEST**). You will see that BASIC.COM was erased but that the **.** and **..** entries remain. You cannot erase a subdirectory with the ERASE command. The only way to remove a subdirectory is to use the RD command.

Remove the directory by typing

  RD TEST

Now call for a listing of the SAMPLES directory. You will see that the TEST directory has been removed.

Step 19. *You are ready to run the MORTGAGE program. First, try to invoke Advanced BASIC, which is in the COMS directory with the mortgage program. Type*

  ..\BASICA MORTGAGE

Advanced BASIC loads into the computer, executes, and then loads and runs the mortgage calculator program. If you haven't tried the program, try it now.

To exit the program, press the Esc key when you see the menu. You will see an `Ok`. Then type the word **SYSTEM**, and press Enter. The DOS prompt reappears.

The command **..\BASICA** tells DOS to move up one directory and get Advanced BASIC. Now try the same command a different way. Type

  \COMS\BASICA MORTGAGE

This command also loads and runs Advanced BASIC and the mortgage calculator. At the menu, press the Esc key. Then type **SYSTEM** to get back to DOS.

Now try to load Advanced BASIC without a path name in front of the word BASICA. Type

  BASICA MORTGAGE

You'll see the message:

  `Bad command or file name`

DOS could not find BASICA.COM. in the directory you specified. The file is not in the SAMPLES directory; it is in the COMS directory.

You could give a path name whenever you wanted to use Advanced BASIC. Another alternative is to put your files "together" in one directory, move to that directory, and run the programs from there. However, there is another way: using the PATH command. The PATH command enables you to tell DOS to search in other subdirectories for the program you want to run. If DOS does not find the program in the current directory, DOS will search the directories you named in the PATH command.

Type the following command:

  PATH C:\BIN

This command tells DOS to look in the BIN subdirectory on drive C if DOS cannot find in the current directory the program you want to run. The last directory named in the path (BIN) is searched, but no other directory is searched (in this case, the root directory of the disk). If you want DOS to search both these directories, you must use the PATH command and type the names of the directories to be searched, separating the names with semicolons. If you want DOS to search both the root directory and the BIN subdirectory, you type

PATH C:\;C:\BIN

Now that the PATH command has been properly set, type

BASICA MORTGAGE

This command should load Advanced BASIC from the C:\BIN directory. BASIC will then load and execute MORTGAGE. Now get out of the menu and back to DOS.

This step is the last instruction for this exercise. The next section discusses the PATH command.

Understanding the PATH Command

Two facts make the PATH command important, for both command-line and DOS Shell users. The first is that the PATH command allows you to use programs that are not stored in the current directory. That is, you can run a program command file (a file with a .COM extension), an executable file (a file with an .EXE extension), or a batch file (a file with a .BAT extension) when the file is not in the current directory. The second fact is that when you use a disk with many subdirectories, you may frequently be in a directory other than the one with the .COM, .EXE, or .BAT file you want to use.

You could solve the problem by leaving whatever subdirectory you are in, going to the directory that contains the desired program file, and using the file there. But, preferably, you would invoke the PATH command to name explicitly the path to the program or batch file you want to use. The convenience of the PATH command is that it lets you automatically use a .COM, .EXE, or .BAT file from any directory.

The PATH command is thus an important command for users of hierarchical directories, particularly those who have created complex arrangements of multiple subdirectories. Because owners of hard disks and high-capacity disks will most likely use hierarchical directories, these persons especially should know how to use the PATH command. You can't directly access the PATH command from the DOS Shell, so if you use the Shell, you should read this section carefully.

The syntax of the PATH command is

PATH = *d1:path1;d2:path2;d3:path3...*

PATH is an internal DOS command and does not need a disk drive name or path name to run the command.

The next part of the command line is an equal sign. A space can precede the equal sign.

The next part of the command line specifies the disk drives and directories that DOS should search to find a program. Each combination is called a *path set* and consists of an optional disk drive name (*d:*), followed by a path name (*path*). The path name is the full name of the chain of directories that lead to the directory to be searched. Only the last directory named in the path is searched.

The disk drive names are optional. If you do not include drive names, PATH will cause DOS to search for the directories on the current disk drive.

You can give one path set or many path sets. The additional path sets are designated by the ... in the syntax. When you give more than one path set, separate each path set with a semicolon. Do not use a space in any path set or between path sets. Only the semi-colon is allowed between path sets.

If you wish to change the PATH, simply issue the PATH command again using the new list of path sets DOS should use. To display the current PATH, type

PATH

DOS displays the list of current paths or the message `No path` if the PATH command has not been used. To clear and disconnect the PATH command, give the command

PATH = ;

The command is the word PATH, followed by an equal sign and a semicolon. This clears the directory paths and instructs DOS to look only in the current directory for programs.

As you have noticed, the PATH command accepts a disk drive name in front of the path name. Use drive names in the path sets. DOS will automatically go to the named floppy disk drive or hard disk drive to find a program in the specified path, regardless of your current disk or directory.

When you use the PATH command, always start paths with the root directory. This way, you can be in any subdirectory on the disk, and DOS will always start at the root direc-tory. If you don't specify the root directory as the beginning of these paths, DOS will try to move down your specified path, starting with the current directory. You will have to give a new PATH command whenever you change subdirectories. The easier way is to start your paths for the PATH command at the root directory with a disk drive name and a backslash. For more information about the PATH command, check the *DOS Command Reference* in Part VI.

The PATH command has one limitation. The PATH command works only when you are running programs or batch files from the DOS system prompt. Your programs must know where to get any additional programs or data files that might be needed. The PATH command does not help your programs locate additional programs or data files. Fortunately, however, DOS V3.3 and V4 feature a PATH-like command for data files— APPEND. APPEND is discussed in Chapter 14.

Summary

In this chapter, you learned the following key points about the hierarchical directory system:

❑ Each disk or hard disk starts with a single root (system) directory.

❑ Each subdirectory (a child) is owned by exactly one directory (a parent). Each child subdirectory (as well as the root directory) can be a parent to many child subdirectories.

❑ The three directory commands are

    a. CHDIR, or CD, which changes a current directory.

    b. MKDIR, or MD, which creates a new subdirectory.

    c. RMDIR, or RD, which removes a subdirectory.

❑ Each disk has a current directory. If you change disks, and the current directory does not exist on the changed disk, the root directory becomes the current directory.

❑ The path character is the backslash (\).

❑ A path is a series of subdirectory names separated by the path character.

❑ When the path character begins the path name, the directory movement starts at the root directory of the disk. If the path character does not start the path, the directory movement starts with the current directory of the disk.

❑ When you place a path name in front of a file name, you must separate the two names with a path character.

❑ When you run a program, you can precede the program name with a drive name followed by a path.

❑ The PATH command enables DOS to execute programs and batch files that are not in the current directory of the current disk drive. However, PATH does not help your programs find additional program or data files.

Chapter 14 expands your knowledge about the hierarchical directory system. In that chapter, you'll learn more about the APPEND command, and I'll show you shortcuts you can use with many DOS commands.

14

Gaining Better Control with Hierarchical Directories

In Chapter 13, you were introduced to hierarchical directories. In this chapter, you will extend your knowledge of how to use multiple directories. Specifically, you will learn some shortcuts for path names. You will also learn how to list the entire directory system with the CHKDSK and TREE commands. And you will read more about the APPEND command—the PATH-like command for data files. This information will be of interest to all personal computer users, especially those whose computers have hard disks.

Shortcuts for Specifying Paths

Recall the comparison of a hierarchical directory to an airline's routing system. The airline has a major hub, minor hubs, and planes going to outlying cities. Analogous to the airline, a hierarchical directory has a root directory, subdirectories, and files. When you instruct DOS, you are giving instructions to the system's "control tower." You communicate how you will reach your destination.

Of the directions that you give DOS, some parts can be viewed as optional, but other parts are essential. The mandatory directions are the minimum information you must give so that DOS will know where to find the files it needs. The optional directions make your instructions more clear, but DOS doesn't absolutely need them. As you learned in Chapter 7, these mandatory and optional instructions are called the command *syntax*.

Using the airline analogy, if the airline's main hub were in Chicago (your current location) and you wanted to go to New York, you would take a "Chicago to New York" plane. Because the tower (DOS) knows the current location (the disk drive and current directory), indicating "Chicago" is optional. The inclusion of "Chicago" in the instructions helps to clarify the planned travel, but it is not essential. Stating the destination (New York), however, is mandatory so that the tower (DOS) will know where the plane is to go.

219

This analogy especially fits the use of DOS's COPY command—a command frequently used with hierarchical directories. The COPY command's syntax is similar to that of many DOS commands. Table 14.1 shows different ways to use directions (paths) with the COPY command to copy files to other locations.

The examples in table 14.1 assume that you are using a personal computer with at least one floppy disk drive and a hard disk. The floppy disk drive is the A drive, and the hard disk drive is the C drive. When you use table 14.1, assume that the hard disk has the subdirectory layout shown in Appendix B.

In the table, the *Current Position* is the current disk drive and directory. (Recall Chapter 5's discussion of the current disk drive and Chapter 13's discussion of the current directory.) The current position (or current location) is the directory in which you are working when you give DOS instructions.

The *Source* column in the table shows the drive and subdirectory from which you want to copy a file. *Destination* is the drive and subdirectory where you want the copy of the file to go. If the name of the file is changed when the file is copied, you will see a *Y* (for yes) in the *Name Change* column. An *N* (for no) in the column indicates that the name is to remain unchanged.

Look carefully at the *Syntax To Use* column. Notice that entries appear in blue and black characters. The black characters are optional: you can leave them out of the syntax and still be able to accomplish the desired operation. The blue characters are mandatory: you must use them to accomplish the operation. The blue- and black-character combination represents the full, formal syntax, which best shows you how the path works. After you understand how each operation works, you can use just the mandatory syntax to perform the task.

To use table 14.1, assume that the root directory of drive C (C:\) has a file named SAMPLE1.TXT. The subdirectory called C:\WORDS\LETTERS has a file named SAMPLE2.TXT. Notice that only the numbers before the extension (.TXT) are different. The directories C:\DOS\BASIC\TEST and C:\DOS\HARDDISK and the disk in drive A have files named SAMPLE3.TXT, SAMPLE4.TXT, and SAMPLE5.TXT, respectively.

The following explanations discuss the syntax for each line in table 14.1. As you study the examples, note the places where you must enter spaces. One place is after the command name (COPY, in this set of examples). Another place is after the source file's extension (.TXT), between the source specification and the destination specification.

1. The first command line shown in the *Syntax To Use* column copies the file SAMPLE1.TXT from the root directory of C (C:\) to the drive C subdirectory named \WORDS\LETTERS. As the table indicates, when the current directory is the root directory, you do not need to enter the characters that appear in italic typeface (the source and destination disk drive name and root directory indicator) in order to accomplish the operation.

If you are not changing the file name, you do not have to give the file name in the destination. If you do not give a name in the destination, DOS keeps the file name the same when it copies the file. Hence the file name in the destination is also optional.

2. The second command line performs the same operation as the first line, except that the file name is changed from SAMPLE1.TXT to NEW1.TXT. Because you give a file name in the destination name, DOS will copy the file and give it the new name.

3. The third command line copies the file named SAMPLE1.TXT from the root directory to the drive C subdirectory named \DOS\BASIC\TEST.

4. The fourth command line performs the same operation as the third line, except that the file name is again changed as it was in the second command line. After the fourth line, no file name changes are illustrated, because the process is as simple as tacking the new file name, preceded by a backslash, onto the destination directory's path name. Each of the preceding examples is useful if you copy a file immediately after you start DOS from the hard disk, because your current directory will normally be the root directory after DOS starts.

5. The fifth command line copies the SAMPLE1.TXT file from the root directory to the \DOS\HARDDISK subdirectory on drive C. Notice that you don't need to type the "\DOS" (pronounced "backslash DOS"), shown in italic characters, to get the file into the \DOS\HARDDISK subdirectory. Your current directory is \DOS, and HARDDISK is a subdirectory of \DOS.

6. The sixth command line copies SAMPLE4.TXT from C:\DOS\HARDDISK to C:\DOS.

   This example is significant because it shows that you need to put a backslash before DOS in order to copy a file to a higher level in this branch (from \DOS\HARDDISK to \DOS).

   At first glance, this requirement may seem inconsistent with the preceding example, but the backslash is necessary.

7. In the seventh command line, the paths of all three subdirectories are different; therefore, you must specify the full name of the source and destination paths. This form of the syntax is the fullest for copy operations on one drive (unless, of course, other subdirectories are at lower levels in the hierarchical directory). If you know the full syntax, you won't have to use the CHDIR (or CD) command to change directories. You can use the full syntax from any subdirectory to copy a file from any subdirectory to any other subdirectory.

8. Line 8 shows you how to copy a file from a subdirectory of one path (\WORDS\LETTERS) to a subdirectory of another path (\DOS\HARDDISK) when you are positioned in a different subdirectory (BASIC) of the \DOS path. Only the drive designation is optional (italic).

Table 14.1
Examples of Full and Mandatory Syntax

Current Position	Source	Destination
(1)C:\	C:\	C:\WORDS\LETTERS
(2)C:\	C:\	C:\WORDS\LETTERS
(3)C:\	C:\	C:\DOS\BASIC\TEST
(4)C:\	C:\	C:\DOS\BASIC\TEST
(5)C:\DOS	C:\	C:\DOS\HARDDISK
(6)C:\DOS\HARDDISK	C:\DOS\HARDDISK	C:\DOS
(7)C:\DOS\HARDDISK	C:\WORDS\LETTERS	C:\SS\123DATA
(8)C:\DOS\BASIC	C:\WORDS\LETTERS	C:\DOS\HARDDISK
(9)C:\WORDS	C:\DOS\BASIC\TEST	C:\WORDS\LETTERS
(10)C:\DOS	C:\WORDS\LETTERS	A:\
(11)C:\DOS	A:\	C:\SS\123DATA
(12)A:\	C:\	C:\DOS
(13)C:\WORDS\LETTERS	C:\DOS\BASIC\TEST	C:\WORDS\LETTERS

Examples of Full and Mandatory Syntax

Name Change	Syntax To Use
N	COPY *C:*\SAMPLE1.TXT *C:*\WORDS\LETTERS*SAMPLE1.TXT*
Y	COPY *C:*\SAMPLE1.TXT *C:*\WORDS\LETTERS\NEW1.TXT
N	COPY *C:*\SAMPLE1.TXT *C:*\DOS\BASIC\TEST
Y	COPY *C:*\SAMPLE1.TXT *C:*\DOS\BASIC\TEST\NEW1.TXT
N	COPY *C:*\SAMPLE1.TXT *C:**DOS*\HARDDISK
N*	COPY *C:**DOS**HARDDISK*\SAMPLE4.TXT *C:*\DOS
N	COPY *C:*\WORDS\LETTERS\SAMPLE2.TXT *C:*\SS\123DATA
N*	COPY *C:*\WORDS\LETTERS\SAMPLE2.TXT *C:*\DOS\HARDDISK
N	COPY *C:*\DOS\BASIC\TEST\SAMPLE3.TXT *C:**WORDS*\LETTERS
N	COPY *C:*\WORDS\LETTERS\SAMPLE2.TXT A:\
N	COPY A:\SAMPLE5.TXT *C:*\SS\123DATA
N	COPY C:\SAMPLE1.TXT C:\DOS
N	COPY *C:*\DOS\BASIC\TEST\SAMPLE3.TXT *C:**WORDS**LETTERS*

9. Line 9 shows the syntax for copying a file from a level-three subdirectory (\DOS\BASIC\TEST) to a subdirectory (LETTERS) of the path where you are positioned (\WORDS).

10. Line 10 shows how to copy a file from a drive C subdirectory (\WORDS\LETTERS) to another drive (A:) when you are positioned in another drive C subdirectory (\DOS).

   This example illustrates two common situations. It shows that the phrasing of path names is identical on all disk drives: floppy, hard, or semireal. When you use path names for another drive, such as drive A in this example, you use a syntax similar to that used for drive C in the preceding examples. This line also illustrates the syntax for copying files to a floppy disk. The only changes are that the source path name and file name will be different for different files.

11. The eleventh line presents the syntax for receiving a file from another disk drive or for installing onto a hard disk a program that has no installation routine. In this example, SAMPLE5.TXT is copied from the root directory in drive A to a drive C subdirectory (\SS\123DATA) when you are positioned in a drive C subdirectory (\DOS).

12. Line 12 shows you how to copy between subdirectories on drive C if you are positioned in drive A.

13. Line 13 shows how to copy a file from a totally different path of subdirectories into the current directory. Note that, except for the drive designation, you must give the entire source. But because the destination is the same as the current position, you don't need to specify the destination at all.

Keep in mind the *rule of currents*: if you don't give DOS the complete position portion of the command syntax, DOS uses the current position.

If you do not give a disk drive name to a DOS command, the current disk drive is used. If you do not give a path name, the current directory is used. If you do not give a file name, either all files are used or the file name used in the preceding part of the command is used. The *rule of currents* yields several guidelines for table 14.1, which are discussed in the rest of this section.

One guideline is that if the current drive is neither the source nor the destination, you must enter the drive name of the source and destination. Another guideline is that if the current directory (the current path) is neither the source nor the destination, you must enter the path name of the source and destination. An important variant is that if the source or the destination is in a subdirectory of your current directory, you need to start the path name with that subdirectory. Example 5 in the table demonstrates this point.

On the other hand, if you can omit part of the full syntax, you have created a shortcut. You need only type the necessary parts of the command. After you have learned what syntax parts you can omit, you will become faster at typing commands and more proficient at using DOS.

One shortcut is to use shorter path names where possible. Notice in table 14.1 the two lines that contain asterisks (see the *Name Change* column). For both of these lines, you can learn even easier ways to tell DOS how to copy the files you want. You have already learned that the current directory is represented by one period and that the parent directory is represented by two periods. To simplify the two command lines, you can use the double-period symbol. Here are the two command lines:

COPY SAMPLE4.TXT ..

COPY \WORDS\LETTERS\SAMPLE2.TXT ..\HARDDISK

In these two examples, the current directory is owned by \DOS. In the first case, you are copying to the DOS directory. The destination is the parent directory (DOS), represented by the **..** symbol. In the second example, you are copying to another subdirectory owned by DOS. Instead of typing **\DOS\HARDDISK**, you can substitute the double-period symbol. The destination becomes **..\HARDDISK** (moving up to DOS and down to HARDDISK).

If you know the layout of your hard disk, type the shortest route for a path. DOS will navigate the directory system by using the long path starting at the root directory or the shorter path starting at the current directory. It makes little difference to DOS. If you are like me, you will want to type the shortest command line you can use. If you take some time to look for shortcuts, you will find that using the computer is more fun.

Listing a Disk's Directories (TREE, CHKDSK /V)

If you are using the DOS Shell, showing a disk's directory tree is a snap. You've already learned how to view the tree from the File System menu. Those who are using the DOS prompt can also access the tree.

The files in your hierarchical directories are probably organized in a manner similar to the way you would physically organize floppy disks. But as the number of directories and files grows, your ability to remember which directory holds what file decreases. Instead of asking yourself which disk holds your file, your question becomes "Which directory holds my file?"

DOS thoughtfully provides a command that will list all the directories of a disk: the TREE command. TREE will also list the files in the directories. Or you can use the CHKDSK command with the /V switch to list all the subdirectories and files on a disk. If you have a hard disk computer, you will find these two commands useful.

TREE's command syntax is as follows:

  *dc:pathc***TREE** *d: /F*

TREE is an external command.*dc:pathc* is the optional disk drive and path name for the TREE command. *d:* is the name of the disk drive that holds the directories you want to list. If you omit *d:*, TREE lists the directories on the current disk drive.

TREE accepts the single switch */F*, which directs TREE to list the *files* in the directories. Use this switch if you are trying to locate a file. If you do not give the switch, you will get only a list of the disk's directories—not the disk's files.

Notice that you do not give a path or file name with the drive name. TREE is not the same as the DIR command. TREE automatically starts its listing with the root directory of the specified or current disk drive, so you don't give TREE the choice of where it starts. Also, you cannot specify a file for which you want to search. With TREE, you get an all-or-nothing listing of the disk's directory.

The following example shows the TREE command used on the practice disk you made in Chapter 13. It provides a display similar to that found with DOS V3.3. For DOS V4, TREE's output uses block graphics and indents to show the hierarchical nature of the directory structure a bit more clearly.

```
C>TREE A:

DIRECTORY PATH LISTING FOR VOLUME PRACTICE

Path: \COMS

Sub-directories:  SAMPLES


Path: \COMS\SAMPLES

Sub-directories:  TEST


Path: \COMS\SAMPLES\TEST

Sub-directories:  None

C>TREE A: /F

DIRECTORY PATH LISTING FOR VOLUME PRACTICE

Files:            None

Path: \COMS

Sub-directories:  SAMPLES

Files:            COMMAND .COM
                  ASSIGN  .COM
                  BACKUP  .COM
                  BASIC   .COM
                  BASICA  .COM
                  CHKDSK  .COM
                  COMP    .COM
                  DEBUG   .COM
                  DISKCOMP.COM
                  DISKCOPY.COM
                  EDLIN   .COM
```

```
                    FDISK    .COM
                    FORMAT   .COM
                    GRAFTABL.COM
                    GRAPHICS.COM
                    KEYB     .COM
                    LABEL    .COM
                    MODE     .COM
                    MORE     .COM
                    PRINT    .COM
                    RECOVER  .COM
                    RESTORE  .COM
                    SELECT   .COM
                    SYS      .COM
                    TREE     .COM
```

```
Path: \COMS\SAMPLES

Sub-directories:  TEST

Files:            MORTGAGE.BAS


Path: \COMS\SAMPLES\TEST

Sub-directories:  None

Files:            BASICA   .COM
```

The CHKDSK command accepts the /V switch, which in this case means give a *verbose* listing of the disk's directories and files. The command syntax for CHKDSK is

    *dc:pathc***CHKDSK** *d:* /*V*

CHKDSK /V is like the TREE command. *dc:pathc* specifies the command's disk drive and path. *d:* is the optional name of the disk drive to be checked. The /*V* switch lists the directories as well as the files. The following sample output shows the results when the CHKDSK command is used on Chapter 13's practice disk:

    C>**CHKDSK A: /V**

```
Volume PRACTICE      created Feb 24, 1989 10:52p
Directory A:\
      A:\PRACTICE
Directory A:\COMS
Directory A:\COMS\SAMPLES
      A:\COMS\SAMPLES\MORTGAGE.BAS
Directory A:\COMS\SAMPLES\TEST
      A:\COMS\SAMPLES\TEST\BASICA.COM
      A:\COMS\COMMAND.COM
      A:\COMS\ASSIGN.COM
```

```
          A:\COMS\BACKUP.COM
          A:\COMS\BASIC.COM
          A:\COMS\BASICA.COM
          A:\COMS\CHKDSK.COM
          A:\COMS\COMP.COM
          A:\COMS\DEBUG.COM
          A:\COMS\DISKCOMP.COM
          A:\COMS\DISKCOPY.COM
          A:\COMS\EDLIN.COM
          A:\COMS\FDISK.COM
          A:\COMS\FORMAT.COM
          A:\COMS\GRAFTABL.COM
          A:\COMS\GRAPHICS.COM
          A:\COMS\KEYB.COM
          A:\COMS\LABEL.COM
          A:\COMS\MODE.COM
          A:\COMS\MORE.COM
          A:\COMS\PRINT.COM
          A:\COMS\RECOVER.COM
          A:\COMS\RESTORE.COM
          A:\COMS\SELECT.COM
          A:\COMS\SYS.COM
          A:\COMS\TREE.COM

 730112 bytes total disk space
      0 bytes in 1 hidden files
   3072 bytes in 3 directories
 361472 bytes in 27 user files
 365568 bytes available on disk

 654336 bytes total memory
 522368 bytes free
```

Notice that CHKDSK performs its normal disk analysis in addition to listing the files and directories.

With CHKDSK /V and TREE, the resulting output can be lengthy. This type of output is ideally suited for redirection. For example, you could use the MORE filter to display one screen's worth of information at a time. The command syntaxes for using MORE for output redirection with CHKDSK or TREE are the following:

CHKDSK /V | MORE
TREE | MORE

You can redirect the output of either TREE or CHKDSK to the printer with these commands:

TREE > PRN
CHKDSK /V > PRN

You can place TREE's or CHKDSK's output into a disk file with these commands:

TREE > **treelist**
CHKDSK /V > **dsklist**

If you store the output in a disk file, you can print the output at any time. I recommend that you occasionally run TREE or CHKDSK /V on your hard disk to get a printed copy of your disk's entire contents, which you can keep near your computer. This type of output is a good road map of your hard disk's structure and can help coworkers or friends when they must use your computer.

Helping Programs Find Their Data Files (APPEND)

In Chapter 13, you learned that the PATH command allows you to run any command (.COM), executable (.EXE), or batch (.BAT) file from any directory. When you type a command that is not preceded by a path name, DOS searches the current directory for the program or batch file. If the file does not appear in the current directory, DOS then searches the directories listed in the PATH command. If the file appears in any of these directories, DOS automatically loads and executes the file.

But PATH works only for files with .COM, .EXE, or .BAT extensions. PATH does not solve another problem: using programs that know nothing about hierarchical directories.

Most software publishers write programs that take advantage of hierarchical directories, making larger-capacity disks and hard disks easier to use. But some older packages that do not use hierarchical directories need special help. If you are using a program that does not take advantage of hierarchical directories, you must keep your programs and data files together in a single directory. You cannot place your programs in one directory and your data files in a subdirectory—an organizational pattern that most hard disk users follow.

You will find that the most problematic software is the type that requires additional program files while the main program is running. WordStar Release 3 is an example of this type of software. This version of WordStar uses two overlay files, WSOVLY1.OVR and WSMSGS.OVR, while WordStar is running. Although you can put the main WordStar program file in the subdirectory that the PATH command uses, you must also keep copies of the two overlay files in each subdirectory you use with WordStar Release 3. (Fortunately, releases 4 and 5 of WordStar incorporate hierarchical directories.)

New with DOS V3.3, APPEND is the PATH command for use with data files. It was changed slightly for DOS V4. If you need to trick main programs into finding other needed files, you can now use APPEND. APPEND is a more complex command than PATH, and its syntax requirements are somewhat more complicated. APPEND's syntax is more complex because the phrasing changes depending on whether you are using it for the first time during a woking session or at some later time in the session.

When you use APPEND for the first time, the syntax is one of the following:

*dc:pathc***APPEND** *d1:path1;d2:path2; . . .*

*dc:pathc***APPEND** */X /E*

For both commands, *dc:pathc* names the disk drive and path that hold the APPEND command. Both the drive name and path are optional.

For the next part of the command line, you specify the disk drive and directories that APPEND should search when a main program is looking for a data file. Each path set is in the following form:

d:path

d: is the drive that holds the directory to search. *path* is the full name of the directory path that leads to the directory to search. Only the last directory specified in each path is searched.

You can specify more than one drive-directory simply by separating each set with a semicolon. As with the PATH command, do not use a space between the paths. For example, to have APPEND search the directory C:\\WORDS\\LETTERS, use this command:

C>APPEND C:\\WORDS\\LETTERS

To search both \\WORDS\\LETTERS and \\WORDS\\CONTRACTS, use the following command:

C>APPEND C:\\WORDS\\LETTERS:\\WORDS\\CONTRACTS

Notice the semicolon that separates the two paths. No spaces appear except between the D in APPEND and the first path.

With APPEND's second form, you can use two optional switches, but you cannot specify a directory path for APPEND to use. You can use one, both, or no switches, but if switches are used, they must appear only the first time you use APPEND during a working session. APPEND's switches are as follows:

/E   Places the paths given to APPEND in the *environment*

/X   Processes *extended* searches using the DOS SEARCH FIRST, FIND FIRST, and EXEC functions

If you use the /E switch, the paths you specify to APPEND are placed in the environment. The *environment* is an area of RAM in which information can be placed. Chapter 16, which discusses batch files, provides a complete description of the environment. For now, you need only know that if you give the /E switch, the paths are placed in the environment. If you do not give the /E switch, APPEND stores the paths internally.

The /X switch handles directory searches. Some programs search the directory for files to use rather than simply load the files into memory. For example, DIR, BACKUP, and TREE search directories for files. To have APPEND intercept these programs, you must use the /X switch. Also, using the /X switch will cause APPEND to trick the DOS EXEC function, which allows a program to run another program. Many applications programs commonly use the EXEC function.

With DOS V4, you can turn this feature on and off at will. The /X switch can be used in the following three ways:

/X	Turns the feature on
/X:ON	Same as /X
/X:OFF	Turns the feature off

Also new with DOS V4 is the capability of commanding APPEND to search for files in the APPEND path even if you have specified a drive or path. That way, if you happen to type the wrong drive or path, DOS will continue to search through the APPEND path you have designated. The switches for this capability are these:

/PATH:ON	Turns the feature on
/PATH:OFF	Turns the feature off

Once you have used APPEND, APPEND becomes part of DOS; it becomes an internal command and remains an internal command until you restart DOS. Therefore, you can use APPEND without designating a path to the command. APPEND's internal form is as follows:

> **APPEND** *d1:path1;d2:path2; . . .*

If you compare this form to the first form for APPEND, you will see that this command is almost identical to the first. Here, you simply indicate the command and the disk drive names and paths you want APPEND to use. If you have specified APPEND once with the /E or /X switch, use this form of the command to specify the directories that APPEND should search.

To clear the APPEND command, you simply type

> C>**APPEND;**

When you use the APPEND command with a semicolon, the command deactivates itself until you issue APPEND again.

To see the current directories that APPEND is using, type the following without any additional information:

> C>**APPEND**

APPEND displays the current set of directories it is using, such as the following:

> `APPEND=C:\WORDS\LETTERS;C:\WORDS\CONTRACTS`

Each path set will be separated by a semicolon.

Some caveats apply to the use of APPEND. First, APPEND cannot trick programs that do absolute reading or writing to the disk.

If your program writes information to files, be cautious in using APPEND. Programs always write information to files in the current directory, regardless of where the original files may be. For example, if the current directory is \WORDS, and APPEND has tricked a program into finding the file MEYER.TXT in the directory \WORDS\CONTRACTS, the program will save the file in \WORDS. However, the original file in \WORDS\CONTRACT remains unchanged. You can be astonished when a program saves files in the current directory and you are not aware of it.

If you use the APPEND and the ASSIGN commands, which are discussed in Chapter 25, use the APPEND command first. APPEND and ASSIGN will have allergic reactions to each other if you use ASSIGN before APPEND.

If you misspell a path that you use with APPEND, or if you delete the directory, APPEND does not notice any error until DOS attempts to use the paths. You will not see any error messages if you specify invalid paths. DOS simply skips any missing or misspelled path names and proceeds to the next path. If you use an invalid path name, APPEND may skip the directory you intended APPEND to use.

To see how APPEND /X can fool you and your programs, here is a sample session demonstrating how I was tricked. I placed a blank, formatted disk in drive A. I invoked APPEND /X and then set APPEND to use a directory. I then tried to get a directory of the disk. The result was astonishing.

```
C>DIR A:

Volume in drive A is TEST DISK
Directory of  A:\

File not found

C>DIR C:\BIN\DRIVERS

Volume in drive C is CHRIS'S DSK
Directory of  C:\BIN\DRIVERS

.              <DIR>      01-01-89    2:14p
..             <DIR>      01-01-89    2:14p
ANSI     SYS    1678      3-17-89   12:00p
COUNTRY  SYS   11285      3-17-89   12:00p
DISPLAY  SYS   11290      3-17-89   12:00p
DRIVER   SYS    1196      3-17-89   12:00p
KEYBOARD SYS   19766      3-17-89   12:00p
PRINTER  SYS   13590      3-17-89   12:00p
VDISK    SYS    3455      3-17-89   12:00p
         9 file(s)  5256794 bytes free

C>APPEND /X

C>APPEND C:\BIN\DRIVERS

C>DIR A:
```

```
Volume in drive A is TEST DISK
Directory of  A:\

.              <DIR>      01-01-89    2:14p
..             <DIR>      01-01-89    2:14p
ANSI      SYS      1678    3-17-89   12:00p
COUNTRY   SYS     11285    3-17-89   12:00p
DISPLAY   SYS     11290    3-17-89   12:00p
DRIVER    SYS      1196    3-17-89   12:00p
KEYBOARD  SYS     19766    3-17-89   12:00p
PRINTER   SYS     13590    3-17-89   12:00p
VDISK     SYS      3455    3-17-89   12:00p
          9 file(s)  5256794 bytes free

C>
```

Instead of DOS's reporting that there were no files to be found on the disk in drive A, the DIR command shows the C:\BIN\DRIVERS directory! When there are no files on the disk, APPEND tricks DOS into searching the first directory specified to APPEND. You get a false answer from the DIR command. It took several minutes for me to understand why a blank disk suddenly held several files. After I disconnected APPEND, everything worked correctly.

If you use APPEND with the /X switch, some programs may react in unexpected ways. The result will be that a perfectly working program will mysteriously not perform correctly. If you encounter this problem, restart DOS and use the APPEND command without the /X switch (or, if you have DOS V4, turn off the feature by typing **APPEND / X:OFF**). If the program then works correctly, remember not to use APPEND with the /X switch with that program. Or restart the computer just before you need to use that program (or, if you have DOS V4, turn APPEND off with a command).

If the program continues to work incorrectly, try using the **APPEND;** command to deactivate APPEND. If the program still doesn't work correctly, your mixing of the program with APPEND is not the problem. Although I have not yet had a problem using APPEND with my applications programs, I suspect that some applications programs that I do not use will not work correctly with APPEND.

Finally, do not mix DOS V3.3's or V4's APPEND with another version of APPEND, such as the ones provided with the IBM PC Network or IBM PC LAN software. The programs are incompatible, and you will have unsatisfactory results.

Despite these caveats, APPEND, like PATH, is a very useful command. With APPEND, you can place your programs in one directory and organize your data files in a subdirectory. What PATH does for command files, APPEND does for data files.

Summary

In this chapter, you learned the following:

❏ The *rule of currents* means that if you omit a disk drive or path name, DOS uses the current disk drive and the current path.

❏ Giving disk drive and path names to a command is optional when the current disk drive and path are involved. If the current disk drive or path is not involved, the drive-path name is mandatory and must be given.

❏ You can use the CHKDSK /V and TREE commands to list all the subdirectories and files of a disk.

❏ You can use the APPEND command to trick programs into using files that are not in the current directory.

In Chapter 15, you will learn how to create and use batch files.

15

Understanding Batch Files

Up to now, you've learned how you can use DOS, but have you ever thought of making DOS use itself? Batch files enable you to make DOS work for you. Learning to use this convenient and time-saving feature is worthwhile for all PC DOS users. At first, the concept may seem elusive to you, but understanding and using batch files can speed up and ease many tedious computer tasks.

A batch file is a series of DOS commands placed in a disk file. When instructed, DOS executes the commands in the file, one line at a time. DOS treats these commands as though they were typed individually from the keyboard.

Batch files have several advantages. Once you have placed the correctly phrased commands in a batch file, you can, by typing the batch file's root name, direct DOS to execute the commands. You can direct DOS to perform one or hundreds of commands in a batch file.

Another advantage is that once a batch file has been invoked, DOS does not need your attention until it has finished running the batch file. This capability comes in handy for programs that may take a long time to run. For example, if you need to run several long programs back-to-back, you ordinarily start each program and wait until it has finished running before you start the next one. But why should you wait for the computer if you don't have to? A batch file will execute commands to run the programs without your intervention. You can do other tasks or just relax while the computer does the hard work.

If a program needs your input—to change disks, for example—the batch file cannot do this task for you. Your attention is still required. You can use a batch file, though, to execute programs or commands without having to type the program or command name each time. By redirecting the input of the program to a file, you can avoid having to answer manually a program's questions.

Batch files are available for your convenience. After a few experiments, you will probably find this DOS facility quite handy. Those who are using the DOS Shell will learn in Chapter 21 how to install batch files as menu selections.

Rules for Creating and Running Batch Files

To create batch files, you must follow certain rules. After you read these rules, look over the rules for running batch files. You need not understand all the rules yet. They will be explained as you read through the chapter. The rules for creating batch files are summarized in the following list:

1. A batch file contains ASCII text. You use the DOS COPY CON command, the DOS line editor EDLIN, or another text editor to create a batch file. If you use a word-processing program, make sure that it is in programming, or nondocument, mode.

2. The root name of a batch file can be one to eight characters long and must conform to the rules for file names.

3. The batch file name must have the extension .BAT.

4. A batch file's root name should be different from the root name of program files in the current directory (files that end with the extension .COM or .EXE). The root name also should not be the same as that of an internal DOS command—COPY or DATE, for example. If you use one of these root names, DOS will not know whether you want to execute the batch file, the program, or the command.

5. You may include in a batch file any valid DOS command you might type at the keyboard. You may also use the *parameter markers* (%0 to %9) and batch subcommands.

6. To use the percent sign (%) in a batch file command, such as in a file name, you enter the percent symbol twice. For example, to use a file called A100%.TXT, you would enter A100%%.TXT. This rule does not apply to the parameter markers (%0 to %9).

The syntax for running a batch file is

*d:path***filename** *parameters*

in which *d:* is the optional name of the disk drive that holds the batch file, and *path* is the optional directory path to the batch file. **filename** is the root name of the batch file, and *parameters* is any additional information to be used by the batch file.

The following list summarizes the rules for running batch files:

1. If you do not give a disk drive name, the current disk drive will be used.

2. If you do not give a path, the current directory will be used.

3. To invoke a batch file, simply type its root name and press Enter. For example, to invoke a batch file called OFTEN.BAT, you type **OFTEN** and press Enter. If there is a file with the same root name and the .COM or

.EXE extension, either in the current directory or in the PATH you have specified, you must explicitly name the batch file, including the .BAT extension. Otherwise, DOS will run the .COM or .EXE program.

4. If the batch file is not in the current directory of the disk drive, and a path name did not precede the batch file name, DOS will search the directory or directories specified by the PATH command to find the batch file.

5. DOS will execute each command, one line at a time. The specified parameters will be substituted for the markers when the command is used.

6. DOS recognizes a maximum of ten parameters. You may use the SHIFT subcommand to get around this limitation.

7. If DOS encounters an incorrectly phrased batch subcommand when running a batch file, the message Syntax error is displayed. DOS ignores the rest of the commands in the batch file, and the system prompt reappears.

8. You can stop a running batch file by pressing Ctrl-Break. DOS will display the following message:

    Terminate batch job (Y/N)?

    If you answer **Y**, the rest of the commands will be ignored, and the system prompt will appear. If you answer **N**, DOS skips the current command but continues processing the other commands in the file.

9. DOS remembers which directory holds the batch file. Your batch file may change directories at any time.

10. Because DOS remembers the disk drive that holds the batch file, you may change current disk drives freely. DOS V3.0 does not remember which disk holds the batch file, however. If you remove the disk that holds the batch file, DOS V3.0 will give you an error message. DOS V3 and V4 request that you reinsert the disk holding the batch file and press a key to continue.

11. You can instruct a batch file to run another batch file after the first batch file has run. When you enter the name of a second batch file as the last command in the first batch file, control of the computer passes to the second batch file unless the COMMAND technique or the CALL subcommand is used. If the CALL subcommand or COMMAND technique is used, the second batch file is executed, and control returns to the first batch file. Both commands are discussed in Chapter 16.

Rules for AUTOEXEC.BAT Files

You must follow certain rules when you use the file AUTOEXEC.BAT. The following list is a summary of these rules:

1. The file must be called AUTOEXEC.BAT and must reside in the boot disk's root directory.

2. The contents of the AUTOEXEC.BAT file must conform to the rules for creating batch files.

3. When DOS is booted, it automatically executes the AUTOEXEC.BAT file.

4. When AUTOEXEC.BAT is executed after DOS is booted, the date and time are not requested automatically. To get the current date and time, you must put the DATE and TIME commands into the AUTOEXEC.BAT file. (This is important only for PCs and for PC XTs, because other IBM computers "remember" the time.)

To better understand batch files, take a look at the following example of an AUTO-EXEC.BAT file, which comes on the Lotus 1-2-3® Release 1 disk (Release 2 omits these files). When you use the TYPE command to display this file, you will see the following:

```
A>TYPE AUTOEXEC.BAT
date
time
lotus

A>
```

When you boot the computer, DOS loads itself into the computer's memory. Next, DOS scans the disk's root directory for the AUTOEXEC.BAT file. After finding the file, DOS starts executing the commands in the file. First, DOS executes the DATE command to get the current date; then it executes the TIME command to get the current time. These steps set DOS's internal clock and calendar. The AUTOEXEC.BAT file then loads and executes the 1-2-3 menu program, LOTUS.COM.

The AUTOEXEC.BAT file is a useful feature. This sample AUTOEXEC.BAT file allows the computer operator to insert a disk into drive A, turn on the computer, and have the computer automatically load 1-2-3. This is called *turnkey* capability—you just turn on the computer's "key" (switch), and the computer automatically starts and runs its programs without additional instructions.

This batch file has one slight disadvantage on some computers. Some PCs, like the standard IBM PC and XT, do not remember dates or time, so you must enter them manually. If you do not set the date and time, DOS date-stamps each 1-2-3 data file 01-01-80, the default DOS date. When you display a directory of disks used on these machines, you won't be able to tell when a 1-2-3 data file was created or changed. That's why the DATE and TIME commands are included in this batch file. You don't need to change 1-2-3; just change the batch file. However, the DATE and TIME commands are unnecessary if you are using a Personal Computer AT or PS/2.

You can easily modify this AUTOEXEC.BAT file to perform different or additional functions. For example, if you use a Personal Computer AT, you could edit this batch file and delete the DATE and TIME commands, because these computers know the current date and time on start-up. You can also insert the DOSSHELL command into the file so that the Shell is loaded each time you boot the computer.

When you have become familiar with 1-2-3, you might want to bypass the Lotus menu and invoke the 1-2-3 program itself when you start your computer. To do that, simply change the line `lotus` to **123**, which is the name of the file that holds the 1-2-3 program. When the computer starts, the 1-2-3 program boots instead of the Lotus menu.

The concept of a batch file is simple. When you invoke such a file, the computer executes the commands from the file as if you were typing them at the keyboard.

The AUTOEXEC.BAT file is different in only one way from any other batch file. DOS automatically executes AUTOEXEC.BAT when you start the computer. You can also execute this batch file at any time by typing **\AUTOEXEC** while the disk that holds the file is in the current disk drive. The only "magic" to this file occurs when DOS starts up. After DOS is up and running, AUTOEXEC.BAT is just another batch file.

You can make your own AUTOEXEC.BAT file by creating a file that contains all the commands required to start your program. A line that hard disk users should include is one concerning the PATH command. I suggest that you add the line

    PATH C:\BIN;C:

to your current AUTOEXEC.BAT file or create another AUTOEXEC.BAT file with this line. If you are using a computer that doesn't have a clock, add the DATE and TIME commands to your AUTOEXEC.BAT file. Otherwise, DOS will not ask for this information, and your files will never have the correct date and time.

If you have programs and batch files that are used frequently, you might copy these to a RAM disk. If you do, you might also add the RAM disk to your path, as in the command line:

    PATH E:\;C:\BIN;C:

where **E:** is the name of the RAM disk. The reason for adding E:\ first is that PATH searches the specified directories in the order given. Therefore, DOS will search E:\ before searching C:\BIN. You can also include in the AUTOEXEC.BAT file the commands to copy files to the RAM disk. For example, I use the commands

    COPY C:\LIGHT\DISK.DIC E:\LIGHT

    COPY C:\LIGHT\THES.DIC E:\LIGHT

to copy my Turbo Lightning™ files to the RAM disk. You can use this basic concept to copy any frequently used program or batch file to the RAM disk.

A batch file is especially convenient for executing a long series of commands you would normally have to type. Let's look at INSTALLH.BAT, the hard disk installation batch file that comes with Borland's Turbo Lightning. The instructions for using this file are to make the hard disk the current disk drive and to make the current directory the directory where the Turbo Lightning files should be placed. The following screen shows the contents of the INSTALLH.BAT file.

```
ECHO OFF
CLS
ECHO This batch file will Install Turbo Lightning onto your hard
ECHO disk. Have all three of your Turbo Lightning disks ready.
ECHO Turbo Lightning will be installed onto the "Default
ECHO Directory" of your hard disk. This means that the Dos
ECHO Prompt should be "C". If you use tree structured
ECHO directories on your hard disk please make sure that you are
ECHO logged in to the directory where you want Turbo
ECHO Lightning files to reside. For more information on this:
ECHO Hold down the [CTRL] key and press [C] and refer to page 9
ECHO in the Owner's Handbook.
PAUSE
COPY A:*.COM
COPY A:*.DIC
COPY A:LIHARD.BAC LIHARD.BAT
LIHARD
```

The first two lines of the file turn off the display of lines from the batch file (ECHO OFF) and clear the screen with the Clear Screen command (CLS). The next lines give instructions. The ECHO subcommand is a batch command that displays on-screen whatever follows it. The message tells you to make sure that the hard disk drive is the current drive and that the current directory is where you want the Turbo Lightning files to be placed.

Another batch file subcommand, PAUSE, writes the message Strike any key when ready ... on the screen and then waits. When a key is pressed, the batch file continues. The PAUSE subcommand is included so that the operator can read a long message or change disks. After the operator has taken the appropriate action, DOS will continue with the batch file.

The next two lines of the file (COPY A:*.COM and COPY A:*.DIC) copy the program and dictionary files to the hard disk. The following two lines are a bit of trickery. The file LIHARD.BAC is copied to the hard disk, and the name is changed to LIHARD.BAT. The final command invokes the LIHARD batch file.

This batch file shows a second batch file being run from a first batch file. That topic will be discussed in Chapter 16.

If you have Turbo Lightning, you can separately execute the last four lines of the batch file by typing each line at the keyboard. Just typing **A:INSTALLH** is much simpler, however.

Making Batch Files Versatile with Parameters

Batch files can perform different operations on different files, even though the commands in the file are fixed. You can use the same batch file with different files by taking advantage of *batch file parameters*.

What is a batch file parameter? In DOS, many commands accept information you type when you run the program. COPY is an example of such a command. The name of the file you want to copy, the destination to copy the file to, and the additional switches you enter are all parameters. A *parameter* is the additional information you type after you type the program name on the command line. Programs, in turn, can use whatever information is in the parameters.

For example, in the command line

   COPY FORMAT.COM B: /V

every word or set of characters that is separated by a space, comma, semicolon, or other valid *delimiter* is a parameter.

FORMAT.COM, B:, and **/V** are parameters. Each parameter tells the COPY command what to do. In this case, the parameters tell COPY to copy the program FORMAT.COM from the default disk to the disk in drive B and to verify that DOS has correctly made the copy.

The term *argument* is a synonym for parameter. Both terms refer to the delimiter information on the command line. (Delimiters were discussed in Chapter 11.)

Batch files also use parameters, but in a manner different from that of commands. To use parameters in your batch file, you insert *markers* to tell DOS where to use the batch file's parameters. A marker is a percent sign (%) followed by a number from 0 to 9. These ten markers tell DOS to substitute for the markers whatever you type on the command line.

The first parameter on the command line is the program or batch file name. This is parameter 0. (Computers usually start numbering with 0, which serves as a true number, not simply a placeholder.)

The second word on the command line is parameter 1, the third word is parameter 2, and so forth. This arrangement works well because we often ignore the name of the program or batch file when counting parameters. We are usually concerned with the items placed after the program or batch file name. The first item placed on the command line after the program or batch file name is usually considered the first parameter. The second item after the program or batch file name is the second parameter, with each additional item on the command line one higher than the previous item.

To practice including parameters in a batch file, use a text editor or the COPY CON technique to create a file called TEST.BAT. Type the following line into the file:

   ECHO Hello, %1

Now type **TEST**, press the space bar, type your first name, and press Enter. When I tried this exercise on my screen, I saw this:

```
A>TEST CHRIS

A>ECHO Hello, CHRIS
Hello, CHRIS
A>
```

Why didn't DOS print Hello, %1? In this example, DOS substituted my name—the second word on the command line—for the %1 in the batch file. That is, my name became the first parameter. When DOS executes a batch file, markers are replaced by the appropriate parameters from the command line. For this reason, the markers are sometimes called *replaceable parameters*.

To see how DOS replaces the parameters, create another batch file called TEST1.BAT, which is also a one-line file. Type the following line:

ECHO %0 %1 %2 %3 %4

After you have created this file, type TEST1, a space, your name, another space, and your street address. Here's how my file looked:

```
A>TEST1 CHRIS 1234 THUNDERBIRD AVENUE

A>ECHO TEST1 CHRIS 1234 THUNDERBIRD AVENUE
TEST1 CHRIS 1234 THUNDERBIRD AVENUE
A>
```

You can see from the batch file command line that DOS was instructed to display on the video screen the parameters 0 through 4. These parameters worked out to be the following:

Word:	**TEST1**	**CHRIS**	**1234**	**THUNDERBIRD**	**AVENUE**
Parameter:	%0	%1	%2	%3	%4

What happens if you don't give enough information on the command line to fill each parameter? Run TEST1 again, but this time give only your first name. In my case, I saw the following:

```
A>TEST1 CHRIS

A>ECHO TEST1 CHRIS
TEST1 CHRIS
A>
```

DOS displayed the batch file name and my name. No other information "echoed" on the video display. I did not give enough parameters on the command line, and DOS replaced the unfilled markers with nothing. In other words, DOS ignores unfilled markers.

One last comment should be made about parameter 0. If you give a drive name with the name of the batch command, the drive name appears with the batch file name. If I had typed **A:TEST1 CHRIS**, the lines on my screen would have been these:

```
A>ECHO A:TEST1 CHRIS
A:TEST1 CHRIS
A>
```

Constructing a Batch File Using Parameters

Let's construct a batch file that takes advantage of parameters. I use several computers, but one of my hard disk systems is my "workhorse" where I store the files I want to keep.

I use disks to move information between computers. Sometimes I edit a file on one computer and then move the information to the hard disk of another computer. Many times, I remove the file from the disk after it has been copied back to the hard disk. The steps required are these:

Step 1. *Copy the file from the disk to the hard disk.*

Step 2. *Erase the file from the disk.*

My batch file is called C&E.BAT (copy and erase) and consists of these commands:

COPY A:%1 C:%2 /V
ERASE A:%1

To use this file, I type

C&E oldfilename newfilename

The first item, **oldfilename**, is the name of the file I want to copy to the hard disk, and **newfilename** is the new name for the copied file (if I want to change the file name as it is being copied).

Now suppose that I put a disk which contains the file NOTES.TXT into drive A and want to copy the file to the hard disk. Here's what the screen looks like.

C>C&E NOTES.TXT

```
C>COPY A:NOTES.TXT C: /V
   1 file(s) copied

C>ERASE A:NOTES.TXT

C>
```

In this example, DOS ignores the empty markers. Because I don't want to change the file name, I didn't give a second parameter. DOS copies NOTES.TXT from drive A to drive C and then deletes the file on the disk in drive A. The %2 parameter is "dropped," and the batch file does not get a new name when it is copied.

One of the benefits of constructing a batch file this way is that I can use a path name as the second parameter and copy the file from the disk into a different directory on the hard disk. For instance, to copy NOTES.TXT to the second-level directory called WORDS, I type **C&E NOTES.TXT \WORDS**. The screen display is

```
C>COPY A:NOTES.TXT C:\WORDS /V
   1 file(s) copied

C>ERASE A:NOTES.TXT

C>
```

Because WORDS is a directory name, DOS knows that it should copy the file NOTES.TXT into the directory WORDS. DOS will not give the new file the name WORDS.

Understanding Your Environment (SET)

The *environment* is a safe area of RAM established by DOS to hold strings. The strings are typically names of directories or frequently used switches for programs, although any information can be used. DOS makes the information placed in the environment available to your programs.

Don't be discouraged if you do not understand the preceding paragraph yet. The use of the environment is a classic example of needing to know something before you can learn something else. In this section, we discuss the environment: how you use it, how your programs use it, and what it can do for you.

There are two reasons for discussing the environment in this chapter. Frequently, you place information in the environment by including commands in the AUTOEXEC.BAT file. The second reason is that DOS provides a mechanism that you use in your batch files to retrieve the information that has been placed into the environment.

To explain what is placed in the environment, we'll look at an example:

```
COMSPEC=C:\COMMAND.COM
```

The object on the left is called an *environmental variable*. It is a name of any length, but one to eight characters is preferred, since the space available for variable names can be limited. The object on the right is a string, a group of arbitrary characters. An equal sign separates the variable name from the information.

Information is placed in the environment in two ways: (1) by DOS or other programs and (2) by you. DOS places information in the environment when you use the PATH, APPEND, or PROMPT commands. Programs or executable files, including batch files, may also put information in the environment. To place your own information in the environment, you use the SET command. SET, which stores strings in the environment, is an internal command and is always available at the system prompt or within batch files. The syntax for SET is

   SET *name* = *information*

where *name* is the environmental variable's name and *information* is any information that can be placed in a string, such as a path name, a file name, or optional switches to programs. When your programs search the environment for *name*, the programs find the *information*

For example, the line

   SET EXAMPLE = C:\WORDS\EXAMPLE

sets the environmental variable EXAMPLE. When programs find and examine EXAMPLE, they find the string C:\WORDS\EXAMPLE. The environment provides a noninteractive method to give your programs information. Later, your programs can locate the variable and use the string associated with the variable.

SET also displays the current environmental variable. If you type **SET** with no arguments, you should see at least one line that looks something like this:

   `COMSPEC=C:\COMMAND.COM`

COMSPEC is the environmental variable for the command interpreter. You see the environmental variable, COMSPEC, followed by the equal sign, followed by the disk drive, path name, and file name for the command interpreter, COMMAND.COM. This line is inserted into the environment by DOS when the system starts.

What is the significance of COMSPEC? This environmental variable tells DOS where to find the command interpreter.

As you learned in Chapter 8, COMMAND.COM does not always remain in RAM. Your programs can free part of the memory COMMAND uses so that the programs can use this memory instead. Then, when the program exits, DOS must reload COMMAND.COM from the disk.

Did you know that COMMAND.COM does not need to be in the root directory of the boot disk? If you use the SHELL directive in your CONFIG.SYS file, COMMAND.COM can be located anywhere on your disk. (SHELL and its other uses are discussed in Chapter 17.) But if COMMAND.COM is not in the root directory, how does DOS know where to find COMMAND.COM?

DOS stores the location in its safe harbor, the environment. Until DOS is restarted (or a program writes into random-access memory that it should not use), the environment is memory-sheltered by DOS for the exclusive use of storing these variables.

To find the command interpreter, DOS searches the environment for COMSPEC. When DOS locates COMSPEC, it uses the full file name stored with COMSPEC (the information on the right side of the equal sign) to reload COMMAND.COM.

When you issue the SET command, you may see other environmental variables. If you see variables other than those created by the PATH, APPEND, or PROMPT commands, these were established by commands included in some other file, such as AUTOEXEC.BAT.

The most popular use for environmental variables is to give programs certain options or information only once. Instead of typing these options or information on the command line each time the program is run, the SET command is used to place the information into the environment. When the program runs, the program finds the environmental variables and adapts.

For example, Brief, my favorite text editor, uses several environmental variables. The variables are BFLAGS (which sets certain options), BHELP (the path to the help files), and BPATH (the path to parts of the editor program). In my AUTOEXEC.BAT file, I have these commands:

```
set bflags=-pr -mCDV
set bhelp=c:\brief\help
set bpath=c:\brief\macros
```

The first line sets up information on my display (-pr) and tells Brief which customized "macro" file to use (-mCDV). The next line sets up the location of the help file. The third line sets where the additional program pieces should be found.

When I invoke Brief, it immediately reads the environment, looking for BFLAGS, BHELP, and BPATH variables. Upon finding the variables, Brief takes the information associated with the variables and knows which options to use and where the Brief files are located. Once the information is SET in the AUTOEXEC.BAT file, I never give it again. Brief automatically adjusts itself. If I change the AUTOEXEC.BAT, Brief will read the new environmental variables when it starts and adjust itself again.

Another example is my favorite spelling corrector, MicroSpell™. I use the line

SET LEX = C:\WORDS\SPELL\LEX

in my AUTOEXEC.BAT file, and MicroSpell automatically knows where to find its LEX (dictionary) files.

A further example is the environmental variable TEMP or TMP, which I usually define as E:\, my RAM disk. Many programs use the TEMP or TMP variable as the location where they will place temporary files. If I designate my fast RAM disk rather than the slower hard disk as the place for temporary files, my programs' throughput can dramatically increase.

Many programs today use environmental variables. You should check your program's documentation to determine whether some environmental variables are appropriate for your use.

Unfortunately, the environment is not unlimited. Each character stored in the environment takes one byte of RAM, and each environmental variable takes one additional byte. Remember that the environment is located in the same memory space your programs could use. For this reason, DOS starts with an environment size of 128 bytes for DOS pre-V3.3 and 160 bytes for DOS V3.3 and DOS V4. You can expand the size of the environment up to 32,767 bytes. Environment size is discussed in Chapter 17.

Since the environment is not unlimited, there are times you might want to eliminate a variable. To do so, use the form

   SET name=

Give the name of the variable you wish to eliminate, followed by an equal sign. DOS removes the variable from the environment.

Although the major use of environmental variables is to leave information for your programs, you can use environmental variables in batch files, also. This technique, which works with DOS V3.1 and later versions, requires that you surround the name of the variable with percent signs. For example, the following one-liner prints the contents of the COMSPEC variable:

   echo COMSPEC is set to %COMSPEC%.

Type this example into a batch file and run it. Just place a percent sign directly before and after the environmental variable name, and DOS will replace the %name% with the appropriate information from the environment. This means that you have two types of replaceable batch file markers: parameters from the command line (%1, %2, etc.) and environmental variables (%name%).

SET's main use is to place information into the environment. This is often done through AUTOEXEC.BAT. However, SET can be used at any time. Environmental variables make programs easier to use, but you rarely use the variables directly. Unfortunately, environmental variables do not make your batch files truly interactive. The missing feature is an ASK subcommand that would ask the user for some information from the keyboard and place it in an environmental variable. With this function missing, the %name% function is not fully usable.

Summary

Batch files can make your computer do the hard work for you. For example, they can replace repetitive typing with commands that execute automatically. As you work with batch files, you should remember the following key points:

- ❏ Batch files must have a .BAT extension.

- ❏ You invoke batch files by typing the root name of the batch file. You may also use an optional disk drive name and path name before the batch file name.

- ❏ You can use in a batch file any command you can type at the DOS prompt.

- ❏ The AUTOEXEC.BAT file automatically executes when DOS starts. Rather than your having to issue a command after DOS starts, you can use an AUTOEXEC.BAT file to run start-up programs.

❑ On a command line, each word (or set of characters) separated by a delimiter is a parameter. When you use a batch file, DOS substitutes for the file markers (%0 to %9) the appropriate parameters.

❑ The SET command can place strings into the environment. You can use environmental variables in batch files by using the form *%name%*.

In Chapter 16, you'll learn about using batch subcommands and how to run batch files from other batch files.

16

Using Batch Subcommands

Chapter 15 discussed how batch files work and showed you some examples of how you might put them to work for you. This chapter focuses on special batch-file subcommands and suggests ways to construct more powerful batch files.

Table 16.1 lists batch subcommands for DOS V3 and V4. You used two of the subcommands, ECHO and PAUSE, in Chapter 15.

Table 16.1
Batch Subcommands for DOS V3 and V4

Subcommand	Function
@	Suppresses the display of a line on the screen (DOS V3.3 and later).
CALL	Runs another batch file and then returns to the original batch file (DOS V3.3 and later).
ECHO	Turns on or off the display of batch commands as they execute. Also can display a message on the screen.
FOR..IN..DO	Allows the use of the same batch command for several files.
GOTO	Jumps to the line after a label in a batch file.
IF	Allows conditional execution of a command.
SHIFT	Shifts the command-line parameters one parameter to the left.
PAUSE	Halts processing until a key is pressed. Can optionally display a message.
REM	Displays a message on the screen or allows for batch comments.

You can use any of the subcommands from the preceding list in a batch file. Most of them can be used at the DOS system level, but not to accomplish anything useful. For example, you can type ECHO at the DOS prompt, with or without an argument. DOS will either display the string you type after ECHO or, if you leave off the argument, tell you whether ECHO is ON or OFF. You can type PAUSE at the DOS prompt and DOS will pause. Neither effect is of much use.

You will see, as we discuss these commands, that you would have no reason to use most of the subcommands at the system level. In this chapter we'll look at examples that show how each command can be used.

Controlling the Display with ECHO and REM

The ECHO command does two things. First, ECHO controls the display of lines from the batch file as the command lines are executed. Turning ECHO off is useful when you don't want to display the commands from the batch file.

Second, ECHO can be used to display messages. In this sense, ECHO is like the REM (remark) command, which also displays messages on the screen. Either subcommand can display a message with a maximum length of 122 or 123 characters, respectively (the 127-character DOS command line limit, minus the length of the command, plus a space).

Note that you may *include* a remark in your batch file that is longer than 123 characters; DOS simply won't display the excess characters. Keep this in mind if you find you do need a long remark, and don't care whether it is displayed or not. Indeed, REM is rarely used to display messages on the screen.

You see, setting ECHO affects REM. If ECHO is off, no REM statement appears on the video screen. If ECHO is on, it unconditionally displays the message. The echoed message *always* appears on the video display, regardless of whether ECHO is on or off. If you always want to display a message in your batch file, use ECHO rather than REM.

You can put both ECHO and REM to good use in a batch file. Often by the time you re-edit a batch file, you may have forgotten why you used certain commands or why you constructed the batch file a particular way. You can leave reminders in your batch file by using REM statements. These comments allow the batch file to be self-documenting, which you and other PC users will appreciate later. If you want to incorporate messages that you always want displayed, use the ECHO subcommand. The echoed message appears on the video display whether ECHO is on or off.

Another way to include a remark in a batch file is through the use of a colon. If the first character on a line is a colon, DOS assumes that the line is a *label* and does not try to carry out any commands on that line. The disadvantage of this approach is that DOS may confuse your "remark" with a true label (labels will be discussed shortly). You must be certain that the first eight characters of such a statement don't match an actual label used later in the file. This will become more clear later.

For now, just keep in mind that the colon can be used to provide a second type of remark—one that is not displayed under any circumstances, whether ECHO is on or off. You can use such labels to mark sections of the batch file where ECHO happens to be turned on. You can also use them to temporarily remove portions of the file that you don't want DOS to carry out—as during debugging or testing the file. Reserve the REM type of remark for statements that you want to remain as remarks.

This use for the colon is not a "standard" DOS practice, but is one that is widely used nonetheless. If you keep the potential danger of confusing DOS in mind, you may safely use the colon to enhance your batch files.

Controlling the Display with @ and CLS

A feature new with DOS V3.3 is controlling the display with the @ sign. Placed at the beginning of a batch-file line, this character suppresses the display of the line on-screen. DOS absorbs the character and executes the remainder of the batch-file line. You can use the @ to hide batch-file lines selectively as they execute, whereas ECHO controls the display of all the lines in a batch file.

The customary first two lines of a *quiet batch file* (one that issues an ECHO OFF command) are

```
ECHO OFF
CLS
```

The first line turns off the display of commands that are executing. The second line invokes the clear-screen command, CLS, which is built into DOS and can be used any-time at the system prompt.

The reason CLS follows the ECHO OFF command is that the ECHO OFF command itself appears on the screen. To keep the screen clear, you need to issue the CLS command. If you have DOS V3.3 or later, you can replace the two lines with this line:

```
@ECHO OFF
```

Because @ is the first character of the line, the ECHO OFF does not appear on the screen, and the ECHO OFF command stays in effect until the end of the batch file. The screen is not cleared, however. If you desire a clean screen when you start a batch file, you must use the CLS command in the file.

Using PAUSE To Interrupt Processing

The PAUSE subcommand performs a series of activities. It stops the batch file's process-ing and displays on-screen any message on the rest of the line (just as the REM subcom-mand does). PAUSE then displays the message Strike a key when ready... and waits for you to press a key. When you press a key, DOS continues to process the batch file. The PAUSE command allows you to change disks while you are processing a batch file. PAUSE also has another use, which is discussed in the section on the GOTO subcommand.

As just mentioned, PAUSE, like REM, can also display a message. And, as with REM, if ECHO is off, the message is not displayed. The message Strike a key when ready is always displayed, however, whether ECHO is on or off, unless you redirect the output of the command. For example,

    PAUSE>NUL

will redirect the message to the NUL device, and prevent it from being displayed to the screen.

Leaping and Looping with GOTO

The GOTO subcommand is similar to the BASIC language's GOTO command. With DOS's GOTO command, you can jump to another part of your batch file. DOS's GOTO command uses a label, not a line number, to specify where to jump. As mentioned above, a *label* is a batch file line that starts with a colon (:) and is followed by a one- to eight-character name. The name can be longer than eight characters (as when you are using the colon to put remarks in your file, or to "comment out" commands you wish to bypass), but only the first eight are significant.

When DOS encounters a GOTO label command in the batch file, DOS starts at the *beginning* of the batch file and searches for a label matching the one specified by GOTO. It then jumps to the line in your batch file *that follows* the line holding the label. The batch file TEST2.BAT is shown in the following screen. This file is similar to the TEST.BAT batch file you created in Chapter 15, with the addition of the GOTO and PAUSE subcommands.

```
:START
ECHO Hello, %1
PAUSE
GOTO START
```

When I invoked the batch file by typing TEST2 CHRIS, my screen showed the following message:

```
A>TEST2 CHRIS
A>ECHO Hello, CHRIS
Hello, CHRIS
A>PAUSE
Strike a key when ready. . .  <space>
A>GOTO START
A>ECHO Hello, CHRIS
```

```
Hello, CHRIS
A>PAUSE
Strike a key when ready. . .^C
Terminate batch job (Y/N)? Y
A>
```

The batch file began by echoing the message with my name in it. The file then paused for me to press a key before it continued. After I pressed a key, DOS executed the GOTO START command. DOS then jumped to the line after :START and continued processing. When DOS paused a second time, I typed a Ctrl-C to stop the batch file. DOS then asked whether I wanted to stop the batch file. I answered Y for yes, and DOS stopped processing the batch file and returned to the system prompt. This type of batch file causes DOS to loop continuously until you type the Ctrl-Break sequence.

You can use this batch file's endless looping to repeat the batch file's contents several times, but you can also repeat the batch file a different number of times each time you invoke the file.

For example, suppose that I want to copy the files CHKDSK.COM, FORMAT.COM, DISKCOMP.COM, and DISKCOPY.COM to several disks. I may want to copy these programs onto one, two, or a hundred disks. With a batch file, I can make DOS do the hard work.

For this example, assume that the computer has two disk drives. The disk that contains the files CHKDSK.COM, FORMAT.COM, DISKCOMP.COM, DISKCOPY.COM, and the new batch file will be in drive A. The disk to receive the programs will go into drive B.

First, I'll create a batch file called FLOPPY.BAT (remember that the @ symbol in line 1 can be used only for DOS V3.3 and DOS V4):

```
(1) @ECHO OFF
(2) :START
(3) ECHO Place the disk to receive CHKDSK.COM, FORMAT.COM,
(4) ECHO DISKCOMP.COM, and DISKCOPY.COM in drive B.
(5) ECHO To quit, type Ctrl-C, then press Y, or
(6) PAUSE
(7) COPY A:CHKDSK.COM B: /V
(8) COPY A:FORMAT.COM B: /V
(9) COPY A:DISKCOMP.COM B: /V
(10) COPY A:DISKCOPY.COM B: /V
(11) ECHO Files are copied.
(12) GOTO START
```

In this file, the GOTO subcommand causes an endless loop. The file also illustrates several batch subcommands.

Line 1 turns ECHO off so that the commands are not displayed. The @ sign at the beginning of the line stops the line from being displayed.

Lines 2 through 5 tell the operator either to put a disk into drive B or to type Ctrl-C to quit.

Line 6 has the PAUSE command that displays the message Strike a key when ready. At this point, if the operator has finished copying the files, he can type **Ctrl-C** and answer **Y** to the Terminate batch job (Y/N)? prompt.

Lines 7 through 10 transfer the four programs to the disk in drive B.

Line 11 is the "reassurance" line. It tells the operator that the files have been transferred. This line is not necessary, but it assures the operator that all has gone well.

Line 12 is the GOTO line that starts the process over again.

Notice the arrangement of lines 2 through 5. The on-screen result is as follows:

```
Place the disk to receive CHKDSK.COM, FORMAT.COM,
DISKCOMP.COM, and DISKCOPY.COM in drive B
To quit, type Ctrl-C, then press Y or
Strike a key when ready...
```

The Strike a key when ready line comes from PAUSE. I see little sense in duplicating what the PAUSE command displays. Rather than inserting my own message, I depend on PAUSE's message to tell the user to just strike any key when ready. You could, however, redirect PAUSE as described above and supply your own message.

The only batch commands that this chapter has not discussed are IF, FOR..IN..DO, SHIFT, and CALL. All four commands are simple, once you understand how they work. The following sections explain these commands.

Using IF

The IF command is a "test and do" command. When a condition is true, IF executes the command on the command line. When the condition is false, IF ignores the line. The DOS IF subcommand works like the IF statement in BASIC. The command can be used to test three conditions:

- The ERRORLEVEL of a program

- Whether a string is equal to another string

- Whether a file exists

Let's look at each condition and at how the command can be used.

The first condition is ERRORLEVEL. A better name for this condition would have been "exit level." *ERRORLEVEL* is a code your program leaves for DOS when the program has finished executing. In DOS V3.3 and later, only the BACKUP, GRAFTABL, KEYB, REPLACE, RESTORE, and XCOPY commands leave an exit code. Many other programs use exit codes, however.

A zero (0) exit code usually means that everything was okay. Any number greater than 0 usually indicates that something was wrong: no files were found, the program encountered an error, or the operator aborted the program. Including an IF command in a batch file lets you test ERRORLEVEL to see whether a program worked properly.

If the exit code your program leaves is equal to or greater than the number you specify in the batch file, the ERRORLEVEL condition is true. You can think of this condition as a BASIC-like statement:

IF ERRORLEVEL > number THEN do this

Suppose, for example, that you wanted to invoke KEYB.COM, the program that changes the keyboard layout and characters to a language other than American English (see Chapter 18). You could test to see whether the KEYB worked successfully by inserting the following lines:

KEYB US, 437
IF ERRORLEVEL 1 ECHO Could not set the keyboard!

These lines test KEYB's exit code. If the exit code is 1 or greater, Could not set the keyboard! is displayed on-screen. If the exit code equals 0, then nothing is displayed. The condition (ERRORLEVEL 1) is false, so the line is skipped.

The best way to test the ERRORLEVEL with a batch file is to use an IF statement to move around the commands that execute if the ERRORLEVEL test fails, as shown in this example:

KEYB
IF ERRORLEVEL 1 GOTO OOPS

.

.

.

GOTO END
:OOPS
ECHO Could not set the keyboard!
:END

The batch file invokes KEYB. If the exit code is 1 or greater, the batch file jumps to the line after the OOPS label. If the exit code is 0, the rest of the batch file is processed. Notice the GOTO END statement placed before the OOPS label. You don't want the batch file to say Could not set the keyboard! when the KEYB *did* work. If the batch file does the rest of the work correctly, DOS jumps to the end of the file, the END label. When DOS reaches this label, it stops processing the batch file.

The **IF string1** = = **string2** condition is normally used with command-line parameters and markers. One simple example is the batch file ISIBM.BAT:

IF %1 = = IBM ECHO I'm an IBM computer

If you type

   ISIBM IBM

you will see

```
I'm an IBM computer
```

If you type anything other than **IBM** as the first parameter, you won't see this line on the screen.

Note two important facts about this part of the IF command. If you don't give enough parameters with the IF subcommand, DOS replaces the parameter marker with nothing. The parameter becomes a *null parameter*. Because DOS does not like to compare null parameters with anything, it displays a Syntax error message and aborts the batch file.

If you type **ISIBM** and do not give any other information, the %1 turns into nothing; the line becomes

```
IF == IBM ECHO I'm an IBM computer
```

The result is the dreaded Syntax error message, and the batch file halts. The way to solve the problem is to first test if a parameter is empty before trying another test. You can see the general technique in this revised version of ISIBM.BAT:

```
IF %1. == . GOTO NOTHING
IF %1 == IBM GOTO IBM
ECHO What computer are you?
GOTO END
:IBM
ECHO I'm an IBM computer
GOTO END
:NOTHING
ECHO Pardon me, I could not hear you.
:END
```

The first line adds a period to the %1 and tests to see if this addition is the same as a single period. If %1 is null (meaning you gave no parameters), the line becomes

```
IF . == . GOTO NOTHING
```

This method succeeds in trapping the error condition of giving too few batch-file parameters. If you need to check for a nonexistent parameter, use the form as I did in line 1 of ISIBM.BAT's revised version.

If the test is false, DOS executes the next line. This line tests to see if IBM was entered at the keyboard. Notice that you use GOTO statements to jump around the batch file parts that should not be executed. If you give no parameter, you see the message Pardon me, I could not hear you. Giving the parameter IBM produces the message I'm an IBM computer. Any other parameter produces the message What computer are you?

Another fact to remember about the IF subcommand is that DOS compares the strings literally. Therefore, uppercase characters are different from lowercase. If I invoke either the old or new ISIBM.BAT with the line

ISIBM ibm

DOS will compare the lowercase "ibm" to the uppercase "IBM" and decide that the two strings are not the same. The IF test will fail, and I'm an IBM computer will not appear on the display.

The IF subcommand's last part is **IF EXIST filename**. This IF condition tests whether the file **filename** is on the disk. If you are testing for a file on a drive other than the current drive, put the disk drive name in front of the file name (for example, B:CHKDSK.COM).

You can also test for the opposite of these conditions. That is, you can test whether a condition is false by adding the word NOT after IF.

IF NOT EXIST filename can be used to check whether a file is not on the disk. The file name to check is placed after IF NOT EXIST.

I'll discuss more uses of IF later in this chapter, after I explain the FOR..IN..DO command. Frequently, you can use the IF and FOR..IN..DO commands together.

Getting Creative with FOR..IN..DO

FOR..IN..DO is an unusual and extremely powerful batch command. The command's syntax is

FOR %%variable IN (set) DO command

where **variable** is a one-letter name. The %% in front of the **variable** is important. If you use a single %, DOS will confuse the symbol with the parameter markers and not work properly. The *command*, not the marker, is the action you want performed.

The set is the name of the item(s), command(s), or disk file(s) you want to use. You can use wild-card file names with this command. You can also use drive names and paths with any file names you specify. If you have more than one file name or other item in the set, use a space or comma between the names.

An interesting example of FOR..IN..DO is a simple batch file that compares file names on a copy of the DOS master disk with those on any other disk. To see how this batch file works, find a working copy of a DOS disk. If you have a two-floppy disk drive computer, place this file, CHECKIT.BAT, on the disk:

**@ECHO OFF
FOR %%a IN (*.*) DO IF EXIST B:%%a
ECHO %%a is on this disk also.**

Now put the disk with the CHECKIT.BAT file into drive A and put a copy of your DOS master disk into drive B. Type CHECKIT, and watch the results.

If you have a hard disk computer, place this version of CHECKIT.BAT in the subdirectory that holds your DOS file (usually BIN):

@ECHO OFF
FOR %%a IN (*.*) DO IF EXIST A:%%a
ECHO %%a is on this
disk also.

Place a disk into drive A, type CHECKIT, and watch what happens.

The first part of the FOR..IN..DO command says, "For every file specified, do the command." Here, because you gave the wild-card file name ***.***, which matches every file on the disk, every specified file corresponds to all the files on drive A. The rest of the command says, "If the file exists on drive A or B (depending on which disk drive you gave for the comparison), display the message that the file is on the DOS disk."

I wrote a simple program in C, called PR.EXE, that produces a line-numbered printout of a text file. To print all my C text files and my macro assembler files, I wrote a simple batch file. All C text files end with a .C extension, and all macro assembler files end with an .ASM extension. The batch file that I created to print all these files contained only this line:

FOR %%a IN (*.C *.ASM) DO PR %%a

The FOR..IN..DO command finds every C and assembler text file and invokes the PR command for every matching file name. I was able to get a numbered listing of 35 C and assembler programs with one batch file command.

FOR..IN..DO also enables you to use wild-card file names with certain commands. For example, the TYPE command does not accept wild-card file names. You must use a specific file name with the command. However, you can make a batch file that uses the FOR..IN..DO command to type a series of files. The batch file TYPER.BAT consists of this command line:

```
@FOR %%d IN (%1 %2 %3 %4 %5) DO TYPE %%d
```

The command places up to five parameters in the FOR..IN..DO command. The batch file substitutes specific file names for wild-card file names and then executes the TYPE command on each file. Running the batch file on my system gave this result:

C>**TYPER *.BAT**
```
C>TYPE AUTOEXEC.BAT
```

(AUTOEXEC.BAT's contents are displayed)

```
C>TYPE TYPER.BAT
```

(TYPER.BAT's contents are displayed)

```
C>TYPE STARTUP.BAT
```

(STARTUP.BAT's contents are displayed)

```
C>
```

One novel use of FOR..IN..DO is to avoid the problem of uppercase and lowercase characters in DOS. The following line is a modification to the second line of the ISIBM.BAT:

FOR %%d In (IBM, ibm) DO IF %1 = = %%d GOTO IBM

The new line says, "For each member of the set IBM and ibm, if the first parameter is equal to a member of the set, go to the label :IBM." This one line replaces the two lines

```
IF %1 == IBM GOTO IBM

IF %1 == ibm GOTO IBM
```

Because IF sees a difference between uppercase and lowercase characters, the two tests are necessary. This FOR..IN..DO command checks both.

One final example of this technique is a little batch file that stops someone from inadvertently formatting the hard disk. In this example, you must place FORMAT.COM in a subdirectory that is not on the PATH or current directory, and you must place this batch file (FORMAT.BAT) on the PATH or in the current directory:

```
@ECHO OFF
IF %1. == . GOTO WHATDRIVE
FOR %%d IN (A:,a:,B:,b:) DO IF %1 == %%d GOTO FORMAT
GOTO BADDRIVE
:FORMAT C:\BIN\DISK\FORMAT %1 %2 %3 %4 %5
GOTO END
:BADDRIVE
ECHO You cannot format %1!
ECHO %1 is not a floppy disk drive
:WHATDRIVE
ECHO Please try again and specify the disk drive you wish
ECHO to use, such as FORMAT A: or FORMAT B:
:END
```

FORMAT.BAT's major worker is the FOR..IN..DO command, which tests whether the first parameter (which should be the disk drive name) is A:, a:, B:, or b:. If the batch file finds a match, the batch file jumps to :FORMAT. If the batch file finds no match, the batch file jumps to :BADDRIVE. Notice the beforehand-check for a missing parameter.

If the batch file finds a matching drive name, the operator executes the FORMAT program, which is located in \BIN\DISK, a subdirectory not on the PATH. I use the additional parameters in case the operator should type some switches for FORMAT. If the operator doesn't type any switches, these parameters change to nothing and do not interfere with FORMAT.

My error messages are a little stingy. In fact, both error conditions (no parameter and the wrong drive name) use the same two lines. However, if you give an improper first parameter, my batch file does display a message that shows the proper parameter so that the operator will know what is wrong.

Before I change the subject and start explaining the SHIFT command, I want to mention one annoying aspect of the FOR..IN..DO command and I/O redirection. The FOR..IN..DO variable is *not* expanded by DOS. Like TYPE, MORE does not accept wild-card file names. (For that matter, MORE does not accept any file name. You must redirect the input of MORE.) I thought that a batch file like TYPER would be perfect for MORE. The line I used was

@FOR %%d IN (%1 %2 %3 %4 %5) DO MORE < %%d

When I ran the file, the result was a `File not found` error message. I removed the @ECHO OFF to see the commands after DOS expanded the argument and got the following:

```
C>MORER *.BAT

C>FOR %%d IN (*.BAT    ) DO MORE  < %d

File not found

C>
```

Rather than expanding %%d to the appropriate file names, DOS immediately attempts to open the file called %d so that MORE's input comes from the file. You cannot use the FOR..IN..DO variable with I/O redirection for either input or output. If you attempt to use >> %%d with some command from within a batch file, the output of the command ends up in a file called %D. If you use %%d instead, the output from the command running ends up in the file %D. (Each time the symbol is encountered, the earlier version of %D is destroyed.)

The FOR..IN..DO command is versatile and allows one command to handle many files. However, for I/O redirection, the command leaves something to be desired.

Finally, you also will be interested to know that FOR..IN..DO works equally well with commands as well as file names. Instead of naming a set of files, you can name a series of commands that you would like DOS to carry out. Consider the following example:

FOR %%a IN (COPY ERASE) DO %%a C:*.* A:

In a batch file, this line will first *copy* all the files on C: to drive A and then *erase* them. You can put a replaceable parameter in the line instead of explicitly naming the drive and file specifications:

FOR %%a IN (COPY ERASE) DO %%a %1 %2

Then, when you invoke this batch file, you would type in the files you want copied and moved on the command line, followed by the destination drive and directory. If the file were called MOVER.BAT, we could type the following:

MOVER C:\WP D:\BAK

The file would copy all the files in the subdirectory C:\WP and put them in D:\BAK, and then erase the files in C:\WP. It would work a lot like our earlier batch file, C&E.BAT.

Moving Parameters with SHIFT

SHIFT moves the command line parameters one parameter to the left. This batch command tricks DOS into using more than ten parameters. The diagram of SHIFT is

%0 ← %1 ← %2 ← %3 ← %4 ← %5 . . .

↓

bit bucket

Parameter 0 is dropped. The old parameter 1 becomes parameter 0. The old parameter 2 becomes parameter 1; parameter 3 becomes 2; parameter 4 becomes 3; and so on.

The SHIFTIT.BAT batch file is a simple example:

```
:START
ECHO %0 %1 %2 %3 %4 %5 %6 %7 %8 %9
SHIFT
PAUSE
GOTO START
```

When you type

SHIFTIT A B C D E F G H I J K L M N O P Q R S T U V W X Y Z

the first time, ECHO shows

```
SHIFTIT A B C D E F G H I
```

After you press a key to continue, ECHO will show

```
A B C D E F G H I J
```

Press any key to keep moving down the line, or type a Ctrl-C when you want to stop.

SHIFT has many uses. We can use it to build a new version of our old friend, C&E.BAT. A modified version of the copy-and-erase batch file, called MOVE.BAT, shows a use for SHIFT:

```
:LOOP
COPY %1 C: /V
ERASE %1
SHIFT
IF NOT %1. == . GOTO LOOP
```

This batch file copies and then erases any file. For this version, I assume nothing about the file I am copying. I can specify a disk drive, a path, and a file name. This batch file will copy the file to my current directory on drive C and then erase the file from its original disk or directory.

The extra lines shift the parameters one to the left, test whether any parameters remain, and then repeat the operation if necessary. What follows are the commands' actions (with blank lines left out):

```
C>MOVE A:SYSI.EXE A:SETUP.BAT \BIN\GROUP.TXT
C>COPY A:SYSI.EXE C: /V
  1 file(s) copied

C>ERASE A:SYSI.EXE
C>SHIFT
C>IF NOT SETUP.BAT. == . GOTO LOOP
C>COPY A:SETUP.BAT C: /V
  1 file(s) copied

C>ERASE A:SETUP.BAT
C>SHIFT
C>IF NOT \BIN\GROUP.TXT == . GOTO LOOP
C>COPY \BIN\GROUP.TXT C: /V
  1 file(s) copied

C>ERASE \BIN\GROUP.TXT
C>SHIFT
C>IF NOT . == . GOTO LOOP
C>
```

Each SHIFT brings the next parameter into action until all parameters (and files) have been processed. Note that you can give no "destination" with the SHIFT batch file. The destination—the place to copy to—would be shifted left. The destination would become the source. COPY would then object (you can't copy a file onto itself). Finally, the file would be erased! Be careful when you design batch files that can "automatically" erase files.

Running Batch Files from Other Batch Files (CALL, COMMAND /C)

On some occasions, you may need to run a batch file from another batch file. In Chapter 15, you saw how the Turbo Lightning hard-disk-installation batch file, INSTALLH, ran LIHARD.BAT, another batch file. This section discusses three ways to run batch files from other batch files. One method is a one-way transfer of control. The other two ways show you how to run a batch file and return control to the first batch file. These techniques are useful if you want to build menus with batch files or use one batch file to set up and start another batch file.

The first method is simple. Include the root name of the second batch file as the final line of the first batch file. The first batch file runs the second batch file as if you had typed the second batch file's root name on the command line. For example, to run BATCH2.BAT, the final line of the BATCH1.BAT file would be

BATCH2

DOS loads and executes the lines from the file BATCH2.BAT. The control passes one-way—from the first batch file to the second. When BATCH2.BAT finishes executing, DOS displays the system prompt. You could consider this technique an inter-batch file GOTO. Control goes to the second file but doesn't come back to the first file.

There is a technique to perform an inter-batch file GOSUB in all versions of DOS. For DOS V3.0 through V3.2, the command is accomplished by using COMMAND, the DOS command processor. In DOS V3.3 and DOS V4, the process is simplified by the use of the CALL subcommand, which is discussed next.

The syntax of the CALL subcommand is

> CALL *d:path***filename** *parameters*

where *d:path*\\ is the optional disk drive and path of the second batch file you want to execute and **filename** is the second batch file's root file name. You may place the line anywhere in the first batch file. DOS executes the batch file named by the CALL subcommand, and then returns and executes the remainder of the first batch file. *parameters* represents the optional command-line parameters that you want to give to the batch file on which you used the CALL command.

The following three batch files demonstrate how CALL works. If you use DOS V3.3 or later, try typing these files into your computer. You can use uppercase or lowercase characters for the lines; I have used uppercase to highlight information.

After you type the batch files, if your printer is ready, press Ctrl-PrtSc to turn on the printer. Then type **BATCH1 first**. Turn the printer off by pressing Ctrl-PrtSc again. If you do not have a printer, press Ctrl-S to pause the screen as needed.

(If you have a version of DOS earlier than V3.3, do not type these files yet. Later, I'll give you directions on how to change the files to make them work for you.)

BATCH1.BAT

```
@ECHO OFF
rem This file does the setup work for demonstrating
rem the CALL subcommand or COMMAND /C.
ECHO This is the STARTUP batch file
ECHO The command line parameters are %%0-%0 %%1-%1
CALL batch2 second
ECHO CHKDSK from %0
chkdsk
ECHO Done!
```

BATCH2.BAT

```
echo This is the SECOND batch file
echo The command line parameters are %%0-%0 %%1-%1
CALL batch3 third
echo CHKDSK from %0
chkdsk
```

BATCH3.BAT

```
echo This is the THIRD batch file
echo The command line parameters are %%0-%0 %%1-%1
echo CHKDSK from %0
chkdsk
```

Look at the number of bytes of available RAM for each time CHKDSK runs. What did you see? The following screen is an abbreviated output from my PS/2 machine:

```
C>BATCH1 FIRST
This is the STARTUP batch file
The command line parameters are %0-BATCH1 %1-FIRST
This is the SECOND batch file
The command line parameters are %0-batch2 %1-second
This is the THIRD batch file
The command line parameters are %0-batch3 %1-third
CHKDSK from batch3
Volume MODEL 60    created Apr 24, 1989 5:10p
   ...

   654336 bytes total memory
   453744 bytes free

CHKDSK from batch2
Volume MODEL 60    created Apr 24, 1989 5:10p
   ...

   654336 bytes total memory
   453840 bytes free

CHKDSK from batch1
Volume MODEL 60    created Apr 24, 1989 5:10p
   ...

   654336 bytes total memory
   453936 bytes free
DONE!
C>
```

So that you will understand the results, take a look at each batch file starting with BATCH1.BAT. The first line of the first batch turns ECHO off. Notice that with DOS V3.3 and V4, when you turn ECHO OFF, it stays off. With DOS V2, ECHO always turns back ON each time a new batch file starts. The next two lines are REM comments. Because ECHO is OFF, the REM statements do not display when the batch file is run.

The following two lines are similar for all three batch files. The first of the two lines identifies which batch file is used. The second of the two lines shows the zero (the name by which the batch file was invoked) and first parameters (first argument) to the batch file. Notice that to display the strings %0 and %1 you must use two percent signs (%%0 and %%1). If you use a single percent sign, DOS will interpret the string as a replaceable parameter and not display the desired result.

The next line in the first and second batch files invokes another batch file. In the first batch file, BATCH2.BAT is invoked. In the second batch file, BATCH3.BAT is invoked. In each case, the batch file passes a single argument: the word second to BATCH2.BAT and third to BATCH3.BAT.

The batch file next displays the name of the file that will run CHKDSK. The CHKDSK program then runs. You use the %0 to display which batch file is running CHKDSK. When DOS encounters the end of each batch file, DOS returns to the invoking batch file.

As illustrated by the sample run, the steps that DOS takes are

1. Run BATCH1.BAT.

2. Display the two ECHO statements.

3. Within BATCH1.BAT, run BATCH2.BAT with the argument second.

4. Display the two ECHO statements.

5. Within BATCH2.BAT, run BATCH3.BAT with the argument third.

6. Display the three ECHO statements.

7. Run CHKDSK.

8. Return to BATCH2.BAT, displaying the single ECHO statement and running CHKDSK.

9. Return to BATCH1.BAT, displaying the single ECHO statement and running CHKDSK.

10. Quit processing the batch files.

These ten steps show why the batch files ran CHKDSK three times, but in "backwards" order. Because of the way the commands are ordered, the first running of CHKDSK comes from BATCH3.BAT, the second from BATCH2.BAT, and the third run from BATCH1.BAT. These batch files show what happens when you use the CALL subcommand and what happens when the batch file you CALL is completed. Control passes back to the line following the CALL subcommand, in the invoking batch file.

Also note the amount of free memory used in each CHKDSK run. The difference between the first and second, and second and third running of CHKDSK is 96 bytes. Each time you use the CALL command, DOS temporarily uses 96 bytes until the called batch file finishes running. Because of this use of free memory, you could run out of memory if you used many batch file CALL commands (possible but not probable). Few people use so many CALL commands in a row in their batch files. This limitation affects only batch files that call other batch files. A single batch file can use the CALL command as many times as desired. The memory usage occurs only when one called batch file calls another.

As mentioned in the preceding chapter, you cannot use I/O redirection when you are invoking a batch file. This caveat includes when you use CALL on another batch file.

If you use a version of DOS prior to V3.3, you can use the command interpreter to perform this batch file GOSUB routine. The syntax is

COMMAND /C *d:path***filename parameters**

One difference between the CALL and COMMAND syntax is that you must use COMMAND's /C switch. The /C switch accepts a single string that can include spaces and any other information. (You still cannot use I/O redirection, however.) DOS loads another copy of the command interpreter and gives it the command line **filename**, as though you had typed the command line at the DOS prompt. The results are *generally* identical to the CALL batch file, except that each copy of COMMAND.COM uses more memory than if you had used the CALL subcommand.

There is one other major difference between these two commands. Since COMMAND loads a new version of COMMAND.COM, any changes you make to the environment are lost when you return to the COMMAND.COM that is running your batch file. However, if you call another batch file with the CALL command and change the environment, those changes are made to the copy of the environment currently used by that batch file. This distinction can be important if you write batch files that make changes to the environment as a way of "flagging" some process that you carry out. With COMMAND /C, your current batch file will be unaware of what happened, and any later batch files you run will also not inherit the changed environment. With CALL, the changes are "permanent" and available to the current batch file later on, as well as to other programs run by the same command processor.

To understand this better, look at the following example:

```
ECHO OFF
SET VAR1=VAR1
COMMAND /C TEST2
CALL TEST3
```

The batch files called by this file, TEST2.BAT and TEST3.BAT, might consist of these lines, respectively:

SET VAR2 = VAR2

or

SET VAR3 = VAR3

When the first file finishes running, if you type **SET**, you will see something like the following:

```
PATH=C:\BATCH;C:\DOS;C:\UTILS;C:\
COMSPEC=C:\DOS\COMMAND.COM
VAR1=VAR1
VAR3=VAR3
```

We're only interested in the last two lines. What happened to VAR2? It was set when COMMAND /C loaded a new command processor, but lost when DOS returned to the old copy to continue to process the batch file.

You can use batch files like the ones described in this section with versions of DOS prior to V3.3 by making two changes. First, delete the @ character in BATCH1.BAT's first line. The @ feature is not available in versions of DOS prior to V3.3. Second, change BATCH1.BAT's and BATCH2.BAT's occurrences of **CALL** to **COMMAND /C.** You will then be able to run the batch files.

The following screen shows the abbreviated output of the batch files' COMMAND /C versions showing just the memory-available lines from CHKDSK:

```
CHKDSK from batch3
446208 bytes free

CHKDSK from batch2
450080 bytes free

CHKDSK from batch1
453952 bytes free
```

You'll note that each DOS V3.3 COMMAND.COM takes slightly more than 3,800 bytes. (Each of DOS's different COMMAND.COM versions uses a different amount of memory.) If you are running many batch files, you will run out of memory much faster using COMMAND /C than you will using CALL. However, you will probably never use enough batch files—20 or more—to cause such a problem.

Summary

In this chapter you learned these major facts:

❑ Several subcommands can be used within batch files. ECHO controls the display of lines on the screen. REM displays messages. PAUSE causes DOS to wait until a key is pressed. GOTO jumps to the line following a label within the batch file. IF can test for a condition or for the opposite condition. SHIFT shifts parameters one to the left. FOR..IN..DO can repeat a batch file command for one or more files or words.

❑ The @ character suppresses the display of a single line from a batch file.

❑ COMMAND /C and CALL can be used to run a second batch file and return control of the computer to the first batch file.

Part IV

Tailoring DOS to Your Use

Includes

Customizing DOS

Making DOS Go International

Customizing the DOS Shell

17

Customizing DOS

To *customize* your system means to alter it for your needs. The steps in altering your system include setting up directories, programs, and data to accommodate your tasks and to suit your style. Another necessary step is configuring your computer.

With some early operating systems, establishing an operating-system configuration meant changing the Basic Input/Output System (BIOS)—a task that was not easy for novices.

Now, Versions 2, 3, and 4 of DOS include a major feature that assists in the configuration process: the CONFIG.SYS file. This special text file lies in the root directory of your boot disk and contains specialized commands that can improve the performance and flexibility of your computer.

DOS starts with certain settings for its functions or features. But some of the settings may not be appropriate for your use of the computer. The only way to change these settings is by using a set of special commands called *directives* in the CONFIG.SYS file.

If you don't yet have this file on your disk, don't worry. By the end of this chapter, you will have made your own CONFIG.SYS file. On the way to making the file, I'll explain each directive, tell you how it works, and suggest some settings that may be appropriate for your use.

What Is CONFIG.SYS?

After DOS starts, but before the AUTOEXEC.BAT file is invoked, DOS looks for the CONFIG.SYS file. This section describes CONFIG.SYS and tells you what it can do for you.

The name CONFIG.SYS stands for *system-configuration* file. CONFIG.SYS is an ASCII text file you can create with a text editor—such as EDLIN—with a word-processing program in the programmer mode, or with the command **COPY CON CONFIG.SYS**. You can change the file by using the text editor or a word-processing program, but you can't use COPY CON to edit the file. COPY CON only creates files. In Chapter 20, you will see how you can use COPY CON + to add new lines to an established CONFIG.SYS file, but you cannot edit the established lines.

271

Inside the CONFIG.SYS file are the directives that alter some of DOS's functions and features. Table 17.1 lists the directives you can use in your CONFIG.SYS file and describes the functions the directives control.

Table 17.1
CONFIG.SYS DIRECTIVES

Directive	Action
BREAK	Determines when DOS recognizes the Ctrl-Break sequence
BUFFERS	Sets the number of file buffers DOS uses
COUNTRY	Sets country-dependent information
DEVICE	Allows different devices to be used with DOS
FCBS	Controls file-handling for DOS V1
FILES	Sets the number of files used at one time
INSTALL	Installs memory-resident programs
LASTDRIVE	Sets the highest disk drive on the computer
SHELL	Informs DOS what command processor should be used and where the processor is located
STACKS	Sets the number of stacks that DOS uses
SWITCHES	Disables extended keyboard functions

If you are a beginner, the directive you will be most interested in is BUFFERS. DEVICE is probably next in importance, then FILES, and FCBS (if you have some older DOS programs). Some of these directives can be used immediately. Others are advanced features you should not use until you are experienced with DOS and comfortable with your computer.

Interestingly, when these directives are assembled alphabetically, the order is generally from the least to the most complex. We will generally discuss the directives in the order they are shown in the table. Note the discussion later in the chapter of three of the five drivers that work with the DEVICE directive, including VDISK, the RAM disk provided with DOS.

The second half of this chapter also has a discussion of several files provided with DOS and some PS/2 computers to enhance the use of your video screen, keyboard, and disk drives. These files are called *device drivers*. I'll explain what each files does and how the file can be used.

Device drivers are very versatile, but with the versatility comes complexity. However, you need not know all aspects of device drivers to utilize their features. Also, you will probably find that some device drivers are not suitable for your computer setup. At the start of the discussion on the device drivers, I'll mention what device drivers are appropriate for different setups.

The changes in DOS V3.3 and V4 concern the CONFIG.SYS file more than any other single part of DOS. The largest changes involve the way the computer handles national language characters. The most affected directives are COUNTRY and DEVICE. If DOS's international features interest you, see Chapter 18, which covers the COUNTRY directive and the parts of the DEVICE directive that pertain to internationalized DOS.

Telling DOS When To Break (BREAK)

The BREAK directive is identical to the normal DOS BREAK command. The directive determines when DOS checks for the Ctrl-Break (or Ctrl-C) sequence to stop running a program.

If BREAK is ON, DOS checks to see whether you have pressed Ctrl-Break whenever a program requests some activity from DOS (performs a DOS function call). If BREAK is OFF, DOS checks for a Ctrl-Break only when DOS is doing work with the video display, keyboard, printer, or asynchronous serial adapters.

For long, disk-bound programs that do a lot of disk accessing but little keyboard or screen work, you may want to set BREAK ON. This setting will allow you to break out of a long program if it goes awry.

The syntax for the BREAK directive is

BREAK ON

to turn BREAK on and

BREAK OFF

to turn BREAK off.

Because DOS starts with BREAK OFF, you do not have to give the directive at all if you want to leave BREAK off.

As a rule, you should generally leave BREAK off and not include the directive in CONFIG.SYS. In that case, DOS checks for a Ctrl-Break command only when it performs keyboard, screen, printer, or modem input and output. If you have a program that performs much disk activity and little screen activity, turn the BREAK directive on before you run the program, and turn BREAK off afterward.

Using BUFFERS To Increase Disk Performance

The BUFFERS directive tells DOS how many disk buffers to use. Of all the directives, BUFFERS potentially has the greatest impact on disk performance. This directive was changed significantly for DOS V4. I'll discuss the older version first and then explain DOS V4 enhancements.

A *disk buffer* is a reserved area of RAM that is set up by DOS. The purpose of disk buffers is to minimize the number of times DOS must use a slow, mechanical device—the disk drive. Although you may consider your disk drives very fast, compared to the internal workings of your computer, disk drives operate very slowly. The idea behind disk buffers is to use random-access memory more and the disk drive less.

The BUFFERS directive controls how many disk buffers you will use. The syntax is

    BUFFERS = nn

in which **nn** is the number of disk buffers you want. You can have any number of buffers, from 1 to 99. If you do not give the BUFFERS directive, DOS starts with a default value from 2 to 15 buffers.

DOS's default starting number of buffers depends on your equipment (disk drive type and amount of memory) and the version of DOS you use. If you have 360K floppy disk drives, DOS starts with two disk buffers. DOS starts with three if you use any other type of disk drive (including a hard disk). If you have more RAM (256K to 512K+), DOS starts with five to fifteen disk buffers. Table 17.2 lists the different buffer configurations.

Table 17.2
Default Number of Disk BUFFERS

DOS Version	Number of BUFFERS	Hardware
DOS pre-V3.3	2	floppy disk drives
	3	hard disk drive
DOS V3.3/V4	2	360K disk drive
	3	any other type of disk drive
	5	more than 128K of RAM
	10	more than 256K of RAM
	15	more than 512K of RAM

You can use fewer BUFFERS than the starting numbers shown in table 17.2. You will probably find, however, that you will want more, rather than fewer, buffers.

Understanding How DOS Uses Disk Buffers

How do disk buffers work? Before you learn the answer to that question, remember that a disk buffer is just slightly larger than a disk sector and can hold the contents of a disk sector. A disk sector is typically 512 bytes; a disk buffer is typically 528 bytes. (The additional bytes in the buffer are used by DOS to track the information in the disk buffer.)

When DOS is asked to get information from a disk or place on a disk information that isn't the same size as a disk sector, DOS reads or writes a full sector of information. DOS cannot read or write less than a sector at a time.

Information can be moved within RAM faster than information can be moved from the disk to RAM. Hence, the object of disk buffers is to use high-speed memory-to-memory movement more often than slower disk-to-memory movement.

When DOS gets information from the disk, DOS conserves the number of times it must access the disk. When part of the disk sector is requested by your programs, DOS reads the full sector and places it into a disk buffer. If the program requests the next group of information, the chances are strong that the needed information is in a disk buffer. Rather than wasting time rereading the sector, DOS shuffles the desired information from the disk buffer in high-speed memory. Only when the information in the buffer is exhausted (when a different disk sector is needed) does DOS return to the disk.

Similarly, DOS conserves disk activity when it writes information to the disk. If less than a full disk sector should be written to the disk, DOS accumulates the information in a disk buffer. When the buffer fills, DOS writes the information to the disk. This writing is called *flushing* the buffer. To make sure that all information is placed into the file, DOS also flushes the buffers when a program "closes" a disk file, which signals that the file is no longer needed.

When a disk buffer becomes full or empty, DOS marks the buffer to indicate that it has been used recently. When DOS needs to recycle the disk buffers due to more disk activity, DOS goes through the list of disk buffers to find the buffer that hasn't been used for the longest time. The term for this buffer is *least recently used*. This process is repeated for any disk activity.

The net effect is that DOS reduces the number of disk accesses by reading and writing only full sectors. By discarding the least recently used buffers, DOS retains the information that is more likely to be needed next. The result is that your programs and DOS run faster.

In some ways, the system of disk buffers is similar to that used for a RAM disk, when a section of memory is used as though it were a real disk drive. The difference is that only strategic parts of the disk (rather than the entire disk) are kept in buffers. (VDISK, which is DOS's RAM disk, is discussed later in this chapter.)

A comfort in using disk buffers is knowing that DOS handles all this activity for you. When your program reads part of a data file, DOS brings this portion of the file into RAM—the disk buffer. As your program writes information to the disk, the information goes into the disk buffer first. Disk buffers can be used with all types of files, including the additional program files used with programs such as 1-2-3 and WordStar. DOS loads these additional program files (called *overlays*) into the buffers and gives them to the main program as needed.

If your program does much *random* disk work (reading and writing information in different parts of a file), you may want a higher number of buffers. The more buffers you have, the better the chance that the information DOS wants is already in memory (the disk buffer).

However, some programs do not benefit much from using disk buffers. If your program mainly performs *sequential* reading and writing (reads and/or writes information from the start of the file straight through to the end), using disk buffers won't give you a large advantage.

The real advantage of disk buffers is evident when your program does much random reading or writing of information in amounts that are not exactly equal to a disk's sector. This advantage applies especially to database or accounting programs. Some word-processing programs can benefit from disk buffers, but many other programs do not.

Determining the Number of Buffers

How many disk buffers should you have? The answer depends on what programs you run on your computer and how much memory you have. If your day-to-day use of the computer does not involve accounting or database work, generally the right number is from 10 to 30 disk buffers. If you use many subdirectories, using more disk buffers also increases your computer's performance.

The memory issue can be important. Each disk buffer takes 528 bytes of memory. This means that every two disk buffers you use will cost you just over 1K of RAM, which could be used by your programs instead.

If you are using a system with 256K or less, you don't have much space to devote to disk buffers. But most people use computers that have at least 512K. If you have this much RAM, you can probably use as many disk buffers as you like, simply leaving as much memory space as your programs need. Otherwise, there is little sense in robbing Peter (reducing the amount of RAM space available for your programs) to pay Paul (increasing the size of DOS's disk buffers).

DOS has a "magic" range for disk buffers. DOS V3 and V4 bog down somewhere between 40 and 60 disk buffers. The reason is that DOS spends more time searching the disk buffers for information than simply reading or writing the disk. Depending on what programs you run, you will find that more than 30 buffers cause the system to become sluggish.

The best advice is to start with 10 disk buffers for floppy disks or 20 buffers for hard disk systems. Fine-tune the number by increasing or decreasing it by 1 to 5 buffers every few hours or once a day. Reboot DOS and examine its performance. Keep doing this until you think you have the best performance. You don't need to be exact, but just get the general "feel" of the computer's performance. (I run 30 disk buffers on both a 640K IBM Personal Computer AT and a 1M PS/2 Model 60 and find that this number is "just right" for what I do.)

New Options with DOS V4

DOS V4 added important options for the BUFFERS directive. First, it increased the number of buffers available to 10,000—if you have expanded memory. In addition, you may now use something called a "look-ahead" buffer to increase disk efficiency. We'll address these enhancements one at a time.

As you will see later in this chapter, expanded memory is a type of memory that is "officially" supported by PC DOS for the first time with the introduction of DOS V4.

As you may know, the Intel 8088 microprocessor chip used by the original IBM PC was able to recognize, or address, no more than one megabyte of RAM, chiefly because a 24-bit number was set aside to track memory locations. The largest address that can be specified by such a number is 111111111111111111111111 in binary, or about 1 million in decimal. The microprocessor cannot address memory beyond that point because it has no way of storing a larger number. It is as though your mailbox had room for only four digits to hold your house number. You could include numbers up to 9999 (decimal) and no larger. If you happened to live at 12345 Thunderbird Rd., you'd simply be unable to put the number on your mailbox.

Later microprocessors were designed with more room to designate memory addresses. However, DOS was built around the 24-bit number limitation. In fact, only the first 640K of memory was deemed necessary for DOS applications. So, DOS can generally use only that 640K of *conventional* memory.

The IBM PC/AT, which was designed around the Intel 80286 microprocessor, can address additional memory that extends beyond one megabyte. DOS programs still cannot access this *extended* memory, but specialized utilities, including RAM disks, have been written to use extended memory.

A consortium of non-IBM vendors that includes Lotus, Intel, Microsoft, and AST has agreed to support a third type of memory called *expanded* memory. A comprehensive discussion of expanded memory is beyond the scope of this book. However, you can consider expanded memory to be a large canvas of memory which can be viewed through a *window* in DOS, one page or frame at a time. Applications written to use expanded memory can move this window around as required to make the desired pages visible to the application. Thus, software like Lotus 1-2-3 can use expanded memory to hold very large spreadsheets.

DOS V4 introduced support for expanded memory, and BUFFERS is one of the features that can use it. If you add the /X switch to the BUFFERS directive in your CONFIG.SYS file, DOS will use expanded memory (rather than your precious DOS memory) to store buffered information.

Look-ahead buffers are an additional enhancement. These are special buffers that DOS uses to store sectors *ahead* of the sector requested by a DOS read operation. You may specify from 0 to 8 look-ahead buffers. If you indicate that five look-ahead buffers should be used, every time DOS reads a sector from your disk, it also reads the following five sectors as well. Doing this is simple, since the entire track passes under the disk's read/write head anyway.

If it turns out that your application or DOS needs one of the sectors already read, DOS will find the sectors in memory and will not need to make another disk access. As you can see, this is potentially a powerful performance enhancer.

Look-ahead buffers require only 512 bytes of memory. The syntax for the two new features is as follows:

> **BUFFERS** = *buffers, look-ahead_buffers* /X

278 Chapter 17: Customizing DOS

For example, the directive **BUFFERS = 1000,8 /X** would direct DOS to set aside 1,000 buffers plus 8 look-ahead buffers, using expanded memory. If enough expanded memory is not available, the directive is ignored, and DOS reverts to its default value.

Installing Device Drivers with DEVICE

The DEVICE directive is the "flexibility" command for DOS V3 and V4. With DEVICE and the proper software, you can make better use of your current computer hardware and use other hardware your computer could not easily use before.

The syntax for the DEVICE directive is

DEVICE = *d:path***filename**.*ext /switches*

in which *d:* is the disk drive holding the device-driver file, *path* is the directory path to the device-driver file, and **filename**.*ext* is the name of the file holding the device driver. */switches* are the switches, if any, needed by the device-driver software.

What is a device driver? As you recall from Chapter 8, a device is any peripheral, such as a disk drive, keyboard, video display, terminal, or printer. A *device driver* is the software that links itself to the operating system, so that the computer can use a particular device.

DOS includes software that controls the peripherals that come with your computer. But what if you want to use a device the operating system knows nothing about? The most common example is a *mouse*, the hand-held device for moving the cursor and inputting data. Before you can use a mouse, DOS needs to know what type of device it is, how to talk to the device, and how to listen to it. Adding the appropriate DEVICE directive to the CONFIG.SYS file solves this problem.

Device-driver software, written according to the specifications in the DOS manual, may be provided by the manufacturer of the device, or you may write your own. The device driver is placed on the system boot disk. Then, to instruct DOS about the device, you include the following line in the CONFIG.SYS file:

DEVICE = **driver_filename**

For **driver_filename**, you substitute the full name—including disk drive and path name if needed—of the file that holds the device-driver software. When DOS boots, it loads and installs the appropriate software. Afterward, the computer system can use the device.

One of the device-driver files provided with DOS V3.3 and V4 is called ANSI.SYS. This software alters the way DOS handles the video screen and the keyboard. The ANSI.SYS file enables you to control the video screen's color and graphics from any program and to reprogram the entire keyboard if you like.

There are only three steps to using the ANSI.SYS device driver. These three steps illustrate how to use any device driver:

Step 1. *Copy the device driver to the appropriate startup disk.*

If you use floppy disks, copy the file to the root directory of a bootable disk. If you are using a hard disk, copy the file to either the root directory of the hard disk or to a standard subdirectory. To keep the root directory uncluttered, I use \SYS or \DRIVERS as the subdirectory to hold my device-driver files.

Step 2. *Add the DEVICE = directive to the CONFIG.SYS file.*

To use the ANSI.SYS file, add this line to the CONFIG.SYS file:

DEVICE = ANSI.SYS

If you use a hard disk system, I suggest that you give the disk drive and path name. For example, if you copied ANSI.SYS to a subdirectory you called \SYS, the line would be

DEVICE = C:\SYS\ANSI.SYS

To use ANSI.SYS on a floppy disk system, the line would be

DEVICE = A:\ANSI.SYS

Step 3. *Restart the computer.*

Remember, CONFIG.SYS is read only when DOS starts. The changes are not activated until you restart DOS. When the computer restarts, DOS follows the new DEVICE directives.

You can load as many device drivers as you need. As each device driver is loaded, DOS extends its control to that device.

Remember that the device driver must be accessible when DOS starts. For convenience, device drivers should be placed in the root directory for floppy disks. Hard disk users should make a special subdirectory called \DRIVERS or \SYS and put the device drivers into this directory, out of the way of daily files. If you put the files in a separate subdirectory, add the directory path name in front of the device-driver file name, as in

DEVICE = C:\DRIVERS\ANSI.SYS

or

DEVICE = \SYS\ANSI.SYS

Later in this chapter, I'll discuss several of DOS V3.3's device drivers.

Accessing Files through File Control Blocks (FCBS)

Many DOS V3 users (I include myself) quickly found the FCBS directive indispensable. The FCBS directive allows useful, but antiquated, programs written for DOS V1 to be used with later versions of DOS.

FCB is an abbreviation for *file control block*. FCBs provide one way for a program to access a file. The method, which has origins in the CP/M operating system, was used in DOS V1. When DOS was directed to work with a file, the programmer asked DOS to create an FCB for each file. DOS used this FCB to communicate with the program and also kept track of each FCB.

Later versions of DOS borrow a UNIX-like method for controlling files, called *handles* (discussed in the FILES directive section). The problem is that, whereas FCBs can be used with any version of DOS, handles can be used only with DOS V2 or V3.

You may have several programs that use the older-style FCB method for accessing files. The FCBS directive regulates how DOS V3 will treat the programs.

The syntax of the directive is

   FCBS = maxopen, *neverclose*

in which **maxopen** is the maximum number of unique FCBs that programs can open at one time. *neverclose* is the number of FCBs that DOS is not allowed to reuse automatically.

You must specify **maxopen**, which can be a number from 1 to 255. The default value is four FCBs. *neverclose;* which is optional, must be a number less than or equal to **maxopen**. If you don't specify *neverclose*, the default value is zero.

When I upgraded to DOS V3.0, my favorite spelling checker, MicroSpell, came to a screeching halt. After some investigation, the author, Bob Lucas, and I found that the program opens 10 FCBs. Because I hadn't given an FCBS directive, I was allowing DOS to reuse FCBs behind MicroSpell's back, and MicroSpell was unable to use the files it needed.

The quick solution was to use the following line, which I placed in my CONFIG.SYS file:

   FCBS = 12,12

This directive tells DOS that my programs will use up to 12 FCBs at a time and not to close any of them automatically. If one of your familiar programs worked fine under DOS V1 or V2, but doesn't work right under DOS V3, try this line. Most programs today do not use FCBs; hence this directive should have decreasing importance in the future.

The IBM documentation states that FCBs are closed only when you use the SHARE command for a local area network. I found that this isn't the case with DOS V3.0 and V3.1. If you use an older program that doesn't support UNIX-like path names, the program uses FCBs. Use the FCBS directive.

You pay a small price in RAM to use the FCBS directive. For each number above 4 that **maxopen** exceeds, DOS takes up about 40 bytes. Considering that most people have 256K or more in their computers, the use of this extra RAM should not be a problem.

Telling DOS How Many FILES To Handle

As the FCBS directive decreases in importance, the FILES directive increases. FILES is the DOS V3 and V4 command for UNIX/XENIX®-like file handling. FILES works this way: Your program gives DOS the name of the file or device you want to use. DOS gives back to your program a *handle*—a two-byte number. From that point on, your programs use the handle, rather than the FCB, to manipulate the file or device.

The syntax for the FILES directive is

FILES = nn

in which **nn** is the number of UNIX/XENIX-like files you want opened at any time. The maximum number is 255, and the minimum is 8. If you give a FILES directive with a number less than 8, or if you omit this directive, DOS makes the number 8. Each additional file over 8 increases the size of DOS by 39 bytes.

The name FILES is somewhat deceiving, as handles are used by files and devices. In the discussion of I/O redirection (Chapter 12), you learned about standard input, standard output, and standard error. DOS automatically uses two other "standard" devices: standard printer (PRN or LPT1:), and standard auxiliary (AUX or COM1:).

These "standard" devices automatically receive one file handle each. If you do not specify the FILES directive, DOS starts with eight file handles and immediately takes five handles for the standard devices, leaving only three handles for your programs.

If you use BASIC, or don't program at all, don't worry about the details on handles. Your concern is that the starting value of 8 may not be enough for your programs. My advice is to include in your CONFIG.SYS file this directive:

FILES = 10

This directive establishes ten file handles, which should be enough for most programs. If a program gives you an error message about file handles, edit your CONFIG.SYS file and increase the number of handles to 15 or 20 (if you are using dBASE III Plus, use 20 files). Those higher numbers are sufficient for most existing programs.

Using LASTDRIVE To Change the Number of Disk Drives

The directive LASTDRIVE informs DOS of the maximum disk drives on your system. Generally, LASTDRIVE is a directive used with networked computers or with the pretender commands, which are discussed in Chapter 25.

If you don't use the LASTDRIVE directive, DOS assumes that the last disk drive on your system is E. If you give DOS a letter that corresponds to fewer drives than are physically attached to your computer, DOS ignores the directive. The LASTDRIVE directive enables you to tell DOS how many disk drives, real or apparent, are on your system.

The syntax for LASTDRIVE is

LASTDRIVE = x

in which x is the alphabetical character for the last disk drive on your system. The letters A through Z, in upper- or lowercase, are acceptable.

Personal Computers and PS/2 computers can immediately recognize a total of four disk drives, which can be a combination of floppy disk drives and hard disk drives. The POST (power-on self-test) checks the number of real disk drives attached to the computer.

Why would you want to use the LASTDRIVE directive? One reason is so that you can use a RAM disk. When you add a RAM disk to your computer, you have a fifth—albeit semi-real—disk drive. Because POST knows nothing about a nonphysical RAM disk, DOS assumes that you want one more disk drive. Hence, having five disk drives makes sense.

Another reason is that LASTDRIVE must be used to establish *logical* disk drives. A logical disk drive can be a nickname for another disk drive (see the ASSIGN command). A logical disk drive may also be the second partition of the hard disk. And, a logical disk drive may actually be part of a disk. A logical disk drive is just a name. DOS "thinks" that the logical disk drive is real. You know that the disk drive is something else.

DOS, via the SUBST command, allows you to use subdirectories as though the subdirectory were a disk drive. This facility is important when you work with programs that know nothing about subdirectories, particularly if you use a local area network. To effectively use the SUBST command, you need to inform DOS that you have additional disk drives.

If you are unsure whether you will use SUBST, omit the LASTDRIVE directive for now. If you use a network, the network documentation should mention the proper value for LASTDRIVE.

If you want to defeat these phantom disk drives, use the directive

LASTDRIVE = C

in your CONFIG.SYS file. This directive says that the last drive on your system is drive C, usually the hard disk. If you add devices that act like disk drives to your computer (such as a cartridge-tape backup unit), you can bump up the last "disk drive" (as high as Z, the 26th drive).

Using the LASTDRIVE directive does not affect the size of DOS. LASTDRIVE is discussed again in Chapter 25.

Playing the SHELL Game

The SHELL directive was originally implemented to allow programmers to replace the DOS command processor (COMMAND.COM) with other command processors. The directive now has two additional functions: You can place the command processor in any directory—not just in the boot disk's root directory. And you can expand the size of the environment.

SHELL is a tricky directive that should be used cautiously. Giving the wrong SHELL directive can "lock up" your system. Until you are familiar with the directive, omit it from your CONFIG.SYS file.

When you do need to use the directive—to move COMMAND.COM from the root directory or to increase the size of the environment—have handy another DOS disk that can start up your computer. If you make a mistake, you'll need to reboot with this disk.

The SHELL directive is slightly different for DOS V3.0, V3.1, and DOS V3.2 and later versions.

The syntax for the SHELL directive in DOS V3.0 is

   SHELL = *d:path***filename**.*ext d:**path* /**P**

The syntax for SHELL for DOS V3.1 through V4 is

   SHELL = *d:path***filename**.*ext d:**path* /**P** /*E:size*

The first item after the equal sign is the file name of the command processor you will use. *d:* is the name of the disk drive that holds the command processor. The *path*\\ is the subdirectory path to the command processor. Both *d:* and *path*\\ are optional, but they should be given. **filename**.*ext* is the name of the directive processor. The root name is required, and the extension is needed if the file does not use the suffix .COM.

The next item is the disk drive and path name to the directive processor. DOS uses this information to set the COMSPEC environmental variable. Normally, this drive and path name duplicate the first disk drive and path name. And, although this drive and path are also marked as optional, they should be given.

SHELL has two switches under versions prior to DOS V4:

   /**P**   Stay permanent

   /*E:size*   Sets the size of the environment

DOS V4 adds a new switch to SHELL:

   /*MSG*   Tells DOS to load DOS messages into RAM when it loads
                            COMMAND.COM. This enhancement can speed up
                            operation somewhat if you have enough memory.

The /P switch instructs DOS to load and keep resident the copy of the command processor. Without the /P switch, DOS loads COMMAND.COM, executes the AUTO-EXEC.BAT file, and immediately exits. You must reboot the system using a different disk if you omit the /P switch.

/*E:size* is the optional switch that sets the amount of random-access memory that will be used for the environment. If you see the message

   ```
   Out of environment space
   ```

you need to use the SHELL directive with the /E switch.

If you use /E, the size of DOS increases by the amount of space you add to the normal starting value for the environment. The SHELL directive does not use any additional memory except when it increases the size of the environment.

Note that the /E switch is not available for DOS V3.0. The size given with the switch is the same for DOS V3.2, V3.3, and V4, but different for DOS V3.1.

DOS V3.2, V3.3, and V4 start with an environment size of 160 bytes. The size can be a number from 160 to 32,767. If you give a size number greater than 32,767, DOS uses 32,767. If you give a number smaller than 160 or give a nonsense size (such as using letters for size), DOS uses 160 bytes for the environment.

However, if *size* is not evenly divisible by 16, DOS adjusts it to the next multiple of 16. For example, if you use the number 322 for size, DOS adjusts up the size to 336. The adjustment is automatic.

DOS V3.1 uses a different system for *size*, which is the number of 16-byte paragraphs for the environment. DOS V3.1 starts with an environment size of 128 bytes. The size can be changed with the SHELL directive from 11 (11 × 16 or 176 bytes) to 62 (62 × 16 or 992 bytes). If you use a number less than 11 or greater than 62, DOS V3.1 will display an error message and ignore the /E switch.

You can reverse the order of the /P and /E switches. You can place a space between the switches. You can also omit the /E switch. If you give the /E switch, however, do not forget to put the colon between the /E and *size* and do not put spaces within any part of the /E switch.

The normal command processor for DOS is COMMAND.COM. If you don't write your own command processor (I would not even attempt such a task), why use the SHELL directive?

As mentioned, the SHELL directive can expand the size of the environment. When your programs need more environment space, you'll need to give the SHELL directive. The other reason is that the command processor can be moved from the root directory of the boot disk.

To keep the root directory as uncluttered as possible, put COMMAND.COM in a separate directory on the hard disk. Then, when you copy a disk that contains another copy of COMMAND.COM, you know you are not placing an outdated version over a more current version.

The other reason to use the SHELL directive is to direct DOS to look for COMMAND.COM on the hard disk. This means that when COMMAND.COM must reload itself, DOS does not give an annoying message to place a disk with COMMAND.COM in the disk drive. DOS knows to get COMMAND.COM from the hard disk. This example may seem obscure, but it works.

By the way, the DOS manual does not mention the second item about SHELL—the drive and path name to the command processor. The DOS manual states that the SHELL directive does not affect the COMSPEC variable. But if you use the second item, DOS *does* set COMSPEC.

Keeping Up with the STACKS Directive

The STACKS directive was added to DOS V3.2 and was changed slightly with DOS V3.3. If you do not have an Enhanced Keyboard, this directive may have little use for you. If you have a PS/2, Personal Computer AT, or PC 286-XT, you may find this directive useful. To understand why, you need to know a few things about your computer's internal operation.

A *stack* is an area of RAM. The CPU (central processing unit, the "brain" of your computer) uses this area to temporarily hold information. High-speed instructions place items onto the stack and remove items from the stack. The IBM's CPU can use a stack anywhere in memory, and each program you use can have its own stack.

The second concept is the *hardware interrupt,* a signal generated by a device that is demanding attention. For example, each time you press a key, the keyboard generates a hardware interrupt. Your disk drives, modem, mouse, or other devices also generate interrupts—demands for the CPU's attention.

When a hardware interrupt occurs, the computer executes the software instructions in a fixed-memory location to satisfy the device. The first step the computer takes is to store the information that was being acted upon when the interrupt occurred. It stores this information in a stack.

The difficulty with interrupts is that they can nest, meaning the computer can be interrupted again, by the same or a different device, while it is handling a hardware interrupt. When additional interrupts occur, DOS must quickly store each level of information on a stack and handle the next interrupt.

Versions of DOS prior to V3.2 used the single-stack method to handle the interrupts. This system usually worked well, but when too many interrupts occurred and the stack overflowed, the system ran into problems. The computer would mysteriously lock up, and no error message would be given.

DOS V3.2 implemented a new method of using a pool of nine stacks. When a hardware interrupt occurs, DOS V3.2 draws another stack from the pool. As DOS successfully answers the interrupt, it returns the stack to the pool for use later when another interrupt occurs.

Lately, as more people use sophisticated peripherals that generate numerous interrupts, the problem of nested interrupts has become increasingly apparent. If the ninth interrupt occurs before DOS can satisfy any of the eight previous interrupts, DOS displays this error message:

```
Fatal: Internal Stack Failure, System Halted
```

When this error message appears on your screen, your computer has "blown" its stack. *You must turn the computer off and on again to restart it.* You will not be able to reboot the system with Ctrl-Alt-Del.

Most stack problems surface when you use an Enhanced Keyboard and certain programs, such as dBASE III Plus. Holding down a key can trigger stack failure.

To prevent the problem of stack overflows, DOS provides the STACKS directive. The syntax is

> STACKS = number, *size*

number is the number of stacks that DOS should establish to handle the interrupts. The value of number should be from 8 to 64. *size* is the size in bytes of each stack. This number can be from 32 to 512.

The default value of the STACKS directive varies from machine to machine. For DOS V3.2, V3.3, and V4, on the PS/2, Personal Computer AT, PC XT, and 286-XT (with the Enhanced Keyboard), and the PC Convertible, DOS starts with 9 stacks of 128 bytes each (equivalent to giving the directive **STACKS = 9, 128**). DOS V3.3 on the PC, PC XT, and PC Portable has a single stack for all interrupts.

To revert to the "single-stack-fits-all" approach for handling interrupts, use the directive

> **STACKS = 0, 0**

Generally, you can ignore the STACKS directive. But if you get a stack error, you have a program that triggers the hardware problem. Immediately change the CONFIG.SYS file to increase the number of stacks without altering the size of the stacks. A comfortable line to use is

> **STACKS 12, 128**

This directive establishes 12 stacks of 128 bytes each.

The preferred way to handle stack failure is to increase the number of stacks and not to increase their size. If, however, you must change the size of the stacks, increase the size. Do not decrease it. The benefits of decreasing the size of the stacks are outweighed greatly by the chance that a program will overflow the smaller stack.

The STACKS directive does affect DOS's size. Considering that DOS starts with approximately 1,200 bytes for the stack pool, increasing the number or size of the stacks correspondingly increases the size of the stack pool. Using only one DOS stack (**STACKS = 0, 0**) decreases DOS's size by approximately 1,000 bytes.

Using Device Drivers for Your Keyboard, Screen, and Disks

A variety of device drivers can be used on your computer with DOS V3.3 or V4 to enhance keyboard function, the display, and/or the disk drives. You can use all of them with the DEVICE = directive. All but one are located on the DOS disks. The other file is located on the Reference disk that comes with the PS/2 Models 50, 60, 70, or 80. The device drivers are shown in table 17.3.

Table 17.3
Device Drivers Provided with DOS

Driver	Action
ANSI.SYS	Extends control over your keyboard and display (All versions of DOS V3)
VDISK.SYS	RAM-disk software (All versions of DOS V3)
IBMCACHE.SYS	A disk-cache program (PS/2 Models 50, 60, and 80 only)
DRIVER.SYS	Extends control over your built-in or external floppy disk drives (DOS V3.2 and V3.3)
DISPLAY.SYS	Provides foreign language font support for the display (DOS V3.3 only)
PRINTER.SYS	Provides foreign language font support for the printer(s) (DOS V3.3 only)
XMA2EMS.SYS	Provides EMS support for 80286 computers (V4 only)
XMAEMS.SYS	Provides EMS support for 80386 computers (V4 only)

DISPLAY.SYS and PRINTER.SYS are part of DOS V3.3 and V4 only. DRIVER.SYS made its debut with DOS V3.2. IBMCACHE.SYS is provided only to owners of PS/2 Models 50, 60, or 80. XMA2EMS.SYS and XMAEM.SYS were introduced with DOS V4.

DISPLAY.SYS and PRINTER.SYS are device drivers that are used in DOS V3.3 and V4's non-English language functions. Chapter 18, which explains how to use DOS internationally, discusses these files.

DOS V3.3 and V4 users receive two additional SYS files on their DOS disks—COUNTRY.SYS and KEYBOARD.SYS. These files are *not* device drivers. Do not attempt to use them in the DEVICE directive.

In the rest of this chapter, you'll read about the remaining device drivers. I'll first discuss ANSI.SYS, followed by VDISK.SYS, IBMCACHE.SYS, DRIVER.SYS, XMA2EMS.SYS, and XMAEM.SYS.

Device drivers vary greatly in how difficult they are to use. The degree of difficulty is based on what the driver does. Drivers that work with very specific hardware, such as ANSI.SYS, are easy to use. You simply use the DEVICE directive to load the driver. Other device drivers, which work with a variety of hardware, have optional and mandatory parameters that increase the degree of complexity. DRIVER.SYS is the most complex of the four device drivers in this chapter.

I rate the various device drivers as follows:

ANSI.SYS - required by many software packages, needed by most users, and the easiest to understand and install.

VDISK.SYS - not required by any software packages, but beneficial to most users whose computers have at least 512K of RAM or any extended memory; somewhat difficult to understand and moderately difficult to install.

IBMCACHE.SYS - not required by any software package, but useful to many users of hard disk systems; moderately difficult to understand and easy to moderately difficult to install.

DRIVER.SYS - required for most external disk drives and optional for users who want to make additional logical disk drives out of a single physical disk drive; moderately difficult to understand and install.

XMA2EMS.SYS - required only if you want to use the officially "blessed" EMS support for DOS V4. Most expanded memory boards come with their own EMS driver that may be more compatible with your applications software. IBM's version can be very difficult to understand and install if you have other software and hardware that could conflict with this driver. For example, I had some difficulty with conflicting memory addresses when I installed an HP ScanJet™ scanner with my PS/2 Model 60. That machine's default driver settings conflicted with XMA2EMS.SYS's expanded memory setup.

XMAEM.SYS - required if you have a PS/2 Model 80 and wish to use some other memory adapter to emulate the IBM Personal System/2 80286 Expanded Memory adapter. Not especially difficult to install.

Because the discussion of these device drivers is somewhat technical and detailed, I *strongly* suggest that you first skim the discussion of the device drivers and then reread the sections of interest. If you find the discussion too difficult, jump to the end of the chapter where I recommend some sample CONFIG.SYS files; simply use the sample file that most closely matches your system.

Using ANSI.SYS To Enhance Your Keyboard and Display

The ANSI.SYS driver replaces DOS's standard way of looking at characters that are going to the keyboard or video screen. With ANSI.SYS, your programs can do any of the following: control the video screen's colors and graphics; move the cursor anywhere on the screen; erase characters anywhere on the screen; reprogram any key, including the special-function keys; and produce many characters at the press of a single key.

Many programs need the capabilities of ANSI.SYS. If any of your programs require ANSI.SYS, you must use the driver, or the program will not display properly. Check your applications programs' manuals for more information.

Usually, ANSI.SYS is copied to the start-up floppy disk's root directory. To use ANSI.SYS on a floppy disk system, add the following line to CONFIG.SYS:

DEVICE = A:\ANSI.SYS

For use with a hard disk, ANSI.SYS is normally copied to the root directory or to a sub-directory dedicated to device drivers, like \BIN or \DRIVERS. Depending on the file's placement, you should add one of these lines to your CONFIG.SYS file:

> **DEVICE = C:\ANSI.SYS**
>
> **DEVICE = C:\SYS\ANSI.SYS**
>
> **DEVICE = C:\DRIVERS\ANSI.SYS**

Use the first line if you have placed ANSI.SYS in your hard disk's root directory. Use the second line if you have placed ANSI.SYS in your \SYS subdirectory. Use the third line if you have placed ANSI.SYS in your \DRIVERS subdirectory.

The name of ANSI.SYS reflects its background. ANSI® is the abbreviation for the *American National Standards Institute,* the agency that formulates and publishes standards affecting items ranging from programming languages to safety shoes. ANSI is a member of the *International Standards Organization* (ISO), a multinational standards group.

Two standards, ANSI 3.64 and ISO 6429, cover terminals and display devices. The standards establish a method to control terminals by transmitting strings of characters from the computer to the terminal. The strings are called *escape sequences*, since the strings start with the ASCII Escape character (27 decimal, 1B hexadecimal). Every terminal complying with these standards understands and reacts to these escape sequences in the agreed manner.

The standard establishes escape sequences to move the cursor up, down, left, right, or to any position on the video screen. The standard also establishes sequences to erase a line or the entire video screen, and to set the mode of the screen (into alphanumeric or dot-by-dot graphics, including the color of the characters or dots and the background).

One application of the ANSI.SYS standards is reprogramming your keyboard. You can define any key on the keyboard to produce a single character or many characters. This capability allows you to create keyboard *macros*, which enable you to make a single keystroke or set of keys (such as Ctrl-1 or Alt-F6) complete a DOS command or produce a frequently typed word.

ANSI.SYS has some limitations. The program is not a substitute for keyboard macro programs like RoseSoft's ProKey™ or Borland's SuperKey®. ANSI.SYS can hold about 128 characters of text for all macros, which is minuscule compared to the 2K to 8K the other macro programs can use.

Nor does ANSI.SYS provide a method to use or control high-resolution color graphics (the 640-by-200- or 640-by-350-dot modes). Also, using ANSI.SYS to display text and graphics is much slower than using programs like WordStar or 1-2-3, which write to the screen directly or use the computer's BIOS.

Regardless of these limitations, ANSI.SYS is an essential device driver for your computer, and many programs depend on it for their video output. Because ANSI.SYS's memory burden is light, including ANSI.SYS in your CONFIG.SYS file is a worthwhile tradeoff of memory resources for video screen control.

For DOS V4, ANSI.SYS was given three new switches: /X, /L, and /K.

/X - Allows you to redefine keys with extended key values (such as F11 and F12). Keyboard redefinition is beyond the scope of this chapter. However, if you have used ANSI.SYS to redefine keys in the past, you probably noted that the extended keys couldn't be redefined in the usual manner. Now they can.

/L - Tells DOS to over-ride any software that resets the number of screen rows to 25, in case you have defined more rows using the MODE command. MODE allows changing the default number of screen rows from 25 to 43 or 50 with the EGA and VGA display adapters, respectively. However, you'll find that many applications reset the value to 25 when they start up. /L prevents this.

However, there is no guarantee that the application will still *use* the increased number of rows. I tried the new capability with a number of packages and found that they did use the smaller character size to display tinier lines, *but used only half the screen*. Not a very useful capability at this time, unless your application can actually use 43 or 50 lines of text.

/K - Turns off the extended keyboard functions of the IBM Enhanced Keyboard. You can use this switch to enable DOS to run programs that refuse to operate correctly with an Enhanced Keyboard. The old-style (10 function-key) keyboard will be mimicked.

Using VDISK To Make a RAM Disk

The VDISK directive creates a *virtual disk*. When you install VDISK, you install what is apparently a floppy disk drive. In reality, you are using a portion of your RAM as though that RAM were a disk drive.

You can benefit greatly from using RAM disks. RAM disks can be ten to fifty times faster than using a floppy disk and five to twenty times faster than using a hard disk.

How does the RAM disk process work? The VDISK device driver tells DOS that the program wants to use some memory. DOS gives the requested RAM to the program until DOS restarts or until the computer is turned off. The software then sets up the memory with a boot record, a file allocation table (FAT), a directory, and locations in which to store files. The memory area becomes a disk device, as accessible as any real disk drive.

VDISK.SYS is the device driver for the RAM disk. The syntax for VDISK is

> **DEVICE** = d:path**VDISK.SYS** bbbb sss ddd /E:max

d: is the disk drive that holds the VDISK.SYS file. *path* is the directory path to VDISK.SYS.

The four options for VDISK are

bbbb	The size (in K) of the RAM disk
sss	The size of the RAM disk sectors
ddd	The number of directory entries (files) for the RAM disk
/E:max	The switch for extended memory use for DOS V3.0

bbbb can range from 1K to the maximum amount of memory available, less 64K that DOS requires you to leave free for use by other programs. For most Personal Computers and for the PS/2 Models 25 and 30, the maximum amount of memory is 640K. Personal Computer ATs and the other PS/2 models can have up to 16 megabytes of RAM. For these computers, you can use more than one VDISK. For example, you could conceivably use three four-megabyte and one three-megabyte virtual disks.

The default value of *bbbb* is 64K. For DOS V3.2, V3.3, and V4, VDISK adjusts the RAM disk's size disk downward if you haven't left 64K of memory free for your programs. For DOS V3.0 and V3.1, if *bbbb* is larger than the amount of your computer's RAM, VDISK uses the 64K size. If you have less than 64K of memory available, VDISK displays an error message and does not install.

When you size your RAM disk, remember that DOS treats the RAM disk as though it were a real disk drive. Because of the boot sector, FAT, and root directory on the RAM disk, the space available for storing your files will be 5K to 24K less than the size you specify. Also remember that the VDISK software itself uses 768 bytes of memory.

sss is the size of the sectors for VDISK. You can specify three sector sizes: 128, 256, or 512 bytes. The default sector size is 128 bytes. DOS disks usually use a sector size of 512 bytes. This size is best if you are storing larger files on the VDISK or if you want to maximize disk speed when you use the RAM disk. If you are storing many small files, a sector size of 256 or 128 will waste less space than a larger sector size.

ddd is the number of directory entries for the RAM disk. Each file you store on the RAM disk uses one directory entry. The volume label VDISK creates takes one of the directory entries. Thus, *ddd* actually specifies the number of files, minus one, that your RAM disk can hold.

The range for *ddd* is from 2 to 512 files, and the default is 64. VDISK may automatically adjust the number of directory entries in two situations: when the directory entries do not fill a complete sector and when you have insufficient space.

First, VDISK may increase the number of directory entries to fill a complete sector. Each directory entry is 32 bytes long. Sector sizes of 256 bytes will have the number of directory entries that are an integer multiple of 8. Sector sizes of 128 will have entries that are an integer multiple of 4. If you are using a sector size of 512, the number of directory entries will be evenly divisible by 16. If you are using 512-byte sectors and you specify 72 directory entries, VDISK automatically adjusts the number of entries to 80. (72 entries require 4.5 sectors of 512 bytes; VDISK rounds the number to the next multiple of 16.)

Second, VDISK decreases the number of directory entries by one sector's worth at a time when you have insufficient space for the FAT, the directory, and two additional sectors. If you specify a small RAM disk (64K to 128K) and have many directory entries, this problem may occur. VDISK will issue an error message and not install. The solution to the problem is to specify a smaller sector size, *sss*, or a larger RAM disk size, *bbbb*

When you start your system, VDISK may make some size adjustments. The adjustments occur when VDISK uses the default values or when special sizes for options conflict with the RAM disk's size. The adjustments are harmless unless VDISK cannot find enough space on the RAM disk in which to fit the FAT and the directory. Harmful adjustments occur when you give improper values to VDISK, such as specifying too large a RAM disk with too small a sector size. In that case, VDISK displays an error message and refuses to install itself.

/E is the switch VDISK uses to access extended memory, that is, memory above the one million-byte point. Computers that can use extended memory—PS/2 computers (except Models 25 and 30) and Personal Computer ATs that have an add-on board which provides more than 1M of memory—can use the /E switch.

PS/2 Models 25 and 30, which use an 8086 CPU, and the PC, which uses an 8088, can use only 1M (megabyte) of memory at a time. PS/2 Models 50 and 60 and the Personal Computer AT use an 80286 CPU, enabling the machines to use more than 1M of RAM. The PS/2 Model 80 uses an 80386 CPU that can also use more than 1M of RAM.

If you have a different computer, including the 286-XT, don't use this switch. Although the 286-XT has a 80286 CPU, the computer cannot accommodate extended memory. VDISK will find that your computer does not have extended memory and will not install itself.

If you use the /E switch, VDISK takes up 768 bytes of regular memory, but places the RAM disk itself in extended memory. With the /E switch, the maximum size of the RAM disk is 4M. You can use multiple RAM disks, limited only by the extended memory that is available and DOS's regular memory. If the 768 bytes that each VDISK uses reduces your regular memory below 64K, the extended VDISK will not install.

DOS V3.0 uses the /E switch alone; later versions add the *max* parameter to the switch. *max* is the maximum number of sectors to transfer at one time from the RAM disk. Certain programs, primarily communications programs, may drop characters if the 80286 or 80386 CPU's attention is kept for too long on the RAM disk. If you have such a problem, set *max* to seven or less. Otherwise, *omit* the max or give eight as the value, as indicated in the next section.

If you have enough extended memory, you can have several RAM disks. Just specify additional DEVICE = VDISK lines in your CONFIG.SYS file. Each line will invoke a fresh copy of VDISK and install additional RAM disks.

If you want to use a RAM disk that mimics a single-sided DOS disk, use the command line

   DEVICE = VDISK.SYS 180 512 64

This command line sets up a 180K disk with 512-byte sectors and 64 directory entries.

To use a RAM disk that appears to be a 360K, double-sided DOS disk, use this command line:

   DEVICE = VDISK.SYS 360 512 112

If you want a RAM disk that uses all the extended memory on a 1M PS/2, use this command line:

   DEVICE = VDISK.SYS 384 512 112 /E:8

The line requests a RAM disk of 384K (384K is the difference between 1M of RAM and 640K DOS memory), 512-byte sectors, and 112 directory entries. The */E:8* switch tells DOS to install the RAM disk in extended memory and transfer 8 sectors to and from the RAM disk at a time. If the /E switch were omitted, DOS would install the RAM disk within the 640K DOS memory.

DOS V4 adds a /X parameter, which allows you to use expanded memory (instead of extended memory) for the RAM disk. You must first load the expanded memory driver (such as XMA2EMS.SYS) and then load VDISK.SYS. You can't use both the /X and /E parameters on the same line. However, you may create *different* RAM disks, some using extended memory and others using expanded memory, if enough is available. Simply create multiple DEVICE = lines in your CONFIG.SYS file.

Determining the Size of the RAM Disk

The amount of RAM in your system, the programs you use, and the RAM disk's convenience determine the size of the RAM disk you can use. On my systems, several programs compete with VDISK for free memory space: SideKick®, SuperKey, and Turbo Lightning, which are from Borland; FLASH™ from Software Masters; and 1-2-3 from Lotus.

Depending on the system, DOS, my buffers, FCBs, and other CONFIG.SYS options use from 56K to 66K of RAM. In the configuration I use on all my computers, SideKick takes about 73K of RAM. SuperKey, the keyboard macro program, uses 58K. Turbo Lightning, the on-line dictionary and thesaurus, uses 68K. FLASH, a disk-caching program, uses from 40K to 200K.

I typically have an average of 360K in use, with 280K memory space left. Lotus 1-2-3 requires about 179K of memory space, leaving a worksheet space of 101K. However, a 64K RAM disk (almost 65K if you include DOS's overhead) leaves only 36K. Very few 1-2-3 models fit into that space.

The point is you must balance your need for RAM workspace with your need for the tools you use. Actually, I balance by using two compromises. The first is to use different boot disks. The CONFIG.SYS file for one disk calls for a 100K RAM disk; another boot disk does not call for any RAM disk at all. I use SideKick, SuperKey, Turbo Lightning, and FLASH with my first disk. The second disk loads only SideKick and FLASH. I boot from the first disk to use the RAM disk and discard it when I need 1-2-3.

The second compromise is simple but slightly more expensive. I installed memory expansion boards that added 2.5 megabytes of RAM. I added the /E switch to the VDISK line in my CONFIG.SYS file so that I can use the extended memory.

Here's an explicit warning for you about RAM disks: RAM is volatile. When the power goes off or DOS is rebooted, everything on your RAM disk is lost! If you store changing files on your RAM disk, get into the habit of copying these files to a "real" disk every 15 minutes to two hours. A power loss destroys in seconds information that has taken hours of work to build. Copying from a RAM disk to a real disk is cheap insurance.

If you are hesitant about putting changing files in volatile memory, try using the RAM disk just for nonchanging program files. If power is lost, you have lost nothing. The real copies of the programs or data files are on floppy disks or hard disks.

By the way, here's a trick that may help you. I used to use two RAM disks. One held the dictionary and thesaurus files for Turbo Lightning. I used the other for fast-access programs and copying files. I was wasting 768 bytes in regular memory by using two RAM disks and wasting about 30K in extended memory by having two boot sectors, two FATs, and two directories, one for each disk.

I now use one RAM disk and place the Turbo Lightning files in a subdirectory on the RAM disk. I have regained the 30K of extended memory through this approach. More important, I have regained almost 1K of regular memory, which is much more valuable than extended memory.

I have one last RAM-disk trick—one that takes advantage of RAM's volatility. My systems are a maze of batch files, which move from one program to another. Frequently, it is useful for the batch file to be able to tell whether or not something has taken place, in order to decide what to do next.

For example, I access a batch file called COM.BAT to run my telecommunications program. Sometimes I run COM.BAT from the DOS prompt. Other times I run it from the DOS Shell. On still other occasions, I run COM.BAT from within a word-processing program that allows you to access DOS. When I am done with telecommunications, I like to return to the program I was using before I called COM.BAT.

My solution is to have each of the batch files that runs an application—including the Shell—create a dummy file when it starts up and erase that dummy file when it ends. For example, my DOSSHELL.BAT file has a line in it that says

```
ECHO DUMMY>H:SHELL.ASC
```

Drive H is a 1 megabyte RAM disk I use on some of my systems. This line redirects the word DUMMY (which could be any word) to a file on drive H. At the end of DOS-SHELL.BAT is another line:

```
ERASE H:SHELL.ASC
```

COM.BAT, or any batch file, can test for the existence of SHELL.ASC and do one thing if the file exists and another if not. For example:

```
IF EXIST H:SHELL.ASC GOTO RELOAD

GOTO END

:RELOAD

EXIT

:END
```

I include several such lines in COM.BAT so it can quickly determine where it "came" from. Since H: is a RAM disk, DOS is able to check it very quickly. Plus, when I turn off the computer, all the dummy files automatically disappear. If I just shut down the system at the end of the day without exiting from the program I am using, DOS will start fresh the following day with no dummy files cluttering up the hard disks.

RAM disks can speed computer operations manyfold. If you have the memory to support RAM disks, they are wonderful improvements.

Making Hard Disk Use Faster with IBMCACHE.SYS

A potential benefit of purchasing a PS/2 computer is that IBM provides a disk-cache program with the computer: IBMCACHE.SYS. IBMCACHE uses RAM to speed the performance of your disks.

A cache (pronounced *cash*) is a safe place for hiding provisions. A disk cache is a safe place for hiding and preserving disk data. Like RAM disks, disk caches operate from a section of RAM that you request from DOS. A disk cache is more similar to a DOS disk buffer than to a RAM disk, however.

Both a disk cache and a disk buffer accumulate information going to the disk or coming from the disk. When information is needed from the disk, the information is placed in a disk buffer or cache and then parceled out to the program. When information is written to the disk, the information is stored in the buffer or cache until the buffer or cache is full. Then the information is written to the disk. The performance of your programs improves because slow disk accesses are replaced by higher speed memory-to-memory transfers.

In theory, a DOS disk buffer is a form of caching. A good caching program can outperform DOS's disk buffers, however. The reason is the intelligence devoted to handling the buffer or cache.

As you recall from the discussion of the BUFFERS directive, DOS recycles disk buffers on a least-recently used basis. When another disk buffer must be used, DOS recycles the disk buffer that has not been used for the longest time. Although this information might be needed soon, DOS reuses this buffer.

A disk cache uses a different scheme to determine what information should be kept or discarded: the cache remembers what sections of the disk have been used most *frequently*. When the cache must be recycled, the program keeps the more frequently used areas and discards the least frequently used.

Given absolute random disk access (program and data files scattered uniformly across the disk), the least *frequently* used method of recycling works better than recycling the least *recently* used sector. The areas of the disk that are most heavily used tend to be kept in memory.

Another feature of the disk cache is *look-ahead*, a technique in which the cache reads more sectors than the program requests. Typically, a program requests DOS to read one or two sectors at a time. These sectors are held in the disk buffer. If the program needs the next sector or two, DOS will have to access the disk again to get the next sectors.

With look-ahead, the cache commands DOS to read the next one to seven sectors at one time. If the program requests information that resides in the next sectors, the cache passes the information to DOS, which gives the information to the program. By reading two to eight sectors at one time, DOS can avoid up to seven individual disk accesses. This technique greatly increases the speed of reading sequential files but decreases slightly the performance of working with completely random files.

Should you use a disk cache? I believe the answer is yes! Given a choice between a RAM disk and a disk cache, the cache is preferable—but not all the time.

A disk cache is preferable because it helps you with all disk activity. A RAM disk helps only with files that are copied to the RAM disk. The cache's activity is transparent and effortless whereas separate directives are required to place the needed files on the RAM disk. Thus, the cache is more convenient to use.

The disk cache is also preferable to a RAM disk because the danger of losing information can be less. Actually, the danger of losing files read from a RAM disk and from a disk cache is identical: nil. The original copies of the files reside on the physical disk.

But there is a greater probability of losing information when files are written to the RAM disk than when files are written to the cache. The cache, like the DOS buffers, holds the information for only a few seconds before writing it to the disk. During this brief period, the information is at risk. If power is lost to the RAM disk, however, all files on the disk are destroyed. A sudden computer power-out is more catastrophic to the RAM disk than to the disk cache.

In two situations, however, a RAM disk is preferred to a disk cache. When you need to copy files between disks on a computer with a single floppy disk drive, copying to and from the RAM disk is convenient. You first copy the files to the RAM disk, change disks, and then copy the files to the second disk. A disk cache does not help you copy files between disks.

The second occasion to prefer a RAM disk is when you frequently use nonchanging files that can be completely placed on the RAM disk. A good example is Turbo Lightning: I place its dictionary and thesaurus files on the RAM disk. Because I access these files very frequently, but seldom at the same spots in the file, having the files on the RAM disk yields better performance than using a disk cache.

I should mention two downsides to the IBM disk cache program. First, the program only works with hard disks. IBMCACHE.SYS does not help when you read floppy disks. Even though most personal-computer work today is done on hard disks, having increased performance for floppy disks would have been pleasant. Second, the cache is not very intelligent. Many third-party, non-IBM disk cache programs offer greater features and performance benefits. But IBMCACHE.SYS is worth the price—free with every PS/2 Model 50, 60, and 80—and worthy of experimentation.

To install IBMCACHE.SYS the first time, you must run the program IBMCACHE from the Reference Diskette. The program, IBMCACHE.COM, and the disk cache, IBMCACHE.SYS, are hidden files on the disk. Thus, you cannot copy the files to your computer using COPY. Running the installation program is painless, however, and does properly set up your CONFIG.SYS file for use with the cache.

The first step is to start up DOS on your PS/2 system. After DOS is running, insert the Reference Diskette that comes with your system into drive A. Then type

   C>**A:IBMCACHE**

Your screen should look something like figure 17.1. The highlighted bar should be over the first option, Install disk cache onto drive C. When you press Enter to select the option, a window pops up giving information as shown in figure 17.2. Press **Y** to install the cache. The window will go away, the floppy and hard disk lights will go on, and a message that the cache is installed will appear in another window (see fig. 17.3). Press Enter to continue.

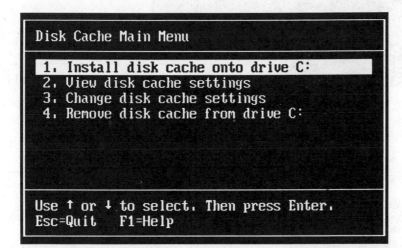

Fig. 17.1

Initial installation screen for IBMCACHE.

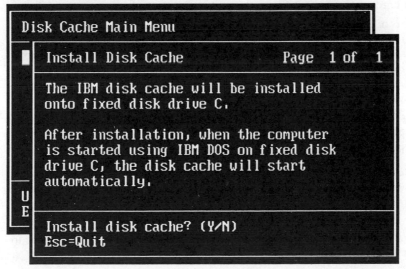

Fig. 17.2

IBMCACHE installation information

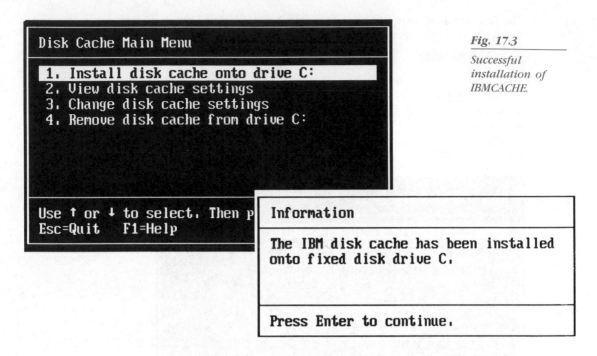

```
Disk Cache Main Menu

 1. Install disk cache onto drive C:
 2. View disk cache settings
 3. Change disk cache settings
 4. Remove disk cache from drive C:




Use ↑ or ↓ to select. Then p
Esc=Quit    F1=Help
```

```
Information

The IBM disk cache has been installed
onto fixed disk drive C.




Press Enter to continue.
```

Fig. 17.3

*Successful
installation of
IBMCACHE.*

If you have extended memory, move the highlighted bar down to option 3, Change disk cache settings, by tapping the down-arrow key twice. Press Enter.

Change the first option, Cache Location, from Low Memory to Extended Memory by pressing either the F5 or F6 special-function key. Your screen will resemble figure 17.4. Do not press Enter yet.

The initial size of the cache is 64K. A one-megabyte computer has 384K of extended memory. You can use this entire memory for your cache or you can use some of this memory for a RAM disk. If you want to change the size of the cache, use the down-arrow key to move to the next option, Cache Size. Pressing the F5 special-function key reduces the cache size. Pressing the F6 special-function key increases the size. Try pressing the F5 and F6 keys to see some of the possible sizes for the cache.

I suggest that if you don't use a RAM disk in extended memory, use a cache size of 384. If you use a RAM disk, use the leftover memory for the cache. Subtract the size of the RAM disk in K from 384 and use the resulting figure as the size of the cache.

You may notice that size choices offered when you press the F5 or F6 keys do not match your calculations. If the program does not have a number that matches your calculations, simply type the number you want.

In using the cache in low memory, you must balance your programs' need for RAM space against the cache's. My advice is leave the cache size at 64K or increase the size to 128K at most. If your cache size is too large, your programs will suffer.

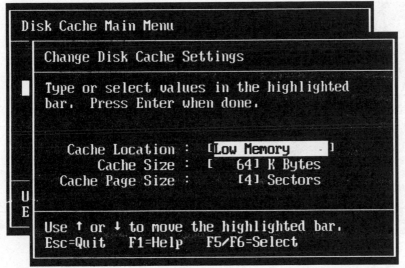

Fig. 17.4

Changing the location of IBMCACHE to extended memory.

The final option is Cache Page Size. This option specifies the number of sectors that should be read from the disk when DOS reads any information from the disk. Regardless of how many sectors a program may request that DOS read, DOS will always read this many sectors at a time. This strategy is excellent for programs that start at the beginning of a file and read to the end. It is not always good for programs that randomly read files.

The starting value for Cache Page Size is four sectors. Do not change this value initially. There is no single optimum value for this option. You and your programs must determine what is the best value. Run your system for several hours or days. If you find the performance of some of your programs declining slightly, rerun IBMCACHE and change this value to two.

Once your options are set up properly, press Enter. You will see a message stating that changes you have made have been saved (see fig. 17.5). Press Enter once more and the DOS prompt should reappear.

To start the cache program, restart DOS. Press Ctrl-Alt-Del and shortly, you should see the following message:

```
Disk Cache  Version 1.0

Copyright 1987 by IBM Corp.

Allocating Cache Buffers

Cache Initialization Complete
```

The cache has been successfully installed.

If you want to change the options once the cache has been installed, you can either rerun IBMCACHE or edit the IBMCACHE line in your CONFIG.SYS file. The syntax for the IBMCACHE.SYS program is

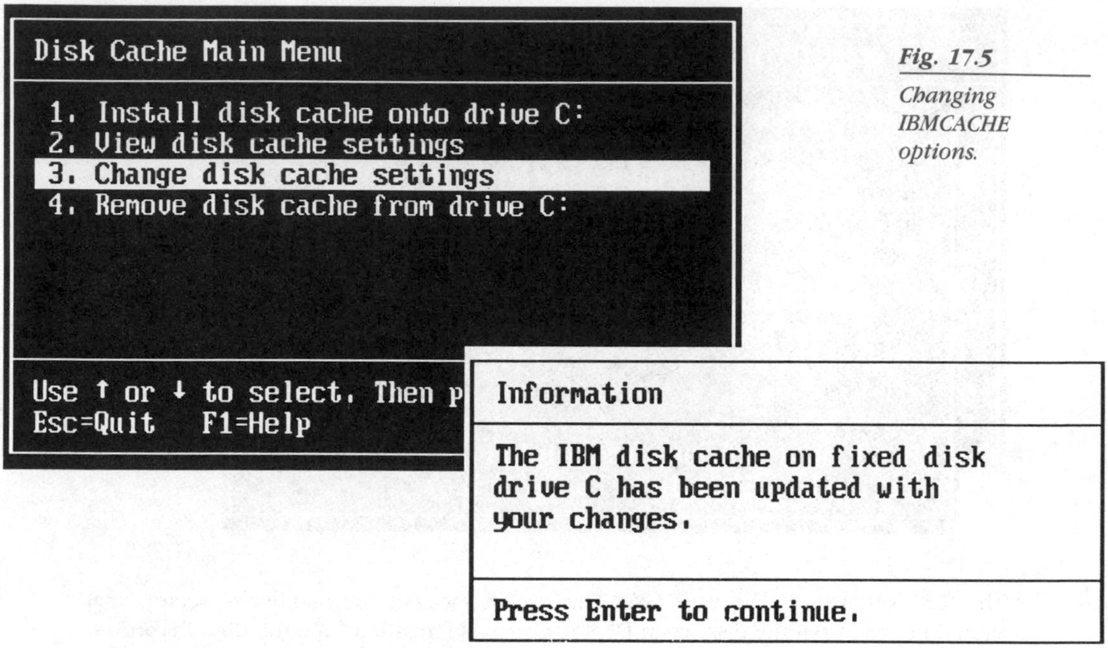

```
┌─────────────────────────────────────────────────┐
│ Disk Cache Main Menu                              │
│                                                   │
│   1. Install disk cache onto drive C:             │
│   2. View disk cache settings                     │
│ ┌───────────────────────────────────┐             │
│ │ 3. Change disk cache settings     │             │
│ └───────────────────────────────────┘             │
│   4. Remove disk cache from drive C:              │
│                                                   │
│                                                   │
│                                                   │
│ Use ↑ or ↓ to select. Then p┌──────────────────────────────────┐
│ Esc=Quit   F1=Help          │ Information                      │
└─────────────────────────────┤                                  │
                              │ The IBM disk cache on fixed disk │
                              │ drive C has been updated with    │
                              │ your changes.                    │
                              ├──────────────────────────────────┤
                              │ Press Enter to continue.         │
                              └──────────────────────────────────┘
```

Fig. 17.5

Changing IBMCACHE options.

DEVICE = *d:path*\ **IBMCACHE.SYS cachesize** /E or /NE /Psectors

d:path\ is the optional disk drive and path name to the IBMCACHE.SYS program. **cachesize** is the size of the cache in kilobytes.

The /E and /NE switches designate where the cache will be placed: /E designates extended memory and /NE designates 640K low memory. You can use either, but not both, switches.

/Psectors designates the number of disk sectors that DOS should read at once. **sectors** should be 2, 4, or 8. Notice that, unlike many DOS switches, no colon is used to separate the P from sectors.

Should you install IBMCACHE.SYS? My opinion is an unqualified "maybe." I do believe you should experiment with the cache. You may find the cache can increase the performance of your system. However, if you use many programs that do a great deal of random accessing of files, the cache could actually be detrimental. Since the cache is easy and quick to install, alter, and remove, the effort of trying the cache is painless and may help speed your operations.

Using DRIVER.SYS To Control Additional Disk Drives

DRIVER.SYS is a device driver for disk drives. On most systems, DRIVER.SYS is an exotic extension. But for some systems that use an external floppy disk drive, DRIVER.SYS is required.

In Chapter 5 you learned that when you have only one floppy disk drive, DOS establishes two logical disk drives, A and B, from the single physical disk drive. You can perform the same kind of "trickery" on any disk drive with DRIVER.SYS.

Other occasions for using DRIVER.SYS arise when you use an external floppy disk drive or a non-IBM hard disk drive that "looks like" (has the same physical characteristics as) the corresponding IBM hard disk drive. You must inform DOS that the additional disk drive is attached to your system. When you invoke DRIVER.SYS for these disk drives, DOS makes the drive an integral part of the system.

You can also load an additional copy of DRIVER.SYS so that DOS will make two logical disk drives out of the single, physical disk drive. With this technique, you can copy files between two disks on the single external disk drive.

You must use DRIVER.SYS if you use an external disk drive with any Personal Computer. You also must use DRIVER.SYS with an external disk drive used with a PS/2 computer that has two internal floppy disk drives. But you do not have to use DRIVER.SYS for the external disk drive on a PS/2 computer that has one internal floppy disk drive.

Before you use DRIVER.SYS, read the information and explanations on the directive's switches, particularly the /D switch. If you do not provide DOS with the needed information, DRIVER.SYS will not work properly.

The syntax for DRIVER.SYS is

    DEVICE = *d:path***DRIVER.SYS** **/D:ddd** */F:f* */T:ttt* */S:ss* */H:hh* **/C /N**

d: is the disk drive that holds DRIVER.SYS, and *path*\\ is the directory path to DRIVER.SYS. Both directives are optional but should be given. DRIVER.SYS has seven switches, which are described in the rest of this section.

/D:ddd is the mandatory physical disk drive number. The allowable numbers for **ddd** are 0 to 255. You use the numbers 0 to 127 for floppy disks. The first physical floppy disk drive, drive A, is 0, the second, drive B, is 1, and the third is 2. The values 3 to 127 for floppy disks are possible in theory, but IBM does not support these additional drives. For hard disk drives, you use the numbers 128 to 255. The first hard disk, drive C, is **128**, the second is **129**, and so on. As with floppy disks, the values 130 to 255 can theoretically be used for additional hard disk drives, but not in fact.

There is one potential source of confusion in giving disk drive numbers. If you have an external minifloppy disk drive for a PS/2 computer that has a single internal floppy disk, the external drive is the second physical disk drive. You use a 1 for the external disk drive.

If you give a number that corresponds to a nonexistent disk drive, DRIVER.SYS will happily install itself with no indication that anything is wrong. When you attempt to use the disk drive through its logical drive name, however, DOS will display a General Failure error. To correct the problem, you will need to edit the incorrect DRIVER.SYS entry and reboot the computer.

The /F:f switch identifies the type of disk drive used. /F:f is called the *form factor* switch. The *f* portion of the switch is a single digit from the following list:

0	160K to 360K minifloppy disk drive
1	1.2M minifloppy disk drive
2	720K microfloppy or other disk drive (any disk drive not on this list)
7	1.44M microfloppy disk drive

If you do not give the /F:f switch, a value of 2 will be used.

The /T:ttt switch indicates the number of tracks per side (or cylinder) for the disk drive. The *ttt* can range from 1 to 999, and if you do not specify the switch, a value of 80 tracks is assumed. (1.2M, 720K, and 1.44M floppy disk drives use 80 tracks.)

/S:ss indicates the number of sectors per track. The range of *ss* is 1 to 99, and if you do not specify the switch, a value of 9 sectors per track is assumed. (360K and 720K floppy disk drives use 9 sectors per track.)

The /H:hh switch indicates the maximum number of recording heads per disk drive. The range of *hh* is 1 to 99, and if you do not specify the switch, two heads per disk drive are assumed. (Except for older, single-sided minifloppy disk drives, this rule is correct for all floppy disk drives.)

Never shortchange your disk drive when you give these switches. Use the correct value. For example, don't give /S:8 or /H:1 to read 8-sector, single-sided disks on a 360K disk drive. Don't give /S:9 to read 720K disks on a 1.44M disk drive. Internally, DOS usually knows how to produce a smaller capacity disk from a higher capacity disk drive. Using settings smaller than is allowable simply shortchanges your computer capacity without adding any capabilities.

The /C switch indicates that the disk drive supports a *changeline*. This means the disk drive "knows" when the microfloppy disk has been ejected or when the minifloppy drive's door has been opened. This switch is used with 1.2M, 720K, and 1.44M disk drives on PS/2, Personal Computer AT, and 286-XT computers.

The /N switch indicates that the disk drive is *nonremovable*. Basically, the /N switch refers to a hard disk. This switch should not be used with floppy disk drives.

Table 17.4 lists the DRIVER.SYS switches for common floppy disk drives.

Here are some examples of using DRIVER.SYS. If you have a PS/2 computer with two internal disk drives, the syntax to use an external minifloppy disk drive is

DEVICE = DRIVER.SYS /D:2 /F:0 /T:40

Table 17.4
DRIVER.SYS Switches for Common Floppy Disk Drives

Disk Drive	Switches
160K/180K	**/F:0** /T:40 /S:9 /**H:1**
320K/360K	**/F:0** /T:40 /S:9 /**H:2**
1.2M	**/F:1** /T:80 /**S:15** /H:2 /**C**
720K	/F:2 /T:80 /S:9 /H:2 /**C**
1.2M	**/F:7** /T:80 /**S:18** /H:2 /**C**

Note: The /C switch is meaningful only with the PS/2, the Personal Computer AT, and PC 286-XTs. The switch should not be used with other PCs.

/D:2 designates the third disk drive. This switch is not needed if you have only one internal microfloppy disk drive. If you do not specify the **/T:40** switch, DOS will assume that the disk drive uses 80 tracks per side—an error that the 360K disk cannot handle. In this case, the switch is required. The **/F:0** is also required.

If you want to use the single external physical disk drive as two logical disk drives, you load the device driver twice. The syntax for this setup is

> **DEVICE = DRIVER.SYS /D:2 /F:0 /T:40**
> **DEVICE = DRIVER.SYS /D:2 /F:0 /T:40**

Each time the driver is loaded, the physical disk drive will be assigned an additional valid drive letter—for example D: the first time and E: the second time. You then may refer to the drive by either of the two new designations.

I will explain more about using DRIVER.SYS for additional logical disk drives later in this chapter.

To use an external 1.2M disk drive on a PS/2 computer, load the driver with this syntax line:

> **DEVICE = DRIVER.SYS /D:2 /F:1 /S:15 /C**

Because the form factor and number of sectors are different from those DOS would establish if you did not specify these switches, you must provide the **/F** and **/S** switches. Notice the /C switch, the changeline support switch. PS/2s, Personal Computer ATs, and 286-XTs can recognize and use the changeline of floppy disk drives, so you specify the /C switch.

The difference in changeline support is the reason this directive would be used for an external 720K microfloppy on a Personal Computer AT or 286-XT. The syntax for this setup is

> **DEVICE = DRIVER.SYS /D:2 /C**

Use this DRIVER.SYS syntax for an external 720K microfloppy disk drive on a PC or PC XT:

DEVICE = DRIVER.SYS /D:2

The PC and XT do not recognize disk drive changelines, so no /C switch is given. Notice that none of the other switches need be given, either. DRIVER.SYS's default settings fit the 720K disk drive.

If the 720K disk drive used in the preceding examples were an internal drive, you would use 1 for the value of the /D switch. For example, to use an internal 720K microfloppy disk drive in a Personal Computer AT, the directive is

DEVICE = DRIVER.SYS /D:1 /C

Regardless of drive type, **/D:1** designates the second internal floppy disk drive.

You can also load a copy of DRIVER.SYS to use with established disk drives. The copy of DRIVER.SYS, with the appropriate switches, will establish a second logical disk drive for the physical disk.

You do not need this technique if you have a single floppy disk drive computer. But you can use the technique when you have two disk drives. For example, suppose that you have a Personal Computer AT with 1.2M and 360K internal minifloppy disk drives. To use drive A as two logical disk drives, the directive would be

DEVICE = DRIVER.SYS /D:0 /S:15 /C /F:1

To use drive B, the 360K drive, as two logical disk drives, the directive would be

DEVICE = DRIVER.SYS /D:1 /T:40 /F:0

You could use both directives and have four logical drives from the two physical disk drives. If you have one hard disk drive, the "second" 1.2M drive would be D and the "second" 360K drive would be E. In this way, you could use either disk drive to copy files between disks.

Cautions about Logical Disk Drives

I should give you two cautions about logical disk drives. Both relate to the order of the DRIVER.SYS directives, the VDISK.SYS directive, and the disk drive names that DOS assigns to the logical disk drives.

The first caution is that the logical disk drive names that DOS assigns to DRIVER.SYS and VDISK depend on the placement of the directives in the CONFIG.SYS file. You may try to use the wrong disk drive name if you do not know how DOS assigns drive names.

Normally, CONFIG.SYS directives are *order independent*. That is, you can give the directives in any order you desire, and the computer will not change how the directive operates.

VDISK.SYS and DRIVER.SYS do not have the same independence, however. The order in which you use these directives can make a difference in how you use your computer. You can load VDISK.SYS and DRIVER.SYS in any order and the device drivers will work.

But the disk drive names will change. Whenever DOS encounters a block-device driver, DOS assigns the next highest drive letter to the device. The order is first come, first assigned.

For example, load a copy of VDISK.SYS on a hard disk system. DOS assigns the disk drive name D: to the RAM disk. If you load a second copy of VDISK.SYS (this works only on a machine that has extended memory), DOS assigns the drive name E: to the second RAM disk.

Instead of VDISK, load a copy of DRIVER.SYS for the external floppy disk drive on the same computer. DOS assigns the external disk drive the name D:. Load another copy of DRIVER.SYS (for example, to copy disks on the external disk drive) and DOS assigns the logical name E: to this disk drive.

Remember that additional hard disks or additional logical disks add to the starting letter. For example, the hard disk drive on a 44M PS/2 system has the drive names C: and D:. Additional partitions of the hard disk always get the next highest available disk drive letters before drives created by CONFIG.SYS directives are considered. Hence, the second partition of the hard disk is named D:. VDISK, if used, is assigned drive E:. DRIVER.SYS, if used instead of VDISK, would be assigned E:.

The potential for further confusion comes when several block device drivers are loaded. The order of loading, which is determined by the order of the directives in the CONFIG.SYS file, determines what disk drive names will be assigned by DOS.

If you load VDISK.SYS first and DRIVER.SYS second, the RAM disk gets the next available disk drive letter (D). DRIVER.SYS will be one letter higher than the RAM disk (E). If you interchange the lines that hold the two directives, the disk drive names will be interchanged. DRIVER.SYS will be named D and VDISK.SYS will be named E.

Load two copies of DRIVER.SYS, for example, for a Personal Computer AT with a 1.2M and a 360K floppy disk drive. The lines are arranged in this order:

    DEVICE = DRIVER.SYS /D:0 /S:15 /C /F:1
    DEVICE = DRIVER.SYS /D:1 /T:40 /F:0

DOS assigns D to the 1.2M disk and E to the 360K disk drive. In other words, drive A and logical disk drive D will be the same physical disk drive. Drive B and logical disk drive E will be the same. Reverse the order of the lines and disk drives A and E are the same physical disk drive; drives B and D are the same disk drive.

Put the line **DEVICE = VDISK.SYS** in your CONFIG.SYS file before the two DRIVER.SYS lines, and the result is that the VDISK is drive D. Drives A and E would be the same; drives B and F would be the same. Put the VDISK line after the DRIVER.SYS lines and VDISK becomes drive F.

When you use DRIVER.SYS and VDISK.SYS or multiple copies of DRIVER.SYS, plan which drive names each logical disk drive should have. Also consider any logical disk drive DOS automatically adds for a partitioned hard disk. Then add the directives in the order of the disk drive letters—lower letter driver before higher letter driver.

For example, I run an external minifloppy disk drive on a 40M PS/2, but I also use VDISK. The hard disk is assigned drives C and D. DOS recognizes the physical minifloppy disk drive as B. To copy files between minifloppy disks without using the hard disk, I invoke DRIVER.SYS once to make two logical disk drives out of the single physical disk drive. However, because I use the copy operation infrequently and I use the RAM disk more, I want VDISK to be drive E, the next letter after the two hard disks. The lines in my CONFIG.SYS file are

DEVICE = VDISK.SYS 360 512 64
DEVICE = DRIVER.SYS /D:1 /T:40 /F:0

VDISK is drive E. The external disk drive is logical drive F (and physical disk drive B). Because VDISK appears first in the CONFIG.SYS file, DOS assigns VDISK the next available drive letter (E). The copy of DRIVER.SYS, which handles the external disk drive, is assigned the next ascending letter (F).

If I wanted the external disk drive to be E and VDISK to be F, I would reorder the lines like this:

DEVICE = DRIVER.SYS /D:1 /T:40 /F:0
DEVICE = VDISK.SYS 360 512 64

The second caution concerns using DRIVER.SYS with an external disk drive. If you have an external disk drive, the DRIVER.SYS line for this drive should appear before any additional DRIVER.SYS lines for other drives. If you reverse the order and use a copy of DRIVER.SYS for any other disk drive, you can "cover up" and lose the use of the external disk drive. This problem occurs if you do not have a system with one internal floppy and one internal hard disk. To simplify the situation, make the first DRIVER.SYS directive the one that concerns the external disk drive.

DRIVER.SYS has two purposes. DRIVER.SYS is a required device driver when you use a non-IBM hard disk drive, or if you use an external disk drive on the PC family of computers. DRIVER.SYS is required on PS/2 computers when two internal floppy disk drives are already in use. DRIVER.SYS can optionally make additional logical disk drives from the one physical disk drive.

I suggest that you use DRIVER.SYS only when you need to: when you use a non-IBM disk drive, when you use an external microfloppy disk drive on a PC-family computer, or when you use an external minifloppy on a PS/2 that has two internal floppy disk drives. Unless you have a compelling reason, I suggest that you avoid using DRIVER.SYS to create additional logical disk drives. If you need to copy files between floppy disks, first copy to the hard disk, and then copy to the second floppy disk. Or use DISKCOPY to make a copy of the entire disk. These methods cause fewer problems than using DRIVER.SYS.

Using Expanded Memory with DOS V4

Two device drivers, XMA2EMS.SYS and XMAEMS.SYS, are provided with DOS V4 to allow you to use expanded memory with your system. While intended for IBM memory adapters, you can successfully use these drivers with other brands, including the Orchid RamQuest™ 50/60 memory add-on.

You can use XMA2EMS.SYS if you have either an expanded memory adapter or an 80386-based computer with the XMAEMS.SYS driver installed.

The syntax is

DEVICE = XMA2EMS.SYS FRAME=xxxx *P254=yyyy P255=zzzz /X:aa*

xxxx can be any page from C000 to E000. Each will be 64K in size. P254 and P255 represent 16K pages of memory used by FASTOPEN and BUFFERS, respectively, to perform their functions in expanded memory. *yyyy* and *zzzz* are memory addresses of the pages you want to use for these functions. */X:aa* is used to limit the driver from using less than the maximum total available memory.

If you substitute a value *aa* in multiples of 16K pages, XMA2EMS.SYS will use only that amount for EMS. For example, if you use /X:8, 128K of EMS memory would be defined from the total memory on your expanded/extended memory board.

Consult the manuals furnished with your applications programs to see how to allocate expanded memory in your system. I had to check the Hewlett-Packard manual that came with my ScanJet to determine how to resolve memory conflicts with that device.

Early users of DOS V4 reported serious problems with IBM's EMS support, because it implements expanded memory in a way that is different from most of the other EMS drivers available. In particular, you can run into trouble when you install FASTOPEN and BUFFERS through CONFIG.SYS, if you tell DOS to use expanded memory for each of these.

I was one of the first victims of this bug. I usually install a new version of DOS and use it daily as a way of gaining familiarity. Unfortunately, I managed to lock up my computer (or I *thought* it was locked up) while testing Ventura Publisher Version 2.0. Since the keyboard didn't respond to Ctrl-Alt-Del, I waited for a few minutes (just in case Ventura was not locked up, but was just writing a file to disk) and then turned off the system.

Surprise. When I turned the computer back on and logged onto drive D, I was unable to access any files. CHKDSK informed me that I had 22 megabytes of free disk space and 22 megabytes' worth of lost clusters in a couple thousand chains. My disk's file allocation table (FAT) had gotten garbled during its sojourn in DOS V4's EMS-based disk buffers.

The thought of sorting through a thousand files to see what was what didn't appeal to me. I also had committed the cardinal sin of not yet purchasing the latest version of the Norton Utilities (Release 4.5), which is compatible with DOS V4. (This latest edition has a nifty program called the Norton Disk Doctor which would have, I think, salvaged the files on the disk.)

What did I do? I reformatted the hard disk. It wasn't as bad as it sounds. That system has 124 megabytes of disk storage (the original IBM 44M Seagate® drive, plus an add-on 80-megabyte Seagate drive), divided into drives C, D, E, F, and G.

Drive D, as it happens, is used only to store applications programs. All data resides on other drives and is backed up regularly. So, all I had to do was restore all the applications programs to drive D.

Later versions of DOS V4 don't have this EMS bug. However, you're well advised to be extra careful in using the IBM driver until all the kinks have been worked out.

XMASYS is designed to be used with 80386-based systems. It allows you to use the extended memory that can be addressed as though it were EMS memory. You can use this driver to define the number of 16K pages of extended memory to be devoted to expanded memory. Use the following syntax:

DEVICE = XMAEM.SYS *aa*

aa is the number of pages to allocate (divide the amount of memory by 16 to calculate this figure). This driver must be loaded *before* XMA2EMS.SYS in your CONFIG.SYS file. Again, you may need to refer to the software and hardware manuals for your system to install this driver properly. (I warned you that these drivers might not be easy for the neophyte!)

New DOS V4 CONFIG.SYS Commands

In addition to the new device drivers, DOS V4 provides three additional CONFIG.SYS directives: REM, SWITCHES, and INSTALL.

REM allows you to insert remarks in your CONFIG.SYS file. You can leave notes to yourself (or others) explaining what particular lines do. This is especially helpful if you need non-DOS device drivers for your hardware. You can also temporarily remove a CONFIG.SYS statement by prefacing it with a REM directive. When you test a new configuration, you can enable only those features you want.

SWITCHES turns off extended keyboard functions. This directive works like the ANSI.SYS /K switch. The syntax is:

SWITCHES = /K

INSTALL allows you to load from CONFIG.SYS certain utility programs that remain in memory. In previous versions of DOS, you had these programs from the DOS prompt or through a batch file, such as AUTOEXEC.BAT. DOS V4 supports loading any of the following using INSTALL:

FASTOPEN.EXE
KEYB.COM
NLSFUNC.EXE
SHARE.EXE

The syntax for using INSTALL is

INSTALL = **program**

program is the name and path of the utility you wish to load. I tried INSTALL with some non-DOS utilities, including SideKick and KEYWORKS, and it seemed to work fine.

Making a CONFIG.SYS File

You may want to use the following major directives with DOS V3: BUFFERS, DEVICE, FCBS, and FILES. You can use any text editor, including EDLIN, or the COPY command to make the CONFIG.SYS file. Remember that the system-configuration file must be called CONFIG.SYS.

Following is my copy of CONFIG.SYS for an IBM PS/2 Model 60 and a Personal Computer AT:

```
DEVICE = C:\SYS\SJDRIVER.SYS /M
DEVICE=C:\SYS\HPSCANER.SYS
REM DEVICE=C:\SYS\RAMQUEST.SYS Slot=7 EMSsize=1024
REM DEVICE=C:\SYS\RQEMM.SYS
DEVICE=C:\SYS\XMA2EMS.SYS FRAME=C000 P254=D000 P255=D400 /X:32
DEVICE=C:\SYS\IBMCACHE.SYS 1900 /E /P8
LASTDRIVE=G
BUFFERS=10,5 /X
COUNTRY=001,,c:\SYS\COUNTRY.SYS
DEVICE=c:\SYS\DISPLAY.SYS CON=(,437,1)
SHELL=C:\DOS\COMMAND.COM /P /MSG
DEVICE=C:\SYS\ANSI.SYS /L
REM DEVICE=C:\SYS\VDISK.SYS 360 /X:8
REM INSTALL C:\DOS\SHARE.EXE
INSTALL C:\DOS\FASTOPEN.EXE C:=(100,50) /X
FILES = 99
```

Examining this specialized file may provide you with some tips useful in building a customized CONFIG.SYS file of your own.

The first two lines load special third-party device drivers needed to operate my HP Scan-Jet scanner. You'll need to consult the syntax recommendations of your software or hardware vendors to see exactly how to phrase your own DEVICE directives when installing such drivers.

The next two lines would install the EMS drivers supplied with my RamQuest memory card if they weren't "commented out" with remarks. Why did I do this? Some applications aren't compatible with DOS V4's EMS support. I don't use such applications often, but when I do, I can remove the remarks from my CONFIG.SYS file, and insert them in front of the XMA2EMS.SYS device directive instead. Then I can reboot and use the new configuration. There is no need to look up the syntax in a manual; the commands are already in the file.

The LASTDRIVE and BUFFERS commands were explained earlier in this chapter. I use only 10 buffers at the moment because I find the IBMCACHE program reduces the need for a larger number of buffers.

The COUNTRY and DISPLAY.SYS commands are explained in Chapter 18. We've already talked about the use of ANSI.SYS and FILES. Note that I've commented out an INSTALL command to load SHARE.EXE. When I first got DOS V4 I repartitioned one of my hard disks to take advantage of the greater-than-32-megabyte disk volumes allowed. SHARE.EXE must be loaded to support this feature. However, I found there were so many compatibility problems with the large volumes that I no longer wished to use them. So, I "temporarily" removed SHARE.EXE from my permanent CONFIG.SYS file. Some of the reasons for this approach arc discussed later in the book along with the changes made in FASTOPEN reflected here.

This sample file assumes that you have a subdirectory called \SYS on your hard disk and that device drivers are in this subdirectory.

I use the following CONFIG.SYS file on my floppy disk Toshiba 1100+(R):

```
BUFFERS = 20
FILES = 20
FCBS = 20,20
LASTDRIVE = F
DEVICE = ANSI.SYS
DEVICE = VDISK.SYS 64 128 64
```

Notice that I have assumed here that the device-driver software is in the root directory of my start-up disk. I also have increased the number of BUFFERS to 20.

Put the appropriate file in the root directory of your DOS boot disk. If you are using a hard disk system, such as the PC XT or Personal Computer AT, put the file in the root directory of the hard disk. If you have included the fifth or sixth lines (**DEVICE = ANSI.SYS** or **DEVICE = VDISK.SYS**), copy the ANSI.SYS file and/or the VDISK.SYS file to the disk you will use for booting.

If you use a 256K PC, you may want to omit the VDISK line and reduce the number of buffers to ten.

After you have saved the file, reboot the system, using your new disk. DOS will read the CONFIG.SYS file and alter itself to accommodate any directives in the file.

If you change the CONFIG.SYS file, the changes will be implemented the next time you boot the system from the disk. Remember that DOS reads CONFIG.SYS only when DOS starts up.

Summary

In this chapter, you learned the following important points:

❏ When DOS starts, it can alter system settings through instructions in the CONFIG.SYS file.

❏ The CONFIG.SYS file must be in the root directory of the boot disk. When you alter CONFIG.SYS, the changes do not occur until DOS is restarted.

❏ VDISK, the DOS RAM-disk software, can speed disk operations if your computer has sufficient random-access memory.

❏ IBMCACHE, the DOS disk cache, can speed up certain disk operations.

❏ DRIVER, the device driver for disk drives, must be used for external or non-IBM hard disk drives. DRIVER can also be used to make additional logical disk drives from one physical disk drive.

In Chapter 18, you'll learn how to make DOS operate in languages other than English.

18

Making DOS Go International

The Personal Computer, PS/2 computers, and MS-DOS, the foundation of PC DOS, are American inventions. But DOS is an international operating system. Vast changes in MS-DOS V2.11 made DOS easier to use in countries outside the United States. Additional changes occurred in each revision of DOS V3, the most radical changes since DOS V2.11 being in DOS V3.3. DOS V4 added some minor enhancements. If you use the computer in a country other than the United States, these changes make the computer more natural to use.

DOS V3 and V4 have several international features seldom noticed by North American users. One feature is that the date and time can be displayed in three different formats. Also, DOS can inform a program on request which characters to use for the decimal point, the thousand separator, and the currency symbol. DOS can even tell the program whether the currency symbol precedes or follows the amount and whether a space should separate the symbol from the amount.

In addition, the display and keyboard of Personal Computers and PS/2s can be changed to produce characters that are appropriate for countries other than the United States. Although users outside the United States have had these programs since DOS V1.1, IBM now distributes the programs as part of DOS V3 and V4.

To make DOS go international, you must alter your CONFIG.SYS and AUTOEXEC.BAT files. These changes are recommended only for those who need international capability. If you do not need this capability, I suggest that you skip this chapter.

To customize DOS for international use, you may need to perform several actions:

1. Add the following items to your CONFIG.SYS file:

    a. the COUNTRY directive

    b. the DEVICE = DISPLAY.SYS directive

    c. the DEVICE = PRINTER.SYS directive

2. Add the NLSFUNC, MODE, CHCP, and/or KEYB commands to your AUTOEXEC.BAT file.

313

To understand how DOS's international character support works, you first need to understand the concept of *code pages*.

Understanding Code Pages

Code pages allow the computer to use, display, and print non-English language characters with minimal effort on your part.

You may recall from earlier discussions that your computer communicates to peripherals using ASCII. ASCII is the standard manner of taking the numeric values 0 to 255 and translating the values into letters, numbers, and symbols. The dots on your screen that form the visible characters are the graphic representations of those ASCII numbers.

Think of your computer as having three punchboards, one each for the keyboard, video display, and printer. Each punchboard has holes arranged in a 16-by-16 square, for a total of 256 holes. You can move to any hole, punch it, and get the message or prize inside. For example, if you punch the hole marked 65, out pops the character whose ASCII value is 65—the letter A.

When you press the A key, your computer punches the video adapter's hole for 65. The adapter, in turn, looks up the numeric value and finds the pattern of dots that corresponds to the character. The adapter turns on the appropriate dots, and the letter A appears on the screen.

Each video adapter displays a dot-formed representation of ASCII characters. The common name for the "shape" of characters is *font*. Depending on the adapter in use, the fonts are switchable, meaning that different character sets can be displayed.

Basically, a code page is a font set. You may recognize names for typewriter and typesetting faces, such as Courier, Elite, and Times Roman. Similarly, code pages allow for different typefaces of English and international language characters.

Five video adapters are available: the Monochrome Adapter, the Color/Graphics Display (CGA), the Enhanced Color/Graphics Adapter (EGA), the Liquid Crystal Display (LCD) of the PC Convertible laptop, and the Video Graphics Array (VGA) of the PS/2. (The LCD and VGA are not truly adapters but are integrated circuitry built into the computers and are responsible for the display of information.)

The VGA, the EGA, and the LCD displays can use the five international font sets listed below. Depending on the punchboard (code page) used, you can display various language characters as indicated in table 18.1. Monochrome and CGA adapters cannot support switchable code pages.

Suppose, for example, that you punch the hole for ASCII character 236. Each font set except the Multilingual code page displays ∞. The Multilingual code page displays ý. Punch position number 157 on the North American set, and you get the ¥. Punch the same position on the Multilingual or Norwegian-Danish sets, and you get an Ø . The Portuguese and French Canadian sets have Ù in this position. Many characters are identical in all five sets, but some are customized for various localities.

Table 18.1
Code Page Numbers

Font	Code Page Number
United States (English)	437
Multilingual	850
Portuguese	860
Canada (French)	863
Nordic	865

Appendix G contains the five code pages used by PCs and PS/2 computers. The major difference between these code pages is the characters whose values are in the range of 128 through 255 (columns 9 through F on the charts). There is no widely used prevailing standard for these characters. DOS sacrifices some of the scientific and graphics characters in this range and substitutes the needed language characters.

Printers also use code pages; therefore, what can be displayed on the screen can be reproduced on the printed page. DOS V3.3 includes code pages for the IBM ProPrinter™ and Quietwriter® III printers. DOS V4 also supports IBM ProPrinters Models 4201, 4202, 4207, and 4208. You can expect other printer manufacturers to follow Microsoft and IBM's lead in building code-page support into DOS and provide code pages for their printers sometime soon.

To use a particular language font, you select a starting code page and you can change code pages freely. However, you may find code page switching completely unnecessary if your video adapter and printer start with the "right" code page. Most North American users will find the built-in DOS code pages adequate and will probably never use code page switching.

However, switching code pages may be important for international users, including those who have files that were established in early versions of DOS. In addition, the capability of changing fonts "on the fly" is valuable to those who need the capability. International users will find that code pages are a logical and powerful way to handle languages.

Using DOS's International Directives

DOS uses directives and device drivers to set up your computer to use a particular character set. The directives are COUNTRY, NLSFUNC, MODE (in three "flavors"), and CHCP. The device drivers are KEYB.SYS, PRINTER.SYS, and DRIVER.SYS. Some directives/device drivers are included in the CONFIG.SYS file. Other commands required for international support may be included in your AUTOEXEC.BAT file so that they are run each time you boot your system.

Changing the CONFIG.SYS File

You include in your CONFIG.SYS file the COUNTRY directive and two drivers that control devices attached to your system: DISPLAY.SYS for the display and PRINTER.SYS for the printer. The next two sections discuss these changes to CONFIG.SYS.

Adding the COUNTRY Directive

The first step in making DOS go international is issuing the COUNTRY directive to inform DOS how to customize itself for your location. When you issue the COUNTRY directive, DOS automatically changes the date and time formats to conform to the practice in the country specified. In addition, DOS can tell inquiring programs which characters to use for lists, currency symbols, thousands, and decimal fractions.

The syntax for COUNTRY differs in different versions of DOS. The syntax for DOS V3.0 through V3.2 is

   COUNTRY = nnn

nnn is a three-digit country code.

The syntax for DOS V3.3 and V4 is

   COUNTRY = countrycode *codepage d:path\filename.ext*

countrycode is the mandatory three-digit code for the country. The default country code is that of the United States, 001.

codepage is the code page number (see table 18.2). North American users of English should use the United States code page (number 437). If you cannot find a code page number for your country, the Multilingual code page (850) is probably your best choice.

d:path\filename.ext is the path and file name for the file that contains country information. If you use the COUNTRY directive, but do not provide this a file name, DOS assumes that the information is in the COUNTRY.SYS file (which is supplied on the DOS Startup/Operating or Startup disk).

As you can see in the syntax, the code page and the country information file need not be specified. To skip one of these optional elements, use two commas between the country code and the COUNTRY.SYS file:

   COUNTRY = 001,,C:\COUNTRY.SYS

The two commas instruct DOS to use the default code page. You may also omit the file name and give either the country code or the country code and code page:

   COUNTRY = 001

or

   COUNTRY = 001 437

Table 18.2
Country Codes

Country/Language	Country Code	Keyboard Code	Existing Code Page	New Code Page
Arabic	785	none	none	none
Australia	061	US	437	850
Belgium	032	BE	437	850
Canada (English)	001	US	437	850
Canada (French)	002	CF	863	850
Denmark	045	DK	865	850
Finland	358	SU	437	850
France	033	FR	437	850
Germany	049	GR	437	850
Israel	972	none	437	850
Italy	039	IT	437	850
Japan*	081	none	437	932
Korea*	082	none	437	934
Latin America	003	LA	437	850
Netherlands	031	NL	437	850
Norway	047	NO	865	850
PRC*	088	none	437	938
Portugal	351	PO	860	850
Spain	034	SP	437	850
Sweden	046	SV	437	850
Switzerland (French)	041	SF	437	850
Switzerland (German)	041	SG	437	850
Taiwan*	086	none	437	936
United Kingdom	044	UK	437	850
United States	001	US	437	850

*Added in DOS V4. Supported only on versions sold in Asia, for use on Asian hardware.

Note that if you use the COUNTRY directive, DOS searches for the file COUNTRY.SYS in the root directory of the boot disk. If DOS cannot find the file, it displays the message

```
Bad or missing \COUNTRY.SYS
```

I strongly recommend that you always give the full file name for COUNTRY.SYS. This step will prevent the possibility that DOS will be unable to locate the file.

Table 18.3 shows how DOS changes the display when you use various country codes.

DOS V3.3 and V4 make additional information about a country available to programs, including information about switching lowercase and uppercase letters and sorting characters' equivalents. DOS maintains information on sorting characters based on the country code and the code page, both of which affect the sorting order.

Table 18.3
Effects of Country Codes on Display

	US-English	UK	Sweden
Country code	1	44	46
Code page*	437	437	437
Currency symbol	$	£	SEK
Digits after decimal separator in currency	2	2	2
Thousand separator	,	,	.
Decimal separator	.	.	.
Data list separator	,	,	;
Date separator	-	-	-
Time separator	:	:	.
Time format	24-hour	24-hour	24-hour
Current date	Tue 3-21-1989	Tue 21-03-1989	Tue 1989-03-21
Current time	16:24:39.01	16:24:39.01	16.24.39,01

*Although the country code currently supports 19 countries (23 with DOS V4), only five code pages are available.

COUNTRY does have some limitations. One is that DOS does not automatically display its prompts in languages other than English. For that refinement, DOS messages must be rewritten.

Adding DISPLAY.SYS

In order to display more than one code page or to print non-English language characters, you must use DISPLAY.SYS and PRINTER.SYS. Using DISPLAY.SYS in your CONFIG.SYS file allows you to switch code pages without restarting DOS. Using PRINTER.SYS allows you to download a font table to certain printers so that they can print non-English language and graphics characters.

The DISPLAY driver allows you to switch code pages on video adapters other than Monochrome or Color/Graphics adapters. The adapters that can be used effectively with DISPLAY.SYS are the PC Convertible LCD, the EGA, and the VGA. In DOS V4, DISPLAY.SYS checks your hardware to determine the type of active display if you don't specify the adapter type.

The line to add to the CONFIG.SYS file is

DEVICE = *d:path* \ **DISPLAY.SYS CON:** = **(type,** *hw_codepage,*
     (added_codepages, subfonts))

d:path \ is the drive name and path to DISPLAY.SYS. If DISPLAY.SYS is not in the root directory of your starting disk, give the disk drive and path name.

CON: is the DOS device name for the console—the keyboard and display. The colon is optional.

The parameters to DISPLAY.SYS are enclosed in two sets of parentheses. The first parameter, the display type, can be any of the following:

MONO	Monochrome Adapter
CGA	Color/Graphics Adapter
EGA	Enhanced Color/Graphics Adapter or PS/2
LCD	Convertible LCD

The second parameter is *hw_codepage*, which stands for the *hardware* code page built into your adapter. The possible values are 437, 850, 860, 863, and 865, the five code pages that IBM provides with DOS V3.3 and V4. If you do not give the *hw_codepage*, DISPLAY.SYS uses the code page given to the COUNTRY directive.

added_codepages is the maximum number of additional code pages the adapter can use. The range is from 0 (if you have a monochrome or CGA adapter) to 12 (if you are using the PC Convertible, an EGA adapter, or the PS/2). *added_codepages* actually refers to the number of code pages you can prepare and use with the MODE command, which is discussed later in this chapter.

subfonts refers to the dot resolution of the character—9 by 14, 9 by 16, or 8 by 8. This number can range from 0 to 2, depending on the adapter. For the Monochrome and CGA adapters, the default *subfonts* value is 0. For the LCD display, the value is 1, and for the EGA or PS/2, *subfonts* can be 1 or 2. For the adapter type EGA, DOS defaults to 2 subfonts if you omit this parameter.

Here is a sample DISPLAY.SYS directive for those who use an EGA or VGA and 437 as the hardware code page:

DEVICE = C:\SYS\DISPLAY.SYS CON = (EGA,437,1)

This command specifies an EGA display (EGA is used for both the EGA and VGA displays), 437 for the the starting code page, and 1 additional code page. This example assumes that the DISPLAY.SYS file is placed in a subdirectory on drive C called \SYS. The following command line assumes that an EGA display is used and that the existing code page (that is, the default code page for the country where the computer is sold) is 863, for French-speaking Canada:

DEVICE = C:\SYS\DISPLAY.SYS CON = (EGA,850,2)

Notice that the existing code page is 863, but that the specified code page is 850. If your existing code page is not 437, always use 850 as the new code page and 2 as the value for added code pages.

Note: If you use both ANSI.SYS and DISPLAY.SYS in your CONFIG.SYS file, the ANSI.SYS directive must appear before the DISPLAY.SYS directive. If the order is reversed, you lose the capability of ANSI.SYS.

Adding PRINTER.SYS

PRINTER.SYS allows the characters shown in the code page sets to be printed on certain printers. DOS V3.3 supports code pages on these two printers:

IBM ProPrinter Model 4201
IBM Quietwriter III Model 5202

DOS V4 adds support for these printers:

IBM ProPrinter Model 4202
IBM ProPrinter Model 4207
IBM ProPrinter Model 4208

To use code page switching with these printers, you must add the DEVICE= PRINTER.SYS line to your CONFIG.SYS file. The syntax for PRINTER.SYS is similar to that for DISPLAY.SYS:

DEVICE = *d:path***PRINTER.SYS LPTx:** = (**type**, *hw_codepage*,
added_codepages) . . .

or

DEVICE = *d:path***PRINTER.SYS LPTx:** = (**type**,
(*hw_codepage1,hw_codepage2*), *added_codepages*) . . .

d:path\\ is the drive name and path to PRINTER.SYS. If PRINTER.SYS is not in the root directory of your starting disk, give the disk drive and path name.

LPTx: is the DOS device name for the line printer. The **x** is the number of the parallel printer: 1, 2, or 3. The colon is optional.

The parameters to PRINTER.SYS are enclosed in parentheses. The printer **type** is the model number for the printer: 4201 for the ProPrinters (with DOS V3.3) or 4202, 4207, or 4208 (with DOS V4) and 5202 for the Quietwriter III.

The second parameter, *hw_codepage*, stands for the *hardware* code page built into your printer. As with DISPLAY.SYS, the possible values are 437, 850, 860, 863, and 865.

There is a difference between the possible *hw_codepage* values for the printers. The ProPrinters have one font built into the device. This font is moved to the printer's RAM. When you change the code page for this printer, DOS overwrites the font that is in memory.

The Quietwriter III, on the other hand, uses hardware font cartridges. Each cartridge holds several code pages in the same type style. To use a particular code page, you must select the correct cartridge. The Quietwriter III cannot inform DOS when a cartridge has been changed; DOS must assume that the correct cartridge is in the printer.

The result is you can specify one hardware code page for the ProPrinters and two for the Quietwriter III. However, if you specify two code pages for the Quietwriter III, you cannot prepare any code pages for the printer—DOS assumes that both code pages are fixed in hardware.

For the ProPrinters, the value for *hw_codepage* follows the same guidelines as for DIS-PLAY.SYS. For the Quietwriter III, follow the same guidelines with one exception. You may specify two hardware code pages, in which case DOS assumes that no code pages should be prepared for the Quietwriter III.

added_codepages is the maximum number of additional code pages that the printer can use. *added_codepages* can range from 0 to 12.

For the ProPrinters, if you either specify 0 or omit *added_codepages*, you get the Pro-Printer's built-in font. If you specify a number other than 0, the number is the maximum number of additional code pages the ProPrinters can use. Generally, use 1 if your hardware code page is 437; otherwise, use 2.

For the Quietwriter III, if you have specified two code pages, you must either omit *added_codepages* or specify a value of 0. The reason is that no code pages can be prepared if you have specified two *hw_codepages*.

An example of the directive to use with a ProPrinter is

DEVICE = C:\SYS\PRINTER.SYS LPT1 = (4201, 437,1)

This directive calls for a ProPrinter connected to the first parallel port (LPT1), for 437 as the starting code page, and for 1 additional code page. As with DISPLAY.SYS, this example assumes that the PRINTER.SYS file is placed in a subdirectory on drive C called \SYS. If PRINTER.SYS is in a different directory, change the disk drive and path information but leave all other information the same.

The following command assumes that the ProPrinter is used and that the existing code page is 863 (Canada-French):

DEVICE = C:\SYS\PRINTER.SYS LPT1 = (4201,850,2)

Notice that the existing code page is 863, but that the specified code page is 850. If your existing code page is not 437, always use 850 as the new code page, and use 2 as the value for added code pages.

Here is an example for the Quietwriter III that uses a 437 and 850 code page cartridge:

DEVICE = C:\SYS\PRINTER.SYS LPT1 = (5202,(437,850),0)

This directive follows the general form of the ProPrinter directive, but with the model number of the Quietwriter III (5202). Notice the parentheses that enclose the two code pages. If you give two code pages, you must surround them with parentheses. Also, the number of added code pages is set to 0.

If you have more than one of these printers attached to your system, you can include that information on one directive line.

Assuming that the ProPrinter is connected to LPT1 and the Quietwriter III is connected to LPT2, the command would be

DEVICE = C:\SYS\PRINTER.SYS LPT1 = (4201,437,2) LPT2 = (5202,(437,850),0)

You simply use a space after the information for LPT1 and before the word **LPT2**. DOS loads PRINTER.SYS and sets up both printers at the same time.

Changing the AUTOEXEC.BAT File

DOS V3.3 and V4 international language support depends not only on the COUNTRY directive and the two device drivers, but also on the following additional directives to set up and switch code pages for your display, printer, and keyboard:

NLSFUNC	Enables the CHCP command
CHCP	Activates (changes) code pages
KEYB	Loads and activates code pages for the keyboard
MODE	Loads and activates code pages for the display and printer

These directives may be included in the AUTOEXEC.BAT file. Table 18.4 summarizes the effect these directives have on DOS, on the console (the CON: device, including both the display and the keyboard), and on the printer. You may want to refer to this table as you read through the rest of the chapter.

Table 18.4
Effects of Various Commands and Device Drivers
on DOS, the Console, and the Printer

Command/Device Driver		*CON*		
	DOS	*Display*	*Keyboard*	*Printer*
DISPLAY.SYS	X	X	O	-
PRINTER.SYS	-	-	-	X
NLSFUNC	X	-	-	-
CHCP	X	X	X	X
MODE PREPARE	-	X	O	X
MODE SELECT	-	X	O	X
MODE REFRESH	-	X	O	X
KEYB	-	O	X	-

Key:
    X Sets or changes
    O Affects but does not set or change
    - No effect

CHCP, NLSFUNC, KEYB, and MODE are closely linked. CHCP depends on NLSFUNC, and KEYB depends on MODE and CHCP. We'll look at each command and explain briefly what it does, how to use it, and what steps must be performed before and after you use the command.

Supporting National Languages with NLSFUNC

NLSFUNC, the *national language support function*, is a DOS V3.3 program that performs two tasks. First, it hooks into DOS and provides programs with extended information about the specified country. Second, the program allows you to use the CHCP (change code page) command. If you will be switching code pages for any device except the keyboard, you need this command. Fortunately, NLSFUNC is one of the easiest commands to use.

The syntax for NLSFUNC is

   dc:pathc**NLSFUNC** *d:path**COUNTRY.SYS*

The *dc:* is the name of the disk drive that holds the command, and *pathc*\\ is the directory path to the command. The single parameter to NLSFUNC is the full file name to the COUNTRY.SYS file. To simplify the use of NLSFUNC, use the COUNTRY directive in your CONFIG.SYS file and give the full file name for the country information file. Also, place the NLSFUNC command in your AUTOEXEC.BAT file. Certain applications programs may require you to run NLSFUNC. These programs use the new extended country information provided by DOS V3.3. Your program's documentation should state whether the program requires NLSFUNC.

Because NLSFUNC becomes part of DOS, using NLSFUNC increases DOS by almost 2,700 bytes. NLSFUNC remains in memory until you turn off the machine or restart DOS. You need to run NLSFUNC only once after you have started DOS. Running NLSFUNC a second time produces an error message.

Changing the Code Page with CHCP

CHCP, or *change code page*, was new in DOS V3.3 and is the simplest method of changing code pages. Because CHCP can affect the keyboard also, those using the KEYB program should be familiar with CHCP.

The syntax for CHCP is

   CHCP *codepage*

where *codepage*—the new code page for DOS and all the devices to use—can be 437, 850, 860, 863, or 865.

Using CHCP sets the code page for DOS and establishes information about sorting and about switching lowercase and uppercase characters. CHCP also sets the code page for devices. If you have included DISPLAY.SYS in your CONFIG.SYS file, CHCP sets the code page for the display. If you have included PRINTER.SYS in CONFIG.SYS, CHCP sets the code page for the printer. If you have used the KEYB program, CHCP sets the keyboard's code page as well. Because of these capabilities, CHCP can be thought of as a *system-wide* program. If you have set up any device to use code page switching, CHCP will set the device.

Before you use CHCP, you must first be sure you have

- issued the NLSFUNC command
- given the COUNTRY directive in the CONFIG.SYS file
- issued the necessary MODE CODEPAGE PREPARE commands

(MODE is covered later in this chapter.)

The command for setting the code pages for DOS and all the devices to 437 is

CHCP 437

You can get the current code page that DOS is using by simply issuing the CHCP command without a code page number:

CHCP

Interestingly, CHCP can report the current code page for DOS even if you have not yet used NLSFUNC. CHCP does not increase the size of DOS and can be issued as often as you want.

Selecting a Language for the Keyboard with KEYB

The KEYB command is a program (or programs) that makes the keyboard of the PS/2, Personal Computer, and compatible systems multilingual. KEYB determines which characters can be typed on the keyboard.

KEYB for DOS V3.3 and V4 has major differences from KEYB for versions of DOS prior to V3.3. DOS pre-V3.3 KEYB programs should not be used with DOS V3.3 or V4. Each version is discussed separately in the following sections.

KEYB for DOS V3.2 and Earlier Versions

The syntax for pre-V3.3 versions of KEYB is

d:path**KEYxx**

d:path\\ is the optional disk drive and path name to the KEYB programs. The **xx**, which can be any one of the keyboard codes in table 18.5, adapts the keyboard and display to the character set of a particular language.

Table 18.5
Keyboard Codes for V3.0 - V3.2 SELECT and KEYBxx

Country	Code
France	FR
Germany	GR
Italy	IT
Spain	SP
United Kingdom	UK
United States	US

The KEYBxx program takes about 2K of memory and becomes a resident program. KEYBxx remains in memory until you reboot DOS or turn off the computer. Once the program is loaded, the native language character set for the KEYBxx program becomes active.

KEYB for DOS V3.3 and V4

The KEYB command for V3.3 and V4 has a different syntax and set of requirements. KEYB alters the code page of the console (CON:, the keyboard and video display). If you will use keyboard layouts that need different code pages, you must "prepare" the console; that is, you must use the MODE CON CODEPAGE PREPARE command before you use KEYB.

The syntax for KEYB V3.3 is

    *d:path***KEYB** *keyboardcode, codepage, d:path\\filename.ext*

DOS V4 allows you to add one more parameter:

    /ID:zzz

keyboardcode is the two-character keyboard code for your country from table 18.5. If your country isn't listed, use the keyboard code that meets your needs most closely. If you want to set the keyboard to use a different language, you must give this parameter.

codepage is the optional code page you want to use with the keyboard. If you don't specify a code page, KEYB uses the default code page.

With DOS V4, the */ID:zzz* parameter may be used to select a specific keyboard layout for those countries that have available more than one enhanced keyboard. These are France (189,120), Italy (141, 142), and the United Kingdom (166, 168). Replace *zzz* with the keyboard ID code for the enhanced keyboard. The manual that came with your computer will let you know the layouts of the various enhanced keyboards so you can select the one you want.

The final parameter of the KEYB command is optional. *d:path\\filename.ext* is the full disk drive, path, and file name for KEYBOARD.SYS, the file that holds the information that KEYB uses to build the various translation tables. KEYB places one restriction on keyboard codes and code pages. The keyboard code, the code page given to KEYB, and the console code page (and the keyboard ID number, if used) must all be compatible. Table 18.6 shows the allowable combinations for the first three parameters.

Table 18.6
Compatible Code Page and Keyboard Code Combinations for KEYB

Code Page	Keyboard Codes
437	FR, GR, IT, LA, NL, SP, SU, SV, UK, US
850	All
860	PO
863	CF
865	DK, NO

The reason for this requirement has to do with the way KEYB works. Basically, KEYB translates the raw on-and-off codes produced by the keyboard hardware into ASCII characters. The ASCII characters built by KEYB are determined by the keyboard code and code page used by KEYB and by the code page used by the console. KEYB builds a table of *keystroke codes to character translations* for each prepared console code page. The different combinations substitute the correct characters for each language. With each set of substitutions some characters "disappear," and other characters appear.

However, KEYB can build these translation tables only for certain keyboard/code-page combinations. Sometimes, graphics characters must be sacrificed for language characters. The characters to type for these languages appear in certain code pages but not in others. Hence, using a keyboard layout with the wrong console code page means you get the wrong characters on the video screen. You type the "right" character, but you see the wrong character. For this reason, the keyboard code and code page that KEYB uses must agree with the console code page.

Avoiding a few traps will help you use keyboard codes and code pages effectively:

- Don't give a keyboard code and code page that do not agree.

- If you are switching code pages, don't give a code page that is not in the list of code pages given to MODE CON CODEPAGE PREPARE.

- Don't give a keyboard code that does not agree with the CON (console) code page used in a CHCP command or in a MODE CON CODEPAGE PREPARE SELECT command.

- Don't use KEYB with a keyboard code or a code page that conflicts with the current console code page. In other words, use MODE CON CODEPAGE SELECT or CHCP to switch the console code page before you use KEYB for a different code page. If you don't, KEYB will mutter a warning about incompatible combinations.

The manual for your computer and the DOS Reference manual have a set of templates showing the different keyboard layouts. If you would like to experiment, you can load the KEYB programs and try typing some characters.

When any version of KEYB is loaded, you can switch easily between the U.S. character set and another language set. The key combination Ctrl-Alt-F1 (the F1 special function key) switches to the U.S. character set. Ctrl-Alt-F2 switches back to the other language set.

The KEYB program stays in memory until you either reboot DOS or turn off the machine. You can use the DOS V3.3 version of KEYB as many times as you want. The first time you use KEYB, it increases the size of DOS by about 7,800 bytes. Using KEYB again does not increase the size of DOS.

If you have a DOS pre-V3.3 version of KEYB, you should load only one KEYBxx program. If you load a second KEYBxx, it assumes control, and the first KEYBxx program is deactivated. The first program, however, is trapped in memory and will continue to eat its 2K of space until you reboot DOS or turn off the computer.

Some computers are manufactured specifically for non-U.S. use. These computers have a different ROM BIOS and multilingual character set. Loading KEYB has no effect on such computers.

Changing the Code Page with MODE

If you want to use different code pages with your computer, you must prepare each code page for each device and then activate that code page. The MODE command prepares and selects code pages for each device.

MODE is the command that controls devices. Before DOS V3.3, MODE consisted of four subcommands. In DOS V3.3, MODE has eight subcommands. The four additional subcommands handle code-page switching. (The remaining functions of MODE are covered in Chapter 23.) Fortunately, you don't need to use every MODE subcommand every time you start DOS. To switch code pages on a device, you must assemble the code pages for use. The MODE CODEPAGE PREPARE command loads code pages into the computer's memory. The MODE CODEPAGE SELECT command downloads any needed code page to the device and tells the device which code page to use. MODE CODEPAGE SELECT also can tell the device to "forget" a software font and switch back to the font built into the device.

Because some fonts are placed in the device's RAM, you might turn the device off and lose the information. Or perhaps a stray program might wipe out the code page information. For these reasons, the MODE command has the ability to remind the device of the font in use. This reminding is the function of MODE CODEPAGE REFRESH.

The MODE CODEPAGE /STATUS command rounds out MODE, displaying the number of the available code pages for a device and which code page is active.

DOS provides some abbreviations for parts of the command. You can use the set of abbreviations in table 18.7 with MODE.

Table 18.7
MODE CODEPAGE Abbreviations

Word	Shorthand
CODEPAGE	CP
PREPARE	PREP
SELECT	SEL
REFRESH	REF
STATUS	STA

Defining Code Pages with MODE PREPARE

The first step in using switchable code pages is to use the MODE PREPARE subcommand to load the disk-based code pages into the computer's memory. The syntax of MODE PREPARE is the most complex of any MODE subcommand, but the command can be tamed. The syntax is

dc:pathc**MODE device CODEPAGE PREPARE** = ((code_page, . . .)
            d:path**filename.ext**)

dc:pathc is the optional disk drive and directory path to the MODE command. **device** is the name of the device for MODE to use. You must specify the device, which can be any of the following:

CON:	console
LPT1:	first parallel printer
LPT2:	second parallel printer
LPT3:	third parallel printer
PRN:	the current system printer, usually a synonym for LPT1:

As with all device names, the colon is optional. The driver for each device specified must have been loaded via the CONFIG.SYS file. To use CON in this command, you must include DISPLAY.SYS in CONFIG.SYS; to use the remaining devices, you must include PRINTER.SYS in CONFIG.SYS.

The **code_page** numbers must be enclosed within a set of parentheses. If you need more than one code page, separate the code page numbers with a comma. The ellipsis (. . .) represents the optional additional code pages. Remember to give a closing parenthesis after the final code page.

For example, to use 850 as a code page, you would use

= (850)

To use the 437 and 850 code pages, you would use

= (437, 850)

Spaces are optional here.

Avoid giving a hardware code page number to MODE PREPARE. In other words, remember the code page you gave to DISPLAY.SYS or PRINTER.SYS. Don't give MODE PREPARE the same code page number. If you used this line in your CONFIG.SYS file:

DEVICE = C:\SYS\DISPLAY.SYS CON = (EGA, 437, 2, 2)

don't give 437 to MODE CODEPAGE PREPARE. The driver already knows that the 437 code page is built into the adapter. Giving 437 to MODE only causes MODE to reload the 437 code page, wasting memory that other fonts could use. You also force the computer to download the font each time the 437 code page is selected—a minor, but avoidable, waste of time.

The final information you must give to MODE CODEPAGE PREPARE is the drive name, path name, and file name for the file that holds the font information for the device. The general form of the file name is **devicename.CPI**. The **devicename** can be any of the following:

EGA	EGA and VGA display adapters
LCD	PC Convertible LCD display
4201	IBM ProPrinter
5202	IBM Quietwriter III

The CPI extension is for *code page information*.

The EGA.CPI and LCD.CPI files, of course, are used with the CON device. The 4201.CPI and 5202.CPI files are used with the PRN or LPT devices.

If the code page information file is not on the current disk or in the current directory, you must provide the needed information. The root name is mandatory. Because all DOS code page files have an extension of CPI, you will usually give both root name and extension.

Note that you cannot prepare more code pages than the number you gave to DIS-PLAY.SYS or to PRINTER.SYS for *added_codepage*. If you need more code pages, you must edit the DISPLAY.SYS or PRINTER.SYS line in your CONFIG.SYS file and then restart DOS.

Remember that if you gave two hardware code pages for the Quietwriter III, you must have given a value of 0 for *added_codepages*. DOS assumes that the two code pages are in the printer. In this case, you don't need to use MODE CODEPAGE PREPARE on the Quietwriter.

If you issue the MODE CODEPAGE PREPARE command more than once, you can skip the code pages you don't want to change. For example, you use this MODE command to load the 850, 860, and 863 code pages:

MODE CON CODEPAGE PREPARE = ((850, 860, 863) C:\EGA.CPI)

If you later want to use the 850 and 863 code pages, but you want the 865 instead of the 860 page, you simply drop the number and insert a comma for the unchanged code pages. To change the 860 code page to the 865, the command would be

MODE CON CODEPAGE PREPARE = ((,865,) C:\EGA.CPI)

A more common example would be first using this command to load the multilingual code page into memory:

MODE CON CODEPAGE PREPARE = ((850) C:\EGA.CPI)

Later, you might want to add another code page to the list. To add the 860 code page, you would use this command:

MODE CON CODEPAGE PREPARE = ((,860) C:\EGA.CPI)

Now either the 850 or 860 code page can be used. Remember that the value for *added_codepages* given to DISPLAY.SYS must be at least 2 for this example to work, and 3 for the preceding example to work.

Now, suppose that you give an incorrect code page number or give the name of an existing file that is not a code page information file. MODE displays a `Font file con-tents invalid` message. The code page at that position is removed from the list. Using the previous example (which has the 850 and 860 code pages prepared), if you issue the command

MODE CON CODEPAGE PREPARE = ((,836) C:\EGA.CPI)

MODE tells you that the code page file does not have the given font. 836 cannot replace the code page in the second position, which was 860. However, 860 is removed from memory. To use 860, you must reload it with the MODE PREPARE command.

Remember that the commands can be abbreviated. Here are two examples:

MODE CON CP PREP = (850, 863) C:\EGA.CPI

MODE LPT1 CP PREP = (860, 863) C:\4201.CPI

Activating Code Pages with MODE SELECT

After code pages are prepared, they can be used. One command to activate the code pages is MODE CODEPAGE SELECT. (The other is CHCP.)

CHCP is the preferred command to activate code pages. You can use CHCP to activate the code pages for DOS and for all the devices at one time. CHCP is also easier to use than MODE SELECT. However, there may be occasions when you don't want the same code page active on all devices. Then you must use MODE SELECT.

Suppose that you have edited a document using code page 437 and have started printing the document in the background. Now you want to edit another document. That document was created using the 850 code page. You need to use the 860 code page for the console (the display and keyboard).

If you use CHCP in this instance, you affect both the display and the printer. Since you do not want that, your only choice is to use MODE SELECT to switch fonts on the display.

The syntax for MODE SELECT is

*dc:pathc***MODE device CODEPAGE SELECT = codepage**

dc:pathc is the optional drive and directory path to the MODE command. **device** is the name of the device whose code page will be activated by MODE. **device** can be CON, LPTx, or PRN. **codepage** is the code page the device will use. **codepage** must be either the hardware code page given to the appropriate device driver or one of the code pages given to the MODE PREPARE command. One, and only one, **codepage** can be given.

Using the MODE SELECT command downloads the appropriate font to the device and activates the font. The device uses this font until you issue another MODE SELECT or CHCP command, or until you turn off the device or restart DOS.

The usual way to type MODE SELECT is

MODE CON CP SEL = codepage

or

MODE LPT1 CP SEL = codepage

Refreshing a Device's Memory with MODE REFRESH

MODE REFRESH reminds the device which font the device should be using. Generally, the command is not needed on the video display, unless a program has affected the video screen in an undesirable manner. The command is used more frequently for the printer. If you turn the printer off and on again, the software code page is lost. Thus,

DOS can lose track of the code page that the printer is using. The printer and DOS must then be resynchronized.

The MODE REFRESH command reloads and activates any needed font. The syntax for MODE REFRESH is

   *dc:pathc***MODE device CODEPAGE REFRESH**

device is the name of the device whose code page should be re-established. Don't give a code page number. MODE uses the last code page used in the MODE SELECT command.

To use MODE REFRESH, you must have used MODE PREPARE and either MODE SELECT for the device, or the CHCP command. MODE REFRESH can be issued as often as needed. Examples of the shorthand form of MODE REFRESH are

   MODE LPT1 CP REF

and

   MODE CON CP REF

Checking Code Pages with MODE /STATUS

You can use the MODE /STATUS command to display various code page information about a device. MODE /STATUS lists this information:

   The number of the active code page, if any
   The number of the hardware code page
   The numbers of any prepared code pages

The syntax for MODE /STATUS is

   *dc:pathc***MODE device CODEPAGE /STATUS**

device is the name of the device whose code page information you want displayed. Notice that this command is a switch. You must give the switch character (the slash), followed by the word **STATUS**.

The following examples display the output of the MODE /STATUS command for the console. DOS was started with this command in the CONFIG.SYS file:

   DEVICE = C:\SYS\DISPLAY.SYS CON = (EGA, 437, 4)

The DISPLAY.SYS file has been set up for an EGA or VGA display (**EGA**), a hardware code page of 437, and 4 additional code pages:

```
C>MODE CON CODEPAGE PREP = (850, 860) C:\EGA.CPI
C>MODE CON CODEPAGE SELECT = 850
C>MODE CON CODEPAGE /STATUS

hardware codepages:
    Codepage 437
prepared codepages:
    Codepage 850
    Codepage 860
```

```
      Codepage not prepared
      Codepage not prepared
  MODE Status Codepage function completed
  C>
```

The first MODE command sets up the console to use the 850 and 860 code pages, in addition to the 437 code page built into the display adapter. The second MODE command activates the 850 code page.

The first line of the MODE /STATUS command's report shows the active code page. The next two lines give the hardware code page based on the DISPLAY.SYS or PRINTER.SYS line in the CONFIG.SYS file. The following lines show the software code pages. The number of lines is based on the *added_codepages* number given to DISPLAY.SYS or PRINTER.SYS. If a code page is prepared, you will see the number listed. The message `Codepage not prepared` indicates that additional areas for code pages are available.

You can use MODE /STATUS at any time. However, you get an error message if the appropriate device driver has not been installed for the device. MODE /STATUS can be abbreviated to

MODE CON CP /STA

for the console or

MODE LPT1 CP /STA

for the first line printer.

Solving Display Problems Using GRAFTABL

There is a minor problem with displaying non-English characters on the IBM Color/ Graphics Adapter (CGA). When you attempt to display characters in the ASCII range of 128 to 255 while in graphics mode, the characters are almost unreadable. Unfortunately, the non-English language characters are in the range of 128 to 255. This problem affects only the CGA. And the problem occurs only in medium-resolution, 320 by 200, 4-color mode, not in normal alphanumeric text mode or in the high-resolution, 640 by 200, 2-color mode.

To get a legible display in medium-resolution graphics mode, use GRAFTABL. This command loads the alternate character set into the computer's memory and then directs the CGA to use this set when it is in graphics mode. The ASCII characters in the 128 to 255 range are thus displayed legibly.

To use GRAFTABL, type

*dc:pathc***GRAFTABL**

GRAFTABL uses about 1,200 bytes of RAM. This memory remains trapped until you either restart DOS or turn off the computer. Running GRAFTABL more than once simply wastes 1,200 bytes of memory each time you run it. If a program you frequently run requires GRAFTABL, add the command to your AUTOEXEC.BAT file.

With DOS V4, GRAFTABL was enhanced to support code page 850, the multilingual code page.

Using SELECT To Set Country Information

In Chapter 3, I covered the new, enhanced version of the utility program SELECT, which was extended to allow installing DOS V4 on a floppy disk or on your hard disk. However, SELECT existed prior to DOS V4 as a program with somewhat more limited capabilities.

In DOS V3.x SELECT is used solely to automate the selection of the country code and keyboard program. SELECT for versions of DOS prior to V3.2 destroys any previously established CONFIG.SYS and AUTOEXEC.BAT files. SELECT for V3.2 and V3.3 runs FORMAT and destroys all the files on the disk! If you have already set up your disk, you should simply edit your existing CONFIG.SYS and AUTOEXEC.BAT files, rather than running SELECT.

If you are using SELECT with floppy disks, you need the correct blank disk for your disk drive. If you have a 1.2M disk drive, you need a 1.2M floppy disk. If you have a 1.44M disk drive, you need a 1.44M disk. Using the wrong capacity disk can cause SELECT to fail.

SELECT for DOS V3.2 and V3.3

SELECT for DOS V3.2 and V3.3 can work on floppy disks or on hard disks. This version of SELECT runs the FORMAT command. *If you use SELECT on your hard disk, you will destroy all information on the disk.* For this reason, I strongly suggest that you do not run SELECT unless the hard disk has no files. You'll gain more by creating or editing your CONFIG.SYS and AUTOEXEC.BAT files than by copying everything back to your hard disk after FORMAT has run.

The syntax for SELECT V3.2 and V3.3 is

   *dc:pathc***SELECT** *ds: dd:\\pathd* **countrycode keyboardcode**

ds: is the name of the disk drive that holds the *source* disk and should hold the DOS Startup or Startup/Operating disk. *ds:* must be a floppy disk drive (either A or B). If you don't specify the source disk drive, SELECT uses drive A.

dd: is the optional *destination* disk, the disk to be set up. The destination disk must be different from the source disk. If you don't give *dd:* and the current disk is not the source disk, SELECT uses drive B. If you don't give *dd:* and the current disk is the source disk, SELECT displays an error message and aborts. To use SELECT on a hard disk, you must specify the hard disk's drive name.

\\pathd is the path to the directory that SELECT copies the DOS files to. You must use an *absolute* path name—that is, you must start with the root directory (\\ ); the **.** and **..** names are not allowed.

If you don't give *\\pathd*, DOS copies the files to the root directory of *dd:*. If the destination is a floppy disk, you generally can omit *\\pathd*. Because of the limited storage space, don't use a destination path if the destination is a 360K disk. If the destination is a hard disk, you should give *\\pathd*. The name I suggest is either BIN or DOS.

countrycode is the three-digit code for your country, and **keyboardcode** is the two-character code for your country.

SELECT runs FORMAT to prepare a hard disk. FORMAT will ask you for a volume label. Putting volume labels on hard disks is a good processing practice. FORMAT requests the existing volume label before it formats a hard disk, so inadvertently formatting a hard disk that has a volume label is almost impossible.

After FORMAT has run, SELECT runs XCOPY, to transfer the files from the start-up disk to the destination disk or hard disk. If you specified a destination path (*pathd*), XCOPY copies the files to the directory. SELECT then creates any needed directories. If you did not specify a destination path, XCOPY copies the files to the root directory of the destination disk.

Finally, SELECT creates a CONFIG.SYS file and an AUTOEXEC.BAT file. The CONFIG.SYS file for SELECT V3.2 and V3.3 holds the single line

    COUNTRY = countrycode,codepage

or

    COUNTRY = countrycode,codepage,d:path\COUNTRY.SYS

This line sets up the COUNTRY directive. The correct code page is based on the country code you gave to SELECT. The first line is used if you do not give a destination path. The second line, which has the full file name for COUNTRY.SYS, is used if you give a destination path. The *d:path* is the destination drive and path name.

If the destination is a floppy disk, the AUTOEXEC.BAT file for V3.2 and V3.3 holds the following lines:

    PATH \;\path
    KEYB keycode codepage
    ECHO OFF
    DATE
    TIME
    VER

If the destination is a hard disk, AUTOEXEC.BAT holds these lines:

    PATH d:\;d:\path
    KEYB keycode codepage
    ECHO OFF
    DATE
    TIME
    VER

d: is the name of the destination disk drive. If you gave a destination path to SELECT, the first line substitutes that destination path for the path variable. If you did not give a destination path to SELECT, the second directory path is dropped. The line becomes either PATH \ or PATH d:\.

The AUTOEXEC.BAT file runs the KEYB program with the keyboard code you gave and inserts the compatible code page for the keyboard code. The batch file then turns ECHO off, asks for the date and time, and displays the DOS sign-on message. The last three commands approximate what DOS does if no AUTOEXEC.BAT file is on the disk.

If you run SELECT on a floppy disk, the disk you produce should be your new DOS working copy. If you run SELECT on a hard disk, your DOS files are copied to the hard disk. Put any additional CONFIG.SYS or AUTOEXEC.BAT command lines you desire into these files.

A Sample COUNTRY Setup

In these examples, I presume that you have a hard disk and that all of the DOS program files are copied to a subdirectory called C:\BIN. I also presume that all .SYS files have been copied to C:\SYS. If this is not true, change the disk drive and path name to match your system. Floppy disk users should omit the path name and use A: in place of C:.

The examples are for DOS V3.3 and V4 only. Consult your DOS manual for your correct setup if you are using an older version of DOS.

Adding International Directives to CONFIG.SYS

To use DOS's international features, start by adding the following line to your CONFIG.SYS file:

COUNTRY = 001, 437, C:\SYS\COUNTRY.SYS

If you have a PC Convertible LCD display, an EGA, or a VGA, use the following DEVICE = DISPLAY.SYS line:

DEVICE = C:\SYS\DISPLAY.SYS CON = (EGA, 437, 1)

This line sets up the display for the 437 code page and 1 additional code page. For a Monochrome Adapter, use the line

DEVICE = C:\SYS\DISPLAY.SYS CON = (MONO, 437, 0)

Remember that the number of added code pages for a monochrome adapter is always 0.

If you use ANSI.SYS, the DRIVER.SYS line must appear after the ANSI.SYS line. Reversing this order causes you to lose the features that ANSI.SYS offers.

If you have either the IBM ProPrinter or the Quietwriter III, you should use PRINTER.SYS. The line for the ProPrinter is

DEVICE = C:\SYS\PRINTER.SYS LPT1 = (4201, 437, 1)

This line sets up the ProPrinter for the first parallel port (LPT1), the 437 code page, and one additional code page.

In the preceding lines, if 437 weren't my existing code page, I would use the existing code page and specify 2 instead of 1 for the added code pages to be used. For example, the DISPLAY.SYS line would be

DEVICE = C:\SYS\DISPLAY.SYS CON = (EGA, 863, 2)

meaning that the French Canadian code page (863) is built into the adapter and that I will use two additional code pages.

Remember that the CONFIG.SYS file must be in the root directory of the boot floppy disk or hard disk, and that you must restart DOS before the change takes place.

Adding International Directives to AUTOEXEC.BAT

Add the following lines to the AUTOEXEC.BAT file of your start-up disk. If the start-up disk is a hard disk, place these additional commands after the line that holds your PATH command. When the commands occur after PATH, DOS automatically finds the commands.

The line to add is simply

NLSFUNC

The next step is to use MODE PREP on each device. If DISPLAY.SYS is installed, use the MODE CON CODEPAGE PREPARE command:

MODE CON CP PREP = (850) C:\BIN\EGA.CPI

This command prepares the 850 code page for use with EGA/VGA-type displays. If your hardware code page is 437, use 850 as the prepared code page. If your hardware code page is not 437, use 850 and the existing code page:

MODE CON CP PREP = (850, 863) C:\BIN\EGA.CPI

This command adds the French Canadian code page to the multilingual code page.

If PRINTER.SYS is installed, use the MODE LPTx CODEPAGE PREPARE command. The line for the ProPrinter is

MODE LPT1 CP PREP = (850) C:\BIN\4201.CPI

which prepares the 850 code page for use with the model 4201, the ProPrinter. If the hardware code page is not 437, I prepare the 850 but add another code page:

MODE LPT1 CP PREP = (850, 863) C:\BIN\4201.CPI

which adds the French Canadian code page to the multilingual code page.

If you gave two hardware code pages for the Quietwriter III, you don't need to issue the MODE PREPARE command for this printer. Otherwise, follow the same form for the ProPrinter, but use 5202.CPI for the code page information file name.

After you add the commands to prepare the code pages, use the CHCP command to activate the pages. The line to be added to AUTOEXEC.BAT is **CHCP codepage**.

The command I type into my AUTOEXEC.BAT is

CHCP 437

437 is the existing code page.

Finally, add a line to enable switching of your keyboard. For me the line is

KEYB US,,C:\SYS\KEYBOARD.SYS

If you use KEYB frequently on the hard disk and follow the suggestion to copy the file to the root directory, add this command to the AUTOEXEC.BAT file instead:

KEYB US,,C:\KEYBOARD.SYS

If you have a Color/Graphics Adapter and use the medium-resolution graphics mode frequently, add the line

GRAFTABL

Now restart DOS and watch your display. If you see any error messages, check the lines in your CONFIG.SYS file and AUTOEXEC.BAT files. You probably simply misspelled a command or forgot to give the correct file name. Correct the mistake and try restarting DOS.

Summary

In this chapter, you learned the following important points:

- Code pages are fonts. Some code pages are built into hardware, and some are loadable from a file.
- You use the CONFIG.SYS COUNTRY directive to tell DOS which international country code and which code page to use.
- DOS adapts the format for the date and time based on the country code.
- The DISPLAY.SYS device driver allows code page switching on some video displays.
- The PRINTER.SYS device driver allows code page switching on some printers.
- The NLSFUNC command provides additional functions that make DOS go international and allows the CHCP command to be used.
- The CHCP command switches code pages for DOS and all devices at one time.
- The MODE CODEPAGE subcommands load, activate, reselect, and display selected code pages.

❏ The KEYB command alters the keyboard for different languages.

❏ The GRAFTABL command enables you to display legibly non-English language characters and certain graphics characters when you use the Color/Graphics Adapter in medium-resolution mode.

In Chapter 19, we finish this section on customizing DOS by looking at customizing the DOS V4 Shell.

19

Customizing the DOS V4 Shell

This final chapter on customizing DOS shows you how to customize the DOS V4 Shell. You'll learn how to change the start-up options that DOS uses when it loads the Shell. Learning to make these changes requires knowing about batch files; if you read Chapters 14 and 15 carefully, however, you should have most of the knowledge you need.

Understanding a Typical DOSSHELL.BAT File

Before you begin customizing the Shell, take a look at a DOSSHELL.BAT file and see what each line does. Here is a typical file:

1. **@ECHO OFF**

2. **C:**

3. **CD \DOS**

4. **SHELLB DOSSHELL**

5. **IF ERRORLEVEL 255 GOTO END**

6. **:COMMON**

7. **@SHELLC /MOS:PCIBMDRV.MOS/TRAN/COLOR/DOS/MENU/MUL**
   /SND/MEU:SHELL.MEUH /CLR:SHELL.CLR/PROMPT
   /MAINT/EXIT/SWAP/DATE

8. **:END**

9. **CD **

Each of the preceding lines is numbered for easy reference. The line numbers are *not* part of the batch file, however, and should not be included if you copy this file or create one of your own from scratch.

You can use EDLIN or the ASCII/nondocument mode of your word processor to edit or create your own DOSSHELL.BAT file. The techniques for creating batch files are discussed in Chapters 15 and 16.

The following is an explanation of what each line of the sample DOSSHELL.BAT file does:

Line 1: Turns off the echoing of commands so that they won't be displayed on-screen as DOS carries them out.

Line 2: Changes the current drive to drive C, in case you happen to be using some other drive at the time you call up DOSSHELL.BAT.

Line 3: Changes the current directory to \DOS, where the SHELL programs are stored.

Line 4: Summons a program called SHELLB.COM, which loads some key functions into memory. These take up a little less than 4K of DOS memory. SHELLB.COM also performs two other tasks, which enable the rest of the SHELL programs to load. First, SHELLB.COM checks for any errors that might prevent the Shell from running properly. If any errors are found, a value of 255 is loaded into the special memory register that stores the current ERRORLEVEL.

Second, SHELLB.COM notes the name of the batch file you want to use to call up the DOS Shell. In this case, that name is DOSSHELL. You may wonder why it's necessary to specify the name. The reason is simple: Many computers are used in network environments, in which several workstations share the same applications programs. It's not necessary for each user to have a copy of each program at his own computer; the programs can be accessed as needed from the network file server.

The workstations in a network can use different kinds of hardware, however. One workstation might use one type of mouse and a CGA display, whereas another might use a different mouse (or no mouse at all) and a VGA monitor. Because the DOSSHELL.BAT file includes information about hardware, if all the workstations accessed the Shell through the DOSSHELL.BAT file, this information would not necessarily be appropriate for all workstations.

You can thus substitute customized batch files, each containing the proper hardware configuration data for a particular workstation. If you specify to SHELLB.COM the name of a certain batch file, SHELLB.COM will "know" what file to use the next time it needs information about configuration. In naming batch files, you can use numbers (SHELL1.BAT, SHELL2.BAT, SHELL3.BAT . . .) or users' names (SHJOHN.BAT, SHJOE.BAT, and so on). The important thing is to make sure that each user knows the correct batch file to use to call up the DOS Shell for a particular workstation.

Line 5: Checks to see whether SHELLB.COM found any errors. If so, control passes to line 8 (:END), and the batch file terminates. If this happens, you may need to run the SELECT program again. You also can check to make sure that all the proper SHELL programs and menu files (which end with .MEU) are available in the subdirectory specified in line 3.

Line 6: Marks the portion of the batch file that calls the SHELLC.COM program. When you run a program from the DOS Shell or leave the Shell to access the DOS prompt, DOS returns to this portion of the batch file to reload the Shell. That's why it's important to (1) specify to SHELLB.COM the name of the file you want to use and (2) use the :COMMON label and no other at this point in the batch file. If you don't specify the name of the file, DOS won't know where to look. If you use some label other than :COMMON, DOS will not find the correct starting place.

Line 7: Does most of the work in setting up your DOS Shell. A detailed examination of this line appears in the following section.

Line 8: Marks the end of the batch file.

Line 9: Changes the current subdirectory to the root directory.

Taking a Closer Look at Shell Options

Although line 7, in the preceding section, doesn't include all the available Shell options, it still provides an excellent basis for a discussion of options. This section first examines the options listed in line 7 and then discusses those that didn't make their way into the sample DOSSHELL.BAT file.

/MOS:

The /MOS: option enables you to specify the mouse driver to be used with the DOS Shell; include this option only if you will be using a mouse with the Shell. One such driver is PCIBMDRV.MOS, used with the IBM mouse. Also provided with the Shell are PCMSDRV.MOS and PCMSPDRV.MOS. The former is a driver for the Microsoft serial mouse; the latter is used with the Microsoft parallel port mouse. One of these three drivers should work with your particular mouse, and each has the advantage of requiring only 1K of memory. DOS deactivates these drivers when the Shell is not active; as a result, they won't conflict with other mouse drivers you may be using.

Although the three drivers discussed in the preceding paragraph enable you to use the mouse for most of your DOS Shell functions, other programs may not use these drivers. To gain mouse functions with other programs, such as PC Paintbrush and Ventura Publisher, you may have to load through the CONFIG.SYS or AUTOEXEC.BAT files the mouse driver supplied with your mouse. Consult the manual that came with your mouse.

/TRAN

Including the /TRAN option activates the transient mode of the Shell. That's fine, you say, but what is *transient mode*? You may recall that in Chapter 8 we discussed the resident and transient parts of COMMAND.COM.

Similarly, the Shell can operate in either resident mode or transient mode. In *resident mode* the DOS Shell and the buffers it uses are loaded into memory and stay there. The buffers grab all available memory (unless you limit their size with the /B: option, described later). The advantage of resident mode is speed. DOS doesn't have to access the hard disk; the entire Shell code is available in memory for instant access. The disadvantage is that you have less free memory for other uses.

In *transient mode* the Shell takes up only 3.5K of memory permanently and uses the hard disk to store the other information it needs. You might select this mode for your system if you want memory available for such programs as Ventura Publisher (which, by the way, works just fine under the DOS Shell).

/COLOR

If you are not using a monochrome monitor, the /COLOR option activates the Change Colors utility in the Main Group. If you omit this option from the DOSSHELL.BAT file, you will not be able to change the colors of the Shell. The Change Colors selection will still appear in the Main Group menu, however, unless you remove the selection by using a technique to be explained later. One reason for disabling the Change Colors utility is to prevent those who use your system from accidentally (or intentionally) changing the color scheme.

/DOS

Including the /DOS option makes the File System selection available from the Main Group. Omitting the /DOS option leaves you unable to perform any of the File System functions, including copying files and viewing directories.

/MENU

The /MENU option activates the Start Programs main menu. If you don't specify this option, you can access only the File System. (If you don't specify the /DOS option as well, you won't be able to do anything.)

/MUL

When the /MUL option is specified, the Shell keeps track of the information it obtains from the last two drives it accesses. Having the Shell keep track of this information can speed up File System operations, such as displaying the directory tree and listing files, because the Shell doesn't have to access the disk drive to recall the information.

/SND

Choosing the /SND option activates sound, which you hear when working in the Shell. Unless you work in a "quiet zone," you'll probably want to have the added feedback that your computer's various beeps can provide.

/MEU:

The /MEU: option enables you to define the name of the menu file used for the Main Group menu. The default is SHELL.MEU. If you want to use the SHELL.MEU file, you don't have to include the /MEU: option at all.

You may choose to use a file other than SHELL.MEU if you want to create a new Main Group menu. For example, you may have deleted the Change Colors utility and now want to remove it from the Main Group menu as well. To do this, create a new subgroup menu that has the headings you want (minus Change Colors) and provide it with a name. Then edit the DOSSHELL.BAT file so that the /MEU: option includes the new menu name. Chapter 20 shows you how to create menus.

/CLR:

The /CLR: option enables you to specify the name of the file containing the DOS Shell color scheme you have selected. The default is SHELL.CLR. If you want to use that file, you don't have to include the /CLR: option at all. Or you can write different versions of DOSSHELL.BAT, each specifying a different color-file so that you can use different color schemes, if you like.

/PROMPT

Including the /PROMPT option enables you to switch from the Shell to the DOS command prompt in order to carry out functions or even run other programs. To return to the Shell, you type **EXIT**.

If you leave out the /PROMPT option, you will be "stuck" inside the Shell with no means of quick access to DOS (other than exiting from the Shell entirely.)

/MAINT

Including the /MAINT option gives you access to the various action bar commands that appear in the Main Group and in each of the subgroups. If /MAINT is omitted, you can use only the commands found in the group listings themselves. Each of the Main Group programs and utilities would be accessible, for example, but you would be unable to add or change programs and groups. In the File System, you would be able to view directories and the directory tree, but you would be unable to copy or delete files, create directories, and so on.

/EXIT

The /EXIT option activates the action bar selection that enables you to unload the Shell and exit to DOS. If /EXIT is not specified, you will be "trapped" in the Shell. If the /PROMPT option is not specified as well, no access to the DOS command prompt is available unless you reboot the system.

/SWAP

The Shell can maintain a file that stores the buffered information about files and directories used by the File System. If you specify the /SWAP option, DOS stores this information on disk in a temporary file. This file helps speed up the reloading of the Shell when you exit from a program.

/DATE

When you specify the /DATE option, the date and time are displayed in the DOS Shell title bar and are updated every minute. One of the few reasons for not wanting this information is that you may have installed the Shell on a computer that has a nonfunctioning clock. Original PCs and PC XT systems don't have clocks accessible to DOS. If you haven't installed the necessary add-on hardware to make the clock available to DOS, you wouldn't want to use the /DATE option.

Although the following Shell options didn't appear in the sample file, you may want to include them in your own Shell start-up file.

/ASC:file.asc

Chapter 22 explains how the DOS Shell's Associate... function works. This function enables you to correlate various file extensions with particular applications programs: you can pair the .DOC extension with your word-processing program, for example, or the .WKQ extension with your Quattro spreadsheet program. Then when you select a data file that has an "associated" extension, the Shell automatically loads the specified application for you.

DOS stores these links in a file called SHELL.ASC. If your computer has several users, you may want to store each one's associations in different files. The /ASC: option enables you to specify another file name. Substitute for **file.asc** the name you want to use.

/B:size

If you use the /B: option, you can limit the amount of memory that the Shell uses in resident mode for its buffers. Specify the size in whole kilobytes; if you want to specify 8K, for example, type **/B:8**. If you don't use the /B: option, DOS will use all available memory.

/CO1, /CO2, and /CO3

To specify which video graphics mode the Shell is to use, choose one of these three options. The mode you choose must be compatible with your display adapter and CRT. The modes are the following:

- /CO1:EGA 640 x 350 16-color mode, which produces an 80-column, 25-line display. Technical types know this as video mode 10H.

- /CO2:VGA 640 x 480 black-and-white mode, which produces an 80-column, 30-row display. In technical terms, this is video mode 11H.

- /CO3:VGA 640 x 480 16-color mode (known as video mode 12H), which produces an 80-column, 30-row display.

/TEXT

The /TEXT option instructs the Shell to use text mode for Color Graphics Adapter (CGA) monitors or Monochrome Display Adapter (MDA) CRTs. These video modes are 3 and 7, respectively.

/COM2

Ordinarily, the Shell uses the COM1 serial port for the mouse. If you include the /COM2 option, the Shell will use COM2 instead.

/LF

The /LF option changes the mouse driver's configuration so that you use the right-hand button instead of the left-hand one. This option is useful for left-handed people.

Summary

This chapter provided you with the information you need to customize the DOS Shell start-up file. You can customize the Shell even more, however, by creating your own menus, adding and removing programs, and even creating your own groups. Because these tasks call for a little more knowledge of how to manage files, the next chapter discusses file management. Chapter 21 resumes the discussion of the Shell and shows you how to manage your system with some of the Shell's specialized features.

Important points covered in this chapter include the following:

❑ You can change the DOS Shell by adapting the DOSSHELL.BAT file.

❑ Many of the features of the Shell can be disabled or activated, as you prefer.

❑ Customized shells can be prepared for different users.

Part V

Managing Your System

Includes

Managing Your Files

Managing the DOS V4 Shell

Using Advanced Features of the
DOS Shell File System

Gaining Control of Drives, Devices,
and the Printer

Backing Up and Restoring the
Hard Disk

Gaining More Control of the
Hard Disk

Migrating between Minifloppy and
Microfloppy Systems

A Few DOS V4 Considerations

Some Final Thoughts

20

Managing Your Files

In this chapter you will learn more about the COPY command. You will also learn how to gain more control over copying with the command XCOPY.

Expanding Your Use of the COPY Command

Both COPY and the DOS Shell COPY utility copy files. With them, you can copy files between disk drives, between devices, or between a disk drive and another device. If you use the DOS prompt, you have some additional options for using COPY. For example, you can copy from a disk file to a device, from a device to a disk file, or from a device to another device. You cannot readily perform these functions from the DOS Shell.

Understanding ˆZ, the End-of-File Marker

ASCII files, usually called text files, use a special character to signal the end of a file. This character is represented as ˆZ, CHR$(26), or 1A in the hexadecimal numbering system. The character is called the end-of-file marker.

Every program recognizes that Ctrl-Z marks the end of an ASCII text or data file. Anything beyond the end-of-file marker is not used. If you press the F6 key at the system prompt, a ˆZ will appear on-screen.

COPY makes one assumption about the files being copied: if a file does not come from a character-oriented device, such as the keyboard, modem, or video display, the file is considered a binary file. When DOS copies binary files, it uses the file size from the directory to determine how much information to copy. Thus, DOS copies everything in the file. DOS also copies ASCII files on the basis of their directory length. The end-of-file marker, which is reflected in the directory size, is copied with the rest of the file's information.

Copying with nondisk devices is different. DOS has no way of knowing how many characters will be involved in copying with these devices. The indicator is the Ctrl-Z. When DOS receives a Ctrl-Z from the console, the serial port, or another nondisk device, DOS knows that all information has been received or sent.

Using COPY's Switches (/A, /B, /V)

COPY has three switches: /A, /B, and /V. You can use the switches to force conditions on the COPY command. The switches /A and /B specify to COPY how much information is to be copied.

The /A switch makes DOS handle the file transfer as ASCII text. For source files, DOS copies all information up to, but not including, the first Ctrl-Z. For a destination file, DOS adds a Ctrl-Z to the end of the file. This method of copying files ensures that a good end-of-file marker is placed in the file. When you copy a file from a device other than a disk drive, DOS assumes that the /A switch is to be used.

The /B switch is the opposite of the /A switch. The /B switch tells DOS to copy binary (program) files on the basis of directory size. For destination files, DOS does not add a Ctrl-Z. When you copy files from one disk to another, DOS assumes that the /B switch is to be used.

You cannot force DOS to copy a binary file from a nondisk device. DOS will have no way of knowing when the information has ended. If you type the /B switch with the source device name, DOS displays the error message Cannot do binary reads from a device and halts the command.

The placement of COPY's switches is important. A COPY switch affects the file or device name that precedes the switch and all file and device names after the switch, until contradicted by another switch. For example, if you use the /A switch after the first file or device name, you affect all files in the command line. If, however, you use the /A switch after the second file name, the switch affects only the second file and files after that. The following examples show how the position of the switch affects command lines:

1. COPY /A ONEFILE.TXT TWOFILE.TXT

    COPY treats ONEFILE.TXT and TWOFILE.TXT as ASCII text files, copying ONEFILE.TXT up to, but not including, the first Ctrl-Z. COPY adds a Ctrl-Z to the end of TWOFILE.TXT.

2. COPY ONEFILE.TXT /A TWOFILE.TXT

    This example's effect is identical to that of the first example. The /A switch affects the file in front of it (ONEFILE.TXT) and all files after the switch (TWOFILE.TXT).

3. COPY ONEFILE.TXT TWOFILE.TXT /A

    COPY treats ONEFILE.TXT as a binary file. COPY takes all information from ONEFILE.TXT (determined by its length in the directory) and copies it to TWOFILE.TXT. COPY adds a Ctrl-Z to the end of TWOFILE.TXT.

4. COPY COM1: TWOFILE.TXT /B

COPY takes information from the first communications adapter (COM1:)
until it encounters the Ctrl-Z. COPY places this information, excluding the
Ctrl-Z, in a disk file called TWOFILE.TXT. COPY does not add a Ctrl-Z.

5. COPY COM1: /B TWOFILE.TXT

This command line is illegal. The /B switch affects the file or device in
front of the switch and all files or devices after it. The problem with this
command line is that the /B switch will affect the communications port,
COM1:. COPY does not allow "binary" copies from a nondisk device, and
DOS displays an error message if you try such an action.

The third switch used with COPY is /V, which verifies that the copies are correct. When
you use /V, you must place it after the last file name. Although the /A and /B switches
affect one another, /V does not affect the /A and /B switches.

Using COPY To Join Files

COPY does more than copy files. The command can also concatenate (join) files. The
syntax is

COPY */A/B d1:path1\filename1.ext1/A/B + d2:path2\filename2.ext2/A/B + ...
dd:pathd\filenamed.extd /A/B/V*

The *d1:, d2:,* and *dd:* are valid disk drive names. The *path1\, path2\,* and *pathd* are
valid path names to the files. The *filename1.ext1, filename2.ext2,* and *filenamed.extd*
are valid file names. Wild cards are acceptable. The ... represents additional files in the
form *dx:pathx\filenamex.extx.* If you give additional file names, separate them with a
plus sign (+) to tell DOS you are joining files. The numbers and the letter *d* are special
notations. The numbered file names, marked 1 and 2, are the source files. Names followed by *d* represent destination files. The source files are those you want to join. The
destination file or files will hold the product of this concatenation.

COPY can produce several destination files. This process is tricky and potentially dangerous; it involves wild-card characters and is discussed later in the chapter.

Source files can be binary files (program files or non-ASCII data files) or ASCII files.
When you concatenate, COPY assumes that you are joining ASCII files and issues an
invisible /A switch.

This assumption is not true when you copy disk-based files. But because non-ASCII files
are rarely concatenated, the assumption is helpful.

Here is an example of this command:

COPY FILE1.TXT + FILE2.TXT + FILE3.TXT FILE.ALL /V

COPY moves the contents of FILE1.TXT to a file called FILE.ALL. COPY then adds the
contents of FILE2.TXT to the end of FILE.ALL. COPY also appends the contents of

FILE3.TXT to FILE.ALL. The /V switch verifies the concatenation. Because no disk drive or path name is given, all of the activity takes place in the current directory on drive C.

Each source file name can have a disk drive name and a path name. The rules about current disk drives and current directory file names apply here.

You can use wild-card characters in the file names. Such characters force COPY to join any files that match the given wild-card name. With one file name, therefore, you can join several files.

The destination file is the last file name on the command line that does not have a + sign in front of its name. If you look at the preceding example, you will see a space, not a plus sign, between FILE.ALL and the last file to be concatenated (FILE3.TXT). DOS adds the second and subsequent files to the end of the first file.

If you use matching wild cards for the root names of both the source and destination file names, you can create multiple destination files. The following command line shows how to accomplish this task.

COPY *.LST + *.REF *.PRN

This line takes each root name that has a .LST extension and joins that file to each file that has a .REF extension. The command line then places the joined result into a file with the same root name but with a .PRN extension. If you use a wild card in the destination file name, the destination files have the same root names as the source files.

Now look at the following set of files:

MYFILE.LST	MYFILE.REF
APROG.LST	APROG.REF
FILE3.LST	FILE3.REF

The command COPY *.LST + *.REF *.PRN will combine these files in the following way:

MYFILE.LST	+	MYFILE.REF	→	MYFILE.PRN
APROG.LST	+	APROG.REF	→	APROG.PRN
FILE3.LST	+	FILE3.REF	→	FILE3.PRN

You can use wild cards with a destination file that is also a source file. This list shows a group of program files in the order in which they appear in the directory:

COUNT.C

PREP.C

DSKTIME.C

VERTEST.C

ALL.C

SWITCHAR.C

To combine these source files into one destination file called ALL.C, I used the command line

   COPY *.C + ALL.C

This command gave me an error message, but the message came too late. COUNT.C had already been placed in the file called ALL.C, followed by PREP.C, DSKTIME.C, and VER-TEST.C. Then the error message appeared.

Why? The destination file is ALL.C. But ALL.C is also a source file. Because the destination file and the first source file have different names, DOS copies the first source file to the destination file. This copy is destructive because the contents of the destination file are lost before the copy is made. Each additional source file is appended to the destination file.

DOS then encounters a source file name that is identical to the destination file name. But DOS has already destroyed the old contents of the original destination file, so DOS cannot copy this file. DOS displays the message

```
Contents of destination lost before copy
```

and proceeds to concatenate the rest of the source files. When you use wild-card names, DOS scans the directory from beginning to end. When DOS encounters a file that matches the wild-card name, DOS operates on the matching file. ALL.C was not the first file in the directory. The first file was COUNT.C. DOS saw that this file name was not the same as ALL.C, the destination file, and created a new ALL.C. Four files later, DOS discovered that ALL.C was also a source file. DOS had already altered this file—hence, the problem and the error message. The command used was not correctly phrased.

The correct command for copying all the *.C files into ALL.C is

   COPY ALL.C + *.C

The last file without a plus sign in front of it is ALL.C. It becomes the destination file. Because ALL.C is also the first source file, DOS skips copying ALL.C. DOS appends all other .C files to ALL.C. Traveling down the list of files, versions of DOS before V3.3 find ALL.C a second time, know that this file has already been "copied," and skip the file again.

DOS V3.3 finds the file a second time and gives the Contents lost warning, but ALL.C is intact. The message is incorrect.

Another use for concatenation is to change the date and time of a file when you copy it to a different disk. When you copy a file, DOS preserves the date and time. To change B:ALL.C's date and time, type the following:

   COPY B:ALL.C+

DOS joins all files by the name ALL.C (in this case, only one) on drive B and places the results on drive C, the default disk drive in this example. DOS changes the date and time because the file on drive C is a "new" file—the product of all the files named ALL.C on drive B. In reality, the contents of the file are unchanged. This DOS quirk is useful. To "copy" the file B:ALL.C without moving it and to change the date and time, type the following line:

COPY B:ALL.C+,, B:

The two commas tell DOS that no other file name is given after the plus sign. You must specify B: to keep the file on drive B. B: is the destination file name. You do not, however, specify a source file to be joined to ALL.C. The two commas tell DOS that it has reached the end of the source file name. DOS usually expects a file name after the + sign. To ensure that DOS does not confuse the destination file name with the non-existent additional source file name, two commas designate the end of the source file name.

The preceding COPY command appends B:ALL.C to a file by the same name on the same drive. When no file name and extension are used for the destination, DOS uses the same file name as that of the source file. What really happens is that DOS leaves the file in place and just changes the date and time.

If you want to concatenate program or non-ASCII data files, do not forget to use the /B switch. If you try either of the preceding command lines on a nontext file, you will not get what you want.

Be careful with wild-card names when you use concatenation to change a file's date and time. If you type

COPY B:*.* + ,, B:

DOS will combine all the files on drive B into the first file found on B! You probably do not want to combine these files.

If you want a quick way to add lines to the end of a batch file, try the following command:

COPY filename.BAT+CON

First create a batch file with the command COPY CON TESTCOPY.BAT. Type this line into the batch file:

ECHO This is the original line

Press Enter, press F6, and then press Enter again. Now type

COPY TESTCOPY.BAT+CON

This line tells DOS to copy the contents of TESTCOPY.BAT and the contents of CON, the keyboard, to the destination file. Because no destination file is stated, DOS assumes that the destination is TESTCOPY.BAT. After you see the word CON appear on the screen, type

ECHO This is the added line

Again, press Enter, press F6, and then press Enter. Use the TYPE command to view the TESTCOPY batch file. You should see the following lines:

```
C>TYPE TESTCOPY.BAT

ECHO This is the original line

ECHO This is the added line
```

You can use this technique when you want to add a few lines to an established .BAT file. COPY CON is a crude way to capture lines from the keyboard, however. If you make a mistake and press Enter, you cannot go back to correct a line. To add more than a few lines, use a text editor or word-processing program.

Gaining More Control of Copying with XCOPY

DOS V3.2 introduced an extended copy command called XCOPY. XCOPY addresses the needs of three principal users: users who have more than one computer, users who have hard disks, and users who need more selectivity than the standard COPY command offers. Almost all PC users fit one or more of these categories, so XCOPY is an important command to know and use.

XCOPY is best described as a hybrid between COPY and BACKUP/RESTORE, the disk-backup commands discussed in Chapter 24. XCOPY and COPY both copy files between disks. But unlike COPY, XCOPY does not copy files to a nondisk device, such as the printer (PRN) or the console (CON). Like BACKUP and RESTORE, XCOPY can selectively copy files and traverse the directory tree to copy files from more than one directory.

Like COPY but unlike BACKUP, XCOPY copies files that are directly usable: you cannot use files processed by BACKUP until you have processed them with RESTORE. XCOPY's syntax is similar to COPY's syntax, but the switches are more complex. XCOPY's syntax is

dc:pathc**XCOPY** *ds:paths**filenames.exts*
dd:path*filenamed.extd* /V /P /W /S /E /A /M /D:*date*

The *dc:pathc*\\ is the XCOPY command's optional path name. The source files, designated by an *s*, are the files to be copied. If you omit the disk drive name (*ds:*), the current disk drive is used. If you omit the path name (*paths*\\), the current directory on the drive is used. You may use wild cards in the file name (*filenames.exts*). If you omit the file name, XCOPY assumes that you want to specify a wild card *.*, and all files in the given path will be copied. If you specify no path and file name, XCOPY issues an error message.

With XCOPY, the destination files are designated by a *d* in the name. File names, disk drives, and path names follow the rule of currents. If you do not specify a drive name (*dd:*), XCOPY uses the current disk drive. If you do not specify a path name (*pathd*\\), XCOPY uses the current disk's directory. If you omit the file name (*filenamed.extd*), the copied files retain their previous names.

If you give a destination name that might be a path name or a file name and the potential path does not exist on the destination, XCOPY asks you whether the destination is a file name or path name. This message was introduced with XCOPY V3.3. To illustrate XCOPY's operation, use the sample hierarchical directory in Appendix B. If you give the command

XCOPY C:\WORDS*.* A:\WORDS

to copy the files from C:\WORDS to the disk in drive A, and the disk does not have a directory called WORDS, XCOPY will display this message:

```
Does WORDS specify a file name
or directory name on the target
(F = file, D = directory)?
```

If the destination is a file name, answer **F**. If the destination is a directory, answer **D**. Unlike COPY, XCOPY creates directories on the destination disk as needed.

XCOPY's Switches

XCOPY has eight switches, as shown in table 20.1.

Table 20.1
XCOPY's Switches

Switch	Function
/V	*Verifies* that the files have been copied correctly (identical to COPY's /V switch).
/W	*Waits* until the disk has been changed. XCOPY prompts you to change disks before it searches for the files to copy.
/P	*Pauses* and asks for confirmation before copying each file.
/S	Copies the files in the source directory and all files in subsequent *subdirectories*. This option is identical to BACKUP's and RESTORE's /S switches.
/E	When given with the /S switch, causes XCOPY to create *empty* subdirectories on the destination if the subdirectory on the source is empty. If you do not give the /E switch, /S ignores empty directories.
/A	Copies files with *archive* flags set to on (the file has been created or modified since the last running of BACKUP or XCOPY). /A does not reset the file's archive flag.
/M	Copies files with archive flags set to on (the file has been created or *modified* since the last running of BACKUP or XCOPY). /M resets the file's archive flag.
/D:*date*	Copies files created or modified since *date*. This option is identical to BACKUP's /D switch.

/V is the familiar *verify* switch. XCOPY verifies that it has copied the files correctly.

/W causes XCOPY to prompt and *wait* for you to insert the source disk. This switch is particularly important to floppy-disk-drive users. XCOPY is an external program that must be loaded from a disk, which normally starts the copying process after the program loads. If you want to copy files between disks that do not have the XCOPY program, use the /W switch. After XCOPY starts, the program prompts you to insert the correct disk. Remove the disk that holds XCOPY, insert the correct disk, and press any key to start the actual copying process.

/P is the *pause and ask* switch. XCOPY displays the name of the file it will copy and asks if the file should be copied. Answer **Y** to copy the file or **N** to skip it. When you answer **Y**, XCOPY immediately copies the file.

The next two switches, */S* and */E*, affect how XCOPY handles additional subdirectories. These two switches show the true power of XCOPY. COPY limits itself to handling the files from one directory. XCOPY starts with the named or current directory and can process the files in all additional subdirectories of the directory, all subdirectories of these subdirectories, and so on. XCOPY traverses the subdirectory tree and can copy complete directory branches from one disk to another.

The /S switch affects the source and destination directories. If you give the /S switch, you are instructing XCOPY to copy all designated files from the current and subsequent *subdirectories* to a parallel set of subdirectories on the destination disk drive. If you use the sample directory system shown in Appendix B, giving the command

   XCOPY C:\WORDS*.* A: /S

first copies all files in WORDS to the current directory on drive A. The command then copies all files from WORDS\LETTERS to a subdirectory of the current directory called LETTERS on drive A and then copies all files from the subdirectory WORDS\CONTRACTS to the subdirectory of the current directory on drive A called CONTRACTS. In essence, XCOPY lifts a copy of the subdirectory tree starting at the source directory and transplants the copy onto drive A.

Note that XCOPY does not place the copied files from the subdirectories into a single directory. XCOPY places files from one subdirectory into a parallel subdirectory. If the subdirectory does not exist on the destination, XCOPY creates the subdirectory.

The */E* switch affects the way the /S switch works. If XCOPY encounters an empty subdirectory on the source drive, XCOPY /S skips the *empty* subdirectory. If you give the /S and /E switches, XCOPY also creates empty subdirectories on the destination drive. If you give the /E switch without giving the /S switch, the /E switch has no meaning.

The next three switches, */A, /M,* and */D:date,* control which files that match the source file name will be copied. The /M switch tells XCOPY to copy any file that has been *modified*. This switch really tells XCOPY to copy a file you have not previously backed up or copied with XCOPY. Remember the archive attribute from Chapter 10? It is stored in the directory with each file name. When you create or change a file, this attribute is turned on. XCOPY checks whether the archive attribute has been set. When you give the /M switch, XCOPY processes this file. If the attribute is not set, XCOPY skips the file.

The /A switch works like the /M switch. XCOPY will process only those files that have the *archive* flag turned on. However, whereas /M clears the archive attribute after XCOPY has copied a file, /A does not. This difference can be important. As you will learn later in this book, the BACKUP command can select files based on the archive attribute. However, if XCOPY has cleared this flag, BACKUP will not process the file. Therefore, if you use XCOPY /M and BACKUP /M (the switches have identical meaning for the two commands), the backup you make using BACKUP may not be complete. Unless you customarily use XCOPY as a backup program, avoid using the /M switch; use the /A switch instead.

The */D:date* switch selects files based on their directory *date,* which is the date of the file's creation or modification. XCOPY copies files that have been created or modified on or after the date specified.

Using XCOPY Effectively

Because XCOPY can control which files should be copied by date or archive attribute, can copy complete subdirectory trees, and can confirm which files should be copied, the command has several ideal uses. One use is to copy files selectively between disks or directories. A second major use is as a "quickie" hard-disk backup command if you want to back up only a few critical files in several subdirectories. The third major use is to keep the directories of more than one computer synchronized—a task that affects more and more computer users each day.

With COPY, control is limited: the only control you have over the files that COPY will process is the source file name. COPY copies all files that match the given name, which is an all-or-nothing approach. If you use the /P switch with XCOPY, you can select all the files that match the source file name, and XCOPY will ask you if each file should be copied. You can give a single "larger" file name (a name that selects more files than necessary but covers all the files you may want to copy), and then you can select individually which files you really want to copy.

The only fault I find with the /P switch is that XCOPY immediately begins copying after you answer **Y** to its query. You have to wait for XCOPY to finish copying each file before XCOPY presents the next file name and asks if that file should be copied. I prefer a program that presents all the file names for you to select from, accepts all the selections, and then copies the selected files.

XCOPY is practical to use if you want to make backup copies of less than a disk full of files from several directories. Rather than using BACKUP, you might prefer to use XCOPY /A to select files that have changed since the last backup.

This technique has one drawback: you should ensure that the files will fit on one disk. When the destination disk fills, XCOPY stops. XCOPY cannot gracefully handle full disks. You must change disks and restart the XCOPY process using the /A and /P switches to skip the files you have already copied. Also, XCOPY cannot handle files that occupy more than one disk. If you need to back up such a file, use BACKUP.

My favorite use of XCOPY is to keep the contents of two computers' hard disks synchronized. More and more people use multiple computers today, especially many people who have one computer at work and another at home. If both computers have hard disks, keeping your copies of programs and data files current is a major task. Which files did you change today? Which machine has the more current version?

XCOPY is a godsend. You will find especially useful the /A switch or the /D:date switch if you use the /S switch on the source and destination computers. The /S switch forces XCOPY to play a hunting game you would otherwise need to perform manually. Which switch you use, /A or /D, depends on how often you copy files between the machines. If you copy files between the machines frequently, you will find that the /A switch is preferable. If you let many days pass between synchronizing your computers' contents, you may find that the /D switch works better. If you run BACKUP on the source machine between the times you use XCOPY, you must use the /D switch. BACKUP resets the archive attribute, and XCOPY will not catch all files that have changed.

Summary

In this chapter, you learned these important points:

❏ When you use COPY to copy files, you can specify the /A (ASCII file) and /B (binary file) switches.

❏ You can use COPY to join, or concatenate, files. The command **COPY filename.ext+CON** is a quick method of adding lines to an established file.

❏ XCOPY can only copy files between disk devices. The command can traverse the subdirectory tree, select files based on their archive attribute or date, and confirm individual files for copying.

Chapter 21 extends the discussion of file management to the DOS Shell, showing you how to efficiently manage files with DOS V4 and customize the Shell to suit your needs.

21

Managing the DOS V4 Shell

This chapter shows you how to manage your DOS V4 Shell system more efficiently. You'll learn how to add programs to the Main Group, and you'll find out how to add new groups, delete some of the default Main Group selections, and further customize the Shell to suit your needs.

Working with the Program Menu

You've already seen in Chapter 4 that you can use the Program menu to start programs listed in the Main Group: you can start any program highlighted in the Main Group by pulling down the Program menu and choosing Start. Because you can run a program even more quickly from the Main Group menu, however, you've probably not used the Start option very much. The Program menu has four other options: Add..., Change..., Delete..., and Copy....

You use the Add... option to put additional programs in the Main Group. The Change... option enables you to modify the guidelines or parameters used to load a specific program from the Shell. You use this option to change certain information (such as the path DOS uses to find the program) about a program already available from the Shell. With the Delete... option, you remove programs from the menu entirely. And with the Copy... option, you duplicate a given program in another menu. (You can then delete that program from the old menu if you want to move the program rather than simply duplicate it.)

Note that each of these menu listings is followed by trailing dots, which indicate that an additional menu is summoned whenever you select that option.

Adding a Program

Adding a program to the DOS Shell is simple. You may have up to 16 entries in a group menu at one time, including programs and other groups (those followed by trailing dots, such as DOS Utilities...). When you select the Add... menu option, the screen shown in figure 21.1 appears.

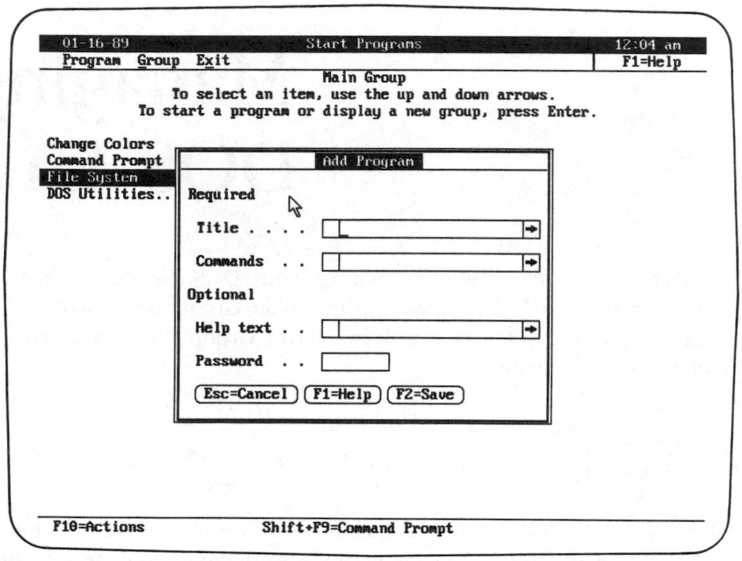

Fig. 21.1

The Add Program menu.

Of the four parameters that you can type, two are required; the other two are optional. The first required parameter is the program's title, the label that will be used in the Main Group menu (or other menu, if you are adding the program to a different group, as you'll see later). This title can have up to 40 characters and may contain spaces, upper-case or lowercase characters, and even graphics characters.

More commonly, you call the new program by a useful name, such as DisplayWrite 4 or dBASE III®. Press Enter when you have finished typing. You also may press the Tab key or use the mouse to move to the next field.

The second required parameter is the set of commands needed to load the program. You have two options here: On the Commands line, you may type in all the commands needed to load your program, using up to 500 characters. Or you may incorporate all the commands into a batch file and CALL that batch file.

If your program has relatively simple parameters, or if you want to use some of the Shell customizing tools introduced shortly, you may want to incorporate the commands into the Add Program file. You'll then find that changing those commands directly from the DOS Shell is relatively simple. Suppose that your word processing program loads with the following commands:

```
C:
CD \WP
WORDRITE
CD \
```

These commands simply make drive C the current drive, instruct the drive to log onto the C:\WP subdirectory, request the loading of the fictitious program WORDRITE, and then instruct the drive to log back to the root directory after the program is finished. If you decide to move WORDRITE to another subdirectory, you can change a single line (by using the Change... menu) and be done.

To enter such a string of commands, type them on the Commands line, pressing F4 to separate each line. A graphics character in the form of a double vertical bar appears between each command. The preceding example would look like this:

**C:‖CD \WP‖WORDRITE‖CD **

Your application might involve much more complex setup commands. The following is a batch file used to load IBM's DisplayWrite 4 word processing program:

```
ECHO OFF
REM RELEASE 2.0
MODE LPT1:,,,P
MODE LPT2:,,,P
CD >D:\dw4\DW4ODIR.BAT
D:
CD \dw4
CD >D:\dw4\DW4DDIR.LST
D:
CD \dw4
DW4PG D:\dw4\PROFILE.PRF,D:\dw4,,,C
D:
CD D:\dw4
IF NOT EXIST DW4ODIR.BAT GOTO LABEL1
DW4ODIR
:LABEL1
```

You could type in all these commands, but creating such a list as a batch file is easier. You could then use a text editor to edit the file if you want to make changes.

If the file were named DW4.BAT, you would load DisplayWrite 4 by typing this command on the Commands line of the Add Programs panel:

CALL DW4

DW4.BAT would have to reside in a subdirectory pointed to by your PATH command. Or you can explicitly name, on the Commands line, the subdirectory where DW4.BAT is located.

If you want, you may add two more items of information to the Add Program panel. First, you can create your own help text, which will be displayed when your new program entry is highlighted and you press F1. Up to 478 characters may be entered. The

Shell neatly displays this information in pages that you can scroll through. You may want your help text to explain what the program is or how it is to be used.

Second, to limit access to a program, you can specify a password of up to eight characters. If you create a password, you must use it in order for the Shell to load, change, copy, or delete that program. Don't forget the password, or you won't be able to perform any of these functions!

Because you can tailor the parameters for each entry you add, you may create menu options for quite specialized operations. The first exercise in this chapter is a simple one: creating a menu selection that will back up to a floppy disk all changed files in your C:\BATCH subdirectory. You'll use the XCOPY command.

For this exercise, you need your computer and a blank, formatted floppy disk. If you don't have a C:\BATCH subdirectory, substitute the name of a directory on your hard disk. Follow these steps:

Step 1. *Insert the blank, formatted disk in drive A.*

Step 2. *From the action bar, pull down the Program menu and select Add....*

Step 3. *Type in the following title:*

Back Up Batch Subdirectory

Step 4. *Press Tab to move to the* Commands *line and type in the following commands. Do not type the characters "<F4>"; rather, press F4 at the ends of the first and second lines.*

ECHO INSERT BACKUP DISK IN DRIVE A:<F4>
PAUSE<F4>
XCOPY C:\BATCH A:\ /M

Step 5. *Press Tab again to move to the* Help text *line; type the following:*

Copies any batch files that have changed since they were last copied. Files are copied to the floppy disk in drive A.

Step 6. *Press Tab once more to move to the* Password *line; enter the following password:*

XCOPY

Step 7. *To save your new entry, press F2 or, using the mouse, choose the F2 box.*

The Back Up Batch Subdirectory selection appears in the Main Group menu.

Test your new menu option by selecting it a few times. You'll need to enter the password, XCOPY, to activate it. In the next section, we'll use the Change... option to remove the password.

The DOS Shell enables you to customize the Add Program entries even more extensively. Because you can create interactive menu selections (which ask you to enter information "on the fly"), the Shell can be even *more* versatile than most batch files. To demonstrate this versatility, let's create a menu entry that enables you to perform much the same backup command but also to specify the source and destination drives and directories.

First you need to learn about the Shell's optional prompt panels. You can insert these on the `Commands` line by typing a pair of square brackets, which look like this: [].

In the preceding example, if you'd wanted to allow yourself to enter the source and destination subdirectories, you could have replaced both C:\BATCH and A:\ with pairs of brackets, like this:

XCOPY [ ] [ ] /M

You would then be asked to substitute parameters for those two sets of brackets. Unfortunately, new users hardly know what parameters are required, and help screens might be too little too late. So the Shell enables you to enter a prompt panel for each of those parameters. These prompt panels replace the default (and somewhat generic) Enter Parameters box that appears if you do not create your own panel.

A prompt panel enables you to enter three options: /T"title," the name of the prompt panel; /I"instructions," your instructions; and /P"prompt," the label for the line itself where the parameters are typed in. The first two options may be up to 40 characters long; the prompt may be 20 characters or fewer. These options will become clearer in the following example, in which you'll create a new Main Group option called Back Up a Directory.

To create a new Main Group option, follow these steps:

Step 1. *Insert a blank, formatted disk into drive A.*

Step 2. *From the action bar, pull down the Program menu and select the Add... option.*

Step 3. *Type the following title:*

Back Up a Directory

Step 4. *Press Tab to move to the* `Commands` *line; type the following line, all as one line, without pressing F4.*

XCOPY [/T"Source Directory" /I"Full drive/path of source directory" /P"Drive/path..."] [/T"Destination Directory" /I"Drive/path of destination directory" /P"Drive/path..."] /M

Step 5. *Press Tab again to move to the* `Help text` *line; type the following:*

Copies to the destination directory any files in the source directory that have changed since they were last copied.

Step 6. *Press Tab once more to move to the* `Password` *line; enter the following password:*

XCOPY

***Step** 7. To save your new entry, press F2 or choose the F2 box by using the mouse.*

The Back Up a Directory selection appears in the Main Group menu.

When you call up this menu option, you'll be prompted with screens like those in figures 21.2, 21.3, and 21.4.

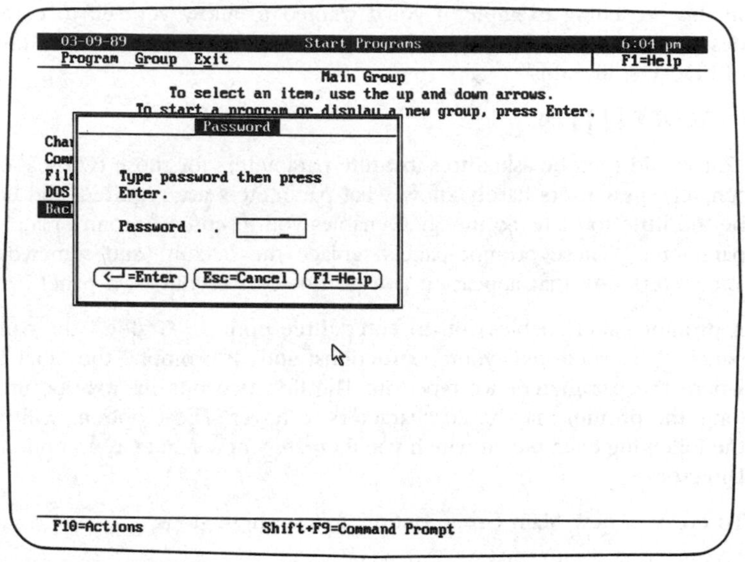
03-09-89
Start Programs
6:04 pm
Program Group Exit
F1=Help
Main Group
To select an item, use the up and down arrows.
To start a program or display a new group, press Enter.
Password
Type password then press
Enter.
Password . .
=Enter
Esc=Cancel
F1=Help
F10=Actions
Shift+F9=Command Prompt

Fig. 21.2

The Password prompt panel.

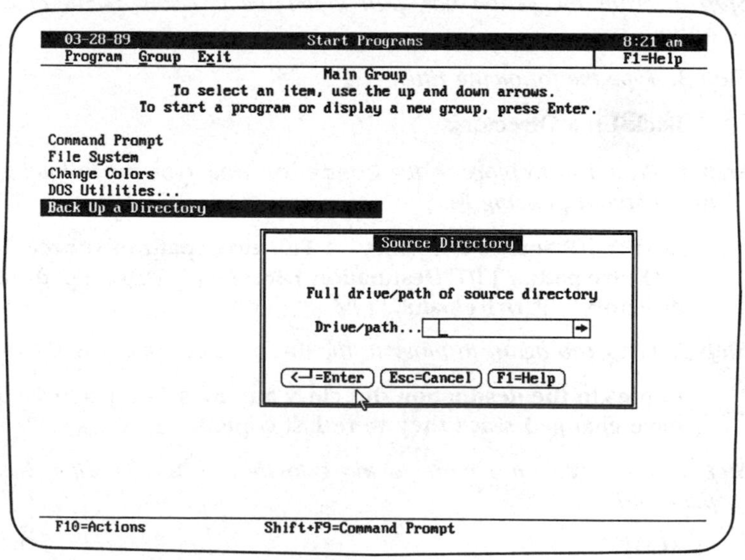
03-28-89
Start Programs
8:21 am
Program Group Exit
F1=Help
Main Group
To select an item, use the up and down arrows.
To start a program or display a new group, press Enter.
Command Prompt
File System
Change Colors
DOS Utilities...
Back Up a Directory
Source Directory
Full drive/path of source directory
Drive/path...
=Enter
Esc=Cancel
F1=Help
F10=Actions
Shift+F9=Command Prompt

Fig. 21.3

The customized Source Directory prompt panel.

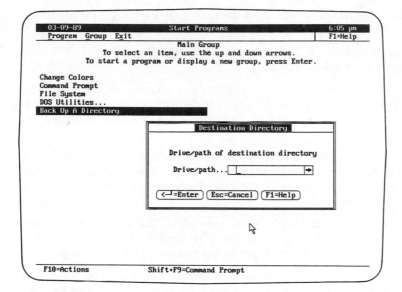

Fig. 21.4

The customized Destination Directory prompt panel.

You're not finished yet. You can use a number of other commands to customize your Add Program parameters. These commands are powerful facilities indeed. Let's run through the other options and then put them to work.

The /F"drive:\path\filename" parameter checks to see that the file specified by drive:\path\filename actually exists before you continue with the procedure. Suppose that you wanted to run a program from a floppy disk. Before continuing, you could check to see that the correct floppy disk was loaded.

The %n parameter is similar to the replaceable parameters used in batch files. You replace the *n* with a whole number from 1 to 10 and enter a value for each of the parameters as they appear in prompt panels. Then the parameters can be placed any-where in the Commands line. The new value will be substituted. Suppose that a com-mand line is as follows:

COPY [/T"Enter filename" /P"Filename..." %1] B: ||ERASE %1

When the program is called from the group, you will be asked to enter a file name. That file name will be stored in %1 and used as a parameter to copy the file (in this case, to drive B). That same file will then be erased by the second command on the line, ERASE %1.

The /D"text" parameter defines an initial or default value for the entry field within the brackets. If you press Enter instead of typing something in the prompt panel, the default text is used. Suppose that the command line is this:

XCOPY [/T"Source directory" /P"Directory..." /D"C:\BATCH"] A:

If you do not enter a value when prompted, the program defaults to C:\BATCH as the source directory.

If you want, you can use /D"%n" to specify as the default value a replaceable parameter defined earlier in the command string. Suppose that the command line is as follows:

COPY [/T"Enter filename" /P"Filename..." %1] B: ||ERASE
[/T"Erasing File" /P"File..." /D"%1"]

This command line prompts you to assign a file name to %1, copies that file to drive B, and then erases that file or enables you to substitute the name of another file to erase instead. Although this example may not be especially useful, it clearly illustrates the concept.

Sometimes, if you choose to type something other than the default value, you don't want to force yourself to erase the default supplied. The Shell provides a parameter to help you out: /R. If you include this parameter, the default value shown is erased as soon as you start to type something else.

The /L"n" parameter defines the length of the entry field. The letter *n* can be any number from 0 to 128. If you don't use /L"n", the entry field is 128 characters long. If you specify 0 for *n*, no characters can be typed in, but you must press Enter to proceed.

Using the /M"e" parameter causes the Shell to check whether the file name entered actually exists. If it doesn't, you will be asked to substitute a different name. Consider the following example:

COPY [/T"Enter filename" /P"Filename..." /M"e" %1] B:

These instructions take effect only if the file name specified by %1 actually exists. Otherwise, the prompt panel is repeated until you enter a valid file.

The /C"%n" parameter passes a variable defined in one section from a given group to another section. The variable must already be defined; that is, the previous menu choice must be used after the computer is turned on but before you use /C"%n." Imagine, for example, that you had the following two Main Group entries:

Copy a Program to Drive A:

ERASE a Program Copied to Drive A:

The first menu option's command line looks like this:

COPY [/T"Enter filename" /P"Filename..." %1] A:

The second menu option's command line looks like this:

ERASE [/C"%1"]

You wouldn't have to enter the name of the program to be erased; it would be supplied as the default. Note that %1 takes on the value of %1 as defined by the most recently used program selection. If you had another menu option that used %1, and that selection was chosen more recently, then its value for %1 would be used. In such a case, you might want to pair the two options so that you have the choice of erasing the file after it has been copied by the first task.

The /# parameter, which must be used outside the brackets, substitutes the drive letter (followed by a colon) from which the Shell was started. The /@ parameter, which also must be used outside the brackets, substitutes the path from which the Shell was started. No backslash is included in the path name that is substituted. You can use both these parameters to default to the drive and directories used to run the Shell.

Changing a Program

Now that you understand how to add a program, changing an existing program should be easy. Follow these steps:

Step 1. *Highlight the program to be changed. For this exercise, use the Back Up Batch Subdirectory program you created earlier.*

You cannot change any of the default DOS entries, such as Command Prompt, File System, DOS Utilities..., or Change Colors. You may change only those entries you have added yourself.

Step 2. *Pull down the Program menu and select Change....*

The Change Program menu appears. It looks like the Add Program menu, except that the title is different and that all the existing information about the program is shown.

Step 3. *Press Tab to move the cursor to the* Password *field. Delete the password.*

Step 4. *Press F2 to save the changed program entry.*

Now you can call Back Up Batch Subdirectory without entering a password.

Deleting a Program

You may want to delete a program that you no longer use. The program itself is not removed, only the menu entry. You cannot delete the default DOS program entries, such as Command Prompt, DOS Utilities..., or Change Colors. To delete other programs, follow these steps:

Step 1. *Highlight the program to be deleted. For this exercise, use the Back Up Batch Subdirectory program you created earlier.*

Step 2. *Pull down the Program menu and select Delete....*

The Delete Program menu appears, asking you to confirm or abort the process. The default option is Delete program.

Step 3. *Press Enter to delete the program.*

The Back Up Batch Subdirectory is removed.

Copying a Program

If you want, you can copy a program menu entry to the same group. Although two programs in the same group may have the same name, there is little point in that. You can also copy a program to a subgroup. In the following exercise, you'll copy the Back Up a Directory entry to another group, DOS Utilities.... Follow these steps:

Step 1. Highlight Back Up a Directory, the program in the Main Group to be copied.

Step 2. Pull down the Program menu from the action bar. Choose Copy....

Step 3. Now highlight the group that the program should be copied to. Move the cursor to the DOS Utilities... selection and press Enter, or double-click with the mouse.

The DOS Utilities menu appears.

Step 4. Press F2 to copy the program to the new group.

Back Up a Directory now appears in both the Main Group and DOS Utilities menus.

Working with the Group Menu

Working with group menus will be easy now that you know how to use the Add..., Change..., Delete..., and Copy... functions on programs in the Main Group. Note the word *menus*; as you'll see, groups beneath the Main Group can have subgroups of their own. You may find yourself building menus several levels deep in order to group a large number of programs conveniently.

Figure 21.5 shows the Group menu. Notice that this menu has four choices. Three are familiar: Add..., Change..., and Delete.... The fourth, Reorder..., enables you to change the arrangement of programs in the group listing.

Adding a Group

You may add a group, provided that fewer than 16 entries appear on the group menu you are working with. To add a group, follow these steps:

Step 1. Pull down the Group menu from the action bar.

Step 2. Choose Add....

The Add Group panel appears, containing, like the Add Program panel, four entries.

Step 3. Enter a title of up to 27 characters. The title is the name that will appear in the group menu. The Shell automatically adds the trailing dots.

Step 4. Enter a file name of up to eight characters. The file name is the name under which the new menu will be stored. The Shell automatically adds the .MEU extension for you.

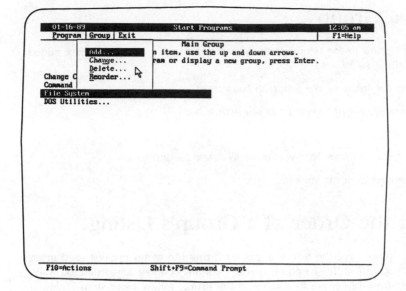

Fig. 21.5

The Group menu.

Step 5. *If you want, add help text and a password.*

Step 6. *Press F2 to save the new group entry.*

The new title appears in the group menu.

Changing a Group

Just as you can change the parameters used to define a program, you can change those used to define a group. Although you may not change the default DOS subgroups, such as the Main Group's File System, DOS Utilities..., and Change Colors options, you can add, change, or delete individual programs within those subgroups. Working within the current group (such as the Main Group), simply highlight the group you want to modify; press Enter or double-click the mouse. You may then access the Program or Group menu within the subgroup.

To change the parameters of a group you have added yourself, follow these steps:

Step 1. *Highlight the name of the group.*

Step 2. *Pull down the Group menu from the action bar.*

Step 3. *Select Change....*

The Change Group panel appears. It looks like the Add Group panel, except that the current information about the selected group is shown.

Step 4. *Using the Tab key, move to the field you want to change; make your changes.*

Step 5. *Press F2 to save the changes.*

Deleting a Group

Using the Delete option in the Group menu, you may remove a group you have added yourself. Follow these steps:

Step 1. Highlight the name of the group to be deleted.

Step 2. Pull down the Group menu from the action bar.

Step 3. Select Delete....

Step 4. Press Enter to confirm that you want to delete the group.

The group is removed from the menu.

Changing the Order of a Group's Listing

You may want to place near the top of a group's listing the menu options used most; doing so enables you to find those options quickly. You may choose any order you want. To move an entry from one place to another in the listing, follow these steps:

Step 1. Highlight the menu option to be moved.

Step 2. Pull down the Group menu.

Step 3. Choose Reorder....

Under the group title appears a prompt telling you to move the highlighting to the new position and press Enter.

Step 4. Use the cursor keys or mouse to move the highlighting to the new position you want the menu option to have. Press Enter.

The menu option is moved.

You can repeat Steps 1 through 4 as often as necessary to produce the order you want for a given group.

Creating a New Main Group Menu

Often, creating an entirely new Main Group menu is desirable. Perhaps you want to move the Command Prompt option to a special subgroup protected by a password. Such an arrangement enables only those users who know the password to use the command prompt.

Or you may find that certain Main Group entries, such as Change Colors, are rarely used.

The DOS Shell won't enable you to delete entries from the Main Group, however. So what do you do? The following exercise shows a way around that roadblock.

You'll create a subgroup that includes all the programs you want in your Main Group, except for the DOS defaults. Then you'll cause the Shell to use this new subgroup as its Main Group instead. You won't have deleted anything from the Main Group; you'll just have scrapped it and substituted a new one containing the files you want. The old Main Group can become a subgroup under your new Main Group.

Creating this subgroup is a lot easier than it sounds. Here are the steps:

Step 1. From the Main Group, pull down the Group menu from the action bar.

Step 2. Choose Add....

Step 3. In the Title *space, enter a name for the new group that will become your Main Group. For this example, type*

> **NEW**

The Shell later substitutes the name Main Group, so the name entered at this point is almost irrelevant.

Step 4. Press Tab to move to the Filename *line. Type*

> **NEW**

as the name to save this menu under. DOS adds the extension .MEU for you automatically.

Step 5. Type in help text if you want. Don't type in a password. Putting a password on the menu that will be your Main Group is generally not a good idea.

Step 6. Press F2 or, using the mouse, point to the F2 box and click.

Your new group appears in the present Main Group listing. Now copy the programs that you want to appear in the Main Group to this new group, called New.

Step 7. Highlight a program you want to copy. The program may be in the current Main Group, or it may be in one of the subgroups you have created. The program may not be one of the default DOS programs, such as Change Colors.

Step 8. Working within the group where the program to be copied is located, pull down the Program menu from the action bar.

Step 9. Choose the Copy... option.

A prompt reminds you to press F2 after the group the program is to be copied to appears on-screen.

Step 10. Move to the New group. If you are copying a program from a subgroup, press Esc to get out of the subgroup and return to the current Main Group; then select the New group with the cursor or mouse. If you are copying a program from the Main Group, simply choose the New group.

Step 11. When the New group is on-screen, press F2.

The program is copied to the group.

Step 12. Repeat Steps 7 through 11 until all the programs to be copied to the new Main Group have been duplicated.

Now you must substitute this new group for the current Main Group, which is stored in a file called SHELL.MEU. Your DOSSHELL.BAT file contains the line /MEU:SHELL.MEU. This line instructs the Shell to load SHELL.MEU as the Main Group when the Shell is started up. To use NEW.MEU instead, you need only edit DOSSHELL.BAT and substitute NEW.MEU for SHELL.MEU in that parameter. You may use EDLIN, or whatever ASCII text editor you work with, to edit batch files.

Step 13. Exit from the Shell (by using the Main Group's Exit option). Now load DOS-SHELL.BAT into your text editor. Find the /MEU:SHELL.MEU line. Replace SHELL.MEU with NEW.MEU and save the file.

Step 14. Reload the DOS Shell by using DOSSHELL.BAT.

The New group is now the Main Group menu and is labeled as such. You don't have access, however, to any of the default DOS functions formerly available from the Main Group. To resolve that problem, add the old Main Group as a new subgroup. Follow these steps:

Step 1. From the new Main Group, pull down the Group menu.

Step 2. Select Add....

Step 3. Type in a name for the old Main Group, such as

Shell Utilities

Step 4. On the `Filename` *line type*

SHELL.MEU

Step 5. Type help text if you want.

Step 6. If you want to protect this group with a password, type one in on the `Pass-word` *line.*

Step 7. Select F2 to save the new group parameters.

A new subgroup appears in your new Main Group. This new subgroup contains old DOS Shell functions such as Change Colors, as well as subgroups such as DOS Utilities....

Summary

This chapter showed you how to customize the DOS Shell even further by adding your own programs, groups, and menus. You learned how to provide your own prompts when creating special commands and program-loading files. Key points to remember in this chapter are the following:

❏ You cannot add or change the default DOS programs, such as Change Colors.

❏ You can create a new Main Group menu.

❏ The order of files within groups can be changed.

❏ Programs can be copied from one group to another.

22

Using Advanced
Features of the DOS
Shell File System

Although you have used the DOS Shell to copy files and perform other tasks, some of the File System's functions have not yet been explained. The reason is that you first needed to develop a background in a few of DOS's more esoteric aspects, such as file attributes, so that these new functions would make sense.

You now have the information you need to tackle the last few features of the DOS Shell. As you know, the File System has four pull-down headings in its action bar: File, Options, Arrange, and Exit. You already know how to use the Exit menu, but you have used the other three menus to only a limited extent. This chapter covers the more advanced functions listed in the File, Options, and Arrange menus.

Working with the File Menu

Figure 22.1 shows the File menu.

As figure 22.1 indicates, the File menu lists 12 options, which are divided into 3 groups. You already know how to use all the options in the third group. Of the middle group's options, you know how to use all but Move..., Change attribute..., and View. These three options, along with those in the first group, are explained in this section.

Moving a File

You can select the Move... option if you need to move a file (or files) quickly from an old subdirectory to a new one or if you need to send a file to a disk for archiving.

The Move... option works just like the Copy... option, except that after you have copied the file to the new directory or disk, the file is erased from the old location. The name of

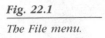

Fig. 22.1

The File menu.

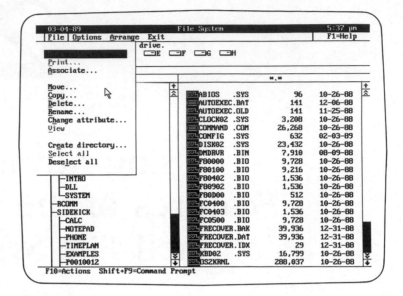

the file(s) you have marked in the file listing will appear on the From: line; you may specify the new location on the To: line.

If you have activated the Confirm on Delete choice in the Options menu, the Shell will ask you for a confirmation before it removes the old file.

Changing a File's Attributes

You can run the Change attribute... utility in batch mode to change several files one after another. You can also use the utility in global mode to change many files all at once in exactly the same way. Or you can use the utility to change only a single file. To change a file's attributes, follow these steps:

Step 1. *From the file listing, select the file(s) you want. Mark them by using the space bar or mouse.*

Step 2. *Pull down the File menu and choose the Change attribute... selection.*

The Change Attribute initial menu appears. You can choose to change all selected files either one at a time or simultaneously.

Step 3. *Choose either (1) One at a time or (2) All selected files at once. Press Enter.*

If you choose to change all selected files one at a time, each of the file names will appear in turn on the File: line of the next panel. If you elect to change all selected files at one time, no file names appear. Either way, the options of the hidden, read-only, and archive attributes will appear.

Step 4. *Choose the attributes you want to change.*

You can move the highlighting by using the mouse or cursor keys. Press the space bar to toggle the attribute on or off. (If the attribute is on, pressing the space bar will turn it off, and vice versa.)

Step 5. *When you have set the attributes as you want them for a given file, press Enter.*

The attributes are changed on the disk. If you have selected more than one file, the next file name will appear in the panel, and you can repeat Steps 3 through 5 until the last file is accounted for.

Viewing a File

The View option enables you to look at the contents of ASCII files. You can page through them by pressing the PgUp and PgDn keys.

To view a file, select it from the file list (either by using the mouse or by pressing the space bar when the file name is highlighted). Then pull down the File menu from the action bar and select View. The File View panel appears, as shown in figure 22.2.

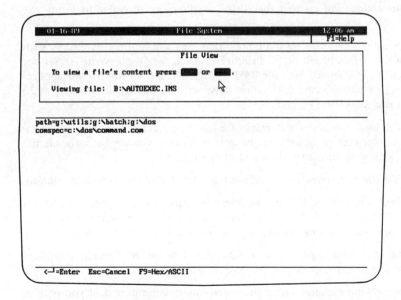

Fig. 22.2

The File View panel.

When you have finished viewing the file, press Esc to return to the File System.

Associating a File

The Associate... option enables you to specify to the Shell which applications programs are associated with various file extensions. After you have associated particular applications programs with particular file extensions, you may automatically start up one of those applications by simply selecting a data file used by it.

This procedure of selecting an associated data file is a third way to start up a program. You've already learned how to start a program from the Main Group or subgroup listings, and you also know how to use the Program menu in the action bar to start a program.

To associate an applications program with specific file extensions, follow these steps:

Step 1. *Choose the applications program that you want to associate with specific extensions.*

The program can be a .COM or .EXE file, or a .BAT batch file that loads a .COM or .EXE file.

Step 2. *Highlight the file by pressing the space bar or by moving the mouse pointer to the file's name and clicking the mouse.*

You may have to change the current disk drive or directory in order to locate the application.

Ideally, your applications program should be one that uses a default file extension, such as .PCX for Publisher's Paintbrush or PC Paintbrush, .DOC for DisplayWrite 4, .WP for WordPerfect, .WKQ for Quattro, .BAS for BASIC programs, and so on. If your applications program uses several different extensions, however, you can specify as many as 20 different ones in the Associate File menu.

Note that 20 is the total number of extensions for *all* the programs you want to associate. The extensions for each program must be unique. That is, you cannot associate the .DOC extension with *both* DisplayWrite 4 and PC-Write.

Step 3. *Pull down the File menu in the action bar and choose the Associate... option.*

If you have marked several files, the first file name appears. If the file does not have a valid extension (.COM, .EXE, or .BAT), you'll be told that the extension is invalid and asked to choose between skipping the file or entering a different extension.

Step 4. *If the file is a valid application or batch file, type on the* Extensions... *line the extension or extensions you want to associate.*

Type only the one to three characters of the extension, not the period. If you type in more than one extension, separate the entries with a space.

Step 5. *When you have typed the extensions for a given application, press Enter.*

The Prompt for Options panel appears. In this panel, you specify whether you want the Shell to (1) pause and ask for options when it loads the application or (2) load the application directly. Some of your programs may enable you to specify something on the command line, such as the file to be edited. You can choose Prompt for options if you want to provide this capability. If your application doesn't enable you to do this, or if you simply don't want this option, select Do not prompt for options.

Step 6. *Choose either Prompt for options or Do not prompt for options; press Enter.*

The Associate information is stored in a file called SHELL.ASC. Any time you try to open a file with an associated extension, the Shell will instead open the application you have tied to that extension.

Note that the Shell won't actually open the data file you have selected. You can type in that file name when prompted, if you have told the Shell to prompt for options when a data file with that extension is selected. At this point, however, no provision enables the DOS Shell to pass the file name directly to the application.

Opening a File

Aside from using the Associate... function, you may start an application by double-clicking the mouse after moving the mouse pointer to the appropriate file entry in the File System's directory listing. If you don't have a mouse, you can press Enter when the file name is highlighted. DOS will run the file if it is a valid .EXE, .COM, or .BAT file (unless it is a data file that has had its extension associated with an application).

The final way of starting a program is to choose the Open... option from the File menu when a file is highlighted in the directory listing. You also may type in a new file's name when the Open File panel appears on your screen (see fig. 22.3). In the Open File panel, you can type in an associated file name as well as options to be passed to the application when the file is opened.

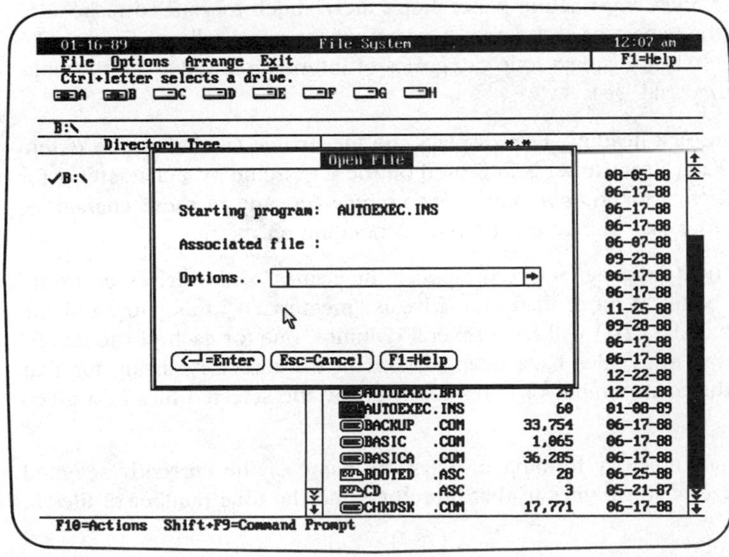

Fig. 22.3

The Open File panel.

Printing a File from the Shell

The DOS Shell includes a Print... option, which is similar to that available from the command prompt except that the switches used from the prompt are not readily available in the Shell. You *could* create a separate program that includes the PRINT command along with parameters that enable you to enter switches. The Shell's Print... option, however, is generally used only to get a quick printout of an ASCII file, so creating such a program is probably not worth your while.

In ASCII mode, the File System's Print... option works quite well. You must have PRINT.COM loaded from the DOS prompt in order for the option to work, though. Once you've done that, here are the steps to follow to print a file:

Step 1. Mark in the File System's directory listing the file(s) you want to print.

Step 2. Pull down the File menu.

Step 3. Choose Print... .

Each file you marked is submitted to DOS for printing. A panel confirming that the file has been submitted for printing appears, displaying the name of each file in turn.

Working with the Options Menu (Show Information...)

Earlier in this book, you learned how to use the three choices listed in the File System's Options menu: Display options..., File options..., and Show information.... At that time, however, some of the Show Information panel didn't mean much to you. To make sure that you understand the import of each entry, a review of the panel follows. Figure 22.4 shows a typical panel, which displays four categories of information under the headings File, Selected, Directory, and Disk.

The section under the first heading, File, displays the file's name (including the extension) and attributes. Each attribute set is indicated on the `Attr` line by a character: *r* for *read-only*, *h* for *hidden*, *s* for *system*, and *a* for *archive bit*. Any of these characters, none of them, or all four may appear on the line, depending on the file.

To the right of the next heading, Selected, appear the names of the drives currently stored in the Shell's buffer. If more than one drive is "memorized," this entry and the two below (`Number` and `Size`) will have several columns, one for each of the drives. `Number` indicates how many files have been marked in the directory listing for that drive. `Size` shows the total number of bytes taken up by the selected files in a given drive.

The section under the Directory heading displays the name of the currently selected directory, the total size of all the files in that directory, and the total number of files in that directory.

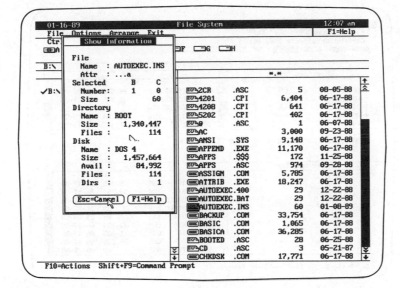

Fig. 22.4

*The Show
Information
panel.*

The last section, labeled Disk, covers information about the disk drive itself. The `Name`
entry is the label applied during formatting or with the LABEL command. The next
entry, `Size`, represents total disk space, and the `Avail` entry signifies free space available for new files. The `Files` entry shows the number of files stored on the disk. The
last entry, `Dirs`, shows the number of subdirectories on the disk.

Although certain utility programs provide the same information as the Show Information
panel, the panel gives DOS users easy access to all this data, in one place.

Working with the Arrange Menu

The Arrange menu, a powerful new tool, enables you to choose files from a single file
listing (the default option) or from multiple windows that show file listings for two disks
or directories. You also can select another option, System file list, that shows only the
DOS system files for the currently selected disk.

Because Single file list is the default option, you'll want to learn how to access the multiple windows. Follow these steps:

Step 1. *Making sure that the File System menu is on-screen, pull down the Arrange
menu and choose Multiple file list.*

The screen shows two panels, one above the other (see fig. 22.5), that each consist of a
directory tree section and a file listing section. The current drive and directory listing
appears in the top panel; the other buffered drive or directory appears in the bottom
panel. Each panel displays fewer lines than its corresponding single file listing would.

Fig. 22.5

The Multiple file list.

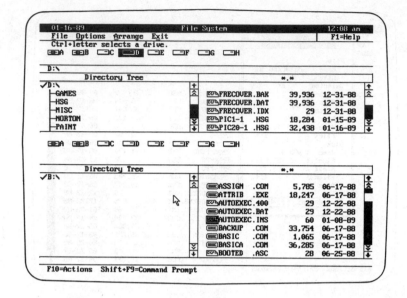

Fig. 22.5

The Multiple file list.

Step 2. *Use the mouse or Tab key to move from one panel to the other.*

You can scroll through each of the listings and manipulate the directory tree of each individually.

Step 3. *If you want to select another drive for an active panel, move the mouse pointer to the drive symbol you want; then click the mouse. Or hold down the control key and press the letter associated with that drive (A, B, C, and so on).*

Each set of panels has a drive-selector line.

Step 4. *To return to the single file list, pull down the Arrange menu and choose Single file list.*

Summary

In this chapter, you learned more techniques for using the DOS Shell File System. Important points to remember include these:

❑ The File System enables you to change the attributes of files.

❑ Files may be erased automatically after they are copied to another disk or directory.

❑ You can associate an application with the file extensions its data files use. As a result, the application will be loaded automatically when you attempt to open the data file.

❑ The Shell provides an extensive Show Information listing.

❑ You may view the directories of more than one disk or subdirectory at one time by using the Multiple file list option.

In Chapter 23, you'll see how to gain more control over your disk drives, printer, and other devices.

23

Gaining Control of Drives, Devices, and the Printer

This chapter discusses some of DOS's fundamental and advanced commands—RECOVER, MODE, and PRINT. RECOVER salvages files that have bad sectors. MODE controls the screen, serial ports, and printer. The PRINT command prints files while you continue performing other work with your computer.

Recovering Files and Disks (RECOVER)

The RECOVER command works with one file or with a complete disk. The form of RECOVER that works with a complete disk is dangerous and should not be run unless you have no alternative. Once DOS has "fixed" the directory, you may spend hours trying to recover from RECOVER. The form of RECOVER you use on a single file is not risky, however.

How do you recover a file with defective sectors on the hard disk? RECOVER is the program to use. With RECOVER, you can make a new copy of a file, minus the data held in the bad sectors. A bonus is that the bad sectors are marked "in use" so that they will not be used again.

The syntax for this form of RECOVER is

   *dc:pathc***RECOVER** *d:path***filename**.*ext*

The *dc:pathc* is the optional disk drive and path name to the RECOVER command. The *d:* is the optional disk drive name if the file is not on the current disk drive. The *path* is the optional path name if the file is not in the current directory. The **filename** is the root name of the file to recover, and *.ext* is the optional extension.

After you use RECOVER on a file, the file you are recovering has the same name as before. The bad sectors on the disk are "removed" from use, but the material in them is lost. This recovery method means that the total capacity of the disk is decreased by the capacity of the bad sectors that have been removed.

The only files you should recover are text and data files. Do not bother recovering program files. When information is lost from such a file, the program may not run at all or, worse, may run erratically when you recover it. Use a backup copy of the program instead.

You will need to edit text or data files after you recover them. For text or ASCII data files, use a text editor to get rid of any garbage or to add lost information. For non-ASCII data files, you may need special programs to restore files to their original states. Many applications programs will refuse to read data files that have been recovered, because essential header or internal pointer information may have been deleted.

There is little reason to recover a file with RECOVER. If you make frequent backup copies of your hard disk or floppy disks, you can usually restore files easily from the backup copies and then re-edit as necessary. You should run RECOVER, though, to "hide" the bad sectors on the disk.

The only way to remove bad sectors is to reformat the disk. If the disk is physically damaged, formatting will not help, however. If the disk is a floppy disk, you should retire it. Hard disks, however, are difficult to retire. You will have to live with any flaws.

Bad sectors are a bad sign. Either the magnetic coating on the disk is damaged, or you have a problem with the electronics of the disk drive. The most likely reasons—in order—are these: (1) mishandling of the floppy disk or hard disk; (2) physical wear from normal use of the floppy disk (seldom applicable to a hard disk because its recording heads do not touch the surface when the drive is in use); (3) mechanical or electronic failure of the disk drive; (4) electronic failure of the disk interface or controller card (the board inside your computer); (5) a damaged disk drive cable; (6) bad random-access memory in the computer.

Bad RAM occurs infrequently. But when it does, the change can cause erratic or disastrous disk performance. The best you can hope for is that DOS will just go "dead in the water." The worst that can happen is that DOS will reformat the disk or make garbage of directories. That is why a *memory-parity error* makes your computer "lock up." IBM wisely chose to stop the computer so that only work in progress is destroyed and not your previous work, programs, and data stored on the disks.

If a floppy disk is physically worn, the time has come to retire it. Look through the access holes at the floppy disk's surface. Dark grooves indicate wear. Dark or dull splotches may indicate spots where the floppy disk has been mishandled or contaminated. If you see a fold or crease, retire the disk.

Mechanical or electronic problems are more difficult to analyze. Run your diagnostics program. For floppy disk drives, use a disk formatted on a drive you know is good. If the problem is in the hard disk, back the disk up immediately!

If problems show up when you run the diagnostics, have your computer or disk drive repaired right away, before other floppy disks are harmed. If a problem with a disk drive shows up in the diagnostics, it may be caused by the disk drive, the interface board inside the computer, the cable that connects the board and the disk drive, the power supply of the disk drives, or possibly something else in the computer's main circuitry. Whatever the problem, have it repaired immediately.

Seldom do you electronically damage a floppy disk or hard disk when you read information. If the problem is not in the floppy disk itself, and you have not written information to it, the floppy disk and its files are probably still intact. There is always a small chance that the disk drive wrote some garbage instead of reading information. Check out all the files or floppies you have used since you first detected the problem. Make sure that the information is intact.

What about bad sectors that can develop in directories? This problem is a serious one. If a bad sector is in the root directory, the problem is grave. The root directory is in a fixed position on the hard disk or floppy disk. Because DOS cannot move the root directory, this condition can be "fatal." The second form of RECOVER, the potentially dangerous form, recovers damaged root directories.

If a subdirectory has bad sectors, the problem is serious, but not fatal. CHKDSK can cope with it. (For more information about CHKDSK, see the *DOS Command Reference*.) Before you run CHKDSK, take the following steps for copying the floppy disk or hard disk. If CHKDSK does not work, RECOVER is your final choice.

First, you should copy or back up all the files you can. Use a different set of floppy disks than the set you used for your last backup copies. Keep your last backup floppy disks intact. You may need to use them if all else fails.

For a faulty floppy disk, use the COPY command to copy each file to a second floppy disk. Then use the DISKCOPY command to copy the bad floppy disk to a third floppy disk. If the offender is the hard disk, use a different set of backup floppy disks. Run BACKUP, keeping your master backups and last daily backups intact.

Because you do not know at this point the cause of any bad sectors, you should suspect that the same problem exists in the backed-up or copied files you have just made. Whatever caused the directory to develop bad sectors may have damaged other areas on the floppy disk or hard disk. Make sure that the files you just copied or backed up are correct before you fully trust them.

(If the problem is in a subdirectory, use CHKDSK first. If CHKDSK does not work, use RECOVER. In either case, you should continue reading the rest of this section.)

The next step is to use RECOVER. The syntax for this form of RECOVER is

    *dc:pathc***RECOVER** *d:*

The *dc:pathc* is the optional disk drive and path name to the RECOVER command. The second *d:* is the optional disk drive name. If the current drive does not hold the disk you want to recover, give the appropriate disk drive name.

DOS will run through the file allocation table (FAT). Remember that the FAT knows the disk clusters (sectors) where each file is stored. But the FAT does not know the previous file name, the file's attributes (system, hidden, etc.), or the file's date and time.

DOS first re-creates the root directory. Then DOS begins to create files with the name FILEnnnn.REC in the root directory. The *nnnn* is a number from 0000 to 9999. Each file that DOS creates represents one of the recovered files from the disk. Every file on the disk becomes a FILEnnnn.REC file: program files, data files, and subdirectories.

Now the detective work begins. Each FILEnnnn.REC can be anything—a normal file or a subdirectory. You must find which FILEnnnn.REC files hold the information you need to keep and which FILEnnnn.REC files (such as subdirectories) hold information you can discard. The files' previous names are lost. Their dates and times are also lost. The best indicator of what is in each file is the file itself.

You will need several tools to help you. The TYPE command can display on-screen the characters in a file. This command will help you identify ASCII text files. Program files and subdirectories are different, however. Most of their information is displayed as gibberish. To display the contents of these files, you will need DOS's DEBUG, NU from the Norton Utilities™, DUMP.EXE from Phoenix Associates, or a similar program.

With one of these tools, you can find the files you were not able to copy or backup. Copy these files to another floppy disk and change their names back to what they were. Make sure that the files are intact. There is a small chance that whatever caused the directory to develop bad sectors may have affected other areas of the floppy disk or hard disk, making other files bad also.

The task of identifying each file is difficult. For practice, I took a backup copy of a good floppy disk and ran RESTORE on the floppy disk. (I also had another backup copy.) I then tried to find the files, using TYPE to type the files and DEBUG and DUMP to identify them. I spent several hours trying to decipher a 360K floppy disk. A full 1.2M or 1.44M floppy disk takes even more hours to restore. You should use RECOVER only as a last resort. Unless your backup copies are extremely out-of-date, you will find that re-creating or re-editing files is better than trying to use RECOVER on a hard disk or floppy disk.

Before you use RECOVER, practice first on a copy of any floppy disk. Then work with a copy of the disk you are attempting to recover. If you botch up the copy, nothing is really lost.

When you try to recover a floppy disk with a flawed directory, again use a copy. If you make a mistake with the copy, you can make another copy of the original, flawed floppy disk. If you work with the flawed floppy disk and do not have a copy, a mistake can be costly.

Remember that this discussion does not apply to the **RECOVER filename** command, in which RECOVER is used on a single file. Because this process works on one file at a time, the worst that can happen is that you will lose part of the file.

After you have re-created your files, you should reformat your floppy disk or hard disk. FORMAT gives a message when it cannot properly format any system area, including the areas for the boot record, the root directory, and the FAT. If you use FORMAT's /S switch, IBMBIO.COM's and IBMDOS.COM's areas are also checked, and DOS gives error messages if these areas are bad. The error messages indicate that the floppy disk or hard disk is currently unusable. You can retire a floppy disk, but you must have a hard disk repaired.

Remember to back up your data frequently. You will have less work and experience less frustration if you back up your floppy disks and hard disk instead of trying to re-create them with RECOVER.

Changing Modes of Operation (MODE)

The MODE command is unique to PC DOS. MODE serves several purposes. In fact, you could say that MODE is eleven commands in one. (MODE is treated this way in the *DOS Command Reference*.)

MODE enables you to customize your computer's setup. The major difference between using MODE and using the CONFIG.SYS file to customize DOS is that what you do with MODE is lost when you turn off your computer or reboot DOS. If you find yourself issuing a MODE command whenever you boot DOS, it is time to put that command in the AUTOEXEC.BAT file.

MODE handles printers, serial adapters, and display adapters. MODE also prepares, selects, and displays font files for international computer users. The information on the international uses of MODE is in Chapter 18. This chapter covers the other uses of MODE, including the three new uses of MODE introduced with DOS V4. This information is important for users of PCs and PS/2 computers.

Controlling Your Printer

For printing, MODE sets the lines per inch and characters per inch, handles timeouts, and indicates whether you are using a serial printer. (*Timeout* is the period that the printer is not ready in a given length of time.) Remember, you can have as many as three printers. The first printer, the primary one, is called LPT1:. (PRN is the pseudonym for whatever printer is LPT1. When you use PRN, you are telling DOS to use whatever has been assigned as LPT1.)

The syntax for this form of MODE is

MODE LPTx *cpl, lpi, P*

The x is the *number* of the printer (1, 2, or 3), and *cpl* is the number of *characters per line*, based on an eight-inch-wide line. This number can be either 80 (10 characters per inch) or 132 (16.5 characters per inch). The *lpi* stands for *lines per inch*, which can be either 6 or 8. And *P* tells DOS to "keep trying" when the printer is not ready.

DOS starts with the printer set at 80 characters per line and 6 lines per inch. To see how your printer is set up, type

MODE LPTx

Substitute the number of the printer (usually 1) for the x.

This form of MODE works best with IBM and Epson® printers or with printers that act like Epson printers. If you do not have such a printer, MODE cannot set the characters per line or the lines per inch. In fact, MODE gives a printer-error message when you try to use MODE with some other type of printer.

If you want DOS to keep trying to send characters to the printer when something is wrong, you must give the full command with the P whenever you use MODE LPTx. If you give MODE LPTx without the P, DOS will not retry but will give an error message when the printer "times out."

If you give the P and your printer "hangs up," your computer will lock up. You can get the computer out of this situation by pressing Ctrl-C or Ctrl-Break. The computer should respond within 20 to 40 seconds.

If you are using a network in which the printer is shared, you should omit the P option. If the printer is busy because another computer is using the printer, the performance of your computer will come almost to a standstill until the printer is free.

The retry option has a new format in DOS V4. You can add the RETRY=x parameter. For x, substitute any of the following:

E	to return an error from a check of a busy port
B	to return a busy signal from a busy port
R	to return a ready message from a busy port
NONE	for no action if the port is busy.

If you do not want to change all the options for MODE, either drop the optional elements from the command line or use a comma and leave out the number. For example, the following command line changes the characters per line to 132 and the lines per inch to 8:

MODE LPT1 132, 8

The following line sets the characters per line to 80 but leaves the lines per inch unchanged:

MODE LPT1 80

Finally, this command line leaves the characters per line unchanged and changes the lines per inch to 6:

MODE LPT1, 6

In these three examples, DOS will not retry on a timeout because the P has been omitted. To get continuous retries, you must add **,P** to the first and third examples and **,,P** to the second example.

Using a Serial Printer

The second form of MODE also involves the printer. The syntax is

MODE LPTx: = COMy:

Here, x is the number of the printer you are reassigning, and COMy: is the communications adapter for your serial printer. This form of MODE tricks DOS into using the serial printer connected to a communications adapter instead of using the normal parallel printer. You may need to check what number is correct for the communications adapter because the number can be either 1, 2, 3, or 4. Use 1 if you have only one communications adapter (serial port). PS/2 users can use as many as four adapters. If you have more than one adapter, check with your dealer or experiment with this command.

Typing the following line directs DOS to use the printer connected to the first communications adapter:

MODE LPT1 = COM1

To reverse this setting, enter **MODE LPTx.** No other information is required.

Before you use this form of the command, you should set up the asynchronous serial adapter, using the form of MODE discussed in the next section.

Controlling the Serial Adapter

This form of MODE sets the communications adapter's characteristics: baud rate, parity, data bits, stop bits, and retries. The syntax is

MODE COMy: baud rate, *parity, data bits, stop bits, P*

The y is the number of the communications adapter (1 through 4 for PS/2s; 1 or 2 for PCs). The colon after the number is optional. The baud rate is mandatory: it can be **110, 300, 600, 1200, 2400, 4800,** or **9600.** If you are using a PS/2, the baud rate can also be **19200.** You can abbreviate the baud rate to just two numbers, such as 30 for 300 baud, 96 for 9600 baud, or 19 for 19200.

The rest of the command's syntax is optional. If you do not include a characteristic, you should use a comma for each characteristic you skip. DOS also expects these parameters to be in the order shown on the syntax line.

parity can be Odd, Even, or None. With DOS V4, you can also use Mark and Space parity. Mark indicates that the parity bit is always 1, whereas Space indicates a 0 parity bit. Only the first character—O, E, N, M, or S—is necessary. Parity starts as even. The number of data bits is either 7 or 8; the number starts as 7. And the number of stop bits is either 1 or 2. If you use 110 baud, the default is 2 stop bits. Any baud rate faster than 110 will default to 1 stop bit.

As with MODE LPTx, the P in MODE COM. is the retry option. If you do not set P, the option is off. Retry is good to use with printers (when the printer is not used on a network), but not when the adapter is used with a modem. You can use Ctrl-C or Ctrl-Break to get out of a retry loop.

With DOS V4, the retry option gained a new format. You can add the RETRY = x parameter. For x you can substitute any of the following:

E	to return an error from a check of a busy port
B	to return a busy signal from a busy port
R	to return a ready message from a busy port
NONE	for no action if the port is busy.

As with MODE and LPT, the default is no retry action if the port is busy.

Look at the following command lines:

MODE COM1 1200
MODE COM1 12

Either line sets the baud rate at 1200 for the first communications adapter. Everything except the retry remains the same. If retry were set before, it is now off because it is not given here.

The following command line sets the first adapter to 19200 baud and 7 data bits:

MODE COM1 19,,7

Everything else except the retry is unchanged. Retry will be turned off.

The following line sets the adapter to 4800 baud and to continuous retries. As before, nothing else is changed.

MODE COM1 48,,,,P

Controlling the Video Display

The next form of MODE controls the video display. The primary use of this form of MODE is to reset the display or to change displays when you have more than one type of video adapter. If you use just the monochrome display, this command will not work.

The syntax for this form of MODE is

MODE *display type, shift, T*

The *display type* can be any of the displays indicated in table 23.1. You can use MODE with either a television set or a monitor. With some monitors, characters "fall off" the edge of the screen. The *shift* option lets you shift the line back into position. This command shifts the display left or right by one character position. You enter either **L** or **R** to accomplish the movement. *T* stands for *test pattern*. When you request it, MODE shows a line of 40 or 80 characters and asks whether the display is okay. You press **Y** if it is. If you press **N**, MODE again shifts the display by one character and repeats the question. In this way, you can adjust your screen without having to use the MODE command repeatedly.

Table 23.1
Types of Video Display

Display Type	Function
40	Uses 40-column lines for the C/G display
80	Uses 80-column lines for the C/G display
BW40	Makes the C/G display the active display, turns off color, and uses 40-character lines
BW80	Makes the C/G display the active display, turns off color, and uses 80-character lines
CO40	Makes the C/G display the active display, turns on color capabilities, and uses 40-character lines
CO80	Makes the C/G display the active display, turns on color capabilities, and uses 80-character lines
MONO	Makes the Monochrome Display the active display

Note: C/G display refers to the monitor or television attached to the Color/ Graphics Adapter (CGA), Enhanced Color/Graphics Adapter (EGA), or Video Graphics Array (VGA). The term *Color/Graphics* can refer to any of these adapters.

An active display is the display that DOS and your programs use to show information. If you have two displays, such as a monochrome display and another monitor attached to a color graphics adapter board, you can use this command to select either display.

Selecting the CO40 or CO80 display enables DOS to display color. Specifying CO40 or CO80 does not guarantee that your programs will be in color, however, because some programs use color and others do not.

Using a MODE color command does not affect BASIC either. If you use a color command in BASIC, specifying BW40, BW80, CO40, or CO80 to MODE makes no difference. BASIC overrides MODE. Whether you see colors will depend on the monitor or TV you use. The size of the screen (40- or 80-column) will remain as you set it, however.

MODE does not change the character set on the Enhanced Color/Graphics Adapter or the Video Graphics Array. The EGA can use the same character set (9 by 14 dots) that the monochrome display uses. The VGA can use the sharper 9 by 16-dot character set. To use the enhanced character sets, you must correctly set the switches on the EGA. Check the installation manual that comes with the Enhanced Color/Graphics Adapter for more information. Fortunately, the VGA automatically adapts to the monitor used and gives the 9 by 16-dot character sets if the appropriate monitor is used.

The most frequent use of this form of the MODE command is to clear the video display and reset the colors after a graphics program has gone awry. Type **MODE CO80** to restore the color display.

Controlling the Lines Per Screen

All monitors used with IBM computers and compatibles will support 25 lines per screen. EGA monitors also allow you to use a special 43-line mode, and VGA screens will support even tinier characters in a 50-line mode.

You can set the current number of lines with these monitors using the new MODE feature provided with DOS V4. You can do this in one of two ways.

First, you can set the number of lines at the same time you set the other video characteristics. You can also use the MODE CON command to set the columns and rows separately. The following examples help clarify the distinction:

MODE CON: COLS=*cols* LINES=*lines*

MODE CON: COLS=80 LINES=50

MODE *mode, lines*

MODE CO80,50

Printing Your Files in the Background (PRINT)

The PRINT command is the background printing facility introduced with DOS V3. PRINT allows you to print a disk file while you are running another program. Essentially, PRINT is a primitive form of multitasking—having your computer do two or more activities at the same time.

The only kind of file you can print in the background is a disk file. You should use the PRINT command only with ASCII text files. Program and non-ASCII data files usually have control characters in them. If you use PRINT on these files, the results are similar to using TYPE on them: the characters appear as nonsense.

Understanding the PRINT Command

The first time you use PRINT, DOS loads part of the PRINT program into memory and hooks the program into DOS. As a result, PRINT steals about 3K of memory. When you reboot DOS or turn your computer off and then on again, this memory will be freed.

The PRINT command works by sharing CPU working time with another program. PRINT V3 is different from PRINT V2. PRINT V2 stole idle time from the CPU. While your programs were running, the computer sometimes waited for you. During these times, PRINT V2 briefly diverted the CPU's attention to the PRINT program, and PRINT sent some characters to the printer.

Whereas PRINT V2 waited until your computer had nothing else to do, PRINT in DOS V3 and V4 demand attention from the CPU. PRINT V3 and V4 "install" a time-slicing module into DOS to get some of your computer's CPU time. PRINT V2 printed little when the CPU had little idle time. PRINT V3 and V4 print more consistently.

Before you use PRINT, you should be familiar with a related term: *queue*. A queue is a line in which one waits for a turn. When you PRINT a file, you place it in a queue to await printing. DOS handles the queue one file at a time. The first file you place in PRINT is put at the front of the queue and is the first file printed. Any files that follow are printed in the order in which they were placed into the line. When we talk about a queue, we are referring to this line-up of files.

The syntax for the PRINT command is

PRINT */B:bufsize /D:device /M:maxtick*
/Q:maxfiles /S:timeslice /U:busytick d:path\filename.ext
/T/C/P . . .

The *d:path\filename.ext* is the name of the file to print and the optional disk drive and path to the file. If you use wild-card characters, one "file name" can queue up several files. The rest of PRINT's syntax is discussed in the next section.

Using PRINT's Switches

PRINT has nine switches (see table 23.2). You can give the first six switches to PRINT, in the form */letter:option*, when you first use the command. PRINT displays an `Invalid parameter` warning if you use these switches at any other time. The other three switches can be given any time you use the PRINT command.

Table 23.2
Switches for the PRINT Command

Switches Used When PRINT Is First Issued	
/B:bufsize	The size of the *buffer*
/D:device	The *device* to use
/M:maxtick	The *maximum* number of clock ticks to use
/Q:maxfiles	The maximum number of files to *queue*
/U:busytick	The number of clock ticks to wait for the printer
/S:timeslice	The number of times per second that PRINT can print (number of *timeslices*)
Switches Used Any Time You Issue PRINT	
/T	*Terminates* printing
/C	*Cancels* the printing of the file
/P	*Prints* this file

Each of the switches starts with the switch character, the slash (/). For the first six switches, after the slash, you add the letter for the option, a colon, and then the appropriate information. Do not use any spaces between any of these elements.

/B: sets the PRINT command's internal buffer size. (The buffer holds sections of the file to be printed.) The buffer's size, *bufsize*, is specified in bytes. The default is 512 bytes. Increasing the buffer size improves performance and the amount of space PRINT takes from DOS.

/D: determines the DOS *device* to be used for printing. You can use any DOS device name, such as LPTx or COMy. Obviously, you should not use devices auch as CON that are not connected to printers. If you do not give the /D switch, PRINT asks for this switch the first time the program runs:

```
Name of list device [PRN]: _
```

If you press Enter, PRINT uses PRN. You could enter LPT1, LPT2, LPT3, COM1, COM2, COM3, COM4, AUX, or PRN. Do not give a device that is not on your system, however. Until you restart DOS, PRINT uses whatever device you specify. To change this device, you must restart DOS.

The next three switches are for performance-tuning. Unless you are dissatisfied with the way PRINT operates, you can ignore them.

/M: determines the maximum number of clock ticks (*maxtick*) that PRINT uses each time it prints. A *clock tick* is 1/18.2 of a second, about 55 thousandths of a second. /M: tells PRINT how much time it has in which to send characters to the printer whenever it is PRINT's turn. A 240-cps parallel printer can get about 4 characters into a clock tick.

The default value of /M: is 2. The range is from 1 to 255. Increasing this number boosts the number of characters that PRINT sends to the printer. If you increase this number too much, however, the keyboard becomes sluggish when PRINT gets control.

/S: determines how many of the available timeslices per second PRINT will get. The starting value is 8. The possible values are from 1 to 255. A second is divided into a number of turns. PRINT gets one turn out of every *timeslice* number of these turns. The effect of timeslice is opposite that of maxtick. Increasing the timeslice gives PRINT fewer turns to PRINT each second. Decreasing this value increases the number of times that PRINT is activated each second. If, however, you decrease this number too much, the keyboard becomes sluggish, and your programs will slow down because PRINT will be called more frequently.

If you are wondering whether to use /M or /S, the following formula determines how much of the CPU's time per second PRINT should get:

$$\text{PRINT's percent of CPU time} = \frac{maxtick}{(1 + timeslice)} * 100$$

At 2 maxticks and 8 timeslices, PRINT's use of CPU time is

$$\frac{2}{(1 + 8)} * 100 = 22\%$$

Increasing maxtick by 2 gives PRINT 44 percent of the CPU's time each second. Keeping maxtick at 2 and increasing timeslice to 10 gives PRINT 18 percent of the CPU's time each second. As you can see, the /M and /S switches give you a wide range of control over the amount of time PRINT can obtain.

/U: is the maximum number of clock ticks PRINT will wait for a busy printer. The starting value is 1. The possible values are from 1 to 255. When PRINT gets control, it waits *busytick* number of clock ticks for the printer to accept more characters. If the printer is not ready in *busytick* time, PRINT relinquishes its turn. The computer can then continue with productive work. You should increase busytick when you have a slow printer—one that works at less than 4800-baud serial or less than 100 cps.

/Q: is the maximum number of files (*maxfiles*) you can place in the queue. The default value is 10. The possible values are from 1 to 32. Increasing this number increases slightly the size of PRINT but allows more files to be put in line for printing.

Remember, you give the preceding six switches only when PRINT is first used. You can give the following three switches whenever you use PRINT:

/T	*Terminates* printing
/C	*Cancels the printing of the file*
/P	*Prints this file*

If you do not give a switch but do give a file name, DOS assumes that you want to use the */P* switch and prints the files on the command line.

The three periods (. . .) that follow the /T, /C, and /P switches in the command syntax represent other files and switches on the command line. You can have several files and switches on the same line.

PRINT's switches work like COPY's switches. A switch affects the file name given before the switch and all files after the switch—until DOS encounters another switch. For the next example, the line

PRINT MYFILE.TXT /P NEXTFILE.TXT

tells DOS to background print MYFILE.TXT and NEXTFILE.TXT. The /P switch affects the file before the switch (MYFILE.TXT) and the file after the switch (NEXTFILE.TXT). Note that giving the /P switch when you are only adding files to the queue is a wasted effort. PRINT automatically adds the files to the printing queue without the switch.

The following command line cancels the printing of MYFILE.TXT and NEXTFILE.TXT and puts FILE3.TXT in the queue:

PRINT MYFILE.TXT /C NEXTFILE.TXT FILE3.TXT /P

The cancel switch, /C, works on the file names before and after the switch. The /P switch works on the file name before the switch (FILE3.TXT). If you typed additional file names after the /P switch, PRINT would print them as well.

Changing disk drives and directories has no effect on PRINT. You can queue up additional files or cancel them regardless of changing your current disk or directory. Do not, however, change a floppy disk that holds a file on which PRINT is being used. If you remove the floppy disk prematurely, PRINT will print an error message and skip the file.

Do not try to use the printer again until PRINT has finished. If you do, the program you are using will issue a `Device not ready` message or a similar error message. Pressing Shift-PrtSc while the printer is printing should produce a similar error message. When you get such an error message from DOS, press A to abort, and DOS will continue.

PRINT is not a sophisticated function. It is not designed to underscore, do boldface printing, set margins, or number pages as a word-processing program can do. PRINT prints only what is in a disk file, exactly as it is. For more information on PRINT, see the *DOS Command Reference*.

Setting the Keyboard Rate

Some keyboards, such as those provided with the Personal Computer AT and compatibles and PS/2 systems allow you to adjust some of their response characteristics. MODE has been modified in DOS V4 to allow you to control how DOS responds when you hold down the keys. You can tell DOS how long to wait before it starts to repeat a key and how many times to repeat that key per second as long as the key is held down. The syntax for the command is as follows:

MODE CON RATE=*r* **DELAY**=*d*

You can replace *r* with a value between 1 and 32. The exact number is not important. But the higher the value for *r*, the more repetitions per second.

The *d* represents the interval DOS should wait before beginning to repeat the key being held down. You may enter a whole number between 1 and 4. A value of 1 will cause DOS to start repeating 1/4 of a second after the key is first held down. Up to four 1/4-second intervals can be specified, for a total delay of one second.

DOS will let you know if your computer does not allow using MODE in this way, with an error message:

```
Function not supported on this computer
```

Summary

In this chapter, you learned these important points:

- ❏ RECOVER can recover a damaged file or a damaged disk. Use extreme caution in running RECOVER on a complete disk.

- ❏ The MODE command sets the characteristics of the printer and the serial adapter and controls the active display and its characteristics. DOS V4 includes three new uses for MODE that affect display screens, the serial adapter, and the keyboard.

- ❏ You use the PRINT command for background printing of a file.

- ❏ PRINT has nine switches: /D, /B, /M, /Q, /S, /U, /T, /C, and /P. If you want to specify the first six switches, you must do so the first time you use PRINT.

Chapter 24 explains how to back up and restore the hard disk.

24

Backing Up and Restoring the Hard Disk

This chapter and the next are directed to most users: those whose systems use a hard disk. Using a hard disk presents certain problems, the solutions to which are the subject of this chapter. In this chapter you will learn how to back up the entire disk, restore disks from backup files, and update a hard disk to a new version of DOS.

Backing Up Your Hard Disk (BACKUP)

BACKUP is a versatile command. You can use it to back up a hard disk onto another hard disk, a hard disk onto floppy disks, or floppy disks onto other floppy disks. The most frequent use of BACKUP is to back up the hard disk onto floppy disks.

BACKUP in DOS V3.0 and V3.1 has quirks. BACKUP V3.0 has an occasional "fatal" problem filling out the *header* file, which contains the backup floppy disk number and the date. In a directory of a backup floppy disk created using releases before DOS V3.3, the first file name should be BACKUPID.@@@. Look at the length of the file. If the length of BACKUPID.@@@ is zero, BACKUP V3.0 goofed, and the backup copy is unusable. You will need to back up again.

BACKUP in DOS V3.2 through V4 has no reported problems to date. However, DOS V3.3 and V4 use a method different from earlier versions to back up files. With the new technique, only two files are placed on the backup disks: a control file and a data file. The control file holds the housekeeping information about the data files. The single data file holds the backup files. The two-file technique makes BACKUP 40 percent faster than previous versions and more disk-efficient, meaning you will use fewer floppy disks for backing up.

An unlikely problem may occur if you bring up DOS with the new version of BACKUP and then need to return to a previous version of DOS. RESTORE V3.3 and V4 can read floppy disks created under all versions of DOS. However, earlier versions of RESTORE cannot read files produced by BACKUP V3.3 and V4. For this reason, if you are upgrading, back up your hard disk with the earlier version of BACKUP. If for any reason you must revert temporarily to your earlier version of DOS, your earlier version of RESTORE can still read the backup floppy disks. If you use the later version of BACKUP, your files will be trapped until you can run DOS V3.3 or V4 again.

Preparing Your Floppy Disks (FORMAT, CHKDSK)

The first step in backing up your hard disk is having enough floppy disks on hand to hold the backup files. Unless you are using BACKUP V3.3 or later—which can format disks on-the-fly—the disks *must* be formatted before you run BACKUP. Once BACKUP starts, you do not want to stop the process until it is finished. If you do not have enough formatted floppy disks on hand, you will have to stop and format more, which usually means starting the BACKUP command again from the beginning.

When you format the backup floppy disks manually, do not use switches. You want the maximum storage capacity from your floppies. Therefore, do not decrease this capacity by placing DOS on the floppy disks or by otherwise limiting the amount of disk space that can be used.

If you are formatting floppy disks or just stacking new disks in a pile to be used later, place a numbered label on each disk. Start with 1 and number each disk sequentially. If you are using several boxes of floppy disks, label each group of 10 floppy disks with a letter as well. Use A for the first group, B for the second group, and so on. Indicate the letter on the label of each floppy disk as well as on the box or holder in which you keep the floppy disks. If you are backing up more than one disk drive, also place the letter of the disk drive (such as C: or D:) on the label. You should always keep a group of floppy disks together. It is quite frustrating to lose the floppy disk that holds the file you need to restore.

How many floppy disks will you need to back up your hard disk? The only answer is two more questions. What exactly are you backing up? And what is the capacity of the floppy disks you are using? Bigger hard disks and lower capacity floppy disks mean that you need more floppy disks.

Table 24.1 shows the maximum number of the various floppy disks needed to back up different sizes of hard disk drives. The figures include "fudge factor" calculations that are necessary to back up a full hard disk.

Are you backing up only part of the hard disk? If so, you will need to approximate the number of floppy disks you will need. The first step is to determine how many bytes are taken up by the files to be backed up.

If you are backing up just one or two files or directories, run DIR and add up the number of bytes in the files. If you are backing up several files, you can use the CHKDSK command to determine the number of bytes in user files and in hidden files. (If the space devoted to hidden files is less than 100K, ignore the hidden files.) Round the number of bytes in your user and hidden files to the nearest thousand and divide this

Table 24.1
Number of Floppy Disks Needed for Backup

Hard Disk Capacity	Floppy Disk Capacity			
	360K	720K	1.2M	1.44M
10M	29	15	9	8
20M	59	29	18	15
30M	83	44	27	22
40M	116	58	35	29
70M	200	100	60	50

number by 1000 to determine the approximate number of kilobytes used. If you have two or more logical disk drives on the hard disk, don't forget to repeat the process for the additional disk drives.

Divide the number of kilobytes in user files by 362,496 if you use 360K disks; by 1,228,800 for 1.2M disks; by 730,112 for 720K disks; or by 1,457,664 for 1.44M disks. Round off the result to the next highest number to determine approximately how many floppy disks you will need. Because BACKUP stores some housekeeping information with the disk files, you may need one more floppy disk than your figure indicates.

Suppose, for example, that CHKDSK reports these holdings for a disk on a PC XT:

```
10592256 bytes total disk space
   28672 bytes in 3 hidden files
   73728 bytes in 18 directories
 4894720 bytes in 331 user files
 5595136 bytes available on disk
```

The hidden files are less than 50K, and you simply ignore them. To achieve an approximate calculation, round off the space in your user files to the nearest thousand. The 4,894,720 becomes 4,895,000. Divide the result by 1,000. The approximate amount of disk space in user files is 4,895 kilobytes.

To calculate the number of floppy disks needed, divide the approximate number of bytes by the backup floppy disk capacity in kilobytes. For 360K floppy disks, the calculation is

$$\frac{4895 \text{ kilobytes used}}{360 \text{ kilobytes per floppy disk}} = 13.60 \text{ floppy disks}$$

Rounded up, the number of 360K floppy disks needed is 14.

For a Personal Computer AT with a 20M drive, suppose that CHKDSK reports the following:

```
21213184 bytes total disk space
   49152 bytes in 5 hidden files
  241664 bytes in 107 directories
19556352 bytes in 1866 user files
 1366016 bytes available on disk
```

If you use 1.2M high-capacity disks, the calculation is

$$\frac{19{,}556 \text{ kilobytes in user files}}{1{,}200 \text{ kilobytes per floppy disk}} = 16.30 \text{ floppy disks}$$

Rounded up, the approximate number of floppy disks needed is 17. Interestingly, it took 16 floppy disks to back up under DOS V3.2 and 14 floppy disks under DOS V3.3. BACKUP in DOS V3.3 and later is usually more efficient in storing files than previous versions of BACKUP; therefore, your floppy disk approximations with V3.3 and V4 may result in a higher number of floppy disks than you actually need.

Suppose that CHKDSK reports the following figures for a PS/2 Model 60 using a 40M disk drive and 1.44M floppy disks. The hard disk is divided into two logical disk drives.

First logical disk drive

```
33419264 bytes total disk space
   53248 bytes in 3 hidden files
  137216 bytes in 66 directories
18536448 bytes in 1021 user files
   30720 bytes in bad sectors
14461632 bytes available on disk
```

Second logical disk drive

```
10993664 bytes total disk space
       0 bytes in 1 hidden files
   40960 bytes in 10 directories
 2985984 bytes in 195 user files
   36864 bytes in bad sectors
 7929856 bytes available on disk
```

Although hidden file space is less than 100K, I will demonstrate how to handle the hidden files. For the two disks, the calculations are as follows:

	First drive	*Second drive*	
	18,536	2,986	kilobytes in user files
+	53	0	kilobytes in hidden files
	18,589	2,986	kilobytes to back up
	18,589	2,986	kilobytes to back up
	1,440	1,440	kilobytes per floppy disk
=	12.91	2.07	Number of floppy disks

Round up each figure; then combine the two. The result is 13 plus 3 floppy disks, a total of 16 floppy disks needed. If your hidden files exceed 100K, the number of floppy disks you will use can change. For less than 100K of hidden file space, however, relying on just the user file space is sufficient. Additional precision is not required because the approximation has enough "fudge factor" to handle less than 100K of hidden files.

If you are unsure or nervous about the number produced by the approximation, have on hand the number of floppy disks indicated by table 24.1.

Starting the Backup Process

When you first use BACKUP, you should back up the entire hard disk. Make the root directory the current directory for the hard disk by typing:

CD C:

As you become accustomed to the BACKUP command, you can start with a different directory and back up only sections of the hard disk. However, for the examples that follow, if you make the hard disk (drive C) the current drive, the next steps will be easier.

Using the BACKUP Command

The complete syntax for the BACKUP command is

*dc:pathc***BACKUP** **ds:***paths\\filenames.exts* **dd:**
  /S /M /A /D:mm-dd-yy /T:hh:mm:ss /F/L:dl:pathl\\filenamel.extl

As with all other DOS commands, you may give a drive name and a path name before the word **BACKUP**. If BACKUP is not in your current directory or on the PATH, give the drive or path name or both (*dc:pathc*) before the word BACKUP.

The **ds:** is the disk to be backed up, the *source*. The *paths* tells DOS which directory to start the backup with. If you begin with the correct directory, you can omit the path name. (For this reason I always move to the root directory of the hard disk.) *filenames.ext* is the name of the file(s) you want to back up. Wild cards are allowed.

For DOS V3.3, you must give a disk drive name for the source. For other versions of BACKUP, you must give at least one part of the full source file name, which can be either the disk drive, path name, or file name. For the older versions of BACKUP, the current drive is used if you omit the disk drive name.

If you omit the path, BACKUP starts with the current directory of the disk. If you omit the file name, BACKUP assumes the name *.*.

The **dd:** is the disk drive, or *destination*, to receive the backup files. You should always give the name of the disk drive that will hold the backup, either the destination hard disk or the floppy disk drive. DOS makes no assumptions about this name. When you back up the hard disk onto floppy disks, you will usually type **A:** as the destination drive name.

Using BACKUP's Switches

The versatility of BACKUP is shown by its switches. Note that some switches can be used together. BACKUP in V3.3 and V4 has seven switches, whereas earlier versions have four switches. Table 24.2 outlines the switches and their functions for BACKUP V3.3.

Table 24.2
Switches for the BACKUP Command

Switch	Function
/S	Backs up all *subdirectories*, starting with the specified or current directory on the source disk and working downward.
/M	Backs up all files *modified* since the last time they were backed up.
/A	*Adds* the file(s) to be backed up to the files already on the specified floppy disk drive.
/D:date	Backs up any files that were created or changed on or after the specified *date*.
/T:time	Backs up any file that was created or changed on or after the specified *time* on the specified date (given with the /D switch).
/F	*Formats* the destination floppy disk if the floppy disk is not formatted. DOS V4 will automatically format the target floppy disks.
/L:dl:pathl\filenamel.extl	Creates a *log* file.

The Subdirectory (/S) Switch

If you have been wondering why you should start at the root directory, the /S switch gives the answer. BACKUP works with the specified directory or the current directory if a directory is not indicated. BACKUP backs up the specified files in that directory. If you give the /S switch, BACKUP uses the directory as a starting point, moves to the subdirectories of the directory and backs up the files, and then moves to the subdirectories of the subdirectories and backs up these files. With the /S switch, BACKUP moves down through all subdirectories on this branch of the directory tree and backs up all the specified files.

If you start with a subdirectory and use the /S switch, you will get all the files in the chain of subdirectories for that side of the directory tree, but you will not get the whole hard disk. For example, look at the sample directory in Appendix B. If you start at the root directory and use the /S switch, you will back up the entire disk. But if you start in the WORDS directory, you will back up the files in WORDS, LETTERS, and CONTRACTS, but not the files on the DOS subdirectory side of the tree. If you start with DOS, you will back up all the files on that side of the tree, but the WORDS subdirectory side of the tree will not be backed up.

To back up the entire hard disk onto floppy disks, begin with the root directory. Type

    BACKUP C:\ A: /S

This command tells DOS to back up the files in the root directory, any subdirectories, any subdirectories of these subdirectories, and so on.

A mistake I made when I first used the BACKUP command was to start in a subdirectory, not specify a path, and think that I had backed up the entire disk. I was wrong. DOS started with the directory I was in and backed up only about a third of my hard disk. When you use BACKUP, watch your starting directory and the path name you give, if any. Make sure that you tell DOS exactly what you mean.

The Format (/F) Switch

The /F switch is the savior of those who do not format enough floppy disks to hold the backup files. When the /F switch is given, BACKUP tests the floppy disk to see if it is formatted. If the floppy disk is not formatted, BACKUP runs FORMAT. When FORMAT is invoked, you can format as many floppy disks as you like. FORMAT acts as though you had invoked the command from the keyboard, but there are two differences. For one, FORMAT invoked by /F does not display any information or warning message about placing a floppy disk into the drive. The only message about changing floppy disks comes from BACKUP. The other difference is that when you leave FORMAT, you return to BACKUP, which continues the backup process.

I have mixed feelings about using the /F switch. On the one hand, giving the /F switch is the "safety play." If you have omitted the /F switch and you happen to run out of format-ted backup floppy disks, you are out of luck. You will need to invoke BACKUP again, and you may need to restart the process from the beginning. Using the /F switch whenever you back up the hard disk is reasonable and will prevent the formatting problem.

On the other hand, I dislike losing control of the options to FORMAT. FORMAT will be run without any switches being set when you use the /F switch. Although I believe that you should normally use FORMAT without any switches (except the /V volume label switch), you might use the /N:9 switch if you are trying to format a 720K floppy disk on a 1.44M disk drive.

If you use the /F switch and BACKUP encounters an unformatted floppy disk, it will invoke FORMAT without the /N:9 switch. The result is that PS/2s with 1.44M disk drives will format 720K floppy disks at a 1.44M capacity. My experience is that this operation is risky. I have seen too many floppy disks that have been pushed to a higher capacity fail at a later date. About half of the time the floppy disk fails to format altogether. In addi-tion, the only way you will discover the problem is when you need the files on the backup floppy disk.

Another problem with using the /F switch to format your floppy disks occurs when FORMAT is not in the current directory or on the path. This problem may strike when you use a batch file to invoke FORMAT (discussed in chapter 15) and expect an option that BACKUP cannot give, or when FORMAT is not placed in a directory on the path. You will find yourself in a "fine kettle of fish" when you have to stop BACKUP, format floppy disks, and repeat the BACKUP process.

For these reasons, I recommend that you give the /F switch only if certain conditions are met: you are unsure you have enough formatted floppy disks, FORMAT is in a directory included in your last PATH command, *and* you use the correct capacity floppy disks for the floppy disk drive. Otherwise, omit the /F switch and format enough floppy disks before you run BACKUP.

The Modified (/M) and Add (/A) Switches

The */M* switch tells DOS to back up any file that has been *modified*. This switch really tells DOS to back up a file you have not backed up before. The archive attribute is stored in the directory with each file name. When you create or change a file, this attribute is turned on. DOS checks whether the archive attribute has been set. When you give the /M switch, DOS backs up the file. Otherwise, DOS skips the file.

This switch enables you to choose the files you want to back up, but there are two hitches. First, the XCOPY command, which was discussed in Chapter 20, also uses the archive attribute and can clear this flag. If you use the /M switch with XCOPY and do not change a file before you back it up, BACKUP /M will not back up the file. That means your backup will be incomplete. If you did not preserve the "XCOPYed" version of the file and the original file is destroyed, the file will be lost.

The other problem occurs when you use BACKUP /M several times a month. Suppose that on the first day, you back up your entire hard disk. Then on the second day, you use the /M switch to back up files selectively. During the next three days (day 3, 4, and 5), you do the same. Did all your files get backed up each time? Maybe. If a file changed each day, it was backed up each day. But what happens if the file changed only on the second and third days? It was backed up on those days only.

Unless you give the */A switch*, DOS erases all files on the backup floppy disks before recording the new files. This provision may be helpful when you have only a few files in one directory or when you have a complete subdirectory chain to back up. But what if you need to restore a file, after using the same backup floppy disks each day, and you have not given the /A switch? Each day, DOS erases the files backed up on the preceding day before backing up the new files. You will succeed in backing up the file twice (on days 2 and 3), but you will still lose the file from the backup floppy disks beginning with day 4.

To prevent this loss, you should have two sets of backup floppy disks, or you should give the /A switch whenever you back up. If you give the /A switch, DOS expects the previously used backup floppy disks to be in the floppy disk drive you specify. Otherwise, DOS will prompt you to put the appropriate floppy disk into the disk drive and press a key to start.

You may still have problems, though. How will BACKUP know which file version is the most recent if you have backed up the file more than once? Which set of backup floppy disks has the most recent version of the file? To avoid these problems, I generally do not use either the /M switch or the /A switch.

There is one occasion when the /M and /A switches should be used, however. When a file is being used by another program or computer, BACKUP cannot back up the file. DOS gives a warning message when a file cannot be backed up. If this happens, I run BACKUP as many times as necessary, using the /M and /A switches to add the files that were not backed up the first time. After the other program or computer is finished, I rerun BACKUP to add the files to my set of backup floppy disks. Usually the command

BACKUP C:\ A: /S/M/A

backs up only those files that were not backed up on the first run of the BACKUP program.

The Date (/D) and Time (/T) Switches

The /D and the /T switches are an alternative to the /M and the /A switches. You can enter a date with the /D switch and a time with the /T switch. BACKUP then backs up all files that have been created or changed on or after the specified date and time. Because of this switch, you should always answer the date and time questions when DOS boots. DOS uses the date and time in the directory in searching for files to back up.

The /D (date) switch tells BACKUP to grab any file that has been created or changed on or after the given date. Although this switch enables you to copy the same files each day, the switch also makes BACKUP run longer. This increase in time, however, makes restoring the hard disk easier.

The /T switch can make the BACKUP process more selective. You can tell DOS to grab any file specified by the date and the time. This switch is most helpful when you must perform the backup process more than once in the same day. You simply give the date and the time of your backup, and BACKUP will find any files created or changed since the time of your last backup.

The form of *time* is *hh:mm:ss* where *hh* is the hour, *mm* the minutes, and *ss* the seconds. A colon usually separates the parts of the *time* switch. The /T switch was introduced with DOS V3.3.

You should not use the /T switch without also giving the /D switch. If you do use the /T switch by itself, you will back up any file created or changed from the time of day you specify to the following midnight, regardless of the day. The result will be a scattering of files that just happen to have been created or modified after the given time on *any* date, not on or after a desired date. DOS will do as bidden; what you get will not be what you want backed up.

The /L switch produces a *log file*, a file that reports the files processed by BACKUP. The first line of the log file holds the date and time of the backup. The remaining lines contain the floppy disk number of the backed up files with the full path and file name of the backed-up file.

The log file can be displayed by TYPE or MORE, or it can be used with any text editor. RESTORE does not use the file. The only reasons to produce a log file are to check what files BACKUP processed and to find which backup floppy disk holds the file you want to restore. Rather than processing each floppy disk through RESTORE, you can search quickly through the log file for the correct starting floppy disk. This process can save some time when you restore a few files.

Previous versions of BACKUP stored the files under their existing file names. Upon finding a name conflict, the earlier versions renamed the extensions of the files. The new BACKUP consolidates all files into one file called BACKUP.nnn, where nnn is the number of the floppy disk. Because you cannot examine directly and ascertain the files that are recorded on the floppy disk, preserving log files may be important to you. BACKUP, upon finding a previous log file, does not erase the log file but adds (appends) the new information to the old file.

The following switch creates a log file.

   /L:dl:pathl\filenamel.extl

The *dl:pathl\filenamel.extl* is the drive path/file name of the log file.

When you use the /L switch, you can omit the complete file name, and the log file will be placed in the root directory of the source disk and given the name BACKUP.LOG. If you omit the full file name, do not give a colon after the /L.

If you do give a file name, a colon must appear directly after the *L* and before the full file name. Using an argument like /L:C:\BIN\BACKUP.LOG, with colons before and after the disk drive name, may look funny, but it is the only way BACKUP will accept a file name with a disk drive.

The rules about the full file name for the /L switch are slightly different from the normal rules. If you omit the disk drive or the path name, the source disk drive and the current directory are used, respectively. However, DOS makes no presumption about the file name. If you specify a drive or path name, you must specify at least the name of the log file. Unlike most DOS commands, the disk drive and the path names cannot be used without specifying the file name, which means that switches like /L:D: or /L:\WORDS (when WORDS is a subdirectory of the root) will not work. (If you give only the switch, the default filename BACKUP.LOG is used and the file is placed in the current directory.) For the latter example, if WORDS were not a subdirectory of the root directory, the log file would be called WORDS and placed in the root directory of the source disk drive. In this example DOS does what you directed, but not what you might have intended.

Making BACKUP a Routine Procedure

You should keep three sets of backup floppy disks for each hard disk, and each set should be kept in a separate box or bin. Each set should also have enough floppy disks to hold the contents of the entire hard disk.

Once every month, back up the entire hard disk, using the first set of floppy disks. Try to do the backup on the same day each month. The first day of the month may be a good choice. If your hard disk is subdivided into two or more logical disk drives, make sure you back up all of the drives.

Each day (or every few days, depending on how often you use the computer), back up the hard disk, using the /D switch. Use the second and third sets of floppy disks for this procedure; alternate the sets each time. The date you give BACKUP should be the day you backed up the entire hard disk. This way, you will back up each file that has changed since the "master" backup of the hard disk.

The monthly backup takes the most time, and the time required for daily backup increases each day. Once you have completed the backup process, the entire hard disk and every file that has changed will be on two sets of floppy disks. The third set is for safety. If you have a problem with a file on a "daily" floppy disk, you can go to the other set. You will lose some work on the file, but that's better than losing a month's work.

BACKUP follows the status of VERIFY. If VERIFY is OFF, BACKUP does not check your backup files to see whether they have been recorded properly. If VERIFY is ON, BACKUP checks the files. Before you do a monthly backup, turn VERIFY on to ensure that your backup files will be recorded correctly. Be sure to turn VERIFY off afterward. VERIFY slows down DOS by more than 90 percent on the floppy disk. You may turn VERIFY off for daily backups because the operation is usually safe.

An important step before you run BACKUP is to disconnect any unneeded resident programs, such as SideKick, before you run BACKUP. This step is necessary with DOS V3.1 and advisable with later versions of BACKUP. Also, break any JOIN, SUBST, or ASSIGN commands that are in effect. These commands are covered in Chapter 25. If any of these commands are in effect, your backup copies may not contain the files you think.

BACKUP V3.0 users should run DIR to get a directory listing of each backup floppy disk after finishing the BACKUP process. Check the BACKUPID.@@@ file. If the file has a size of 0, the backup is no good, and you will need to back up again.

Running a backup like the one outlined here requires a little more work each day, but a lot less work when a crisis comes. And a crisis will come some day, from one of two different hardware failures:

First, all disk drives fail eventually. When I first used a hard disk in 1979, my disk failed after two months. The last good backup copy I had was several weeks old. It took me more than a week to restore most of the files. Some files were lost permanently.

I am pleased to say that I have had only one other hard disk failure since 1979 and lost only a few unimportant files. Hard disks are increasingly reliable, but they are not everlasting. Do not get lured into a false sense of security.

The more common hardware failure, a "screw loose in the operator," has caught me more frequently. My failures range from overwriting good files with out-of-date files to erasing all files in the wrong directory. I have found this personal failure to be more frequent, more insidious (you typically do not discover the mistake until later), and almost as devastating as losing the entire hard disk. For this reason, BACKUP is even more important.

Restoring Backup Files (RESTORE)

The RESTORE command is the opposite of BACKUP. RESTORE takes the files from your backup floppy disks or hard disk and places (restores) these files on the destination floppy disk or hard disk. To restore the entire hard disk, you should run RESTORE twice—first with the monthly set of backups and then with the daily set. If you have lost a file or two, try to restore the file from the last daily backup. If the file is not there, it has not changed all month. Using the monthly backup set, run RESTORE again to retrieve the missing file.

The syntax for RESTORE is similar to BACKUP's:

> *dc:pathc***RESTORE ds:** *dd:pathd\\filenamed.extd*
> */S /P /M /N /B:date /A:date /L:time /E:time*

As with all other DOS commands, if RESTORE is not in your current directory, you can give a disk drive and path name before command RESTORE (the *dc:pathc*).

The **ds:** is the disk drive that holds the backup information (usually the drive for the backup floppy disks), and *dd:* is the hard disk drive. (If the current disk drive is the hard disk drive, you can omit *dd*.)

The *pathd* is the optional path to the directory that will receive the restored files. RESTORE uses the current directory for the hard disk if you do not specify a path.

The *filenamed.extd* is the name of the file(s) to be restored. Wildcards are permitted. For DOS V3.3, DOS assumes all files (*.*) if you do not give a file name *and* a path name. If you give a path name, then you must give a file name. Otherwise BACKUP does not find any file to restore.

Several switches have been added to RESTORE to make the restoration process faster and more convenient.

The switches are shown in table 24.3.

The */S* switch is helpful when you restore the entire disk or many subdirectories. The /S switch tells RESTORE to travel through the starting directory and subsequent subdirectories to restore files.

The /P, the /M, and the /N switches selectively restore files based on the archive or read-only flags kept by DOS.

The */P* switch causes RESTORE to ask if a read-only or subsequently modified file should be replaced with its backup copy. You answer **Y** for yes or **N** for no.

Table 24.3
Switches for the RESTORE Command

Switch	Function
/S	Restores files in the specified directory and in all other *subdirectories* below it. This switch is identical to BACKUP's /S switch.
/P	*Prompts* and asks whether a file should be restored if it is marked as read-only or has been changed since the last backup.
/N	Restores all files that *no longer* exist on the destination disk. This switch is like the /M switch, but /N processes only the files deleted from the destination since the backup set was made.
/M	Restores all files *modified* or deleted since the backup set was made. This switch is like the /N switch because /M processes files that no longer exist on the destination, but /M also restores files that have been modified since the last backup.
/A:date	Restores all files created or modified on or *after* the *date*. The format of date is the same as the /B switch.
/B:date	Restores all files created or modified on or *before* the *date*.
/L:time	Restores all files modified at or later than the specified *time*. The form of time is *hh:mm:ss*, where *hh* is the hour, *mm* the minutes, and *ss* the seconds.
/E:time	Restores all files modified at or *earlier* than the specified *time*.

If a file is set to read-only, it has probably not been altered—and probably will not be. IBMBIO.COM and IBMDOS.COM are two examples of read-only files. However, beginning with RESTORE V3.3, neither these files nor the third system file, COMMAND.COM, is processed. If you are using RESTORE V3.3 or later, these names should not appear when you restore files.

If a file has changed since it was last backed up, you usually will not want to restore the file. The backup copy is probably out-of-date. The only reason to restore an out-of-date file is if the current file is trashed (corrupted). In any case, DOS will ask whether you want to restore such a file.

The /P switch does not limit the selection of files; all files matching the destination name are eligible for restoration. The /P switch allows you to choose which updated or read-only files should or should not be replaced.

The /N switch, which was new with DOS V3.3, instructs RESTORE to search for files on the backup floppy disks that have been erased or renamed since the backup was made. If you have deleted a set of files you need to restore, /N is the switch to use. Only the files on the backup floppy disk that have been erased will be restored. Watch out for renamed files, however. If you rename a file after the last time you backed up, DOS will not see that name in the directory and will restore the version of the file with the previous name. If this happens, simply delete the unwanted file.

The /M switch, which was introduced with DOS V3.3, acts like the /N switch in that /M restores deleted files, but /M also selects files in the backup set that have been modified since the last backup. The /M switch replaces those files that were backed up but have been changed. I nicknamed the /M switch the surprise switch when some "surprise" corrupted several files in a directory or two of mine. Generally, I would not replace current files with out-of-date files unless the current files are worthless. If something has undesirably altered your files, as it did mine, you can replace the current, but worthless files, with the out-of-date but worthwhile files. In this case, give the /P switch with the /M switch. RESTORE will ask before replacing files, reducing the chances of destroying a good file.

The next four switches, /A, /B, /L, and /E, control which files will be restored, based on the file's date and time. These switches were introduced with DOS V3.3.

The /A:*date* switch selects files created or modified on or *after* a given date. The /B:*date* switch selects files created or modified on or *before* the given date. These switches limit the files that RESTORE processes, particularly if you have been using the /A and /M switches with BACKUP.

The /A switch prevents RESTORE from processing several previous revisions of the files. Specify the date that you last changed the file, and RESTORE processes only the copies that were backed up on or after that date. It is better to be too early with the date than too late. If too early, RESTORE restores several versions of the file, but only the most recent version remains. RESTORE will overwrite previous versions.

I think of the /B switch as the tragic-accident-recovery switch. When something "explodes" unnoticed inside the computer and corrupts your files, the /B switch works well. Use the /B switch when the current or more recent backup files are wrong and you need an earlier backed-up version. First, specify the date of the file that you know is good. RESTORE processes all backup files that were modified or created on or before the given date for that file name. The given date should be your best guess of when the problem occurred. Unfortunately, you may need to use RESTORE several times before you can get the "best" out-of-date copy.

The /A and /B switches can be used together to form a range of dates. Give the earlier date to the /A switch and the later date to the /B switch. For example, to restore the files modified or created between June 1 and July 15, 1988, the switches would look like this:

/A:06-01-88 /B:07-15-88

The /L:*time* and the /E:*time* switches permit the fine-tuning of the /A and the /B switches. The /L switch includes files that were created or modified at or later than the given time; the /E switch works on those files created or modified at or earlier than the given time. These switches were introduced with DOS V3.3.

As with the /T switch of BACKUP, using either the /L or the /E switch without the /A or the /B switch is usually meaningless. If you do use the time switches alone, you will get a scattering of files that were created or modified before, on, or after the given time, with no consideration for dates.

The starting directory is important when you use the RESTORE program. You must be in the right part of the directory tree to restore a file.

When a file is backed up or restored, the path and the file name appear on the screen. This information is stored in each backup file and is used when you restore files. If you have erased a subdirectory, DOS re-creates it. This feature is useful when you are restoring a faulty section of the disk drive or when the hard disk has been erased.

When you use RESTORE, you must always start with the first backup floppy disk of the set and work sequentially, even if you are restoring only a few files. DOS prompts you to change floppy disks.

Caution: RESTORE and APPEND do not mix. If you must use APPEND, give the command after you RESTORE your files, particularly if you use the /M or the /N switches. If you do not clear APPEND first, RESTORE may search for files in the directories given to the APPEND command rather than searching the real directory. You can avoid this potential confusion by clearing the APPEND command before using RESTORE.

BACKUP and RESTORE are two powerful utility programs for hard disk users. Study them carefully and use BACKUP frequently. If you are lucky, you will need to use RESTORE only a few times.

Knowing When To Use BACKUP

The suggestion that you back up your floppy disks frequently to protect your files applies also to the hard disk. You should also back up your complete hard disk at two other times: when you reorganize your hard disk, and when your hard disk is heavily fragmented.

Reorganizing a hard disk involves copying many files to different directories. Reorganizing may also involve creating new directories, deleting unused directories, and deleting old copies of files. After you have reorganized the hard disk, you will want to make a "snapshot" (a captured image—in this case, a binary image) of the hard disk. In other words, you will want to back up your hard disk. By backing up the hard disk, you will not need to repeat the work you did in reorganizing the hard disk in case the disk should "crash."

Fragmentation occurs when a file is not stored in contiguous sectors on the surface of the hard disk. After you have deleted and added many files, a new file can be scattered across the entire hard disk. This hurts neither DOS nor the file, but DOS must work longer to retrieve such a file. The hard disk's recording heads must move across the disk several times to read the file. As a result, the performance of the hard disk decreases. Fragmentation can also occur after a major reorganization of the hard disk.

The solution to the problem of fragmentation is to back up your entire hard disk, reformat it, and then restore your files. Formatting will erase from the hard disk all the files and subdirectories. As you restore each file and subdirectory, the information will be stored on consecutive sectors, thus increasing the performance of the hard disk.

To accomplish this task, you will need to complete the following steps. These steps back up the hard disk completely, reformat it, and then restore all the files.

Step 1. Make certain that you have a floppy disk that contains the operating system (formatted with the /S switch) and the following programs and files:

> COMMAND.COM
> BACKUP.COM
> FORMAT.COM
> RESTORE.COM

If BACKUP.COM is already on the hard disk, you may use the version on the hard disk instead. But you will still need a floppy disk-based copy of FORMAT.COM and RESTORE.COM.

Step 2. Be sure that you have a sufficient number of floppy disks.

Use the guidelines in table 24.1 to determine the number of floppy disks you will need. If you are using a version of BACKUP released before V3.3, the floppy disks must be formatted before you start BACKUP.

Step 3. Uninstall any copy-protected programs.

Backed up, copy-protected programs will not work after the programs have been restored. You must uninstall the programs and then reinstall them after you have restored the hard disk. Follow the publisher's directions for uninstalling a particular program.

Step 4. Turn VERIFY on.

Having VERIFY on will almost double the time required for the backup, but you do not want anything to go wrong. Skipping this step can be risky.

Step 5. Make sure that you have turned off any resident programs like SideKick and any ASSIGN, JOIN, or SUBST commands.

These can interfere with the backup. Also, clear APPEND if you are using it.

Step 6. Run BACKUP by typing

> C>**BACKUP** C:\ A: /S /F

You can use this command line if BACKUP is in the current directory or in one of the subdirectories specified by the PATH command. In any other instance, you should invoke BACKUP from the floppy disk or specify the directory holding BACKUP. If you are using an earlier version of BACKUP than V3.3, omit the /F switch.

On one of my hard disks, BACKUP is in a subdirectory called \BIN\DISK. For my backups, I type a slightly different command:

C>**\BIN\DISK\BACKUP C:\ A: /S /F**

Regardless of where BACKUP is, you should specify the hard disk and root directory, which is where you want BACKUP to start.

DOS will prompt you to put your first floppy disk into drive A. Insert your backup floppy disk 1 (the floppy disk with the number 1 on the gummed label), close the door if you are using minifloppy disk drives, and press a key. Coordinate the numbers on the labels of the backup floppy disks with the numbers that DOS assigns. That way, the floppy disks will be easy to store and use.

When DOS prompts for the next floppy disk, take disk 1 out of the drive and put it back in the envelope. Insert disk 2 and repeat the procedure, continuing with each additional floppy disk until you are finished. (You can stack the floppy disks at the side of the computer as you use them. When you are finished, the stack of floppy disks makes up the copy of your hard disk.)

If you get an error message from the floppy disk drive during the backup procedure, abort the program and reformat the offending floppy disk. If any bad sectors show up, retire the floppy disk and format a replacement. If you get an error message indicating that a file cannot be backed up, correct the problem and restart BACKUP. If you run out of formatted floppy disks and you are using DOS V3.3 or higher, FORMAT automatically runs and you can format additional floppy disks.

Remember that the backup copy of the hard disk must be correct. If you allow errors, information will be lost.

Step 7. *(For BACKUP V3.0 users.) Check the BACKUPID.@@@ file on each floppy disk. Starting with disk 1, put each floppy disk into the drive and type*

C>**DIR A:BACKUPID.**@@@

Look at the length of each file. If one of these files has a length of zero or if DOS reports that no file was found, you have a "trashed" backup set. Go back to step 6 and again back up your hard disk. You should also check to be sure that you do not have a resident program running that is causing interference.

After you have typed this directory line the first time and have looked at its results, change floppy disks, press the F3 special-function key to have DOS repeat the last command you issued, and press Enter.

Step 8. *(For DOS V3.2 or later users.) Know the volume label of the hard disk you will format. If necessary, perform a DIR or CHKDSK and write down the volume name.*

Step 9. *Reformat the hard disk.*

This is the point of no return. You must have a good backup copy of the hard disk, or you will lose information.

Put the floppy disk that contains DOS, FORMAT.COM, and RESTORE.COM into drive A. Make drive A the current disk drive (type **A:**) and then type

   A>**FORMAT C: /S /V**

This command reformats the hard disk, takes DOS from the floppy disk and puts it onto the hard disk, and allows you to put a volume label on the hard disk drive. Remembering the rules for volume labels (see Chapter 11), type your volume label when DOS prompts you.

With DOS V3 and later releases, FORMAT will warn you that you are formatting a hard disk. The message is a reminder that 10 or 20 megabytes of information are about to be destroyed. This warning is your last chance to back out of the procedure.

If you are using DOS V3.2 or later, FORMAT will ask for the volume label of the hard disk you are formatting. This question is a triple check that indeed you are formatting the hard disk. Enter the volume label and press Enter.

Step 10. *To restore the hard disk, type*

   A>**RESTORE A: C:\ /S**

This command tells DOS to start at the root directory of the hard disk drive and restore all files in this directory as well as all files in the subdirectories. You do not have to make subdirectories again. DOS will do it for you when the first file from an erased subdirectory is restored, which is why the path name is included in each backed-up file.

Remove the DOS and program floppy disk from drive A, put in backup floppy disk #1, and press a key. Then, following DOS's prompts, take the next floppy disk from the pile and restore the next series of files. Continue this process until the system prompt reappears.

Step 11. *Turn VERIFY off. (This step is optional.)*

Step 12. *Reinstall any copy-protected programs that were on the hard disk. Again, follow each publisher's directions.*

You are done! You have backed up the entire hard disk, erased it, and restored it. This procedure takes from 30 minutes to a few hours, depending on how large and how full your hard disk is.

If you get a floppy disk out of order while using RESTORE, you are prompted to put the correct floppy disk into the disk drive. If you number your floppy disks, you should not have this problem. You can tell by the label whether the floppy disks are in the correct numerical sequence. Remember also to store your backup floppy disks in a safe place.

The floppy disks will be your monthly backup set until the next time you back up the entire hard disk. If you use the /D switch for both monthly and daily backup procedures, change the switch's date to reflect the current date.

Updating a Hard Disk to a New Version of DOS (REPLACE)

In the course of using a personal computer, you may find yourself upgrading the version of DOS you use. The method you use to upgrade varies, depending on the version of DOS you are upgrading to. I will show how you can upgrade to DOS V3.3 first and then how to upgrade to V4.

First, no matter what version of DOS you are using, make copies of the original disk(s). You may do so by using DISKCOPY. If you have a computer with one floppy disk drive, start the computer, and type

   A>**DISKCOPY A: A:**

Duplicate each disk, labeling the copy. Even though you have booted your computer with an earlier version of DOS, DISKCOPY will make exact duplicates of the disks holding the new version of DOS.

Replacing your old DOS files with new ones is easy with the REPLACE command. REPLACE can both replace old files with newer versions or add files that do not already exist on a disk. See the *DOS Command Reference* for REPLACE's syntax.

You probably have a directory on your hard disk that contains all of your DOS programs. The directory that I have is C:\BIN. For the purpose of this discussion, I will assume that your directory is also called C:\BIN.

Upgrading to V3.3

To upgrade your hard disk to use DOS V3.3, place the Startup disk in drive A and reboot the computer. Make sure the date and time are correct, pressing Enter for each prompt. You will see the A> system prompt. The next task is to replace the current DOS utilities from the old version of DOS with utilities from V3.3. To do so, issue the following command:

   A>**REPLACE A:*.* C:\ /S**

This command causes DOS to search every subdirectory on drive C, including the root directory and all subsequent subdirectories, for files that match those on drive A. If files with matching names are found, the files on drive C are replaced with the files from drive A.

Using the /S switch to include subdirectories is recommended so that REPLACE will replace all the appropriate files. You may, for example, have separate directories for DOS utilities, device drivers, and other types of DOS files. REPLACE with the /S switch searches the entire hard disk for matching files.

There is one caution you should heed before you issue this command. If, for some reason, you have other programs or utilities on your hard disk with the same name as the utilities provided with DOS, these will be replaced. You may want to verify that you do not have files with the same names as *any* DOS command.

The next step is to copy any new files that may have been added with this version of DOS to the hard disk. The command is

    A>**REPLACE A:*.* C:\BIN /A**

REPLACE examines the names of files in the \BIN directory and on drive A. If a file exists on drive A but not in \BIN, the file is copied to \BIN. The /A flag *adds* files to the destination.

If you are using minifloppy disks, insert the Operating disk into drive A and issue the two commands again. This time, however, you must precede the REPLACE command with the path leading to REPLACE.EXE. The commands are:

    A>**C:\BIN\REPLACE A:*.* C:\ /S**
    A>**C:\BIN\REPLACE A:*.* C:\BIN /A**

This technique is ideal for users who keep all DOS files in one or more subdirectories. The first REPLACE command replaces old DOS files with their new counterparts. Because the REPLACE command can examine all subdirectories of the given subdirectory, REPLACE automates the "search and replace" mission that is needed. The second command adds the new files to the \BIN subdirectory.

The next step requires the SYS command. Place the Startup disk in drive A once again and type

    A>**SYS C:**

This command places the operating system on the hard disk. There is no need to copy COMMAND.COM to the hard disk. It was copied with the first REPLACE command.

At this point, the hard disk is ready with the new version of DOS. Remove the floppy disk from the disk drive and reboot DOS from the hard disk. If all is well, the new DOS boots properly.

Now, because you have reorganized the disk, it is time to make a master backup of the hard disk. Follow instructions for the BACKUP command.

Upgrading to V4

Upgrading to V4 of DOS is much easier than upgrading to V3.3. First, insert the V4 Install disk into drive A and boot your computer. Follow the procedure outlined in Chapter 3 for installing DOS V4.

As DOS V4 is being installed, you will need to type the name of the directory you use to contain your DOS files—for example, C:\BIN. This step places the new DOS utilities in the appropriate directory. Old DOS utilities on your hard disk will be replaced with the new utilities.

The current versions of your AUTOEXEC.BAT and CONFIG.SYS files will be preserved. Two new files will be added—AUTOEXEC.400 and CONFIG.400. These files contain suggested statements for your AUTOEXEC.BAT and CONFIG.SYS files. You may wish to view the new files and add any new statements to your current AUTOEXEC.BAT or CONFIG.SYS files.

Once the installation is complete, remove the disks from your floppy disk drive and reboot your computer. And, since you have reorganized your computer, make sure that you do a complete backup.

Summary

In this chapter, you learned the following key points:

❏ The BACKUP command makes backup copies of floppy disks or the hard disk.

❏ The RESTORE command restores files that have been backed up. You use RESTORE after you use BACKUP.

❏ To prevent the loss of information, you must follow certain procedures for backing up and restoring a hard disk.

❏ The REPLACE command can replace existing files on a disk or add new files to the disk in one of many subdirectories.

Chapter 25 covers more DOS commands for hard disk users. Some of the commands are also beneficial to users with floppy disk drive computers.

25

Gaining More Control of the Hard Disk

This chapter covers ASSIGN, JOIN, and SUBST—three commands especially worthwhile for users whose computers have hard disks. Computer users with floppy disk systems will occasionally have use for these commands as well. This chapter also covers DOS's FASTOPEN command, a command that can improve the speed of finding and using files.

Using the Pretender Commands

ASSIGN, JOIN, and SUBST are DOS's "pretender" commands. When you use these commands, the disk drive or the disk's subdirectory masquerades as a different disk drive. The program you are running "thinks" that it is using a certain disk drive, even though it is using a different physical disk drive or subdirectory. ASSIGN originated with DOS V2. SUBST and JOIN started with DOS V3.1.

Why use these commands? Some older accounting and word-processing programs assume that a computer uses only two disk drives: the minifloppy disk drives A and B. Such programs are ignorant of hard disk drives, RAM disks, external floppy disk drives, and the hierarchical directory system. You need a way to trick these programs into using different disk drives.

The pretender commands are usually effective; however, these commands can have side-effects that are not always benign. Read the cautions at the end of this chapter, which explain how pretender commands can cause confusion.

Pretending That One Disk Drive Is Another (ASSIGN)

ASSIGN is the whole-disk reroute command. The syntax for ASSIGN is

*dc:pathc***ASSIGN** *d1 = d2 . . .*

Because ASSIGN is an external command, *dc:pathc* is the disk drive and path name to the command. The *d1* is the single-character name of the disk drive to be rerouted. *d2* is the single-character name of the disk drive that will be used in place of *d1*. You should not use a colon after either disk drive name, but you must use an equal sign between the disk drive letters. Putting a space before and after the equal sign is optional.

You can give more than one assignment in a single line. If you do, separate each additional assignment from the others with a space. The most frequent assignment is

ASSIGN A = C B = C

This line assigns drives A and B to drive C, the hard disk. Whenever a program tries to use either of the two floppy disk drives, DOS will trick the program into using the hard disk instead.

I frequently use ASSIGN to redirect a program that is attempting to use drive A to use my RAM disk, drive E, instead. I use the line

ASSIGN A = E

To undo the assignments, type **ASSIGN** without any drive assignments.

Pretending That a Subdirectory Is a Disk Drive (SUBST)

SUBST, the second pretender command, is similar to ASSIGN. But for hierarchical directory users, SUBST is more useful than ASSIGN. The difference between the two commands is that ASSIGN reroutes all disk activity to another disk. SUBST reroutes the activity to a subdirectory on another disk. SUBST is the better choice for programs that don't use subdirectories—usually programs written to run under DOS prior to V2.

SUBST lets you give a subdirectory a nickname using a disk drive name. The nickname or *alias* is used like any disk drive name. While SUBST is in effect, you can access the subdirectory normally (by its "real" disk drive/path name) or by its disk drive name alias.

SUBST's syntax is

*dc:pathc***SUBST d1:** *d2:***pathname**

d1: is a valid disk drive name that becomes the alias. *d2:***pathname** is the optional disk drive name and mandatory directory path that will be nicknamed d1.

To see the current active substitutions, type SUBST with no parameters. You will see a list of each current alias with the corresponding "real" disk drive and subdirectory.

To remove a substitution, type

> *dc:pathc***SUBST d1: /D**

You can also use SUBST to substitute an alias for a real disk drive. Give the disk drive letter with the name of the path to the subdirectory for which you want an alias. For example, giving the following command reroutes any activity intended for drive A to the subdirectory WORDS on drive C:

> **SUBST A: C:\\WORDS**

However, until you disconnect the substitution with the /D switch, you cannot use the real disk drive; you can use only the substituted disk drive and subdirectory.

If the disk drive name you give to SUBST is "higher" than E, you must use the LASTDRIVE directive in your CONFIG.SYS file. This command enables you to use disk drive names F through Z.

If you organize disk files into subdirectories, you will find the SUBST command more useful than the ASSIGN command.

Pretending That Two Disk Drives Are One (JOIN)

On a computer that has only one floppy disk drive, DOS uses the single disk drive as if it were two different disk drives: A and B. The JOIN command works in the opposite way, letting you combine two different disk drives into one disk drive.

The most frequent use of JOIN is to join two "logical" hard disk drives into a larger combined drive. However, you can join any two disk drives, including joining a floppy disk drive to another disk drive. If you have a computer with two physical or logical hard disks, such as the PS/2 with a 40M or larger disk drive (or one hard disk and one floppy disk drive), you can join them. You use the JOIN command to join the second disk to an empty subdirectory on the first.

The syntax for JOIN is similar to that for SUBST. To join two disk drives, use the following command:

> *dc:pathc***JOIN d1:** *d2:***path**

The *dc:pathc* is the optional disk drive and path name to the JOIN command. To clarify the designations for joined drives, I will use the terms *guest* and *host*. The guest disk drive (d1:) is the disk drive that will be joined to another drive. The host is the disk drive that will make the guest drive look logically like part of the host. In the syntax phrasing, *d2:* represents the host disk drive's optional name. The path, which is mandatory, is an empty subdirectory at which point the two disk drives are logically connected.

The following example shows what happened when I joined my floppy disk drive (drive A) to my hard disk.

```
C>DIR A:              {Get a directory of the
                       floppy disk.}

Volume in drive A has no label

Directory of A:\

CO2     PCD     46336    4-22-85    4:55p
CO3     PCD     15744    4-16-85    7:12p
CO4     PCD     44288    4-22-85    3:57p
CO5     PCD     35968    4-23-85   10:44a
CO6     PCD      8192    4-23-85   11:03a
CO7     PCD     12288    4-23-85   11:58a
CO8     PCD     53120    4-25-85    8:42a
7 File(s)    143360 bytes free
```

C>**MD C:\JOIN**   {Make the subdirectory.}
C>**DIR C:\JOIN**   {Show the JOIN directory.}

```
Volume in drive C is MORE DOS
Directory of  C:\JOIN

.            DIR       52485    2:55p

. .          DIR       52485    2:55p

2 File(s)   2101248 bytes free
```

C>**JOIN A: C:\JOIN**   {Join the floppy and hard disk drives.}
C>**JOIN**   {Have JOIN display the
                            connection.}

```
A: = C:\JOIN
```

C>**DIR C:\JOIN**   {Show the new directory.}

```
Volume in drive C is MORE DOS
Directory of  C:\JOIN

CO2     PCD     46336    4-22-85    4:55p
CO4     PCD     44288    4-22-85    3:57p
CO5     PCD     35968    4-23-85   10:44a
CO6     PCD      8192    4-23-85   11:03a
CO7     PCD     12288    4-23-85   11:58a
CO8     PCD     53120    4-25-85    8:42a
7 File(s)   2101248 bytes free
```

```
C>DIR A:                          {DOS no longer recognizes A:.}

Invalid drive specifier

C>JOIN A: /D                      {Break the connection.}
C>DIR A:                          {Show the floppy disk
                                   directory again.}

Volume in drive A has no label
Directory of   A:\
C02    PCD     46336    4-22-85    4:55p
C03    PCD     15744    4-16-85    7:12p
C04    PCD     44288    4-22-85    3:57p
C05    PCD     35968    4-23-85   10:44a
C06    PCD      8192    4-23-85   11:03a
C07    PCD     12288    4-23-85   11:58a
C08    PCD     53120    4-25-85    8:42a
7 File(s)     143360 bytes free

C>
```

In this process, my first step was to create an empty directory, which I called JOIN. Then I "JOINed" drive A: to drive C:\JOIN, the empty subdirectory. I performed the DIR command before and after the action to show that DOS had made the two disks into one larger disk.

While JOIN was active, I attempted to get a directory of drive A. DOS denied this request. This happened because you cannot access the joined disk except through the connecting subdirectory. In this example, the only way to use drive A is to use its new alias, \JOIN. When you issue the JOIN command without any arguments, JOIN prints the current subdirectory and disk drive on which you have used the command. JOIN also recognizes the /D *disconnect* switch. To undo the action, you give the real disk drive name with the switch.

JOIN restricts the subdirectories you can use as the host. The subdirectory must be empty. In addition, for versions of DOS through V3.3, the subdirectory must be held by the root directory. You cannot use a subdirectory of a subdirectory. V4 will allow you to join a drive to a second-level subdirectory. For ease of use, though, join a drive only to a first-level subdirectory.

If the subdirectory you name does not exist, JOIN will create the subdirectory for you. JOIN does not remove the subdirectory, however. You must remove the subdirectory by using the RMDIR command.

A frequent use of JOIN is to join a second hard disk drive to the first, or a RAM disk to a hard disk. To join the second hard disk to the first using a subdirectory called JOIN, the command would be

JOIN D: C:\JOIN

Presuming that the RAM disk is drive E, the command to join the RAM disk to drive C using a subdirectory called VDISK is

JOIN E: C:\VDISK

Important Warnings about All Pretender Commands

The ASSIGN, JOIN, and SUBST commands and the PATH and APPEND commands (discussed in Chapters 13 and 14) all trick DOS and other programs into using different disk drives or subdirectories. Because of the rerouting, you should be aware of certain problems that can occur. Most of these problems are obvious, but some are not.

The APPEND, ASSIGN, JOIN, and SUBST commands do not work with all programs, particularly those that are copy protected. A copy-protected program makes a special request to DOS to read a specific part of the disk in the floppy disk drive. APPEND, ASSIGN, JOIN, and SUBST cannot intercept and reroute this special request. In such cases, your only choice is to have the correct floppy disk in the correct disk drive.

You should not use ASSIGN, SUBST, or JOIN to reroute a real disk drive to a nonexistent disk drive. If you try, most DOS commands immediately display an `Invalid parameter` or `Invalid drive specification` error message.

The highest disk drive on which you can use ASSIGN or SUBST is based on the LASTDRIVE directive you have in your CONFIG.SYS file. You must properly set up the LASTDRIVE command to use higher-letter disk drive names.

Although JOIN creates a host subdirectory if one does not exist, SUBST requires an existing subdirectory. You will get an error message if you try to use SUBST with a nonexistent subdirectory.

While ASSIGN, SUBST, and JOIN are active, you should use some DOS commands with caution and avoid others altogether. Be cautious with the following commands when you specify an ASSIGN, SUBST, or JOIN command:

CHDIR	LABEL
MKDIR	APPEND
RMDIR	PATH

When you are changing, creating, and removing subdirectories, you are operating on the physical disk drive that is the recipient of the rerouting. Although you specify one disk drive to create or remove a subdirectory, DOS actually uses another disk drive if you have used a pretender command. Keep in mind the physical disk drive that is being affected by these commands.

If you attempt to use LABEL on a disk drive on which you have used ASSIGN, SUBST, or JOIN, you can receive some astonishing results. The "real" disk drive is actually labeled, not the alias disk drive you specified. Remember that search paths follow ASSIGN, JOIN, and SUBST substitutions. Using these commands to hide a path used by PATH causes DOS to display a warning message about invalid paths in DOS versions released before DOS V3.2. For PATH and APPEND in DOS versions after DOS V3.2, no warning is given at all. DOS simply will not find your programs or data files.

The DIR and CHKDSK commands work differently (or not at all) with ASSIGN, SUBST, and JOIN. DIR gives an error message when you attempt to display the directory of the JOIN command's guest disk drive. You must either break the JOIN before you can get a directory of the "JOINed" drive or get a directory using the alias path name.

When you use DIR with a SUBST directory, DIR displays a proper list of files. The volume label reflects the real disk drive used. The disk drive name and the directory reflect the rerouting. For the ASSIGN command, DIR always displays the rerouted disk drive's files. For example, if drive A is assigned to drive B, a directory of either drive shows the files on drive B.

CHKDSK will not process the rerouted disk drive involved in the ASSIGN or JOIN command. Nor will CHKDSK process the substituted disk drive (which is actually a directory). CHKDSK will process the host disk drive of a JOIN command but skip the guest portion of the disk drive. You can use CHKDSK to analyze the subdirectory you have used in a SUBST command if you use the subdirectory name instead of the alias disk drive name.

Both DIR and CHKDSK show the free disk space on the "real" disk. DOS does not attempt to give new statistics on the combined disk space for JOIN. DIR and CHKDSK will report free space and similar statistics on the joined-to (host) disk drive only. You have no way to find the free space on the disk that has been joined (the guest) unless you disconnect it from the second disk and then run DIR or CHKDSK.

Do not use the following commands on the disk drives involved in an ASSIGN, SUBST, or JOIN command:

DISKCOPY	FORMAT
DISKCOMP	BACKUP
FDISK	RESTORE
PRINT	

Most of these commands immediately issue an error message when you attempt to use them with ASSIGN, SUBST, or JOIN. The reason is that you may operate inadvertently on a disk drive that is physically different from the drive you specify on the command line. DOS simply protects you (and itself) from such operations. PRINT, BACKUP, and RESTORE do not issue warning messages. Using these commands while rerouting is in effect is risky. To use these commands, first break the assignment, joining, or substitution. Then run the commands.

Finally, you should not mix the pretender commands. You could, for example, join disk drives, use SUBST on the "JOINed" directory, and then use ASSIGN to direct the whole thing to a different disk drive. DOS will happily reroute the disk activity, but where the rerouted activity ultimately goes may be difficult to determine. To avoid "spaghetti" rerouting, do not reroute something that is already rerouted.

Gaining More Speed with FASTOPEN

FASTOPEN, which was introduced with DOS V3.3, can be used only with hard disk drives. FASTOPEN partially solves a performance problem not solved by CONFIG.SYS's BUFFERS command. BUFFERS helps when your computer reads or writes information to several files. BUFFERS helps most when the disk activity is isolated to a file's few key portions.

If you use many of the same files during the day, particularly small files that DOS can read or write in one cluster, BUFFERS is not a major benefit. The time DOS spends traversing the subdirectory system and opening the files may take more time than actually reading or writing the files.

FASTOPEN basically caches directory information, holding in memory the locations of frequently used files and directories. Directories are a type of file, not accessible by users, that DOS reads and writes in a manner similar to other files. A part of the directory entry for a file or subdirectory holds the starting point for the file in the file allocation table. Because DOS typically holds the FAT in the disk buffers, FASTOPEN was developed to hold directory entries in memory.

FASTOPEN is not a complex command, but you will have to do a small amount of work before you can effectively use it. FASTOPEN's syntax is

   dc:pathc**FASTOPEN d:** = *nnn*

The *dc:pathc*\\ is the disk drive and path to the FASTOPEN command. The **d:** is the name of the hard disk drive you want FASTOPEN to aid. *nnn* is the number of directory entries that FASTOPEN should cache. Each file or subdirectory requires one entry. If you do not specify *nnn*, the number defaults to 34. The allowable range of *nnn* is 10 to 999.

For DOS V4, additional syntax is

   dc:pathc**FASTOPEN d:** = *(nnn,mmm)* /X

The *mmm* refers to the number of fragmented entries (the DOS manual calls it "continuous space buffers") for the drive. Using this parameter improves performance when files on your hard disk become fragmented. The values you may use for *mmm* range from 1 to 999. There is no default value for fragmented entries. If a value is not given, the feature is not active.

The /X switch is similar to the /X switch of other commands. This switch allows FASTOPEN information to reside in expanded memory.

You can use FASTOPEN on as many disk drives as you want. Note, however, that the total number of directory entries or fragment entries FASTOPEN can handle is 999. If you issue the command for several disk drives, *nnn*'s and *mmm*'s sum cannot exceed 999. This limit is FASTOPEN's physical limit.

The practical limit of *nnn* is between 100 and 200 per disk drive. If you use many entries above this number, DOS will wade through the internal directory entries slower than it reads information from the disk. Also, each directory entry stored in memory takes 35 bytes. Considering the speed-versus-memory tradeoff, the 100-to-200 limit yields adequate performance.

However, using too small a number for *nnn* can be a disadvantage. When directory entries are recycled, the least recently used entry is discarded if a new entry is needed. The object is to have enough entries in memory so that FASTOPEN operates efficiently, but not so many that the time FASTOPEN spends wading through directory entries exceeds any gains in performance.

The *nnn* must exceed the number of subdirectories you must travel through to get to your "deepest" subdirectory. In many cases, however, the minimum value FASTOPEN will accept for *nnn* (10) will exceed the number of levels in your directory organization. For example, in the sample hierarchical directory in Appendix B, the deepest "level" is three (\DOS\BASIC\TEST and \DOS\BASIC\SAMPLES). If the deepest level were nine, you could use ten, but using that small a number also nullifies the improvements that FASTOPEN can offer. My not-terribly-scientific guideline is start with 100 and fine-tune up or down by 5 until you "feel" the right performance.

The number of *mmm*s you use is dependent on how fragmented your files are. Use CHKDSK *.* in subdirectories where you store data files to get a report of fragmentation. A general rule is to use twice the number of *nnn*s as your *mmm* entry.

You should observe two restrictions about using FASTOPEN. First, the disk drive you name to FASTOPEN cannot be one on which you have used JOIN, SUBST, or ASSIGN. Second, if you use a disk drive device driver that is loaded through your AUTO-EXEC.BAT file rather than through the CONFIG.SYS file (some manufacturers provide a driver in the form of a program rather than a device driver), you must use FASTOPEN after you have defined all disk drives. FASTOPEN can become confused if you add additional disk drives after you have invoked the program.

Issue the FASTOPEN command only once per disk drive. The best way to invoke FASTOPEN is to place the command in your AUTOEXEC.BAT file. In this way, the command runs automatically whenever you invoke DOS.

As I noted in Chapter 17, you can also install FASTOPEN through the CONFIG.SYS file using the INSTALL configuration command if you are using DOS V4. The syntax to install FASTOPEN through CONFIG.SYS is basically the same as installing FASTOPEN from the DOS prompt. The major difference is that when FASTOPEN is installed through CONFIG.SYS, you must include the extension, i.e., FASTOPEN.EXE. The caveat about using DOS V4's expanded memory support noted in Chapter 17 applies if you install FASTOPEN from the DOS command line.

Summary

In this chapter, you learned the following important points:

- [ ] The ASSIGN command reroutes the activity for one disk drive to another disk drive.

- [ ] The SUBST command enables you to give a disk drive name to a subdirectory.

- [ ] The JOIN command joins two disk drives into a single disk drive.

- [ ] The FASTOPEN command speeds the finding of files on the hard disk.

In Chapter 26, you will learn how to transfer information between minifloppy and microfloppy systems.

26

Migrating between Minifloppy and Microfloppy Systems

This chapter describes a new problem: *migration*, the transfer of information between computers that use 5 1/4-inch disks (minifloppies) and computers that use 3 1/2-inch disks (microfloppies). I examine the problem and suggest some solutions. This chapter also discusses using a minifloppy-based desktop computer and a microfloppy-based laptop or portable.

When the PC Convertible was announced in August of 1986, few industry watchers were surprised that the machine used microfloppy disk drives and disks. Although IBM did not announce that other new machines would use microfloppy disk drives, sharp-eyed computer users could see the writing on the wall. Actions speak louder than words.

When the PS/2 systems were announced in April of 1987, suspicions were confirmed. Every machine used microfloppy disk drives. All subsequent new machines would have microfloppy disk drives, too, was the educated guess. The current PC family someday would be withdrawn.

If you have a PC-XT, Personal Computer AT, XT-286, PC*jr*™, or PC Portable, your machine uses 5 1/4-inch minifloppy disks. If you have a PC Convertible or a PS/2 computer, your machine uses 3 1/2-inch disks. Because you can't use minifloppy disks in a microfloppy disk drive or microfloppy disks in a minifloppy disk drive, you face some challenges.

If your first computer is a PS/2 and you don't use any other computer, this chapter probably is not for you. You might want to skim it, however, because almost everyone I know has some need to get information from a minifloppy-based machine.

Determining Your Migration Needs

Assume that you do need to transfer files from one system to another. The first logical step in satisfying your needs is determining those needs. Here are some questions to ask:

- What and how much information must be moved?
- Will you continue to use your old computer?
- How frequently will you move information?

Finding the answers to these questions involves looking at both your minifloppy-based and microfloppy-based systems and planning the future use of your computers. These answers are the key to which migration solution works best.

What and How Much Information Must Be Moved?

If you answer "everything" to the question about what information must be moved, you fail the test. After examination, you may find that only a small percentage of files must be moved. Amazingly, a study of corporate management information services departments shows that only 5 percent of a computer's files are moved when a new system is brought in. I suspect that a greater number of files are moved when a new personal computer arrives, but that number typically amounts to less than 50 percent of all files.

You don't need to move all your files. First, you don't need to move DOS itself because you have a microfloppy copy of DOS. Second, you don't have to move copy-protected software because you'll need new microfloppy versions of the software. (However, you may have to move the data files you use with this software.) Third, you may have to replace older versions of programs with new versions. As with copy-protected software, only the data files may need to be moved.

Fourth, some utilities fall by the wayside. Some programs that fit only your old computer may not or will not work with your new system. If you have a new printer, for example, some older printer utilities do not need to be moved. Examine your old utilities to determine what should be moved and what should stay.

Fifth, you may have some old data files you don't use any more. I haven't met the hard disk on a mature computer (one that's more than six months old) that does not have some abandoned relics.

Two of your best aids in determining the files that need to be moved are the TREE /F and DIR commands. Get a complete road map of your hard disk by entering **TREE /F >PRN**. Use the resulting list to see what files you have. Then use the DIR command and look at each file's date and time stamp for clues to the use of that file. Data files more than one year old should be suspect. Don't apply this same standard to program files, however, because the dates of these files don't change when you use the program. Therefore, you must run the programs to determine whether they have a life on your new machine.

Which method should you use to move files to your new computer? If your files will fit on one or two 360K disks, almost any method can work. I'd choose the lowest-cost method. If the number is larger—as many as ten disks—your choices are more limited. You might spend a little more money to make the transfer process faster and more convenient. If the number is larger than ten 360K disks, or if you don't plan to abandon your old computer, only a few choices are available.

Will You Continue To Use Your Old Computer?

Before I explain the methods of migration, you need to consider another question: what are your plans for your old machine? The answer to this question helps you choose your solution. After your new computer is set up and running, will you abandon your old computer? Will you keep your old system as a backup? Will you take it home or give it to your children? Will it stay at work and move to a co-worker's office?

Basically, you have three possible answers. One, you'll never see your minifloppy-based system again—your old workhorse is going to pasture. Two, your old machine will supplement your new computer. You will have constant access to your old computer. Three, your computer is going to another person nearby, or it is going to your home. You'll have occasional access to your old machine.

If you will never see your minifloppy-based system again, you just need to move files to your new computer. The transfer is one-way: old computer to new. After you complete that task, the files on your minifloppy disks or old hard disk won't matter; both will disappear. In one-way migration, if you have any question about whether a file should be moved to your new computer, move the file.

If you will be using both machines, chances are good that the file movement will be bidirectional. In this case, you must find a convenient—almost casual—method of moving files between your computers. If you keep both machines, you can be more lax about what files must be moved. If you need a file on your other computer later, you can move that file then.

If your minifloppy-based computer is staying "in the family," you have several options. If your former computer will be located nearby at the office or at home, you still have access to the machine. However, tying the old and new computers together may not be convenient if one machine is at home.

How Often Will You Move Information?

How often will you move files between the systems? If the frequency is high, convenience is important. If you spend more time or energy moving your files than creating or editing them, why bother moving them? You'd be better off re-creating the edited file than moving the file.

Examining the Migration Solutions

To summarize the preceding section, here are the migration issues:

- What and how much information must be moved?
- Is the movement one-way or two-way?
- How often will the movement take place?

Based on the answers to these questions, you have three choices:

- the IBM Migration Facility
- communications programs
- dual floppy disk drives

The IBM Migration Facility

The IBM Migration Facility is a software/hardware combination that moves files through the parallel ports of two computers. One of your computers must be a PS/2, and you must have the parallel cable. The package comes with a disk and a device that plugs into the parallel port of the PS/2 computer and accepts the 36-pin "printer" end of the cable. The other end of the cable is plugged into the 25-pin parallel port of your minifloppy-based computer.

A program called RECV35.COM is on the PS/2 Reference disk, and a program called COPY35.COM is on the disk provided with the Migration Facility. You run RECV35 on your PS/2, and you run COPY35 on your minifloppy-based machine. The result is a fast and fairly convenient method of moving files from your minifloppy-based machine to your PS/2.

The Migration Facility has several advantages and one major disadvantage. If you already have the parallel cable, the Migration Facility, at less than $40, is inexpensive. Its information transfer is fast, and the copy-receive programs send information over parallel ports several times faster than files are sent over serial adapters. The copy-receive programs are fairly easy to use. The COPY35 program works in a manner similar to the DOS COPY command. You can use wild-card file names and with one command send all the files from a directory. You also specify the destination name to COPY35. You start RECV35 on your PS/2 and tell COPY35 on your minifloppy-based computer where the files should go on your new machine. You can send the files to a microfloppy or hard disk. The entire process is fairly convenient.

The Migration Facility has only one major limitation. Its file movement is only from your minifloppy-based computer to your PS/2. You can't reverse directions. Although the PS/2 parallel port is capable of sending or receiving information, the parallel ports on the other computers can only send information. If you want to send information from your PS/2 to your minifloppy-based computer, the Migration Facility is not the solution for you.

The Migration Facility has some minor disadvantages, too. The process is convenient, but not exceptionally convenient. After you start RECV35 on your PS/2, the program stays active and does not return to DOS until you press Esc on your PS/2. Therefore, you can run COPY35 several times and not touch your PS/2. RECV35 actively receives all files sent by COPY35. But this advantage is offset by the fact that RECV35 does not make subdirectories automatically on your PS/2. You must manually create any needed directories on your PS/2. Although the transfer commands are issued on the minifloppy computer, you must occasionally leave RECV35 on your PS/2 and make subdirectories on the disk.

The Migration Facility copies only one subdirectory at a time. COPY35 has no /S (subdirectory) switch. Because RECV35 can't make needed subdirectories, the program can't copy files from multiple directories with one command.

Another disadvantage is that your machines must be within cable reach. Parallel cables are usually 25 feet long or less. Distance usually is no problem when you first transfer files. When you want to move files later and your other machine is in a different location, however, you must retrieve the other computer. This hassle may be more work than you'd like to do frequently.

Basically, the Migration Facility is good for moving information from a minifloppy computer to a PS/2. The program is fairly painless to use. However, if you need bi-directional file movement, two other solutions may work better for you.

Communications Programs

A second choice is the communications solution, which uses the serial ports of the two machines to move files between computers. The communications solution involves both hardware and software. The software is the communications program which makes possible the two-way flow of information. The hardware consists of the cable and modems. If your machines are located within a few feet of each other, all you need is the right communications program on each machine and a serial cable. If your machines are farther apart, you may need modems on both.

Like the Migration Facility, the communications solution has both advantages and disadvantages. The principal advantage is that files can be moved both ways. Another advantage is that this method can be used if the machines are not near each other. Serial cables can be as long as 200 feet, so the distance between the systems can be greater. If modems are used on both machines, the two machines can be located almost anywhere.

You will find some trade-offs with this solution, however. First, serial communications are slower than parallel communications. Unless a very high baud rate for the serial ports is used, the file transfer takes longer. Because you can't use very high baud rates with modems, only computers connected directly by a serial cable are fast. If you want to move several files, you may spend several minutes or hours waiting for your two computers to finish their conversation.

The ease of use for this method depends on your communications software. With most programs, you can send a group of files at one time. If you can send only one file at a time on your communications program, you must endure the tedious process of typing at both computers the name of every file you transmit.

Communications programs do not create subdirectories on the receiving machine. For this reason, you must manually create the needed subdirectories on your receiving machine. With some communications programs, you can control your receiving computer. If you use this type of program and transfer files only to your hard disk, you can issue the necessary commands at your sending machine only. If you send information to microfloppy disks, however, someone must be at the receiving machine to change disks. Unattended operation of your receiving computer is not an option.

The communications solution can range from inexpensive to expensive. You will have to acquire a special serial cable, called a *null modem* cable. Basically, the second and third lines on the cable are reversed so that the two computers "talk" and receive on separate lines. Fortunately, a null modem cable costs about the same amount as any other serial cable.

Communications programs can cost almost nothing, or they can be very expensive. You can use public-domain programs, which are available free from many user groups and community bulletin boards. Also available are shareware programs, whose costs amount to a donation or registration fee you should send the author. Shareware programs are usually cheaper than their commercial counterparts and can be of good quality.

The other solution is to use commercial communications programs, which range in price from $50 to $400. The programs are worth the money, but they may be more than you need. Remember that you need compatible communications programs on both machines. This requirement can double the cost of the programs.

You don't have to have the same program on both machines, but the programs must understand how to talk to each other and must use the same type of special protocol to handle program files. If the programs don't agree, you cannot move the files.

The communications solution is an inexpensive-to-more-expensive solution. Files can be moved both ways, but the process is slower and may require more effort. The distance between machines is unlimited if you increase the cost by buying and using modems. The more cost-effective method is to use a long serial cable. The ease of use depends on the communications programs you use.

The Floppy Disk Drive Solution

The third solution is installing an additional floppy disk drive on your computer. This solution, which may be the most expensive (from $160 to $500), has some exclusive advantages.

Basically, you put on your computer an internal or external disk drive opposite the type you have: a minifloppy disk drive on your PS/2 or a microfloppy disk drive on your

Personal Computer. After the disk drive is installed properly, the drive becomes a regular part of your computer. You use the disk drive like any other, to copy files to and from the disks.

To move files between your computers, you copy files to the disk by using XCOPY, COPY, or BACKUP. Then you take the disk from the disk drive and put it in the disk drive of your other computer. You use XCOPY, COPY, or RESTORE to retrieve the files. You can move files in either direction.

The advantage is that the new drive is a regular part of your system. All DOS commands work with the disk drive. You don't need any other programs, you get the additional use of the drive to store and retrieve files, and the computers can be located anywhere. You have only to transport the floppy disks between your computers—not bring the computers to each other.

The major disadvantage of this solution is cost. The price of the disk drive and any needed adapter is more than the price of the Migration Facility and can be more than that of the communications solution.

The minor disadvantage is storage capacity. IBM sells a 360K minifloppy disk drive for the PS/2. But if you use high-capacity 5 1/4-inch disk drives, reverting to 360K floppies is a painful pullback. Some outside vendors sell 1.2M floppy disk drives, which appear to be the best solution. Fortunately, IBM also sells a 720K microfloppy disk drive for Personal Computers.

If the disk drive solution seems desirable, you have two other considerations. Which machine gets the disk drive? Will the drive be internal or external?

The machine you choose as your workhorse will be the base computer for your operations. Most files will either originate on or return to this machine. Also, this machine is the one you will keep for the longest time. For this reason, your best investment is complementing your workhorse with the opposite type of disk drive.

Do you need an internal or an external drive? External disk drives are slightly more expensive (from $30 to $100 more) than internal disk drives because an external disk drive may require a separate power supply and cabinet for the disk drive.

Can you use an internal disk drive in your computer? If you have a PC that already has two floppy disk drives, the answer is yes. You can replace the second minifloppy disk drive with a microfloppy disk drive. If you don't want to remove a floppy disk drive, however, you need an external disk drive.

Are you placing a minifloppy disk drive on your PS/2? You may have a choice between internal and external disk drives also. IBM's minifloppy disk drive for the PS/2 is external. Third-party vendors, however, have developed a minifloppy disk drive that fits in the slot for a second hard disk on the Models 60 and 80. If you won't use a second hard disk on one of these models, you can buy an internal minifloppy drive. If you have a different PS/2 model or will use both hard disks, your only option is an external disk drive.

Installing a disk drive involves some hardware and software tinkering. You may have to install an adapter in your computer. You must connect the disk drive, which could involve opening your computer and playing around with the cables. On a Personal Computer, you alter your CONFIG.SYS file. If your disk drive is external, you copy a file or two from the disk provided with the disk drive. On your PS/2, you run the configuration option from the Reference disk. The process of installing a disk drive is not difficult or very complex, but if you are wary of these steps, have your dealer or a computer-literate friend install the drive for you.

The disk drive approach may be the most expensive, but it is the most natural to use. The speed of the transfers is the time needed to copy the disk twice—once from your sending machine to the disk and once from the disk to the receiving machine.

Choosing the Best Migration Solution

Based on your needs and your budget, your migration problem can be solved in several ways. The following are my suggestions.

The Migration Facility is the best solution if you are abandoning your minifloppy-based computer. You need to move information only one way, and you can move any amount of information. The cost of the Migration Facility is small, and the speed is acceptable.

The communications solution is best if you need to move several files to your microfloppy-based computer and later must occasionally move small files or a few files back to your minifloppy-based computer. Because you need to move files both ways, you need a bi-directional link between your machines. This link is furnished by the communications solution.

This solution is good if both machines usually are connected, will remain close, or will be used for other types of computer-to-computer communications. To talk to other computers, you must make an investment in communications software. You get the additional capability from the communications software to talk to your old computer also.

If you frequently must move many files between your machines, installing *floppy disk drives* is the solution for you. It is good also if your machines are in different locations—when you have a laptop computer, for example.

Transfer frequency and the number of files is the key. If you move files between your machines frequently, you want the most casual method possible. The extra disk drive makes the copying process easy, and your two machines can be anywhere. Instead of transporting your computers, you simply transport the information on disks.

By the way, I should mention an even less expensive solution than the three I have given. Find a friend, a company, or a users group that has one of these setups, and use it. (One of the technical editors of this book calls this the "Mooch Solution.") If you need the setup only occasionally, borrowing someone else's hardware and software makes sense.

My Personal Solution

Any of the recommended solutions should work for you. However, you might be wondering how I solved the problem personally. Actually, I adopted two solutions that are slightly different from what you might expect.

When I first got my PS/2 Model 60, I didn't have any software available for it, so I needed a quick fix. Since money is no object for wealthy authors, I purchased IBM's add-on 3 1/2-inch disk drive for my old PC-XT. This external drive plugs right into the back of the floppy controller on the PC-XT and gets its power from a special connector that takes only a minute to plug in. A quick DRIVER.SYS command in the CONFIG.SYS file tells the XT that it has a new disk drive.

Although the drive is a 720K rather than 1.44M, it still allows me to copy files onto a disk that can be read by my PS/2 Model 60. Yet, this was not my long-term solution.

Eventually I discovered a program called Lap-Link that is intended for high-speed data exchange between computers through their serial ports. By high speed, I mean about 119,000 bits per second. That is *fast*. At about the same time, Radio Shack introduced a nifty adapter that plugs into the computer's serial port and has a socket for a standard six-conductor telephone cable on the back. I wired one of these adapters as a null modem and ran telephone wire from my PS/2 Model 60 down into the wall, under the floor, and up to my XT.

I can turn on the XT through a remote control at my desk. Its AUTOEXEC.BAT file automatically loads Lap-Link. Since the two computers are connected through their respective COM2 ports, all I need to do is load Lap-Link on my Model 60 to start exchanging files.

Lap-Link provides a split screen display that shows the directory of the host computer on the left side of the screen. On the right side is the directory of the remote computer. From either computer you may log onto other directories, mark files for copying, and start the copy process.

Copying a file from my XT to my Model 60 is almost as fast as writing it from the XT to the 720K floppy disk—and I'm not limited to 720K per copy operation. In fact, I can use wild cards to copy dozens of files in a few minutes.

This is not only an efficient migration tool, but may be the best backup method I've ever come up with. I can back up files from my PS/2 to the XT in a few minutes. It's almost as fast as a tape drive, and it's not limited to the capacity of a floppy disk.

Recommended Migration Techniques

One favorite technique for the whole computer-file transfer is to use BACKUP and RESTORE or XCOPY. I back up on microfloppy disks the directories holding the files to be moved, and then I use RESTORE to transfer them to my other machine. This solution is the fastest. Afterward, however, be careful to remove files you don't need and be sure not to wipe out new versions of software when you RESTORE. If you are unsure, back up your receiving hard disk before you move the software. If you make a mistake, you can restore the right file.

If you copy only a few files or subdirectories, use XCOPY to copy the files and their subdirectories to the floppy disk. Then take the disk to your other computer and use XCOPY again. If you copy more than one subdirectory, you can use the /S switch on XCOPY each time.

If I think that I might fill up my transfer disk, I use ATTRIB and XCOPY. ATTRIB turns on the archive attribute for the files I copy. The command is

> **ATTRIB +A filename**

in which **filename** is the full name for the files to be moved. Then, I copy the files in which the archive attribute is turned on by giving the command

> **XCOPY filename B: /M**

If the disk fills up, I move to my other computer, issue XCOPY to copy the files from the disk to the hard disk, erase the files on the disk, and then return the disk to my original computer. I give the same XCOPY command again. Because XCOPY turned off the archive attribute on the files it copied, only uncopied files are processed.

If you copy from more than one subdirectory, add the /S switch to the ATTRIB and XCOPY commands. To avoid copying more files than you want, add the /P switch to the XCOPY command. XCOPY asks which files should be copied. Answer **Y** to any files that should be copied and **N** for files that should not be transferred.

Summary

This chapter discussed the problems of transferring information between minifloppy and microfloppy disks and examined three solutions:

- ❏ the IBM Migration Facility
- ❏ communications programs
- ❏ the floppy disk drive solution

You learned how to decide which solution is the best for you, and you also learned some migration techniques. This chapter's discussion of how to solve problems resulting from hardware innovations is followed by a discussion of issues related to software innovations. Chapter 27 explores some of the differences between DOS V3 and V4 that you might not have thought about.

27

A Few DOS V4 Considerations

By now, I've covered just about everything you need to know to use DOS. However, there are some other considerations for using DOS V4 that need to be addressed. One key topic is the larger logical hard disks—greater than 32 megabytes—that DOS V4 can handle. You need not know how the 32-megabyte barrier was demolished, but you should understand the implications. In addition, this chapter covers miscellaneous command tips that you may find useful.

Large Disk Partitions

If you had asked a group of DOS V3 users for a "wish list" of new features, the capability of partitioning hard disks into logical disk drives larger than 32 megabytes would probably rank second. (I would guess that the number one "dream" feature would be access to more than 640K memory for ordinary DOS programs.)

Now, IBM's PC DOS V4 and some non-IBM versions of DOS after V3.2 provide for larger partitions. So, will everyone who has a large hard disk jump on the bandwagon? Will users abandon DOS V3.3 just to gain this feature? Oddly enough, I think they won't. Mammoth disk partitions are not all they have been cracked up to be. Let's look at some of the pros and cons, so you can decide whether big logical disks are for you.

Who Needs Large Partitions?

Of course, some users simply must have large partitions—those who have a single, mammoth data file that occupies more than 32 megabytes of disk space, for example. Without a large logical disk drive, such files must be split into sections. That makes accessing and processing tedious.

With such large data files, you can quickly fill up even a 300-megabyte or larger hard disk. And hard disks in this size are becoming quite common. If a workstation and its hard disk are dedicated to a database application, it is entirely practical to work with a huge file using a fast PC. This is particularly true if the disk can be partitioned as one large logical drive.

Another use for large disk partitions is in desktop publishing and graphics. Files created for programs like Ventura Publisher and PageMaker can be very large. Moreover, if you don't have a PostScript printer, the *font* files for these programs can be massive. For example, type sizes larger than 30 points require 200,000 bytes per size. So, a set of 32-point characters for normal, bold, italic and bold italic could themselves take up almost a megabyte of space. A single graphics file can easily amount to 150K. An 8 1/2 by 11-inch image scanned at 300 dots per inch amounts to a megabyte (8 1/2 * 300 * 11 * 300 = 8.4 million bits or about 1 megabyte). If you're doing any desktop publishing at all or have extensive graphics applications, you may find that 32 megabytes is far too little to store even your basic active files.

Other monolithic applications with smaller data files may benefit from a large hard disk partition if keeping all the files on a single hard disk is convenient. However, as you will see later, splitting these files among several logical disks may actually be more practical. I'll describe a method for organizing files shortly that is more useful than using a single large partition.

Even if you think hard, you'll find that there are not many applications which absolutely must have large partitions, and only a few more that can benefit from large partitions. Let's look at some of the possible problems.

Potential Problems with Large Partitions

Since no earlier version of PC DOS offered large disk partitions, it stands to reason that any such partitions you create on your hard disk will be incompatible with previous editions of DOS. Thus, if you choose to partition your hard disk into logical drives greater than 32 megabytes, you won't be able to access those logical drives at all with an earlier version of DOS.

I've already run into this problem. DOS V4 takes up twice as much memory—approximately 128K—as DOS V3.3. My favorite applications and memory-resident utilities (which take up their own portions of DOS memory while other programs run) cumulatively require more memory than DOS V4 leaves available. For example, I have a large number of device drivers loaded by CONFIG.SYS, which control my PS/2 Model 60's mouse, scanner, and second hard disk. In addition, I like to use Keyworks macros to customize the commands of my various applications. With these programs loaded, DOS V4 simply doesn't have enough memory left over to run Ventura Publisher. So, once a week when I plan to use Ventura Publisher in addition to my other applications, I boot DOS V3.3.

However, if I had partitioned either my 44-megabyte drive 1, or my 80-megabyte drive 2 hard disks with logical drives larger than 32M, DOS V3.3 would refuse to recognize the partitioned disk. The same is true of other operating systems that are designed for the partitioning scheme of earlier versions of DOS. Included are OS/2 Standard Edition 1.0 and Extended Edition 1.0. Later versions of OS/2 Presentation Manager do recognize larger disk volumes.

There are other potential problems with larger hard disk partitions. First, you may find that some of the software utilities you own, particularly older versions, won't work with the larger drives. I found, for example, that my version of the Norton Utilities, and a favorite program I used to sort, hide, and manipulate subdirectories, were incompatible with the larger partitions. I've since upgraded to the latest version of the Norton programs (Version 4.5 at this writing), which does fully support DOS V4. However, you may not be willing to pay the added expense if the number of programs involved is significant.

Another problem derives simply from trying to manage large hard disk partitions. You may find that you need so many subdirectories to properly divide the disk into logical units that you might as well have used separate, smaller disk partitions in the first place.

Finally, you may find that a very large hard disk partition provides reduced performance. That's generally because a larger disk will likely have more files, and be prone to performance-robbing fragmentation. You'll be less likely to optimize such a fragmented disk as often as you should, too, because it will take so much time. Smaller disks, in contrast, contain fewer files and are less likely to be fragmented.

A Solution to Partition Problems

If you allow enough room, dividing the large hard disk into partitions smaller than 32 megabytes can be the best compromise. Let me describe the organization of one of my own computers, which is equipped with one 44-megabyte drive and one 80-megabyte drive. 124 megabytes may be a lot more disk storage than you need, but you'll agree that such a disk is a candidate for larger disk partitions. However, I prefer to set up my system as shown in tables 27.1 and 27.2.

Table 27.1
Organization of Hard Disk 1 - 44 Megabytes

Drive/Directory	Contents
C - 22 megabytes	Key operating-system programs and utilities used on a daily basis
C:\DOS	All DOS files for DOS V4, including COMMAND.COM
C:\DOS3	All DOS files for DOS V3.3, including COMMAND.COM
C:\SYSAll	DOS V4 device drivers such as ANSI.SYS, as well as non-IBM device drivers used by both DOS V4 and V3.3
C:\SYS3	DOS V3.3-only device drivers
C:\BATCH	Batch files
C:\UTILS	Small utility programs
C:\ASCII	Files such as Sidekick, phone directory, and menu files displayed by batch files
C:\WINDOWS	Microsoft Windows and applications

Table 27.1—*Continued*

Drive/Directory	Contents
D - 22 megabytes	Other frequently used programs and utilities
D:\NORTON	The indispensable Norton Utilities
D:\PAINT	Publisher's Paintbrush
D:\GAMES	Miscellaneous games
D:\QUATTRO	A spreadsheet program
D:\TURBO	Turbo BASIC
D:\DBASE	dBASE III
D:\MISC	Miscellaneous programs and utilities
D:\BAK	Used as a temporary backup site for files from second hard disk until they are copied to floppy disk

Table 27.2
Organization of Hard Disk 2 - 80 Megabytes

Drive/Directory	Contents
E - 31 megabytes	Ventura Publisher and its files
E:\VENTURA	
E:\TYPESET	
E:\FONTS	
E:\	Files I am uploading or downloading with a telecommunications program. (Since nothing normally resides in the root directory of drive E, I use it for temporary storage.)
F - 31 megabytes	DisplayWrite 4 files
F:\LETTERS	
F:\PROPOSALS	
F:\USINGPC	
....etc.	
G - 18 megabytes	Backup copies of key files
G:\DOS	
G:\DOS3	
G:\BATCH	
G:\ASCII	
G:\UTILS	
G:\BAK	

I also use a 1-megabyte RAM disk, drive H, for overflow files generated by various applications that can't use expanded memory directly.

One interesting point: My AUTOEXEC.BAT file includes several lines that automatically copy any new or revised files from key subdirectories to a set of backup subdirectories *on the other hard disk* each time I boot the computer. Other batch files can be used to perform this task at any time. I use the XCOPY command to do this backup. For example, word processing files stored on drive F are copied to a subdirectory on drive D. Any batch files or ASCII files I might have updated on drive C are copied to drive G—automatically.

In effect, I have a daily, no-decision automatic backup system that copies key files to a different hard disk. If one of my hard disks crashes, those files are available on the other disk. If the first drive dies, I can boot DOS V4 from a special floppy I have prepared. For convenience, that floppy includes a SHELL command in the CONFIG.SYS file and a COMSPEC command in the AUTOEXEC.BAT file that tell DOS to look for COM-MAND.COM in G:\DOS. That way, I can remove the boot disk from the drive and use the computer normally.

(I do much the same thing when I boot DOS V3.3 from a floppy, only DOS is told to look for COMMAND.COM in C:\DOS3 or G:\DOS3.)

Some "Techie" Background

In this book, I've dealt with some aspects of DOS on a semi-technical level. If details like the FAT don't interest you, you can skip this section. But if you want a bit more detail about how the 32 megabyte barrier was passed, I offer the following explanation.

Prior to DOS V4, a 16-bit number was used to number individual sectors on a hard disk. All the numbers in binary from 0000000000000000 (0 decimal) to 1111111111111111 (65,535 decimal) could be used. Since disk sectors contain 512 bytes each, 65,535 of them will contain 32 megabytes of information.

DOS V4 uses a 32-bit number, which allows keeping track of 2 million megabytes (two *terabytes*) of information. However, we must also take into account the file allocation table (FAT) structure of the disk, which numbers and sets aside individual clusters, or groups of sectors. DOS allocates a number to track clusters as well: a 12-bit number for hard disk partitions of about 16 megabytes or smaller, and a 16-bit number for partitions that are larger than 16 megabytes. That translates into 4096 different FAT entries for 16M and smaller disks and 65,535 entries for larger disk partitions. The actual number of clusters that can be allocated is a little smaller, since DOS reserves some FAT entries for its own special uses.

If DOS uses four-sector clusters (of 2048 bytes each) for larger disks, and only about 65,000 entries are available to number them, you can see that the largest partition possible would be 128 megabytes. That's a long way from 2 terabytes of disk storage, even if 2 terabytes is more disk capacity than most of us have available.

Since DOS is locked into the FAT scheme, the only answer was to increase the cluster size. The 2048-byte cluster size is used only for disks sized between 16M and 32M. Disks in the 33M to 256M range use 4096-byte clusters. The same 65,535 FAT entries can then be spread across twice as many possible sectors.

Even larger disk partitions use 8192-byte clusters—the same size used with DOS V2 and with current versions for partitions smaller than 16M. A quick calculation shows that this brings us support for "only" 512 megabytes. However, larger partitions, if they are needed, can be accomplished simply by using even larger cluster sizes. As we've noted, this tends to waste disk space if many small files are created, but speeds disk access somewhat.

You may note in the *DOS Command Reference* that SHARE is used with larger disk partitions. Do you wonder why this is? One key reason is that some programs don't recognize one special new feature of DOS V4: the disk serial number. SHARE is used primarily on networked systems to lock and unlock files so that one user can't access a file that may be in the process of being changed by another user. For DOS V4, SHARE was given the ability to recognize disk serial numbers. If a disk is changed in the middle of an I/O operation, DOS will recognize that from the unique serial number. Remember, this wasn't possible before, since you could provide two disks with the same label if you wanted. SHARE's ability to keep such information about individual files is also used by DOS V4 to store data about files in larger disk partitions.

New and Undocumented Commands

Although DOS V4 has new configuration commands, enhancements to existing commands, and significant new features in the DOS Shell, all-new DOS prompt commands are few and far between.

A few commands were relatively undocumented in early releases of DOS V4 and, as such, should be used with caution. There may be good reasons why a command is not discussed in the documentation. The /H switch for the FORMAT command is a perfect example. If you use this parameter with the FORMAT command, DOS V3.3 immediately begins to format a disk, without waiting for you to insert a new disk or asking for confirmation that you want to format the disk. That's certainly a convenience, but it also can lead quickly to disaster. So, you won't find FORMAT /H discussed much, and it isn't available at all in DOS V4. Nondocumented features can quickly become nondocumented *non*features.

Such a nondocumented feature is TRUENAME. It is an "unknown" DOS V4 command that reports the actual name for an "aliased" disk or directory. Suppose, for example, that you used SUBST to create a false disk drive, say drive H, which actually was C:\FILES. If you typed **TRUENAME H:**, DOS would report

```
C:\FILES
```

Since SUBST itself can also be used to report on the status of substituted drives, there isn't a lot of use for a command like TRUENAME. That's probably why IBM hasn't called attention to it. This command could easily vanish in later versions of DOS. One use I can think of for the command would be within batch files. For example, suppose that a batch file allowed the user to enter a drive letter as a command-line parameter, and this letter could vary depending on how SUBST had been set up. If your batch file needed to know the identity of the real subdirectory, you could include a line like this:

TRUENAME>REAL.ASC

The output of TRUENAME would be redirected to a file called REAL.ASC for you to use as you wished.

Happily DOS V4's *documented* new DOS command, MEM, is a lot more useful than TRUENAME. MEM will provide you with a wealth of information about the contents of your computer's memory. MEM reports on conventional memory (the first megabyte, only 640K of which DOS can use for applications), extended memory (memory available on 80286 and 80386-based computers from 1M to 15M), and expanded memory (usually up to 24M with the appropriate hardware). MEM can be used on the command line alone, or with two optional parameters. The syntax is

```
MEM
MEM /DEBUG
MEM /PROGRAM
```

The first command produces a report like the following:

```
 655360 bytes total memory
 654336 bytes available
 335808 largest executable program size
 524288 bytes total EMS memory
 393216 bytes free EMS memory
2490368 bytes total extended memory
  86016 bytes available extended memory
```

MEM shows that of the 655,360 bytes of conventional memory (640K), all but 1024 bytes are available for DOS programs once the system is booted. Memory-resident utilities and other programs in memory when MEM was executed take up some additional memory, so only 335,808 bytes are available for another program.

If you want more detail from MEM, you can use the /PROGRAM parameter, which provides you a list of all the programs in memory. For my computer, these include COMMAND.COM, DisplayWrite 4 (which I used to write this chapter), COMMAND.COM again (I used DisplayWrite 4's DOS Commands feature to load another copy of COMMAND.COM in order to test out MEM), and MEM itself. MEM/PROGRAM also shows the space required for other directives, such as FILES, FCBS, BUFFERS, LASTDRIVE, and STACKS.

If you ever doubted that each copy of a program of COMMAND.COM inherited its own copy of the environment block, MEM will dispel that notion for you. It *shows* a listing for that block each time a program is loaded. Check it out yourself.

Much of the information supplied by MEM is of little interest to most users. That's particularly true of MEM with the /DEBUG parameter. In addition to providing the same information as MEM/PROGRAM, MEM/DEBUG also shows information about IBMBIO.COM's built-in device drivers (such as COM1, etc.) and handles available for EMS memory. There are 255 entries in the full display.

Summary

In this chapter, you learned about DOS V4's capability of using disk partitions greater than 32M. We also covered some of the reasons why you would—or would not—want to use this feature and finished with a few new features of DOS V4 that may prove of some use to you.

Chapter 28 discusses some of the better utility programs and gives you some final thoughts about using PC DOS.

28

Some Final Thoughts

This final chapter looks at many subjects already discussed in this book. I offer some thoughts about how to make DOS easier to use and how to avoid certain pitfalls. These pitfalls are experiences based on my own encounters.

Avoiding Dangerous Commands

In several chapters in this book, some commands are labeled "dangerous." Such commands are not dangerous to you personally, of course, but to the data recorded on your disk. If you do not use these commands properly, they can erase or destroy files.

Recording data on a disk takes time and work and may represent the heart of your business or livelihood. Common sense should tell you that these data must be protected. If you apply this common sense, you should have few problems.

FORMAT and DISKCOPY are the two most dangerous commands. If you use FORMAT or DISKCOPY on the wrong disk, you can destroy several files in just a few seconds. ERASE (DEL) is dangerous also because it deletes files. Although these three commands appear to do the same thing, they have differences.

When you erase a file, you do not remove it from your disk. DOS simply marks the directory entry holding the file name as "erased" and frees the file allocation table (FAT) sectors that held the file. When you add to or extend another file, the new file either takes over the directory entry for the erased file or uses the sectors that held it. With an appropriate program, you can "unerase" a file as long as the sectors have not been reused. (The best unerase program I have seen is part of the Norton Utilities by Peter Norton, described later in this chapter.)

FORMAT and DISKCOPY record new information on the entire floppy disk and, depending on your version of DOS, FORMAT may wipe clean your hard disk. When you format a disk, dummy information is recorded. When you use DISKCOPY, every bit of information from your first disk is copied to your second disk. If you use either FORMAT or DISKCOPY on a disk that has useful files, the information is no longer usable; it is lost.

Thankfully, DOS V4 can use SHARE and the unique serial numbers given to each disk to make sure that you do not accidentally write over your source disk when you meant to copy to the target disk.

With early versions of DOS, if you run FORMAT while the hard disk is the current disk drive and you do not specify a disk drive name to FORMAT, you see the following emphatic message:

```
WARNING, ALL DATA ON NON-REMOVABLE DISK
DRIVE C: WILL BE LOST!
Proceed with Format (Y/N)?_
```

Ignoring the message given by FORMAT V3 and earlier versions can quickly destroy many megabytes of hard disk information. DOS V3.2 and later versions insist that you type the volume label of the hard disk before you format the disk drive. The additional precaution is welcome. *Carefully read the messages on your screen whenever you use FORMAT.* A momentary lapse can have disastrous results.

SELECT prior to DOS V4 is also a dangerous command because it runs FORMAT. Do not use SELECT on a hard disk that holds any useful files. The files will be gone after SELECT has run.

COPY and XCOPY too can be problematic commands. If you use either command to copy an old version of a file to a disk holding a new version and you do not change the file name, you are in trouble. The new version of your file will be destroyed. Be careful when you use COPY or XCOPY.

The RECOVER command can be troublesome too. For a single file, RECOVER is easy and simple to use, but when you use RECOVER to recover a complete disk, you may need hours or days to recover files. Practice before you use RECOVER on "live" disks.

Knowing the Secret

A professional magician used to appear on television commercials all over the United States for a product called "TV Magic Cards." After performing a few tricks, he told viewers that they could easily do the card tricks "once you know the secret."

I feel the same way about computers and DOS. The concepts of hierarchical directories and I/O redirection may seem difficult to grasp at first. But with a little practice, these facilities are easily mastered once you "know the secret."

After you know how a command operates, you know the secret. After you have learned how to use the commands and know a little about how your computer operates, you can imagine what actually goes on when you invoke DOS and use its commands. Computers are "mystical" only when no one bothers to explain what really happens inside them. I hope that this book has helped you understand how your computer operates.

DOS really is a friendly operating system. You can learn by doing. Just be sure to watch what you are doing. Even experienced users make mistakes, which occur most often when users get over-confident or sloppy.

After a while, you may develop "advanced user's syndrome." Your fingers fly across your keyboard. You know exactly what you want to do before you do it. Then you make an "experienced mistake." You use FORMAT or DISKCOPY on the wrong disk or copy the wrong files over correct ones. You do not check to see whether the proper floppy disks are in the disk drives. You do not read the messages completely, or you make a typing error and do not see it. You will get so good at using your computer that you do not notice a mistake until it is too late.

To avoid some of these problems, always proofread your typing and check your messages. Make sure that the correct floppy disks are in the right disk drives. Use write-protect tabs on important floppy disks, even if you plan to remove the tabs after you have formatted or used DISKCOPY on them. Run DIR to be certain that no useful files will be destroyed by COPY, XCOPY, DISKCOPY, or FORMAT. Label your floppy disks.

Forgetting to save frequently while you revise a copy of a document, a spreadsheet, or a program also can be an "experienced mistake." You may be confident that you will not forget to save your information before you are finished, so you keep adding to, editing, or revising your document, spreadsheet model, or program without saving. At such times, Murphy's Law—Whatever can go wrong will go wrong—strikes.

To give you an idea of the necessity of frequently saving and backing up your files, I will relate some experiences of my own. I told the first story in the first edition of this book.

I once worked on a spreadsheet model for more than an hour. Several times I felt my subconscious nagging me to save my work, but I ignored the feeling. Then, in a half-second loss of power, the model I had been working on was destroyed. Restoring it took only half an hour, but that time would not have been wasted if I had taken just 10 seconds to save it.

Lesson One: Save your work frequently.

Lesson Two: Save your work more frequently if a storm is near.

The next few lessons came during the summer I was writing the second edition of this book.

Waves of strong thunderstorms swept across Indianapolis late one afternoon. When I noticed the sky darkening and the wind growing stronger, I marked my place in the text, saved my work, and turned off my computer. Within minutes, torrential rains soaked the area—and my car, on which the sunroof was wide open. After dashing from my door to my car, I was thoroughly drenched and found I could squeegee water from the car seats. Needless to say, my general humor when I returned to the desk was darker than the skies.

The power flickered several times. I felt relieved for having had the foresight to abandon my work during the height of the storm. Then, as quickly as the storm came, the skies cleared.

Impatient to begin working again, I started my computer and continued writing. The skies were almost clear when a brief power flicker paralyzed my computer. I lost 15 minutes of work. After impugning my computer, the local power company, and my stupidity for not following my own advice, I quickly re-entered the lost material.

Lesson Three: You cannot beat Mother Nature if she's out to get you.

Later that evening, I went to dinner with a friend. After returning home, I squeezed in a couple more hours of work. When I write, time passes quickly. My last glance at my watch told me that it was 10:45 p.m. The next time I looked at my watch, I was in total darkness. The power had gone out for five seconds. My watch read 12:10 a.m. I restarted my computer and checked the time for the chapter I was working on: 11:14 p.m. Another hour of work had been blissfully slung into the bit-bucket. I resisted my strong desire to drown my system and myself in the pond outside my window and began to re-enter my work.

Lesson Four: If you work late, keep a clock in sight so you will remember when to save your work.

Lesson Five: If you do not save your work every 10 to 15 minutes, regardless of weather conditions, you deserve to be up until 2 a.m. re-entering it.

The Most Important Lesson: Save your work frequently and often.

Finally, always back up your hard disk and floppy disks. Let me relate two true "horror" stories. Both stories demonstrate that the impossible can happen.

A computer user had issued an ASSIGN command on a computer not made by IBM. Remember that this command tricks your programs into using a disk drive different from the one that the programs intend to use. The command was

ASSIGN A = C

The command tricked all his programs into using the hard disk instead of the floppy disk drive A.

A half hour later, he issued the command

FORMAT A:

The normal DOS messages appeared. He put a floppy disk in drive A and then pressed Enter. After 30 seconds, he noticed that the light on his floppy disk drive had not gone on, which meant that the floppy drive was not in use. He then looked at the light on his hard disk: it was on.

He quickly pressed Ctrl-C and looked at his hard disk directory, which reported that his 10M hard disk "thought" it was a 360K floppy. He had lost more than 8 megabytes of data. FORMAT had written over his directory and his file allocation table. Recovering his data would be like rebuilding the side of a mountain after it had been dynamited.

The tragedy was not that FORMAT did something it should never do. FORMAT, under IBM PC DOS, is never fooled by the ASSIGN command, although the computer manufacturer was fooled in the command's MS-DOS V2 implementation. The real tragedy was that the man had to spend three weeks recovering his files from a 30-second mistake because he had never made a backup of his hard disk.

Now, I remind you that I am a very experienced computer user. I entered the home-stretch of writing this book after returning from a trip to the West Coast. Cautious person that I am, I backed up my hard disk before I left. After I returned, I worked furiously at my machine for 10 to 12 hours a day. The end was in sight.

Something had my end in sight also. To this day, I do not know what happened, although I use some experimental and rather exotic software combinations that may have been the cause. The temperature on those sunny days was high, and my air conditioning was not handling the problem well. Maybe the heat caused the failure. My machine is trustworthy, and the problem has not recurred. Whatever the electronic mischief was, the outcome was a scrambled file allocation table on the hard disk holding my book.

I first noticed the problem when I found a file that contained the wrong information. I corrected the problem file. I then ran a disk test program, which reported that the disk had no bad sectors. After finding nothing wrong, I continued my work.

The problem was insidious. No physical damage had occurred, but parts of my file allocation table had become electronic spaghetti. The damage was purely logical, affecting only the electronic information that DOS stored on files. The housekeeping information was stored correctly, but the information was wrong. The problem showed on only a few files I was using. As I continued to use my computer, I created more havoc on my disk.

When I discovered the extent of logical damage to my disk, I was shocked. CHKDSK reported so many crossed-up files that it actually aborted. When I cleaned up this mess, rerunning CHKDSK caused it to lock up my system. CHKDSK, which had found a circular chain in my file allocation table, was endlessly chasing its tail. I had to restart DOS to get to my disk. I finally was able to back up a few changed files before I had to reformat my hard disk. However, most of my work from the past three weeks was ruined.

The damage in this event was self-inflicted. I had not made a backup for more than three weeks. I spent the next four weeks recovering from my mistake. Even my 12-year-old nephew berated me for not following my own advice.

And yes, there is the chance that one of the backups you make may be bad. For this reason, you should rotate sets of backup disks. If you have a bad backup set, you can restore from your previous set. The goal is to lose as little work as possible.

Back up, back up, back up, back up! Backups are your cheapest form of insurance. I cannot emphasize enough the need to back up your hard disk. If your business or personal life depends on the information on your computer, you cannot afford not to back up.

Introducing Some Favorite Programs

I have found that a few programs are indispensable in my daily DOS use. I describe these programs in this section.

The "granddaddy" of the DOS add-on utility programs is the Norton Utilities by Peter Norton, who has been a regular columnist for *PC Magazine, PC Week*, and *PC Tech Journal*, a model for a widely seen beverage advertisement, as well as a respected book author (and a respected competitor, I might add).

The Norton Utilities, which have undergone several revisions, are a set of programs that can sort the names of your files in a directory, set the foreground and background colors for your screen, test floppy disks and disk drives for bad sectors, report technical information about your system, display or change a file's attributes, time a program or an activity, and search for text among all the files in a directory or on a disk.

The most important program in the set is called NU. With this program, you can examine the contents of a file, directly alter the file, examine the directory, and "unerase" a file. NU is menu-driven, simple to operate, and effective. I took a copy of a 360K disk and erased all the files on it. Using NU, I needed only 10 minutes to restore 20 files.

The latest version, V4.5, includes a quick "unerase" program. If you have an earlier version, Version 4.5 is worth the small update fee. An Advanced Version, which includes even more useful programs, also is available. It includes something called the Norton Disk Doctor, which can perform seeming miracles of repair work—automatically!

The program price is about $100 for the regular utilities; the advanced version is more. However, either version is well worth five times that amount if you ever have to "unerase" even one file. The Norton Utilities is a must for every PC owner. You will find the program in many computer and software stores. If you do not have and cannot find the Norton Utilities, you can write to the author:

Peter Norton
2210 Wilshire Blvd.
Santa Monica, CA 90403

Another excellent group of utilities comes from SDA Associates, of San Jose, California. One set of programs is called FilePaq(C) ($39.95); another set is called FilePath(C) ($34.95).

FilePaq has four utility programs. One of these, SDADIR, is a directory program that can show normal files, hidden and system files, and subdirectories, or subdirectories only. SDADIR shows the actual file size and the allocated file size (based on clusters) and totals the figures for all displayed files. Like the /S switch for BACKUP and RESTORE, the /T switch for SDADIR traverses subdirectories.

SDADEL erases files. This command has a /P switch that tells SDADEL to display each matching file name, one by one, and to ask whether the file should be deleted. This utility is one of the few I know about that allows you to erase selected files.

SDARD removes subdirectories. Unlike RD, SDARD erases all files in the subdirectory (and all subdirectories in the subdirectory) before the command removes the subdirectory. With SDARD, you can type one command to remove a directory without first having to erase all your files and subdirectories. Needless to say, use SDARD with caution.

SDACHMD is a program that can change a file's attributes. Unlike ATTRIB (before V3.3), in which you can change only the read-only attribute, SDACHMD and Norton's FA (File Attribute) program can toggle the hidden, archive, and read-only system attributes for any file. Although some of FilePaq's functionality is duplicated in the Norton Utilities, FilePaq is a useful addition on any computer.

FilePath is an extensive version of the APPEND command. For machines that are not running DOS V3.3 or later, you load FilePath through your AUTOEXEC.BAT file whenever you boot DOS. FilePath sits in memory and tricks the program into looking for files in different directories.

FilePath is a worthy addition for any hard disk user who does not use DOS V3.3 or later. Because these products may not be available in computer stores, you can call or write the company:

> SDA Associates
> P.O. Box 36152
> San Jose, CA 95158
> (408) 281-7747

A "resident" program, SideKick, from Borland International, is one of my favorites. The program has a calculator, an appointment calendar, a phone dialer, a WordStar-like memo pad, and an ASCII chart. A new version, SideKick Plus, lets you keep multiple memo pads and adds other features. Admittedly, I use only the autodialer, calculator (which has a binary and hexadecimal—base 16—mode) and the ASCII chart. The rest are just frills for me. When I move to a UNIX or OS/2 system, however, I usually miss SideKick within a few minutes. I recommend SideKick. The program costs $89.95, and you can buy it at many computer and software stores or directly from Borland. Sidekick Plus costs more, but does more, too.

> Borland International
> 4113 Scotts Valley Drive
> Scotts Valley, CA 95066
> (408) 438-8400

You also can buy many other "backgrounders" or memory-resident programs. Software Arts, now part of Lotus Development Corporation (of 1-2-3 fame), offers Metro. BELLESOFT of Bellevue, Washington, has Pop-Up programs. Both programs have an alarm clock, which SideKick does not have.

I mention these particular programs because I spend a fair amount of time writing and programming. SideKick suits my style. Because your needs may be different from mine, a different backgrounder may suit you better. You may want to check these and similar programs at your local computer or software store. One of these backgrounders will make your life easier.

The final must-have-if-you-have-a-hard-disk program is a jewel called FASTBACK. If hard disk drives have any problem, it is the problem of backup. I don't back up my hard disk as frequently as I should because of the time required for backing up. I recognize the danger of this attitude—witness my earlier confession. And I know I am not alone in my attitude. After using FASTBACK, though, my thinking has changed.

FASTBACK is a hard-disk backup utility from Fifth Generation Systems. The utility works with all PC and PS/2 computers and many close clones. FASTBACK is an extremely fast backup program. It presents a series of questions about which files should be backed up, which floppy disk drives to use, and whether to back up all files or only changed files.

You insert a floppy disk into the drive and let the program go. If you have two floppy disk drives, the program uses both drives to back up your hard disk.

The results of FASTBACK are spectacular. The program took 20 minutes and 15 seconds to back up almost 19 megabytes of files (a total of 1,940 files) onto 14 HC floppy disks. At least one minute of that time I spent changing floppy disks. I also had used unformatted floppy disks, which FASTBACK formatted "on the fly." When I ran FASTBACK a second time, on formatted floppy disks, the backup time dropped to just less than 12 minutes.

With DOS's BACKUP, the hard disk backup took about an hour and a half. If you include the time for formatting the floppy disks, add about 15 minutes. FASTBACK, even when it formatted floppy disks, was more than five times faster than FORMAT and BACKUP. When FASTBACK was not formatting floppy disks, it was 7 1/2 times faster than BACKUP.

FASTBACK costs $179, and site licensing and dealer discounts are available. Although FASTBACK is more expensive than DOS's BACKUP (BACKUP is included with DOS), I consider FASTBACK infinitely more valuable. By using the program just four times, I have already saved the equivalent of its cost in time.

FASTBACK is available in many computer stores, or you can write directly to the manufacturer:

Fifth Generation Systems
11200 Industriplex Boulevard
Baton Rouge, LA 70809
(800) 225-2775

FLASH is a program that can improve your disk performance. DOS includes three tools to improve disk performance: the BUFFERS directive, included with DOS V2.0 and later; FASTOPEN, included with DOS V3.3; and IBMCACHE, included with some PS/2 models. If you want to get more performance out of your disk drives, I strongly suggest a third-party disk-cache program. Some of these programs greatly out-perform the DOS tools.

My favorite is FLASH. FLASH can cache floppy or hard disks; IBMCACHE handles only hard disks. FLASH buffers directories better than FASTOPEN can. FLASH is faster than DOS's disk buffers.

FLASH, like any good disk-cache program and like DOS disk buffers, buffers as much information from the disk as possible into its cache. When a program wants information that resides in the cache, FLASH hands this information to DOS, which relays the information to the program. FLASH, like DOS disk buffers, minimizes the number of times the disk must be read. FLASH, however, regulates the cache more efficiently than DOS regulates its disk buffers. The result is that FLASH is 50 percent faster than DOS.

Another attractive feature of FLASH is that the program overrides DOS when DOS attempts to write disk sectors that have not changed. For example, a program reads four sectors into memory. The contents of two sectors are altered. The program instructs DOS to write all four sectors back to the disk. FLASH looks at the disk sectors to be written. If the information has not changed, FLASH instructs DOS not to write the unchanged sectors. Since writing information to the disk is more time-consuming than reading it, this feature vastly improves disk performance.

I enjoy several other features of FLASH. The cache can be placed in expanded (EMS) memory or extended (80286/80386) memory. If you have either type of memory, you can use a very large cache area and not impinge heavily on the precious 640K of DOS memory. FLASH automatically uses full-track reading and writing of disk information, which greatly speeds sequential disk operations without greatly slowing random disk operations.

(IBMCACHE handles multiple disk sector reading and writing, but cannot automatically adapt as FLASH does. The result is that sequential disk operations are faster and random operations are much slower.)

FLASH has other features that I will not mention. I will mention that several other disk-cache programs are available. The price and major features of all disk-cache programs vary only slightly. I will also state that FLASH boosts my disk performance by 35 percent.

FLASH costs $69.95 and is available from

> Software Masters
> 6352 Guilford Avenue
> Indianapolis, IN 46220
> (317) 253-8088

Looking Ahead

This book has described most DOS commands, features, and functions. You have learned how to use DOS effectively, and you also have had some hands-on practice. You now should feel comfortable with your system.

In addition to the switches described in the main chapters, some additional switches appear in the *DOS Command Reference,* which offers helpful hints. The *Command Reference* also has some additional information about several commands not covered in the first parts of the book. Read that section, and return to it whenever you are "stuck" on a command.

Getting More Information

User groups are invaluable resources. You may find you are not the first person to have a problem with a program. Members of user groups often can help each other with problems or projects. Find a group in your area and join it. The benefits of membership will be worth your money.

If you are looking for more information about using your hard disk, I recommend *Managing Your Hard Disk,* written by Don Berliner and Chris DeVoney (and published by Que Corporation). The book has detailed discussions about hard-disk organization and DOS tools and describes a number of outside programs that make using your hard disk more enjoyable and effective.

Finally, try to enjoy. You learn by doing, as well as from friends, classes, user groups, and books. I hope that the time you have spent with this book was both useful and enjoyable. Here's to pleasant experiences.

Part VI

DOS Command Reference

Includes

DOS Survival Guide
DOS Messages
DOS Commands

DOS Survival Guide

Note: An asterisk (*) designates a CONFIG.SYS directive.

To	*Use*
Analyze a disk	CHKDSK
Automatically find files	APPEND, PATH
Automatically run a file at start-up	AUTOEXEC.BAT
Back up files	BACKUP, COPY, XCOPY
Back up disks	BACKUP, DISKCOPY
Change a code page	CHCP, KEYB, MODE
Change the active display	MODE
Change the baud rate	MODE
Change the console	CTTY
Change the current directory	CHDIR (CD)
Change the current disk drive	**d:**
Change disk buffers	BUFFERS*
Change the disk label	LABEL
Change the environment	SET
Change file attributes	ATTRIB
Change a file name	RENAME (REN)
Change/set location of the command interpreter	SHELL*
Change program input	<
Change program output	>, >>
Clear the video display	CLS
Combine disks	JOIN
Combine files	COPY
Compare disks	DISKCOMP
Compare files	COMP
Concatenate files	COPY
Connect disk drives	JOIN
Control Ctrl-Break	BREAK, BREAK*
Control verification of files	VERIFY
Copy backup files	RESTORE
Copy disks	DISKCOPY, COPY, XCOPY
Copy files	COPY, REPLACE, XCOPY
Create a subdirectory	MKDIR (MD)
Display available RAM	CHKDSK, MEM
Display the current code page	CHCP, MODE
Display the date	DATE
Display enviroDisplay a list of files	DIR, CHKDSK /V, TREE /F
Display national-language characters	CHCP, GRAFTABL, KEYB, MODE
Display the time	TIME
Display the version of DOS	VER
Display the volume label	VOL, LABEL, DIR, CHKDSK
Erase a character	←
Erase a directory	RMDIR (RD)

Erase a disk label	LABEL
Erase files	DEL, ERASE
Execute several DOS commands with one command	Batch file
Find disk free space	CHKDSK, DIR
Find a file	CHKDSK /V, TREE /F
Find a word or phrase in a file	FIND
Freeze the video display	Ctrl-Num Lock, Pause
Ignore a line	Esc
Load file-sharing software	SHARE
Pause the display	Ctrl-Num Lock, Pause, Ctrl-S
Pipe output between programs	|
Place DOS on a disk	SYS, FORMAT /S
Prepare a disk	FORMAT, FDISK
Print the display	Shift-PrintSc, GRAPHICS
Print graphics	GRAPHICS
Print on the display and the printer	Ctrl-PrintSc
Print a file	PRINT, >, >>
Print from the background	PRINT
Reassign disk drives	ASSIGN, JOIN, SUBST
Reassign printers	MODE
Restore backup files	RESTORE
Repair a file	RECOVER
Remove a directory	RMDIR (RD)
Remove files	DEL, ERASE
Repair a disk	RECOVER, CHKDSK
Run a program	**program_name**
Set alternative directories for data files	APPEND
Set alternative directories for programs	PATH
Set the country code	COUNTRY*
Set/change a code page	MODE, KEYB
Set/change checks on file writing	VERIFY
Set/change communications ports	MODE
Set/change displays	MODE
Set/change an environmental variable	SET
Set/change internal stacks	STACKS*
Set/change printers	MODE
Set/change the system date	DATE
Set/change the system prompt	PROMPT
Set/change the system time	TIME
Sort a file	SORT
Speed DOS	BUFFERS*, FASTOPEN
Stop a running program	Ctrl-Break, Ctrl-C
Stop a running program and reset the computer	Ctrl-Alt-Del
Unfreeze the video display	Any key
Update files	REPLACE
Use a different disk drive	**d:**, ASSIGN, SUBST
Use a new device	DEVICE*
Use a subdirectory in place of a disk	SUBST

Introduction to the Command Reference

This *DOS Command Reference* includes in reference form all of PC DOS's commands. Each command is presented in this format: the command name appears first, followed by the version of DOS to which the command applies. Asterisks (**) indicate that the command's functions are different in the newest versions of DOS.

The terms *Internal* and *External* indicate whether the command is built into DOS (internal) or is disk-resident (external). Each command entry discusses the command's purpose, followed by the syntax required to invoke the command. Exit codes, if any, are listed. For some commands, examples are given.

The "Messages" section is an alphabetical listing of three types of messages that commands produce:

- INFORMATION: This message informs the user that an activity is taking place or prompts the user for a response.

- WARNING: This message warns the user of a possible problem. The command continues to function.

- ERROR: This message indicates that an error has occurred. The command terminates (aborts) after an error message.

Notation

The common notation used to represent a file specification is

    *d:path***filename.ext**

The *d:* is the name of the disk drive that holds the file, and *path* is the directory path to the file. The **filename** is the root name of the file, and **.ext** is the file-name extension.

If any part of this notation does not appear in the file specification (under "Syntax"), the omitted part is not allowed with the command. For example, the notation **d:filename.ext** indicates that path names are not allowed in the command.

In most cases, a device name may be substituted for a full file specification.

If a notation under "Syntax" appears in **this typeface**, it is mandatory and must be entered. If a notation appears in *this typeface*, it is optional and is entered only when appropriate.

Notation for External Commands and Batch Files

DOS V3 and later versions can execute external commands (which are simply program files) and batch files residing in different subdirectories, as well as program and batch files on different disks.

The syntax used in this summary has a *c* added to the disk drive name and path. The notation is *dc:pathc***command_name**. The *dc:* is the name of the disk drive holding the command, *pathc* is the directory path to the command, and **command_name** is the name of the program or batch file to execute.

This notation is valid only for external commands—those disk-resident commands that are not part of COMMAND.COM (DOS's command processor). The notation may be used also for batch files, but it is not valid for internal commands—those that are part of COMMAND.COM.

In this command notation, the following rules apply:

- If you do not give a disk drive name for the command (*dc:*), DOS will search for the command on the current disk drive.

- If you do not give a path (*pathc*), DOS will search for the command in the current directory of the current disk (or the current directory of the specified disk drive if one was given).

- If you do not give a drive name and a path name, DOS will search the current directory of the current disk for the command. If the command is not found, DOS will search the list of paths specified by the PATH command. If DOS does not find the command after searching the path, DOS displays the error message `Bad command or file name` and gives the DOS system prompt (usually A>).

Using Upper- and Lowercase Letters

Words that appear in uppercase letters under "Syntax" are the words you type. Words that appear in lowercase letters are variables. Be sure to substitute the appropriate disk drive letter or name, path name, file name, etc., for the lowercase variable when you type the command.

Commands, as well as all parameters and switches typed with them, may be entered in either upper- or lowercase. The exceptions are FIND and the batch subcommands; for these commands, the use of upper- or lowercase for certain parameters may be important. (See the sections on FIND and the batch subcommands for more information about using upper- and lowercase letters.)

DOS Messages

DOS messages fall into two groups: general DOS messages and DOS device error messages. The larger group, general DOS messages, is listed here alphabetically, followed by the device error messages.

General DOS Messages

The following messages may appear when you are starting DOS or using your computer. Messages that occur only when you are starting DOS are marked (start-up). Most start-up errors mean that DOS did not start and you must reboot the system.

Most of the other error messages mean that DOS terminated (aborted) the program and returned to the system prompt (A>).

The messages are listed in alphabetical order for easy reference.

```
Bad command or filename
```

ERROR: The name you entered is not valid for invoking a command, program, or batch file. The most frequent causes are the following: (1) you misspelled a name; (2) you omitted a needed disk drive or path name; or (3) you gave the parameters without the command name, such as typing **myfile** instead of **ws myfile** (omitting the **ws** for WordStar).

Check the spelling on the command line. Make sure that the command, program, or batch file is in the location specified (disk drive and directory path). Then try the command again.

```
Bad or missing Command Interpreter
```

ERROR (start-up): DOS cannot find COMMAND.COM, the command interpreter. DOS does not start.

If you are starting DOS, this message means that COMMAND.COM is not on the start-up disk or that a version of COMMAND.COM from a previous version of DOS is on the disk. If you have used the SHELL directive in CONFIG.SYS, the message means that the SHELL directive is improperly phrased or that COMMAND.COM is not where you specified. Place another disk that contains the operating system (IBMBIO.COM, IBMDOS.COM, and COMMAND.COM) in the floppy disk drive, and then reset the system.

After DOS has started, copy COMMAND.COM to the original start-up disk so that you can boot DOS.

If this message appears while you are running DOS, there are several possible explanations: COMMAND.COM has been erased from the disk and directory you used when starting DOS, a version of COMMAND.COM from a previous version of DOS has overwritten the good version, or the COMSPEC entry in the environment has been changed. You must restart DOS by resetting the system.

If resetting the system does not solve your problem, use a copy of your DOS master disk to restart the computer. Copy COMMAND.COM from this disk to the offending disk.

Bad or missing filename

WARNING (start-up): The device driver `filename` was not found; an error occurred when the device driver was loaded; a break address for the device driver was out of bounds for the size of RAM memory being used in the computer; or DOS detected an error while the driver was being loaded into memory. DOS will continue its boot but will not use the device driver `filename`.

If DOS loads, check your CONFIG.SYS file for the line `DEVICE=filename`. Make sure that the line is spelled correctly and that the device driver is where you specified. If this line is correct, reboot the system. If the message appears again, copy the file from its original disk to the boot disk and try starting DOS again. If the error persists, contact the dealer or publisher who sold you the driver, because the device driver is bad.

Batch file missing

ERROR: DOS could not find the batch file it was processing. The batch file may have been erased or renamed. For DOS V3.0 only, the disk containing the batch file may have been changed. DOS aborts the processing of the batch file.

If you are using DOS V3.0 and you changed the disk containing the batch file, restart the batch file and do not change the disk. You may need to edit the batch file so that you will not need to change disks.

If you renamed the batch file, rename it again, using the original name. If required, edit the batch file to ensure that the file name does not get changed again.

If the file was erased, re-create the batch file from its backup file, if possible. Edit the file to ensure that the batch file does not erase itself.

Cannot load COMMAND, system halted

ERROR: DOS attempted to reload COMMAND.COM, but the area where DOS keeps track of available and used memory was destroyed, or the command processor was not found in the directory specified by the `COMSPEC=` entry. The system halts.

This message indicates either that COMMAND.COM has been erased from the disk and directory you used when starting DOS, or that the `COMSPEC=` entry in the environment has been changed. Restart DOS from your usual start-up disk. If DOS does not start, the copy of COMMAND.COM has been erased. Restart DOS from the DOS start-up or master disk and copy COMMAND.COM onto your usual start-up disk.

Another possible cause of this message is that an erroneous program corrupted the memory allocation table where DOS tracks available memory. Try running the same program that was in the computer when the system halted. If the problem occurs again, the program is defective. Contact the dealer or publisher who sold you the program.

Cannot start COMMAND, exiting

ERROR: You or one of your programs directed DOS to load an additional copy of COM-MAND.COM, but DOS could not load it. Either your CONFIG.SYS FILES directive is set too low, or you do not have enough free memory for another copy of COMMAND.COM.

If your system has 256K or more and FILES is less than 10, edit the CONFIG.SYS file on your start-up disk and use FILES = 15 or FILES = 20. Then restart DOS.

If the problem occurs again, either you do not have enough memory in your computer, or you have too many resident or background programs competing for memory space. Restart DOS again and do not load any resident or background programs you do not need. If necessary, eliminate unneeded device drivers or RAM-disk software. Another alternative is to increase the amount of RAM memory in your system.

Configuration too large

ERROR (start-up): DOS could not load itself because either you specified in your CON-FIG.SYS file too many FILES or BUFFERS, or you specified too large an environment area (/E switch) to the SHELL command. This problem should occur only on systems with less than 256K.

Restart DOS with a different disk; then edit the CONFIG.SYS file on your boot disk, lowering the number of FILES, BUFFERS, or both. You could also edit the CONFIG.SYS file to reduce the size of the environment, either in addition to lowering the number of FILES and BUFFERS or as an alternative solution. Restart DOS with the edited disk.

Another alternative is to increase the RAM memory in your system.

Current drive is no longer valid

WARNING: You have set the system prompt to PROMPT $p. At the DOS system level, DOS attempted to read the current directory for the disk drive and found the drive no longer valid.

If the current disk drive is set for a floppy disk, this warning appears when you do not have a disk in the disk drive. DOS reports a Drive not ready error. Give the **F** command to fail or the **I** command to ignore the error. Then insert a floppy disk into the disk drive.

The invalid-drive error also can happen if you have a current networked or SUBST disk drive that has been deleted or disconnected. Simply change the current drive to a valid disk drive.

Disk boot failure

ERROR (start-up): An error occurred when DOS tried to load itself into memory. The disk contained IBMBIO.COM and IBMDOS.COM, but one of the two files could not be loaded. DOS did not start.

Try starting DOS from the disk again. If the error recurs, try starting DOS from a disk you know is good, such as a copy of your DOS start-up or master disk. If this action fails, you have a disk-drive problem. Contact your dealer.

Divide overflow

ERROR: A program attempted to divide by zero. DOS aborts the program. Either the program was incorrectly entered, or it has a logic flaw. With well-written programs, this error should never occur. If you wrote the program, correct the error and try the program again. If you purchased the program, report the problem to the dealer or publisher.

This message can also appear when you are attempting to format a RAM disk under DOS V3.0 and V3.1. Make sure that you are formatting the correct disk, and try again.

Error in COUNTRY command

WARNING (start-up): The COUNTRY directive in CONFIG.SYS is either improperly phrased or has an incorrect country code or code page number. DOS continues its start-up but uses the default information for the COUNTRY directive.

After DOS has started, check the COUNTRY line in your CONFIG.SYS file. Refer to Chapter 18 and make sure that the directive is correctly phrased (using commas between country code, code page, and COUNTRY.SYS file) and that any given information is correct. If you detect an error in the line, edit the line, save the file, and restart DOS.

If you do not find an error, restart DOS. If the same message appears, edit your CONFIG.SYS file. Re-enter the COUNTRY directive and delete the old COUNTRY line. The old line may contain some nonsense characters that DOS can see but are not apparent to your text-editing program.

Error in EXE file

ERROR: DOS detected an error while attempting to load a program stored in an .EXE file. The problem is in the relocation information DOS needs to load the program. This problem can occur if the .EXE file has been altered in any way.

Restart DOS and try the program again, this time using a backup copy of the program. If the message reappears, the program is flawed. If you are using a purchased program, contact the dealer or publisher. If you wrote the program, use LINK to produce another copy of the program.

Error loading operating system

ERROR (start-up): A disk error occurred while DOS was loading itself from the hard disk. DOS does not start.

Restart the computer. If the error keeps occurring after several tries, restart DOS from the floppy disk drive. If the hard disk does not respond (that is, you cannot run DIR or CHKDSK without getting an error), you have a problem with the hard disk. Contact your dealer. If the hard disk does respond, use the SYS command to put another copy of DOS onto your hard disk. You also may need to copy COMMAND.COM to the hard disk.

EXEC failure

ERROR: Either DOS encountered an error while reading a command or program from the disk, or the CONFIG.SYS FILES directive has too low a value.

Increase to 15 or 20 the number of FILES in the CONFIG.SYS file of your start-up disk. Restart DOS. If the error recurs, you may have a problem with the disk. Use a backup copy of the program and try again. If the backup copy works, copy it over the offending copy.

If an error occurs in the copying process, you have a flawed floppy disk or hard disk. If the problem is a floppy disk, copy the files from the flawed disk to another disk and reformat or retire the original disk. If the problem is the hard disk, immediately back up your files and run RECOVER on the offending file. If the problem persists, your hard disk may be damaged.

```
File allocation table bad, drive d
Abort, Retry, Fail?
```

WARNING: DOS encountered a problem in the file allocation table of the disk in drive d. Enter **R** for Retry several times. If this does not solve the problem, use **A** for Abort.

If you are using a floppy disk, attempt to copy all the files to another disk and then reformat or retire the original disk. If you are using a hard disk, back up all files on the disk and reformat it. The disk will be unusable until it has been reformatted.

```
File creation error
```

ERROR: A program or DOS attempted to add a new file to the directory or to replace an existing file, but failed.

If the file already exists, use the ATTRIB command to check whether the file is marked as read-only. If the read-only flag is set and you want to change or erase the file, use ATTRIB to remove the read-only flag; then try again.

If the problem is not the read-only flag, run CHKDSK without the /F switch to determine whether the directory is full, the disk is full, or some other problem exists with the disk.

```
File not found
```

ERROR: DOS could not find the file that you specified. Either the file is not on the current disk or in the current directory, or you specified incorrectly the disk drive name, path name, or file name. Check these possibilities and try the command again.

```
filename device driver cannot be initialized
```

WARNING (start-up): In CONFIG.SYS, either the parameters in the device driver filename are incorrect, or the DEVICE line is in error. Check for incorrect parameters, and check for phrasing errors in the DEVICE line. Edit the DEVICE line in the CONFIG.SYS file, save the file, and restart DOS.

```
Incorrect DOS version
```

ERROR: The copy of the file holding the command you just entered is from a different version of DOS.

Get a copy of the command from the correct version of DOS (usually from your copy of the DOS start-up or master disk), and try the command again. If the disk you are using has been updated to hold new versions of the DOS programs, copy the new versions over the old ones.

```
Insert disk with batch file
and strike any key when ready
```

INFORMATION: DOS is attempting to execute the next command from a batch file, but the disk holding the batch file is not in the disk drive. This message occurs for DOS V3.1 and later versions. DOS V3.0 gives a fatal error when the disk is changed.

Put the disk holding the batch file into the disk drive and press a key to continue.

```
Insert disk with \COMMAND.COM in drive d
and strike any key when ready
```

INFORMATION and WARNING: DOS needed to reload COMMAND.COM but could not find it on the start-up disk.

If you are using floppy disks, the disk in drive d (usually A:) probably has been changed. Place a disk holding a good copy of COMMAND.COM in drive d and press a key.

```
Insert diskette for drive d and strike
any key when ready
```

INFORMATION: On a system with one floppy disk drive or a system using DRIVER.SYS that makes more than one logical disk drive out of one physical disk drive, you or one of your programs specified the tandem disk drive d (such as A: or B:). This drive is different from the current disk drive.

If the correct disk is in the disk drive, press a key. Otherwise, put the correct disk into the floppy disk drive and then press a key.

```
Insufficient disk space
```

WARNING or ERROR: The disk does not have enough free space to hold the file being written. All DOS programs terminate when this problem occurs, but some non-DOS programs continue.

If you think that the disk has enough room to hold this file, run CHKDSK to see whether the disk has a problem. Sometimes when you terminate programs early by pressing Ctrl-Break, DOS is not allowed to do the necessary clean-up work. When this happens, disk space is temporarily trapped. CHKDSK can "free" these areas.

If you simply have run out of disk space, free some disk space or use a different disk. Try the command again.

```
Insufficient memory
```

ERROR: The computer does not have enough free RAM memory to execute the program or command.

If you loaded a resident program like PRINT, GRAPHICS, SideKick, or ProKey, restart DOS and try the command before loading any resident program. If this method fails, remove any unneeded device driver or RAM-disk software from the CONFIG.SYS file and restart DOS again. If this action fails, your computer does not have enough memory for this command. You must increase your RAM memory to run the command.

Intermediate file error during pipe

ERROR: DOS is unable to create or write to one or both of the intermediate files it uses when piping (|) information between programs. The disk is full, the root directory of the current disk is full, or DOS cannot find the files. The most frequent cause is running out of disk space.

Run the DIR command on the root directory of the current disk drive. Make sure that you have enough free space and enough room in the root directory for two additional files. If you do not have enough room, create room on the disk by deleting or copying and deleting files. You may also copy the necessary files to a different disk with sufficient room.

One possible cause of this error is that a program is deleting files, including the temporary files DOS uses. If this is the case, you should correct the program, contact the dealer or program publisher, or avoid using the program with piping.

Internal stack overflow
System halted

ERROR: Your programs and DOS have exhausted the stack, the memory space that is reserved for temporary use. This problem is usually caused by a rapid succession of hardware devices demanding attention (interrupts). DOS stops, and the system must be turned off and on again to restart DOS.

The circumstances that cause this message are generally infrequent and erratic, and they may not recur. If you want to prevent this error from occurring at all, add the STACKS directive to your CONFIG.SYS file. If the directive is already in your CONFIG.SYS file, then increase the number of stacks specified. See Chapter 17 for more information on the STACKS directive.

Invalid COMMAND.COM in drive d

WARNING: DOS tried to reload COMMAND.COM from the disk in drive d and found that the file was from a different version of DOS. You will see a message instructing you to insert a disk with the correct version and press a key. Follow the directions for that message.

If you frequently use the disk that was originally in the disk drive, copy the correct version of COMMAND.COM to that disk.

Invalid COMMAND.COM, system halted

ERROR: DOS could not find COMMAND.COM on the hard disk. DOS halts and must be restarted.

COMMAND.COM may have been erased, or the COMSPEC variable in the environment may have been changed. Restart the computer from the hard disk. If you see a message indicating that COMMAND.COM is missing, the file was erased. Restart DOS from a disk and recopy COMMAND.COM to the root directory of the hard disk or to wherever your SHELL directive indicates if you have used this command in your CONFIG.SYS file.

If you restart DOS and this message appears later, a program or batch file is erasing COMMAND.COM or is altering the COMSPEC variable. If a batch file is erasing COMMAND.COM, edit the batch file. If a program is erasing COMMAND.COM, contact the dealer or publisher who sold you the program. If COMSPEC is being altered, either edit the offending batch file or program, or place COMMAND.COM in the subdirectory your program or batch file expects.

Invalid COUNTRY code or code page

WARNING (start-up): Either the COUNTRY code number or the code page number given to the COUNTRY directive in the CONFIG.SYS file is incorrect or incompatible. DOS ignores the COUNTRY directive and continues to start.

Check the COUNTRY directive in your CONFIG.SYS file. Refer to Chapter 18 and make sure that the correct and compatible country code and code page numbers are specified. If you detect an error, edit and save the file and restart DOS.

Invalid directory

ERROR: One of the following errors occurred: (1) you specified a directory name that does not exist, (2) you misspelled the directory name, (3) the directory path is on a different disk, (4) you forgot to give the path character (\) at the beginning of the name, or (5) you did not separate the directory names with the path character. Check your directory names, make sure that the directories exist, and try the command again.

Invalid disk change

WARNING: The disk in the 720K, 1.2M, or 1.44M disk drive was changed while a program had open files to be written to the disk. You will see the message Abort, Retry, Fail.

Place the correct disk in the disk drive and type **R** for Retry.

Invalid drive in search path

WARNING: Either a specification you gave to the PATH command has an invalid disk drive name, or a named disk drive is nonexistent or hidden temporarily by a SUBST or JOIN command.

Use PATH to check the paths you instructed DOS to search. If you gave a nonexistent disk drive name, use the PATH command again and enter the correct search paths. If the problem is temporary because of a SUBST or JOIN command, you can again use PATH to enter the paths, but leave out or correct the wrong entry. Or you can just ignore the warning message.

Invalid drive or file name

ERROR: Either you gave the name of a nonexistent disk drive, or you mistyped the disk drive, file name, or both.

Remember that certain DOS commands (such as SUBST and JOIN) temporarily hide disk drive names while the command is in effect. Check the disk drive name you gave, and try the command again.

Invalid drive specification

ERROR: This message is given when one of the following errors occurs: (1) you have entered the name of an invalid or nonexistent disk drive as a parameter to a command; (2) you have specified the same disk drive for the source and destination, which is not permitted for the command; or (3) by not giving a parameter, you have defaulted to the same disk drive for the source and the destination. Remember that certain DOS commands (such as SUBST and JOIN) temporarily hide disk drive names while the command is in effect. Check the disk drive names. If the command is objecting to a missing parameter and defaulting to the wrong disk drive, explicitly name the correct disk drive.

Invalid drive specification
Specified drive does not exist,
or is non-removable

ERROR: One of the following errors occurred: (1) you gave the name of a nonexistent disk drive, (2) you named the hard disk drive when using commands for floppy disks only, (3) you did not give a disk drive name and defaulted to the hard disk when using commands for floppy disks only, or (4) you named or defaulted to a RAM-disk drive when using commands for a "real" floppy disk only.

Remember that certain DOS commands (such as SUBST and JOIN) temporarily hide disk drive names while the command is in effect. Check the disk drive name you gave, and try the command again.

Invalid environment size specified

WARNING: You have given the SHELL directive in CONFIG.SYS.

The environment-size switch ($</E:size$) contains either nonnumeric characters or a number that is less than 160 or greater than 32768.

If you are using the SHELL /E:size switch of DOS V3.1, size is the number of 16-byte paragraphs, not the number of bytes.

Check the form of your CONFIG.SYS SHELL directive; the form needs to be exact. There should be a colon between /E and size; there should be no comma or space between or within the /E: and the size characters; and the number in size should be greater than or equal to 160 but less than or equal to 32768.

Invalid number of parameters

ERROR: You have given either too few or too many parameters to a command. One of the following errors occurred: (1) you omitted required information, (2) you forgot a colon immediately after the disk drive name, (3) you put a space in the wrong place or omitted a needed space, or (4) you forgot to place a slash (/) in front of a switch.

Invalid parameter Incorrect parameter

ERROR: At least one parameter you entered for the command is not valid. One of the following errors occurred: (1) you omitted required information, (2) you forgot a colon immediately after the disk drive name, (3) you put a space in the wrong place or omitted a needed space, (4) you forgot to place a slash (/) in front of a switch, or (5) you used a switch that the command does not recognize. For more information, check the explanation of this message in the *Command Reference* under the command you were using when the message occurred.

Invalid partition table

ERROR (start-up): While you were attempting to start DOS from the hard disk, DOS detected a problem in the hard disk's partition information.

Restart DOS from a floppy disk. Back up all files from the hard disk, if possible. Run FDISK to correct the problem. If you change the partition information, you must reformat the hard disk and restore all its files.

Invalid path

ERROR: One of the following errors has occurred: (1) the path name contains illegal characters, (2) the name has more than 63 characters, or (3) one of the directory names within the path is misspelled or does not exist.

Check the spelling of the path name. If needed, do a DIR of the disk and make sure that the directory you have specified does exist and that you have the correct path name. Be sure that the path name contains no more than 63 characters. If necessary, change the current directory to a directory "closer" to the file and shorten the path name.

Invalid STACK parameter

WARNING (start-up): One of the following errors has occurred to the STACKS directive in your CONFIG.SYS file: (1) a comma is missing between the number of stacks and the size of the stack, (2) the number of stack frames is not in the range of 8 to 64, (3) the stack size is not in the range of 32 to 512, (4) you have omitted either the number of stack frames or the stack size, or (5) either the stack frame or the stack size (but not both) is 0. DOS continues to start but ignores the STACKS directive.

Check the STACKS directive in your CONFIG.SYS file. Edit and save the file, and restart DOS.

`Invalid switch character`

WARNING: You have used VDISK.SYS in your CONFIG.SYS file. VDISK encountered a switch (/), but the character immediately following it was not an *E* for *extended* memory. DOS loaded VDISK and attempted to install it in low (nonextended) memory. Either you misspelled the */E* switch, or you left a space between the / and the *E* . Edit and save your CONFIG.SYS file, and restart DOS.

`Memory allocation error`
`Cannot load COMMAND, system halted`

ERROR: A program destroyed the area where DOS keeps track of in-use and available memory. You must restart DOS.

If this error occurs again with the same program, the program has a flaw. Use a backup copy of the program. If the problem persists, contact the dealer or program publisher.

`Missing operating system`

ERROR (start-up): The DOS hard disk partition entry is marked as "bootable" (able to start DOS), but the DOS partition does not have a copy of DOS on it. DOS does not start.

Start DOS from a floppy disk. Use the **SYS C:** command to place DOS on the hard disk, and then copy COMMAND.COM to the disk. If this command fails to solve the problem, you must back up the existing files, if any, from the hard disk; then issue **FORMAT /S** to put a copy of the operating system on the hard disk. If necessary, restore the files that you backed up.

`No free file handles`
`Cannot start COMMAND, exiting`

ERROR: DOS could not load an additional copy of COMMAND.COM because no file handles were available.

Edit the CONFIG.SYS file on your start-up disk to increase the number of file handles (using the FILES directive) by five. Restart DOS and try the command again.

`Non-System disk or disk error`
`Replace and strike any key when ready`

ERROR (start-up): Either your disk does not contain IBMBIO.COM and IBMDOS.COM, or a read error occurred when you started the system. DOS does not start.

If you are using a floppy disk system, put a bootable disk in drive A and press a key.

The most frequent cause of this message on hard disk systems is that you left a nonboot disk in drive A with the door closed. Open the door to disk drive A and press a key. DOS will boot from the hard disk.

`Not enough memory`

ERROR: The computer does not have enough free RAM memory to execute the program or command.

If you loaded a resident program like PRINT, GRAPHICS, SideKick, or ProKey, restart DOS and try the command again before loading any resident program. If this method fails to solve the problem, remove any unneeded device driver or RAM-disk software from the CONFIG.SYS file and restart DOS again. If this option fails also, your computer does not have enough memory for this command. You must increase your RAM memory to run the command.

Out of environment space

WARNING: DOS is unable to add any more strings to the environment from the SET command. The environment cannot be expanded. This error occurs when you load a resident program, such as MODE, PRINT, GRAPHICS, SideKick, or ProKey.

If you are running DOS V3.1 or a later version, refer to the SHELL directive in Chapter 17 (on customizing DOS) for information about expanding the default space for the environment. DOS V3.0 has no method to expand the environment.

Path not found

ERROR: A file or directory path that you named does not exist. You may have misspelled the file name or directory name, or you may have omitted a path character (\ ) between directory names or between the final directory name and the file name. Another possibility is that the file or directory does not exist in the place you specified. Check these possibilities and try again.

Path too long

ERROR: You have given a path name that exceeds the 63-character limit of DOS. Either the name is too long or you omitted a space between file names. Check the command line. If the phrasing is correct, you must change to a directory that is closer to the file you want and try the command again.

Program too big to fit in memory

ERROR: The computer does not have enough memory to load the program or the command you invoked.

If you have any resident programs loaded (such as PRINT, GRAPHICS, or SideKick), restart DOS and try the command again without loading the resident programs. If this message appears again, reduce the number of buffers (BUFFERS) in the CONFIG.SYS file, eliminate unneeded device drivers or RAM-disk software, and restart DOS again. If these actions do not solve the problem, your computer does not have enough RAM memory for the program or command. You must increase the amount of RAM memory in your computer to run this command.

Sector size too large in file filename

WARNING: The device driver filename is inconsistent. The device driver defined a particular sector size for DOS but attempted to use a different size. Either the copy of the device driver is bad, or the device driver is incorrect. Make a backup copy of the device driver on the boot disk and then reboot DOS. If the message appears again, the device driver is incorrect. If you wrote the driver, correct the error. If you purchased the program, contact the dealer or software publisher.

Syntax error

ERROR: You phrased a command improperly by (1) omitting needed information, (2) giving extraneous information, (3) putting an extra space in a file name or path name, or (4) using an incorrect switch. Check the command line for these possibilities and try the command again.

Too many block devices

WARNING (start-up): There are too many DEVICE directives in your CONFIG.SYS file. DOS continues to start but does not install any additional device drivers.

DOS can handle only 26 block devices. The block devices created by the DEVICE directives plus the number of block devices automatically created by DOS exceed this number. Remove any unnecessary DEVICE directives in your CONFIG.SYS file and restart DOS.

Top level process aborted, cannot continue

ERROR (start-up): COMMAND.COM or another DOS command detected a disk error, and you chose the **A** (Abort) option.

DOS cannot finish starting itself, and the system halts.

Try to start DOS again. If the error recurs, use a floppy disk (if starting from the hard disk) or a different floppy disk (if starting from floppy disks) to start DOS. After DOS has started, use the SYS command to put another copy of the operating system on the disk, and copy COMMAND.COM to the disk. If DOS reports an error during the copying, the disk is bad. Either reformat or retire the floppy disk, or back up and reformat the hard disk.

Unable to create directory

ERROR: Either you or a program has attempted to create a directory, and one of the following has occurred: (1) a directory by the same name already exists; (2) a file by the same name already exists; (3) you are adding a directory to the root directory, and the root directory is full; or (4) the directory name has illegal characters or is a device name.

Do a DIR of the disk. Make sure that no file or directory already exists with the same name. If adding the directory to the root directory, remove or move (copy, then erase) any unneeded files or directories. Check the spelling of the directory name and make sure that the command is properly phrased.

`Unrecognized command in CONFIG.SYS`

WARNING (start-up): DOS detected an improperly phrased directive in CONFIG.SYS. The directive is ignored, and DOS continues to start; but DOS does not indicate the incorrect line. Examine the CONFIG.SYS file, looking for improperly phrased or incorrect directives. Edit the line, save the file, and restart DOS.

DOS Device Error Messages

When DOS detects an error while reading or writing to disk drives or other devices, one of the following messages appears:

> *type* error reading *device*
> *type* error writing *device*

The *type* is the type of error, and *device* is the device at fault. If the device is a floppy disk drive, do not remove the disk from the drive. Refer to the possible causes and corrective actions described in this section, which lists the types of error messages that may appear.

`Bad call format`

A device driver was given a requested header with an incorrect length. The problem is the application software making the call.

`Bad command`

The device driver issued an invalid or unsupported command to *device*. The problem may be with the device driver software or with other software trying to use the device driver. If you wrote the program, it needs to be corrected. For a purchased program, contact the dealer or publisher who sold you the program.

`Bad format call`

The device driver at fault passed an incorrect header length to DOS. If you wrote this device driver, you must rewrite it to correct the problem. For a purchased program, contact the dealer or publisher who sold you the driver.

`Bad unit`

An invalid subunit number was passed to the device driver. The problem may be with the device driver software or with other software trying to use the device driver. Contact the dealer who sold you the device driver.

`Data`

DOS could not correctly read or write the data. Usually the disk has developed a defective spot.

Drive not ready

An error occurred while DOS tried to read or write to the disk drive. For floppy disk drives, the drive door may be open, the microfloppy disk may not have been inserted, or the disk may not be formatted. For hard disk drives, the drive may not be properly prepared—you may have a hardware problem.

FCB unavailable

With the file-sharing program (SHARE.EXE) loaded, a program that uses the DOS V1 method of file handling attempted to open concurrently more file control blocks than were specified with the FCBS directive.

Use the Abort option (see the end of this section). Increase the value of the FCBS CONFIG.SYS directive (usually by four), and reboot the system. If the message appears again, increase the number again and reboot.

General failure

This is a catchall error message not covered elsewhere. The error usually occurs for one of the following reasons: (1) you are using an unformatted disk; (2) the disk drive door is open; (3) the floppy disk is not seated properly; or (4) you are using the wrong type of disk in a disk drive, such as formatting a 360K disk in a 1.2M disk drive.

Lock violation

With the file-sharing program (SHARE.EXE) or the network software loaded, one of your programs attempted to access a file that is locked. Your best choice is **Retry**. Then try **Abort**. If you choose **A**, however, any data in memory will be lost.

No paper

The printer is either out of paper or not turned on.

Non-DOS disk

The FAT has invalid information. This disk is unusable. You can **Abort** and run CHKDSK to learn whether any corrective action is possible. If CHKDSK fails, your other alternative is to reformat the disk. Reformatting, however, will destroy any remaining information on the disk.

If you use more than one operating system, the disk has probably been formatted under the operating system you are using and should not be reformatted.

Not ready

The device is not ready and cannot receive or transmit data. Check the connections, make sure that the power is on, and check to see whether the device is ready. For floppy disk drives, check to make sure that the disk is formatted and is properly seated in the disk drive.

Read fault

DOS was unable to read the data, usually from a disk. Check the disk drive doors and be sure that the disk is inserted properly.

Sector not found

The disk drive was unable to find the sector on the disk. This error is usually the result of a defective spot on the disk or of defective drive electronics. Some copy-protection schemes also use this method (a defective spot) to prevent unauthorized duplication of the disk.

Seek

The disk drive could not find the proper track on the disk. This error is usually the result of a defective spot on the disk, an unformatted disk, or drive-electronics problems.

Write fault

DOS could not write the data to this device. Perhaps you inserted the disk improperly or you left the disk drive door open. Another possibility is an electronics failure in the floppy or hard disk drive. The most frequent cause is a bad spot on the disk.

Write protect

The disk is write-protected.

Note: One of the previously listed messages (usually Data, Read fault, or Write fault) appears when you are using a double-sided disk in a single-sided disk drive or a 9-sector disk (V2 and later) with a version of DOS V1. DOS will display one of these error messages, followed by the line

Abort, Retry, Fail?

for DOS V3.3 or

Abort, Retry, Ignore?

for versions of DOS before V3.3.

If you press **A** for Abort, DOS ends the program that requested the read or write condition. Typing **R** for Retry causes DOS to try the operation again. If you press **F** for Fail or **I** for Ignore, DOS skips the operation and the program continues. Some data may be lost, however, when you use **Fail** or **Ignore**.

The order of preference, unless stated differently under the message, is **R**, **A**, and **F** or **I**. You should retry the operation at least twice. If the condition persists, you must decide whether to abort the program or ignore the error. If you ignore the error, data may be lost. If you abort, data still being processed by the program and not yet written to the disk will be lost.

APPEND
(Set directory search order)   *V3.3, V4—External*

Purpose

Instructs DOS to search the specified directories on the specified disks for non-program/nonbatch files.

Syntax

To establish the data-file search path the first time, use

   *dc:pathc***APPEND** *d1:path1;d2:path2;d3:path3;. . .*

dc: is the name of the disk drive that holds the command.

pathc is the path to the command.

d1:, d2:, d3: are valid disk drive names.

path1, path2, path3 are valid paths to the directories you want DOS to search for nonprogram/nonbatch files. The three periods (. . .) represent additional disk drive and path names.

To use either of APPEND's switches, use

   *dc:pathc***APPEND** */X /E*

DOS V4 users may also use this syntax for the /X switch:

   *dc:pathc***APPEND** */X:OFF*
   *dc:pathc***APPEND**   */X:ON*

To change the data-file search path, use

   APPEND *d1:path1;d2:path2;d3:path3; . . .*

For DOS V4, the default state for a search for files that have the drive or path specified is as follows:

   APPEND */PATH:ON*

To turn off a search for files that have the drive or path specified (for DOS V4 only), use

   APPEND */PATH:OFF*

To see the search path, use

   APPEND

To disconnect the data-file search, use

   APPEND;

Switches

/X	Redirects programs that use the DOS function calls SEARCH FIRST, FIND FIRST, and EXEC.
/X:ON	Same as /X (DOS V4 only).
/X:OFF	Turns this feature off (DOS V4 only).
/E	Places the disk drive paths in the *environment.*
/PATH:ON	Turns on search for files that have drive or path specified (DOS V4 only).
/PATH:OFF	Turns off search for files that have drive or path specified (DOS V4 only).

Reference

See Chapter 14.

Messages

1. `APPEND/ASSIGN Conflict`

   `APPEND/TopView Conflict`

   ERROR: You attempted to use APPEND after you loaded either TopView or ASSIGN. If you are using TopView, exit TopView, give the APPEND command, and then restart TopView. If you are using ASSIGN, break the assignment, issue the APPEND command, and then issue the ASSIGN command again.

2. `APPEND already installed`

   WARNING: You attempted to load APPEND again by giving a disk drive or path name for a command. You need to load APPEND only once. Give the command again without the command's drive or path name.

3. `Incorrect APPEND Version`

   ERROR: You are using a version of APPEND from a different version of DOS. Check to be sure that you are not using the version of APPEND from the IBM Local Area Network program. The problem may be that the wrong version of APPEND is being loaded first from a PATHed directory.

4. `Invalid parameter`

   ERROR: You used a switch that APPEND did not recognize when you first ran the command. The only valid switches for APPEND are /X and /E. Try the command again using the correct switches.

5. Invalid path

ERROR: The path you gave to APPEND was not valid for one of these reasons: (1) you used illegal characters, (2) you forgot to separate multiple path sets with semicolons, or (3) you gave a path name that exceeded 63 characters. Check the spelling of each path set, the semicolons that separate multiple paths, and the length of each path. Then try the command again.

6. Invalid path or parameter

ERROR: After you installed APPEND, you made one of the following errors: (1) you used a switch with the command, (2) you used a misspelled path name, or (3) you used a path that exceeded 63 characters. Check the spelling of the paths and the semicolons that separate multiple paths. Then try the command again. To use a different switch with APPEND, you must restart DOS and give the APPEND command with the appropriate switch.

7. No Append

INFORMATION: You typed APPEND to see the current path, and APPEND is currently inactive.

ASSIGN
(Assign disk drive)   *V2, V3, V4—External*

Purpose

Instructs DOS to use a disk drive other than the one specified by a program or command.

Syntax

To reroute drive activity, use

    *dc:pathc***ASSIGN d1 = d2 . . .**

dc: is the name of the disk drive that holds the command.

pathc is the path to the command.

d1 is the letter of the disk drive that the program or DOS normally uses.

d2 is the letter of the disk drive you want the program or DOS to use instead of the usual drive. The three periods (. . .) represent additional disk drive assignments.

To clear the reassignment, use

    *dc:pathc***ASSIGN**

Reference

See Chapter 25.

Messages

1. Invalid parameter

   ERROR: You made one of the following errors: (1) you put a colon after one or more drive letters; (2) you did not type all the information that ASSIGN required; (3) you used a letter for a nonexistent disk drive; or (4) you did not correctly phrase the command.

2. Incorrect DOS Version

   ERROR: The version of ASSIGN you are using does not match the version of DOS the computer is using. Make sure that your machine is running the correct version of DOS and that the proper version of your utility programs is on your disk.

ATTRIB
(Change/show a file's read-only and archive attributes)   *V3, V4—External*

Purpose

Displays, sets, or clears a file's read-only and archive attributes.

Syntax

To set the file's attributes on, use

  *dc:pathc***ATTRIB** +**R** +**A** *d:path***filename**.*ext* /S

To clear the file's attributes, use

  *dc:pathc***ATTRIB** −**R** −**A** *d:path***filename**.*ext* /S

To display a file's read-only and archive status, use

  *dc:pathc***ATTRIB** *d:path***filename**.*ext* /S

dc: is the name of the disk drive that holds the command.

pathc is the path to the command.

R is the read-only attribute.

A is the archive attribute (DOS V3.2 and later).

+ turns on the attribute (the file becomes read-only or marked as created/changed).

− turns off the attribute (the file is writeable or marked as not created/changed).

d: is the name of the disk drive that holds the files for which the read-only or archive attribute will be displayed or changed.

path is the starting path to the files for which the read-only or archive attribute will be displayed or changed.

filename.*ext* is the name of the file(s) for which the read-only or archive attribute will be displayed or changed. Wild cards are allowed.

Switch

/S   Sets or clears the attributes with the files in the current or specified directory and all subsequent subdirectories, continuing downward through the subdirectories (DOS V3.3 and later).

Reference

See Chapter 10.

Messages

1. Access denied

   ERROR: You cannot change the read-only attribute of this file. The file may be temporarily unavailable because another computer or program is using the file, or the file may be in a directory on a networked disk that you do not have permission to change.

2. Incorrect DOS Version

   ERROR: The version of ATTRIB you are using does not match the version of DOS the computer is using. Make sure that your machine is running the correct version of DOS and that the proper version of your utility programs is on your disk.

3. Invalid drive specification

   ERROR: You specified a disk drive that does not exist. Check your phrasing of the command and try again.

4. Invalid number of parameters

   ERROR: You did not specify a file name.

5. Invalid path or file not found

   ERROR: You specified a directory or file name that does not exist. Check the spelling of the names, and be sure that the files are in the directory you specified.

6. Syntax error

   ERROR: One of the following errors occurred: (1) you gave a switch other than /S to ATTRIB; (2) you gave a poorly formed **R** and/or **A** command (omitting the + or −, or the **R** or **A** itself, or giving both the + and − for attributes); or (3) you gave more than one file name.

BACKUP
(Back up disks)   *V2, V3, V4—External*

Purpose

Backs up one or more files from a hard disk or floppy disk onto a floppy disk or another hard disk.

Syntax

*dc:pathc***BACKUP** **d1:***path\\filename.ext* **d2:** */S /M /A /D:date*

         /T:time /F /L:dl:filenamel:extl

dc: is the name of the disk drive that holds the command.

pathc is the path to the command.

d1: is the name of the hard disk or floppy disk drive to be backed up.

path is the starting directory path for backup.

filename.ext specifies the name(s) of the file(s) you want to back up. Wild cards are allowed.

d2: is the hard disk or floppy disk drive that will receive the backup files.

Switches

See table 24.2, Chapter 24.

Exit Codes

```
0 = Successful backup
1 = No files found to be backed up
2 = Some files not backed up because of sharing problems
3 = Aborted by the user (Ctrl-Break or Ctrl-C)
4 = Aborted because of an error
```

Examples

For the following examples, refer to the sample hierarchical directory in Appendix B. The directory is used as the directory of the hard disk to show the effects of the different commands. For each set of examples (lettered A through J), the current directory is indicated.

Example A. *Current directory: root*

Commands	*What They Back Up*
(1) **BACKUP C: A:**	IBMBIO.COM, IBMDOS.COM,
	COMMAND.COM
(2) **BACKUP C:*.* A:**	AUTOEXEC.BAT, CONFIG.SYS,
(3) **BACKUP C:\ A:**	VDISK.SYS, COUNTRY.SYS,
(4) **BACKUP C:*.* A:**	and KEYBOARD.SYS

These four commands all have the same effect. They back up only the files in the root directory.

Example B. *Current directory:* \ *WORDS* \ *LETTERS*

Commands	What They Back Up
(1) **BACKUP C: A:**	IBM.BAK, IBM.LET, JACK.BAK,
(2) **BACKUP C:*.* A:**	JACK.LET, and DOUG.LET
(3) **BACKUP C:.*.* A:**	
(4) **BACKUP C:\WORDS\LETTERS A:**	
(5) **BACKUP C:\WORDS\LETTERS*.* A:**	
(6) **BACKUP . A:**	

These six commands all have the same effect. They back up all files in the directory LETTERS.

Examples A-1 and B-1 tell DOS to back up onto drive A all the files in the current directory on drive C. These examples are based on the assumption that you are using the directory you want to back up. Because you have not given a file name, BACKUP "assumes" that all files should be backed up.

The only difference between A-1/B-1 and A-2/B-2 is that the *.* wild card is given in A-2 and B-2. Giving the *.* in these commands is the same as not giving a file name. If you do not give a drive name or path name, you must use **BACKUP *.* A:** because BACKUP must have a source name.

Examples A-3 and B-3 are phrased differently and have different meanings. Example A-3 explicitly tells DOS to back up all files in the root directory. A backslash (\ ) at the beginning of the path name tells DOS to start with the root directory of the disk. Because the root directory is the only specified directory on the path, only the root directory's contents are backed up. Example B-3 tells DOS to back up the files in the current directory. When a period (current directory symbol) is used as a path name, the effect is the same as giving no path.

The main difference between A-3 and B-3 is that A-3 is an absolute path reference and B-3 is a relative reference. No matter what directory you are using on drive C, A-3 always backs up the root directory, and B-3 always backs up the current directory.

Example A-4 is the same as A-3, except that in A-4 the *.* wild-card file name is used. Examples B-5 and B-4 are also the same. Both back up all files in the LETTERS subdirectory on the disk. Examples B-4 and B-5 have the same characteristics as A-3. All three commands explicitly state the directory to be used for the backup (the last named directory in the chain, or path).

Example C. *Current directory: LETTERS*

Commands	What They Back Up
(1) **BACKUP C:*.LET A:**	IBM.LET, JACK.LET,
(2) **BACKUP C:\WORDS\LETTERS*.LET A:**	and DOUG.LET

Examples C-1 and C-2 back up all files with the file-name extension .LET in the directory LETTERS. The difference between C-1 and C-2 is that C-2 can be issued while you are using a directory other than LETTERS. To use C-1, your current directory must be LETTERS.

Example D. *Current directory: root*

Commands	What They Back Up
(1) **BACKUP C: A: /S**	All files on drive C
(2) **BACKUP C:\ A: /S**	

These examples use the /S switch, which tells DOS to start with the current directory and move down through all the subdirectories. Examples D-1 and D-2 perform the same action: they back up all the files on drive C. The commands have one main difference, however. Example D-2 backs up all the files on drive C because the backslash causes the root directory and all directories below it to be backed up, regardless of what the current directory is. But D-1 backs up all the files on drive C only if the current directory is the root directory.

Example E. *Current directory: DOS*

Commands	What They Back Up
(1) **BACKUP C:\ A: /S**	All files on the disk
(2) **BACKUP C: A: /S**	All files in the DOS, BASIC, UTIL, HARDDISK, SAMPLES, and TEST directories

Examples D-2 and E-1 are identical, as are D-1 and E-2. D-2 and E-1 back up all the files on the disk. The key is the indicated path. In D-2 and E-1, the root directory symbol is given for the path. No matter which directory is current on drive C, BACKUP starts at the root directory. This condition is not true in D-1 or E-2. Because no path is given, BACKUP starts with the current directory and works downward through all of its subdirectories.

A common mistake occurs when you are working in a subdirectory and you try to use D-1 or E-2 to back up the entire disk. To back up the entire disk, use D-2 or E-1.

Example F. *Current directory: root*

Commands	What They Back Up
(1) **BACKUP C:\ A: /S /D:08/21/88**	All files created or or changed since August 21, 1988
(2) **BACKUP C:\ A: /S /D:08-21-88**	

In both command lines, BACKUP backs up in every directory on drive C all files created or changed since August 21, 1988. Examples F-1 and F-2 are different forms that achieve the same result. Slashes or hyphens are acceptable between the numbers, and leading zeros are not necessary with one-digit months or days. Do no put spaces between the starting slash of the switch and the ending number in the *date*.

Example G. *Current directory: root*

Commands	What They Back Up
(1) **BACKUP C:\ A: /S /D:08/21/88**	All files created or changed since August 21, 1988
(2) **BACKUP C:\ A: /S /D:08-21-88 /T:12:45**	All files created or changed since 12:45 p.m., August 21, 1988

In both lines, BACKUP backs up in every directory on drive C all files created or changed since August 21, 1988. However, G-2 processes files changed or altered after 12:45 p.m.; G-1 processes files changed or altered at any time since August 21. The /T switch restricts BACKUP to finding files changed or altered after a given time. The time is based on a 24-hour clock. For example, 2:00 p.m. would be entered as 14:00.

Example H. *Current directory: root*

Command	What It Backs Up
BACKUP C:\ A: /S /D:08-21-88 /A	All files created or changed since August 21, 1988

Like F-1, this command backs up all hard disk files created or changed since the given date. The difference is that the /A switch directs BACKUP to add these files to the backup disk without deleting the old files. Without the /A switch, any files in the \BACKUP subdirectory (if you are backing up onto another hard disk) or on the backup disk will be erased.

When you give the /A switch and back up onto floppy disks, you should have a backup disk in the disk drive; otherwise DOS requests that you Insert last backup disk. The disk must be a backup disk. BACKUP checks the disk for the special file BACKUP.xxx (xxx is the number assigned to backup disks in order of insertion during a backup). If this file is not on the disk, BACKUP notifies you that you have the wrong disk and then aborts.

Example I. *Current directory: root*

Command	What It Backs Up
BACKUP C:\ A: /S /M	All files created or changed since the last time you ran BACKUP

The /M switch tells BACKUP to back up any files that do not have the archive bit set. An archive bit is a special area kept in the directory for each file. When you create or modify a file, the archive bit is off. When you back up a file, BACKUP turns on the archive bit.

When you use the /M switch, BACKUP skips any file with an archive bit that is turned on. This switch setting allows BACKUP to back up any file or version of a file you have not backed up previously.

Obviously, if you create a file, BACKUP selects that file for backup. If you change a file, BACKUP selects that file. Suppose, however, that you back up only part of the disk and later back up the complete disk, using the /M switch. In this case, using the /M switch, BACKUP will back up the following:

1. All files in the portion of the disk you had not backed up earlier;

2. All files in the previously backed-up portion that were modified or created since you first used BACKUP.

On the second running (backing up the complete disk), BACKUP will probably select more files than on the first running (backing up only a part of the disk). Do not be alarmed; BACKUP is simply doing what you requested.

Example J. *Current directory: root*

Commands	What They Back Up
(1) **BACKUP C:\ A: /S /F**	All files on the disk, running FORMAT if the backup disk is not formatted
(2) **BACKUP C:\ A: /S /F /L**	Same as J-1, but creates a log file
(3) **BACKUP C:\ A: /S /F /L:082188.LOG**	Same as J-2, but places the log in a file called 082188.LOG

J-1 through J-3 show examples of backing up the entire disk using the /F and /L switches. Use J-1 when you want to back up the entire disk but you are unsure you have enough formatted disks. If BACKUP encounters an unformatted disk, BACKUP will automatically run FORMAT.

J-2 and J-3 show how to create a log file. For J-2, BACKUP places the log file in the root directory of drive C (the source directory) under the name BACKUP.LOG. For J-3, BACKUP places the log on drive C in the current directory under the name 082187.LOG, the specified name. If you specify a disk drive, the log file will be placed on the specified disk. If you specify a path, the log file will be placed in the specified directory.

Reference

See Chapter 24.

Messages

1. `***Backing up files to target drive; d: ***`
   `diskette Number: nn`

   INFORMATION: BACKUP displays this message as the program archives the files from the source disk to the receiving disk in disk drive d or to the receiving hard disk drive d. If you are using floppy disks to back up, nn is the backup disk's sequential number, starting with 1. After you see the message shown in item 1, DOS will display a list of the files that it is backing up. DOS displays the complete path and file name for each file.

2. Cannot execute FORMAT

WARNING: BACKUP could not execute FORMAT because (1) FORMAT is not in the current directory or in a directory specified to the PATH command; or (2) you do not have enough memory to run FORMAT. When you see this error message, FORMAT does not run. If you have no formatted disks, abort BACKUP, format additional disks, and rerun BACKUP. If you have formatted disks, insert one into the disk drive and continue the backup process.

3. Cannot FORMAT nonremovable drive d:

ERROR: The destination disk to receive the backup files is a hard disk or networked disk drive, and you used the /F switch to request formatting. When you see this message, BACKUP aborts. To recover from this error, issue the BACKUP command again without the /F switch, or use a floppy disk drive as the destination.

4. Disk full error writing to BACKUP Log File
   Strike any key to continue

WARNING: The disk that holds the BACKUP log file is full. Press any key to continue backing up your files. However BACKUP will not write any new information to the log file.

5. Error opening logfile

ERROR: BACKUP could not open the log file. You may have made one of the following errors: (1) you may have omitted the file name; (2) you may have given an improperly phrased file name; (3) you may have given an incorrect disk drive name (remember that you cannot place the log file on the destination disk); (4) you may have given an incorrect path; (5) the log file may be in use by another program; or (6) the disk's root directory may not have additional directory entries available.

If you have used the /L switch without a file name, check to see whether you have sufficient room in the root directory for the log file. If necessary, delete or move a file from the root directory and try again. If you specified a file name, make sure that you spelled and punctuated the name correctly. Make sure that the file name is correct and try the command again.

6. Fixed Backup device is full

ERROR: The hard disk you specified to receive the backed-up files is full. To remedy the error, begin the backup process again using floppy disks, or delete unwanted files from the target hard disk. Then try BACKUP again.

7. `Insert backup diskette nn in drive d:`
`Strike any key when ready`

INFORMATION: This message appears when the source of the backup is a floppy disk, not a hard disk. Insert the proper disk number `nn` in drive `d:` and press a key to start or continue the backup process.

8. `Insert backup diskette nn in drive d:`
`Warning! Files in the target drive d:\ root directory`
`will be erased`
`Strike any key to continue`

INFORMATION and WARNING: This message appears during the backup process when you are backing up onto floppy disks. When you use the /A switch, the message does not appear for the first target disk but appears for subsequent disks. This message appears for all disks when you are not using the /A switch.

The message instructs you to put the first or next backup disk (disk number `nn` in the series) into drive `d:` and press any key to continue. The message also warns that BACKUP will delete any existing files in the root directory of the receiving disk before transferring any files. Be sure that the proper disk is in the disk drive and then press any key to start.

9. `Insert last backup diskette in drive d:`
`Strike any key when ready`

INFORMATION: This message appears only when you are using the /A switch and invoking BACKUP without having placed the backup set's final disk in the correct disk drive. Put the proper disk into the disk drive and press any key to start.

10. `Insert backup source diskette in drive d:`
`Strike any key when ready`

INFORMATION: You have specified a floppy disk drive as the source for BACKUP. BACKUP is instructing you to insert the source disk and press any key when you are ready to begin the backup process.

11. `Invalid date`

ERROR: You made one of two errors: (1) you inserted a space between the /D switch and the date; or (2) you gave an impossible date. Make sure that the date you gave is correct and try the command again.

12. `Invalid path`

ERROR: You made one of two errors: (1) you specified a directory path for the source drive that contains invalid characters; or (2) your directory path is too long. Check the PATH command's spelling and phrasing and try the command again.

13. `Invalid time`

    ERROR: You made one of two errors: (1) you inserted a space between the /T switch and the time; or (2) you gave an impossible time. Check the time you gave and try the command again.

14. `Invalid drive specification`

    ERROR: You made one of the following errors: (1) you specified a non-existent disk drive as the source or destination for BACKUP; (2) you did not specify a source disk drive name; (3) you specified a disk drive that is currently being used by an ASSIGN, SUBST, or JOIN command; or (4) you allowed a resident program like SideKick to remain active and thus interfere with BACKUP. Check the disk drive names that you specified and inactivate any interfering memory-resident programs. If necessary, restart DOS and try the command again.

15. `Last backup diskette not inserted`

    WARNING or ERROR: This message appears when you use the /A switch and the disk in the disk drive is not the last disk from a previously made backup set. If you used a disk previously processed by BACKUP, this message appears with the `Insert last backup disk in drive d:` message. If the disk has not been processed by BACKUP before, BACKUP aborts.

16. `*** Last file not backed up ***`

    ERROR: The hard disk used as the recipient for the backed-up files is full. The file not backed up is the last file in the list that is displayed on the screen. BACKUP deletes this backup file. The original source file is left intact and not marked as having been backed up.

    To correct the problem, either back up onto floppies or delete unwanted files from the target hard disk. Then try the backup again.

17. `Logging to file filename`

    INFORMATION: You have used the /L switch, and BACKUP is recording information to the log file called `filename`.

18. `No source drive specified`

    ERROR: You did not give a disk drive name for the source. Retry the command and give a disk drive name for the source and destination.

19. `No target drive specified`

    ERROR: You did not give a disk drive name for the destination disk, or you forgot to give the source disk drive name. Retry the command and give a disk drive name for the destination.

20. `Source and target drives are the same`

    ERROR: You specified the same disk drive to be the source of the backup and to receive the backup files. Issue the command again and use a different disk drive for either the source or the target.

21. `Target can not be used for backup`

    ERROR: BACKUP could not place files on the destination disk. The disk is flawed. If you are using floppy disks, try a different one. If you are using a hard disk, try backing up to a different disk drive or restart DOS and reissue the BACKUP command.

22. `Warning! Files in the target drive d:\BACKUP direc-`
    `tory will be erased`
    `Strike any key when ready`

    INFORMATION and WARNING: This message appears during the backup process when you are backing up onto a hard disk. You have not used the /A switch, and BACKUP will erase the files in the BACKUP subdirectory. Before you proceed, check to be sure that you have selected the proper directory.

23. `Warning! No files were found to back up`

    WARNING: No files on the disk you designated for BACKUP matched the file specifications you gave. Check the spelling of the path and file names. Then get a listing of the disk's directory to learn whether the files you want to back up are there.

Batch Command

V1, V2, V3, V4—Internal

Purpose

Executes one or more commands contained in a disk file.

Syntax

*dc:pathc***filename** *parameters*

dc: is the name of the disk drive that holds the batch file.

pathc is the path to the batch file.

filename is the batch file's root name.

parameters are the parameters to be used by the batch file.

Reference

See Chapter 15.

Batch Subcommand—CALL

V3.3, V4

Purpose

Runs a second batch file and then returns control to the first batch file.

Syntax

CALL *dc:pathc***filename** *parameters*

dc: is the name of the disk drive that holds the called batch file.

pathc is the path to the called batch file.

filename is the root name of the called batch file.

parameters are the parameters to be used by the batch file.

Reference

See Chapter 16.

Batch Subcommand—ECHO

V1, V2, V3, V4

Purpose

Displays a message and allows or inhibits the display of batch commands and messages by other batch subcommands as DOS executes them.

Syntax

To display a message, use

ECHO *message*

To turn off the display of commands and messages by other batch commands, use

ECHO OFF

To turn on the display of commands and messages, use

ECHO ON

To see the status of ECHO, use

ECHO

message is the text of the message to be displayed on the video screen.

Reference

See Chapter 16.

Message

```
ECHO is status
```

INFORMATION: ECHO's *status* is displayed as either ON or OFF.

Batch Subcommand—FOR..IN..DO

V2, V3, V4

Purpose

Allows iterative (repeated) processing of a DOS command.

Syntax

FOR %%variable IN (set) DO command

variable is a single letter.

set is one or more words or file specifications. The file specification is in the form *d:path***filename**.*ext*. Wild cards are allowed.

command is the DOS command to be performed for each word or file in the set.

Reference

See Chapter 16.

Message

```
FOR cannot be nested
```

ERROR: More than one FOR command was found on a command line in the batch file. Edit the batch file to correct this problem and try executing the batch file again.

Batch Subcommand—GOTO

V2, V3, V4

Purpose

Jumps (transfers control) to the line after the label in the batch file and continues batch file execution from that line.

Syntax

GOTO label

label is the name used for one or more characters, preceded by a colon. Only the first eight characters of the label name are significant.

Reference

See Chapter 16.

Message

```
Label not found
```

ERROR: DOS cannot find the label specified in the GOTO command. The batch file is aborted, and the system prompt reappears.

Batch Subcommand—IF

V2, V3, V4

Purpose

Allows conditional execution of a DOS command.

Syntax

IF *NOT* **condition command**

NOT tests for the opposite of the **condition** (executes the command if the condition is false).

condition is what is being tested. It may be one of the following:

ERRORLEVEL number—DOS tests the exit code (0 to 255) of the program. If the exit code is greater than or equal to the number, the condition is true.

string1 = = **string2**—DOS tests whether these two alphanumeric strings are identical.

EXIST *d:path***filename**.*ext*—DOS tests whether *d:path***filename**.*ext* is in the specified drive or path (if you give a drive name or path name) or is on the current disk drive and directory.

command is any valid DOS batch file command.

Reference

See Chapter 16.

Batch Subcommand—PAUSE
(Pause execution)   *V1, V2, V3, V4*

Purpose

Suspends batch-file processing until a key is pressed; optionally displays a user's message.

Syntax

PAUSE *message*

message is a string of up to 121 characters.

Reference

See Chapter 16.

Batch Subcommand—REM
(Show remark)   *V1, V2, V3, V4*

Purpose

Displays a message within the batch file.

Syntax

REM *message*

message is a string of up to 123 characters.

Reference

See Chapter 16.

Batch Subcommand—SHIFT
(Shift parameters)   *V2, V3, V4*

Purpose

Shifts one position to the left the parameters given on the command line when the batch file is invoked.

Syntax

> **SHIFT**

Reference

> See Chapter 16.

BREAK

(Ctrl-Break)   *V2, V3, V4—Internal*

Purpose

> Determines when DOS looks for a Ctrl-Break sequence to stop a program.

Syntax

> To turn on BREAK, use
>
> **BREAK ON**
>
> To turn off BREAK, use
>
> **BREAK OFF**
>
> To find out whether BREAK is on or off, use
>
> **BREAK**

Reference

> See Chapter 17.

Message

> `Must specify ON or OFF`
>
> WARNING: You gave the BREAK command with some word other than ON or OFF.

CHCP

(Change code page)   *V3.3, V4—Internal*

Purpose

> For as many devices as possible, changes the code page (font) that DOS uses.

Syntax

To change the current code page, use

CHCP codepage

To display the current code page, use

CHCP

codepage is a valid three-digit code page number.

Reference

See Chapter 18.

Messages

1. Code page nnn not prepared for all devices

   ERROR: CHCP could not select the code page nnn because of one of the following errors: (1) you did not use MODE to prepare a code page for this device; (2) an I/O error occurred while DOS was sending the new font information to the device; (3) the device is busy (for example, a printer is in use or off-line); or (4) the device does not support code-page switching.

   Check that the MODE CODEPAGE PREPARE command has been issued for the appropriate devices and that the devices are on-line and ready. Then try CHCP again.

2. Code page nnn not prepared for system

   ERROR: CHCP could not select the code page nnn because of one of the following errors: (1) you have not yet run NLSFUNC; (2) you have specified an invalid code page for your country; or (3) you have not prepared a code page, using the MODE command.

   Be sure that you have run NLSFUNC and that you have used the MODE CODEPAGE PREPARE command to prepare the code page for the appropriate devices.

3. File not found

   ERROR: CHCP could not find the COUNTRY.SYS file. One of two errors occurred: (1) you did not specify COUNTRY.SYS's location when you gave the NLSFUNC command; or (2) COUNTRY.SYS is not in the current disk drive's root directory.

CHDIR or CD
(Change directory)   V2, V3, V4—Internal

Purpose

Changes the current directory or shows the path of the current directory.

Syntax

To change the current directory, use either of these forms:

CHDIR *d:***path**

CD *d:***path**

To show the current directory path on a disk drive, use either of these forms:

CHDIR *d:*

CD *d:*

d: is a valid disk drive name.

path is a valid directory path.

Reference

See Chapter 13.

Message

```
Invalid directory
```

ERROR: A directory you specified does not exist. This error can occur for several reasons: (1) you may have spelled the directory name incorrectly; (2) you may have forgotten or misplaced the path character (\) between the directory names; or (3) the directory may not exist in the path you specified. When this error occurs, CHDIR aborts and DOS remains in the current directory.

CHKDSK
(Check disk)   V1, V2, V3, V4—External

Purpose

Checks the directory and the file allocation table (FAT) of the disk and reports disk and memory status. CHKDSK can also repair errors in the directories or the FAT.

Syntax

dc:pathc **CHKDSK** *d:path\\filename.ext/F/V*

dc: is the name of the disk drive that holds the command.

pathc is the path to the command.

d: is the name of the disk drive to be analyzed.

path is the directory path to the files to be analyzed.

filename.ext is a valid DOS file name. Wild cards are allowed.

Switches

/F   *Fixes* the file allocation table and other problems if errors are found.

/V   Shows CHKDSK's progress and displays more detailed information about the errors the program finds. (This switch is known as the *verbose* switch.)

Reference

See Chapters 6 and 14.

Messages

1. `All specified file(s) are contiguous`

   INFORMATION: The files you specified are stored in contiguous sectors on the disk, and you are getting the best performance from this disk or disk subdirectory.

2. `filename`
   `Allocation error for file, size adjusted`

   WARNING: The file `filename` has an invalid sector number in the file allocation table (FAT). CHKDSK truncates the file at the end of the last valid sector.

   Check this file to ensure that all information in the file is correct. If you find a problem, use your backup copy of the file. This message is usually displayed when the problem is in the FAT, not in the file. Your file should still be good.

3. `Cannot CHDIR to root`

   ERROR: CHKDSK could not return to the root directory during its scan of the disk's subdirectories. When this message appears, CHKDSK aborts. Try CHKDSK again. If the message reappears, restart DOS and try CHKDSK again. If the message appears yet again, the disk is damaged, and CHKDSK cannot fix the damage. Try to copy as many files as possible to another disk and then reformat or retire the damaged disk.

4. Cannot CHKDSK a network drive

   ERROR: You attempted to run CHKDSK on a disk drive that is part of a network. You must run CHKDSK on the computer attached to the disk drive and pause or disconnect the computer from the network when you run CHKDSK.

5. Cannot CHKDSK a SUBSTed or ASSIGNed drive

   ERROR: You attempted to run CHKDSK on a disk drive that is actually a subdirectory (SUBST) or a different disk drive (ASSIGN). If you are trying to analyze a subdirectory, rerun CHKDSK, giving the real disk drive and path name. You cannot analyze a disk on which you have used the ASSIGN command. You must break the assignment by giving the ASSIGN command without parameters and then rerun CHKDSK on the disk.

6. directoryname
   Cannot recover direntry
   entry, processing continued

   WARNING: CHKDSK cannot recover direntry, which is either the . (current directory entry) or the .. (parent directory entry) in the named subdirectory, *directoryname*. This subdirectory may be so badly damaged that CHKDSK cannot recover the directory.

   If possible, copy all the files from this subdirectory to another disk or subdirectory. Then erase the files in the original subdirectory and remove the subdirectory (using the RD command). Most likely, you have lost the files in the subdirectory that CHKDSK reported to be faulty. You may need to restore the files from backup copies.

   If the problem is in the disk's subdirectory, copy all the files from the offending disk to another disk. Either reformat or retire the offending floppy disk.

7. CHDIR .. failed trying alternate method

   ERROR: CHKDSK cannot change directories to return to a parent directory. This error is internal to CHKDSK or DOS (or both) and does not mean that your disk drive or disk is bad.

   The best approach is to restart DOS and rerun CHKDSK. If you see this message a second time, get another copy of CHKDSK from your DOS master disk. The copy of CHKDSK you are using is probably bad. Restart DOS and run CHKDSK a third time. If you still get this error, your disk has a serious flaw. Copy whatever files you can from the floppy disk or hard disk. Retire or reformat the floppy disk or reformat the hard disk.

8. filename
   Contains invalid cluster, file truncated

   WARNING: The file filename has a bad pointer to a section in the FAT on the disk. If you gave the /F switch, CHKDSK will truncate the file at the last valid sector. If you did not use the /F switch, CHKDSK will take no action.

Check this file to see whether all information is intact. If it is, CHKDSK can usually correct this problem without any loss of information in the file.

9. `filename`
   `Contains xxx noncontiguous blocks`

   INFORMATION: The file `filename` is not stored contiguously on the floppy disk or hard disk, but is stored in xxx number of pieces. If you find that many files on a floppy disk are stored in noncontiguous pieces, copy the floppy disk to another floppy disk to increase disk performance. If you are using a hard disk, backup the hard disk, format it, and then restore it.

10. `directoryname`
    `Convert directory to file (Y/N)?`

    WARNING: The directory `directoryname` contains so much bad information that the directory is no longer usable as a directory. If you respond **Y**, CHKDSK converts the directory into a file so that you can use DEBUG or some other tool to repair the directory. If you answer **N**, CHKDSK takes no action.

    Respond **N** the first time you see this message. Try to copy any files you can from this directory to another disk. Check the copied files to see whether they are usable. Then rerun CHKDSK to convert the directory into a file and try to recover the rest of the files.

11. `directoryname`
    `Directory is joined,`
    `tree past this point not processed`

    WARNING: CHKDSK encountered a directory that is actually a disk on which you have used JOIN to attach it to the currently processed disk. CHKDSK will not process this subdirectory, but will continue to process the remaining portion of the real disk or floppy disk.

12. `Disk error reading FAT n`

    WARNING: CHKDSK encountered a disk error while attempting to get information from FAT 1 or FAT 2 (shown by the number n). The probable cause is a premature shutdown while the computer was trying to write to the disk—for example, a power failure or system lockup—or you pulled the floppy disk from the drive too soon).

    If this message appears for FAT 1 or FAT 2 on a floppy disk, copy all the files to another floppy disk. Then retire or reformat the bad floppy disk. If this message appears for the hard disk, backup all files on the hard disk. Then reformat and restore the hard disk.

    If the message appears for both FAT 1 and FAT 2, the floppy disk is unusable. Copy the files to another floppy disk and retire or reformat the floppy disk after you have removed all the information you can.

13. `Disk error writing FAT n`

    WARNING: CHKDSK encountered a disk error while attempting to put information into FAT 1 or FAT 2 (shown by the number).

    If this message appears for FAT 1 or FAT 2 on a floppy disk, copy all the files to another floppy disk. Then retire or reformat the bad floppy disk. If this message appears for the hard disk, backup all files on the hard disk, reformat it, and then restore it.

    If the message appears for both FAT 1 and FAT 2, the floppy disk is unusable. Copy the files to another floppy disk and retire or reformat the floppy disk after you have removed all the information you can.

14. `. or`
    `..`
    `Entry has a bad attribute or`
    `Entry has a bad size or`
    `Entry has a bad link`

    WARNING: The link to the parent directory (..) or the current directory (.) has a problem. If you gave the /F switch, CHKDSK will attempt to repair the problem. This procedure is normally a safe one and does not carry the risk of losing files.

15. `Error found, F parameter not specified`
    `Corrections will not be written to the disk`

    INFORMATION: CHKDSK found an error. This message tells you that CHKDSK will go through the motions to repair (fix) the disk, but will not actually make any changes to it because you did not give the /F switch.

    If you see this message, you can freely answer yes to any CHKDSK message, knowing that the disk will not be changed. However, you can see what actions CHKDSK would have to take to correct the error.

    This message also means that your disk does have problems. You will have to run CHKDSK with the /F switch to fix the disk.

16. `filename`
    `First cluster number is invalid,`
    `entry truncated`

    WARNING: The file `filename`'s first entry in the FAT refers to a non-existent portion of the disk. If you gave the /F switch, the file will be truncated.

    Try to copy this file to another floppy disk before CHKDSK truncates the file. You may not get a useful copy, however, and the original file will be lost.

17. `filename`
`has invalid cluster, file truncated`

INFORMATION and WARNING: A part of the file's (`filename`) chain of FAT entries points to a nonexistent part of the disk. If you gave the /F switch, the file is truncated at its last valid sector. If you did not give the /F switch, no corrective action is taken. Try to copy this file to a different disk and rerun CHKDSK with the /F switch. You may lose part of the file.

18. `filename1`
`Is cross linked on cluster x`
`filename2`
`Is cross linked on cluster x`

WARNING: Two files—`filename1` and `filename2`—have an entry in the FAT that points to the same area (cluster) of the disk. In other words, the two files "think" that they own the same piece of the disk.

CHKDSK will take no action on this problem. You must correct the problem yourself by completing the following steps: (1) Copy both files to another floppy disk; (2) Delete the files from the original floppy disk; (3) Edit the files as necessary. Both files may contain some garbage.

19. `Insufficient room in root directory`
`Erase files from root and repeat CHKDSK`

ERROR: CHKDSK has recovered so many "lost" clusters from the disk that the root directory is full. CHKDSK will abort at this point.

Examine the FILExxxx.CHK files. If you find nothing useful, delete them. Then rerun CHKDSK with the /F switch to continue recovering "lost" clusters.

20. `directoryname`
`Invalid current directory`

WARNING: The directory `directoryname` has invalid information in it. CHKDSK will attempt to repair this directory. For more specific information about the problem with the directory, do *one* of the following:

● Enter **CHKDSK /V**

● Move into the faulty directory, if possible, and enter **CHKDSK *.* /V**

The "verbose" mode will tell you more about what is wrong.

21. directoryname
    Invalid subdirectory entry

    WARNING: The directory directoryname has invalid information in it. CHKDSK will attempt to repair this directory. For more specific information about the problem with the directory, do *one* of the following:

    - Enter **CHKDSK /V**
    - Move into the faulty directory, if possible, and enter **CHKDSK *.* /V**.

    The "verbose" mode will tell you more about what is wrong.

    If you need to, copy the files from this directory and repeat CHKDSK with the /F switch to fix the problem.

22. Probable non-DOS disk
    Continue (Y/N)?

    WARNING: The special byte in the FAT indicates that your disk is a DOS disk, but that the disk was not formatted, was formatted under a different operating system, or is badly damaged.

    If you used the /F switch, answer **N**. Recheck the disk without the /F switch, and then answer **Y** in response to the prompt. See what action DOS takes. Then, if your disk is a DOS disk, run CHKDSK again with the /F switch.

    If you did not use the /F switch, press **Y** and watch what action DOS takes. Then decide whether you want to rerun **CHKDSK /F** to correct the disk.

23. Processing cannot continue,
    message

    This error message indicates that CHKDSK is aborting because of an error; message tells you what the problem is. The likely culprit is a lack of enough random-access memory to check the floppy disk. This message occurs most often with 64K systems. Because most systems have 256K or more, you should see the message infrequently. If DOS displays this message, you may have to increase the amount of memory in your computer or "borrow" another computer to check the floppy disk.

24. Tree past this point not processed

    WARNING: CHKDSK cannot continue down the indicated directory path because the system has found a bad track or the subdirectory is actually a disk on which you have used the JOIN command.

    If the fault is not that you have used the JOIN command, copy all files from the floppy disk to another floppy. The original disk may not be usable any more, and you may have lost some files.

25. `xxxxxxxxxx bytes disk space freed`

    INFORMATION: CHKDSK regained some disk space that was improperly marked as "in use." `xxxxxxxxxx` tells you how many additional bytes are now available. To free this disk space, review and delete any FILExxxx.CHK file that does not contain useful information.

26. `xxx lost clusters found in yyy chains`
    `Convert lost chains to files (Y/N)?`

    INFORMATION: Although CHKDSK has found `xxx` blocks of data allocated in the FAT, no file on the disk is using these blocks. They are lost clusters, which CHKDSK normally safely frees if no other error or warning message is given.

    If you have given the /F switch and answer **Y**, CHKDSK will join each set of lost chains into a file, called FILE0000.CHK, placed in the root directory of the disk. Examine the files and delete any that do not contain useful information.

    If you answer **N** and have used the /F switch, CHKDSK simply frees the lost chains so the disk space can be reused by other files. No files are created.

    If you answer **Y** and have not given the /F switch, CHKDSK displays the actions it would take, but does not take any action.

CLS
(Clear screen)   *V2, V3, V4—Internal*

Purpose

Erases the display screen.

Syntax

CLS

COMMAND
(Invoke secondary
command processor)   *V2, V3, V4—External*

Purpose

Invokes a second copy of COMMAND.COM, the command processor.

Syntax

*dc:pathc***COMMAND** */E:size /P /C string*

dc: is the name of the drive where DOS can find a copy of COMMAND.COM.

pathc is the DOS path to the copy of COMMAND.COM.

string is the set of characters you pass to the new copy of the command interpreter.

Switches

/E:size	Sets the size of the *environment*. Size is a decimal number from 160 to 32,768, rounded up to the nearest 16-byte multiple.
/P	Keeps this copy *permanently* in memory (until the next system reset).
/C	Passes the string of commands (the *string*) to the new copy of COMMAND.COM.

Reference

See Chapters 16 and 17.

COMP
(Compare files)   *V1, V2, V3, V4—External*

Purpose

Compares two sets of disk files to see whether they are the same.

Syntax

*dc:pathc***COMP** *d1:path1\\filename1.ext1*

d2:path2\\filename2.ext2

dc: is the name of the disk drive that holds the command.

pathc is the path to the command.

d1: is the drive that contains the first set of files to be compared.

path1 is the path to the first set of files.

filename1.ext1 is the file name for the first set of files. Wild cards are allowed.

d2: is the drive that contains the second set of files to be compared.

path2 is the path to the second set of files.

filename2.ext2 is the file name for the second set of files. Wild cards are allowed.

d1 and *d2* may be the same.

path1 and *path2* may be the same.

filename1.ext1 and *filename2.ext2* may be the same.

Special Terms

d1:path1\filename1.ext1 is the *primary* file set.

d2:path2\filename2.ext2 is the *secondary* file set.

Rules

1. If you do not enter a file name for a file set, all files for that set (primary or secondary) are compared (which is the same as entering *.*). However, only the files in the secondary set with names matching file names in the primary set are compared.

2. Only normal disk files are checked. Hidden or system files and directories are not checked.

Examples

1. **COMP A:IBM.LET C:IBM.LET**

   The file in the current directory on drive A, IBM.LET, is compared to the file in the current directory on drive C, IBM.LET.

2. **COMP *.TXT *.BAK**

   Files with the extension .TXT are compared to files that end with the extension .BAK on the current disk in the current directory.

3. **COMP A:\WORDS\LETTERS\DOUG.LET B:DOUG.LET**

   The file DOUG.LET in the subdirectory LETTERS on drive A is compared to the file DOUG.LET in the current directory on drive B.

Messages

1. `Compare error at offset xxxxxxxx`

   INFORMATION: The files you are comparing are not the same. The difference occurs at xxxxxxxx bytes from the beginning of the file. (The number given is in hexadecimal format, base 16.) The values for the differing bytes in the files are displayed also in hexadecimal format.

2. `EOF mark not found`

   INFORMATION or WARNING: This message is informational if the files you are comparing are program files, but the message is a warning if the files you are comparing are text files. The message indicates that COMP could not find the customary end-of-file marker (EOF marker, which is Ctrl-Z or 1A hex). COMP got to the end of the file before it found the EOF marker.

This problem does not occur when you compare program files and some data files. The absence of an EOF is a problem for text files. COMP always compares the files on the basis of each file's length in the directory. Sometimes files are saved with extraneous information after the end-of-file marker. As a result, you may get a compare error for the extra bytes. Check that the text files are intact. If the files are all right, COMP was comparing the extraneous part of the files.

3. `d:path\filename.ext`
   `File not found`

   ERROR: The file `d:path\filename.ext` was not found. Check the spelling of the drive, path, and file names. Make sure that the correct floppy disk is in the disk drive and try the command again.

4. `Files are different sizes`

   WARNING: You have asked COMP to compare two files that are of different lengths. Because COMP compares only files that are the same size, COMP skips the comparison.

5. `Invalid drive specification`

   ERROR: You gave a disk drive name that does not exist. Check the disk drives and the command line you typed and try again.

6. `d:path\filename.ext Invalid path`

   ERROR: You specified a directory path that does not exist. Check that your spelling is correct, the correct floppy disk is in the floppy disk drive, and the directory path you specified does exist. Then try the command again.

7. `10 Mismatches--ending compare`

   WARNING: COMP found 10 mismatches between the two files you were comparing. COMP therefore assumes that it has no reason to continue and aborts the comparison of the two files.

COPY

(Copy files)   *V1, V2, V3, V4—Internal*

Purpose

Copies files between disk drives and/or devices, either keeping the same file name or changing it. COPY can concatenate (join) two or more files into another file or append one or more files to another file. Options support special handling of text files and verification of the copying process.

Syntax

To copy a file, use

> **COPY** /A/B *d1:path1***filename1**.*ext1*/A/B *d0:path2*/
> **filename0**.*ext0*/A/B/V

You may also use

> **COPY** /A/B *d1:path1***filename1**.*ext1* /A/B/V

To combine several files into one file, use

> **COPY** /A/B *d1:path1***filename1**.*ext1*/A/B +
> *d2:path2***filename2**.*ext2*/A/B + . . .
> *d0:path0***filename0**.*ext0* /A/B/V

d1:, d2:, and *d0:* are valid disk drive names.

path1\, *path2*\, and *path0*\ are valid path names.

filename1.*ext1*, **filename2**.*ext2*, and **filename0**.*ext0* are valid file names. Wild cards are allowed.

The three periods (. . .) represent additional files in the form *dx:pathx*/**filenamex**.*extx*.

Special Terms

The file that is being copied from is the *source* file. The names containing **1** and **2** are the source files. The file that is being copied to is the *destination* file. It is represented by a **0**.

Switches

/V   *Verifies* that the copy has been recorded correctly.

The following switches have different effects for the source and the destination.

For the source file:

/A   Treats the file as an *ASCII* (text) file. The command copies all the information in the file up to, but not including, the end-of-file marker (Ctrl-Z). Anything after the end-of-file marker is ignored.

/B   Copies the entire file (based on its size, as listed in the directory) as though it were a program file (*binary1*). Any end-of-file markers (Ctrl-Z) are treated as normal characters, and the EOF characters are copied.

For the destination file:

/A   Adds an end-of-file marker (Ctrl-Z) to the end of the ASCII text file after it is copied.

/B   Does not add the end-of-file marker to this binary file.

Reference

See Chapters 5, 7, and 20.

Messages

1. Cannot do binary reads from a device

   ERROR: This message tells you one of two things:

   - You used a /B switch when you tried to copy something from a binary device. When DOS is copying from a device, DOS must have some way of determining the end of the information to be transferred. This indication is made with an end-of-file marker, the Ctrl-Z. Without an end-of-file marker, DOS has no way of knowing when to complete the transfer and, therefore, will wait forever.

   - You used a /B (binary) switch somewhere on the command line in front of the device name, probably just after the word COPY. Use the /B switch after the file name or omit the /B completely.

2. Content of destination lost before copy

   WARNING: A destination file was not the first source file. The previous contents were destroyed. COPY continues concatenating the remaining files, if any.

3. File cannot be copied onto itself

   ERROR: You attempted to COPY a file to the same disk and directory containing the same file name. This usually happens when you misspell or omit parts of the source or destination drive, path, or file name. Check your spelling and the source and destination names, and then try the command again.

4. Invalid path or file name

   ERROR: You gave a directory name or file name that does not exist, used the wrong directory name (a directory not on the path), or mistyped a name. COPY aborts when it encounters an invalid path or file name. If you used a wild card for a file name, COPY transfers all valid files before it issues the error message.

   Check to see which files already are transferred. Determine whether the directory and file names are spelled correctly and whether the path is correct. Then try again.

CTTY
(Change console)   *V2, V3, V4—Internal*

Purpose

Changes the standard input and output device to an auxiliary console, or changes the input and output device back from an auxiliary console to the keyboard and video display.

Syntax

CTTY device

device is the name of the device you want to use as the new standard input and output device. This name must be a valid DOS device name.

DATE
(Set/show date)   *V1, V2, V3, V4—Internal*

Purpose

Displays and/or changes the system date.

Syntax

DATE *date_string*

date_string is in one of the following forms:

> *mm-dd-yy* or *mm-dd-yyyy* for North America
> *dd-mm-yy* or *dd-mm-yyyy* for Europe
> *yy-mm-dd* or *yyyy-mm-dd* for East Asia

mm is a one- or two-digit number for the month (1 to 12).

dd is a one- or two-digit number for the day (1 to 31).

yy is a one- or two-digit number for the year (80 to 99). The 19 is assumed.

yyyy is a four-digit number for the year (1980 to 2099).

The delimiters between the day, month, and year can be hyphens, periods, or slashes. The resulting display varies, depending on the country code set in the CONFIG.SYS file.

Reference

See Chapter 1.

Message

```
Invalid date
```

ERROR: You gave an impossible date or used the wrong kind of character to separate the month, day, and year. This message is also displayed if you enter the date by using the keypad when the keypad is not in numeric mode.

DEL
(Delete files)   *V1, V2, V3, V4—Internal*

Purpose

Deletes files from the disk.

DEL is another term for ERASE. See ERASE for a complete description.

DIR
(Directory)   *V1, V2, V3, V4—Internal*

Purpose

Lists any or all files and subdirectories in a disk's directory.

The DIR command displays the following:

> Disk volume name (if any)
> Name of the directory (its complete path)
> Name of each disk file or subdirectory
> Number of files
> Amount, in bytes, of free space on the disk

The DIR command, unless otherwise directed, also shows the following:

> Number of bytes occupied by each file
> Date/time of the file's creation/last update

Syntax

DIR *d:path\filename.ext /P/W*

d: is the drive that holds the disk you want to examine.

path is the path to the directory you want to examine.

filename.ext is a valid file name. Wild cards are allowed.

Switches

/P	*Pauses* when the screen is full and waits for you to press any key.
/W	Gives a *wide* (80-column) display of the names of the files. The information about file size, date, and time is not displayed.

Reference

See Chapter 6.

Message

```
File not found
```

ERROR: The path or file name you gave does not exist. The path may be incorrect, the file may not exist in the directory, or your spelling may be incorrect.

If you were listing a directory of another directory, you can move to the other directory (using CHDIR) and try the command again. If you still believe that the file is in the directory, enter **DIR /P** to display the complete directory and check the file name.

DISKCOMP

(Compare floppy disks)   *V1, V2, V3, V4—External*

Purpose

Compares two floppy disks on a track-for-track, sector-for-sector basis to see whether their contents are identical.

Syntax

    *dc:pathc***DISKCOMP** *d1: d2: /1 /8*

dc: is the name of the disk drive that holds the command.

pathc is the path to the command.

d1: and *d2:* are the disk drives that hold the floppy disks to be compared. (These drives may be the same or different drives.)

Switches

/1	Compares only the first side of the floppy disk, even if the floppy disk or disk drive is double-sided.
/8	Compares only 8 sectors per track, even if the first floppy disk has 9, 15, or 18 sectors per track (DOS V2 and V3 formats).

Example

DISKCOMP A: B:

DOS compares the floppy disk in drive A with the floppy disk in drive B.

Notes

DISKCOMP compares the contents of two compatible floppy disks. The command compares the files track-for-track. Although you can use this command with any two compatible (or nearly compatible) floppy disks, its most effective use is in comparing original and duplicate floppy disks that have been duplicated with DISKCOPY.

Using DISKCOMP to compare an original floppy disk with a duplicate that has been duplicated with the COPY command can be meaningless. Because COPY copies files one at a time, the copied files may not reside in exactly the same spots on the duplicated floppy disk and the source floppy disk. DISKCOMP seldom works in this situation because DOS reports that the contents of the tracks of each floppy disk are not the same when, in fact, the files themselves are identical. To compare floppy disks that have been duplicated with COPY (not DISKCOPY), use the COMP command.

Messages

1. Compare error(s) on
   Track tt, side s

   WARNING: The floppy disks you are comparing are different at track number tt, side s. DISKCOMP does not specify which sectors are different, only that one or more sectors differ between the two floppy disks.

   If you have just duplicated these floppy disks with DISKCOPY and DISKCOPY did not report a problem, the second floppy disk probably has a flaw. Reformat this floppy disk and try DISKCOPY again. Otherwise, assume that the floppy disks are different.

2. Comparing tt tracks,
   xx sectors per track, s side(s)

   INFORMATION: DISKCOMP states how many tracks (40 or 80), sectors per track (8, 9, 15, or 18), and sides (1 or 2) the program is comparing.

3. Compare process ended

   INFORMATION: DISKCOMP indicates that the comparison of the floppy disks is completed.

4. disknumber diskette bad or incompatible

   WARNING: The first or second floppy disk (disknumber) either is bad or is incompatible with the other floppy disk. The file allocation table of the disknumber floppy disk indicates that the floppy disk is the wrong type for this comparison.

5. Diskettes compare OK

   INFORMATION: DISKCOMP compared the two floppy disks and found that they match.

6. Drive or diskette types not compatible

   ERROR: The disk drives or floppy disks are different. The first floppy disk was read successfully on both sides. However, the second floppy disk or disk drive is not identical to the first floppy disk or drive.

   You cannot compare 1.2M floppy disks with non-1.2M floppy disks or compare 1.2M floppy disks on 360K floppy disk drives. You cannot compare 1.44M floppy disks with non-1.44M floppy disks or on 720K disk drives. You cannot compare double-sided floppy disks with single-sided floppy disks or compare double-sided floppy disks on single-sided disk drives. You cannot compare 9-sector floppy disks (DOS V2 and V3) with 8-sector floppy disks (DOS V1).

   Run a CHKDSK on both floppy disks, and use the disk drive with the highest capacity. For each floppy disk, look at the number on the line bytes total disk space. If the numbers are different for the floppy disks, you cannot compare them. If the numbers are the same, the disk drive that holds the second floppy disk is the wrong type or has a hardware problem.

   If the numbers are the same, compare both floppy disks on the same floppy disk drive. If this message appears again, you are using a bad copy of DISKCOMP, or the second floppy disk is faulty. If this message does not appear again and the second drive is the correct type for the floppy disk, you have a hardware problem.

7. Invalid drive specification
   Specified drive does not exist,
   or is nonremovable

   ERROR: One (or both) of the disk drive names you gave for the comparison (1) does not exist on your system; (2) is a RAM disk; (3) is a disk drive used in a JOIN or SUBST command; or (4) is a networked drive or a hard disk. You also may have omitted the colon following the disk drive letter. Check the disk drive name you entered. Make sure that the disk drive is "real" and try the command again.

8. Invalid parameter
   Do not give filename(s)
   Command format: DISKCOMP d: d:[/1][/8]

   ERROR: You gave on the command line a switch that DISKCOMP does not recognize, gave a file or path name after the disk drive name, or omitted a colon after a disk drive name. Check your typing and try the command again.

9. `Drive d: not ready`
   `Make sure a diskette is inserted into`
   `the drive and the door is closed`

   WARNING: DISKCOMP is having difficulty reading the floppy disk in drive d. The disk drive door may be open, an unformatted or non-DOS floppy disk may have been placed in the drive, or the floppy disk is not inserted properly in the disk drive. Check these conditions and then try DISKCOMP again.

10. `Unrecoverable read error on drive x`
    `Track tt, side s`

    WARNING: Four attempts were made to read the data from the floppy disk in the specified drive. The error is at track number `tt`, side `s`. If drive x is the floppy disk that holds the destination (copied) floppy disk, the copy probably is bad. (The floppy disk has a "hard" read error.) If drive x holds the original floppy disk, the floppy disk had a flaw when it was formatted, or the floppy disk has developed a flaw.

    Run CHKDSK on the original floppy disk and look for the line `bytes in bad sectors`. If this line is displayed, the original floppy disk and the copy may actually be good. When you are formatting a floppy disk, FORMAT detects bad sectors and "hides" them. However, DISKCOMP attempts to compare the tracks even if bad sectors are present. If CHKDSK shows that the original floppy disk has bad sectors, the destination floppy disk may actually be good despite this message. In either case, you eventually should retire the original floppy disk.

    If CHKDSK doesn't show anything for bad sectors, the original floppy disk has a bad spot or the disk drive that holds the floppy disk is faulty. The floppy disk probably is the source of the error. Run the diagnostics on your disk drive. If it passes this test, your floppy disk is faulty and should be retired.

DISKCOPY
(Copy entire floppy disk)   *V1, V2, V3, V4—External*

Purpose

Copies the entire contents of one floppy disk to another floppy disk on a track-for-track basis (making a "carbon copy"). DISKCOPY works only with floppy disks.

Syntax

   *dc:pathc***DISKCOPY** *d1: d2: /1*

dc: is the name of the disk drive that holds the command.

pathc is the path to the command.

d1: is the floppy disk drive that holds the source (original) floppy disk.

d2: is the floppy disk drive that holds the target floppy disk (floppy disk to be copied to).

Switch

/1   Copies only the first side of the floppy disk.

Special Terms

The floppy disk you are copying from is the *source* floppy disk.

The floppy disk you are copying to is the *target* floppy disk.

Reference

See Chapters 1 and 7.

Messages

1. Drive d: not ready
   Make sure a diskette is inserted into
   the drive and the door is closed

   WARNING: DISKCOPY is having difficulty reading or writing the floppy disk in drive d. The floppy disk was not properly inserted, the source floppy disk was not formatted or is a non-DOS floppy disk, or the drive door is open. Check each of these possibilities and press a key to continue.

2. Drive types or diskette types not compatible

   INFORMATION or ERROR: The disk drives or the floppy disks are not compatible for the copying. If the problem is the disk drives, the message indicates an error. The message contains information if the problem is the floppy disks.

   For disk drives, the message indicates that the drive types you attempted to use are different and cannot handle the operation. The first floppy disk was read successfully, but the drive specified to make the copy (target) floppy disk is not the right type. You cannot DISKCOPY 1.2M floppy disks on non-1.2M disk drives or copy 1.44M floppy disks on 720K disk drives. See the identical message under DISKCOMP for remedial action.

   If the destination floppy disk was formatted previously with a capacity that is different from that of the source floppy disk, this message precedes the Formatting while copying message. DISKCOPY reformats the destination floppy disk to match the source floppy disk's format. No other action is necessary.

3. `Invalid drive specification`
`Specified drive does not exist,`
`or is non-removable`

ERROR: You made an error in giving one or both of the disk drive names you gave for the copy. One of the following problems occurred: (1) the disk drive does not exist on your system; (2) the disk drive is a RAM disk; (3) the disk drive is being used in a JOIN or SUBST command; (4) the disk drive is a networked drive on another computer; or (5) the disk drive is a hard disk. You also may have omitted the colon after a disk drive name. Check the disk drive names you entered. Determine that each disk drive is "real" and try the command again.

4. `Invalid parameter`
`Do not specify filenames`
`Command format: DISKCOPY d: d: [/1]`

ERROR: You gave a path and/or a file name with, or in place of, a disk drive name, or you gave a switch that DISKCOPY does not recognize. Check the command line to ensure that you typed the command correctly and try the command again.

5. `Read error on drive d:`
`Write error on drive d:`

WARNING: DISKCOPY is having difficulty reading or writing the floppy disk in drive d. The floppy disk is not properly inserted, the source floppy disk is not formatted or is a non-DOS floppy disk, or the drive door is open. Check these possibilities.

6. `SOURCE diskette bad or incompatible`
`TARGET diskette bad or incompatible`

WARNING: DISKCOPY has detected errors while reading the source floppy disk (first message) or writing the target floppy disk (second message). The error may be caused by bad sectors on either floppy disk, or the floppy disk may be in the wrong type of disk drive (a 1.2M floppy disk in a 360K drive or a 1.44M floppy disk in a 720K disk drive).

Determine whether either floppy disk has bad sectors. If either has bad sectors, use neither floppy disk with DISKCOPY. If the source floppy disk is bad, use **COPY *.*** to copy files from the source floppy disk. If the target floppy disk is bad, use a different floppy disk or try to format the floppy disk again and then use DISKCOPY. If the problem is a suspect disk drive, determine which disk drive is the known, good drive, and use only that single disk drive to DISKCOPY the disks.

7. `Target diskette is write-protected`
`Press any key when ready...`

WARNING: The target floppy disk has a write-protect tab (for minifloppies), or the write-protect switch is up (not covering the hole) for microfloppies.

Before removing or moving the tab, make sure that the correct floppy disks are in the disk drives and check the manner in which you invoked the DISKCOPY command. If you used the write-protect notch to protect the wrong floppy disk, make sure that you DISKCOPY the intended source floppy disk to the right target floppy disk.

8. `Unrecoverable read error on drive d:`
   `Side s, track tt`
   `Target diskette may be unusable`

   `Unrecoverable write error on drive d:`
   `Side s, track tt`
   `Target diskette is unusable`

WARNING: These two messages indicate that the source floppy disk, destination floppy disk, or disk drives used for the DISKCOPY are flawed. The error occurred on `d:`, side s, track `tt`. The destination (target) floppy disk may not be an exact copy of the original and therefore is unusable.

When the message indicates a read error, the source floppy disk and the source drive are suspect. If you have not experienced any difficulties with the disk drive, the source floppy disk may have a bad sector or track.

A read error occurs on source floppy disks with any bad sectors. A floppy disk that has been formatted and has shown bytes lost to bad sectors also produces a read error when you use DISKCOPY on the floppy disk. DISKCOPY attempts to copy the bad sectors, even though no useful information resides in them. In this case, the target floppy disk is good and may be used. However, some disk space on the target floppy disk still is lost to the "bad sectors" on the source floppy disk. This loss occurs because the FAT of the source floppy disk, which has the bad sectors marked out, is copied to the target floppy disk. The corresponding sectors on the target floppy disk are good but are lost for use.

Run CHKDSK to see if the source floppy disk has bad sectors. If the source floppy disk shows no bad sectors when you run CHKDSK, a recent flaw in the source floppy disk has caused the bad sector. The target floppy disk probably is unusable.

You should use COPY rather than DISKCOPY on source floppy disks that have bad tracks.

If the message indicates a write error, suspect the target floppy disk or disk drive that is holding the target floppy disk. If, during previous use of the disk drive, you've experienced no other problems and if the disk drive is in good working condition, the problem is with the target floppy disk.

To solve the problem with the target floppy disk, exit from DISKCOPY and then format the intended target disk. If the floppy disk has bad sectors when it is formatted, you cannot use this disk with the DISKCOPY command. When FORMAT does not show any bad sectors, repeat the DISKCOPY. If more problems occur, try to DISKCOPY from drive B to drive A and suspect that one disk drive may be at fault.

ERASE
(Erase files) *V1, V2, V3—Internal*

Purpose

Removes one or more files from the directory.

Syntax

ERASE *d:path\filename.ext*

or

DEL *d:path\filename.ext*

with DOS V4 you can add the /P switch:

ERASE *d:path\filename.ext* /P

or

DEL *d:path\filename.ext* /P

d: is the name of the disk drive that holds the file(s) to be erased.

path is the directory of the file(s) to be erased.

filename.ext is the name of the file(s) to be erased. Wild cards are allowed.

If you have DOS V4 or later and use the /P switch, DOS will present one at a time the filename(s) matching *filename.ext* and ask you to type **Y** or **N** to confirm whether or not the file is to be deleted.

Reference

See Chapter 7.

Messages

1. Access denied

ERROR: Either you attempted to erase a file marked as read-only, or the file is being used by another program or computer and is marked temporarily as read-only.

If the file you intend to erase has the read-only attribute set, use the ATTRIB command to turn off the read-only flag. If this file is being used by another program or computer, wait until the other program or computer is done and then erase the file. If the file is on another computer in a network and you do not have permission to erase the file, ask the operator to erase the file for you.

2. `File not found`

   ERROR: The file name you gave does not exist on the current or specified disk drive or directory. You also receive this message if you have an incorrect directory name as part of the file name. Check your typing of the names, make sure that the correct floppy disk is in the drive, and try again.

3. `Invalid drive specification`

   ERROR: You entered an ill-formed disk drive name (a colon is missing) or a nonexistent disk drive name. Check your spelling and try again.

4. `Invalid number of parameters`

   ERROR: You made one of the following errors: (1) you did not specify a disk drive name, path name, or file name; (2) you have spaces in the file specification; or (3) you have extraneous characters on the command line.

EXE2BIN

(Change .EXE files into .BIN
or .COM files)   *V1.1, V2, V3—External*

Purpose

Changes suitably formatted .EXE files into .COM files.

Syntax

*dc:pathc***EXE2BIN** *d1:path1***filename1**.ext1
d2:path2\\filename2.ext2

dc: is the name of the disk drive that holds the command.

pathc is the path to the command.

d1: is the name of the disk drive that holds the file to be converted.

path1 is the directory of the file to be converted.

filename1 is the root name of the file to be converted.

.ext1 is the extension name of the file to be converted.

d2: is the name of the disk drive for the output file.

path2 is the directory of the output file.

filename2 is the root name of the output file.

.ext2 is the extension name of the output file.

Special Terms

The file to be converted is the *source* file. The output file is the *destination* file.

FASTOPEN
(Fast opening of files)   *V3.3, V4—External*

Purpose

Keeps directory information in memory so that DOS can quickly find and use files you frequently need.

Syntax

    *dc:pathc***FASTOPEN d:**=*nnn* . . .

For DOS V4, additional syntax is

    dc:pathc **FASTOPEN d:**= *(nnn,mmm)* . . . */X*

dc: is the name of the disk drive that holds the command.

pathc is the path to the command.

d: is the name of the disk drive whose directory information should be held in memory.

nnn is the number of directory entries to be held in memory (10 to 999).

mmm is the number of fragmented entries for the drive (1 to 999).

. . . designates additional disk drives in the form **d:**=*nnn* or **d:**= *(nnn,mmm)*.

/X tells DOS to use expanded memory to store the information buffered by FASTOPEN.

Reference

See Chapter 23.

Messages

1. `Cannot use FASTOPEN for drive d:`

   ERROR: You have attempted to use FASTOPEN on drive `d:`, which is part of an ASSIGN, JOIN, or SUBST command. You cannot use FAST-OPEN on these drives.

   Make sure you have given the correct disk drive name and try the command again.

2. `FASTOPEN installed`

INFORMATION: The FASTOPEN command was successful.

3. `FASTOPEN already installed`

ERROR: The FASTOPEN command already has been issued successfully and/or the command you gave was unsuccessful. This message may appear after another error message.

4. `Incorrect number of parameters`

ERROR: You omitted the disk drive name given to the FASTOPEN command.

5. `Insufficient memory`

ERROR: Insufficient memory is available for issuing the FASTOPEN command. Either remove any unneeded resident programs or modify your CONFIG.SYS file to free more RAM. Then restart DOS.

6. `Invalid drive specification`

ERROR: You gave the name of a floppy disk drive to FASTOPEN. You can use FASTOPEN on only nonremovable disks. Check the command line and try the command again.

7. `Invalid parameter`

ERROR: You made one of the following errors: (1) you gave a switch to FASTOPEN; (2) you forgot the = between the disk drive name and the number of entries to hold; (3) you forgot to give a disk drive name; or (4) you forgot the colon after the disk drive name. Check the command line and try the command again.

8. `Same drive specified more than once`

ERROR: You already have issued the FASTOPEN command on the specified disk drive. After you have given the FASTOPEN command for a disk drive, you cannot alter the number of directory entries for that drive. To alter the number, you must restart DOS and give the FAST-OPEN command with the desired number of entries to hold.

9. `Too many drive entries`

ERROR: You gave too many disk drive names to FASTOPEN. FASTOPEN was not installed for any of the disk drives named. Repeat the command and use fewer disk drive names.

10. `Too many name entries`

ERROR: Either the sum of directory entries for all FASTOPEN commands exceeds 999 or the command for a single drive exceeds 999. FASTOPEN is not installed for the disk drives you have just named. Try the command again and reduce the number of entries or restart DOS and try the command again.

FIND
(Find string filter)   *V2, V3, V4—External*

Purpose

Displays from the designated files all the lines that match (or do not match) the specified string. This command also can display the line numbers.

Syntax

*dc:pathc***FIND** */V/C/N* **"string"** *d:path\\filename.ext . .*

dc: is the name of the disk drive that holds the FIND command.

pathc is the path to the command.

string is the set of characters for which you want to search. As indicated, string must be enclosed in quotation marks.

d: is the name of the disk drive for the file.

path is the directory that holds the file.

filename.ext is the name of the file you want to search.

Switches

/V	Displays all lines that do not contain **string**.
/C	Counts the number of times that **string** occurs in the file but does not display the lines.
/N	Displays the line number (number of the line in the file) before each line that contains **string**.

Rules

1. You may use more than one file specification. All file specifications must appear after string and be separated by spaces.

2. For each file specification:

   - If you do not give a disk drive, the current drive is used;

   - If you do not give a path name, the current directory is used.

3. If you do not give any file specifications, FIND "expects" information from the keyboard (standard input).

4. If you use switches with FIND, you must locate them between the word **FIND** and the **string**. (Most DOS commands require that you place switches at the end of the command line.)

5. You must enclose **string** in quotation marks. To use the quotation-mark character in the string, use two quotation marks in a row.

Reference

See Chapter 12.

Messages

1. `FIND: Access denied filename`

   ERROR: The file named `filename` is being used by another program or networked computer that has an exclusive-use lock on the file. FIND cannot read the file. Try the command later.

2. `FIND: File not found filename`

   WARNING: FIND cannot find the file named `filename` because of one of the following problems: (1) the file does not exist; (2) the file is not in the location you specified (you gave a wrong drive or path); or (3) you made a spelling error.

   If you give a switch after **string**, FIND thinks that the switch is a file name and gives you this warning message. Afterward, FIND continues to process any other files you have specified.

3. `FIND: Invalid number of parameters`

   ERROR: You didn't give FIND enough information. You must type at least the following:

   FIND "string"

   Most likely, you didn't supply a string.

4. `FIND: Invalid parameter x`

   WARNING: You gave FIND an incorrect switch. FIND recognizes only the /C, /N, and /V switches. FIND prints this warning message and continues.

5. `FIND: Read error in filename`

   ERROR: FIND encountered an error while it was reading the file named `filename`. Try FIND again. If the read error occurs a second time, copy the file to a different disk or subdirectory and try the command again. If an error occurs during the copy process, follow the directions for the COPY command to recover the file.

6. `FIND: Syntax error`

   ERROR: You did not phrase the command correctly. You probably didn't put quotation marks around the string for which you were searching.

FORMAT
(Format disk)   *V1, V2, V3**, V4—External*

Purpose

Initializes a disk to accept DOS information and files. FORMAT also checks the disk for defective tracks and (optionally) places DOS on the floppy disk or hard disk.

Syntax

*dc:pathc***FORMAT d:** */S/1/8/V/B/4/N:ss/T:tt*

With DOS V4 you also may add the */V:label* and */F:size* switches:

*dc:pathc***FORMAT d:** */S/1/8/V/B/4/N:ss/T:tt /V:label /F:size*

dc: is the name of the disk drive that holds the command.

pathc is the path to the command.

d: is a valid disk drive name.

Switches

/S	Places a copy of the operating *system* on the disk so that it can be booted.
/1	Formats only the *first* side of the floppy disk.
/8	Formats an *eight-sector* floppy disk (V1).
/V	Writes a *volume* label on the disk.
/B	Formats an eight-sector floppy disk and leaves the proper places in the directory for any version of the operating system, but does *not* place the operating system on the floppy disk.
/4	Formats a floppy disk in a 1.2M disk drive for double-density (320K/360K) use.
/N:ss	Formats the disk with *ss number* of sectors. *ss* ranges from 1 to 99.
/T:ttt	Formats the disk with *ttt* number of *tracks* per side. *ttt* ranges from 1 to 999.
/F:size	Formats the disk to less than maximum capacity, with *size* being one of the following values:

Drive	Allowable Values for size
160K, 180K	160, 160K, 160KB, 180, 180K, 180KB
320K, 360K	All of above, plus 320, 320K, 320KB, 360, 360K, 360KB
1.2M	All of above, plus 1200, 1200K, 1200KB, 1.2, 1.2M, 1.2MB
720K	720, 720K, 720KB
1.44M	All of above, plus 1440, 1440K, 1440KB, 1.44, 1.44M, 1.44MB

/V:label   Transfers volume label to formatted disk. Replace *label* with 11-character name for new disk.

Exit Codes

0   Successful completion of last format
1   Not defined
2   Not defined
3   Aborted by user (Ctrl-Break)
4   Aborted due to error
5   Aborted due to **N** response on a hard disk format

Reference

See Chapters 5, 11, and 24.

Messages

1. `Attempted write-protect violation`

   WARNING: The floppy disk you are trying to format is write-protected. If the disk is the one you want to format, remove the write-protect tab (for minifloppies) or move the write-protect tab down (for microfloppies). If the floppy disk in the drive is the wrong floppy disk, put the correct floppy disk in the drive and try the command again.

2. `Bad Partition Table`

   ERROR: FORMAT displays this message only when it formats the hard disk. FORMAT has detected that the hard disk's partition table does not have a valid DOS partition or any DOS partition.

   If the hard disk is new, the message indicates that you have not run FDISK on the disk. Run FDISK to establish a DOS partition and then repeat the FORMAT command. If the hard disk has been in use, the loss of the partition table is a grave sign. An error has caused the disk to lose the essential information at the start of the disk. Run FDISK, reestablish the DOS partition, and then rerun FORMAT. Another partition error indicates that the hard disk is in error and needs repair.

3. Cannot format an ASSIGNed
   or SUBSTituted drive

   ERROR: This disk drive is being rerouted with the ASSIGN command or is being used as part of a SUBST command. You cannot format a floppy disk in a disk drive that is part of an assignment or a substitution.

   If you are trying to format a drive on which you have used the ASSIGN command, clear the assignment by giving ASSIGN with no additional information. If you are trying to format a drive on which you have used a SUBST command, clear the substitution by entering **SUBST d: D**, in which **d:** is the floppy disk drive. Then try formatting again.

4. Disk unsuitable for system disk

   WARNING: FORMAT detected on the floppy disk one or more bad sectors in the area where DOS normally resides. Because DOS must reside on a specified spot on the disk, and this portion is unusable, you cannot use the floppy disk to boot (load and start) DOS.

   Try reformatting this floppy disk. Some floppy disks format successfully the second time. If FORMAT gives this message again, you cannot use the floppy disk as a boot floppy disk.

5. Drive letter must be specified

   ERROR: You did not give a disk drive name to FORMAT. Check the command line and try the command again.

6. Enter current Volume Label for drive d:

   WARNING: You are attempting to format a hard disk that has a volume label. Enter the exact volume label to proceed with the format; if you do not want to enter a volume label, press Enter.

7. Error reading partition table
   Error writing partition table

   ERROR: FORMAT could not successfully read or write the hard disk's initial sectors. The error probably is a hardware failure. Run FDISK again. Delete and reestablish the DOS partition. Run FORMAT again. If the problem recurs, the fixed disk has failed and needs to be repaired.

8. Format failure

   WARNING: FORMAT encountered a disk error that the program could not handle. This message usually comes after another error message and indicates that FORMAT has aborted.

   One cause of this error may be a floppy disk that has bad sectors where DOS normally records the boot sector, FAT, or root directory. You cannot use a floppy disk or disk with flaws in any of these areas.

9. `Format not supported on drive d:`

   ERROR: The disk drive or RAM disk drive cannot be used by the DOS FORMAT command. This error should not occur if you are using IBM disk drives, but it does occur with most RAM disk programs.

   If you are using an IBM-compatible disk drive, run a different copy of FORMAT. If the message reappears, reboot your system and try again. If the message appears a third time, you may have a hardware problem.

   If your drive is not compatible, use the format program provided by your drive's vendor or simply use a different disk drive for FORMAT.

10. `Insert DOS disk in d:`
    `and strike any key when ready`

    INFORMATION: Before formatting a floppy disk with the /S switch, FORMAT reads into memory the DOS system files IBMBIO.COM, IBMDOS.COM, and COMMAND.COM. This message indicates that DOS cannot find these files. To correct the problem, put a DOS floppy disk containing these three files into drive d: and press any key to continue.

11. `Insert new diskette for drive d:`
    `and strike ENTER when ready`

    INFORMATION: FORMAT is waiting for you to insert into drive d: the floppy disk to be formatted. After you put the correct floppy disk in the drive, press Enter to start the formatting process. Before you press Enter, check the prompt again to ensure that d: is the drive you are using for FORMAT and that the correct floppy disk is in the drive.

12. `Insufficient memory for system transfer`

    WARNING: The disk you are attempting to format has insufficient space to accept a copy of the DOS system files. Because no DOS floppy disk has a total capacity of less than 75K, this message indicates that something else is wrong. Your copy of the DOS system files may be in error, or the floppy disk may have so many bad sectors that it cannot be used.

    Take the floppy disk out of the disk drive, reinsert the floppy disk, and try FORMAT again. If this message reappears, try a different floppy disk (if FORMAT reports a large number of bad sectors) or restart DOS and try again. If this message appears a third time, you have either a disk drive failure or a bad floppy disk.

13. `Invalid characters in volume label`

    WARNING: At least one character in the label name you gave is invalid. Type the name again, and make sure that the characters are appropriate for a volume name. The most common mistake is to use a period (.) in the volume name. DOS asks you to try again.

14. `Invalid device parameters from device driver`

    ERROR: When DOS was partitioning the fixed disk, the DOS partition did not start on a track boundary; it started in the middle of a track instead. DOS cannot handle a partition starting in the middle of a track. Because FDISK does not allow DOS to start in the middle of a track, either the disk has a problem or the program you used is defective.

    Try running FDISK or the partitioning program again and make sure that the DOS partition starts on a track boundary. Run FORMAT again.

15. `Invalid media or track 0 bad`
    `disk unusable`

    WARNING: Track 0 holds the boot record, the FAT, and the directory. This track is bad, and the floppy disk is unusable. Try formatting the floppy disk again. If the error recurs, the floppy disk is bad, and you cannot use it.

    This error can occur when you format 720K floppy disks as 1.44M floppy disks (if you forget to give the /N:9 switch when you formatted on a 1.44M disk drive), or when you format 360K floppy disks as 1.2M floppy disks (if you forget the /4 switch).

    This error can occur also when you format 1.2M floppy disks at lower capacities, such as 360K, and give the /4 switch. In this case, try using a floppy disk rated for double-sided, double-density use.

16. `Invalid parameter`

    ERROR: You have given an invalid disk drive name or an unrecognized switch. Check the command line and try the command again.

17. `Parameters not compatible`

    ERROR: You gave two or more switches that are not compatible. Check FORMAT's rules to see which switches you can use together. Then try running FORMAT again.

18. `Parameter not compatible with fixed disk`

    ERROR: You gave the /1, /4, /8, /B, /N, or /T switch when you attempted to format the hard disk. Be sure that you are formatting the correct disk drive. If you are formatting the fixed disk, the only switches you *may* need to use are /N and /T.

19. `System transferred`

    INFORMATION: FORMAT has successfully written the DOS system files (IBMBIO.COM and IBMDOS.COM) and COMMAND.COM onto the formatted disk.

20. `Unable to write BOOT`

    WARNING: Either the first track of the floppy disk or the DOS portion of the hard disk is bad. DOS cannot write the bootstrap loader (BOOT program) to the floppy disk or hard disk. The floppy disk or DOS portion of the hard disk cannot be used. Try reformatting. If the error occurs again, you cannot use the floppy disk or hard disk drive.

21. `Volume label (11 characters, ENTER for none)?`

    INFORMATION: FORMAT is requesting the volume name that you want to give to the newly formatted floppy disk or hard disk. Enter a valid volume name (a maximum of 11 characters) and press Enter. If you do not want a volume label, simply press Enter.

22. `WARNING! ALL DATA ON NONREMOVABLE`
    `DISK DRIVE d: WILL BE LOST`
    `Proceed with Format (Y/N)?_`

    WARNING: FORMAT is warning that you are about to format a hard disk. Answer **Y** and press Enter if you want to format the hard disk. If you do *not* want to format the hard disk, press **N** and then press Enter.

GRAFTABL
(Load graphics table)   *V3, V3.3**, V4—External*

Purpose

Loads into memory the tables of additional character sets to be displayed on the Color/Graphics Adapter.

Syntax

To install or change the table used by the Color/Graphics Adapter, use

    *dc:pathc***GRAFTABL** *codepage*

To display the number of the current table, use

    *dc:pathc***GRAFTABL /STATUS**

To show the options to GRAFTABL, use

    *dc:pathc***GRAFTABL ?**

dc: is the name of the disk drive holding the command.

pathc is the path to the command.

codepage is the three-digit number of the code page for the display.

Exit Codes

0 = GRAFTABL installed successfully for the first time
1 = The code page used for GRAFTABL has been successfully changed, or, if no new code page was specified, there is an existing code page
2 = GRAFTABL has been installed; no previous code page was installed or is installed

3 = Incorrect parameter, no change in GRAFTABL
4 = Incorrect version of DOS

Reference

See Chapter 18.

Messages

1. Incorrect parameter

   ERROR: You have used a code page that GRAFTABL does not recognize, forgotten the / in front of STATUS, or entered more than one code page.

2. name version of Graphics Character Set is already loaded
   name version of Graphics Character Set has just been loaded

   INFORMATION: GRAFTABL displays which character set was previously used and which set is now active. name is the name of the character set (Can. French, Nordic, Portuguese, USA, Multilingual, or No for none).

GRAPHICS
(Graphics screen print)   V2, V3**, V4—External

Purpose

Prints the graphics-screen contents on a suitable printer.

Syntax

*dc:pathc***GRAPHICS** *printer /R /B /LCD*

With DOS V4, you can add the name of a file containing printer information:

*dc:pathc***GRAPHICS** *printer /R /B /LCD filename*

dc: is the name of the disk drive holding the command.

pathc is the path to the command.

printer is the type of IBM Personal Computer printer you are using. The printer can be one of the following:

COLOR1	Color Printer with a black ribbon
COLOR4	Color Printer with an RGB (red, green, blue, and black) ribbon, which produces four colors
COLOR8	Color Printer with a CMY (cyan, magenta, yellow, and black) ribbon, which produces eight colors

COMPACT	Compact Printer
GRAPHICS	Graphics Printer and IBM ProPrinter
THERMAL	PC Convertible Printer

With DOS V4, you also may specify the following printer:

GRAPHICSWIDE	Graphics Printer and IBM ProPrinter with 11-inch-wide carriage

filename is the name of the file containing printer information (DOS V4 only). If no file name is specified, DOS uses the name GRAPHICS.PRO.

Switches

/R	*Reverses* print colors so that the image on the paper matches the screen (that is, produces a white-on-black image).
/B	Prints the *background* color of the screen. You can use this switch only when the printer type is COLOR4 or COLOR8.
/LCD	Prints the image as displayed on the PC Convertible's *LCD* display.
/PRINTBOX:id	Prints the image and uses the print box size *id*. This value must match the first entry of a Printbox statement in the printer profile (DOS V4 only).

Message

```
Invalid parameter
```

ERROR: One of the following errors occurred: (1) you gave a printer type that GRAPHICS does not recognize; (2) you used the /B switch with a printer other than COLOR4 or COLOR8; (3) you gave the /LCD switch on a computer other than the PC Convertible; or (4) you gave a switch that GRAPHICS does not recognize.

Check the command line to be sure that the correct printer type is specified and that the switches can be used with the printer. Try the command again.

JOIN
(Join disk drives)   *V3.1 and later—External*

Purpose

Produces a single directory structure by connecting a disk drive to a subdirectory of a second disk drive.

Syntax

To connect disk drives, use

> *dc:pathc***JOIN d1:** *d2:***directoryname**

To disconnect disk drives, use

> *dc:pathc***JOIN d1:** **/D**

To show currently connected drives, use

> *dc:pathc***JOIN**

dc: is the name of the disk drive holding the command.

pathc is the path to the command.

d1: is the name of the disk drive to be connected.

d2: is the name of the disk drive to which **d1:** is to be connected.

\\directoryname is the name of a subdirectory in the root directory of *d2:* (the host). **\\directoryname** holds the connection to **d1:** (the guest).

Switch

/D   *Disconnects* the specified guest disk drive from its host.

Special Terms

The disk drive being connected is called the *guest disk drive*.

The disk drive and the subdirectory to which the guest disk drive is connected are the *host disk drive* and the *host subdirectory*.

Reference

See Chapter 25.

Messages

1. `Cannot JOIN a network drive`

   ERROR: You attempted to connect a networked disk drive with another disk drive. If the disk drive you are trying to use is not a networked disk drive, check your spelling and try the command again.

2. `Directory not empty`

   ERROR: The host subdirectory you attempted to use is not empty (it contains files other than the **.** and **..** entries). Either delete all files in the host subdirectory, specify a subdirectory that is empty, create a new subdirectory, or give a name for a host subdirectory that does not exist. Then try the command again.

3. `Incorrect number of parameters`

   ERROR: You omitted the guest disk drive name or the host disk drive name and subdirectory name. Check the command line you typed and try again.

```
4. Invalid parameter
```

ERROR: One of the following errors occurred: (1) you omitted the colon after a disk drive name; (2) you gave the name of a disk drive that does not exist; (3) you failed to give a host subdirectory name or omitted the path character (\ ) before the name; (4) you gave a subdirectory name not owned by the root directory; or (5) you gave a subdirectory name or host disk drive name when you used the /D (disconnect) switch. Another possibility, for JOIN V3.1 or V3.2, is that the current directory of the host disk drive is the intended host subdirectory.

Check the command line to be sure that the proper parameters are given and that the current directory of the host disk drive is not the intended host subdirectory. Then try the command again.

KEYB
(Enable foreign-language keys)   *V1, V2, V3**,*
                                             V4—External

Purpose

Changes the keyboard layout and characters to one of five languages other than American English.

Syntax

To change the current keyboard layout, use

   *dc:pathc***KEYB** *keycode, codepage, d:path***KEYBOARD.SYS**

To specify a particular keyboard identification code, use

   *dc:pathc***KEYB** *keycode, codepage, d:path***KEYBOARD.SYS** **/ID:***code*

To display the current values for KEYB, use

   *dc:pathc***KEYB**

dc: is the name of the disk drive holding the command.

pathc is the path to the command.

keycode is the two-character keyboard code for your location.

codepage is the three-digit code page to be used (437, 850, 860, 863, or 865).

*d:path***KEYBOARD.SYS** is the drive and path to the KEYBOARD.SYS file.

/ID:code is the code of the Enhanced Keyboard type you want to use.

Exit Codes

0 = KEYB ran successfully

1 = Invalid keycode type, code page, or other syntax error

2 = Bad or missing KEYBOARD.SYS file

3 = KEYB could not create a keyboard table in memory

4 = KEYB could not communicate successfully with CON (the console)

5 = The specified code page has not been prepared

6 = The internal translation table for the selected code page could not be found; the *keycode* and *codepage* are incompatible

Reference

See Chapter 18.

Messages

1. `Active code page not available from CON device`

   INFORMATION: The KEYB command, issued to display the current setting, could not determine what code page is being used. Either the `DEVICE=DISPLAY.SYS` directive has not been given in CONFIG.SYS, or there is no currently loaded CON code page.

   If the DISPLAY.SYS line has been included in your CONFIG.SYS file, you must give the MODE CON CODEPAGE PREPARE command to load the font files into memory. See the MODE command for further information.

2. `Bad or missing Keyboard Definition File`

   ERROR: Either the keyboard definition file, usually KEYBOARD.SYS, has been corrupted or KEYB could not find the file. If you did not specify a disk drive and path name, KEYB looks for the file in the root directory of the current disk drive.

   Either copy the file to the root directory or give the full disk drive and path name for the file to KEYB. If this message reappears, the copy of KEYBOARD.SYS is bad. Copy the KEYBOARD.SYS file from your DOS start-up diskette to the root directory of the start-up disk and try the command again.

3. `Code page requested (codepage) is not valid for given keyboard code`

   ERROR: You have given a keyboard code to KEYB, but you did not give a code page. The keyboard code given does not match the currently active code page (`codepage`) for the console. KEYB does not alter the current keyboard or code page. Either choose a new code page for the console that matches the keyboard code (by using the MODE CON CODEPAGE SELECT command), or specify the appropriate matching code page when you give the KEYB command again.

4. `Code page specified is inconsistent with the selected code page`

WARNING: You have specified a keyboard code and a code page to KEYB. However, a different code page was active for the console (CON). The code page specified to KEYB is now active for the keyboard but not for the video display. You may notice that the characters you type are nonsense, because the keyboard and screen do not always "agree" on the characters you have typed.

Use the MODE CON CODEPAGE SELECT command to activate the correct code page (the one specified to KEYB) for the video screen.

5. `Code page specified has not been prepared`

ERROR: The `DEVICE=DISPLAY.SYS` directive has been included in your CONFIG.SYS, but the keyboard code you have used with KEYB needs a code page that has not been prepared. Use the MODE CON CODEPAGE PREPARE command to prepare the code page appropriate for the keyboard code you want to use.

6. `Current CON code page: codepage`

INFORMATION: The current code page used by the console (video display) is designated by the number `codepage`.

7. `Current keyboard code: keycode`
`code page: codepage`

INFORMATION: The current keyboard code is the two-character `keycode`, and the code page (font file) used by the keyboard is the three-digit `codepage`.

8. `Invalid code page specified`

ERROR: You have specified a code page that does not exist. Check the number you have used for the code page and try the command again.

9. `Invalid keyboard code specified`

ERROR: You have specified a keyboard code that does not exist. Check the two-character keyboard code used and try the command again.

10. `Invalid syntax`

ERROR: You have phrased the command in a manner that KEYB could not understand. You either omitted part of the command (such as giving the code page but forgetting the keyboard code); forgot part of the punctuation for the KEYBOARD.SYS file; or forgot to place a space or comma between the keyboard code, the code page, and the full file name of the KEYBOARD.SYS file. Check your typing and try the command again.

11. KEYB has not been installed

   INFORMATION: You have used the KEYB command without any parameters (which request the current status of KEYB), and KEYB reports that
   it has not yet been installed. If KEYB should be installed, give the command again with the appropriate parameters.

12. One or more CON code pages invalid for given keyboard
    code

   WARNING: You have used the MODE command to prepare several code
   pages for the console (CON), and the keyboard code given to the KEYB
   command is not compatible with one or more console code pages.
   KEYB creates the necessary information to work with those keyboard
   and code pages that are compatible. The incompatible keyboard and
   code pages combinations are not honored.

13. Unable to create KEYB table in resident memory

   ERROR: When KEYB is first installed, it fits within a predetermined
   amount of RAM. You have used other commands to add additional code
   pages to the console (CON), and you have attempted to use KEYB
   again. KEYB, which cannot expand past the predetermined amount of
   RAM, cannot adapt to the additional code pages. To use the additional
   code pages, restart DOS and give any needed MODE code page commands before you issue KEYB.

LABEL

(Volume label)   *V3, V4—External*

Purpose

Creates, changes, or deletes a volume label for a disk.

Syntax

   *dc:pathc***LABEL** *d:volume_label*

dc: is the name of the disk drive holding the command.

pathc is the path to the command.

d: is the name of the disk drive for which the label will be changed.

volume_label is the new volume label for the disk.

Reference

See Chapter 11.

Messages

1. Cannot LABEL a network drive

   ERROR: You attempted to put a volume label on a disk drive on your computer or on another computer used by a network. If this disk drive is "owned" by your computer, pause or disconnect from the network and try the LABEL command again.

2. Delete current volume label (Y/N)?

   INFORMATION and WARNING: You did not enter a volume label when you were requested to. DOS is asking whether the current label should be deleted or left unaltered. Pressing **Y** deletes the current label. Pressing **N** leaves the current label intact.

3. Invalid characters in volume label
   Volume label (11 characters, ENTER for none)?

   WARNING: You used a character not permitted in a volume label (usually some punctuation symbol, such as a period or comma). Check to see whether the characters you entered for the label are valid and then enter the volume label again.

4. Invalid drive specification

   ERROR: You gave the name of a disk drive that does not exist, gave a disk drive name that is part of a JOIN command, or omitted the colon in the disk drive name. Check these conditions and try the command again.

5. No room in root directory

   ERROR: The root directory of the disk is full and cannot hold the new volume label. This error should not occur when you change or delete a volume label—only when you add a new volume label. Delete, or copy and then delete, a file in the root directory of the disk and try the command again.

6. Volume in drive d: is label_name
   Volume in drive d: has no label

   INFORMATION: If the first message appears, the floppy disk in drive D or disk drive D has the volume label called label_name. If the second message appears, the floppy disk/disk drive has no volume label.

MEM

(Show memory usage)   *V4—External*

Purpose

Displays the amount of used memory, unused memory, allocated and open memory areas, and all programs currently in the system.

Syntax

*dc:pathc***MEM** */PROGRAM* */DEBUG*

dc:pathc is the optional drive and/or path to the command.

Switches

/PROGRAM	Shows programs that are currently in memory, including the address, name, size, and type of file for each program. Also shows current free memory.
/DEBUG	Displays programs that are currently in memory, including the address, name, size, and type of file for each program. Also displays system device drivers and installed device drivers, as well as all unused memory.

Reference

See Chapter 27.

MKDIR or MD

(Make directory)   *V2, V3, V4—Internal*

Purpose

Creates a subdirectory.

Syntax

MKDIR *d:path***directoryname**

or

MD *d:path***directoryname**

d: is the name of the disk drive for the subdirectory.

path is a valid path name for the path to the directory that will hold the subdirectory.

directoryname is the name of the subdirectory you are creating.

Reference

See Chapter 13.

Message

```
Unable to create directory
```

ERROR: One of the following errors occurred: (1) the directory you tried to create already exists; (2) one of the path names you gave is incorrect; (3) the root directory of the disk is full; (4) the disk is full; or (5) a file already exists by the same name.

Check the directory in which the new subdirectory was to be created. If a conflicting name exists, either change the file name or use a new directory name. If the disk or the root directory is full, delete some files, create the subdirectory in a different directory, or use a different disk.

MODE
(Change/set mode)   V1, V2, V3, V3.3**, V4—External

Purpose

Sets the mode of operation for the printers, the video display, and the Asynchronous Communications Adapter; controls code page switching for the console and printer; with DOS V4, adds capability of controlling typematic rate of keyboard, number of lines on screen, and additional asynchronous parameters.

Reference

See Chapter 23.

MODE
(Set parallel printer characteristics)   V1, V2, V3, V4—External

Purpose

Sets the IBM printer characteristics.

Syntax

*dc:pathc***MODE LPTx:** *cpl, lpi, P*

With DOS V4, you can specify the number of columns and lines, as well as retries, by using a different format:

*dc:pathc***MODE LPTx: LINES** = *lpi,***COLS** = *wid,***RETRY** = *action* *dc:* is the name of the disk drive holding the command.

pathc is the path to the command.

x: is the printer number (1, 2, or 3). The colon is optional.

cpl is the number of characters per line (80 or 132).

lpi is the number of lines per inch (6 or 8).

P specifies continuous retries on time-out errors.

wid is the number of columns per line.

action is the action you want when DOS checks a busy printer port. Substitute for *action* one of the following:

E	Return *error* from check of busy port
B	Return *busy signal* from check of busy port
R	Return *ready signal* from check of busy port

Reference

See Chapter 23.

MODE
(Set display adapter and display characteristics)   *V2, V3, V4—External*

Purpose

Switches the active display adapter between the Monochrome Display and a graphics adapter/array (Color/Graphics Adapter, Enhanced Color/Graphics Adapter, or Video Graphics Array) on a two-display system; sets the characteristics of the graphics adapter/array.

Syntax

   *dc:pathc***MODE dt**

or

   *dc:pathc***MODE** *dt*, **s**, *T*

With DOS V4, you can enter the number of screen lines and columns in one of these three ways:

   *dc:pathc***MODE** *dt*, **s**, *T, lines*

   *dc:pathc***MODE CON LINES** = *lines*

   *dc:pathc***MODE CON COLS** = *cols*

dc: is the name of the disk drive holding the command.

pathc is the path to the command.

dt is the display type, which may be one of the following:

40	Sets the display to 40 characters per line for the graphics display.
80	Sets the display to 80 characters per line for the graphics display.
BW40	Makes the graphics display the active display and sets the mode to 40 characters per line, black and white (color disabled).
BW80	Makes the graphics display the active display and sets the mode to 80 characters per line, black and white (color disabled).
CO40	Makes the graphics display the active display and sets the mode to 40 characters per line (color enabled).
CO80	Makes the graphics display the active display and sets the mode to 80 characters per line (color enabled).
MONO	Makes the Monochrome Display the active display.

s shifts the graphics display right (**R**) or left (**L**) one character.

T requests alignment of the graphics display screen with a one-line test pattern.

lines is the number of screen lines. The number may be 25 or 43 with EGA monitors, 25 or 50 with VGA monitors, and 25 only with all other monitors.

cols is the number of columns. The number may be 40 or 80 characters per line.

Special Terms

The *graphics display* is any display connected to the Color/Graphics Adapter (CGA), Enhanced Graphics Adapter (EGA), PC Convertible, or Video Graphics Array (VGA). The type of video monitor connected to the adapter or array can be color or monochrome.

Reference

See Chapter 23.

MODE

(Set Asynchronous Communications Adapter characteristics)   V1.1, V2, V3, V3.3**, V4—External

Purpose

Controls the protocol characteristics of the Asynchronous Communications Adapter.

Syntax

*dc:pathc***MODE COMy: baud**, *parity, databits, stopbits, P*

With DOS V4, you may set these parameters by using the following syntax:

*dc:pathc***MODE COMy: BAUD** = *baud* **PARITY** = *parity* **DATA** = *databits*
STOP = *stopbits* **RETRY** = *action*

y: is the adapter number (1, 2, 3, or 4). The colon after the number is optional.

baud is the baud rate (110, 150, 300, 600, 1200, 2400, 4800, 9600, or 19200).

parity is the parity checking (None, Odd, or Even). For DOS V4, you also may specify Mark or Space parity.

databits is the number of data bits (7 or 8).

stopbits is the number of stop bits (1 or 2).

P represents continuous retries on time-out errors.

action is the action you want when DOS checks a busy serial port. Substitute for *action* one of the following:

E	Return *error* from check of busy port
B	Return *busy signal* from check of busy port
R	Return *ready signal* from check of busy port

Reference

See Chapter 23.

MODE
*(Redirect printing
from a parallel printer
to a serial printer)*　　　　　　*V2, V3, V4—External*

Purpose

Forces DOS to print to a serial printer rather than to a parallel printer.

Syntax

　　*dc:pathc***MODE LPTx: = COMy:**

dc: is the name of the disk drive holding the command.

pathc is the path to the command.

x: is the parallel printer number (1, 2, or 3). The colon is optional.

y: is the Asynchronous Communications Adapter number (1, 2, 3, or 4).

Reference

See Chapter 23.

MODE
(Prepare code page for use)　　　　　*V3.3—External*

Purpose

Prepares (chooses) the code pages to be used with a device.

Syntax

　　*dc:pathc***MODE device CODEPAGE PREPARE** = *((***codepage**,
　　codepage, . . .)dp:pathp***pagefile.ext)**

or

　　dc:pathc***MODE device CP PREP** = *((***codepage**, codepage, . . . **)**
　　　　*dc:pathp***pagefile**.*ext)*

dc: is the name of the disk drive holding the command.

pathc is the path to the command.

device is the name of the device for which code page(s) will be chosen. Valid devices are these:

CON:	The console
PRN:	The first parallel printer
LPTx:	The first, second, or third parallel printer (**x** is 1, 2, or 3)

codepage is the number of the code page(s) to be used with the device. The numbers are the following:

437	United States
850	Multilingual
860	Portugal
863	French Canadian
865	Denmark/Norway

The ellipsis (. . .) represents additional code pages.

dp: is the name of the disk drive holding the code page (font) information.

pathp is the path to the file holding the code page (font) information.

pagefile.*ext* is the name of the file holding the code page (font) information. Currently, the DOS-provided code page files are these:

4201.CPI	The IBM ProPrinter
5202.CPI	The IBM Quietwriter III Printer
EGA.CPI	EGA/VGA kinds of displays
LCD.CPI	IBM Convertible LCD display

Reference

See Chapter 18.

MODE
(Select code page for use)   *V3.3, V4—External*

Purpose

Activates the code page used with a device.

Syntax

*dc:pathc***MODE device CODEPAGE SELECT** = **codepage**

or

*dc:pathc***MODE device CP SEL** = **codepage**

dc: is the name of the disk drive holding the command.

pathc is the path to the command.

device is the name of the device for which code page(s) will be chosen. Valid devices are the following:

CON:	The console
PRN:	The first parallel printer
LPTx:	The first, second, or third parallel printer (**x** is 1, 2, or 3)

codepage is the number of the code page(s) to be used with the device. The numbers are the following:

437	United States
850	Multilingual
860	Portugal
863	French Canadian
865	Denmark/Norway

Reference

See Chapter 18.

MODE
(Reestablish the current code page) V3.3, V4—External

Purpose

Reloads and reactivates the code page used with a device.

Syntax

*dc:pathc***MODE device CODEPAGE REFRESH**

or

*dc:pathc***MODE device CP REF**

dc: is the name of the disk drive holding the command.

pathc is the path to the command.

device is the name of the device for which code page(s) will be chosen. Valid devices are the following:

CON:	The console
PRN:	The first parallel printer
LPTx:	The first, second, or third parallel printer (**x** is 1, 2, or 3)

Reference

See Chapter 18.

MODE

(Displays code page status)   *V3.3, V4—External*

Purpose

Displays the status of code pages for a device.

Syntax

*dc:pathc***MODE device CODEPAGE** */STATUS*

or

*dc:pathc***MODE device CP** */STA*

dc: is the name of the disk drive holding the command.

pathc is the path to the command.

device is the name of the device for which code page(s) will be chosen. Valid devices are the following:

CON:	The console
PRN:	The first parallel printer
LPTx:	The first, second, or third parallel printer (**x** is 1, 2, or 3)

Switch

/STATUS	Displays the *status* of the device's code pages.

Reference

See Chapter 18.

MODE

(Control typematic rate)   *V4—External*

Purpose

Adjusts rate at which keyboard repeats keys.

Syntax

*dc:pathc***MODE CON RATE**=*rate* **DELAY**=*delay*

dc: is the name of the disk drive holding the command.

pathc is the path to the command.

rate is the approximate number of repetitions per second.

delay is the amount of time DOS waits before starting to repeat a key.

Reference

See Chapter 23.

MODE
(General)

Reference

See Chapter 23.

Messages

1. `Active code page for device devicename is codepage`

   INFORMATION: The MODE /STATUS command displays the number of the active code page (`codepage`) for the device `devicename`.

2. `Codepage not prepared`

   INFORMATION or ERROR: If you used the MODE /STATUS command, it displays this message if a space is available for a prepared code page but no code page has been prepared for this space.

   If you used the MODE SELECT command, the code page you have selected for this device is not prepared. If you issue the command for the console device (CON:), the selected code page may not have the correct font for the current video mode. MODE SELECT aborts.

   Use MODE PREPARE to reload the desired code page; then reissue the MODE SELECT command. If the error occurs again, edit the DEVICE=DISPLAY.SYS line to increase the number of *subfonts*, and restart DOS.

   This message may precede other MODE error messages.

3. `Codepage operation not supported on this device`

   ERROR: When you use either the MODE PREPARE or MODE SELECT command, one of the following has occurred: (1) you gave a nonsense device; (2) you misspelled the device name; (3) you gave the name of a device that does not exist on your system; (4) you gave the name of a device that does not have the proper device driver installed (DISPLAY.SYS for the console; PRINTER.SYS for the printer); (5) you incorrectly phrased the directive for the device driver; or (6) you gave the name of a device that cannot switch code pages.

   First check the spelling of the name of the device you specified to the MODE command. If the device name is correct, make sure that you have the right phrasing for the device driver in CONFIG.SYS. Check the CONFIG.SYS file for the DISPLAY.SYS line (if the problem is in the CON device) or the PRINTER.SYS line (if the problem is in the LPTx or PRN devices). Be sure to specify the number for LPT that is correct for your printer. If you change the CONFIG.SYS file, restart DOS and try the command again.

4. `Code pages cannot be prepared`

ERROR: You have used the MODE PREPARE command and have either specified more code pages than the device driver allows or duplicated a code page for the Quietwriter III printer. MODE does not prepare any code pages, and it deletes the previously prepared code pages that are in the same position as the code pages in this command.

If you use Quietwriter III, you cannot duplicate a hardware code page. If you use any other device, use the MODE /STATUS command to check the number of prepared code pages allowed. If you need more code pages than are listed in the prepared code page lines, edit the *added_codepages* parameter in the DISPLAY.SYS or PRINTER.SYS line in your CONFIG.SYS file. Restart DOS and try the command again.

5. `COMy bbbb,p,d,s,t initialized`

INFORMATION: The Asynchronous Communications Adapter was initialized successfully. `y` is the adapter number, `bbbb` is the baud rate, `p` is the parity, `d` is the number of data bits, `s` is the number of stop bits, and `t` is the retry on time-out.

6. `Current keyboard does not support this Codepage`

WARNING: You have issued the KEYB command previously. You have issued a MODE SELECT command, and a conflict exists between the current code page for the keyboard and the code page you just specified to MODE for the console. The code page for the console is set to the specified code page, but the keyboard code page is not changed. You get nonsense characters when you type on the keyboard.

To use this new code page on the console, issue the KEYB command with the correct, compatible keyboard code. When you issue the KEYB command, KEYB automatically switches the keyboard's code page.

7. `Device error during Prepare`
`Device error during Refresh`
`Device error during Select`
`Device error during Status`
`Device error during write of font file to device`

ERROR: During a MODE CODEPAGE operation, a device error was detected. The error occurs for one of the following reasons: (1) the device does not support code page switching; (2) the CONFIG.SYS file does not have the line for including the proper device driver; (3) the number of *added_codepages* is too low to allow for additional code pages; (4) the code page information file is ruined; (5) you forgot to give the full file name of the code page information file for a MODE

PREPARE command; (6) an incorrect code page number was given; (7) the device detected a transmission error; (8) the device may be turned off or not selected; or (9) you used the MODE REFRESH command before you gave a MODE SELECT or CHCP command.

If you use MODE REFRESH, issue the MODE SELECT command instead. Be sure that you have given the proper device name, code page number, and full file name for the code page file and that the device is turned on and ready. Then try the command again.

If you get the error message again, first examine the CONFIG.SYS file to ensure that the proper device driver (DISPLAY.SYS for the console; PRINTER.SYS for the printers) has been included and that the proper parameters have been given. If the line is included and properly phrased, check the number of additional code pages. If this number is too low, edit the line and increase the number of added code pages. Restart DOS and try the command again.

If the message reappears, you probably have a hardware problem. For the printer only, be sure that printer connections are secure and that the printer is receiving characters. Try Shift-PrintScreen. If nothing prints, your printer has a problem. If the screen's contents print and the MODE command still does not work, your printer has an internal electronics malfunction.

8. `Device or codepage missing from font file`

ERROR: By using the MODE PREPARE command, you have specified a correct possible code page, but the code page information file does not have the font. This error can result from attempting either to prepare a hardware code page or to use a font that the device does not support. All existing code pages for this device are discarded and must be prepared again.

Try the command again, and use a different correct code page number. If this step works, the device can use code pages, but the code page originally specified cannot be used. Also, be sure that you have specified the correct hardware code page to the appropriate device driver. If the hardware code page is incorrect, edit the CONFIG.SYS file, restart DOS, and try the command again.

9. `Do you see the leftmost ▯? (Y/N)`
`Do you see the rightmost ꟼ? (Y/N)`

INFORMATION: You are adjusting the display connected to the Color/Graphics Adapter. Answer **N** or press any other key to shift the display left or right (depending on how you invoked MODE). Answer **Y** if the display is centered properly. This answer ends the MODE command.

10. `Error during read of font file`

ERROR: DOS read the code page information file during a MODE PRE-PARE command and detected a disk error. The most likely cause is a bad sector on the disk. MODE aborts and does not change the prepared fonts.

Run RECOVER on the file. If RECOVER reports any bad sectors for a floppy disk, reformat or retire the floppy disk. If the problem is a hard disk, RECOVER "hides" the bad sectors, and the code page information file is ruined. Copy the .CPI file from a copy of your DOS start-up floppy disk to the hard disk and try the command again.

11. `Failure to access Codepage Font File`

ERROR: You have used the MODE PREPARE command, and MODE could not find the code page information file you specified. You omitted a drive or path name, misspelled the file name, or gave a nonsense file name. Be sure that the code page information file name is spelled correctly and that it is on the correct disk and directory. Try the command again.

12. `Failure to access device: devicename`

ERROR: MODE CODEPAGE could not open the device `devicename`. You have given the wrong device name, the proper device driver is not installed in CONFIG.SYS, or the device is turned off or disconnected.

If you gave the wrong device name, try the command again with the correct device name. If the device is a printer, make sure that the printer is connected and turned on. Be sure that the proper device driver (DISPLAY.SYS for the console; PRINTER.SYS for the printer) is loaded via CONFIG.SYS and phrased properly. If you detect an error in CONFIG.SYS, edit the file, restart DOS, and try the command again.

13. `Font file contents invalid`

ERROR: During a MODE PREPARE command, MODE found the file you specified as the code page information file, but the file's contents are incorrect. Either you specified the name of an existing file that is not a code page information file, or the code page information file has been ruined. All existing prepared code pages for the device are discarded.

Be sure that you have given the correct file name to MODE and try the command again. If the error occurs again, the code page file is damaged. Copy the code page information file from your copy of the DOS start-up floppy disk and try the command once more.

14. `Illegal Device Named`

ERROR: One of the following errors occurred: (1) you did not specify a number with LPTx: or COMy:; (2) you used a number that is not in the correct range (for the PC: 1, 2, or 3 for LPTx: or 1 or 2 for COMy:; for PS/2 computers: 1, 2, 3, or 4); (3) you put no spaces between LPTx: or

COMy: and the next parameter; (4) you put more than one space between LPTx: or COMx: and the next parameter; or (5) the specified adapter is not connected to your system.

Check each possibility, make the needed correction in the command, and try again.

15. `Infinite retry on parallel printer timeout`
`No retry on parallel printer timeout`

    INFORMATION: You have used the MODE LPTx or COM commands. The first message appears if you specify the **,P** option. The second message appears if you do not specify the **,P** option.

16. `Infinite retry not supported on Network printer`

    ERROR: You have used the **,P** option of the MODE LPTx command, and the printer you specified is owned by another computer or is part of a network. You cannot use **,P** on this printer. Either give the command again without the **,P** or specify a printer owned by your computer and not used by a network.

17. `Invalid baud rate specified`

    ERROR: You gave an incorrect baud rate. The baud rate must be 110, 150, 300, 600, 1200, 4800, 9600, or 19200 (or the first two characters for one of these numbers).

18. `Invalid parameter 'string'`

    ERROR: MODE detected an error in your phrasing for a code page command. The objectionable word is `string`, which might be abbreviated to three or four letters. You may have (1) forgotten the equal sign or the code pages in parentheses in a MODE PREPARE command; (2) reversed the order of words; (3) forgotten to give the word CODEPAGE (or CP); (4) forgotten to give the device name; or (5) used a word that MODE does not recognize.

    Check your spelling and punctuation of the command, and try it again.

19. `Invalid parameters`

    ERROR: One of the following errors occurred: (1) you forgot to give a necessary parameter; (2) the first parameter (for the printer or communications adapter) did not start with L or C; (3) you gave a wrong parameter with the command; or (4) the display adapter you are referencing is not connected to your system. Check your spelling and punctuation and try the command again.

20. `LPTx: not rerouted`

    INFORMATION: The specified printer adapter is getting its normal data. Any previous reassignment (LPTx: = COMy:) has been canceled. This message appears when you set or reset the characters per line or the lines per inch for the printer.

21. `LPTx: rerouted to COMy:`

    INFORMATION: The output that usually goes to the specified printer adapter now goes to the specified communications adapter.

22. `LPTx: set for 80`
    `LPTx: set for 132`

    INFORMATION: The specified printer is set for 80 or 132 characters per line.

23. `MODE action Codepage function completed`

    INFORMATION: MODE has completed its function, `action`. This message appears after one of the MODE CODEPAGE functions has run successfully. `action` can be `Prepare`, `Refresh`, `Select`, or `Status`.

24. `Must specify COM1, COM2, COM3 or COM4`

    ERROR: You have given an invalid number for COMy in a MODE LPTx-=COMy command. Check the number you gave and try again.

25. `No codepage has been SELECTED`

    INFORMATION: You have used the MODE /STATUS command, and you have not yet used the MODE SELECT command on this device.

26. `Printer error`

    ERROR: You used the MODE LPTx command, and MODE could not set the printer. The printer may be turned off, not selected, not connected, out of paper, or not IBM-compatible. Check your printer and try the command again.

27. `Printer lines per inch set`

    INFORMATION: You specified a parameter for the lines per inch (six or eight). If your attempt to set the lines per inch fails, a `Printer error` message usually follows this message.

28. `Resident portion of MODE loaded`

    INFORMATION: A section of MODE has been loaded and become a resident part of DOS. This message appears when you use the continuous retry option for MODE LPT#: or MODE COMx:, when you shift the display left or right, or when you reroute printers (MODE LPT#: = COMx). MODE stays resident until you restart DOS.

29. `Unable to shift screen left`
    `Unable to shift screen right`

    ERROR: You used the MODE display command and requested the display to shift for a Monochrome Adapter, an Enhanced Color/Graphics Adapter, or a Video Graphics Display. You cannot shift the display connected to either of these adapters.

MORE
(More output filter)   *V2, V3, V4—External*

Purpose

Displays one screenful of information from the standard input device and pauses while displaying the message --More--. When you press any key, MORE displays the next screenful of information.

Syntax

    *dc:pathc***MORE**

dc: is the name of the disk drive holding the command.

pathc is the path to the command.

Reference

See Chapter 12.

NLSFUNC
(National language support)   *V3.3, V4—External*

Purpose

Provides support for extended country information in DOS and allows the use of the CHCP command.

Syntax

    *dc:pathc***NLSFUNC** *d:path***filename**.*ext*

dc: is the name of the disk drive holding the command.

pathc is the path to the command.

d: is the name of the disk drive holding the country information file.

path is the path to the country information file.

filename.*ext* is the name of the file holding the country information. In DOS V3.3 and V4, this information is contained in the file COUNTRY.SYS.

Reference

See Chapter 18.

Messages

1. `File not found`

   ERROR: NLSFUNC could not locate the country information file, COUN-TRY.SYS. Either you forgot to specify the disk drive, path, or file name for COUNTRY.SYS; or you omitted the complete full file name, and COUNTRY.SYS is not in the root directory of the current disk drive. Either copy COUNTRY.SYS to the root directory of the disk or give the full path and file name for COUNTRY.SYS; then try the command again.

2. `NLSFUNC already installed`

   WARNING: NLSFUNC has already been installed. NLSFUNC should be used only one time after DOS has started.

PATH
(Set directory search order)   *V2, V3, V4—Internal*

Purpose

Tells DOS to search the specified directories on the specified drives if a program or batch file is not found in the current directory.

Syntax

PATH *d1:path1;d2:path2;d3:path3; . . .*

d1:, *d2:*, and *d3:* are valid disk drive names.

path1, *path2*, and *path3* are valid path names to the commands you want to run while the system is logged to any directory.

The ellipsis (. . .) represents additional disk drives and path names.

Reference

See Chapter 13.

Message

`Invalid drive in search path`

WARNING: You specified a nonexistent disk drive name in one of the paths. This message appears when DOS searches for a program or batch file, not when you give the PATH command.

Use PATH or SET to see the current path. If the disk drive temporarily is invalid because of a JOIN or SUBST command, you can ignore this message. If you have specified the wrong disk drive, issue the PATH command again and give the complete set of directory paths you want to use.

PRINT
(Background printing)   *V2, V3, V4—External*

Purpose

Prints a list of files on the printer while the computer performs other tasks.

Syntax

> *dc:pathc***PRINT** */D:device /B:bufsiz /M:maxtick /Q:maxfiles*
> */S:timeslice /U:busytick d1:path1\\filename1.ext1 /P/T/C*
> *d2:path2\\filename2.ext2/P/T/C . . .*

d1: and *d2:* are valid disk drive names.

path1 and *path2* are valid path names to the files for printing.

filename1.ext1 and *filename2.ext2* are the names of the files you want to print. Wild cards are allowed.

The ellipsis (. . .) represents additional file names in the form *dx:pathx\\filenamex.extx.*

Switches

You can specify any one of the following switches only the first time you start PRINT:

/D:device	Specifies which device should be used for printing. *device* is any valid DOS device name. (When this switch is used, it must be listed first.)
/B:bufsiz	Specifies the size of the memory *buffer* to be used while the files are printing. *bufsiz* can be a number from 1 to 32,767.
/M:maxtick	Specifies in clock ticks the maximum amount of time that PRINT has for sending characters to the printer every time PRINT gets a turn. *maxtick* can be a number from 1 to 255.
/Q:maxfiles	Specifies the number of files that can be in the queue (line) for printing. *maxfiles* can be a number from 1 to 32.
/S:timeslice	Specifies the number of slices in each second. *timeslice* can be a number from 1 to 255.
/U:busytick	Specifies in clock ticks the maximum amount of time for the program to wait for a busy or unavailable printer. *busytick* can be a number from 1 to 255.

You can specify any one of the following switches whenever you use PRINT:

/P	Queues up the file (*places* the file in the line) for printing.
/T	*Terminates* the background printing of any or all files, including any file currently being printed.
/C	Cancels the background printing of the file(s).

Special Terms

A *tick* is the smallest measure of time used on Personal Computers and Personal System/2 computers. A tick happens every 1/18.2 (0.0549) seconds.

Reference

See Chapter 23.

Messages

1. Access denied

   ERROR: You attempted to print a file for which another computer or program has exclusive use. Try the command later.

2. All files canceled by operator

   INFORMATION: You used the /T switch to terminate all queued files.

3. Cannot use PRINT - Use NET PRINT

   ERROR: You attempted to print a file to a networked printer, either on your own computer or on another computer. You must use NET PRINT, not PRINT, to print to this printer. You may pause or disconnect from the network and use PRINT on your own printer.

4. Errors on list device indicate that it may be off-line. Please check it.

   WARNING: The device used for PRINT is probably not selected, connected, or turned on. Check your printer and cable, and check to see that all connections are correct.

5. File filename canceled by operator

   INFORMATION: This message appears on the printout to remind you that the printout of the file filename is incomplete because you canceled the printing of the file.

6. filename File not found

   WARNING: PRINT didn't find the specified file, filename. PRINT skips this file and processes any remaining file names on the command line. Check the disk drive, path, and file names for this file. Make sure that the file exists where you specified and then try the command again.

7. `filename File not in PRINT queue`

   WARNING: You requested that PRINT cancel (with the /C switch) a file (`filename`) that PRINT did not have in its queue. Either the file has been printed already or the file name is misspelled. If you meant to cancel one or more files and to print others (that is, if you intended to give both /C and /P), either you gave the /C switch out of order or you omitted the /P switch to print a file. Check each of these possibilities and try the command again.

8. `Invalid drive specification`

   WARNING: Either you specified a disk drive that doesn't exist or you omitted the colon after a disk drive name. PRINT skips this file and processes any remaining files named on the command line. Check your spelling of the file names and try the command again.

9. `Invalid parameter`

   ERROR: You gave a switch that PRINT does not recognize; or you gave the /B, /D, /M, /Q, /S, or /U switch when you ran PRINT the second or subsequent time. If you gave an unknown switch, try the command again. If you attempted to use one of the mentioned switches, you must restart DOS and run PRINT again with the switch.

10. `filename is currently being printed`
    `filename is in queue`

    INFORMATION: This message tells you what file is being printed and what files are in line to be printed. This message appears whenever you use PRINT with no parameters or when you queue additional files.

11. `List output is not assigned to a device`

    ERROR: The device you gave PRINT is not a recognized device; PRINT aborts. To solve this problem, reissue PRINT and give a correct device name when requested.

12. `filename Pathname too long`

    WARNING: The length of the file specification for `filename` exceeded the 63-character limit. PRINT skips this file and processes any other file name on the command line. You also may have omitted a space. In that case, type the command again. If the 63-character limit was exceeded, create a new subdirectory closer to the root subdirectory, move the file to the new subdirectory (so that there are fewer subdirectories in the chain to the file), and try the PRINT command again.

13. `PRINT queue is empty`

    INFORMATION: No files are in line to be printed by PRINT.

14. `PRINT queue is full`

    WARNING: You attempted to add too many files to PRINT and exceeded the maximum number accepted. The request to add more files fails for each file past the limit. You must wait until PRINT processes a file before you can add another file to the queue.

15. `Resident part of PRINT installed`

    INFORMATION: The first time you use PRINT, this message indicates that PRINT has installed itself in DOS and has increased the size of DOS by about 5,500 bytes.

16. `Disk-error-type error on file filename`

    WARNING: This message appears on the printout. A disk error (`disk-error-type`) occurred when DOS tried to read the file `filename`. PRINT uses its procedure for handling disk errors.

PROMPT
(Set the System Prompt)   *V2, V3, V4—Internal*

Purpose

Customizes the DOS system prompt (A>, or the A prompt).

Syntax

PROMPT *promptstring*

promptstring is the text to be used for the new system prompt.

Meta-Strings

A *meta-string* is a group of characters transformed into another character or characters. To use certain characters (for example, the < or > I/O redirection symbols), you must enter the appropriate meta-string to place the desired character(s) in your *promptstring*. Otherwise, DOS immediately attempts to interpret the character.

All meta-strings begin with the dollar sign ($) and have two characters, including the $. The following list contains metastring characters and their meanings:

Character	What It Produces
$	$, the dollar sign
_ (underscore)	New line (moves to the first position of the next line)
b	|, the vertical *bar*
e	The *e*scape character, CHR$(27)

d	The *d*ate, like the DATE command
h	The backspace character, CHR$(8), which erases the previous character
g	>, the *g*reater-than character
l	<, the *l*ess-than character
n	The curre*n*t disk drive
p	The current disk drive and *p*ath, including the current directory
q	=, the e*q*ual sign
t	The *t*ime, like the TIME command
v	The *v*ersion number of DOS
Any other	Nothing or null; the character is ignored

RECOVER

(Recover files or disk directory)   V2, V3, V4—External

Purpose

Recovers a file with bad sectors or a file from a disk with a damaged directory.

Syntax

To recover a file, use

> *dc:pathc***RECOVER***d:path/filename.ext*

To recover a disk with a damaged directory, use

> *dc:pathc***RECOVER d:**

dc: is the name of the disk drive holding the command.

pathc is the path to the command.

d: is the name of the disk drive holding the damaged file or floppy disk.

path is the path to the directory holding the file to be recovered.

filename.ext is the file to be recovered. Wild cards are allowed, but only the first file that matches the wild-card file name is RECOVERed.

Reference

See Chapter 23.

Messages

1. `Cannot RECOVER a Network drive`

   ERROR: You attempted to run RECOVER on a disk drive that is part of a network. You must pause or disconnect from the network and then rerun RECOVER.

2. `File not found`

   ERROR: RECOVER cannot find the file you specified to be recovered. Check the spelling of the file name, make sure that the file exists on the specified disk drive and directory, and try the command again.

3. `Invalid drive or file name`

   ERROR: One of the following errors occurred: (1) you specified a disk drive that does not exist; (2) you omitted a semicolon in the file name; (3) you misspelled the directory path to the file name; or (4) you failed to give a disk drive name or file name. Check each possibility and try the command again.

4. `Invalid number of parameters`

   ERROR: You specified more than one argument for RECOVER. Perhaps you inserted a space between the disk drive name and path name or between the path name and file name, or you used an illegal character. Check the command line and try the command again.

5. `Press any key to begin recovery of the file(s) on drive d:`

   INFORMATION and WARNING: RECOVER is asking you to confirm that you want to recover a file or all files on disk drive d. If you want RECOVER to attempt the recovery of the file(s) on the disk drive, press any key. If you don't want to RECOVER the file(s) from the disk drive, press Ctrl-Break or Ctrl-C. Be sure to check the command line before pressing the key to begin. RECOVER displays this message for the recovery of a single file or all files.

6. `Warning - directory full`
   `nnn file(s) recovered`

   ERROR: The root directory on the disk is full. No more files can be RECOVERed, and RECOVER stops. You should erase or copy to another disk the files in the root directory in order to free more directory space. Then rerun RECOVER.

RENAME or REN
(Rename file) V1, V2, V3, V4—Internal

Purpose

Changes the name of the disk file(s).

Syntax

RENAME *d:path***filename1**.*ext1* **filename2**.*ext2*

or

REN *d:path***filename1**.*ext1* **filename2**.*ext2*

d: is the name of the disk drive holding the file(s) to be renamed.

path is the path to the file(s) to be renamed.

filename1.*ext1* is the current name of the file. Wild cards are allowed.

filename2.*ext2* is the new name for the file. Wild cards are allowed.

Reference

See Chapter 7.

Messages

1. `Duplicate filename or File not found`

   ERROR: Either you attempted to change a file name to a name that already exists, or the file to be renamed does not exist in the directory. Check the directory for conflicting names. Make sure that the file name exists and that you have spelled it correctly. Then try again.

2. `Invalid number of parameters`

   ERROR: You gave too few or too many file names. You must give two file names. Perhaps you used spaces between the disk drive name and path name or between the path name and file name for the first file. Or you may have used an invalid character in one or both file names.

3. `Missing file name`

   ERROR: You forgot to enter the new name for the file.

REPLACE

(Replace/update files)   *V3.2 and later—External*

Purpose

Selectively replaces files with matching names from one disk to another; selectively adds files from one disk to another.

Syntax

*dc:pathc***REPLACE** *ds:paths***filenames**.*exts dd:pathd* /A/P/R/S/W

With DOS V4, you may add a /U switch:

*dc:pathc***REPLACE** *ds:paths***filenames**.*exts dd:pathd*
/A/P/R/S/W/U

dc: is the name of the disk drive holding the command.

pathc is the path to the command.

ds: is the name of the disk drive holding the replacement files.

paths is the path to the replacement files.

filenames.*exts* is the name of the replacement file(s). Wild cards are allowed.

dd: is the disk drive whose files will be replaced.

pathd is the path to the directory to receive the replacement file(s).

Special Terms

The file(s) that will be added to or that will replace another file(s) is the *source*, represented by an *s* in the term *ds:paths***filenames**.*exts*.

The file(s) that is replaced or the disk and directory that will have the file(s) added is the *destination*, represented by the letter *d* in the term *dd:pathd*. DOS refers to the destination as the *target*.

Switches

/A	*Adds* files from sources that do not exist on the destination.
/P	*Prompts* and asks whether the file should be replaced or added to the destination.
/R	Replaces *read-only* files also.
/S	Replaces files in the current directory and all other *subdirectories* beneath this directory.
/W	Causes REPLACE to prompt and *wait* for the source floppy disk to be inserted.

/U   *Updates* only those files that have a date and time more
                         recent than the date and time of the target file being replaced
                         (DOS V4 and later).

Exit Codes

REPLACE returns the DOS error code. A zero exit code indicates successful
completion. A nonzero exit code indicates an error. Common exit levels are
these:

    2 = No source files were found
    3 = Source or target path is invalid
    5 = Access denied to the file(s) or directory(ies)
    8 = Out of memory
   11 = Invalid parameter, incorrect number of parameters
   15 = Invalid disk drive
   22 = Incorrect version of DOS

Reference

See Chapter 24.

Messages

1. `Access denied filename`

   ERROR: REPLACE has attempted to replace the file `filename` that is
   marked as read-only, and the /R switch was not used; or the file is being
   used by another program or computer and is marked temporarily as
   read-only. In both cases, the problem is with the destination file. If
   `filename` is the source file, another computer or process temporarily
   has marked the source file as write-only.

   If the file you intend to replace has the read-only attribute set, either
   reissue the REPLACE command by using the /R switch or use the
   ATTRIB command to turn off the read-only flag of the file that will be
   replaced (the destination file, not the source file). If this file is being
   used by another program or computer, wait until the other program or
   computer is finished and then run the REPLACE command again.

2. `Add filename? (Y/N)`
   `Adding filename`

   INFORMATION and WARNING: These messages appear if the /A and /P
   switches are used. In the first message, REPLACE asks whether the file
   `filename` should be added to the destination directory. If you type **Y**
   for yes, REPLACE adds the file. The second message then informs you
   that REPLACE is adding `filename`. If you answer **N** for no, REPLACE
   does not add the file, and the second message does not appear.

3. `File cannot be copied onto itself filename`

   WARNING: The source and destination disk and directories are identical. Either you forgot to specify a destination, and the source disk and

directory are the current disk and directory, or you have specified the same disk drive and directory twice. REPLACE does not process `file-name`, but continues.

Check the command line to be sure that you have specified the correct source and destination for REPLACE, and then try the command again.

4. `nnn file(s) added`
   `nnn file(s) replaced`

   INFORMATION: REPLACE indicates how many files were successfully added or replaced. The first message appears when the /A switch is used; the second message appears when the /A switch is not used. The message does not indicate that all potential files were added or replaced successfully. This message appears when at least one file has been added or replaced successfully, regardless of any errors that occurred later.

5. `Invalid parameter`

   ERROR: You have either given a switch that REPLACE does not recognize or forgotten to type the switch character (\ ). Check the command line and try the command again.

6. `Invalid drive specification d:`

   ERROR: You have given for the source or destination a disk drive name (`d:`) that does not exist. Check the command line and try again.

7. `Insufficient disk space – filename:`

   WARNING: The file `filename` could not be added or replaced. If the /A switch was given, there was not enough room on the destination disk to add the file. If the /A switch was not given, the replacement file was larger than the old file and the available free space on the destination disk. REPLACE skips this file and continues.

   To solve this problem, erase any unwanted files from the destination disk and COPY the files that REPLACE did not copy. To add new files, erase any unwanted files from the destination disk and give the REPLACE /A command again.

8. `No files found filename`

   ERROR: REPLACE could not find any files that matched the source file name `filename`. You may have misspelled the source file name, given the disk drive and/or directory name but omitted the file name, given the wrong disk drive or directory name for the source, or put the wrong floppy disk in the disk drive. Check the command line to see whether the correct floppy disk is in the disk drive and then try the command again.

9. `No files added`
   `No files replaced`

   ERROR: REPLACE did not add or replace any files. The first message appears if you give the /A switch; the second message appears if you did not give the /A switch. You may have misspelled the source file name or the destination name, given the wrong source name, given no destination name or the wrong one, or put the wrong floppy disk in the disk drive. Also, because of insufficient disk space, REPLACE might not have been capable of adding or replacing files.

   Be sure that the command line is properly phrased, that the correct floppy disk is in the disk drive, and that sufficient room is on the destination disk for the files. Then try the command again.

10. `Parameters not compatible`

    ERROR: You have given both the /A switch and the /S switch, but they cannot be used in the same REPLACE command. To replace files, omit the /A switch. You cannot add files to more than one directory at a time. To add files to more than one directory, you must issue separate REPLACE commands and specify a different directory to which files should be added each time.

11. `Path not Found pathname`

    ERROR: REPLACE could not find the destination directory path, `pathname`. Either the destination directory name is misspelled or you gave the wrong disk drive name. Try the command again and give the correct destination disk drive name and directory name.

12. `Press any key to begin adding file(s)`
    `Press any key to begin replacing file(s)`

    INFORMATION: You have used the /W switch, and REPLACE is waiting for you to strike a key to begin reading the source files. The first message (adding files) appears if the /A switch is used; the second message (replacing files) appears if the /A switch is not used. Press any key to make REPLACE continue.

13. `Replace filename? (Y/N)`
    `Replacing filename`

    INFORMATION and WARNING: These messages appear if the /P switch but not the /A switch is used. The first message queries whether the file name should be replaced on the destination directory. If you type **Y** for yes, REPLACE replaces the old file with the file from the source and then displays the second message. If you answer **N** for no, REPLACE does not add the file, and the second message does not appear.

14. `Source path required`

    ERROR: You either mistyped the command or omitted the source file name. You must specify a source file name to REPLACE. Check the command line and try again.

RESTORE
(Restore backed-up files)   *V2, V3, V4—External*

Purpose

Restores one or more backup files from a floppy disk or hard disk onto another floppy disk or hard disk. This command complements the BACKUP command.

Syntax

dc:path**RESTORE d1:** *d2:path/filename.ext /S /P /M /N*
    B:date /A:date /L:time /E:time

dc: is the name of the disk drive holding the command.

path\\ is the path to the command.

d1: is the name of the disk drive holding the backup file(s).

d2: is the disk drive to receive the restored file(s).

path\\ is the path name of the path to the directory to receive the restored file(s).

filename.ext is the name of the file you want to restore. Wild cards are allowed.

Switches

/S	Restores files in the current directory and all other *subdirectories* beneath this directory.
/P	Causes a *prompt* to ask whether to restore a file that has been changed since the last backup or a file that is marked as read-only.
/M	Restores all files *modified* or deleted since the backup set was made.
/N	Restores all files that *no longer* exist on the destination.
/B:date	Restores all files created or modified on or *before* the date.
/A:date	Restores all files created or modified on or *after* the *date*.
/L:time	Restores all files created or modified at or *later* than the specified *time*.
/E:time	Restores all files modified at or *earlier than* the specified time.

Exit Codes

0 = Normal completion
1 = No files were found to restore
3 = Terminated by the operator (through Ctrl-Break or Esc)
4 = Terminated by an encountered error

Reference

See Chapter 24.

Messages

1. `*** Files were backed up mm/dd/yy ***`

   INFORMATION: RESTORE displays the date the files were backed up. The format of the date varies, depending on the setting of your country code. (See Chapter 17 on CONFIG.SYS.)

2. `filename`
   `File creation error`

   ERROR: DOS found an error while attempting to restore the file `file-name`, and RESTORE stops. You should run CHKDSK on the receiving disk to see whether it has physical problems. For any messages that appear, follow the directions under CHKDSK in the *Command Reference*.

3. `Insert backup diskette nn in drive d:`
   `Strike any key when ready`

   INFORMATION: RESTORE wants the next floppy disk in sequence. This message appears when you are restoring files that were backed up onto floppy disks. Insert the next floppy disk in drive d and press any key.

4. `Insert restore target in drive d:`
   `Strike any key when ready`

   RESTORE is asking you to place in drive d the floppy disk to receive the restored files. This message appears only when you are restoring files onto floppy disks. Insert the target floppy disk in drive d and press any key.

5. `Invalid drive specification`

   ERROR: You failed to specify the disk drive holding the backup files, gave the name of a disk drive that does not exist, or have a resident (background) program that is interfering with RESTORE. Check each of these possibilities and try the command again.

6. `Invalid number of parameters`

   ERROR: You failed to specify the disk drive holding the backup files, or you gave too many drive or file names. A possible cause is a space or other illegal character in a file name. Check the command line and try again.

7. `Invalid parameter`

   ERROR: You gave a switch that RESTORE did not recognize, or you gave a path and/or file name for the disk drive holding the backup files (**d1:**). Check the command line and try again.

8. `Invalid path`

   ERROR: RESTORE was unable to create or use a subdirectory in another subdirectory. Run CHKDSK and follow the directions in the *Command Reference*.

9. `*** Not able to restore file ***`

   WARNING: Either the file listed before this message could not be restored because another computer or program is using the file, or you stopped RESTORE with a Ctrl-Break sequence.

   If you did not stop RESTORE, then after the program is finished, have the other computer or program stop; rerun RESTORE for just this file.

10. `*** Restoring files from drive d: ***`

    INFORMATION: RESTORE is getting the backup files from the disk or floppy disk in drive d.

11. `Source does not contain backup files`

    ERROR: RESTORE could not find any files that were backed up with the BACKUP command. BACKUP malfunctioned when it was backing up files, you inserted the wrong floppy disk (if you were restoring from floppy disks), or BACKUP could not find the \BACKUP subdirectory (if you were restoring files from a hard disk).

    Run DIR to get a directory listing of the floppy disk or hard disk. Look for the file BACKUPID.@@@ on the floppy disk. If this file is missing, either the floppy disk is not a backup or BACKUP malfunctioned (DOS V3.0 only). If the floppy disk is a backup, you cannot restore the files. Use your previous backup set.

    Look for the \BACKUP subdirectory in the root directory on the hard disk. If this subdirectory is missing, the backup files are missing also. Restart DOS and check again. Run CHKDSK if necessary. If the directory is still missing, the backup files have been lost.

12. `Source and target drives are the same`

    ERROR: RESTORE "believes" that the disk drive holding the backup files is the same as the drive designated to receive the restored files. You may have forgotten to specify the disk drive holding the backup files or the target disk. If you have a system with one floppy disk drive and you're attempting to RESTORE files onto a floppy disk, specify drives A and B.

13. `System files restored`
`Target disk may not be bootable`

WARNING: You have restored the three system files (IBMBIO.COM, IBMDOS.COM, and COMMAND.COM) from the backup floppy disks. If these files are from a previous version of DOS, the receiving disk cannot be used to start (boot) DOS. If you know that the system files were from DOS V3.x (the version you are currently using), ignore this message. Otherwise, run SYS on the disk to put current versions of these three files on the disk.

14. `Target is full`
`The last file was not restored`

ERROR: RESTORE was stopped before the current file (listed in the line above this message) was fully restored, because the receiving disk is full. RESTORE deletes the partially restored file.

15. `Warning! Diskette is out of sequence`
`Replace the diskette or continue if okay`
`Strike any key when ready`

WARNING: You inserted a backup floppy disk out of order. Place the correct floppy disk in the drive and continue. You may continue with the wrong floppy disk if you do not want to restore any files and if you are not in the middle of a large file (backed up onto two or more floppy disks) that has been partially restored. If a file was partially restored, RESTORE will want to restore the rest of the file. RESTORE will continue to display this message until the right floppy disk is inserted.

16. `Warning! File filename`
`was changed after it was backed up`
`or is a read-only file`
`Replace the file (Y/N)?`

WARNING: This message appears when you give the /P switch. The file `filename` already exists on the hard disk and is marked as read-only, or the file's date is later than that of the backup copy, which means that the backup copy may be out of date. Answer **Y** to replace the preexisting file with the backup copy or **N** to skip that file.

17. `Warning! No files were found to restore`

WARNING: No files matching the file specifications you gave were found on the backup floppy disks. This message also can occur if you reset SWITCHAR.

18. `Unrecoverable file sharing error`

WARNING: With SHARE.EXE loaded, RESTORE cannot restore a file because another program is using the file or because the file-sharing table is full. The file is not restored.

RMDIR or RD
(Remove directory)   *V2, V3, V4—Internal*

Purpose

Removes a subdirectory.

Syntax

    RMDIR *d:***path**

or

    RD *d:***path**

d: is the name of the drive holding the subdirectory.

path is the name of the path to the subdirectory. The last path name is the subdirectory you want to delete.

Reference

See Chapter 13.

Message

```
Invalid path, not directory
or directory not empty
```

RMDIR did not remove the specified directory because one of the following occurred: (1) you gave an invalid directory in the path; (2) the subdirectory still has files in it other than the **.** and **..** entries; or (3) you misspelled the path or directory name to be removed. Check each possibility and try again.

SELECT
(Select country configuration)   *V3, V4—External*

Purpose

Creates a hard disk or floppy disk with the DOS files and prepares CONFIG.SYS and AUTOEXEC.BAT files configured for your country. For DOS V4, SELECT was changed into a full-featured, menu-oriented DOS installation utility.

Syntax

For DOS V3.x:

    *dc:pathc***SELECT** *ds: dd:pathd* **countrycode keycode**

dc: is the name of the disk drive holding the command.

pathc is the path to the command.

ds: is the country code (see listing).
dd: is the keyboard code (see listing).

The country and keyboard codes for SELECT are listed in table 18.2 in Chapter 18.

Reference

See Chapters 3 and 18.

Messages

1. `Cannot execute A:program_name`

   ERROR: SELECT could not find `program_name` on disk drive A. The file `program_name` may be FORMAT or XCOPY for DOS V3.2 and later; DISKCOPY for DOS V3.1 and earlier; and DISKCOMP.COM for DOS V3.0. You most likely started SELECT without the DOS Startup or master floppy disk in drive A. Check the floppy disk in drive A and try again.

2. `File creation error`

   ERROR: SELECT could not create the CONFIG.SYS or AUTOEXEC.BAT file. This error usually occurs because the target floppy disk (the floppy disk created by SELECT) has a flaw. Run SELECT again. If the problem occurs again, use a different blank floppy disk as the target.

3. `Failure to access COUNTRY.SYS`
   `Failure to access KEYBOARD.SYS`

   ERROR: SELECT could not open the COUNTRY.SYS file (first message) or the KEYBOARD.SYS file (second message) on the source floppy disk to verify the country or keyboard code. Either the wrong floppy disk is in the disk drive, or you specified the wrong source disk drive. If you gave the wrong source disk drive, try the command again.

   If you believe that the correct floppy disk is in the disk drive, issue a DIR command and look for the COUNTRY.SYS and KEYBOARD.SYS files. If these files do not appear, you'll need a copy of your DOS Startup floppy disk. Put the correct floppy disk in the drive and try the command again.

4. `Incorrect number of parameters`

   ERROR: You omitted the country code and/or the keyboard code, or forgot to leave a space between the disk drive names, the country code, and the keyboard code. Be sure that the command line was phrased properly and that you have given both the country and keyboard code; then try the command again.

5. `Invalid country code`
   `Invalid keyboard code`

   ERROR: You omitted the country or keyboard code, or you forgot to leave a space between the disk drive names, the country code, and the keyboard code. Be sure that the command line was phrased properly and that you have given both the country and keyboard code; then try the command again.

6. `Invalid drive specification`

   ERROR: You have given a nonexistent disk drive name for the source or destination, used a disk drive name other than A: or B: for the source disk drive, omitted the source disk drive and named A: as the destination disk drive, or specified the same disk drive as the source and destination. Check the disk drive names and try the command again.

7. `Invalid parameter`

   ERROR: You forgot to place a colon after the source or destination disk drive name. Check the command line and try the command again.

8. `Invalid Path`

   ERROR: The path you gave for the destination directory is misspelled, has incorrect characters, or is longer than 63 characters. Check the destination path name used and try the command again.

9. `Invalid signature in COUNTRY.SYS file`
   `Invalid signature in KEYBOARD.SYS file`

   ERROR: While verifying the country or keyboard information in the COUNTRY.SYS or KEYBOARD.SYS file, SELECT determined that the named file was incorrect. The COUNTRY.SYS or KEYBOARD.SYS file exists, but it has been damaged. The floppy disk holding the file or files is bad, the file has been altered, or another file has been copied over the COUNTRY.SYS or KEYBOARD.SYS file.

   Get another copy of your original DOS Startup floppy disk. Attempt to copy the correct .SYS file over the invalid file. If no error occurs when you copy the file, try the SELECT command again. If an error occurs, reformat or retire the copy of your DOS Startup floppy disk. If the `invalid signature` message appears again, you probably have a bad copy of DOS. See your dealer for a replacement.

10. `Read error, COUNTRY.SYS`
    `Read error, KEYBOARD.SYS`

    ERROR: While reading the COUNTRY.SYS or KEYBOARD.SYS file to verify country or keyboard information, SELECT encountered a disk error. The floppy disk holding the file is bad, or the floppy disk drive is bad.

    Get another copy of your original DOS Startup floppy disk. Attempt to copy the correct .SYS file over the invalid file. If no error message is displayed when you copy the file, try the SELECT command again. If an error message is given, reformat or retire the old copy of your DOS Startup floppy disk and make another copy of the original Startup floppy disk. If you can make a copy of the original Startup floppy disk, the disk drive works correctly, and you should try the SELECT command again with this copy. If DISKCOPY reports an error with the source floppy disk, the disk drive is probably bad.

11. `SELECT is used to install DOS the first time. SELECT erases everything on the specified target and then installs DOS. Do you want to continue (Y/N)?`

   INFORMATION and WARNING: This message appears when you start SELECT. The message informs you that SELECT will format a disk and copy the needed files to the disk. Be sure that the DOS Startup floppy disk is in the correct disk drive. Answer **Y** if you want to continue, **N** if you do not want to continue.

12. `Unable to create directory`

   ERROR: SELECT has formatted the destination disk but was unable to create the destination directory. The most probable reason is that the path name given for the destination directory contains invalid characters or is a reserved device name. Check the spelling of the destination path name and try the command again.

SET
(Set/show environment)   *V2, V3, V4—Internal*

Purpose

Sets or shows the system environment.

Syntax

To display the environment, use

    SET

To add to or alter the environment, use

    SET name = *string*

name is the name of the string you want to add to the environment.

string is the information you want to store in the environment.

Special Terms

The *environment* is an area in RAM reserved for alphanumeric information that may be examined and used by DOS commands or user programs. For example, the environment usually contains COMSPEC, which is the location of COM-

MAND.COM; PATH, the additional paths for finding programs and batch files; and PROMPT, the string defining the DOS system prompt.

Reference

See Chapter 15.

SHARE

(Check shared files)   *V3, V4—External*

Purpose

Enables DOS support for file and record locking. For DOS V4, also used to support large disk partitions.

Syntax

*dc:pathc***SHARE** */F:name_space /L:numlocks*

dc: is the name of the disk drive holding the command.

pathc is the path to the command.

Switches

/F:name_space	Sets the amount of memory space (*name_space* bytes large) used for file sharing.
/L:numlocks	Sets the maximum number (*numlocks*) of file/record locks to use.

Messages

1. `Incorrect parameter`

   ERROR: You gave a switch that SHARE does not recognize, or you put a space between the colon and the letter of the switch or between the switch and the number. Other possible causes are that you omitted the number that goes with the switch, or you omitted the colon.

2. `SHARE already loaded`

   ERROR: You attempted to load SHARE a second time. SHARE simply ignores any attempt to load itself more than once.

SORT
(Sort string filter)   *V2, V3, V4—External*

Purpose

Reads lines from the standard input device, performs an ASCII sort of the lines, and then writes the lines to the standard output device. The sorting may be in ascending or descending order and may start at any column in the line.

Syntax

> *dc:pathc***SORT** */R* */+c*

dc: is the name of the disk drive holding the command.

pathc is the path to the command.

Switches

/R — Sorts in *reverse* order. Thus the letter Z comes first, and the letter A comes last.

/+c — Starts sorting with column number *c*.

Reference

See Chapter 12.

Messages

1. `Invalid parameter`

   ERROR: You gave a switch that SORT does not recognize, forgot the plus sign for the column-sorting switch, or forgot to enter the number for the column-sorting switch. Check the command line and try again.

2. `SORT: Insufficient disk space`

   ERROR: SORT ran out of disk space for its temporary files or ran out of disk space when writing the output file. Free some disk space by deleting unneeded files, or move the file to a disk with more space. Try the command again.

   If you believe you have sufficient room on the disk, run CHKDSK to see whether a problem exists on the disk. If CHKDSK detects a problem, follow the directions for CHKDSK in the *Command Reference*.

3. `SORT: Insufficient memory`

   ERROR: You do not have enough free memory to run SORT on this file. See the entry `Insufficient memory` under "General Messages" at the beginning of the *Command Reference*.

SUBST
(Substitute path name)   *V3.1, V4—External*

Purpose

Creates an alias disk drive name for a subdirectory; used principally with programs that do not use path names.

Syntax

To establish an alias, use

    *dc:pathc***SUBST d1:** *d2:***pathname**

To delete an alias, use

    *dc:pathc***SUBST d1:** **/D**

To see the current aliases, use

    *dc:pathc***SUBST**

dc: is the name of the disk drive holding the command.

pathc is the path to the command.

d1: is a valid disk drive name that becomes the alias (or nickname). **d1:** may be a nonexistent disk drive.

*d2:***pathname** is the valid disk drive name and directory path that will be nicknamed **d1:**.

Switch

/D   *Disconnects* the alias.

Reference

See Chapter 25.

Messages

1. `Cannot SUBST a network drive`

   ERROR: You have attempted to use as the alias or nicknamed disk drive a disk drive owned by another computer. You cannot use a networked disk drive with SUBST, nor can you "cover" a network disk drive with a SUBST command.

2. `Invalid Parameter`

   ERROR: One of the following errors occurred: (1) the alias disk drive name exceeded the limit set by the LASTDRIVE command; (2) the alias disk drive name is the same as the current disk drive name; (3) you did not give a correct disk drive with the /D (disconnect) switch; (4) you specified a switch that SUBST doesn't recognize; or (5) you used the /D switch on the current disk drive.

3. `Invalid path`

ERROR: The directory path you specified does not exist. Make sure that the disk drive name is correct and that the path name does exist.

4. `Incorrect number of parameters`

ERROR: You omitted a parameter when you gave the command. Perhaps you forgot to give the alias or the disk drive name and path name, or you omitted the /D switch. Check the command line and try again.

SYS
(Place the operating system on the disk)　　　*V1, V2, V3, V4-External*

Purpose

Places a copy of DOS on the specified floppy disk or hard disk.

Syntax

*dc:pathc***SYS d:**

For DOS V4 you also may specify a source drive for the system files:

*dc:pathc***SYS d: d2:**

dc: is the name of the disk drive holding the command.

pathc is the path to the command.

d: is the disk drive to receive the copy of DOS.

d2: is the source drive for the system films (DOS V4 only).

Messages

1. `Cannot SYS to a Network drive`

ERROR: You cannot put the system on a networked disk drive. If the disk drive is owned by another computer, use a different disk drive. If your disk drive is being shared, pause the disk drive, perform the command, and then continue.

2. `Incompatible system size`

ERROR: Although the floppy disk or hard disk previously accepted IBMBIO.COM and IBMDOS.COM, DOS cannot put the new version of the files onto the floppy disk. These two files are larger in DOS V3 and V4 than in DOS V1 or V2. This message usually appears when you are putting the system files on DOS V1 floppy disks but occasionally is displayed when you are placing the two files on a DOS V2 floppy disk.

FORMAT a new floppy disk with the /S (system) switch and COPY files from the old floppy disk to the new floppy disk. Be sure that you don't copy the old COMMAND.COM file.

3. `Invalid drive specification`

ERROR: You gave a disk drive name that does not exist.

4. `Invalid parameter`

ERROR: You failed to specify the name of the disk drive to hold the system files.

5. `No room for system on destination disk`

ERROR: The floppy disk or hard disk was not formatted with the necessary reserved space for DOS. You cannot put the system on this floppy disk.

6. `No system on default disk drive`
   `Insert system disk in drive d:`
   `and strike any key when ready`

INFORMATION: DOS tried to load itself into memory but could not find IBMBIO.COM, IBMDOS.COM, and/or COMMAND.COM. Loading these files into memory is a required step before SYS can place the operating system on a floppy disk or hard disk. Put the floppy disk that holds all three programs into drive d and press a key.

7. `System transferred`

INFORMATION: DOS successfully placed IBMBIO.COM and IBMDOS.COM on the target floppy disk.

TIME

(Set/show the time)   *V1.0—External*
                    V1.1, V2, V3, V4—Internal

Purpose

Sets and shows the system time.

Syntax

TIME *hh:mm:ss.xx*

hh is the one- or two-digit number for hours (0 to 23).

mm is the one- or two-digit number for minutes (0 to 60).

ss is the one- or two-digit number for seconds (0 to 60).

xx is the one- or two-digit number for hundredths of a second (0 to 99).

Note: Depending on the setting of the country code in your CONFIG.SYS file, a comma may be the decimal separator between seconds and hundredths of seconds.

Reference

See Chapter 1.

Message

```
Invalid time
```

ERROR: You entered a nonsense time or did not punctuate the time correctly. Check your typing and try again.

TREE
(Display all directories)   *V2, V3, V4—External*

Purpose

Displays all the subdirectories on a disk and optionally displays all the files in each directory.

Syntax

*dc:pathc***TREE** *d: /F*

dc: is the name of the disk drive holding the command.

pathc is the path to the command.

d: is the name of the disk drive holding the disk you want to examine.

Switch

/F   Displays all *files* in the directories.

Reference

See Chapter 14.

Messages

1. `Invalid drive specification`

   ERROR: You gave the name of a nonexistent disk drive. Be sure that the disk drive exists (is not part of a SUBST command) and that the drive letter is correct.

2. Invalid path

   ERROR: TREE could not use a subdirectory because something is wrong with the directory file. Run CHKDSK without the /F switch to determine what is wrong with the hard disk or floppy disk; then take the necessary corrective actions.

3. Invalid parameter

   ERROR: You entered a switch that TREE does not recognize, or you omitted a colon from the disk drive name.

4. No sub-directories exist

   INFORMATION: The root directory of the disk you specified has no sub-directories. If you know that the disk should have subdirectories, issue DIR for the hard disk or floppy disk, or run CHKDSK.

TYPE
(Type file on screen)   *V1, V2, V3, V4—Internal*

Purpose
Displays the contents of the file on the screen.

Syntax
TYPE *d:path***filename**.*ext*

d: is the name of the disk drive holding the file to TYPE.

path is the DOS path to the file.

filename.*ext* is the name of the file to TYPE. Wild cards are not permitted.

Reference
See Chapter 11.

VER
(Display version number)   *V2, V3, V4—Internal*

Purpose
Shows the DOS version number on the video display.

Syntax
VER

VERIFY

(Set/show disk verification)   *V2, V3, V4—Internal*

Purpose

Sets the computer to check the accuracy of data written to a disk to ensure that information is recorded properly; shows whether the data has been checked.

Syntax

To show the verify status, use

> **VERIFY**

To set the verify status, use either

> **VERIFY ON**

or

> **VERIFY OFF**

Reference

See Chapter 24.

Message

`Must specify ON or OFF`

ERROR: You entered a word other than ON or OFF after the VERIFY command.

VOL

(Display volume label)   *V2, V3, V4—Internal*

Purpose

Displays the volume label of the disk, if the label exists.

Syntax

> **VOL** *d:*

d: is the name of the disk drive whose label you want to display.

Messages

1. `Invalid drive specification`

   ERROR: You have given a nonexistent disk drive name. Be sure that the disk drive exists (is not part of a SUBST command) and that you have given the correct disk drive name.

2. `Volume in drive d has no label`

INFORMATION: The hard disk or floppy disk does not have a volume label.

XCOPY
(Extended COPY)   *V3.2 and later—External*

Purpose
Selectively copies files from one or more subdirectories.

Syntax
dc:pathc**XCOPY** *ds:paths**filenames.exts*
    dd:pathd*filenamed.extd* /A/D/E/M/P/S/V/W

dc: is the name of the disk drive holding the command.

pathc\\ is the path to the command.

ds: is the disk drive holding the files to be copied (the source).

paths\\ is the starting directory path to the files to be copied.

filenames.ext is the name of the file(s) to be copied. Wild cards are allowed.

dd: is the disk drive that will receive the copied files (the destination). DOS refers to the destination drive as the *target*.

pathd\\ is the starting directory that will receive the copied files.

filenamed.extd is the new name of the files that are copied. Wild cards are allowed.

Switches
/A	Copies files whose *archive* flag is on, but does not turn off the archive flag (similar to the /M switch).
/E	Creates parallel subdirectories on the destination disk even if the created subdirectory is *empty*.
/D:date	Copies files that were changed or created on or after the specified *date*. The form of *date* depends on the setting of the COUNTRY directive in CONFIG.SYS.
/M	Copies files whose archive flag is on (*modified* files) and turns the archive flag off (similar to the /A switch).
/P	Causes XCOPY to *prompt* and ask whether a file should be copied.

/S	Copies files from this directory and all subsequent *subdirectories*.
/V	*Verifies* that the copy has been recorded correctly.
/W	Causes XCOPY to prompt and *wait* for the correct source floppy disk to be inserted.

Reference

See Chapter 20.

Messages

1. Access denied

   ERROR: You attempted to copy over a file marked as read-only, the destination file is being used by another program or computer and is temporarily marked as read-only, or the source and destination files are the same.

   If the file you intend to copy over has the read-only attribute set, use the ATTRIB command to turn off the read-only flag. If this file is being used by another program or computer, wait until the other program or computer is done and then copy the file. If the file is on another computer and you do not have permission to copy over the file, ask the operator to copy the file for you. Check the command line to make sure that the source and destination file specifications are not identical.

2. Cannot perform a cyclic copy

   ERROR: You have used the /S switch, and one or more of the destination directories are subdirectories of the source directories. Using the files in Appendix B, the command

   XCOPY C:\BIN C:\HARDDISK /S

   would cause this error message to appear. BIN and its subsequent subdirectories are the source. HARDDISK is a subdirectory of BIN. When the /S switch is given, XCOPY will not copy to destination directories that are part of the source directories. If you must copy files from more than one directory, issue individual XCOPY commands to copy the directories one at a time.

3. Cannot XCOPY from a reserved device
   Cannot XCOPY to a reserved device

   ERROR: The source or destination file name is a device name. XCOPY cannot copy to or from devices. You may have misspelled one of the file names.

4. Does %s specify a file name
or directory name on the target
(F = file, D = directory)?

INFORMATION: You have given a destination file name in which the final name does not exist as a directory. XCOPY does not know whether the final name in the destination is a file name of a directory.

If the destination name is a directory, answer **D** for directory. XCOPY creates the needed directory and begins copying files to it. If the destination name is a file name, XCOPY copies files to this file.

5. File cannot be copied onto itself

ERROR: You attempted to copy a file back to the same disk and directory with the same file name. This message usually is displayed after you misspell or omit parts of the source or destination drive, path, or file name. Check your spelling and the source and destination names; then try the command again.

6. File creation error

ERROR: XCOPY cannot create the copy of the file. Either a file exists in the destination disk and directory by the same name and is marked read-only, or the directory is full.

See whether a file by the same name exists and whether it is read-only (use **ATTRIB filename**). If the file is marked read-only, either clear the flag by using ATTRIB or give the source file a new name when you COPY or XCOPY.

If you copy to the root directory of the disk, the root directory may not be able to hold additional entries. Delete or move (copy and then erase) files from the root directory and try the command again. If you copy to a subdirectory, run CHKDSK without the /F switch to determine whether the subdirectory has a problem.

7. filename File not found

ERROR: XCOPY cannot find any files that match the source file name, filename. Either you gave a directory name of a file that does not exist or you mistyped a name.

Check to see which files are transferred already. Determine whether the directory and file names are spelled correctly and whether the path is correct. Then try again.

8. nnn File(s) copied

INFORMATION: XCOPY has copied nnn files to the destination disk. This message appears regardless of any errors that may have occurred.

9. `Insufficient disk space`

ERROR: XCOPY has run out of room on the destination disk. The file being copied when the error is encountered is erased from the destination. Either delete any unneeded files from the destination disk or use a different floppy disk; then try the command again.

10. `Invalid date`

ERROR: You have given an improperly phrased or nonsense date.

11. `Invalid drive specification`

ERROR: You specified a nonexistent disk drive in the source or destination, or you have forgotten the colon after the disk drive name. Check the spelling on the command line and try the command again.

12. `Invalid number of parameters`

ERROR: You omitted the source and destination file name. Check the spelling and the spacing of the command line and try the command again.

13. `Invalid parameter`

ERROR: You have given a switch that XCOPY does not recognize, forgotten to give the switch character before a switch, or given too many file names. Check the spelling on the command line and try the command again.

14. `Invalid path`

ERROR: The directory path has an illegal character, or your entry for the source or destination is more than 63 characters long. You either forgot a space between the source and destination file names or mistyped a name. Check the spacing and spelling on the command line and try the command again.

15. `Look Violation`

ERROR: XCOPY attempts to read a file being used by another computer or process, and the file is locked. Try to find the computer or process that has the locked file; try the command again when the file is free.

16. `Path not found`

ERROR: You have given a source directory name that does not exist, used the wrong directory name (a directory not in the path), or mistyped a name. Issue a DIR command to ensure that the directory you have specified is correct; check the spelling on the command and try the command again.

17. `Path too long`

ERROR: A directory path name for the source or destination exceeds 63 characters. A space may be missing between the source and destination file name. Check the command line. If the line is improperly phrased, try the command again with the correct phrasing. If the path has too many characters, move to the lowest possible subdirectory and try the command again with a shorter path name.

18. Press any key to begin copying file(s)

    INFORMATION: You have used the /W switch, and WXCOPY is waiting for you to press a key. If necessary, change floppy disks. Press any key for XCOPY to continue.

19. Reading source file(s) . . .

    INFORMATION: XCOPY is reading the directories of the source for file names.

20. Sharing Violation

    ERROR: Another computer or process is using the file that XCOPY is attempting to copy. The file is marked so that XCOPY cannot read or write to the file. Wait for the other computer or process to finish with the file; then try the command again.

21. Too many open files

    ERROR: XCOPY attempted to open the file whose name appears above this message but was prohibited by DOS because not enough file handles were available. Either another process on your computer is using all available file handles, or your setting of FILES= in CONFIG.SYS is too low.

    If no other process is active on your computer, edit your CONFIG.SYS file and increase the number of files given to the FILES directive. Restart your system and try the command again. If another process is active, wait for it to finish and then try the command again.

22. Unable to create directory

    ERROR: XCOPY cannot create a subdirectory on the destination disk. Part of the path name for the destination is wrong or misspelled, the root directory of the disk is full, the disk is full, a file by the same name as the created directory already exists, or the directory name is a device name.

    Be sure that the destination name is correct. Check the destination disk by using the DIR command. If the disk or the root directory is full, erase files or use another destination disk. If a file exists that has the same name as the intended directory, either rename the file or change the name of the directory when you issue the XCOPY command.

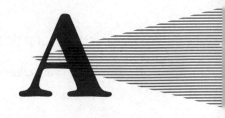

A

Changes between Versions of DOS

Several major changes occurred between DOS V2 and V3. Additional revisions occurred between DOS V3-3.3 and between V3.3 and V4. All these changes are described briefly in this appendix.

Changes between DOS V2.x and DOS V3.0

DOS V3.0 offers several new commands, changed commands, and changed features.

New CONFIG.SYS Features

The following CONFIG.SYS directives are available in V3.0:

COUNTRY	Allows DOS to change its date, time, and other characteristics for international use
FCBS	Controls DOS's reactions to a program's use of PC DOS V1 file handling
LASTDRIVE	Sets the last real or nonreal disk drive that DOS will use
VDISK.SYS	Provides additional RAM (virtual) disk space

The undocumented SWITCHAR directive was dropped.

New Commands

The following commands were added to PC DOS V3.0:

ATTRIB	Enables the user to set the read-only attribute of a file
GRAFTABL	Allows legible display of some graphics characters if you use the Color/Graphics Adapter in medium-resolution graphics mode
KEYBxx	Changes the keyboard layout for different languages
LABEL	Enables a user to add, change, or delete a disk's volume label
SELECT	Enables a user to customize the start-up disk for use with languages other than English
SHARE	Provides file sharing (file and record locking)

Changed Commands

The following commands were changed between DOS V2 and V3:

BACKUP and RESTORE	Includes the backing up of floppy disks and enables backups to be placed on another hard disk
DATE and TIME	Supports international date and time formats
FORMAT	Includes the /4 switch to format 360K floppy disks on 1.2M disk drives; also warns when a hard disk is to be formatted
GRAPHICS	Includes support for the IBM Personal Computer Compact and Color Printers

Changed Features

With PC DOS V3.0, a drive name and a path name can now be specified before an external command or program name. You can run programs that do not reside in the current directory or in a directory specified in the PATH command.

Changes between DOS V3.0 and V3.1

The following changes were made between DOS V3.0 and V3.1.

New Commands/Features

The following commands are available under PC DOS V3.1:

JOIN   Enables the user to connect the directory structures of two different disk drives, thus creating "one" disk drive

SUBST   Enables a subdirectory to be used as though it were a disk drive

DOS V3.1 supports the IBM PC Network commands.

Changed Commands

The following commands were changed in V3.1:

LABEL   Prompts the user before deleting a volume label

SHELL   Includes the */E:size* switch; size in 16-byte paragraphs

TREE   Displays files in the root directory when the */F* switch is used

Changes between DOS V3.1 and V3.2

The following changes were made between DOS V3.1 and V3.2.

New CONFIG.SYS Features

STACKS   Sets the number and size of the DOS internal stacks

The DRIVER.SYS device driver was added to support various-sized floppy disks, particularly 720K microfloppy drives on Personal Computers.

New Feature

Support for the IBM Token Ring was added.

New Commands

REPLACE   Selectively updates files in one or many directories; adds missing files to a directory

XCOPY   Copies files from one or more directories to another; selectively copies files

Changed Commands/Directives

ATTRIB	+*A*/-*A* switch added; controls the archive attribute of files
COMMAND	/*E* switch added; supports the environment size
DISKCOPY/DISKCOMP	Support for 720K floppy disks
FORMAT	Supports formatting of 720K floppy disks; requests verification before formatting a nonremovable disk that has a volume label; disk drive name required
SELECT	Formats the hard disk and copies DOS files
SHELL	/*E:size* switch specifies the environment size in bytes, not 16-byte paragraphs

Changes between DOS V3.2 and V3.3

The following changes were made between DOS V3.2 and V3.3.

New CONFIG.SYS Options

The following device drivers for use with the DEVICE directive were added:

DISPLAY.SYS	Supports code pages (multiple fonts) on EGA, VGA, and PC Convertible displays
PRINTER.SYS	Supports code pages (multiple fonts) on the IBM ProPrinter and Quietwriter III printers

New Features

Support was added for 1.44M microfloppy disks, for COM4: and 19,200 baud rates, and for switchable code pages (international character fonts).

New Commands

The following commands were added to PC DOS V3.3:

APPEND	A PATH-like command for data files
CHCP	Provides code page changing
FASTOPEN	Provides a directory-caching program for hard disks
NLSFUNC	Provides support for additional character sets (code pages) and for country-dependent information

Changed Commands/Directives

The following commands and CONFIG.SYS directives were changed for DOS V3.3:

ATTRIB
: /S switch added to allow changing the attributes of files in subdirectories

BACKUP
: Has the /F switch to format floppy disks, the /T switch to back up files based on their time, and the /L switch to produce a log file; also places all backed-up files into a single file

batch files
: Adds support for using the environment variable (%variable%), @ for suppressing display of a line, and the CALL subcommand for running a second batch file and returning control to the first batch file

BUFFERS
: Default buffers based on random-access memory in the computer

COUNTRY
: Adds support for code pages and a separate country information file (COUNTRY.SYS)

DATE and TIME
: Sets the computer's clock/calendar

DISKCOPY/DISKCOMP
: Supports 1.44M floppy disks

FDISK
: Supports multiple logical disks on a large hard disk

FORMAT
: Adds the /N switch for number of sectors and the /T switch for number of tracks

GRAFTABL
: Supports code pages; also supports additional devices and higher baud rates

KEYB
: Replaces the KEYBxx programs and supports additional layouts

MODE
: Supports code pages; also supports additional devices and higher baud rate

RESTORE
: Adds the /N switch to restore erased or modified files, the /B switch to restore files modified before a given date, and the /L and /E switches to restore files modified after or before a given time

SHELL
: Default environment size changed to from 128 to 160 bytes

Changes between DOS V3.3 and V4

The following changes were made between DOS V3.3 and DOS V4.

New CONFIG.SYS Features

INSTALL	Allows loading of terminate-and-stay-resident programs that were previously loaded from the DOS command prompt or in the AUTOEXEC.BAT file; includes FASTOPEN.EXE, KEYB.COM, NLSFUNC.EXE, and SHARE.EXE
REM	Allows the insertion of remarks in a CONFIG.SYS file, which DOS will ignore when the computer boots
SWITCHES	Disables Enhanced Keyboard functions so that software that cannot use those functions will remain compatible
XMA2EMS.SYS	A new device driver for expanded memory
XMAEM.SYS	Allows emulation of an expanded memory adapter on 80386 machines

New Features

A new user interface, the DOS Shell, allows the running of programs and the management of files using a graphics- or text-oriented menu system. Many error messages were changed, and error checking was refined.

New Commands

MEM	Provides a report on available conventional, extended, and expanded memory and lists how much of each is unused
TRUENAME	Lists the actual name of a drive or directory affected by a JOIN or SUBST command

Changed Commands/Directives

The following commands and CONFIG.SYS directives were changed between DOS V3.3 and V4:

ANSI.SYS	Gained three new parameters: /X, which redefines keys added to Enhanced Keyboards; /L, which tells DOS to override applications program that reset the

	number of screen rows to 25; and /K, which turns off extended keyboard functions to comply with noncompatible software
APPEND	Can ignore file operations that already include a drive or path in the original specification
BACKUP	Automatically formats target floppy disks if necessary
BUFFERS	Allows the /X switch, which tells DOS to use expanded memory. You can specify up to 10,000 buffers and 1 to 8 *look-ahead* buffers
CHKDSK	Shows the disk's serial number and tells the size and number of allocation units
COUNTRY	Provides support for Japanese, Korean, and Chinese characters—on special Asian hardware only
DEL/ERASE	Includes /P, which allows you to verify each file name before it is deleted
DIR	Shows the disk's serial number
DISPLAY.SYS	Checks hardware and automatically chooses the most appropriate type of active display if you don't specify an adapter type
FASTOPEN	May be loaded from CONFIG.SYS, and has the /X parameter, which tells DOS to use expanded memory
FDISK	Supports larger disk partitions and has easier-to-use menus and displays
FORMAT	Has a /V:*label* parameter, which lets you specify the label on the command line as you start to format a disk, and a new /F:*size* parameter, which allows you to indicate the size of a floppy disk when you want to format the disk for less than its maximum capacity
GRAFTABL	Supports code page 850
GRAPHICS	Supports EGA and VGA adapters and can support more printers
KEYB	Has a /ID.*nnn* parameter, which can be used to choose a specific keyboard for countries like France, Italy, and Great Britain that have more than one Enhanced Keyboard
MODE	Lets you specify the keyboard rate and number of lines displayed on the screen; has parameters for the COM ports
PRINTER.SYS	Has enhanced support for the IBM ProPrinter

REPLACE	Has the /U parameter, which tells DOS to update files that have a date and time more recent than that of a file with the same name on the target disk
SELECT	Enhanced to install DOS
SYS	Changed to allow specification of an optional source drive
TIME	Allows either a 12-hour or 24-hour clock, depending on the country code in use
TREE	Includes graphics and indentations to show various subdirectory levels
VDISK.SYS	Has the /X parameter, which tells DOS to use expanded memory, and the /E parameter, which tells DOS to use extended memory

Sample Hierarchical Directory

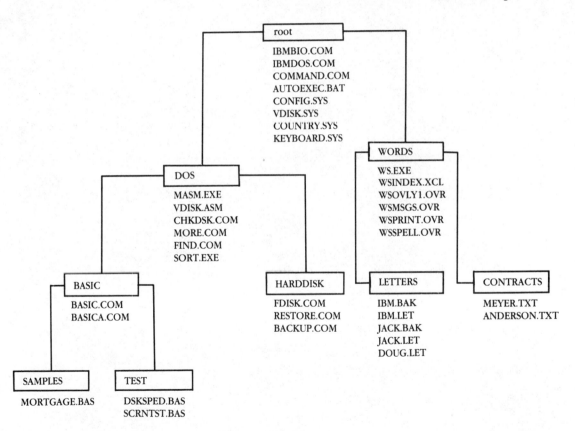

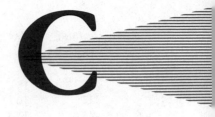

ASCII and Extended ASCII Codes

This appendix presents the ASCII, Extended ASCII, and Extended Function ASCII codes. In the tables, a ^ represents the Control (Ctrl) key. For example, ^C represents Ctrl-C.

ASCII Codes

The standard codes for the American Standard Code for Information Interchange (ASCII) are presented in the following table.

Decimal	Hex	Octal	Binary	ASCII Meaning
0	00	000	00000000	^@ NUL (null)
1	01	001	00000001	^A SOH (start-of-header)
2	02	002	00000010	^B STX (start-of-transmission)
3	03	003	00000011	^C ETX (end-of-transmission)
4	04	004	00000100	^D EOT (end-of-text)
5	05	005	00000101	^E ENQ (inquiry)
6	06	006	00000110	^F ACK (acknowledge)
7	07	007	00000111	^G BEL (bell)
8	08	010	00001000	^H BS (backspace)
9	09	011	00001001	^I HT (horizontal tab)
10	0A	012	00001010	^J LF (line feed—also ^Enter)
11	0B	013	00001011	^K VT (vertical tab)
12	0C	014	00001100	^L FF (form feed)
13	0D	015	00001101	^M CR (carriage return)
14	0E	016	00001110	^N SO
15	0F	017	00001111	^O SI
16	10	020	00010000	^P DLE
17	11	021	00010001	^Q DC1
18	12	022	00010010	^R DC2

Decimal	Hex	Octal	Binary	ASCII Meaning
19	13	023	00010011	^S DC3
20	14	024	00010100	^T DC4
21	15	025	00010101	^U NAK
22	16	026	00010110	^V SYN
23	17	027	00010111	^W ETB
24	18	030	00011000	^X CAN (cancel)
25	19	031	00011001	^Y EM
26	1A	032	00011010	^Z SUB (also end-of-file)
27	1B	033	00011011	^[ESC (escape)
28	1C	034	00011100	^\ FS (field separator)
29	1D	035	00011101	^] GS
30	1E	036	00011110	^^ RS (record separator)
31	1F	037	00011111	^_ US
32	20	040	00100000	Space
33	21	041	00100001	!
34	22	042	00100010	"
35	23	043	00100011	#
36	24	044	00100100	$
37	25	045	00100101	%
38	26	046	00100110	&
39	27	047	00100111	'
40	28	050	00101000	(
41	29	051	00101001	)
42	2A	052	00101010	*
43	2B	053	00101011	+
44	2C	054	00101100	,
45	2D	055	00101101	-
46	2E	056	00101110	.
47	2F	057	00101111	/
48	30	060	00110000	0
49	31	061	00110001	1
50	32	062	00110010	2
51	33	063	00110011	3
52	34	064	00110100	4
53	35	065	00110101	5
54	36	066	00110110	6
55	37	067	00110111	7
56	38	070	00111000	8
57	39	071	00111001	9
58	3A	072	00111010	:
59	3B	073	00111011	;
60	3C	074	00111100	<
61	3D	075	00111101	=
62	3E	076	00111110	>
63	3F	077	00111111	?

Decimal	Hex	Octal	Binary	ASCII Meaning
64	40	100	01000000	@
65	41	101	01000001	A
66	42	102	01000010	B
67	43	103	01000011	C
68	44	104	01000100	D
69	45	105	01000101	E
70	46	106	01000110	F
71	47	107	01000111	G
72	48	110	01001000	H
73	49	111	01001001	I
74	4A	112	01001010	J
75	4B	113	01001011	K
76	4C	114	01001100	L
77	4D	115	01001101	M
78	4E	116	01001110	N
79	4F	117	01001111	O
80	50	120	01010000	P
81	51	121	01010001	Q
82	52	122	01010010	R
83	53	123	01010011	S
84	54	124	01010100	T
85	55	125	01010101	U
86	56	126	01010110	V
87	57	127	01010111	W
88	58	130	01011000	X
89	59	131	01011001	Y
90	5A	132	01011010	Z
91	5B	133	01011011	[
92	5C	134	01011100	\
93	5D	135	01011101	]
94	5E	136	01011110	^
95	5F	137	01011111	_
96	60	140	01100000	`
97	61	141	01100001	a
98	62	142	01100010	b
99	63	143	01100011	c
100	64	144	01100100	d
101	65	145	01100101	e
102	66	146	01100110	f
103	67	147	01100111	g
104	68	150	01101000	h
105	69	151	01101001	i
106	6A	152	01101010	j
107	6B	153	01101011	k
108	6C	154	01101100	l
109	6D	155	01101101	m

Decimal	Hex	Octal	Binary	ASCII Meaning
110	6E	156	01101110	n
111	6F	157	01101111	o
112	70	160	01110000	p
113	71	161	01110001	q
114	72	162	01110010	r
115	73	163	01110011	s
116	74	164	01110100	t
117	75	165	01110101	u
118	76	166	01110110	v
119	77	167	01110111	w
120	78	170	01111000	x
121	79	171	01111001	y
122	7A	172	01111010	z
123	7B	173	01111011	{
124	7C	174	01111100	|
125	7D	175	01111101	}
126	7E	176	01111110	~
127	7F	177	01111111	Del

Extended ASCII Keyboard Codes

Certain keys cannot be represented by the standard ASCII codes. To represent the codes, a two-character sequence is used. The first character is always an ASCII NUL (0). The second character and its translation are listed in the following table. Some codes expand to multi-keystroke characters.

If an asterisk (*) appears in the column *Enhanced Only*, the sequence is available only on the Enhanced Keyboards (101/102-key keyboards).

Enhanced Only	Decimal	Hex	Octal	Binary	Extended ASCII Meaning
*	1	01	001	00000001	Alt-Esc
		03	003	00000011	Null (null character)
*	14	0E	016	00001110	Alt-Backspace
	15	0F	017	00001111	Shift-Tab (back-tab)
	16	10	020	00010000	Alt-Q
	17	11	021	00010001	Alt-W
	18	12	022	00010010	Alt-E
	19	13	023	00010011	Alt-R
	20	14	024	00010100	Alt-T
	21	15	025	00010101	Alt-Y
	22	16	026	00010110	Alt-U
	23	17	027	00010111	Alt-I
	24	18	030	00011000	Alt-O
	25	19	031	00011001	Alt-P
*	26	1A	032	00011010	Alt-[

Enhanced Only	Decimal	Hex	Octal	Binary	Extended ASCII Meaning
*	27	1B	033	00011011	Alt-]
*	28	1C	034	00011100	Alt-Enter
	30	1E	036	00011110	Alt-A
	31	1F	037	00011111	Alt-S
	32	20	040	00100000	Alt-D
	33	21	041	00100001	Alt-F
	34	22	042	00100010	Alt-G
	35	23	043	00100011	Alt-H
	36	24	044	00100100	Alt-J
	37	25	045	00100101	Alt-K
	38	26	046	00100110	Alt-L
*	39	27	047	00100111	Alt-;
*	40	28	050	00101000	Alt-'
*	41	29	051	00101001	Alt-`
*	43	2B	053	00101011	Alt-\
	44	2C	054	00101100	Alt-Z
	45	2D	055	00101101	Alt-X
	46	2E	056	00101110	Alt-C
	47	2F	057	00101111	Alt-V
	48	30	060	00110000	Alt-B
	49	31	061	00110001	Alt-N
	50	32	062	00110010	Alt-M
*	51	33	063	00110011	Alt-,
*	52	34	064	00110100	Alt-.
*	53	35	065	00110101	Alt-/
*	55	37	067	00110111	Alt-* (keypad)
	57	39	071	00111001	Alt-space bar
	59	3B	073	00111011	F1
	60	3C	074	00111100	F2
	61	3D	075	00111101	F3
	62	3E	076	00111110	F4
	63	3F	077	00111111	F5
	64	40	100	01000000	F6
	65	41	101	01000001	F7
	66	42	102	01000010	F8
	67	43	103	01000011	F9
	68	44	104	01000100	F10
	71	47	107	01000111	Home
	72	48	110	01001000	↑
	73	49	111	01001001	PgUp
	74	4A	112	01001010	Alt- − (keypad)
	75	4B	113	01001011	←
	76	4C	114	01001100	Shift-5 (keypad)

Enhanced Only	Decimal	Hex	Octal	Binary	Extended ASCII Meaning
	77	4D	115	01001101	→
	78	4E	116	01001110	Alt-+ (keypad)
	79	4F	117	01001111	End
*	80	50	120	01010000	↓
*	81	51	121	01010001	PgDn
*	82	52	122	01010010	Ins (Insert)
	83	53	123	01010011	Del (Delete)
	84	54	124	01010100	Shift-F1
	85	55	125	01010101	Shift-F2
	86	56	126	01010110	Shift-F3
	87	57	127	01010111	Shift-F4
	88	58	130	01011000	Shift-F5
	89	59	131	01011001	Shift-F6
	90	5A	132	01011010	Shift-F7
	91	5B	133	01011011	Shift-F8
	92	5C	134	01011100	Shift-F9
	93	5D	135	01011101	Shift-F10
	94	5E	136	01011110	Ctrl-F1
	95	5F	137	01011111	Ctrl-F2
	96	60	140	01100000	Ctrl-F3
	97	61	141	01100001	Ctrl-F4
	98	62	142	01100010	Ctrl-F5
	99	63	143	01100011	Ctrl-F6
	100	64	144	01100100	Ctrl-F7
	101	65	145	01100101	Ctrl-F8
	102	66	146	01100110	Ctrl-F9
	103	67	147	01100111	Ctrl-F10
	104	68	150	01101000	Alt-F1
	105	69	151	01101001	Alt-F2
	106	6A	152	01101010	Alt-F3
	107	6B	153	01101011	Alt-F4
	108	6C	154	01101100	Alt-F5
	109	6D	155	01101101	Alt-F6
	110	6E	156	01101110	Alt-F7
	111	6F	157	01101111	Alt-F8
	112	70	160	01110000	Alt-F9
	113	71	161	01110001	Alt-F10
	114	72	162	01110010	Ctrl-PrtSc
	115	73	163	01110011	Ctrl-←
	116	74	164	01110100	Ctrl-→
	117	75	165	01110101	Ctrl-End
	118	76	166	01110110	Ctrl-PgDn
	119	77	167	01110111	Ctrl-Home

Enhanced Only	Decimal	Hex	Octal	Binary	Extended ASCII Meaning
	120	78	170	01111000	Alt-1 (keyboard)
	121	79	171	01111001	Alt-2 (keyboard)
	122	7A	172	01111010	Alt-3 (keyboard)
	123	7B	173	01111011	Alt-4 (keyboard)
	124	7C	174	01111100	Alt-5 (keyboard)
	125	7D	175	01111101	Alt-6 (keyboard)
	126	7E	176	01111110	Alt-7 (keyboard)
	127	7F	177	01111111	Alt-8 (keyboard)
	128	80	200	10000000	Alt-9 (keyboard)
	129	81	201	10000001	Alt-0 (keyboard)
	130	82	202	10000010	Alt- − (keyboard)
	131	83	203	10000011	Alt- = (keyboard)
	132	84	204	10000100	Ctrl-PgUp
*	133	85	205	10000101	F11
*	134	86	206	10000110	F12
*	135	87	207	10000111	Shift-F11
*	136	88	210	10001000	Shift-F12
*	137	89	211	10001001	Ctrl-F11
*	138	8A	212	10001010	Ctrl-F12
*	139	8B	213	10001011	Alt-F11
*	140	8C	214	10001100	Alt-F12
	141	8D	215	10001101	Ctrl-↕/8 (keypad)
	142	8E	216	10001110	Ctrl- − (keypad)
	143	8F	217	10001111	Ctrl-5 (keypad)
	144	90	220	10010000	Ctrl- + (keypad)
	145	91	221	10010001	Ctrl-↓/2 (keypad)
	146	92	222	10010010	Ctrl-Ins/0 (keypad)
	147	93	223	10010011	Ctrl-Del/. (keypad)
	148	94	224	10010100	Ctrl-Tab
*	149	95	225	10010101	Ctrl-/ (keypad)
*	150	96	226	10010110	Ctrl-* (keypad)
*	151	97	227	10010111	Alt-Home
*	152	98	230	10011000	Alt-↑
*	153	99	231	10011001	Alt-PgUp
*	155	9B	233	10011011	Alt-←
*	157	9D	235	10011101	Alt-→
*	159	9F	237	10011111	Alt-End
*	160	A0	240	10100000	Alt-↓
*	161	A1	241	10100001	Alt-PgDn
*	162	A2	242	10100010	Alt-Insert
*	163	A3	243	10100011	Alt-Delete
*	164	A4	244	10100100	Alt-/ (keypad)
*	165	A5	245	10100101	Alt-Tab
*	166	A6	256	10100110	Alt-Enter (keypad)

Extended-Function ASCII Codes

The following extended codes are available only with Enhanced Keyboards (101/102-key keyboards); they are available for key reassignment only under DOS V4. The keys include the six-key editing pad and the four-key cursor-control pad. To re-assign these keys, you must give the DEVICE = ANSI.SYS /X directive or the enable-extended-function-codes escape sequence (Esc[1q). All extended codes are prefixed by 224 decimal (E0 hex).

Enhanced Function	Decimal	Hex	Octal	Binary	Extended ASCII Meaning
*	71	47	107	01000111	Home
*	72	48	110	01001000	↑
*	73	49	111	01001001	PgUp
*	75	4B	113	01001011	←
*	77	4D	115	01001101	→
*	79	4F	117	01001111	End
*	80	50	120	01010000	↓
*	81	51	121	01010001	PgDn
*	82	52	122	01010010	Insert
*	83	53	123	01010011	Delete
*	115	73	163	01110011	Ctrl-←
*	116	74	164	01110100	Ctrl-→
*	117	75	165	01110101	Ctrl-End
*	118	76	166	01110110	Ctrl-PgDn
*	119	77	167	01110111	Ctrl-Home
*	132	84	204	10000100	Ctrl-PgUp
*	141	8D	215	10001101	Ctrl-↑
*	145	91	221	10010001	Ctrl-↓
*	146	92	222	10010010	Ctrl-Insert
*	147	93	223	10010011	Ctrl-Delete

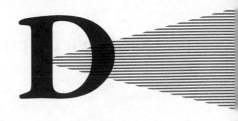

ANSI Terminal Codes

All ANSI terminal codes are preceded by an Escape (ESC) character and a left bracket ([). The Escape character is 27 decimal or 1b hexadecimal.

Cursor-Control Sequences

For the cursor-control sequences, if a value is omitted, the default value of 1 is used.

Cursor Position

Horizontal and Vertical Position

ESC[#;#H	The first # is the row (vertical coordinate);
ESC[#;#f	the second # is the column (horizontal coordinate). The starting value for either coordinate is 1 (also the default value).

Cursor Up

ESC[#A   # is the number of rows to move up.

Cursor Down

ESC[#B   # is the number of rows to move down.

Cursor Forward

ESC[#C   # is the number of columns to move forward (right).

Cursor Backward

ESC[#D   # is the number of columns to move backward (left).

Device Status Report

ESC[6n "Inputs" through the keyboard a cursor report on the current cursor position.

Cursor Position Report

ESC[#;#R Reports the current cursor position. The string is returned by the ANSI console and is eight characters long. The first # is the two-digit row number; the second # is the two-digit column number.

Save Cursor Position

ESC[s "Saves" the current cursor position in the driver. The position can be restored by using ESC[r.

Restore Cursor Position

ESC[r Sets the cursor to the horizontal and vertical position that was "saved."

Erasing

Erase Display

ESC[2J Erases the display and also moves the cursor to the Home position (the upper left corner of the screen).

Erase to End of Line

ESC[K

Modes of Operation

For all ANSI-operation-mode control codes, if a value is omitted, the default value of 0 is used.

Set Graphics Rendition

ESC[#;...;#m   Sets the character attributes by the following parameters. The attributes remain in effect until the next graphics rendition command.

Parameter	Meaning
0	All attributes off (normal white on black)
1	Bold on (high intensity)
4	Underscore on (IBM Monochrome Display only)
5	Blink on
7	Reverse (inverse) video on
8	Cancel on (invisible characters)
30	Black foreground
31	Red foreground
32	Green foreground
33	Yellow foreground
34	Blue foreground
35	Magenta foreground
36	Cyan foreground
37	White foreground
40	Black background
41	Red background
42	Green background
43	Yellow background
44	Blue background
45	Magenta background
46	Cyan background
47	White background

Set Screen Mode

(for parameter 7 only)

ESC[= #h   Sets the screen width or type based on #.

ESC[?71

Reset Screen Mode

(for parameter 7 only)

ESC[= #1   Resets the screen width or type based on #.

ESC[?71

Parameter	Meaning
0	40 x 25 black and white
1	40 x 25 color
2	80 x 25 black and white
3	80 x 25 color
4	320 x 200 color
5	320 x 200 black and white
6	640 x 200 black and white
7	Wrap at end of line (set mode), or do not wrap and discard characters past end of line (reset mode)

Keyboard Key Reassignment

ESC[#;#;...;p   or

ESC["string"p   or

ESC[#;"string";#;#;"string";#p

The first ASCII code (the first #) defines which key or keystrokes (such as a Ctrl-character combination) are being reassigned. However, if the first code in the sequence is 0 (ASCII Nul), the first and second codes designate an Extended ASCII key sequence. See Appendix C for the set of ASCII codes and the set of Extended ASCII codes.

The remaining numbers (#) or characters within the "string" are the replacement characters "typed" when that key or keystroke combination is pressed. Any nonnumeric characters used in the replacement must be placed within double quotation marks.

Preparing Your Hard Disk

IMPORTANT: Some dealers install the DOS operating system and applications programs on your hard disk before you receive your computer. If only DOS has been installed, you may skip the steps in these first two sections, which describe two of the processes for setting up the hard disk. If, however, you choose to complete the steps in these sections, you must complete both sections before proceeding to the final section.

If your dealer has installed some applications programs, such as an accounting package, a word processor, or a data management program, you should not complete the steps outlined in the first and second sections in this appendix.

Before you can use your hard disk, you must perform three distinct processes: (1) assign the disk one or more partitions by using FDISK, (2) format the hard disk by using FORMAT, and (3) set up the hard disk for daily operations using several DOS commands. Before doing these processes, you must have DOS up and running on your computer.

If you have an IBM Personal Computer AT, you must run the SETUP program before doing the steps outlined in the sections of this appendix. The information on SETUP is located in the Installation and Setup manual for your Personal Computer AT. In the setup procedure, you will be asked for the disk drive type. Currently, all IBM 20-megabyte disk drives are type 2, and all IBM 30-megabyte disk drives are type 20. If you are unsure of your disk drive type, remove the cover of your AT and read the large number on the front of the disk drive.

If you have an IBM PS/2 Micro Channel computer (Model 50, 50Z, 60, 70, or 80), you should boot the system from the Reference Disk. Follow the instructions, and the system will automatically configure itself for the hard disk and adapter cards you have installed.

FDISK is slightly different for DOS V3 and DOS V4. Each is addressed in separate sections in this appendix.

Using FDISK with DOS V3.2 and Earlier Versions

FDISK works a little differently with DOS V3.2 and earlier versions than it does with DOS V3.3. I'll point out the differences as they occur in the following instructions.

The hard disk of your computer can be used by more than one disk operating system. To accommodate the people who use more than one operating system, IBM provides the FDISK program, which divides the hard disk into partitions. Each partition is used with a different operating system.

Most people use only DOS. The instructions given in this first section are for setting up your hard disk for a single DOS partition.

Step 1. Insert your DOS start-up disk (one of the disks that came with your DOS program) into the first disk drive.

This drive will be the left or top disk drive. Close the disk drive door. Start your computer by either turning on the power if the computer is off or pressing Ctrl-Alt-Del if the computer is on. (Hold down the Ctrl and Alt keys and then press the Del key.)

Step 2. If you are not using a Personal Computer AT, type the correct date and press Enter. Separate the month, day, and year with hyphens.

If you are using an AT, check the date. If the date is incorrect, enter the correct date and then press Enter. Remember that the date was incorrect.

Step 3. If you are not using an AT, enter the correct time.

Because DOS uses a universal, 24-hour clock, add 12 to afternoon and evening hours. Separate the hours, minutes, and seconds with colons. You don't need to enter the hundredths of seconds.

If you are using an AT, check the time. If the time is incorrect, enter the correct time and press Enter. If the time is off by more than a minute or two, remember this fact.

You should now see the DOS prompt:

```
A>
```

Step 4. Type FDISK and press Enter.

The screen should look something like the following:

```
IBM Personal Computer
Fixed Disk Setup Program Version 3.20
(C)Copyright IBM Corp. 1983, 1985
FDISK Options
Current Fixed Disk Drive: 1
```

```
Choose one of the following:
        1. Create DOS Partition
        2. Change Active Partition
        3. Delete DOS Partition
        4. Display Partition Data
        5. Select Next Fixed Disk Drive
Enter choice: [1]
```

Step 5. *Choose option 1 by pressing Enter.*

For DOS V3.2 and earlier, if the following message appears, a DOS partition has already been created on your hard disk:

```
DOS partition already exists
```

You should skip this section and the next one on formatting your disk. Press the Esc key to return to DOS.

If this message does not appear, and you have DOS V3.2 or an earlier version, your screen should look something like this:

```
Create DOS Partition

Current Fixed Disk Drive: 1

Do you wish to use the entire fixed

disk for DOS (Y/N)............? [Y]
```

Step 6. *Press Enter to inform FDISK that DOS should use the entire hard disk.*

The red light for the hard disk should go on briefly, and the following message should appear:

```
System will now restart

Insert DOS disk in drive A:

Press any key when ready...
```

Step 7. *Press any key.*

Because the DOS disk is already in drive A, DOS will restart. Answer the date and time questions again (steps 2 and 3) and then proceed to the next section on formatting the hard disk.

Using FDISK with DOS V3.3 and V4

Step 1. *After you have booted DOS, load the disk with FDISK in drive A.*

For DOS V3.3 this will be the Operating disk; for DOS V4, the Install Disk. At the A>
prompt type

FDISK

You'll see a screen like this one:

```
            IBM DOS Version 4.00
            Fixed Disk Setup Program
      (C) Copyright IBM Corp. 1983, 1988

                  FDISK Options

Current fixed disk drive:1

Choose one of the following:

      1. Create DOS Partition or Logical DOS Drive
      2. Set active partition
      3. Delete DOS Partition or Logical DOS Drive
      4. Display partition information
      5. Select next fixed disk drive

Enter choice:[ ]

Press Esc to exit FDISK
```

For DOS V3.3, option 2 in this display reads Change Active Partition, and option
4 reads Display Partition Date. DOS V3.3 allows you to have more than one
bootable partition, so it is possible to use FDISK to change the active (bootable) partition from one to another. DOS V4 only allows you to activate the primary DOS partition.

With either version of DOS, option 5 is displayed only if your system has more than one
hard disk.

Step 2. *Choose option 1.*

A menu appears, which looks like this one:

```
            Create DOS Partition or Logical DOS Drive

Current fixed disk drive:1

      1. Create Primary DOS Partition
      2. Create Extended DOS Partition
      3. Create Logical DOS Drive(s) in the
         Extended DOS Partition

Enter choice:[ ]
```

The heading will be slightly different with DOS V3.3, but the menu choices are the same. The primary DOS partition is the bootable partition (under DOS V4), and cannot be divided into more than one logical drive. If you wish to have more than one logical drive you must divide your disk into both primary and extended DOS partitions. Submenu option 3 will let you create those logical drives.

DOS V4 also will let you to create a primary DOS partition that is larger than 32 megabytes. The extended DOS partition can also be larger than 32 megabytes, and the logical drives there *also* may be larger than 32 megabytes. Note that you cannot create a partition of exactly 32 megabytes; if you choose 32, FDISK will substitute 31.

Step 3. *Choose option 1 to create the primary DOS partition.*

The screen you will see will look like the one that follows.

```
            Create Primary DOS Partition

Current fixed disk drive: 1

Do you wish to use the maximum available size for a Primary
DOS Partition and make the partition active (Y/N).....? [Y]

Press Esc to return to FDISK options.
```

Step 4. *Decide how much of your hard disk you want to allocate to the primary partition.*

If you want to use the entire hard disk for a single partition, even if you are using DOS V4 and the partition is more than 32 megabytes, type **Y**. If you enter **N**, DOS will report on available space and ask you to enter the amount to be set aside for this partition. With DOS V3.3, enter the number of megabytes to be allocated. With DOS V4, you may enter either the number of megabytes or the percentage. For example, with a 44-megabyte disk, you could type either 22 or 50% to allocate half for the primary partition. When you have selected the amount of space to allocate, press Enter. You'll be returned to the main menu.

Step 5. *Choose option 2 from the main menu to make the primary partition active, so you'll be able to use it to boot your computer.*

If you want to create additional DOS partitions, because you have another physical hard disk or have not set aside the entire disk as the primary partition, follow the next four steps. Otherwise, press the Esc key and you are finished with FDISK. Go to the section "Using FORMAT To Prepare Your Hard Disk" to format your hard disk.

If additional partitions can be created on your disk, FDISK will automatically take you to the next menu, which looks like this:

```
            Create Extended DOS Partition

Current fixed disk drive:1

Partition Status  Type   Size in Mbytes  Percentage of Disk Used
C:1        A      PRI DOS      22               50%

Total disk space is 22 Mbytes (1 Mbyte = 1048576 bytes)
Maximum space available for partition is 22 Mbytes (50%)
```

```
Enter partition size in Mbytes or percent of disk space (%) to
create an Extended DOS Partition...................[22]

Press Esc to return to FDISK Options
```

C:1 in the first column indicates the drive letter and the number assigned to the DOS partition. The A indicates that the partition is active; PRI DOS shows that it is the primary DOS partition. The Size and Percentage columns show the amount of space already used for the primary partition and any other DOS partitions you may already have created.

***Step* 6.** *Enter the amount of space to be allocated to the next partition.*

Just as you did when you created your primary partition, you may enter the size of the extended partition(s) in megabytes or (with DOS V4) in percentages.

***Step* 7.** *Now create logical disk drives in the partition if you want to divide it into separate drives.*

Each time you create an extended partition, FDISK will show you the following menu:

```
    Create Logical DOS Drive(s) in the Extended DOS Partition

No logical drives defined

Total Extended DOS Partition size is 22 Mbytes
(1 MByte = 104857 bytes)
Maximum space available for logical drive is 22 Mbytes (50%)

Enter logical drive size in Mbytes or percent of disk space
(%)...[ ]

Press Esc to return to FDISK options.
```

DOS V3.3 does not show all the information provided in this DOS V4 screen, such as the size of a megabyte, or the percentage of the disk used. However, the concept is the same. Enter the space in megabytes only, rather than percentages, if you have DOS V3.3.

***Step* 8.** *Repeat steps 5-7 to create additional partitions.*

When you have created all the partitions and logical drives you want, press Esc to return to the FDISK menu. You may exit to DOS from there.

Using FORMAT To Prepare Your Hard Disk

The FORMAT command performs several functions. It lays out individual sections of the disk that DOS uses to store your programs and data. FORMAT creates the housekeeping areas so that DOS can keep track of your programs and files. The command also places the key parts of DOS on your hard disk.

To do its job, FORMAT permanently removes any files stored on the hard disk. *If you have on your hard disk any files you want to keep, do not perform the steps in this section.*

Step 1. *With the DOS start-up disk in the floppy disk drive and the door closed, start the FORMAT program.*

You do so by typing

FORMAT C: /S /V

Then press Enter. The light on the floppy disk drive should go on for a few seconds. You should see this message:

```
WARNING, ALL DATA ON NON-REMOVABLE DISK

DRIVE C: WILL BE LOST! Proceed with Format (Y/N)?
```

Step 2. *Because you do want to format the hard disk, press Y and then press Enter.*

You should see the following message:

```
Formatting...
```

The red light for the hard disk will stay on for two to four minutes, depending on the type of hard disk you have.

After FORMAT has completed its first stage, the message Format complete will appear. Within a few seconds, FORMAT will provide the message System trans-ferred. This informs you that DOS has been placed on the hard disk.

Then you should see the following message:

```
Volume label (11 characters, ENTER for none)?
```

Step 3. *Type a volume name that contains up to 11 characters.*

This name will appear whenever you display a list of files on the hard disk and at several other times also. After you have typed the name, press Enter.

Step 4. *Test the setup of your computer.*

Open the floppy disk drive door and press the Ctrl-Alt-Del keys (hold down the first two keys while pressing the Del key). This sequence should restart DOS from the hard disk.

The floppy disk drive light should come on, followed by the hard disk drive light. Then the computer should beep. The computer will attempt to load DOS from the floppy disk drive. Several seconds later, the computer will try to load DOS from the hard disk. Within 20 seconds, DOS should ask you for the date.

Answer the date and time messages if they appear, as you did in steps 1 and 2 in the first section. You have now successfully prepared the hard disk to start DOS. Go to the next section on setting up files on your hard disk for daily use.

If you don't see a message about the date, either you did not press the Ctrl, Alt, and Del keys correctly, or you were not successful in preparing your hard disk. Try pressing Ctrl-Alt-Del again. If you do not see the date and time messages within 30 seconds, close the disk drive door, restart DOS from the floppy disk (press Ctrl-Alt-Del again), return to step 1, and repeat the instructions in this section again.

Setting Up the Hard Disk for Daily Use

Because only basic setup commands are used for this set-up procedure, the procedure will work for DOS V2, V3, and V4. However, some of the special capabilities of DOS V3 and V4 are not used. You can learn more about customizing DOS in Chapters 17 and 18. (If you have DOS V4, you may prefer to set up your hard disk using SELECT. Chapter 3 describes using DOS's SELECT program.)

Your hard disk is now ready to store and retrieve information under DOS. In this section, you will copy the DOS programs to the hard disk and also create some files for customizing DOS. If your computer uses minifloppy disk drives, you will have extra steps in this section because DOS comes on more than one minifloppy disk.

First, you'll restart DOS to ensure that your computer is working properly. In this section, remember to end each line you are asked to type by pressing Enter.

Step 1. Check that the DOS start-up disk is in the floppy disk drive and that the disk drive door is closed.

Step 2. Make the hard disk the current disk drive.

You do so by typing **C:**. Don't forget to press the Enter key afterward. The DOS prompt should look like this:

    C>

Step 3. Create a subdirectory called BIN by typing

   MKDIR \BIN

Later you will place the DOS programs in this subdirectory.

Step 4. Create a subdirectory in BIN called SYS by typing

   MKDIR \BIN\SYS

Here you will place the DOS device-driver software (files ending in SYS).

Step 5. Create another subdirectory in BIN called SAMPLES by typing

   MKDIR \BIN\SAMPLES

This subdirectory is where you will place the BASIC programs on the DOS Supplemental Programs or Operating disk.

Step 6. Make BIN the current directory by typing

   CHDIR \BIN

Step 7. Copy all files from the DOS start-up disk to the current directory (BIN) on the hard disk by typing

   COPY A:*.* C: /V

You will see the name of each file as it is copied. Then you'll see a message like the following:

```
36 files copied
```

Remember that the number of files on the disk (and the number of files copied) will vary, depending on your version of DOS.

Step 8. *Copy all files ending with SYS to the SYS directory by typing*

> **COPY *.SYS SYS /V**

You will see a message indicating that two files have been copied.

Step 9. *Remove the two SYS files from the BIN subdirectory by typing*

> **ERASE *.SYS**

Because you have safely copied (in step 8) the files to the SYS subdirectory, you can remove them from BIN.

Step 10. *Take the DOS start-up disk out of drive A. Put the disk back into its protective envelope. Put the DOS Operating disk into drive A and close the drive door.*

Step 11. *Copy to the current directory (BIN) the program files with .COM extensions on the Operating disk by typing*

> **COPY A:*.COM C: /V**

Step 12. *Copy to the current directory (BIN) the program files with .EXE extensions on the Operating disk by typing*

> **COPY A:*.EXE C: /V**

Step 13. *Copy the BASIC sample programs to the SAMPLES subdirectory of the hard disk by typing*

> **COPY A:*.BAS \SAMPLES /V**

You should see a message indicating that 13 files have been copied.

You have now copied most of the files from the DOS disk to the hard disk. The files you did not copy are not important.

Step 14. *Remove the Operating disk and store it and the start-up disk in a safe place. (Remember that if you have DOS V4, your disks have other names, such as Install and Operating 1, Operating 2, and Operating 3.)*

Step 15. *Make the root (topmost) directory of the hard disk the current directory by typing*

> **CD **

Step 16. *Begin to create a CONFIG.SYS file by typing the following command:*

> **COPY CON CONFIG.SYS**

The DOS prompt (C>) will disappear.

Step 17. Now type the following lines. Be sure to check your typing before you press Enter at the end of each line. If you make a mistake and you have already pressed Enter, perform step 20 and then return to step 16.

> **BUFFERS = 20**
> **DEVICE = c:\bin\sys\ansi.sys**
> **FILES = 20**
> **FCBS = 12,12 LASTDRIVE = F**

Step 18. If you live in the United States or the English-speaking provinces of Canada, type the following line:

> **COUNTRY = 001**

If you live somewhere else, look at table 18.1 in Chapter 18 for the number you should use in place of 001. Then type the following line, replacing the **xxx** with the correct three-digit code:

> **COUNTRY = xxx**

Step 19. If you want to use a RAM disk on a PC XT or an AT with 640K of memory or less, type the following line:

> **DEVICE = c:\bin\sys\vdisk.sys 180 512 64**

If you want to use a RAM disk on a Personal Computer AT with more than 640K of memory, type the following line instead:

> **DEVICE = c:\bin\sys\vdisk.sys 180 512 64 /e:8**

If you do not want to use a RAM disk, skip this step and continue with step 20.

Step 20. The cursor should be at the beginning of a blank line. If not, press Enter. Then press the F6 special-function key.

A ^Z should appear. Press Enter again. The hard disk light should come on briefly, and you will see the message 1 file(s) copied. The DOS prompt will reappear.

You have just created a CONFIG.SYS file for your computer.

Step 21. To begin creating an AUTOEXEC.BAT file, type the following line:

> **COPY CON AUTOEXEC.BAT**

The DOS prompt should disappear again.

Step 22. Now type the following lines:

> **ECHO OFF**
> **PATH = C:\BIN;C:**

As before, check your typing before you press Enter at the end of each line (for this step and the next two steps). If you notice a mistake after you have pressed Enter, perform step 25 and then return to step 21.

Step 23. *If you are in the United States or the English-speaking provinces of Canada, go to step 24. Otherwise, see Chapter 18 for the number to use for the keyboard code. Type the following line, replacing the **xx** with the correct two-letter code:*

KEYBxx

Step 24. *If you have an IBM Color/Graphics Adapter (CGA) on your computer, type the following line as well:*

GRAFTABL

Step 25. *If you have a Personal Computer AT, continue with step 26. Otherwise, type the following lines:*

DATE
TIME

Step 26. *The cursor should be at the beginning of a blank line. If not, press Enter. Then press the F6 special-function key.*

A ^Z should appear. Press Enter again. The hard disk light should come on briefly, and you will see the message 1 file(s) copied. The DOS prompt (C>) will reappear.

You have just created an AUTOEXEC.BAT file for your computer.

Step 27. *Test the setup you have just created. Make sure that the floppy disk drive door is open. Press the Ctrl-Alt-Del sequence to restart DOS. In one minute, you should see the following lines if you used the VDISK line in your CONFIG.SYS file:*

```
VDISK   Version 2.0 virtual disk D:
VDISK Buffer size:        180 KB
VDISK Sector size:        512
VDISK Directory entries:   64
VDISK Transfer size:        8
```

If you are not using a Personal Computer AT or PS/2, DOS will ask for the date and time. Provide this information. The DOS prompt, C>, should appear. If you are using a Personal Computer AT, the DOS prompt should appear; you should not see a request for the date or time.

If you see a message about a file not found, a syntax error, or some other problem, repeat steps 16-27. If the same message appears again, repeat the entire procedure, beginning at the point where you create the \BIN directory.

The final test is to run the CHKDSK program. Type **CHKDSK**. If you see a message that says something about a bad command or a file not found, return to step 21 and try creating your AUTOEXEC.BAT file again. If, after restarting DOS and typing CHKDSK, you get the same message, the DOS files did not get copied correctly. Try repeating steps 6, 7, and 9.

You're done! DOS is set up on your computer and is ready to go. When you start your computer, make sure that the door to the floppy disk drive is open. When you turn on the power or press Ctrl-Alt-Del, DOS will automatically start from the hard disk.

A Note to Personal Computer AT Owners

If you discovered that the date or time for your computer was incorrect, the incorrect date or time you gave to DOS is kept until the computer is turned off or until DOS is restarted. When you use DOS's DATE and TIME commands to set the computer's date and time, DOS versions prior to V3.3 do not set the battery-backed clock/calendar of the AT.

To change the internal date and time of the Personal Computer AT, you must run the SETUP program again. Directions for using SETUP are in the Installation and Setup manual that comes with your computer.

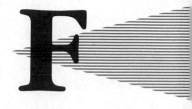

DOS Control and Editing Keys

Command-Line Function Keys

Control Keys

Enter, Return or ↵	Tells DOS to act on the line you just typed
←	Backs up and deletes one character from the line
Ctrl-C Ctrl-Break	Stops a command
Ctrl-Num Lock Ctrl-S	Freezes the video display; pressing any other key restarts the display
PrtSc Print Screen	Prints the contents of the video display (print-screen feature)
Ctrl-PrtSc Ctrl-Print Screen Ctrl-P	Echoes lines sent to the screen to the printer also; giving this sequence a second time turns off this function (printer echo feature)
Ctrl-Alt-Del	Restarts DOS (system reset)

Editing Keys

When you type a line and press Enter, DOS copies the line into an input buffer. By using certain keys, you can use the same line over and over again. The following keys enable you to edit the input buffer line. When you press Enter, the new line is placed into the primary input buffer as DOS executes the line.

631

|← →|	Moves to the next tab stop
Esc	Cancels the current line and does not change buffer
Ins	Enables you to insert characters in the line
Del	Deletes a character from the line
F1 or →	Copies one character from the previous command line
F2	Copies all characters from the previous command line up to, but not including, the next character you type
F3	Copies all remaining characters from the previous command line
F4	Deletes all characters from the previous command line up to, but not including, the next character you type (opposite of F2)
F5	Moves the current line you are typing into the buffer but does not allow DOS to execute the line
F6	Produces an end-of-file marker when you copy from the console to a disk file

Function Keys within the DOS Shell

DOS V4 assigns special functions to some of the keys used with the Start Programs menu.

Special Key Definitions

Enter or ↵	Places the information you select or type into memory
Esc	Cancels the current function
F1	Displays a series of text screens with help information
PgUp PgDn	Scrolls through "pages" of information
F2	Saves the information typed in an entry field and completes the copy operation in Start Programs

F3	Returns you to the DOS command prompt from Start Programs and the File System; cancels copying operations in Start Programs
F4	Creates the ‖ marker that separates the commands used to start a program
F9	Displays key assignments within HELP; returns an entry field to its original value; switches the View function between ASCII and hexadecimal format
Shift-F9	Takes you to the DOS command prompt; typing **EXIT** returns you to the DOS Shell
F10	Moves the cursor to the action bar if the cursor is located in the Main Group or to the Main Group if the cursor is located in the action bar
Space bar	Selects or deselects a file name
Tab	Moves the selection cursor to different areas of the File System screen

Key Assignments within HELP

DOS V4 provides a context-sensitive help feature for all selectable items and entry fields. Within HELP, special-function key assignments assist you in using HELP.

Esc	Returns you to the menu
F1	Provides instructions on how to use HELP
F9	Lists the special key definitions in HELP
F11 or Alt-F1	Displays an index of available HELP screens

Code Page Tables

Code page 437 (United States)

Hex Digits 1st→ 2nd↓	0-	1-	2-	3-	4-	5-	6-	7-	8-	9-	A-	B-	C-	D-	E-	F-
-0		►		0	@	P	`	p	Ç	É	á	▒	└	╨	α	≡
-1	☺	◄	!	1	A	Q	a	q	ü	æ	í	▓	┴	╤	β	±
-2	☻	↕	"	2	B	R	b	r	é	Æ	ó	▓	┬	╥	Γ	≥
-3	♥	‼	#	3	C	S	c	s	â	ô	ú	│	├	╙	π	≤
-4	♦	¶	$	4	D	T	d	t	ä	ö	ñ	┤	─	╘	Σ	⌠
-5	♣	§	%	5	E	U	e	u	à	ò	Ñ	╡	┼	╒	σ	⌡
-6	♠	▬	&	6	F	V	f	v	å	û	ª	╢	╞	╓	µ	÷
-7	•	↨	'	7	G	W	g	w	ç	ù	º	╖	╟	╫	τ	≈
-8	◘	↑	(	8	H	X	h	x	ê	ÿ	¿	╕	╚	╪	Φ	°
-9	○	↓	)	9	I	Y	i	y	ë	Ö	⌐	╣	╔	┘	Θ	∙
-A	◙	→	*	:	J	Z	j	z	è	Ü	¬	║	╩	┌	Ω	·
-B	♂	←	+	;	K	[	k	{	ï	¢	½	╗	╦	█	δ	√
-C	♀	∟	,	<	L	\	l	¦	î	£	¼	╝	╠	▄	∞	ⁿ
-D	♪	↔	-	=	M	]	m	}	ì	¥	¡	╜	═	▌	φ	²
-E	♫	▲	.	>	N	^	n	~	Ä	Pt	«	╛	╬	▐	ε	■
-F	☼	▼	/	?	O	_	o	⌂	Å	ƒ	»	┐	╧	▀	∩	

Code page 860 (Portugal)

Hex Digits 1st → 2nd ↓	0-	1-	2-	3-	4-	5-	6-	7-	8-	9-	A-	B-	C-	D-	E-	F-
-0		►		0	@	P	`	p	Ç	É	á	▦	└	╨	α	≡
-1	☺	◄	!	1	A	Q	a	q	ü	À	í	▨	┴	╤	β	±
-2	●	↕	"	2	B	R	b	r	é	È	ó	▥	┬	╥	Γ	≥
-3	♥	‼	#	3	C	S	c	s	â	ô	ú	│	├	╙	π	≤
-4	♦	¶	$	4	D	T	d	t	ã	õ	ñ	┤	─	╘	Σ	⌠
-5	♣	§	%	5	E	U	e	u	à	ò	Ñ	╡	┼	╒	σ	⌡
-6	♠	▬	&	6	F	V	f	v	Á	Ú	ª	╢	╞	╓	μ	÷
-7	•	↨	'	7	G	W	g	w	ç	ù	º	╖	╟	╫	τ	≈
-8	◘	↑	(	8	H	X	h	x	ê	Ì	¿	╕	╚	╪	Φ	°
-9	○	↓	)	9	I	Y	i	y	Ê	Õ	Ò	╣	╔	┘	Θ	•
-A	◙	→	*	:	J	Z	j	z	è	Ü	¬	║	╩	┌	Ω	·
-B	♂	←	+	;	K	[	k	{	Ì	¢	½	╗	╦	█	δ	√
-C	♀	∟	,	<	L	\	l	|	Ô	£	¼	╝	╠	▄	∞	ⁿ
-D	♪	↔	-	=	M	]	m	}	ì	Ù	¡	╜	═	▌	ø	²
-E	♫	▲	.	>	N	^	n	~	Ã	Pt	«	╛	╬	▐	ε	■
-F	☼	▼	/	?	O	_	o	△	Â	Ó	»	┐	╧	▀	∩	

Code page 850 (Multilingual)

Hex Digits 1st → 2nd ↓	0-	1-	2-	3-	4-	5-	6-	7-	8-	9-	A-	B-	C-	D-	E-	F-
-0		►		0	@	P	`	p	Ç	É	á	▓	└	ð	Ó	-
-1	☺	◄	!	1	A	Q	a	q	ü	æ	í	▒	┴	Đ	ß	±
-2	☻	↕	"	2	B	R	b	r	é	Æ	ó	▓	┬	Ê	Ô	=
-3	♥	‼	#	3	C	S	c	s	â	ô	ú	│	├	Ë	Ò	¾
-4	♦	¶	$	4	D	T	d	t	ä	ö	ñ	┤	─	È	õ	¶
-5	♣	§	%	5	E	U	e	u	à	ò	Ñ	Á	┼	ı	Õ	§
-6	♠	▬	&	6	F	V	f	v	å	û	ª	Â	ã	Í	µ	÷
-7	•	↨	'	7	G	W	g	w	ç	ù	º	À	Ã	Î	þ	˛
-8	◘	↑	(	8	H	X	h	x	ê	ÿ	¿	©	╚	Ï	Þ	°
-9	○	↓	)	9	I	Y	i	y	ë	Ö	®	╣	╔	┘	Ú	¨
-A	◎	→	*	:	J	Z	j	z	è	Ü	¬	║	╩	┌	Û	·
-B	♂	←	+	;	K	[	k	{	ï	ø	½	╗	╦	■	Ù	¹
-C	♀	∟	,	<	L	\	l	|	î	£	¼	╝	╠	▬	ý	³
-D	♪	↔	-	=	M	]	m	}	ì	Ø	¡	¢	=	¦	Ý	²
-E	♫	▲	.	>	N	^	n	~	Ä	×	«	¥	╬	Ì	¯	■
-F	☼	▼	/	?	O	_	o	△	Å	ƒ	»	┐	¤	▬	´	

Code page 863 (Canada-French)

Hex Digits 1st→ 2nd↓	0-	1-	2-	3-	4-	5-	6-	7-	8-	9-	A-	B-	C-	D-	E-	F-
-0		►		0	@	P	`	p	Ç	É	¦	░	└	╨	α	≡
-1	☺	◄	!	1	A	Q	a	q	ü	È	´	▒	┴	╤	β	±
-2	●	↕	"	2	B	R	b	r	é	Ê	ó	▓	┬	╥	Γ	≥
-3	♥	‼	#	3	C	S	c	s	â	ô	ú	│	├	╙	π	≤
-4	♦	¶	$	4	D	T	d	t	Â	Ë	¨	┤	─	╘	Σ	⌠
-5	♣	§	%	5	E	U	e	u	à	Ï	¸	╡	┼	╒	σ	⌡
-6	♠	▬	&	6	F	V	f	v	¶	û	³	╢	╞	╓	µ	÷
-7	•	↨	'	7	G	W	g	w	ç	ù	¯	╖	╟	╫	τ	≈
-8	◘	↑	(	8	H	X	h	x	ê	¤	Î	╕	╚	╪	Φ	°
-9	○	↓	)	9	I	Y	i	y	ë	Ô	⌐	╣	╔	┘	Θ	•
-A	◙	→	*	:	J	Z	j	z	è	Ü	¬	║	╩	┌	Ω	·
-B	♂	←	+	;	K	[	k	{	ï	¢	½	╗	╦	█	δ	√
-C	♀	∟	,	<	L	\	l	|	î	£	¼	╝	╠	▄	∞	ⁿ
-D	♪	↔	-	=	M	]	m	}	‗	Ù	¾	╜	═	▌	ø	²
-E	♫	▲	.	>	N	^	n	~	À	Û	«	╛	╬	▐	ε	■
-F	☼	▼	/	?	O	_	o	△	§	ƒ	»	┐	╧	▀	∩	

Code page 865 (Norway)

Hex Digits 1st → 2nd ↓	0-	1-	2-	3-	4-	5-	6-	7-	8-	9-	A-	B-	C-	D-	E-	F-
-0		►		0	@	P	`	p	Ç	É	á	▓	└	╨	α	≡
-1	☺	◄	!	1	A	Q	a	q	ü	æ	í	▒	┴	╤	β	±
-2	☻	↕	"	2	B	R	b	r	é	Æ	ó	▓	┬	╥	Γ	≥
-3	♥	‼	#	3	C	S	c	s	â	ô	ú	│	├	╙	π	≤
-4	♦	¶	$	4	D	T	d	t	ä	ö	ñ	┤	─	╘	Σ	⌠
-5	♣	§	%	5	E	U	e	u	à	ò	Ñ	╡	┼	╒	σ	⌡
-6	♠	▬	&	6	F	V	f	v	å	û	ª	╢	╞	╓	μ	÷
-7	•	↨	'	7	G	W	g	w	ç	ú	º	╖	╟	╫	τ	≈
-8	◘	↑	(	8	H	X	h	x	ê	ÿ	¿	╕	╚	╪	Φ	°
-9	○	↓	)	9	I	Y	i	y	ë	Ö	⌐	╣	╔	┘	Θ	∙
-A	◙	→	*	:	J	Z	j	z	è	Ü	¬	║	╩	┌	Ω	·
-B	♂	←	+	;	K	[	k	{	ï	ø	½	╗	╦	█	δ	√
-C	♀	∟	,	<	L	\	l	|	î	£	¼	╝	╠	▄	∞	ⁿ
-D	♪	↔	-	=	M	]	m	}	ì	Ø	¡	╜	═	█	φ	²
-E	♫	▲	.	>	N	^	n	~	Ä	Pt	«	╛	╬	▐	ε	■
-F	☼	▼	/	?	O	_	o	△	Å	ƒ	¤	┐	╧	▀	∩	

Index

N

O

P

More Computer Knowledge from Que

LOTUS SOFTWARE TITLES

1-2-3 QueCards	21.95
1-2-3 QuickStart	21.95
1-2-3 Quick Reference	6.95
1-2-3 for Business, 2nd Edition	22.95
1-2-3 Command Language	21.95
1-2-3 Macro Library, 2nd Edition	21.95
1-2-3 Tips, Tricks, and Traps, 2nd Edition	21.95
Using 1-2-3, Special Edition	24.95
Using 1-2-3 Workbook and Disk, 2nd Edition	29.95
Using Symphony, 2nd Edition	26.95

DATABASE TITLES

dBASE III Plus Handbook, 2nd Edition	22.95
dBASE IV Handbook, 3rd Edition	23.95
dBASE IV Tips, Tricks, and Traps, 2nd Edition	21.95
dBASE IV QueCards	21.95
dBASE IV Quick Reference	6.95
dBASE IV QuickStart	21.95
dBXL and Quicksilver Programming: Beyond dBASE	24.95
R:BASE Solutions: Applications and Resources	19.95
R:BASE User's Guide, 3rd Edition	19.95
Using Clipper	24.95
Using Reflex	19.95
Using Paradox, 2nd Edition	22.95
Using Q & A, 2nd Edition	21.95

MACINTOSH AND APPLE II TITLES

HyperCard QuickStart: A Graphics Approach	21.95
Using AppleWorks, 2nd Edition	21.95
Using dBASE Mac	19.95
Using Dollars and Sense	19.95
Using Excel	21.95
Using HyperCard: From Home to HyperTalk	24.95
Using Microsoft Word: Macintosh Version	21.95
Using Microsoft Works	19.95
Using WordPerfect: Macintosh Version	19.95

APPLICATIONS SOFTWARE TITLES

CAD and Desktop Publishing Guide	24.95
Smart Tips, Tricks, and Traps	23.95
Using AutoCAD	29.95
Using DacEasy	21.95
Using Dollars and Sense: IBM Version, 2nd Edition	19.95
Using Enable/OA	23.95
Using Excel: IBM Version	24.95
Using Managing Your Money	19.95
Using Quattro	21.95
Using Smart	22.95
Using SuperCalc4	21.95

HARDWARE AND SYSTEMS TITLES

DOS Programmer's Reference	24.95
DOS QueCards	21.95
DOS Tips, Tricks, and Traps	22.95
DOS Workbook and Disk	29.95
IBM PS/2 Handbook	21.95
Managing Your Hard Disk, 2nd Edition	22.95
MS-DOS Quick Reference	6.95
MS-DOS QuickStart	21.95
MS-DOS User's Guide, 3rd Edition	22.95
Networking IBM PCs, 2nd Edition	19.95
Programming with Windows	22.95
Understanding UNIX: A Conceptual Guide, 2nd Edition	21.95
Upgrading and Repairing PCs	24.95
Using Microsoft Windows	19.95
Using OS/2	22.95
Using PC DOS, 2nd Edition	22.95

WORD-PROCESSING AND DESKTOP PUBLISHING TITLES

Microsoft Word Techniques and Applications	19.95
Microsoft Word Tips, Tricks, and Traps	19.95
Using DisplayWrite 4	19.95
Using Microsoft Word, 2nd Edition	21.95
Using MultiMate Advantage, 2nd Edition	19.95
Using PageMaker IBM Version, 2nd Edition	24.95
Using PFS: First Publisher	22.95
Using Sprint	21.95
Using Ventura Publisher, 2nd Edition	24.95
Using WordPerfect, 3rd Edition	21.95
Using WordPerfect 5	24.95
Using WordPerfect 5 Workbook and Disk	29.95
Using WordStar, 2nd Edition	21.95
WordPerfect Macro Library	21.95
WordPerfect QueCards	21.95
WordPerfect Quick Reference	6.95
WordPerfect QuickStart	21.95
WordPerfect Tips, Tricks, and Traps, 2nd Edition	21.95
WordPerfect 5 Workbook and Disk	29.95
Ventura Publisher Tips, Tricks, and Traps	24.95
Ventura Publisher Techniques and Applications	22.95

PROGRAMMING AND TECHNICAL TITLES

Assembly Language Quick Reference	6.95
C Programming Guide, 3rd Edition	24.95
C Quick Reference	6.95
DOS and BIOS Functions Quick Reference	6.95
QuickBASIC Quick Reference	6.95
Turbo Pascal Quick Reference	6.95
Turbo Pascal Tips, Tricks, and Traps	19.95
Using Assembly Language	24.95
Using QuickBASIC 4	19.95
Using Turbo Pascal	21.95
AutoCAD Quick Reference	6.95

Que Order Line: 1-800-428-5331

All prices subject to change without notice. Prices and charges are for domestic orders only.
Non-U.S. prices might be higher.

SELECT QUE BOOKS TO INCREASE
YOUR PERSONAL COMPUTER PRODUCTIVITY

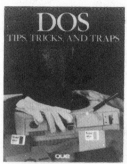

DOS Tips, Tricks, and Traps

by Chris DeVoney

Learn how to get the most from DOS—while avoiding potential problems—with *DOS Tips, Tricks, and Traps*. DOS master Chris DeVoney, author of Que's *MS-DOS User's Guide* and *Using PC DOS*, shows you how to progress beyond basic DOS use to become a true DOS power user. The series of tips and techniques presented in this handy reference includes information on batch files, printer operation, use of floppy and hard disks, I/O redirection, and other important subjects. Whether you use MS-DOS or PC DOS, whether you use a desktop or laptop computer, *DOS Tips, Tricks, and Traps* is your ideal second DOS book!

Managing Your Hard Disk, 2nd Edition

by Don Berliner

Proper hard disk management is the key to efficient personal computer use, and Que's *Managing Your Hard Disk* provides you with effective methods to best manage your computer's hard disk. This valuable text shows you how to organize programs and data on your hard disk according to their special applications, and helps you extend your understanding of DOS. This new edition features detailed information on DOS 3.3, IBM's PS/2 hardware, and new application and utility software. If you own a personal computer with a hard disk, you need Que's *Managing Your Hard Disk*, 2nd Edition!

DOS QueCards

Developed by Que Corporation

When you have trouble remembering important operating system commands, use *DOS QueCards*. Housed in a sturdy 3-ring binder, QueCards are 5″ × 8″ cards that show the proper usage of DOS commands and functions, as well as helpful hints and tips on avoiding treacherous traps. Complete with convenient section tabs, the cards can be either used with the built-in easel or removed and placed next to your computer keyboard. Commands for both PC DOS and MS-DOS 3.3 are included. Every PC user needs *DOS QueCards*—the fast and comprehensive DOS reference!

Upgrading and Repairing PCs

by Scott Mueller

A comprehensive resource to personal computer upgrade, repair and maintenance, and troubleshooting. All types of IBM computers—from the original PC to the new PS/2 models—are covered, as are major IBM compatibles. You will learn about the components inside your computers, as well as how to use this information to troubleshoot problems and make informed decisions about upgrading.

ORDER FROM QUE TODAY

Item	Title	Price	Quantity	Extension
882	Upgrading and Repairing PCs	$24.95		
837	Managing Your Hard Disk, 2nd Edition	22.95		
847	DOS Tips, Tricks, and Traps	22.95		
828	DOS QueCards	21.95		

Book Subtotal
Shipping & Handling ($2.50 per item)
Indiana Residents Add 5% Sales Tax
GRAND TOTAL

Method of Payment

☐ Check   ☐ VISA   ☐ MasterCard   ☐ American Express

Card Number _____ Exp. Date _____

Cardholder's Name _____

Ship to _____

Address _____

City _____ State _____ ZIP _____

If you can't wait, call **1-800-428-5331** and order TODAY.
All prices subject to change without notice.

FOLD HERE

Place
Stamp
Here

Que Corporation
P.O. Box 90
Carmel, IN 46032

REGISTRATION CARD

Register your copy of *Using PC DOS*, 3rd Edition, and receive information about Que's newest products. Complete this registration card and return it to Que Corporation, P.O. Box 90, Carmel, IN 46032.

Name _____ Phone _____

Company _____ Title _____

Address _____

City _____ State _____ ZIP _____

Please check the appropriate answers:

Where did you buy *Using PC DOS*, 3rd Edition?
- ☐ Bookstore (name: _____)
- ☐ Computer store (name: _____)
- ☐ Catalog (name: _____)
- ☐ Direct from Que _____
- ☐ Other: _____

How many computer books do you buy a year?
- ☐ 1 or less
- ☐ 2–5
- ☐ 6–10
- ☐ More than 10

How many Que books do you own?
- ☐ 1
- ☐ 2–5
- ☐ 6–10
- ☐ More than 10

How long have you been using DOS?
- ☐ Less than 6 months
- ☐ 6 months to 1 year
- ☐ 1–3 years
- ☐ More than 3 years

What influenced your purchase of *Using PC DOS*, 3rd Edition?
- ☐ Personal recommendation
- ☐ Advertisement
- ☐ In-store display
- ☐ Price
- ☐ Other: _____
- ☐ Que catalog
- ☐ Que mailing
- ☐ Que's reputation

How would you rate the overall content of *Using PC DOS*, 3rd Edition?
- ☐ Very good
- ☐ Good
- ☐ Satisfactory
- ☐ Poor

How would you rate *Chapter 1: Using DOS the First Time*?
- ☐ Very good
- ☐ Good
- ☐ Satisfactory
- ☐ Poor

How would you rate *Chapter 8: Understanding DOS and Devices*?
- ☐ Very good
- ☐ Good
- ☐ Satisfactory
- ☐ Poor

How would you rate the *Command Reference Section*?
- ☐ Very good
- ☐ Good
- ☐ Satisfactory
- ☐ Poor

What do you like *best* about *Using PC DOS*, 3rd Edition?

What do you like *least* about *Using PC DOS*, 3rd Edition?

How do you use *Using PC DOS*, 3rd Edition?

What other Que products do you own?

For what other programs would a Que book be helpful?

Please feel free to list any other comments you may have about *Using PC DOS*, 3rd Edition.

_____

_____

_____

_____

_____

_____

FOLD HERE

Place
Stamp
Here

Que Corporation
P.O. Box 90
Carmel, IN 46032